PSYCHOLOGY AND
PERSONAL GROWTH

edited by   ABE ARKOFF   university of hawaii

PSYCHOLOGY AND PERSONAL GROWTH

Allyn and Bacon, Inc.
Boston · London · Sydney · Toronto

LIBRARY OF CONGRESS CATALOGING IN PUBLICATION DATA

Arkoff, Abe.
  Psychology and personal growth.

  Includes bibliographies.
  1. Psychology—Addresses, essays, lectures. 2. Maturation (Psychology)—Addresses, essays, lectures. 3. Humanistic psychology—Addresses, essays, lectures. I. Title. [DNLM: 1. Mental health. 2. Personality. 3. Psychology. WM100 A721p]

BF149.A73   155'.08   74-23362

ISBN 0-205-04682-7

Third printing . . . July, 1976

For my fellow growers
Susie, Amy, and Ty

Contents

Thanks

I am grateful to the following for writing so rousingly on psychology and personal growth and for allowing me to include their work in this book:

Arthur W. Combs, Donald L. Avila, and William W. Purkey. "Self-Concept: Product and Producer of Experience," in *Helping Relationships: Basic Concepts for the Helping Professions.* Boston: Allyn and Bacon, Inc., 1971, pp. 39–51. Reprinted by permission.

Louis A. Zurcher. "The Mutable Self," *The Futurist* (October, 1972), 181–185. Reprinted by permission of *The Futurist,* published by the World Future Society, P.O. Box 30369, Bethesda Branch, Washington, D.C. 20014.

Thomas A. Harris. "The Four Life Positions," from *I'm OK—You're OK: A Practical Guide to Transactional Analysis.* New York: Harper & Row, Publishers, pp. 60–77. Copyright © 1967, 1968, 1969 by Thomas A. Harris. By permission of Harper & Row, Publishers and Jonathan Cape Limited.

Seymour Fisher. "Experiencing Your Body: You Are What You Feel," *Saturday Review* (July 8, 1972), 27–32. Copyright 1972 by Saturday Review Co. This article first appeared in *Saturday Review* on July 8, 1972. Used by permission.

Don E. Hamachek. "Body Image and Self-Concept," from *Encounters With the Self.* New York: Holt, Rinehart and Winston, Inc., 1971, pp. 101–113. Copyright © 1971 by Holt, Rinehart and Winston, Inc. Reprinted by permission of Holt, Rinehart and Winston, Inc.

Bernard Gunther. "Sensory Awakening and Relaxation," from *Ways of Growth: Approaches to Expanding Awareness* edited by Herbert A. Otto & John Mann. New York: Grossman Publishers, 1968, pp. 60–68. Copyright © 1968 by Herbert Otto and John Mann. Reprinted by permission of Grossman Publishers.

Alan Graebner. "Growing Up Female," from *After Eve: The New Feminism* by Alan Graebner. Minneapolis: Augsburg Publishing House, 1971. Copyright © 1971 Augsburg Publishing House, Minneapolis, Minnesota. Used by permission.

Patricia Cayo Sexton. "Schools Are Emasculating Our Boys," *Saturday Review* (June 19, 1965), 57. Copyright 1965 by Saturday Review Co. This article first appeared in *Saturday Review* on June 19, 1965. Used with permission.

James Lincoln Collier. "Are Men Really Men Anymore?" *Reader's Digest* (August, 1972), 154–156, 158. Reprinted with permission from the August 1972 *Reader's Digest.* Copyright 1972 by The Reader's Digest Assn., Inc.

Carlfred B. Broderick. "The Importance of Being Ernest—or Evelyn," *J. C. Penney Forum* (Spring/Summer, 1973), 16–17. Reprinted by permission.

Lois Gould. "X: A Fabulous Child's Story," Ms. Magazine (December, 1972), 74–76, 105–106. Reprinted by permission of International Famous Agency and Lois Gould. Copyright © 1972 by Ms. Magazine.

John W. Gardner. "The Idea of Excellence," in *Excellence: Can We Be Equal and Excellent Too?* New York: Harper & Row, Publishers, 1961. Copyright © 1961 by John W. Gardner. Reprinted by permission of Harper & Row, Publishers, Inc.

Robert J. Fisher and Hannelore Wass. "What Price Excellence?" *College Student Survey*, 4(3) (1970), 89–92. Reprinted by permission.

Harvey P. Mandel and Jim Uebner. "If You Never Chance for Fear of Losing . . . ," *Personnel and Guidance Journal,* 50(3) (1971), 192–197. Copyright 1971 American Personnel and Guidance Association. Reprinted with permission.

Marc H. Hollender. "Perfectionism," *Comprehensive Psychiatry,* 6(2) (1965), 94–103. Reprinted by permission of Grune & Stratton, Inc., and the author.

Wayne E. Oates. "On Being a 'Workaholic' (A Serious Jest)," *Pastoral Psychology* (October, 1968), 16–20. Reprinted by permission.

Elton B. McNeil. "Violence Today," *Pastoral Psychology* (September, 1971), 21–30. Reprinted by permission.

Suzanne K. Steinmetz and Murray A. Straus. "The Family as Cradle of Violence," published by permission of Transaction, Inc., from *Society* vol. 10, #6 (September/October, 1973), 50–56.

George R. Bach and Peter Wyden. "Why Intimates Must Fight," in *The Intimate Enemy.* New York: William Morrow & Company, Inc., 1969, pp. 17–33. Copyright 1968, 1969 by George R. Bach and Peter Wyden. Reprinted by permission of William Morrow & Company, Inc. and Sterling Lord Agency.

Arthur Guiterman. "Sex," poem used by permission of Mrs. Arthur Guiterman.

Andrew M. Barclay. "Sex and Personal Development in the College Years," in *Sexuality: A Search for Perspective* edited by D. Grummon and A. Barclay. Princeton, N.J.: D. Van Nostrand Co., 1971, pp. 311–332. Copyright © 1971 by D. Grummon and A. Barclay. Reprinted by permission of D. Van Nostrand Company.

James Ring Adams. "Sex Revolution Casualties," *The Wall Street Journal* (October 1, 1973), p. 10. Reprinted with permission of *The Wall Street Journal,* © 1973 Dow Jones & Company, Inc. All rights reserved.

Andrew H. Malcolm. "Sex Goes to College," *Today's Health* (April, 1971), 27–29. Reprinted by permission of the author and *Today's Health,* published by the American Medical Association.

Albert Ellis and David Mace. "The Use of Sex in Human Life: A Dialogue between Albert Ellis and David Mace," *Journal of Sex Research* 5(1) (February, 1969), 41–49. Reprinted by permission.

Abraham H. Maslow. "Lessons from the Peak-Experiences," reprinted by permission from the *Journal of Humanistic Psychology,* 2(1) (1962), 9–18. (Originally delivered as a public lecture June 30, 1961, La Jolla, California.)

David F. Ricks and Alden E. Wessman. "Winn: A Case Study of a Happy Man," reprinted by permission from the *Journal of Humanistic Psychology,* 6(1) (1966), 2–16.

Daniel A. Sugarman and Lucy Freeman. "The Positive Face of Anxiety," in *The Search for Serenity.* New York: The Macmillan Company, 1970, pp. 317–333. Reprinted by permission of The Macmillan Publishing Co., Inc. and Curtis Brown, Ltd. Copyright © 1970 by Daniel A. Sugarman and Lucy Freeman.

Albert Ellis and Robert A. Harper. "Conquering Anxiety," in *A Guide to Rational Living.* By Albert Ellis, Ph.D. & Robert A. Harper, Ph.D. Englewood Cliffs, N.J.: Prentice-Hall, Inc., 1961, pp. 132–143. © 1961 by Institute for Rational Living, Inc. Reprinted by permission of the Institute for Rational Living, Inc., and the publisher.

G. Donald MacClean and Robert W. Graff. "Behavioral Bibliotherapy: A Simple Home Remedy for Fears," originally printed in *Psychotherapy: Theory, Research, and Practice,* 7(2) (1970), 118–119. Reprinted by permission.

Martin Katahn. "Alleviating the College Student's Anxiety," *NEA Journal,* 57(1) (1968), 17–18. Reprinted by permission.

Elliot Aronson. "The Rationalizing Animal," reprinted from *Psychology Today* Magazine (May, 1973), 46, 48–50, 52. Copyright © Ziff-Davis Publishing Company. Reprinted by permission.

Sidney M. Jourard. "Healthy Personality and Self-Disclosure," *Mental Hygiene,* 43 (1959), 499–507. Reprinted from *Mental Hygiene,* Quarterly Magazine of the National Association for Mental Health, by permission.

Herbert A. Otto. "New Light on Human Potential," reprinted by permission from *Families of the Future,* Iowa State University Home Economics Department (1972), pp. 14–25. © 1972 by Iowa State University Press, Ames, Iowa.

Sidney M. Jourard. "Growing Experience and the Experience of Growth," from *Disclosing Man to Himself* by Sidney Jourard. Princeton, N.J.: D. Van Nostrand Co., 1968, pp. 152–167. © 1968 by D. Van Nostrand Company. Reprinted by permission.

Theodora Wells and Lee S. Christie. "Living Together: An Alternative to Marriage," *The Futurist,* 4(4) (April, 1970), 50–51. Reprinted by permission of *The Futurist,* published by the World Future Society, P.O. Box 30369, Bethesda Branch, Washington, D.C. 20014

Donald Bremner. "Bob & Barbara & Mike & . . . ?" *Los Angeles Times* (June 17, 1973). Copyright 1973 by the Los Angeles Times. Reprinted by permission.

Sandra D. Sandell and Jack E. Rossmann. "College Freshmen View Their Parents," *Personnel and Guidance Journal,* 49(10) (1971), 821–826. Copyright 1971 by the American Personnel and Guidance Association. Reprinted by permission.

Joyce Maynard. "My Parents Are My Friends," *McCall's* (October, 1972), 79, 146, 148, 150, 152. Copyright © 1972 by Joyce Maynard. Reprinted by permission of Curtis Brown, Ltd.

Urie Bronfenbrenner. "Parents Bring Up Your Children!" from *Two Worlds of Childhood: US and USSR* by Urie Bronfenbrenner. New York: Russell Sage Foundation, 1970. © 1970 by the Russell Sage Foundation, New York. Reprinted by permission.

Richard Farson. "Birthrights," *Birthrights.* New York: The Macmillan Company, 1974. Copyright © 1974 by Richard Farson. Abridged and reprinted with permission of The Macmillan Publishing Co., Inc. Originally appeared in *Ms.* Magazine (March, 1974), 67ff.

Jane Whitbread. "A New Way to Raise Kids," *Look* (February 24, 1970), pp. 64ff. Copyright © 1970 by Cowles Communications, Inc. Reprinted by permission.

Emanuel M. Berger. "Vocational Choices in College," *The Personnel and Guidance Journal,* 45 (1967), 888–894. Copyright 1967 by the American Personnel and Guidance Association. Reprinted by permission.

Mildred Henry with Harriet Renaud. "Examined and Unexamined Lives," *Research Reporter,* 7(1) (1972), 5–8. Reprinted by permission.

Robert E. Potter. "The Quality of Life Within the Rat Race," *Honolulu Advertiser* (March 1, 1970), page B2. Reprinted by permission.

David Steinberg. "Work Notes," from *Working Loose* by The New Vocations Project, American Friends Service Committee, 1971, pp. 14–31. Copyright 1971 by David Steinberg. Reprinted by permission of the author.

Letty Cottin Pogrebin. "If You Can't Stand the Heat, Get Back to the Kitchen," in *How to Make It in a Man's World.* Garden City, N.Y.: Doubleday & Company, Inc., 1970, pp. 233ff.

I am also grateful for permission to use the following special materials:

1. An excerpt from a letter by Abraham Maslow through the kindness of his wife Bertha G. Maslow.

2. The "Elation vs. Depression Scale," in Alden E. Wessman and David F. Ricks, *Mood and Personality*. New York: Holt, Rinehart & Winston, Inc., 1966. Copyright © 1966 by Holt, Rinehart & Winston, Inc. Reprinted by permission of Holt, Rinehart & Winston, Inc.

3. A condensation of a case study from William A. Westley and Nathan B. Epstein, *The Silent Majority*. San Francisco: Jossey-Bass, 1969.

4. An excerpt from P. Ebersole, "Effects of Nadir Experiences," *Psychological Reports*, 27 (1970), 208. Reprinted by permission of the author and publisher.

5. Excerpts from David Whittaker, "College Student Needs and Identity as Indicated by Their Self-Reported, Peak Experiences." Paper presented at the meeting of the American Orthopsychiatric Association, San Francisco, March, 1970.

6. Excerpts from Abe Arkoff, "The Desirable Self," "An Introduction to Anxiety," and "Some Common Defenses," in *Adjustment and Mental Health*. New York: McGraw-Hill Book Company 1968, by permission of McGraw-Hill Book Company.

7. Excerpt reprinted from *Introduction to Psychiatry* by O. Spurgeon English, M.D., and Stuart M. Finch, M.D. By permission of W. W. Norton & Company, Inc. Copyright © 1954, 1957, 1964 by W. W. Norton & Company, Inc.

And More Thanks

I am indebted to the many students who have worked with me over the years in my teaching psychology course and my adjustment and personal growth seminars. I cannot thank them enough for suggesting readings, exercises, and questions, for trying them out in their own groups to see if they work, and for helping me make the final selections. Thanks, thanks, thanks. Here are the names of those who have worked most closely with me on the materials which appear in this book:

THOMAS BENTON	MARY HUDAK	MYRON NAKAMOTO
JERRY BERGER	LES IHARA, JR.	EDWIN NAKAYA
CAROL BOHR	HARRIET KIRIHARA	RUSSELL OHTA
RICHARD CARMICHAEL	CATHERINE LARUE	PAM OTA
PAUL CHOCK	JACK LARUE	KIM PAYTON
STEVEN CHOY	WILMA LAU	FRANK SNOW
PHILIP CLEMMER	FRANK LEAVENS	LESTER SUEHIRO
MALCOLM DODSON	GREGG LEE	KENNETH SWEARINGEN
DONNA FEY	M. DAVID LENHOFF	SANDRA TOMIKAWA
SUSAN FUJIMOTO	CAROLE LITTLEJOHN	JOHN TSUKANO
SHARON FUJITANI	JAMES LOWE	CHRISTINE WINSKOWSKI
WENDY HAEDRICH	SABINA MILAN	COLLEEN WONG
JOSEPH HARVEY	STEVEN MIYAKE	EVELYN YANAGIDA
BARBARA HATA	TERESA MULLEN	BARBARA YEE
DAVID HOLT	DAVID NADA	JUNE YIM

And a special note of thanks to M. David Lenhoff for his extra-special assistance with these materials and to Judith Bywater and Susan Arkoff for their very great help in preparing the manuscript.

Abe Arkoff

To the Reader

Who are you? You singly, not you together.
When did it start—that long day's journey into self?
When do you really begin to know what you believe
  and where you're going?
When do you know that you are unique—separate—alone?

—Marya Mannes

Who in the world am I?
Oh, that's the great puzzle.

—Lewis Carroll

"WHO AM I?"

This is a question we may seldom ask—at least in this form—but all
through life we strive to find out who we are and to make some sense of
our existence. Our search can be a happy exploration or a painful struggle. We seek to understand our many puzzling thoughts and feelings. We
seek to assemble the many bits of our behavior to somehow make a whole.
And—with encouragement—we may try to get behind the defenses we
have so carefully erected to keep us from seeing ourself and being ourself.

"WHO AM I BECOMING?"

This is perhaps a more important question. One reason we have trouble knowing ourself is that we are constantly changing. At the end of even the most uneventful day we are different than we were at the beginning. Some of us are eager to change and to cast off the old and try on the new. Others fear change and try to freeze themselves into what they already are. But eager or fearful, we are all caught up in a process of change— a journey of becoming that continues throughout life.

"WHO COULD I BE?"

This may be the most important question of the three. Within each of us are more powers than are ever tapped and developed. And within society today are more pathways to choose among than ever before. Who will we be 5 years, 10 years, 20 years from now? Who *could* we be if we are free to grow and know how to grow and know what to grow into?

The topics and readings in this book have been selected to help you in your search for answers to these questions and others like them. The readings concern some important human problems: being, behaving, feeling, becoming, and belonging. Taken together, the readings provide an introduction to the psychology of personhood or personal growth. I hope that these materials may help you gain a deeper insight into the processes and problems of becoming a person.

Abe Arkoff

PART I

Being: Problems in Identity

There are nearly 4 billion people in the world today, and no two are exactly alike. You are unique. No one else looks exactly like you. No one else thinks or feels or acts the way you do. The qualities that distinguish you as a person and differentiate you from every other person make up your identity.

Identity is a key concept or idea in the study of human beings. Once we humans gain some sense of our identity, we tend to behave in accordance with it. We think of ourself as a person who can do certain things but who can't do certain other things. We think of ourself as someone who should behave in this way and who must not behave in that way.

Generally speaking, we are most comfortable when we are being ourself. We are upset when our thoughts and feelings and actions are not in harmony with the person we think we are. And we are also upset when we are cast in situations or roles that demand behavior inconsistent with our concept of ourself.

A strong sense of identity is a highly valued attribute. A person with this sense knows who he is and this, in turn, is related to who he has been and who he is becoming. There is change, but amid this change there is a core of sameness and continuity.

Erik H. Erikson, who has written extensively on the concept of identity, notes two problems especially prominent in adolescence and young adulthood. The first problem, identity diffusion, describes a person who is unable to define himself. He does not know who he is. He cannot hit upon a style of life, a way of relating to others, or a career direction.

The second problem, closely related to the first, is called identity crisis. This term can apply to a person who is in an acute stage of identity dif-

fusion. But it is also an apt description of the individual whose concept of himself has become grossly unacceptable or out of keeping with the roles and goals he faces. As a result, it becomes abruptly necessary for him to redefine himself to fit his life or redesign his life to fit himself.

Today's society is changing at a dizzying pace and calling upon its members to change too. We are in for some interesting identity problems in the times ahead. Traditional ideas of what it means to be a male or a female, a student or a teacher, an employer or an employee, a child, a parent, or a spouse—the list could go on and on—are under assault. We may be called upon continually to redefine ourself or at least to arrive at a definition more open to change.

The topics in Part I of the book relate closely to identity and have been selected to give the reader a fuller understanding of this important idea. The first topic, self image, *pertains to the picture or view we have of the total self. The second topic,* body image, *concerns our concept of the physical self, which is of course a salient part of the self image. And the last topic in Part I is the* sex-role image, *which concerns our sense of maleness or femaleness that—from the moment of birth—is an inescapable aspect of who we are.*

TOPIC 1

Self Image

O wad some Pow'r the giftie gie us
To see oursels as others see us!
                    —Robert Burns

If we could see ourselves as others see us,
We might never speak to them again.
                    —Anonymous

Our *self image* is the conception or picture we have of ourself. It is the way we see ourself. It is what we think ourself to be.

Our self image begins to form very early in life. In infancy, we constantly explore ourself and the world around us. We learn what is "me" and what is "not me" and discover we are a separate being. We learn to respond to our own name and acquire a sense of our own identity.

As we grow, we develop an increasingly complex and sophisticated image of who we are. Our self image is heavily influenced by certain "significant others"—the persons with whom we are in close interaction. In our earlier years, these influential persons almost certainly include our mother and father, our siblings, and perhaps other family members such as grandparents or uncles, aunts, and cousins. Later, neighborhood persons and teachers and schoolmates help shape our image of ourself.

In our interaction with these significant others we come, to a large extent, to see ourself as others see us. We learn from others' reactions what our qualities are and the value or worth attached to these qualities. We learn the areas of endeavor in which we do well and those in which we do poorly. We learn how competent, how attractive, how acceptable, how lovable we are.

With increasing age, we become less vulnerable to others and to the forces of our our environment. We arrive at a firmer sense of self that is less open to challenge and change. But we also may become more adept at masking undesirable personal qualities—hiding them from ourself as well as from others—until we become strangers to ourself and scarcely know who we are.

Some psychologists believe that the basic human force or tendency is our striving to maintain and enhance our concept of ourself. Other workers in this area do not assign the same preeminence to the self image, but clinical and experimental evidence suggests that this image pervades each person's thoughts, attitudes, feelings, and actions. Once there is an understanding of who a person thinks he is, it becomes possible to better understand that individual's present behavior, relate the present to the past, and even make some predictions about the future.

The stable self

In the lead article, Arthur Combs and his colleagues hold that the "core" of our self image or self concept—and by core they mean the most important beliefs we have about ourself—becomes quite resistant to change. Our experience tells us who we are, but once we think we know, we shape our further perceptions and behavior accordingly. For example, believing we can't do something, we avoid it or do it badly and prove to ourself what we believed. Believing we *can* do something, we give it a good try and prove we can. In brief, we tend to validate our beliefs about ourself. Combs calls this circular aspect of the self concept "self-corroborative" and "self-perpetuating."

The mutable self

Louis Zurcher, in the second selection, writes that rapid changes occurring in present-day society may reshape the relatively stable human self into one more mutable or changeable. His research, which is based on twenty answers subjects gave to the "Who am I?" test, suggests the self image that previously tended to be anchored to institutionalized and stable roles and statuses ("I am a professor," "I am a U.S. citizen," "I am a housewife") is now increasingly linked to characteristic ways of thinking, feeling, and acting ("I am a happy person," "I worry too much," "I am very religious"). This trend can result in a more mutable self—one that changes with changing conditions. Zurcher finds evidence of the mutable self in poor and "hip" subcultures that already must cope with uncertain and changing environments.

The OK self

All our relationships are strongly influenced by our images of ourself and others. Very early in life, writes Harris in the third article, we sense our inferiority and our dependence upon superior adult figures. We are led to depreciate ourself and conclude, in effect, "I'm not OK—You're OK." This is the first and most common of four possible life positions. As children some of us find adults largely unrewarding, and we depreciate others as well as ourself as reflected in the second position: "I'm not OK—You're not OK." A child who finds adult figures brutal may depreciate and reject them, taking refuge in himself: "I'm OK—You're not OK." The fourth and most hopeful position, one in which we see ourself as a worthy person surrounded by worthy others, is "I'm OK—You're OK."

The desirable self

In the last reading, Abe Arkoff notes that each of us has not one but a number of selves that define us in our own eyes and in the eyes of other people. This number includes the *subjective self* (how we see ourself), the *objective self* (how others see us), the *social self* (how we think others see us), and the *ideal self* (how we would like to be). Related to these several selves is a set of qualities that are generally valued or considered desirable. These qualities include *self insight* (an understanding of oneself), *self identity* (a clear and stable picture of oneself), *self acceptance* (a favorable attitude toward oneself), *self esteem* (a pride in oneself), and *self disclosure* (a willingness to let oneself be known).

FOR PERSONAL APPLICATION

1. Who are you? At the top of a sheet of paper write, "Who am I? I am . . ." Then below quickly complete 20 answers to this question. Afterwards analyze your answers. Also analyze your answering behavior, that is, how freely did your answers flow, how and why did you censor your answers, and so on.
2. Who are the "significant others" in your life? Discuss the persons who have most influenced your self image and the ways in which this has occurred.
3. How stable has your self image been over the years? Relate your present image of yourself to the images you had of yourself as a child and as an adolescent.
4. How is your self image presently anchored? Discuss the extent to which your conception of yourself is anchored or tied to institutionalized roles and statuses.
5. How mutable will your future self be? Discuss the extent to which you expect your self image to be influenced by the rapid changes occurring in our society.
6. Do others see you as you see yourself? Contrast your subjective self with your objective or social selves.
7. How much discrepancy is there between who you are and who you want to be? Contrast your subjective and ideal selves.
8. How much insight do you have into yourself? How much of a puzzle are you? Discuss an aspect of yourself which remains a mystery to

you or a situation or event which gave you some important insight into yourself.

9. How clear and stable is your present self image? Have you ever experienced identity diffusion or gone through an identity crisis? Discuss this aspect of yourself.

10. How accepting are you of yourself? How accepting are you of others? Discuss these two qualities and the relationship between them as you see them in yourself.

11. How much pride do you have in yourself? Discuss this quality in yourself, including the personal characteristics from which your pride arises.

12. How willing are you to disclose yourself and let yourself be known to others? Discuss this aspect of yourself.

13. Write down a discussion item (not given above) which seems particularly relevant to this topic and you, and discuss it.

FOR SMALL GROUPS

1. *Portraying the self.* Each member puts together two collages, one representing his image of himself as he is (the subjective self) and the other as he would like to be (the ideal self). He explains each collage to the group.

2. *Symbolizing the self.* Each member writes down the names of two non-human items, one representing himself as he is (the subjective self) and the other as he would like to be (the ideal self). These two representations are explained to the group.

3. *Validating the self: personal notes.* One member (or several in turn) volunteers to be the focus. He writes down the impression he thinks the group has of him (the social self). At the same time, the other members write down the impressions they have of the focal person (the objective self). Then the focal person and the other members read and discuss the congruence or incongruence of their separate images.

4. *Validating the self: the hot seat.* Members sit in a circle with one person in the center (the "hot seat"). Without speaking, this person faces each member in turn, who then gives his impressions of the person in the center. After one person has faced all the members of the circle, another person takes over the center spot. After everyone has had a turn in the hot seat, the members may respond to the comments they have received.

5. *Searching the self.* The group is divided into pairs. "Who are you?" asks the first member of the second. When the second member responds, the first member asks the same question again and keeps asking it, pausing only for the response. When the second member runs out of responses (or when a prearranged time limit has been reached), the two members exchange roles and proceed as before. Afterward, the pair discusses what they have learned from this technique, or the larger group reassembles for this discussion.

FOR FURTHER READING

Banks, J. A., and J. D. Grambs, eds. *Black Self-concept: Implications for Education and Social Science.* New York: McGraw-Hill Book Company, 1972.

Erikson, E. H. *Identity: Youth and Crisis.* New York: W. W. Norton & Company, Inc., 1968.

Gergen, K. J. *The Concept of Self.* New York: Holt, Rinehart and Winston, Inc., 1972.

Gordon, C., and K. J. Gergen, eds. *The Self in Social Interaction. Vol. 1: Classic and Contemporary Perspectives.* New York: John Wiley & Sons, Inc., 1968.

Hamachek, D. E. *Encounters With the Self.* New York: Holt, Rinehart and Winston, Inc., 1971.

Harris, T. A. *I'm OK—You're OK.* New York: Harper & Row, 1969.

James, M., and D. Jongeward. *Born to Win.* Reading, Mass.: Addison-Wesley, 1971.

Yamamoto, K., ed. *The Child and His Image: Self Concept in the Early Years.* Boston: Houghton Mifflin Company, 1972.

SELF-CONCEPT: PRODUCT AND PRODUCER OF EXPERIENCE

Arthur W. Combs,
Donald L. Avila,
and William W. Purkey

The most important single factor affecting behavior is the self-concept. What people do at every moment of their lives is a product of how they see themselves and the situations they are in. While situations may change from moment to moment to place to place, the beliefs that people have about themselves are always present factors in determining their behavior. The self is the star of every performance, the central figure in every act. . . .

WHAT IS THE SELF-CONCEPT?

By the self-concept is meant all those aspects of the perceptual field to which we refer when we say "I" or "me." It is that organization of perceptions about self which seems to the individual to be who he is. It is composed of thousands of perceptions varying in clarity, precision, and importance in the person's peculiar economy. Taken altogether these are described by the perceptual psychologist as the self-concept.

Each of us has literally thousands of ideas or concepts about himself: who he is, what he stands for, where he lives, what he does or does not do, and the like. A particular person might see herself as Mrs. Sally Blanton—wife, mother, part-time social worker; American, white; young; resident of Tampa, Fla.; measurements 34-25-34; good swimmer; poor tennis player. All these and many other perceptions or beliefs about herself make up the personal and unique self-concept of Mrs. Sally Blanton. To be sure, not all the concepts about herself are equally important to Mrs. Blanton. Some concepts of herself may be recognized as transitory. Others, like her concept of herself as a woman and a "Mrs.," are probably extremely important aspects of herself and are difficult to change.

Descriptions like those Mrs. Blanton has of herself serve to distinguish her self as unique from all other selves. But self-description does not stop there. We are seldom content with description alone. Even more important are the values a person places upon his various qualities of self. People do not regard themselves only as fathers or mothers, but as "good" or "bad" fathers and mothers. They see themselves not simply as people, but as attractive or ugly, pleasant or unpleasant, fat or thin, happy or sad, adequate or inadequate people. These, too, are perceptions of self and, taken together with the thousands of other concepts of self, make up the persons' self-concept.

The self-concept, it should be understood, is not a thing but an organization of ideas. It is an abstraction, a Gestalt, a peculiar pattern of perceptions of self. Despite being no more than an abstraction, however, these ideas are terribly important for the person who holds them. They may seem only like ideas to outsiders but, for the person himself, they have a feeling of absolute reality. In fact the self-concept is even more important to its owner than the body in which it exists. The body, according to Earl Kelley, is but "the meat house we live in," the vehicle in which the self rides. We recognize the distinction between body and self when we complain that "the spirit is willing but the flesh is weak," or "I would have come to the meeting, Joe, but my old body let me down and I had to stay in bed with the flu."

This distinction between the self-concept and the physical self may be observed in other ways. For example, the self-concept may be defined in such a way as to include matters quite outside the skin. This often happens with respect to one's most cherished possessions. A man may regard his desk as so much a part of him that he treats interference with it as a personal violation. Consequently, his reaction to a secretary who has intruded upon his territory by disturbing things in or on the desk may be so angry and forceful as to bewilder her. She exclaims to the other girls in the office, "You'd think I'd wounded him, or something!" Of course, she had. What appears to be only a piece of furniture to the secretary seems to be an extension of self to the owner of the desk.

The extension of self is observable even more often with respect to persons or groups. Psychologists refer to this experience as a feeling of "identification." By this, they mean the feeling of oneness we have with those persons or groups who have come to have special value for us. The self of a father, for instance, may be extended to include his son or daughter. When they are insulted, he almost literally behaves as though he were himself offended. The feeling of oneness with those we love and cherish has been experienced by almost everyone. Sometimes it may be so very strong, in fact, that awareness of physical separation may be temporarily lost. In the following excerpt from a letter, a young mother describes this feeling with respect to her newborn child:

When they brought my baby to me I unwrapped her and lay for a while in awe examining the marvelous way she was made. Then, after a while, I placed her on my stomach with her head between my breasts and lay there with a curious feeling of triumph and exquisite peace. Now and then I would raise the covers a little and peek down at her. As she lay there I honestly couldn't tell where she began and I left off. I remember I wept a little because I was so happy. I'll never forget the moment as long as I live.

While few of us are privileged to experience the depth of identification felt by this young mother, almost everyone has some feelings of identification with other people somewhere. It is one of those things that makes us human.

The expansion of self-concept also extends to feelings about groups. In fact, one of the reasons groups come together in the first place is to have the experience of oneness with each other. In becoming a member of a group, the self-concept is expanded to include the other members. Thereafter the individual begins to behave as though the members are an extension of his self. He speaks of "my gang," "my school," "my friend," "my church," "my neighborhood," "my state," or "my country." Depending upon how strong the identification, he behaves with respect to them as though they were part of self. He may even begin to call the members of his fraternity, church, or racial group "brothers" or "sisters."

The Self: Center of the Universe

For each person, his self-concept is who he is. It is the center of his universe, the frame of reference from which he makes his observations. It is his personal reality and the vantage point from which all else is observed and comprehended. We speak of things as "right" or "left," "near" or "far," and, of course, we mean from ourselves. The self is also used as a yardstick for making judgments. We regard others as taller, shorter, smarter, more unscrupulous, more handsome, faster, older, or younger than ourselves. As the self changes, furthermore, the yardstick changes and what we believe to be true changes with it. What is considered "old" is likely to be quite differently defined at ages six, sixteen, thirty-six, or sixty.

Generally speaking, we feel quite at home with "what is me." Toward what is "not me," we are likely to be indifferent, even repelled. Allport points out, for example, that when a person cuts his finger he may put it in his mouth and, in doing so, drinks his own blood without the slightest concern. Once the finger has been bandaged, however, any dried blood on the bandage is no longer regarded as "me"; a suggestion to lick the blood from the bandage would likely be regarded with revulsion. Similarly, everyone is continuously engaged in swallowing the saliva which collects in his mouth. This same saliva, collected in a glass and offered to the person to drink, is a very different matter indeed! Experiences consistent with the existing self-concept are accepted quite readily. They are treated as though they belong even when accepting them may be painful. A failing grade for a student who already believes he is a failure may not concern him at all. It only represents a further corroboration of what he already believes. It fits. On the other hand, incongruous experiences may produce feelings of great discomfort. When a man who believes he is highly attractive is told in no uncertain terms by a beautiful girl what a heel he really is, the shock to the self is likely to be considerable. Doctors and nurses often find it very difficult to get patients newly diagnosed as "diabetic" to care for themselves properly. Such patients often find it very difficult to accept this new concept of self and the use of insulin and dietary prescriptions they must follow. It takes time to assimilate their new definitions of self. The disturbing effect of inconsistent experiences will occur even if the new thought is something the person would like to believe. This can be observed in the embarrassment a person feels when after long periods of failure, he is told he has done something very well. He may even suspect that the teller is being sarcastic!

SELF-CONCEPT DETERMINES BEHAVIOR

The importance of the self-concept in the economy of the individual goes far beyond providing his basis of reality. Its very existence determines what else he may perceive. The self-concept has a selective effect on perceptions. People tend to perceive what is congruent with their already existing concept of self. People who see themselves as men perceive what is appropriate for men to perceive, while people who see themselves as women see what is appropriate for women to perceive. So it happens that on the way home from a party, Mrs. Adams may say to her husband, "John, did you notice what Helen was wearing?" John is quite likely to reply, "No, I didn't notice that." But, being a man, there were other things he noticed which, almost certainly, his wife will not think to ask him about!

It is notorious how a man's behavior may change when he puts on a uniform and becomes "a soldier." With this self-concept he is free to behave in ways he would not dream of as a civilian. Students have been known to fail in school because of unfortunate beliefs about themselves, as in this example reported by Coach Darrel Mudra of Western Illinois University:

What a boy believes about himself is really important. We had a student at Greeley who scored in the 98 percentile on the entrance test, and he thought that he had a 98 IQ. And because he thought he was an average kid, he knew college would be hard for him. He almost failed in his first term. He went home and told his parents, "I don't believe I'm college caliber," and the parents took him back to school and talked with the college counselor. When he found out that 98 percentile score meant that he had a 140 IQ, he was able to do "A" work before the year was over.

Once established, the self-concept thereafter provides a screen through which everything else is seen, heard, evaluated, and understood. Architects do not look at buildings in the same way the rest of us do. Similarly, the view of the world is different as seen by dressmakers, plumbers, house painters, nuclear physicists, or people who see themselves as Russian, Chinese, white, black, Hindu, or Muslim. Each person perceives the world around him filtered through his own self-conceptions; and this occurs whether he is aware of what is happening or not. Even when the businessman goes on vacation, he may find it very difficult to forget his business. In any vacation resort, men can be observed by the hundreds seeking each other out to discuss the comfortable things of the world they know while their wives equally uncomfortable so far from home, find comfort in talking housewifely things with people they never knew before.

The psychological literature is overflowing with learned articles and research studies dealing with the effects of the self-concept on a great variety of behaviors including failure in school, levels of aspiration or goal-setting, athletic prowess, mental health, intelligence, delinquency and criminality, ethnic groups, the socially disadvantaged, and industrial productivity. In every aspect of human existence the self-concept exerts its influence upon what people do and how they behave. When we know how a person sees himself, then much of his behavior becomes clear to us and it is often possible to predict with great accuracy what he is likely to do next.

Circular Effect on the Self-Concept
The selective effect of the self-concept has another important result. It corroborates and sup-

ports the already existing beliefs about self and so tends to maintain and reinforce its own existence. This circular characteristic of the self-concept may often be observed at work in the problems of children in learning arithmetic, spelling, public speaking, physical education, history, music, or any of the rest of the school subjects. Take the case of reading, for example: It now seems clear that many children who cannot read are unable largely because they *believe* they cannot read. It is comparatively rare these days that the child coming to the reading clinic has anything wrong with his eyes. With modern methods of testing children's health, sight deficiencies are usually discovered routinely. Instead, the youngster who comes to the reading clinic is much more likely to be handicapped because he believes he cannot read. For one reason or another he has developed an idea that he is unable to read. Thereafter, he is caught in a vicious circle which goes something like this: Because he believes he can't read, he avoids it. In this way he avoids the very thing that would be helpful for him. Because he avoids reading, he doesn't get any practice and so he doesn't read very well. Then, when his teacher asks him to read, he reads very poorly and she says, "My goodness, Jimmy, you don't read very well!" This, of course, is what he already believed in the first place! Then, to make matters worse, a report card is often sent home telling his parents how badly he reads and so they, too, join the act confirming the child's belief that he is indeed a very poor reader. In this way a poor reader is frequently surrounded by a veritable conspiracy in which all of his experience points out his deficiency to him. This conspiracy, moreover, is produced for the most part by persons whose intentions were excellent. They *wanted* the child to be a good reader, even though the net effect of their pressures was to prove to him he was not.

The reader himself may be one of those thousands of people who believes he cannot do mathematics, make a speech, or spell. With such a belief, he probably shuns those occasions where it is necessary to use the skill and so avoids the opportunity to practice it. Then, of course, his failure experiences when he is forced to act corroborate what he already firmly believes! Many research studies are now available showing the effects of student beliefs upon achievement in a wide variety of school subjects. There is even evidence to suggest that the self-concept may be a better predictor of a child's success in school than the time-honored IQ score.

The self-perpetuating effect of the self-concept is by no means limited to success or failure in academic subjects. It extends to every aspect of human experience. The same dynamics may be seen at work in all walks of life. The juvenile delinquent, for example, who has come to believe that nobody likes him, wants him, cares about him, and who thinks he is not much good, often comes to the conclusion that other people are his enemies. Thereafter, he may find delight in confounding authority. He builds up his feelings of self-esteem and value by taunting the police, and enjoys finding ingenious ways of frustrating and embarrassing them. Such behavior is hardly likely to endear him to others. Almost certainly, it will cause others to behave toward him in ways which confirm and support his already unhappy views of himself.

Dr. Walter Reckless and his colleagues at Ohio State University carried out a series of studies on the self-concepts of delinquent and nondelinquent boys. Among their findings are the following: The 12-year old "good" boy in a slum area perceives himself as staying out of trouble, of his friends as keeping out of trouble, of himself as going to finish school, and of his family as a good family. The mothers of the "good" boys also had favorable perceptions and prognostications of their sons. On the other hand, the so-called "bad" boy, spotted by his sixth-grade teacher as headed for trouble and for dropout, has the opposite perception of himself. He perceives himself as headed for trouble, of his friends as delinquents, and of his family as a "bum" family. The "bad" boy's mother echoed his perceptions. In a follow-up study at the end of four years, these investigations found that the "good" boy was practically delinquency free, while 40 percent of the "bad" boys were in the juvenile court one to seven times.

Fortunately, the circular effect of the self-concept operates equally well in positive directions. Persons with positive self-concepts are quite likely to behave in ways that cause others to react in corroborative fashion. People who believe they *can* are more likely to succeed. The very existence of such feelings about self creates conditions likely to make them so. The nurse who feels sure of herself behaves with dignity and certainty, expecting positive response from other people. To those with whom she works, this in turn calls forth responses which tend to confirm the beliefs she already holds. So, the circular effect of the self-concept creates a kind of spiral in which "the rich get richer and the poor get poorer." The self-corroborating character of the self-concept gives it a high degree of stability and makes it difficult to change once it has become firmly established.

Self-Concept and Social Problems

The self-perpetuating characteristic of the self-concept makes it of special concern in attempting to deal with the great social problems of our time. Millions of people everywhere in the world are caught in a vicious circle in which their experience seems always to confirm their unhappy or disastrous concepts of self. "Like mirrors locked face to face, in an infinite corridor of despair," they are trapped in a way of life from which there seems no escape. Having defined themselves in ways that preclude much hope of success, they remain forever victims of their own self-perceptions. Believing they are only X much, that is all the much they do. Other people seeing them do only X much then learn to expect that much from them and describe them as "X much people" which, of course, only confirms what the person felt in the first place! Many Negroes, for example, have been so thoroughly brainwashed by generations of experience into believing that they are unable, incapable, and second-rate citizens that they often continue to behave so, even in conditions where it is no longer appropriate. Poverty-stricken men in Appalachia who have lived too long without jobs or hope for the future eventually give up trying altogether. White men who have grown up with serious doubts about themselves but feeling superior to "niggers" resist with violence ideas of social equality. Their self-concepts are so negative and their world so full of hopelessness that they must have some belief that makes them better than something. How to help these and thousands of other desperate victims of their own perceptions off the treadmill of self-corroboration is one of the great problems faced by our generation.

The self-concept also plays its part in the social and philosophical problems posed by our great international dilemmas. People who see themselves as Americans behave like Americans, while people who see themselves as Russians, Chinese, Japanese, German, British, or Ghanians behave in ways appropriate to their conceptions of themselves. So also, people who see themselves as Buddhists, Taoists, Jews, Moslems, or Christians tend to think and behave in terms of their beliefs. Sometimes diverse ways of seeing even create differences and misunderstandings where none really exist if it were possible to penetrate to the basic issues beneath the surface of differences. U Thant, as Secretary-General of the United Nations, once expressed this in a description of his own growth and philosophy which had brought him to a point where he could see himself as a "person in the world" rather than a representative of Thailand, his native country. Feeling so, he said that he could watch a wrestling match between a man from his own and a different country and rejoice for whomever won. For most of us, more is the pity, such a "citizen of the world" self-concept is still beyond our experience.

HOW THE SELF-CONCEPT IS LEARNED

The self-concept, we have said, is an organization of beliefs about the self. These concepts are learned in the same fashion in which all other perceptions are acquired—as a consequence of experience. Before a child is born, he has already begun to make differentiations about himself and the world he lives in. This process continues after birth. A very large part of the infant's waking hours are spent in continuous exploration. Everything is smelled, felt, tasted, listened to, and looked at. Very early he begins to distinguish between what is "me" and "not me." With continued exploration, these perceptions in turn become increasingly differentiated into more and more explicit definitions. As language use develops, it soon becomes possible to give "me" a name, and the whole process of differentiation and concept formation is immensely accelerated. Before long the child is in possession of large numbers of perceptions about himself and his world, and a sense of his identity emerges. He becomes aware of himself as a unique person of many qualities and values all together having a feeling of personness. A new self has come into being. Once established, this self will exert its influence on every behavior for the rest of its owner's life.[1]

Some of the things people learn about self are discovered from interaction with the physical world. From these experiences they learn how big or how little they are, how fast they can walk or swim, or where they are located in the space they live in. They also learn what they can lift or not lift, what they can control, what dangers they must avoid or protect themselves from, what things are good or enhancing, and thousands of other perceptions more or less useful for getting along in the physical world we all live in.

Role of Significant Others

Of much more importance to the growth of the self, however, are the concepts we acquire from interaction with other human beings. Man is primarily a social animal, and it is from experiences with other people that his most crucial concepts of self are derived. People learn who they are and what they are from the ways they are treated by the important people in their lives— sometimes called "significant others" by psychologists. From interactions with such people, each of us learns that he is liked or unliked, acceptable or unacceptable, a success or failure, respectable or of no account. We learn very little from unimportant people even if they are called teachers, parents, social workers, counselors, priests, or rabbis. Only the significant people have much effect on the self-concept. The nurse, for example, is not very disturbed by what the casual acquaintance says about her skill. She is very much concerned about what her supervisor or doctor has to say (providing, of course, that she believes they know their business). What is learned about the self is a product of the peculiar experience occurring in the private world of the individual. What he

---

[1] The full story of concept development and the growth of the self is a fascinating field of exploration far beyond the treatment possible here. . . . [Interested readers are referred to the reading list on page 7, especially Erikson (1968), Gergen (1972), Gordon and Gergen (1968), Hamachek (1971), and Yamamoto (1972)—Ed.]

learns from any event may be quite different from the way it appears to the outside observer.

Because the self-concept is primarily learned from experience with significant others, it should not be assumed that this is simply a matter of what one is told by the important people in his life. So much of our daily interaction with one another occurs through verbal communication that it is easy to fall into the belief that what people say to each other has immense importance. Sometimes, of course, it may. The effect of words does not lie in what was said, however, but how it was read by the hearer. Understanding this fact is especially important for persons in the helping professions because so much of these people's work is dependent upon verbal interaction in one form or another. Believing that words are terribly important or that any matter can be solved by talk can result in making the helper ineffective. Certainly, talking is one of the most valuable tools we have at our disposal for influencing the behavior of others, but it is easy to exaggerate its contribution. It is not enough to be told one is loved; it is necessary to *feel* he is loved, and by someone who matters. One need only remind himself how seldom he takes "good advice" from others. Telling may be a way of affecting a change in another's self-concept. It is by no means infallible and is often vastly overrated.

From whatever source the self-concept is acquired, what is learned is a matter of the individual's own experience, not what seems to some outsider to be happening to him. A parent who scolds a child for not doing well in school may do so with the best of intentions, hoping to motivate his child to greater effort. To the child the meaning of this event may only be that he is stupid, unacceptable, or not much good. This kind of unintended learning is called "incidental learning" by psychologists and is often far more important in determining behavior than what the counselor or teacher or social worker expected to convey. Children learn about themselves, for example, from the atmosphere of the classroom, from the moods of teachers, and from the overt or covert indications of success or failure implied by approval or disapproval of teachers and classmates. This unplanned learning is likely to be much more significant and permanent than what the teacher taught. The child in fifth grade who is reading at second-grade level has a daily diet of failure imposed upon him by the rigidity of a system which insists on teaching all children at a given level as though they were alike. In the face of this daily experience, telling him he is "a good boy" is like a drop of water in a dry lake bed. Or, trying too hard to teach the young mother all she should know to care for her sick child may result in convincing her how inadequate she really is.

Place of Trauma in the Growth of Self

Many people believe the self-concept is primarily a product of the dramatic events occurring to the child in the process of growing up. This idea has come about very largely because of the concepts introduced to our thinking by Sigmund Freud and his students. As he listened to his patients retrace the steps of their growth and development in the course of psychoanalysis, Freud found them repeatedly bringing to light shocking events which had happened to them in the past. It was natural to assume that these events had had deep and powerful influences on the formation of personality and the creation of the problems his patients carried into adult years. This impression was further confirmed by the patients themselves, who frequently spoke of these events as having had a critical effect upon them.

In more recent years we have come to see the role of early trauma in a different way. We now understand that the most important changes in the self-concept probably come about only as a consequence of many experiences repeated over long periods of time. It is the little day to day things repeatedly chipping away at an individual's feelings about himself that produce the most permanent, pervasive effects on the self. A child learns that he is acceptable or unacceptable—not so much from the dramatic events as from the thousands of little every day nuances of attitude and feeling picked up from those about him, often so subtle and indistinct at the time they occurred as to make it quite impossible in later life for the grownup to put his finger upon the particular event which produced his current feeling.

If the self-concept is learned only slowly as a consequence of many experiences, why should we have the feeling that dramatic events in the past have so deeply influenced us? The reason seems to be that dramatic events are easier to recall and become symbols which crystallize and bring into clear figure the essence of a particular feeling. The event has tremendous significance, not because the experience was that crucial in its own right but because the experience became symbolic making explicit, many implicit feelings developed over a long period of time. Many a child has known the death of a grandfather with little or no feeling of loss, and many are quite unable in later days to remember the event at all. For the lonely, rejected child whose grandfather was an island of care and concern, the same event has a far different meaning. Looking backward down the years of our growth, dramatic events provide the hooks on which we can hang accumulated meanings. As a consequence the adult may recall how shy he was as a child and how devastated he was the day in third grade "when all the children laughed at me!" What makes the difference in human personality is not the trauma itself, but the multitude of other experiences which hammered and molded its meaning into being.

Stability of the Self-Concept

We have described the self-concept as composed of thousands of concepts of self varying in importance to the person. We have also observed that the core of the self-concept has a high degree of permanence and stability once it has become established. Unimportant aspects of the self can often be acquired or changed fairly quickly. These are generally peripheral aspects of the self, or matters of comparatively little concern. Thus, it may be possible to teach a person a game so that he comes to think of himself as a person who knows how to play that game. By taking a person for a ride in an airplane, we may produce a change in his self-concept to "one who has been in a plane." While these kinds of changes are comparatively simple to bring about, they are seldom enough to produce important changes in personality. Most of the truly important changes in the self-concept, such as those related to values, attitudes, or basic beliefs, occur much more slowly and sometimes only after very long periods of time. This is often very frustrating to those who like to help people quickly or easily. Frustrating as it is, however, we need to remind ourselves that this same resistance to change is also our very best guarantee against being taken over by a demagogue. It is a good thing people do not change easily!

Generally speaking, the more important the aspect of self in the economy of the individual, the more experience will be required to establish it and the more difficult it will be to change it. Fritz Redl once illustrated this slow development of individual feelings about self in the course of a lecture on juvenile delinquency. Delinquents, he pointed out, are not made by any one thing:

It takes fourteen years to make a good delinquent. Before that you can't really be sure you have one. To make a good delinquent everything has to go wrong, not once, but over and over again. The home has to go wrong, the school has to go wrong, the church has to go wrong, the community has to go wrong, his friends have to let him down, not once, but over and over again. They have to make a habit of it! Then, after 14 years of that you may have a good delinquent.[2]

After fourteen years of such experience it is also understandable why it takes time to change such a child's beliefs about himself and the world.

[2] From notes taken at Dr. Redl's lecture by A. W. Combs. Since Dr. Redl was speaking ex tempore, the accuracy of the quotation cannot be checked. The illustration, however, is superb.

THE MUTABLE SELF

Louis A. Zurcher

Socio-cultural change is occurring in contemporary industrial societies at an increasingly accelerated rate. Technical changes, often implemented at dizzying speed, are dramatically altering accustomed roles and values and changing the nature of work, school, family and community. They also may be changing the basic character of the human self.

My curiosity about the state of the self during adaptation to accelerated socio-cultural change was stimulated by a series of investigations which did not yield the expected results.

At the University of Texas I gave a seminar in which each student was to conduct a modest piece of research concerning self-conception, using the Kuhn and McPartland Twenty Statements Test (TST) as a measure. This test is an open-ended, relatively unstructured procedure, in which a respondent is asked to answer 20 times the question, "Who am I?"

The students were to use a TST scoring protocol which establishes four categories for responses.

The categories are:

"A" statements are the most concrete statements, and refer to the self as a physical entity. "I am five feet ten inches tall. I weigh 150 pounds. I have blue eyes."

"B" statements identify the self clearly and specifically with institutionalized statuses or roles. "I am a professor." "I am a U.S. citizen." "I am a housewife."

"C" statements present characteristic ways of acting, feeling, or responding in social interactions: "I am a happy person." "I worry too much." "I am very religious." These state-ments indicate that the self is not closely identified with an institutional context of norms and roles, but is relatively "situation-free."

"D" statements imply no particular context, act, or attitude indicating identification with social structure or interpersonal networks. They indicate that the self is removed from interactive commitment, and are vague and not differentiating. "I am a being." "I am one with the universe."

My seminar students had considerable difficulty completing their assignment, because the overwhelming majority of the freshmen and sophomore respondents were "C" mode on the TST. There were not enough "A," "B," or "D" modes to fill the cells adequately for statistical analysis. By contrast, a random sampling of students at the University of Iowa in 1957 showed that most students were in the "B" mode. When the problem came to my attention, I wondered if the TST's had been miscoded, but independent coding showed that they had not.

Since ours was not a random sample, we wondered if there might not be something unusual or atypical about the students we had sampled which would influence them toward the "C" mode, that is, toward a self-conception that was more loosely anchored in the social structure.

Apparently not. We were unable to get a significant number of "B" modes even among business students whose self-concepts were supposed to be closely linked with the establishment. The business students also responded with a large majority of "C" statements.

What had happened? Why did so many students have self-conceptions that did not reflect an identification with the social structure? Could it be that the self-conception of young people had evolved from a "B" mode tendency in 1957 to a "C" mode tendency in 1970? If so, could it be that accelerated socio-cultural change, which young people in particular were experiencing, had necessitated a self-conception that was not so wedded to the increasingly changeable social forms in our society?

Shortly after my seminar was over, I worked on two other studies specifically hypothesizing the presence of "C" mode self-conception among individuals who were in the midst of social disruption: dissident priests and recently paroled felons.

1. I am *waiting for an answer*.
2. I am *frustrated*.
3. I am *somewhat confused*.
4. I am *useless to many people*.
5. I am *impatient*.
6. I am *angry*.
7. I am *not fulfilling my calling*.
8. I am *bored*.
9. I am *searching*.
10. I am *at a crossroads*.
11. I am *not fully satisfied*.
12. I am *questioning many accepted forms*.
13. I am *becoming more withdrawn*.
14. I am *becoming mentally and physically lazy*.
15. I am *afraid of the future with the unknown ahead*.
16. I am *sorry this whole mess seems so unnecessary*.
17. I am *full of pity that those in authority cannot see the obvious trends of change*.
18. I am *reevaluating my own beliefs*.
19. I am *in the process of change*.
20. I am *sorry I cannot start over from the beginning, many years ago*.

The Twenty Statements Test asks a person to write 20 sentences beginning with the words I am. *The result gives a picture of how the person sees himself. On the test form above, the respondent has answered almost exclusively in the "C" mode—his characteristic ways of acting, feeling, or responding in social situations. The one sentence not classified by author Louis Zurcher as a "C" statement is Number One—a "D" statement, implying no particular context, act, or attitude indicating an identification with a social network.*

Both the priest and felon groups had a very high percentage of "C" mode TST's and seemed to have adopted that self-conception in order to adjust to the social turmoil they perceived around them.

These fragments of research, plus the observations of my colleague Louis Schneider and others,

lead me to suggest that the "C" mode of self-conception is concomitant with individual adaptation to accelerated social change, and reflects *the adaptive self* within contemporary industrial societies. The "B" mode self-conception, representing a self drawn from and dependent upon identification with relatively stable and acceptable social structure, is not functional when that structure is unacceptable or unstable.

When a social structure is undergoing change, a "C" mode self-conception makes a person more fluid in his willingness and ability to change roles, more able to accommodate shifts or conflicts in value orientations, more tolerant of short-lived interpersonal encounters, more open to new experience, more reflective, and consequently more readily able to adapt to change.

The kind of self revealed by "C" mode self-conception is at least a rudimentary form of what I call the *Mutable Self*.

As socio-cultural change continues to accelerate it may be that the "C" mode self will—like the "B" mode before it—cease to be functional. The "D" mode self-conception would then represent the adapting self. The "D" mode indicates a self divorced from physical being, from social structure, and from social interaction. Going beyond any concrete social situation or social structure, "D" mode individuals identify with such abstractions as "the cosmos" or "the eye of existence."

The Mutable Self represents many of the characteristics that have been suggested as being necessary or desirable for adaptation and growth in contemporary society. For example, the anthropologist Edward Sapir suggested in 1937 that in a period of rapid change "the individual tends to be unconsciously thrown back upon himself and demands more and more novel affirmation of his effective reality." When he is thrown back upon himself, he begins to rediscover himself and to engage in "a series of petty truancies from the officially socialized self."

In their book *The Temporary Society,* Warren Bennis and Philip Slater have described the healthy individual in a changing world as being essentially uncommitted to social structure and searching for no new stability; he is comfortable with perpetual transition, constant alteration, and ceaseless change. He has become separated from those permanent groups which traditionally provided him with ready-made values, traits, and self-concept. His ability to say, "I am such-and-such" has, in fact, diminished. For such an individual, say Bennis and Slater, a "consistent self-concept is itself a disease." Other authors have argued for sweeping changes from a distorted, destructive, and rigidly externalized self (developed in a flawed society) to a more phenomenological self

which, one way or another, would make it more feasible to realize human potential.

Our experience with the Twenty Statements Tests at the University of Texas suggests that the Mutable Self may in fact now be developing. Accelerated socio-cultural change and the increasing ephemerality of the social structure may already be ripping away the "me," the *persona*, the facade, or that presentation of self that we deliberately manipulate for social reward. As the sense of identity based upon previously stable social structures (the "B" mode) crumbles, what is left prepotent are the *processes* of self—the phenomenological experiences, the perceiving, thinking, planning, evaluating, intuiting, feeling, creating, etc. The balance of self thus shifts from a sense of identity linked with social structure to a sense of identity based on the existential phenomena experienced by the individual. Since these processes are always changing (with each new experience), the rate of socio-cultural change (now essentially external to the individual) has minimum impact. The self has become mutable.

Further evidence for the development of the Mutable Self may be found among certan subcultures which already have experienced in an especially intense form the changeable environment into which the society as a whole is moving.

The kinds of stresses that the poor and the hip have experienced and the coping mechanisms (social innovations and psychological adaptations) that they have evolved may be indications of how the bulk of the populations of complex societies will cope with accelerating technical and social change in the future. The social innovations and psychological adaptations manifest in these subcultures may be examples of what I call *cultural lead*.

This phrase, *cultural lead,* is developed from the classic "cultural lag" hypothesis formulated by sociologist William F. Ogburn back in the 1920s. Ogburn noted that a given aspect of culture may fail to keep pace with changes in technology; for example, it was some time after the automobile became widespread that retailers began to enlarge their outlets and lower their prices to take advantage of the larger number of people who now could easily come to a store several miles from their homes.

As a corollary to Ogburn's thesis, the hypothesis of cultural lead proposes that small but significant innovations in social forms may take place somewhat in advance of the full impact of a technological change upon society. These social innovations, which may be likened to anticipatory pseudopods, are implemented by a few individuals (often viewed as deviants) who actually are showing the general population alternative ways of adapting to the demands of change. Such reacting individuals or groups are for some reason more sensitive to the changes that have already begun and have tended to act more quickly than the general population.

I would like to suggest that the poor and hip subcultures may offer examples of culture lead: Some of the psychological adaptations and social innovations that have occurred in these subcultures may be functional for the society as a whole in the fast-changing world of tomorrow.

To understand how this might be, let us summarize some of the speculations of scholars who have been analyzing the future of complex industrial societies.

To begin with, there seems to be a general consensus among the forecasters that complex societies in the future will be marked by accelerated technical and social change. Such authors as Alvin Toffler, Donald N. Michael, Robert Theobald, Gardner Murphy, Dennis Gabor, Kenneth Boulding, Alvin C. Eurich, and many others have rather consistently described 21st Century society in terms of such motifs as impermanence, transience, ephemerality, marginality, instability, novelty, and value conflict. These forecasters generally anticipate dramatic developments in mechanical, electronic, chemical, and medical technology, all of which will have affected people's life styles. Significant changes will have at least begun in social institutions.

Other common forecasts:

- Work and work organizations will be less influenced by the Protestant ethic and more by considerations of service to society and the well-being of the worker. It will be more acceptable to move from job to job, and even to change one's profession several times. The guarantee of a minimum annual income and the institution of shorter and more variable work periods will have given individuals considerably more leisure time.

- Geographical mobility will escalate, and there will be a trend toward renting rather than owning one's living space.

- The traditional nuclear family structure will have been found wanting, because of the new mobility, the changing role of women, and medical developments concerning reproduction; as a consequence, there will be widespread experimentation with alternative family units.

- Complex organizations in general will be restructured along less hierarchical patterns, and will have become organized less for stability and more for change.

- Education will be more oriented towards the individual, with students no longer marching in lock-step with their age-mates. There will be a greater emphasis on experiential rather than book learning.

- The trend toward megalopolises will have continued, with accompanying crowding, lack of privacy, noise, pollution, and other forms of urban pathology.

- The changes in technology and social organization will have greatly altered the values, norms, roles and statuses which had been supported by the older technology and social organization. At the same time, the changes in values, norms, roles and statuses will be encouraging further modifications in technology and social organization.

- The sum total of the changes will have moved society more toward an "empirical, this-worldly, secular, humanistic, pragmatic, utilitarian, contractual, epicurean or hedonistic culture." (See *The Year 2000* by Herman Kahn and Anthony J. Wiener, Macmillan, 1967.)

- In the midst of this vortex of change, the individual will have increasingly become challenged to organize his life around transience, to endure discontinuities and disjunctions, and to maintain his ego in an environment explosive with sensory stimulation. His personality will have begun to become change-oriented, and he will be evolving a Mutable Self.

Though speculative, the picture of the future presented by the forecasters seems reasonably consistent. What I should like to suggest is:

1. The environments now experienced by the poor and the hip contain stressful elements, some of which are similar to those anticipated on a massive basis in the larger society of the future.

2. Some of the social innovations and psychological adaptations of the poor and the hip may

point to ways in which the general population may cope with the future.

(The reader is cautioned that, in order to illustrate cultural lead, the existence of subcultures of poor and hip has been assumed, although that assumption can be and has been challenged. The illustrations, while making the point for cultural lead, also tend to obscure the wide variety of individual differences among the poor and among the hip.)

Let us look first at the condition of poverty and how it affects the people who experience it.

CULTURAL LEAD
AMONG THE POOR

When compared with the world of the higher socio-economic classes, the social and physical world of the poor is whimsical, unpredictable, and beyond their control. The poor lack the economic resources and status needed to control arbitrary changes in important aspects of their lives (for example, housing, work, education, government assistance, etc.). Occupying a marginal position in society, they manifest what has been termed by Hyman Rodman a "value stretch" or bi-culturalism; that is to say, they have a wider set of values than do others within the society. The wider set of values creates a heightened condition for value conflict.

The mother-headed family, within which children are cared for by several relatives, particularly older siblings, is not uncommon among the poor. The responsibility for the care of both themselves and younger children equips the older siblings early with resources to meet extra-familial environmental demands, and to cope with the unsettling conditions of poverty.

To accommodate to crowded quarters, lack of privacy, and diverse work or activity schedules, the typically predictable time patterning of the middle class family (for example, a set time for meals, recreation, etc.) is suspended in favor of a more impromptu patterning.

Observers have commented on the fluidity and frailty of personal relationships (especially non-kin) among the poor. As if in anticipation of the ephemerality of personal encounters, individuals hurry each relationship toward maximum intensity, thereby getting as much emotional satisfac-

tion as possible. In such a setting, people are judged more by their personal characteristics than by their status in the social system.

Among the poor, the institution of marriage is diminished in importance and is less rigidly the "acceptable" state for procreation or child rearing. Sexual encounters are more casual and non-binding. Formal education is less valued, both because of the lack of opportunity for higher education and uncertainty as to its usefulness; instead, the children of the poor develop an adaptive preference for *ad hoc* education which is self-directed, action-oriented and pragmatic.

Blocked opportunity in work, meager rewards, and the probability of job obsolescence lessen the relevance of the traditional economic institution. With their work impermanent and low in status, the poor adaptively develop little interest in careerism or competition-based productivity for its own sake. They feel, instead, that work should be action-filled, fun, and tangibly and immediately rewarding. Since complex organizations are socially distant from and a source of arbitrariness for the poor, they cope with those organizations by avoiding them if possible and, when avoidance is not possible, by interacting with them cautiously and skeptically.

Researchers have reported an array of psychological characteristics among poor people: an orientation to the present, low achievement motivation, lack of impulse control or ability to delay gratification, sensual orientation, feelings of powerlessness and alienation, a sense of resignation and fatalism, experiential world view, preference for "being" over "doing," preference for harmony with or subjugation to nature rather than mastery over it, preference for feelings rather than emotional neutrality, preference for evaluating people by their individual characteristics rather than their status, damaged or faulty self-concept.

All of these characteristics can be interpreted as functional adaptations to the stresses of poverty. When the environment is replete with changes that impinge upon one's life but over which one has no control, when the future is unpredictable and uncertain, a set of values which encourages enjoyment of the here and now is a reasonable adjustment. A syndrome of powerlessness, alienation, resignation and fatalism is consistent with reality. Such a world view is, under the circumstances, not weak, but adaptive. The so-called damaged or "faulty" self-concept or identity can be interpreted as not being impaired at all in the context of a poverty environment. A "strong" self-concept or a "good" identity usually means that the individual has lodged his self-conception in a stable "generalized other" or derives his identity from association with or membership in a stable organization. But in an unstable environment, such "strong" self-conceptions and "good" identities would be distressing indeed, since they would be dependent upon a state of permanence which hardly exists. A "fragmented" self-concept—based more upon phenomenological experiences than upon social structure—is better equipped to cope with the vagaries of poverty.

The stresses that we will experience in the complex society of the future will result from patterns of accelerated technical and social change, whereas the stresses of today's poor people result from an inequitable economic system and status structure. However, the conditions lead in both cases to marginality and uncertainty, and for this reason the social innovations and psychological adaptations of the poor now may suggest something of the coping mechanisms of the general citizenry then.

Let us now turn to the counter-culture:

CULTURAL LEAD AMONG THE HIP

A number of recent authors have suggested that the counter-culture is a reaction of young people to the stressful perception of discontinuities, hypocrisy, distortions and dangers in industrial societies. These young people, the "hip," are repulsed by the values, norms, roles and statuses of contemporary society. They perceive the middle-class-oriented technical and social world to be whimsical, beyond their control, and filled with arbitrary and noxious changes which touch upon nearly every aspect of their daily lives. Though the hip have some access to economic resources, they have little power. They are not obstructed from taking a rewarded place in the status system, but they choose not to. They have been socialized into the life style of middle America, but they reject it. By "dropping out" to pursue what they feel to be a more promising and satisfying life style, the hip come to possess a wide set of values, some of which are residues from middle class socialization and some of which are drawn from the new-found counter-culture. Like the poor, the hip manifest "value stretch" and become more subject to value conflict.

The hip actively experiment with alternative domestic units, replacing the traditional nuclear family with serial dyads (temporary pairs), small group arrangements, and full-scale communes. Marriage is devalued; sexual freedom tends to be normative. Within whatever domestic unit is adopted, there are numerous deliberate explorations of different role assignments, daily schedules, eating patterns, leisure pursuits, and so on. The traditional male-female household division of labor is rejected. The socialization of children is shared by many members of the domestic unit.

Life in the domestic units of the hip seems to foster a positive attitude toward change, training for change, a tolerance for and expectation of impermanence, but at the same time to provide each member with a sense of belonging, control and stability.

The hip disclaim the "permanent" role relationships in "straight" society and replace them with interpersonal transiencies. The transiency is supported by an elaborate ideological stance: the hip are "one family" or "the Woodstock nation," and they share love for each other. Interpersonal mobility is seen as consistent with the orientation. Encounter group techniques and other sensitivity devices are used to facilitate affective expression, thus maximizing the intensity of the probably brief interaction of two or more people.

The hip abhor the status-consciousness of the middle class world, and instead accept other people on the basis of their personal characteristics. The hip abhor the formal education process, preferring the unstructured learning experiences to be found in the free universities and store-front schools that they have developed. Knowledge is not valued for its own sake, but only as it applies to the growth, well-being, interpersonal encounters and sensory delight of the individual and his fellows.

The hip reject the institutionalized work system and hold that work should be an integrated part of one's life, not too demanding, more like play than toil. Work should not be based upon competition nor on production as an end in itself. The hip typically refuses to prepare for and remain permanently in a single typical career, since that role path would restrict his freedom for expression, diversity and change. Complex organizations, bureaucratic procedures and hierarchies, and "memberships" in voluntary associations distress the hip; in reaction, they situate themselves in loose, informal, highly modifiable social structures.

Studies of the counter-culture have reported a set of psychological characteristics, some of which are similar to those found among the poor. The hip are oriented toward the present, unwilling to delay gratification, sensually oriented, alienated and spontaneous in emotional expression, existentially oriented, personalistic, prone to passivity, struggling with identity, agonizingly self-reflective.

All of these characteristics may be considered as helping the hip to adapt, since they have rejected the opposite characteristics as manifested among individuals in "straight" society. These hip psychological characteristics are suited to life within the social innovations that the hip have developed.

The identity struggle and intense self-reflection among the hip can be interpreted as a process of transition from a self-concept based in the stability of "straight" society to one based in the individual's own phenomenological experiences—Mutable Self.

ARE HIPPIES SUFFERING FROM "FUTURE SHOCK"?

Like the society foreseen for the future, the counter-culture includes marginality, value conflict, transiency and uncertainty. These characteristics may have come about because the hip have renounced the values and relatively stable social structures of straight society. An alternative interpretation would be that the hip are among the earliest casualties of "future shock" in a society already experiencing distressingly accelerated social change. Under either interpretation, the hip must cope with the stresses of impermanence.

Certain adaptive characteristics among both the poor and the hip are worth noting: the reported confusion of sexual identity, tolerance for idiosyncrasy and deviance, and accommodation to lack of ownership. Each of those characteristics may be examples of cultural lead—an adaptation to the societal future when sex roles may be thoroughly blurred, myriad life styles abound, and ownership of material goods may be little valued.

The level of social organization within the culture of poverty and the counter-culture has often been pejoratively assessed as "primitive." Similarly, the level of personality organization of individuals belonging to those subcultures often has been adjudged "underdeveloped." These negative judgments arise from a positive attitude toward the complex division of labor, hierarchical structure, specificity, and emotional neutrality of middle-class social organization, and the personality that goes with it. But the characteristics that earn the negative labels can be interpreted as quite functional adaptations to the marginalty, impermanence, and other life stresses of the poor and the hip.

Rather than simply condemning these subcultures, we might respectfully study their social innovations and psychological adaptations for their cultural lead potential. Other subcultures and social movements might also give cultural lead information useful for planning public policy.

What does the surfer subculture reveal about the use of abundant leisure time? What does the women's liberation movement divulge about the future role of women when family structures have changed and sex roles are blurred? What does the encounter group subculture disclose about adaptation to interpersonal transiency?

I have said much about adaptation to the stresses associated with technical and social change and little about the desirability of the mechanisms for controlling the societal patterns which allow or encourage the change and thus necessitate adaptation. The question of control raises basic questions about the nature of man, the ideal society, and the actualizing personality. Is the Mutable Self more suitable for the development of human potential than the old self, more securely anchored in social structure? Should the trends leading to the Mutable Self be encouraged or discouraged?

Such questions will become increasingly crucial in complex societies caught up in accelerating social change.

THE FOUR LIFE POSITIONS

Thomas A. Harris

For the sadness in legitimate humor consists in the fact that honestly and without deceit it reflects in a purely human way upon what it is to be a child.

—Søren Kierkegaard

Very early in life every child concludes, "I'm not OK." He makes a conclusion about his parents, also: "You're OK." This is the first thing he figures out in his life-long attempt to make sense of himself and the world in which he lives. This position, I'M NOT OK—YOU'RE OK, is the most deterministic decision of his life. It is permanently recorded and will influence everything he does. Because it is a decision it can be changed by a new decision. But not until it is understood.

In order to support these contentions I wish to devote the first part of this chapter to an examination of the situations of the newborn, the young infant, and the growing child, in both the preverbal and verbal years. Many people insist they had a "happy childhood" and concluded nothing like I'M NOT OK—YOU'RE OK. I believe strongly that *every* child concludes it, "happy childhood" notwithstanding. First, I wish to examine the situation of his entry into life and to point to the evidence that the events of his birth and his infant life are recorded, even though they are not remembered.

In this connection we note again Penfield's conclusions that the brain performs three func-

tions: (1) recording, (2) recalling, and (3) reliving. Although *recall* from the earliest period of life is not possible, we have evidence that we can and do *relive* the earliest experiences in the form of returning to the feeling state of the newborn infant. Because the infant cannot use words, his reactions are limited to sensations, feelings, and perhaps vague, archaic fantasies. His feelings are expressed by crying or by various body movements that indicate either distress or comfort. His sensations and fantasies, though ineffable because of his wordlessness at the time they were recorded, do replay occasionally in dreams in later life.

To illustrate: A patient reported a dream that had recurred throughout her life. Each time she had this dream, she awoke in a state of extreme panic, with rapid heartbeat and heavy breathing. She struggled to describe the dream but she could not find words for it. In one attempt at description she said she thought she felt as if she were "just a tiny, little, small speck, and big, huge, round, cosmic things were swirling around me, like great spirals, getting bigger and bigger, and threatening to engulf me, and I just seemed to disappear in this vast, enormous thing." Though her report was accompanied by her observation about losing her identity, the nature of the extreme panic would seem to indicate there may have been a fear of losing her life, as a primary biological reaction to the threat of death.

Some time later she again reported the dream. It was the first time she had dreamed it for about a year. She had been traveling, and she and her husband had eaten lunch in an out-of-the-way restaurant with an atmosphere of a higher quality than the food's. She did not feel well when they returned to their hotel, so she lay down for a nap. She fell asleep. It was not long before she awoke in the panic of this same dream. She also had severe stomach cramps, which "had me all doubled up in pain." No recent event had been particularly anxiety-provoking, and the panic dream seemed to have some direct connection with the extreme, primordial gut pain. The dream was still indescribable, however, she did report another sensation, the feeling that she was suffocating.

Certain information about the patient's mother helped to suggest a possible origin of this dream. The mother, a large, plump woman, had breast-fed her children and had held to the idea there was no problem that eating would not cure. Her idea of well-cared-for children was well-fed children. She also was an aggressive, domineering woman. We deduced (which is all we can do) that the dream had its origin in a time before the patient had words, since she could not describe the content. The association with the belly cramp suggested some connection with an early eating experience. The probability is that if, as an infant, the patient had had enough, or had had a full feeling and quit nursing, the mother would insist she have more. (This was before the era of demand-feeding: "Fill up now, it will have to last you.") Feelings of "dream-state" sleepiness, suffocation, and stomach cramps could have been present. The content (the small thing being engulfed by huge, cosmic things) could have been a replay of the infant's perception of her situation—herself, the small speck, being engulfed by the huge, round things, mother's breasts, or the huge presence of the mother herself.

This type of dream material lends support to the assumption that *our earliest experiences, though ineffable, are recorded and do replay in the present.* Another indication that experiences are recorded from the time of birth is the retention of past gains. The infant's responses to external stimuli, although at first instinctual, soon reflect conditioned or learned (or recorded) experience. For instance, he learns to look in the direction of mother's footsteps. If all experiences and feelings are recorded, we can understand the extreme panic, or rage, or fear we feel in certain situations today as a reliving of the original state of panic or rage or fear that we felt as infants. We can think of this as a replay of the original tape.

To understand the implications, it is important to examine the situation of the infant. In reference to Figure [1], we see a line representing a span from the moment of conception to the age of five. The first block of time is the nine months between conception and biological birth. During these nine months there occurred a beginning of life in the most perfect environment the human individual may ever experience. This way of life is referred to as a state of symbiotic intimacy.

Then, at biological birth, the little individual, within the brief span of a few hours, is pushed

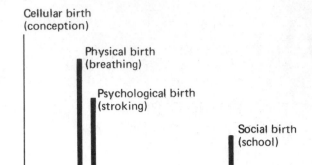

FIGURE 1. *Births of the individual from conception to age five.*

out into a state of catastrophic contrast in which he is exposed to foreign and doubtless terrifying extremes of cold, roughness, pressure, noise, nonsupport, brightness, separateness, and abandonment. The infant is, for a short time, cut off, apart, separate, unrelated. Common to the many theories about the birth trauma is the assumption that the feelings produced by this event were recorded and reside in some form in the brain. This assumption is supported by the great number of repetitious dreams of the "drainage pipe" variety which so many individuals experience following situations of extreme stress. The patient describes a dream in which he is swept from a body of water of relative calm into a sewer or drainage pipe. He experiences the feeling of increasing velocity and compression. This feeling also is experienced in the state of claustrophobia. The infant is flooded with overwhelming, unpleasant stimulations, and the feelings resulting in the child are, according to Freud, the model for all later anxiety.[1]

Within moments the infant is introduced to a rescuer, another human being who picks him up, wraps him in warm coverings, supports him, and begins the comforting act of "stroking." This is the point (Figure [1]) of Psychological Birth.

[1] Sigmund Freud, *The Problem of Anxiety* (New York: Norton, 1936).

This is the first incoming data that life "out there" isn't all bad. It is a reconciliation, a reinstatement of closeness. It turns on his will to live. Stroking, or repetitious bodily contact, is essential to his survival, without it he will die, if not physically, then psychologically. Physical death from a condition known as marasmus once was a frequent occurrence in foundling homes where there was a deprivation of this early stroking. There was no physical cause to explain these deaths except the absence of essential stimulation.

This painful on-again-off-again keeps the infant in a constant state of disequilibrium. During the first two years of life he does not have conceptual "thinking" tools—*words*—to construct an explanation of his uncertain status in his world. He is, however, continually recording the feelings which grow from the relationship between himself and others, primarily mother, and these feelings are directly related to stroking and nonstroking. Whoever provides stroking is OK. His estimate of himself is unsure because his OK feelings are transitory and continually being replaced by NOT OK feelings. Finally the uncertainty convinces him I'M NOT OK. At what point does the child make final his decision as to the position, I'M NOT OK—YOU'RE OK?

Piaget,[2] on the basis of meticulous observations of infants and small children, believes that the development of causality (what follows what) begins in the early months of life and is acquired by the end of the second year. In other words, data, in the form of a jumble of impressions, begin accumulating in certain sequential patterns, to a point where a preverbal position, or conclusion, is possible. Piaget says: "In the course of the first two years of childhood the evolution of sensorimotor intelligence, and also the correlative elaboration of the universe, seem to lead to a *state of equilibrium* bordering on rational thought." I believe this state of equilibrium, evident at the end of the second year or during the third year, is the product of the child's conclusion about himself and others: *his life position*. Once his position is decided he has something solid to work with, some basis for predictability. Piaget says that

these early mental processes are not capable of "knowing or stating truths" but are limited to desiring success or practical adaptation: If I'M NOT OK and YOU'RE OK, what can I do to make you, an OK person, be good to me, a NOT OK PERSON? The position may seem unfavorable, but it is a true impression, to the child, and it is better than nothing. Thus the state of equilibrium. The Adult in the little person has achieved its first mastery in "making sense of life," in solving what Adler called "life's central problem"—the attitude toward others and what Sullivan called the "self-attitudes which are carried forever by the individual."

One of the clearest statements on the development of positions is made by Kubie:

It is possible to make one certain deduction: namely, that early in life, sometimes within the earliest months and sometimes later, *a central emotional position is frequently established. . . .* The clinical fact which is already evident is that once a central emotional position is established early in life, it becomes the affective position *to which that individual will tend to return automatically for the rest of his days.* This in turn may constitute either the major safeguard or the major vulnerability of his life. In fact the establishing of a central emotional position may turn out to be one of the *earliest among the universals* in the evolution of the human neurotic process, since it may start even in the pre-verbal and largely pre-symbolic days of infancy. . . . Whenever the central emotional position is painful . . . the individual may spend his whole life defending himself against it, again using conscious, pre-conscious, and unconscious devices whose aim it is to avoid this pain-filled central position.[3] [Italics mine.]

Kubie then raises the question as to whether or not these positions are alterable later in life. I believe they are. Although the early experiences which culminated in the position cannot be erased, I believe the early positions can be changed. *What was once decided can be undecided.*

[2] Jean Piaget, *The Construction of Reality in the Child* (New York: Basic Books, 1954).

[3] L. S. Kubie, "The Neurotic Process as the Focus of Physiological and Psychoanalytic Research," *The Journal of Mental Science,* Vol. 104, No. 435 (1958).

Transactional Analysis constructs the following classification of the four possible life positions held with respect to oneself and others:

1. I'M NOT OK—YOU'RE OK
2. I'M NOT OK—YOU'RE NOT OK
3. I'M OK—YOU'RE NOT OK
4. I'M OK—YOU'RE OK

Before I elaborate each position I wish to state a few general observations about positions. I believe that by the end of the second year of life, or sometime during the third year, the child has decided on one of the first three positions. The I'M NOT OK—YOU'RE OK is the first tentative decision based on the experiences of the first year of life. By the end of the second year it is either confirmed and settled or it gives way to Position 2 or 3: I'M NOT OK—YOU'RE NOT OK or I'M OK—YOU'RE NOT OK. Once finalized, the child stays in his chosen position and it governs everything he does. It stays with him the rest of his life, unless he later consciously changes it to the fourth position. People do not shift back and forth. The decision as to the first three positions is based totally on stroking and nonstroking. The first three are nonverbal decisions. They are conclusions, not explanations. Yet they are more than conditioned responses. They are what Piaget calls intellectual elaborations in the construction of causality. In other words, they are a product of Adult* data processing in the very little person.

I'M NOT OK—YOU'RE OK

This is the universal position of early childhood, being the infant's logical conclusion from the situation of birth and infancy. There is OK-ness in this position, because stroking is present. Every

* [In this material, the terms *Parent, Adult,* and *Child* (when capitalized in this fashion) refer to three ego states or ways of thinking, feeling, and acting. We are in the Parent state when we are behaving like our parents or other authority figures (frequently in a judgmental or critical way). We are in the Child state when we behave as we did as children (typically with spontaneity and feeling). In the Adult state we are like a computer—receiving, processing, and acting upon information rationally and unemotionally.—Ed.].

child is stroked in the first year of life simply by the fact that he had to be picked up to be cared for. Without at least minimal handling the infant would not survive. There is also NOT-OK-ness. That is the conclusion about himself. I believe the evidence points to the overwhelming accumulation of NOT OK feelings in the child, making logical (on the basis of the evidence *he* has) his NOT OK conclusion about himself. In explaining Transactional Analysis to patients and nonpatients I have found a generally *that's it!* response to the explanation of the origin and existence of the NOT OK Child. I believe that acknowledging the NOT OK Child in each of us is the only sympathetic, thus curative, way games can be analyzed. Considering the universality of games, the universality of the I'M NOT OK is a reasonable deduction. Adler's break with Freud was over this point: sex was not at the basis of man's struggle in life, but rather feelings of inferiority, or NOT OK, which were apparent universally. He claimed that the child, by virtue of his small size and helplessness, inevitably considered himself inferior to the adult figures in his environment. Harry Stack Sullivan was greatly influenced by Adler, and I was greatly influenced by Sullivan, with whom I studied for the five years preceding his death. Sullivan, whose central contribution to psychoanalytic thought was the concept of "interpersonal relationships," or transactions, claimed that the child built his self-estimate totally on the appraisal of others, what he called "reflected appraisals." He said:

The child lacks the equipment and experience necessary to form an accurate picture of himself, so his only guide is the reactions of others to him. There is very little cause for him to question these appraisals, and in any case he is far too helpless to challenge them or to rebel against them. He passively accepts the judgments, which are communicated empathetically at first, and by words, gestures, and deeds in this period . . . thus the self-attitudes learned early in life are carried forever by the individual, with some allowance for the influence of extraordinary environmental circumstances and modification through later experiences.[4]

[4] From G. S. Blum, *Psychoanalytic Theories of Personality* (New York: McGraw-Hill, 1953), pp. 73, 74.

In the first position the person feels at the mercy of others. He feels a great need for stroking, or recognition, which is the psychological version of the early physical stroking. In this position there is hope because there is a source of stroking—YOU'RE OK—even if the stroking is not constant. The Adult has something to work on: What must I do to gain their strokes, or their approval? There are two ways in which people may attempt to live out this position.

The first is to live out a *life script*[5] that confirms the NOT OK. It is written unconsciously by the Child. The script may call for a life of withdrawal, since it is too painful to be around OK people. These people may seek stroking through make-believe and engage in an elaborate wish-life of *if I* and *when I*. Another person's script may call for behavior which is provoking to the point where others turn on him (negative stroking), thus proving once again, I'M NOT OK. This is the case of the "bad little boy." *You say I'm bad so I'll be bad!* He may kick and spit and claw his way through life and thus achieve a fraudulent integrity with at least one constant he can count on: I'M NOT OK—YOU'RE OK. There is a kind of miserable sense in this, in that the integrity of the position is maintained, but it leads to despair. The ultimate resolution of this position is giving up (institutionalization) or suicide.

A more common way to live out this position is by a *counterscript* (also unconscious) with borrowed lines from the Parent: YOU CAN BE OK, IF. Such a person seeks friends and associates who have a big Parent because he needs big strokes, and the bigger the Parent, the better the strokes. (OK strokes can only come from OK people, and the Parent is OK, as it was in the beginning.) This person is eager, willing, and compliant to the demands of others. "Some of our best people" are where they are because of these efforts to gain approval. However, they are committed to a lifetime of mountain climbing, and when they reach the top of one mountain they are confronted by

still another mountain. The NOT OK writes the script; the YOU'RE OK (and I want to be like you) writes the counterscript. Neither works in producing happiness or a sense of lasting worth, however, because the position has not changed. "No matter what I do, I'm still NOT OK."

Once the position is uncovered and changed, the achievements and skills that have resulted from the counterscript can serve the person well when he builds a new and conscious life plan with the Adult.

I'M NOT OK—YOU'RE NOT OK

If all children who survive infancy initially conclude I'M NOT OK—YOU'RE OK, what happens to produce the second position, I'M NOT OK and NEITHER ARE YOU? What happened to the YOU'RE OK? What happened to the source of stroking?

By the end of the first year something significant has happened to the child. He is walking. He no longer has to be picked up. If his mother is cold and nonstroking, if she only put up with him during the first year because she had to, then his learning to walk means that his "babying" days are over. The stroking ceases entirely. In addition punishments come harder and more often as he is able to climb out of his crib, as he gets into everything, and won't stay put. Even self-inflicted hurts come more frequently as his motility sends him tripping over obstacles and tumbling down stairs.

Life, which in the first year had some comforts, now has none. The stroking has disappeared. If this state of abandonment and difficulty continues without relief through the second year of life, the child concludes I'M NOT OK—YOU'RE NOT OK. In this position the Adult stops developing since one of its primary functions—getting strokes—is thwarted in that there is no source of stroking. A person in this position gives up. There is no hope. He simply *gets through* life and ultimately may end up in a mental institution in a state of extreme withdrawal, with regressive behavior which reflects a vague, archaic longing to get back to life as it was in the first year during which he received the only stroking he ever knew—as an infant who was held and fed.

It is hard to imagine anyone going through life

[5] Script Analysis is the method of uncovering the early decisions, made unconsciously, as to how life shall be lived. My reference to script and Counterscript is general. Definitive studies of the origins and analysis of scripts are being conducted by a number of Transactional Analysts, notably Berne, Ernst, Groder, Karpman, and Steiner.

without any stroking. Even with a nonstroking mother there most certainly appeared persons who were capable of caring for a person in this position and who, in fact, did stroke. However, once a position is decided, all experience is selectively interpreted to support it. If a person concludes YOU'RE NOT OK, it applies to all other people, and he rejects their stroking, genuine though it may be. He originally found some measure of integrity or sense in his early conclusion; therefore new experiences do not readily break it down. This is the deterministic nature of positions. Also, the individual in this position stops using his Adult with regard to his relationships with others. Therefore, even in treatment, it is difficult to reach his Adult, particularly in view of the fact that the therapist also occupies the category YOU'RE NOT OK.

There is one condition in which I'M NOT OK—YOU'RE NOT OK may be the initial position, rather than secondary to the first. This is the condition of the autistic child. The autistic child remains psychologically unborn. Infantile autism appears to be the response of the immature organism to catastrophic stress in an external world in which there is no stroking *which gets through to him*. The autistic child is one who, in the critical early weeks of life, did not feel himself to be rescued. It is as if he found "nobody out there" after his catastrophic expulsion into life.

Schopler[6] concludes there is a physiological factor which combines with insufficient stroking to produce the autistic child. The factor is thought to be a high stimulus barrier so that the stroking which is given does not register. He may not be totally deprived of stroking, but he may be deprived of his sensation of it, or an "accumulation" of his sensations of it. The infant is then seen by the parents as a nonresponsive child (he doesn't like to be held, he just lies there, he's different), and then even the stroking which has been given is withheld because "he doesn't like to be held." It is possible that vigorous stroking (more than is given ordinarily) may have overcome the barrier.

Once I observed an eleven-year-old, nonverbal, autistic boy evidence the seeming perception of

[6] E. Schopler, "Early Infantile Autism and Receptor Processes," *Archives of General Psychiatry*, Vol. 13 (October, 1965).

the I'M NOT OK—YOU'RE NOT OK position by an intense, repeated hitting with his fist, first his counselor, and then his own head. It was as if he were acting out his view of life: YOU'RE NOT OK and I'M NOT OK. Let's smash both of us.

I'M OK—YOU'RE NOT OK

A child who is brutalized long enough by the parents he initially felt were OK will switch positions to the third, or criminal, position: I'M OK—YOU'RE NOT OK. There is OK-ness here, but where does it come from? Where is the source of stroking if YOU'RE NOT OK?

This is a difficult question considering that the position is decided in the second or third year of life. If a two-year-old concludes I'M OK, does this mean his OK is the product of "self-stroking," and, if so, how does a small child stroke himself?

I believe this self-stroking does in fact occur during the time that a little person is healing from major, painful injuries such as are inflicted on a youngster who has come to be known as "the battered child." This is the child who has been beaten so severely that bones and skin are broken. Anyone who has had a broken bone or massive bruises knows the pain. Common in battered children are extremely painful injuries such as broken ribs, smashed kidneys, and fractured skulls. How does the every-breath agony of broken ribs or the excruciating headache from blood in the spinal fluid feel to a toddler? Every hour five infants in this country receive injuries of this kind at the hands of their parents.

I believe that it is while this little individual is healing, in a sense "lying there licking his wounds," that he experiences a sense of comfort alone and by himself, if for no other reason than that his improvement is in such contrast to the gross pain he has just experienced. It is as if he senses, I'll be all right if you leave me alone. I'M OK by myself. As the brutal parents reappear, he may shrink in horror that it will happen again. You hurt me! You are NOT OK. I'M OK—YOU'RE NOT OK. The early history of many criminal psychopaths, who occupy this position, reveals this kind of gross physical abuse.

Such a little person has experienced brutality, but he has also experienced survival. What has happened can happen again. I did survive. I will survive. He refuses to give up. As he grows older he begins to strike back. He has seen toughness and knows how to be tough. He also has permission (in his Parent) to be tough and to be cruel. Hatred sustains him although he may learn to conceal it with a mask of measured politeness. Caryl Chessman said, "There is nothing that sustains you like hate; it is better to be anything than afraid."

For this child the I'M OK—YOU'RE NOT OK position is a life-saving decision. The tragedy, for himself and for society, is that he goes through life refusing to look inward. He is unable to be objective about his own complicity in what happens to him. It is always "their fault." It's "all them." Incorrigible criminals occupy this position. They are the persons "without a conscience" who are convinced that they are OK no matter what they do and that the total fault in every situation lies in others. This condition, which at one time was referred to as "moral imbecility," is actually a condition in which the person has shut out any incoming data that anyone is OK. For this reason treatment is difficult, since the therapist is NOT OK along with everyone else. The ultimate expression of this position is homicide, *felt* by the killer to be justifiable (in the same way that he felt justified in taking the position in the first place).

The person in the I'M OK—YOU'RE NOT OK position suffers from stroking deprivation. A stroke is only as good as the stroker. And there are no OK people. Therefore there are no OK strokes. Such a person may develop a retinue of "yes men" who praise and stroke him heavily. Yet he knows they are not authentic strokes because he has had to set them up himself, in the same way he had to produce his own stroking in the first place. The more they praise him the more despicable they become, until he finally rejects them all in favor of a new group of yes men. "Come close so I can let you have it" is an old recording. That's the way it was in the beginning.

I'M OK—YOU'RE OK

There is a fourth position, wherein lies our hope. It is the I'M OK—YOU'RE OK position. There is a qualitative difference between the first three posi-

tions and the fourth position. The first three are unconscious, having been made early in life. I'M NOT OK—YOU'RE OK came first and persists for most people throughout life. For certain extremely unfortunate children this position was changed to positions two and three. By the third year of life one of these positions is fixed in every person. The decision as to position is perhaps one of the first functions of the infant's Adult in the attempt to make sense out of life, so that a measure of predictability may be applied to the confusion of stimuli and feelings. These positions are arrived at on the basis of data from the Parent and Child. They are based on emotion or impressions without the benefit of external, modifying data.

The fourth position, I'M OK—YOU'RE OK, because it is a conscious and verbal decision, can include not only an infinitely greater amount of information about the individual and others, but also the incorporation of not-yet-experienced possibilities which exist in the abstractions of philosophy and religion. *The first three positions are based on feelings. The fourth is based on thought, faith, and the wager of action.* The first three have to do with *why.* The fourth has to do with *why not?* Our understanding of OK is not bound to our own personal experiences, because we can transcend them into an abstraction of ultimate purpose for all men.

We do not drift into a new position. It is a decision we make. In this respect it is like a conversion experience. We cannot decide on the fourth position without a great deal more information than most persons have available to them about the circumstances surrounding the original positions decided on so early in life. Fortunate are the children who are helped early in life to find they are OK by repeated exposure to situations in which they can prove, to themselves, their own worth and the worth of others. Unfortunately, the most common position, shared by "successful" and "unsuccessful" persons alike, is the I'M NOT OK—YOU'RE OK position. The most common way of dealing with this position is by the playing of *games.*

Berne defines a game as

. . . an ongoing series of complementary ulterior transactions progressing to a well-defined, predictable outcome. Descriptively it is a recurring set of transactions, often repetitious, super-ficially plausible, with a concealed motivation; or, more colloquially, a series of moves with a snare, or "gimmick."[7]

I believe all games have their origin in the simple childhood game, easily observed in any group of three-year-olds: "Mine Is Better Than Yours." This game is played to bring a little momentary relief from the awful burden of the NOT OK. It is essential to keep in mind what the I'M NOT OK—YOU'RE OK position means to the three-year-old. I'M NOT OK means: I'm two feet tall, I'm helpless, I'm defenseless, I'm dirty, nothing I do is right, I'm clumsy, and I have no words with which to try to make you understand how it feels. YOU'RE OK means: You are six feet tall, you are powerful, you are always right, you have all the answers, you are smart, you have life or death control over me, and you can hit me and hurt me, and it's still OK.

Any relief to this unjust state of affairs is welcome to the child. A bigger dish of ice cream, pushing to get first in line, laughing at sister's mistakes, beating up little brother, kicking the cat, having more toys, all give momentary relief even though down the road is another disaster like a spanking, getting hit by little brother, being clawed by the cat, or finding someone who has more toys.

Grownups indulge in sophisticated variations of the "Mine Is Better" game. Some people achieve temporary relief by accumulating possessions, by living in a bigger, better house than the Joneses, or even reveling in their modesty: I am humbler than you are. These maneuvers, which are based on what Adler called "guiding fictions," may provide a welcome relief even though down the road may be a disaster in the form of an oppressive mortgage or consumptive bills, which commit the person to a life of perpetual drudgery. In Chapter 7 [of Harris' book I'm OK—You're OK] games are explained in detail as a misery-producing "solution" which compounds the original misery and confirms the NOT OK.

[7] E. Berne, *Games People Play* (New York: Grove Press, 1964), p. 48.

The aim of this book is to establish that the only way people get well or become OK is to expose the childhood predicament underlying the first three positions and prove how current behavior perpetuates the positions.

Finally, it is essential to understand that I'M OK—YOU'RE OK is a *position and not a feeling.* The NOT OK recordings in the Child are not erased by a decision in the present. The task at hand is how to start a collection of recordings which play OK outcomes to transactions, successes in terms of correct probability estimating, successes in terms of integrated actions which make sense, which are programmed by the Adult, and not by the Parent or Child, successes based on an ethic which can be supported rationally. A man who has lived for many years by the decisions of an emancipated Adult has a great collection of such past experiences and can say with assurance, "I know this works." The reason I'M OK—YOU'RE OK works is that instant joy or tranquility is not expected.

One day a young divorcée in one of my groups complained angrily, "You and your damned OK bit! I went to a party last night and I decided to be just as nice as could be, and I decided everyone else there was OK. And I went up to this woman I know, and I said, 'Why don't you come over and have coffee with me sometime?' and she cut me down to two feet tall with 'Well, I would like to, but you know everybody doesn't have the time to sit around and gas all day the way you do.' It's for the birds . . . won't work!"

Personal or social storms are not going to subside immediately when we assume a new position. The Child wants immediate results—like instant coffee, thirty-second waffles, and immediate relief from acid indigestion. The Adult can comprehend that patience and faith are required. We cannot guarantee instant OK feelings by the assuming of the I'M OK—YOU'RE OK position. We have to be sensitive to the presence of the old recordings; but we can choose to turn them off when they replay in a way that undermines the faith we have in a new way to live, which, *in time,* will bring forth new results and new happiness in our living. The Adult also can recognize the Child responses in others and can choose not to respond in kind. . . .

THE DESIRABLE SELF

Abe Arkoff

The idea of self frequently occurs in discussions of adjustment and mental health. Workers in this area find it useful to describe not one but a number of selves or concepts which relate to a person and then a number of qualities which apply to these several selves. There is some consensus concerning the kinds of self-qualities which constitute good adjustment or mental health. The discussion below considers these self-concepts and self-qualities in turn.

SOME SELF-CONCEPTS

Each of us has a number of self-concepts or self-pictures. Each concept or picture is a particular view. We have a view of ourselves as we think we really are, another as we think others see us, and still another as we would like to be.

The Subjective Self
The term *subjective self* refers to our own private view of ourselves. It is the way we see ourselves. It is what we think ourselves to be.

The subjective self is built up of all the ideas that we have concerning our own characteristics. Some of these ideas have been heavily influenced by our parents. Others have been hammered out in interaction with our peers and our larger social environment.

There is some evidence that children tend to see themselves as they assume their parents see them. In short, their view of themselves is influenced by what they believe is their parents' view. When they perceive that their parents are not in accord—when they assume that their father sees them in one way and their mother in another—their adjustment suffers (Wylie, 1961).

We tend to perceive greater similarity between ourselves and our friends than we do between ourselves and nonfriends or nonpreferred people. We tend to see our friends as we see ourselves or, maybe it is the other way around, we tend to see ourselves as we see our friends. But, interestingly enough, there is no substantial evidence that we are actually more similar to our friends than to our nonfriends (Izard, 1963; Wylie, 1961).

The Objective Self
The *objective self* refers to others' views of us. It is the self that others see. It is the person they think us to be.

The objective self also includes the data provided by various tests and measurements. Height as measured by a yardstick, weight as measured by a scale, intelligence as measured by an IQ test, academic ability as measured by an aptitude or achievement test—all are germane to the objective self.

Of course, not all people or all measurements will picture us in the same light. Nor are we the same in the light of every situation. We may behave one way at home, another at school, yet another at work, and the people in each of these environments may have varying perceptions of us.

The Social Self
The term *social self* is used to describe the picture that we think other people have of us. It is the way we think we look to others. It is our view of others' views of us.

How others see us (or how we think they see us) influences our own view. If others value us, it is easier for us to value ourselves. If others depreciate us, our self-estimation may suffer. In such a case, we may defend ourselves by depreciating them (Goldfried, 1963).

Some of us need to be liked by almost everyone; if anyone seems to dislike us or appears indifferent, we are bothered and uncomfortable. A few of us seem little concerned with the opinions of others. Almost all of us, however, are sensitive to the approval and disapproval of certain people who play important parts in our lives.

The Ideal Self

The *ideal self* is our concept of the person we would like to be. It is our ultimate goal. It is the self we would like to become.

It would be hard to imagine a person who was perfectly content with himself. Almost all of us would admit to wishing that we were different in some respects from what we are. Some of us might like to have a nearly whole new self.

A certain amount of idealization is necessary. Our ideals set the guidelines and form the goals of our self-development. Some of us, however, set extremely high goals for ourselves. In the struggle to reach them, we wear ourselves out. Or in contemplation of the wearing struggle, we give up.

SOME SELF-QUALITIES

Many self-qualities have been valued and considered desirable. These self-qualities incorporate the basic concepts which were just introduced. The following discussion presents a number of these qualities, including self-insight, self-identity, self-acceptance, self-esteem, and self-disclosure.

Self-insight

Self-insight means possession of knowledge or understanding of oneself. Self-insight is frequently mentioned as a quality of good adjustment or mental health. A commonly stated goal of psychotherapy is to assist the person who comes for help toward a fuller and more accurate self-insight.

How do we know if we have full and accurate self-insight? How do we know if we are as we think we are? In research, a person's self-insight is commonly assessed by comparing his view of himself (the subjective self) with the views that others have of him (the objective self). For example, the person may be asked to rate himself on certain personal qualities, and friends or acquaintances or trained observers also rate him. The smaller the discrepancy between the two sets of ratings, the more self-insight the person is credited with.

A second approach is to have the person report how he thinks others see him (the social self). This may or may not be how he actually sees

himself (the subjective self). Then an assessment is made of how he actually appears to others or to a trained observer. Again, a small discrepancy between the two views is considered evidence of self-insight.

How good is our self-insight? Apparently pretty good if we do say so ourselves. One psychology professor reports that 96 percent of the students whom he asked claimed that their self-insight was average or better; only 4 percent expressed some doubts about their self-insightfulness (Allport, 1961).

How good is our self-insight? Apparently not so good according to the bulk of research that has been done (but some of the research is not so good either so we must be careful about accepting it at face value). Wylie (1961), who reviewed and qualified the evidence, found that the correlations between self-ratings and ratings by others were generally quite low. There was usually some agreement, but it was far from perfect.

How good is our self-insight? Are we as good as we think we are? A considerable amount of evidence suggests that we're not. Self-overestimation is more common than self-underestimation (Wylie, 1961). In general, we don't take a dim view of ourselves—at least not for publication.

Self-identity

Self-identity refers to the clearness and stability that mark a set of images concerning a person. A sharp sense of self-identity has generally been considered a desirable quality. A person with a clear and stable identity knows who he is and what he values and what he is likely to do under a particular set of circumstances. Other people, too, know what the person stands for and what to expect of him.

A well-developed self-identity seems to presume a well-formulated self-knowledge. There is some evidence that persons who do not maintain stable conceptions of their subjective, social, and ideal selves also do poorly on self-insight measures (Smith, 1958). Other evidence suggests that unstable self-images are associated with heightened anxiety (Rosenberg, 1962).

Block hypothesizes that the optimal condition is one in which our identity is neither too rigidly nor too diffusely defined. He speaks of an aspect of identity called "role variability" which is characterized at one extreme by "role diffusion" and at the other by "role rigidity." He writes:

The meaning of role variability is perhaps most readily indicated by describing its extremes. At one end of this dimension, there is "role diffusion," where an indivdual is an interpersonal chameleon, with no inner core of identity, fitfully reacting in all ways to all people. This kind of person is highly variable in his behaviors and is plagued by self-doubts and despairs for he has no internal reference which can affirm his continuity and self-integrity. At the other extreme, there is what might be called "role rigidity," where an individual behaves uniformly in all situations, disregarding the different responsibilities different circumstances may impose. Here the core of identity is hollow, based not on a genuine and unquestioned sense of personal integrity but rather upon deep seated fear of any amount of self-abandon. Somewhere in between, presumably, a proper balance can be struck in the struggle both for identity and the capacity for intimacy (1961, p. 392).

Similarly, Erikson (1959) writes of "identity diffusion" which is a danger in late adolescence. No longer a child but not an adult, the adolescent may flounder about, trying on one identity, then another. Identity diffusion is well-illustrated in White's case of Joseph Kidd. At the time that Joseph Kidd wrote the following description of himself he was eighteen years old and at "the lowest point" of his life:

I began trying to fit a personality to my make-up. I began "acting" out personalities and tried observing people and copying them, but I realized what I was doing and so carried that "how'm I doing attitude," that is, continually looking at and thinking about what I'd said or done, what impression I had made. But these personalities were all short-lived because they pleased some and not others and because they didn't produce that underlying purpose of making people like me; and every time unconsciously I would resort to my childish attitude to make myself noticeable. Examples of these "personalities" are independence (but I couldn't keep it up); arrogance (but people were only arrogant back at me); big shot in sex (but people weren't so much in love with it as I

thought); hatefulness (people paid no attention to me); extreme niceness (people took advantage of it, kidded me about it because I did it to an ultra degree); humorous nature (but I was only being childish, silly); quiet and studious (but people were only passing me by and I kept feeling I was missing something). I became a day-dreamer so intensively that up to the present I find I'm day-dreaming almost all the time. I became conscious of a person's approach and would become fluttered, flustered, would try to make a friend of him no matter who he was but I overdid it (1942, p. 154).

Erikson has also written of "positive" and "negative" identities. Unlike positive identities, negative ones are built up of patterns of behavior which others have held out as wrong or perverse. Negative identities may stem from the conviction that one cannot amount to much, and rather than being "not quite somebody" it is better to be nobody or somebody bad.

As was already indicated, a frequent goal of psychotherapy is to help the person gain self-insight. Another common aim is to help the person establish or clarify his self-identity. He is helped to discover himself or to discover how the many fragments of his identity may be fitted together to make a self.

This statement, written by a woman in therapy, illustrates, to use the therapist's words, "the discovery of self":

You know, it seems as if all the energy that went into holding the arbitrary pattern together was quite unnecessary—a waste. You think you have to make the pattern yourself; but there are so many pieces, and it's so hard to see where they fit. Sometimes you put them in the wrong place, and the more pieces mis-fitted, the more effort it takes to hold them in place, until at last you are so tired that even that awful confusion is better than holding on any longer. Then you discover that left to themselves the jumbled pieces fall quite naturally into their own places, and a living pattern emerges without any effort at all on your part. Your job is just to discover it, and in the course of that, you will find yourself and your own place. You must even let your own experience tell you its own meaning; the minute you tell it what it means, you are at war with yourself (Rogers, 1961, p. 114).

Self-acceptance

Self-acceptance refers to a generally favorable or positive attitude toward one's own personal qualities. Self-acceptance generally implies some self-insight and self-identity. If we are self-accepting, we have some knowledge of our personal assets and our personal liabilities, and there is not undue pride in the former or undue shame or guilt about the latter (English and English, 1958).

Self-acceptance is considered a very important quality, and the concept has been studied and written about a great deal. In research, a frequent approach has been to obtain two measures, one assessing the person's subjective self, the other his ideal self. If there is little difference between the two—if the person sees himself as not too different from what he wants to be—he is considered self-accepting (Wylie, 1961).

Extreme self-dissatisfaction is generally considered an undesirable condition. However, not all who are esteemed by others show self-acceptance. In some people, very high disparity between subjective and ideal selves accompanies a high degree of social competence as evidenced by their educational, occupational, and marital histories (Achenbach and Zigler, 1963).

Self-satisfaction is generally considered a desirable quality, but not all of us who have a lot to be modest about show a discrepancy between our subjective and ideal selves. There is, of course, the possibility that we may be well-satisfied with ourselves without sufficient cause—because we haven't faced the facts or because we have distorted them (Block and Thomas, 1955). Or we may be well satisfied because we are very undemanding of ourselves; in this regard, some writers have suggested that a small discrepancy between objective and ideal selves is better than no discrepancy at all (Wylie, 1961).

Many writers have suggested that people who accept themselves are also more accepting of others. There is some research evidence to support this contention (Wylie, 1961). Those of us who accept and respect ourselves tend to respect others. Those of us who depreciate and reject ourselves reject and depreciate others as well.

It has been suggested that there may be an element of projection in the relationship between the acceptance of self and the acceptance of others. If we depreciate ourselves, we may assume that others depreciate us too. In retaliation, we reject and depreciate them in order to bolster our own feelings (Goldfried, 1963).

The proper acceptance of ourselves seems to be vital to our acceptance of others and to our getting along with them. In psychotherapy there is frequently an attempt to get the person to be more accepting of himself. As therapy progresses, the person may see himself as more worthy and closer to his ideal self. And he may revise his ideal self, making it more congruent with his objective self. . . .

Self-esteem

Self-esteem denotes that a person has pride in himself. The difference between self-acceptance and self-esteem is one of degree. Both terms imply a sense of worthiness, but self-esteem connotes a greater degree.

Just as self-acceptance and acceptance of others go together, self-esteem and esteem for others appear to be related. Fromm speaks of "self-love" which he feels is closely related to love for others. He says, "The idea expressed in the Biblical 'Love thy neighbor as thyself!' implies that respect for one's own integrity and uniqueness, love for and understanding of one's own self, cannot be separated from respect and love and understanding for another individual. The love for my own self is inseparably connected with the love for any other being" (1956, pp. 58–59).

The whole idea of self-esteem or self-love is a bothersome one for many of us. We have been taught to be modest about our own qualities. We have been taught not to be conceited or infatuated with ourselves.

It is readily apparent in the writings on this subject that self-esteem and self-love have little in common with self-conceit and self-infatuation. The two sets of terms are poles apart in their implications. Fromm illustrates this point nicely in his contrast of selfishness and self-love. He writes:

Selfishness and self-love, far from being identical, are actually opposites. The selfish person does not love himself too much but too little; in fact he hates himself. This lack of fondness and care for himself, which is only one expression of his lack of productiveness, leaves him empty and frustrated. He is necessarily unhappy and anxiously concerned to snatch from life the satisfactions which he blocks himself from attaining. He seems to care too much for himself, but actually he only makes an unsuccessful attempt to cover up and compensate for his failure to care for his real self. Freud holds that the selfish person is narcissistic, as if he had withdrawn his love from others and turned it toward his own person. It is true that selfish persons are incapable of loving others, but they are not capable of loving themselves either (1956, pp. 60–61).

Self-disclosure

Self-disclosure refers to the process of making oneself known to other people (Jourard, 1964). It refers to our ability and willingness to let others know us as we are—to share our thoughts and feelings with them. Are we able to leave ourselves unconcealed and undefended?

Jourard holds that self-disclosure is an important aspect of mental health. Mentally healthy persons, he says, have the ability to make themselves known to at least one significant other. In disclosing himself to another, the person comes to know himself better and he becomes a better self.

By contrast, the less healthy person is unable or unwilling to drop his guard. He is alienated from others and from his own self as well. Jourard (1964, p. 26) writes, "Every maladjusted person is a person who has not made himself known to another human being, and in consequence does not know himself. Nor can he be himself. More than that, *he struggles actively to avoid becoming known by another human being.* He *works* at it ceaselessly, 24 hours daily, and it is work!"

None of us is completely transparent or completely opaque, nor should we be. Too much disclosure, like too little, is undesirable. Disclosure requires the appropriate time and place and person (Jourard, 1963). The important thing is to have a person or persons with whom we can be ourselves, see ourselves, and become ourselves.

One way of measuring self-disclosure is to compare the subjective self with the social self. Do we see ourselves as we see others see us? Do we struggle to construct public selves incongruent with our private images?

People can learn to disclose themselves. In the warmth and security of certain relationships, we can dare to be ourselves. We let down our guard and let others see us and we see ourselves. In the material below, a woman in psychotherapy describes her struggle to know herself and to let her therapist know her:

As I look at it now, I was peeling off layer after layer of defenses. I'd build them up, try them, and then discard them when you remained the same. I didn't know what was at the bottom and I was very much afraid to find out, but I *had* to keep on trying. At first I felt there was nothing within me—just a great emptiness where I needed and wanted a solid core. Then I began to feel that I was facing a solid brick wall, too high to get over and too thick to go through. One day the wall became translucent, rather than solid. After this, the wall seemed to disappear but beyond it I discovered a dam holding back violent, churning waters. I felt as if I were holding back the force of these waters and if I opened even a tiny hole I and all about me would be destroyed in the ensuing torrent of feelings represented by the water. Finally I could stand the strain no longer and I let go. All I did, actually, was to succumb to complete and utter self pity, then hate, then love. After this experience, I felt as if I had leaped a brink and was safely on the other side, though still tottering a bit on the edge. I don't know what I was searching for or where I was going, but I felt then as I have always felt whenever I really lived, that I was moving forward (Rogers, 1961, pp. 110–111).

REFERENCES

ACHENBACH, T., and E. ZIGLER. "Social Competence and Self-image Disparity in Psychiatric and Nonpsychiatric Patients," *Journal of Abnorml and Social Psychology,* **67**(3) (1963), 197–205.

ALLPORT, G. W. *Pattern and Growth in Personality.* New York: Holt, Rinehart & Winston, Inc., 1961.

BLOCK, J. "Ego Identity, Role Variability and Adjustments," *Journal of Consulting Psychology,* **25**(5) (1961), 392–397.

———, and H. THOMAS. "Is Satisfaction with Self a Measure of Adjustment?" *Journal of*

Abnormal and Social Psychology, **51**(2) (1955), 254–259.

ENGLISH, H. B., and A. C. ENGLISH. *A Comprehensive Dictionary of Psychological and Psychoanalytical Terms.* New York: Longmans, Green, 1958.

ERICKSON, E. H. "Identity and the Life Cycle," *Psychological Issues,* **1**(1) (1959), Monograph 1.

FROMM, E. *The Art of Loving.* New York: Harper & Row, Publishers, 1956.

GOLDFRIED, M. R. "Feelings of Inferiority and the Depreciation of Others. A Research Review and Theoretical Reformulation," *Journal of Individual Psychology,* **19**(1963), 27–48.

IZARD, C. E. "Personality Similarity and Friendship: A Follow-up Study," *Journal of Abnormal and Social Psychology,* **66**(6) (1963), 598–600.

JOURARD, S. M. *Personal Adjustment,* 2nd ed. New York: The Macmillan Company, 1963.

———. *The Transparent Self.* Princeton, N.J.: Van Nostrand, 1964.

ROGERS, C. R. *On Becoming a Person.* Boston: Houghton Mifflin Company, 1961.

ROSENBERG, M. "The Association between Self-esteem and Anxiety," *Journal of Psychiatric Research,* **1**(2) (1962), 135–152.

SMITH, G. M. "Six Measures of Self-concept Discrepancy and Instability: Their Interrelations, Reliability, and Relations to Other Personality Measures," *Journal of Consulting Psychology,* **22**(2) (1958), 101–112.

WHITE, R. W. *Lives in Progress.* New York: Holt, Rinehart & Winston, Inc., 1952.

TOPIC 2

Body Image

There is no more fascinating sight than your own image looking back at you in a mirror. You are drawn to it in a half-embarrassed way, excited and intensely involved. Do you remember the last time someone showed you a photograph of yourself? Wasn't there a surge of feeling and a deep curiosity about "How do I look?"

—Seymour Fisher

Our *body image* is our view or concept of our own body. This image includes what we see or think we see when we look at ourself from the outside, so to speak, our reflection in a mirror perhaps or our impression on the bathroom scales. And this image is also based on how we sense or experience our body from the inside.

Our body image is a salient part of our self image. Research has shown a close relationship between these two concepts. If we accept our body, we tend to accept or esteem ourself generally. Those of us who reject our physical self are likely to reject our psychological self.

Our body image has a considerable effect on our thoughts, feelings, and actions. By understanding body image we can understand a good deal else about personality. Seymour Fisher, a prominent researcher in this area, writes, "A person's experiences with his body, as a psychological object, intrude widely into his life. His body is a perceptual object from which he cannot escape. Being an inevitable accompaniment of his awareness, it has great influence on him."

While the body image has a considerable effect on the rest of the self concept, the self concept also has a considerable influence on body image. If we feel unloved and unlovable, we may think of ourself as ugly no matter what the mirror tries to tell us. When we are deeply anxious or guilty, we not infrequently displace our concerns to our body and imagine we are ill or diseased in some way.

The image we project is under our control to some extent. We each have a personal style, a way of dressing, adorning, grooming, and using our body which relates to the person we are or want to be. Our style may have symbolic or even political significance, announcing a personal definition of ourself and what we stand for. For example, a seemingly simple matter such as hair length or hair fashion can be an important emblem of our identity.

Our body constantly changes throughout the life span, and our image of it changes too. However, perception may lag behind or outpace bodily change. The growth spurt during the adolescent years can be upsetting to the teenager (not to mention his parents), who in some ways seems to be a child in the body of an adult. Bodily changes occurring in middle and old age may be denied, resisted, or insistently camouflaged or, at the other extreme, they may be grossly overexaggerated into a one-foot-in-the-grave panic or depression.

Research suggests that body perceptions are frequently distorted or faulty. We may believe ourself to be ugly even though others see us as quite attractive (or it can be the other way around). Or we may think we are in precarious health, even seriously ill, although all medical findings are negative. Or, if we have been taught to focus on intellectual activities, we may be little aware of our body, and out of touch with ourself below the neck or inside the skin.

Many personal growth or human potential movements these days emphasize the need for increased bodily awareness. Workers in these movements maintain that until we know our body we cannot know ourself or be in full possession of ourself. A number of approaches have been devised for awakening, enlivening, and relaxing the body and for increasing bodily awareness—both outside and in.

Body landmarks

In the lead article in Topic 2, Seymour Fisher laments that little study has been made of body image although this area provides important clues to self understanding. He notes the difficulty we have in building up an accurate image of our body but emphasizes the influence this image—accurate or not—has on our behavior. Research demonstrates that body experience can shape interpretation of the outside world. Fisher's own research intriguingly suggests that individuals tend to focus attention on certain sectors (landmarks) of their bodies and some sectors are tied to fairly distinct psychological conflicts.

Body stereotypes

Don Hamachek presents evidence in the second reading that body appearance is an important determiner of self esteem and body build is related to personality. He also demonstrates there are certain stereotypes associated with certain kinds of body build. To some extent these body stereotypes determine how other people value and react to us, and this in turn influences how we regard our own body and ourself as a person.

Body awareness

Although Fisher feels present facts are insufficient to provide well-founded techniques for improving body experience, some pathways have been suggested by various professionals and creative laymen involved in personal growth movements. In the third selection Bernard Gunther, a teacher of body awareness at Esalen Institute, describes a method the goal of which is "heightened awareness, contact, and experience." Relaxation, breathing, listening, movement, and touch techniques are used to bring a person "back to his senses" and distribute his attention throughout his body rather than localizing it in his head, as usually seems to happen.

FOR PERSONAL APPLICATION

1. Contrast your body image and your body ideal. What effect does the discrepancy between these two concepts have on you?
2. Discuss your efforts to camouflage or enhance your body to lessen the discrepancy between your body image and your body ideal.
3. How has your body appearance or body build influenced other people's response to you?
4. How do other people's body appearance or body build influence your response to them?
5. Discuss an experience or set of experiences that has had an important effect on your body image.
6. Discuss the relationship between your body image and your self image or self esteem.
7. Discuss the effect of your body image upon your personality and behavior.
8. Discuss one of your body landmarks, that is, a body area of which you are particularly aware or one that has special significance for you.
9. Discuss the importance of your appearance or body build to your future plans or career.
10. Are you in accord with Gunther's encouragement of sensory awakening or do you share Fisher's cautions? Explain your position.
11. Try a method advocated by Gunther and discuss your reactions to it.
12. Write down a discussion item (not given above) that seems particularly relevant to this topic and you, and discuss it.

FOR SMALL GROUPS

1. *Picturing the self.* Each member draws a picture of himself and shares this picture and his feelings about drawing it with the group. Artistic talent is not important in this exercise. More important are each per-

son's feelings as he draws himself and as he views the picture he has drawn. How much does he resist the task? How well does he know his body? What parts of his body is he sensitive about and perhaps has trouble drawing? How worried is he about how others regard his picture?

2. *Projecting the self.* Each of us has a personal style which includes the way we dress, adorn, and groom ourself and also the way we speak and move our body; this style is related to the person we are or wish to be. In this activity, everyone in the group writes down his view of each member's personal style (including his own). Each description is written on a separate slip of paper, and these (except for the member's view of himself) are gathered by the leader and distributed to the person concerned. Then, each member in turn reads his slips aloud and compares his perceptions of his own personal style with those of the group. Afterwards, the group discusses the feelings and insights that result from this exercise.

3. *Body over mind.* Divide into pairs, designating one partner in each pair the masseur (or masseuse) and the other the subject. For a minute or so each masseur massages the face of his subject into a frown, using a slow, gentle, and repetitive downward motion. Then each masseur massages the face of his subject into a smile, using a similar upward motion. What effect does each of these two motions have on the subject? Finally the partners change roles and now each subject is to think a happy thought while his face is being massaged into a frown and a sad thought while his face is massaged into a smile. What effect does the massage have on the subject's moods?

FOR FURTHER READING

Fast, J. *Body Language.* New York: M. Evans and Lippincott, 1970.

Feldenkrais, M. *Awareness Through Movement: Health Exercises for Personal Growth.* New York: Harper & Row, Publishers, 1972.

Fisher, S. *Body Experience in Fantasy and Behavior.* New York: Appleton-Century-Crofts, Inc., 1970.

Fisher, S. *Body Consciousness: You Are What You Feel.* Englewood Cliffs, N.J.: Prentice-Hall, Inc., 1973.

Gunther, B. *Sense Relaxation Below Your Mind.* New York: Crowell-Collier & Macmillan, Inc., 1968.

Gunther, B. *What to Do Until the Messiah Comes.* New York: The Macmillan Company, 1971.

Scheflen, A. *Body Language and Social Order: Communication as Behavioral Control.* Englewood Cliffs, N.J.: Prentice-Hall, Inc., 1972.

EXPERIENCING YOUR BODY: YOU ARE WHAT YOU FEEL

Seymour Fisher

There is no more fascinating sight than your own image looking back at you in a mirror. You are drawn to it in a half-embarrassed way, excited and intensely involved. Do you remember the last time someone showed you a photograph of yourself? Wasn't there a surge of feeling and a deep curiosity about "How do I look?" Perhaps, too, you have noticed the strange entrancement even animals display at the sight of their mirror double.

Your body encompasses a sector of space that is uniquely your own. It represents your base of operations in the world, the outward manifestation of your being and identity. No other object is so persistently with you. Unceasingly, even when you are asleep, you receive enormous quantities of information from your body. Your decisions, fantasies, even your dreams are influenced by the sensations emanating from it. Yet it is only in the last two decades that serious scientific attention has been given to the study of the body as a psychological phenomenon.

For centuries scientists have studied the body as an anatomical structure and a biological system, leaving its psychological aspects to other disciplines. Artists and writers, for example, traditionally have devoted great energy to capturing the "feel" of the body in dramatic contexts. Eastern philosophies such as yoga have enjoyed a considerable measure of Western popularity in recent years, in part because of their supposed power to put the individual closer to his own body. Similarly, the so-called "drug culture" has

drawn on body experience; LSD users, for example, report that the chemical frequently produces the feeling that parts of the body have become detached or that the boundary between the body and the outside world has dissipated.

But even the average person must admit to a curiosity about his body and a preoccupation with the psychological experiences it presents to him. He is concerned about the impression his body makes on others; he experiences anxiety about the potential vulnerability of his body to disease and trauma; he uses "gut" cues to help him decide whether or not to get involved with certain people or confront certain situations; he puts out large sums of money to shape and camouflage his appearance so that it will conform to his idealized concept of the "good body." Indeed, a major portion of advertising is devoted to products that claim to improve the individual's relationship with his body—by making it cleaner, more fragrant, stronger, sexier.

The task of making sense of our own bodies is not as simple as we might hope or expect. As each individual matures, he is confronted with the problems of integrating an endless barrage of sensations and assimilating the meanings adults ascribe to various sectors of his frame. He discovers complicated rules prescribing the areas he can touch, talk about, look at, and even think about. He is puzzled by the multiple, and often opposed meanings, assigned to the same body area. He learns, for example, that the back of his body is simultaneously a spatial dimension, a place where punishment is applied, and a locus for concern about anal sphincter control; yet the same area also remains obscure because he cannot get a direct view of it.

The child's attempt to construct a complete psychological map of his body is further hindered by the negative messages he receives from others about such an enterprise. His parents are reluctant to talk about body events and, in fact, become angry or embarrassed when he explicitly mentions certain organs or orifices. He learns that the available vocabulary for describing his own body experiences is sparse and tinged with an illicit flavor. Moreover, the child soon realizes that the culture does not trust body experiences; his education focuses on cultivating intellectual capacities, but his teachers insist that he control body impulses that are likely to "break out" if not closely monitored. Growing up in such an atmosphere, a child finds it almost impossible to examine or codify his body experiences realistically. Hasty glimpses of body terrain and fragments of anatomical information must be pieced together with little or no outside help. For these reasons, the individual is inclined to view his body as having alien qualities and to entertain numerous irrational notions about it.

In fact, although an individual experiences his body more often and in far greater depth than he does any other object in his environment, his perceptions of this, his dearest possession, remain distorted throughout his life. For example, when the average person is called upon to describe or make judgments about his body, he displays considerable inaccuracy. In studies in which persons have been asked to indicate the sizes of various body parts (e.g., head, arms), they often grossly over- or underestimate their true proportions. In one experiment Leo Schneiderman asked subjects to stand in front of a novel full-length mirror consisting of multiple panels that could be moved in such a way as to distort their mirror image in known quantitative terms. When subjects were confronted with the distorted image and asked to reconstruct their true appearance by manipulating the movable mirror panels, they frequently erred. They were indeed surprised to discover how vague their knowledge of their own appearance really was.

Other investigators have found that it is not very difficult to arrange conditions in which the individual fails to recognize pictures of himself. For example, if you take a picture of an individual's shadow profile without his knowledge and subsequently show him a series of shadow profile pictures that include his own as well as those of several other individuals, he will rarely recognize his own. But if you ask him to guess about the personal qualities of each profile pictured, he will say more favorable things about his own silhouette than he will about the others. This repeatedly validated finding suggests that even where there is lack of conscious recognition, one's own image still elicits defensive ego involvement (in the form of self-praise) at the unconscious level. Lack of conscious recognition has also been demonstrated with respect to pictures of one's

hands, and even one's face, if presented for only a brief duration.

Freud was one of the first to note, anecdotally, the difficulty we have in identifying our own image when we come across it unexpectedly. The eminent doctor was sitting in a train sleeping car when a sudden jolt opened the door of the washroom and "an aged man, wearing a dressing gown and a cap" entered his compartment. Just as he was about to inform this stranger that he was intruding, Freud discovered that the stranger was actually his own image reflected in the mirror.

One of the problems of maintaining an accurate picture of your own body is that the image needs to be repeatedly revised. There is often a lag between the occurrence of change in your body and the incorporation of this change into your body model. Consider the effects of aging. Many people have been startled to discover on meeting an old friend after a long separation that the friend perceives much greater signs of aging than the individual had recognized in himself. This lag is especially apparent in the blind. For example, a man of middle age who had lost his sight when he was young told me that his image of himself was still that of the child he had last seen in the mirror years ago. Although others responded to him as a middle-aged adult, he could only visualize himself physically in the form of a young boy.

The so-called "phantom limb" provides another striking example of the difficulty in keeping one's body image up to date. When a person loses a projecting body part such as an arm or a nose because of trauma or surgery, he often continues to experience that part as if it were still present. The sensations that seem to emanate from beyond the stump are often so vivid that he may momentarily forget about his loss and try to use the missing part. After a while, however, the phantom limb fades and usually disappears permanently. This phenomenon has been attributed by some to the fact that the sudden loss of a major body sector is too radical a change to "accept." Only gradually does the new pattern of body sensations become assimilated, and the body concept therefore becomes more accurate.

Although the oblique way in which the individual builds up and maintains a model of his body makes it difficult for him to use body cues rationally, there is no doubt that whatever model he *does* evolve strongly influences his behavior. The individual's body concept is an influential intermediary in his transactions with what is "out there." A person who regards his body as weak and fragile will behave less boldly than one who perceives his body as a well-defended place. Similarly, a person who turns away from his body because he experiences it as bad and ugly may turn to intellectual activities as compensation.

Many sophisticated and reliable procedures for evaluating a person's body concept now are available. Reactions to one's mirror image, inkblot interpretations, drawings of the human figure, estimates of body size—such measures of body feelings have proven to be diversely correlated with personality traits, ability to tolerate stress, conduct in intimate group situations, and even psychosomatic symptoms.

Some of the most interesting work being done today by body image researchers is aimed at demonstrating that body experiences can shape an individual's interpretations of the outside world. In a rather ingenious study, Stuart Valins asked men in a laboratory setting to judge the attractiveness of a series of pictures of seminude girls. The men were told that while they were making these judgments their heart rate would be recorded. However, it was added, because of a "defect" in the equipment, they would be able to hear the sound of the heartbeat as it was being picked up. Valins proceeded to manipulate the faked audible heartbeat so that it changed perceptibly while each man was judging certain of the pictures, but remained unchanged for all the others. The final judgments were significant; the men decided that the most attractive pictures were those of the girls they were looking at when they thought their heart rate had changed. The findings of this study, replicated by other investigators, demonstrated that each man's perception of what seemed to be going on within his own body had a definite impact on his opinions of the world around him.

Another experiment found that a person's mood can be influenced by artificially molding his facial muscles. Explaining to his experimental subjects that he was studying the activity of facial muscles, James D. Laird manipulated these muscles so that to an external observer the subjects seemed either to be "smiling" or "frowning."

The subjects had no idea what expression the experimenter had "put on" their face by means of his manipulations. Yet when measures of mood were obtained, the "frown" and "smile" conditions were found to produce opposite mood effects. Somehow, the position of the facial muscles was perceived and interpreted, causing a significant shift in how happy or sad the individual felt.

Rorschach inkblots provide another illustration of the influence that one's body sensations have on his perception of the outside world. The Rorschach, of course, is based on a long-standing psychological theory that one's interpretations of ambiguous stimuli will reveal hidden problems that the individual does not consciously recognize or is afraid to talk about freely. But in studies conducted in my own laboratory, Sidney Cleveland and I discovered that feelings about the body alone can influence the way a person interprets the vague patterns presented to him. The way an individual experiences the outer, peripheral regions of his body will be expressed in the peripheral regions of the objects he creates from the inkblots. For example, people differ in how clearly they perceive their body to have a defensive sheath capable of protecting them from intrusion. Some feel open and vulnerable; others feel well-fortified. The more secure an individual feels about his body boundaries, we discovered, the more he produces Rorschach images with protective sheltering qualities: caves with rocky walls, turtles with hard shells, tanks, shields, persons covered with blankets.

An individual's feelings of boundary security are correlated with how clearly he is aware of his boundary sheath—skin and muscle. Heightened awareness of this sheath seems to contribute to a sense of being adequately bounded and thus more secure. Many of us have employed this trick in fearful surroundings. Lying in bed, a home owner becomes anxious about a break-in and pictures the enclosing walls of his house. A driver entering a storm assures himself of his safety by glancing at the walls of his metal cocoon. Perhaps even more common is the preference many people have for small bedrooms or tight-fitting clothing.

With this notion of body security in mind, we conducted several experiments to determine if heightened awareness of the body sheath would have an effect on the interpretation of inkblots. In one experimental condition, subjects were exposed to experiences that caused them to focus on their skin and muscle. They were asked to report the occurrence of sensations in these areas while various stimuli, such as stroking, were applied to the skin. In the second condition, attention was drawn away from the outside of the body and focused upon the interior, with subjects reporting such phenomena as heart sensations or the feel of swallowing a glass of water. The results of these manipulations validated our assumption that awareness of certain body areas will affect one's feeling of security and, in turn, the perceptions of the outside world. When attention was focused on the skin and muscles, the number of protected inkblot images, such as a man in armor, rose; when attention was directed toward the interior, such inkblot fantasies decreased.

A person's body experiences may permeate his outlook in a number of unique ways. Studies have shown that if a subject is asked to compose imaginative stories, his tales will be affected by whether he is lying down or sitting up; his judgment of how far away an object is will depend on whether or not he feels the object has a meaningful relationship to his body; his beliefs about how friendly others are toward him may depend upon his faith in the security of his body boundaries, and so forth.

All of these body experiences will affect the activities of normal, healthy individuals. But what happens to the body model during psychological breakdown? For years psychiatric literature has suggested that schizophrenics suffer gross fragmentation of the body model. Vivid case histories have been published about schizophrenics who fancy that they have lost important chunks of their anatomy or who perceive their bodies as grotesquely altered—"dead," or transformed into the opposite sex, for example. However, more systematic studies have revealed that the body model stands up pretty well to the impact of the schizophrenic process. In fact, investigators have had a difficult time demonstrating truly impressive differences between psychiatric patients and normals in their mode of body experience. When one sifts through the scientific literature about this matter, only a few limited conclusions seem warranted. Schizophrenic patients *do* report a greater number of distorted and unusual body sensations than do normal persons, but the difference is small. And, somewhat surprisingly, schizophrenics do not exceed neurotic patients in this respect. Even in the throes of severe disturbance, the body concept seems to remain relatively well preserved.

One specific dimension that *has* shown promise in differentiating psychiatric patients from normal persons is perception of body size. Psychiatric patients are concerned about sensations of body shrinkage and smallness. They feel reduced in stature or perceive one or more body parts to be smaller than they should be. When asked to make numerical estimates of the sizes of various body parts, they usually overreact, either underestimating or compensatorily overestimating the true proportions.

I have suggested that these perceptions of shrinkage represent a view of self that is depreciated and devalued. The psychiatric patient is often one who, in his own eyes, has failed or suffered major rejection by the culture. He feels lowly and unwanted, and his Lilliputian sensations reflect his down-graded view of himself.

In the course of probing the nature of abnormal body experiences, we have learned that certain body feelings, once considered extremely pathognomic, are actually quite normal. A good example is provided by the phenomenon of *depersonalization*. Early psychiatric literature asserted that the patient who reports that his body feels alien, as if it did not belong to him, had a particularly poor prognosis for recovery. Depersonalization was supposed to be a mark of advanced pathology. However, several investigators have recently reported that depersonalization is a common reaction to stress among normal persons. For example, depersonalization has been prominently detected in normal persons who become anxious when swallowing an unknown drug during an experiment. There seems to be adaptive value in responding to stress-induced anxiety by getting "distance" from your own body, thereby decreasing personal involvement with it. Furthermore, normal persons who differ in their use of depersonalization also differ in other aspects of their behavior. For example, they have contrasting ways of responding to certain kinds of sexual stimulation. I have found that women who prefer vaginal stimulation to manual clitoral stimulation in reaching orgasm have an unusually strong depersonalized perspective toward their own body. I have described these findings in detail in *The Female Orgasm: Personality, Physiology, Fantasy*, published by Basic Books.

It would be impossible for anyone to attend simultaneously to all of the things happening in his body. He would be overwhelmed and ultimately confused. Just as one learns to attend to only certain auditory stimuli, each person must learn to attend to the various sectors of his body in some pattern that is meaningful and useful to him. Each individual, we have found, actually is rather consistent in his style of distributing body attention, although such consistency holds true more for men than for women. One man may be unusually aware of his head, another of his legs, and still another of the right as compared with the left side of his body. What is an outstanding body landmark for one may be almost invisible for another. Also, we have learned that each body sector is associated with a fairly distinct conflict or tension theme.

Specific conflict themes turn out to be linked to the following areas: head, back versus front, mouth, eyes, stomach, heart, right versus left. For example, the male with heightened awareness of his back (as compared to the front of his body) is often preoccupied with urges to express hostile soiling feelings toward others that evoke alarm in him because they are experienced as dirty and indicative of loss of self-control (perhaps in a way reminiscent of the child who fails to control his anal sphincter as expected by his parents). The male with heightened awareness of his heart is religiously oriented and especially conflicted about guilt feelings. One of the most intriguing patterns we discovered indicated that the male who is grossly more aware of the right as compared with the left side of his body is in conflict about his sexual relationship with women. He feels inhibited in the presence of women, is less likely to date, and gets anxious when confronted by stimuli with sexual connotations. From such findings we concluded that when an individual habitually concentrates a large amount of attention upon a body sector he is doing so because that sector is linked with a conflictual issue that persistently troubles him. What utility might such an association have? Most likely, the individual's

investment of attention in specific body areas has some adaptive or control function. This is somewhat analogous to the piece of string that is tied around a child's finger when he is sent to the store so that he will remember what he is supposed to buy when he gets there. An individual's long-term focus of attention on a body area could serve, therefore, as a kind of "string around the finger" reminding him that certain things should or should not be done.

The persistent concentration of attention upon a body area provides a guiding signal to the individual to restrain the expression of conflictual impulses associated with that area. For example, heightened back awareness would signal that control should be maintained over hostile besmirching urges; or magnified awareness of the right side of the body would warn against heterosexual involvement. Within this framework an individual's style of perceiving his body can be regarded as a part of the elaborate system he evolves to control his behavior. As he develops attitudes toward basic issues in the world, they become coded in terms of differential awareness of specific body parts.

The regulatory function of this concentration of awareness is apparent in the much simpler case of monitoring the muscles of an arm to keep it rigid or the sphincter muscles of a full bladder to inhibit urination. There is also interesting anecdotal information in the psychiatric literature about instances in which patients, having been psychotherapeutically relieved of a preoccupation with sensations or minor symptoms in a body part, suddenly show a dramatic release of affect upon some theme. The investment of concern in the body area apparently served to inhibit awareness of the underlying anxiety that came to the surface when the superficial concern was removed.

We have also completed experiments in which we artificially altered the individual's awareness of a body part to demonstrate the control function of concentration on that region. The greater the amount of attention a man habitually directs to his heart, the greater his religiosity and anxious concern over feelings of guilt. In one experimental procedure a group of men were given exercises designed to heighten their heart awareness; immediately afterward they were briefly exposed to a series of words, half of which referred to guilt themes (e.g., wrong, fault, judge) and half of which did not. They then were asked to recall as many of these words as possible. The purpose of the learning task was to detect defensive emotional attitudes toward the guilt words in terms of the relative proportion of guilt and non-guilt words recalled. Groups of control subjects went through the same procedure, but their degree of heart awareness was not altered. It was found that the group that was made more heart aware had a significantly greater tendency to forget the guilt words. By concentrating a man's attention on his heart, we were able to alter his receptivity to guilt themes.

In view of the obvious differences between male and female bodies, it would be logical to expect that men and women would construct quite different images of their bodies. We do, in fact, find radically different styles of body perception related to sex. At this moment in history the question of body superiority–inferiority most naturally arises. Freud did little for the women's movement by explicitly declaring that the female has a depreciated, inferior concept of her body. A little girl is traumatized, he reasoned, upon discovering that her genital organ is different from the male's, whose phallic attributes are equated with power and strength. Presumably, this trauma leaves indelible scars; she is destined to interpret her lack of a penis as a sign of body inferiority. Thus the idea grew that the average woman is less secure and more disturbed about her body than is the average man.

Body image research, however, indicates that precisely the opposite is true. For example, we put a series of male and female rubber masks on the faces of men and women and requested the subjects to describe each mask as they glimpsed it in a mirror when a light flashed on. To our surprise, the men were made much more anxious than the women by this procedure. They were flustered by the female masks and made significantly more errors when trying to describe the characteristics of their disguised appearance. The solidity of these observations was affirmed by a second study that produced the same results. It was apparent that the men were less able to cope adequately with the change in body concept imposed by the experimental condition.

Other scientific evidence indicates a similar trend. It has been demonstrated that the average woman perceives her body to be better protected and enclosed by a more secure boundary than does the average man. In one study we found that the male was more disturbed by the threat of injecting adrenaline into his body than was the female. Other investigators have observed that men are relatively more preoccupied with themes of body destruction. Even in their dreams men portray themselves as threatened by imminent body damage more often than do women. Several appraisals of males and females hospitalized for surgery reveal greater anxiety in men than in women about the body-threatening implications of the situation. Men may carefully control their open expression of such anxiety, but inwardly they are more disturbed than women.

In addition to the perception of body threat, there is another important difference in the way males and females experience their bodies. Diverse sources have noted that women are more aware of their body feelings than are men and that they are more positive in accepting these experiences. David J. Van Lennep reported that female children not only display greater body awareness than male children, but the magnitude of this difference between the sexes becomes larger after adolescence. In addition, the degree of body awareness in women is known to be correlated with positive attributes such as a clear sense of identity, while in men it is linked with certain categories of conflictual preoccupation. This confirms what we already observe in everyday life. Girls and women invest much more open interest in the body than do their male counterparts. They feel free to study their own appearance and to experiment with techniques for altering it by means of clothing and cosmetics. A male who displays much direct or open interest in his body (except with reference to athletic activities) is regarded as a deviant.

A woman apparently sees a clearer and more meaningful relationship between her body and her life role than a man. Despite the influence of Women's Liberation, the chief goals of most women still revolve about being attractive, entering into marriage, and producing children. Such aims readily permit the female to see her body as a vehicle for her life career. This is not true for the man. Unless he becomes a professional athlete, he can perceive little connection between his body attributes and the requirements for status and success. Male power and accomplishment are increasingly defined in terms of intellect, cleverness, business acumen, and so forth. The low status jobs are the ones that require body strength. As I have reported in *Body Experience in Fantasy and Behavior* (Appleton-Century-Crofts), an important contribution of the research on body experience is that it has cast serious doubt on stereotyped ideas about the inferiority of the feminine body concept.

Our expanding knowledge about the body as a psychological object encourages thought about the potential practical and therapeutic applications of this knowledge. Intriguing possibilities are becoming visible. For example, efforts are under way in both Europe and the United States to evaluate the potentialities of treating psychological disturbance by altering body experience. Austin M. Des Lauriers has suggested that a major problem of the schizophrenic is that he has lost an articulated image of his body; without it he has little individuality or ability to test reality. Des Lauriers has devised therapeutic techniques to make the schizophrenic more aware of his body, particularly its boundary, and claims considerable clinical success with this approach. Others have indirectly affirmed Des Laurier's concepts by demonstrating that exercise and systematic stimulation that highlight muscle and skin sensations in the schizophrenic individual do, indeed, increase his boundary security.

Alterations of body experience also are being explored with "emotionally disturbed" children and those with serious learning problems. Preliminary findings suggest that certain types of learning difficulties may be improved by giving the child a more realistic image of his body, especially its spatial dimensions.

Research analyses of body feelings may prove to be of value in clarifying puzzling complications that arise when people must adapt to body disabilities and medical procedures. We now know that fantasies of body vulnerability may cause an individual to respond with grossly inappropriate distress to minor body trauma and to fail completely to adjust to more serious chronic disablement. We have leads that suggest that the amount and kind of psychological disturbance evoked by an injury may depend upon subtle differences in its location upon the body. An injury on the right side may pose a different form of threat than one on the left side; trauma to the back may arouse different kinds of anxieties than if it involved the front. Body attitudes also seem to play a role in the perplexing problem of why people delay in seeking medical treatment after they discover a serious symptom in themselves. Often the delay is so great that a disease process will have advanced to a point where it is no longer amenable to treatment. Paradoxically, it appears that the individual who feels secure about his body is most inclined toward such irrational delay. Finally, it should be noted that we are beginning to see body attitudes as potentially powerful predictors of the psychological effects produced by various drugs. This is quite logical if we remember that an important part of the impact of drugs involves alterations of body sensations.

Various individuals and cults currently acknowledge the importance of the experienced body as a basic component of life adjustment. It is interesting that heightened concern with body experience has coincided with the investigation of body image in the psychological laboratories and clinics. Here, however, the similarity ends: Those involved with these cults or movements are unwilling to wait for the facts to come in. Instead, they have embarked on impulsive quests via drugs and meditation, for example, in the hope of hitting upon new principles that will make possible "revolutionary" innovations in the body model and overall well-being. But the odds are against these haphazard approaches. Only systematic study will provide sound principles and realistic techniques for altering body experience in helpful ways. Indeed, there is little doubt that the body image is one of the most important—and, ironically, most neglected—phenomena in the scientific quest for understanding of our psychological selves.

BODY IMAGE AND SELF-CONCEPT

Don E. Hamachek

How a person feels about himself is related to how he feels about his body. The self-image is first and above all a body image. In fact, it is very likely that a child's first distinction between "me" and "you," between "I am running" and "he is running,' is formed on the basis of his sensitivity to his own muscular reactions, his own viscera, his own bumps and falls. These internal sensory imputs may provide the nucleus for an emerging self.

A person's height, weight, girth, eye color, hair color, complexion, and general body proportions are very much related to his feelings of personal adequacy. The pace of a boy's total growth in relation to other boys in his class, or the extent of a girl's overall development in comparison to other girls her age play an important part in how they feel about themselves. In this chapter our attention turns to an examination of the relationships between self-concept variables and physical growth and developmental outcomes.

PHYSICAL TYPOLOGIES AND PERSONALITY

For thousands of years, philosophers and physicians and, more recently, anthropologists and developmental psychologists have speculated about and researched the relationships between physical factors and personality. Efforts to classify body types date back as early as 400 B.C. when Hippocrates wrote about the "humors" of the body and the effect of these "humors" on person-

ality. In their review of the literature dealing with physical factors and personality, Sheldon and others state: "It is a curious and perhaps significant fact that 2500 years ago Hippocrates said that there are two roots of human beings. The long thins and the short thicks. Almost all simple classifications of type since that time have nearly the same basis, despite variety of nomenclature and detail of description."[1] Kretschmer[2] used a somewhat similar classification of body type in his controversial but influential hypotheses about the relations of body build to temperament and mental illness. For example, he said that any given body can be typed as *asthenic* (thin and frail), *pyknik* (short, soft, rounded), *athletic* (muscular), or *dysplastic* (one type in one segment and another type somewhere else). He asserted that if the asthenic type becomes mentally ill, he tends to develop schizophrenic symptoms. The normal version of these symptoms, such as idealism, introversion and withdrawal, were supposed to be found in normal people with asthenic bodies. Normal people with pyknik bodies, he said, tend to exhibit traits such as fluctuating moodiness, extroversion, joviality, and realism; mentally ill persons of this type were said to develop manic-depressive symptoms.

Among the more recent attempts to develop a method of classifying personality on the basis of physical characteristics, the efforts of Sheldon[3] has attracted the most attention from contemporary psychologists. He rejected the idea that individuals can be divided into distinct physical types and so he devised a method of classifying them according to three basic components. The terms used to describe the components are analogous to the names of the cell layers in the embryo from which different body tissues originate. The first or *endomorphic* component refers to the prominence of the intestines and other visceral organs. Obese individuals typically fit this category. The second or *mesomorphic* component refers to bone and

[1] W. H. Sheldon, S. S. Stevens, and W. B. Tucker, *The Varieties of Human Physique* (New York: Harper & Row, Publishers, 1940), p. 419.

[2] E. Kretschmer, *Physique and Characters*, 2nd ed., W. J. H. Sprott, trans. (New York: Harcourt, Brace & World, Inc., 1925).

[3] W. H. Sheldon, *Atlas of Men: A Guide for Somatotyping the Adult Male at All Ages* (New York: Harper & Row, Publishers, 1954).

muscle. The wide-shouldered, narrow-hipped, muscular athlete fits this category. The third or *ectomorphic* component is based on delicacy of skin, fine hair, and sensitive nervous system. Tall thin, stoop-shouldered individuals fit this category.

In rating a person's physical characteristics, Sheldon's system assigns one digit between 1 and 7 for each component in the order endomorph, mesomorph, and ectomorph with high numbers indicating more of a component. For example, a football fullback might be rated 3-6-2, which would suggest that he was low in respect to endomorphy, athletically powerful (with a 6 in mesomorphy), and low in the more delicate features of ectomorphy. A rating of 5-4-2 would describe a rounded but relatively muscular and sturdy individual and so on. Figures 1 and 2 will give you an idea of the differences among these three components as they are seen in boys at two different age levels.

To each of these physical components Sheldon assigned a corresponding syndrome of psychological characteristics. For example, the predominately endomorphic person is classified as one who loves to eat, seeks bodily comforts, is sociable and outgoing. The predominately mesomorphic person is energetic, likes exercise, and is direct in manner. The ectomorph is classified as sensitive, given to worrying, fears groups, and needs solitude.

Sheldon's system for "somatotizing" individuals has not been universally accepted among developmental psychologists and, in fact, his technique of classifying and describing body build has been strongly criticized.[4,5] The fact is endomorphs (obese, heavy) are *not all* large eaters, outgoing, and sociable. Mesomorphs (athletic, muscular) are *not all* energetic and athletically inclined. Ectomorphs (tall, thin) are *not all* sensitive, introverted, and fearful. (Indeed, some ectomorphs are aggressive, fearless basketball players whose sensitivity, if that's what you could call it, is apparent only by the pained expression on their faces when caught on the tailend of an opposing team's fast break.) As we shall see, there *are* relationships between physical factors and personality, although it is doubtful that these relationships can be packaged as easily as suggested by Sheldon's numerical somatotizing system.

In considering the notion that certain personality characteristics are related to dimensions of physique, we are, of course, going beyond the mere description of what behaviors are associated with what body builds and are touching upon explanatory matters. The association between physical dimensions and behavioral characteristics at least suggests that the enduring attributes we see here are due to basic physiological processes, the same physiological processes that produce the structure of the body. If such a relationship could be demonstrated, we would be making heady progress toward an explanation of the unique organization of an individual's personality make-up. At the moment, however, the best we can do is speculate that the properties of the inherited physique help determine not only what a person can do, *but what he and those who are close to him expect that he should be able to do.*

Let us turn our attention now to what research says about the relationships between body structure and personality.

BODY BUILD AND PERSONALITY CORRELATES

Most of us don't have to go any further than our own personal experiences to know that different body proportions in men and women elicit different feelings, attitudes, and stereotypes in us. When we meet someone for the first time part of our response to that person is influenced by his physical features and proportions. An ingenious study by Brodsky[6] has demonstrated very nicely that there are indeed different social reactions to different body builds. He prepared five 15-inch silhouettes of males, representing: (1) endomorph (obese); (2) endomesomorph (muscular, but short and heavy); (3) mesomorph (athletic, muscular); (4) ectomesomorph (muscular, but

[4] W. H. Hammond, "The Status of Physical Types," *Human Biology*, 29 (1957), 223–241.

[5] L. G. Humphreys, "Characteristics of Type Concepts with Special Reference to Sheldon's Typology," *Psychological Bulletin*, 54 (1957), 218–228.

[6] C. M. Brodsky, *A Study of Norms for Body Form-Behavior Relationships* (Washington, D.C.: Catholic University of America Press, 1954).

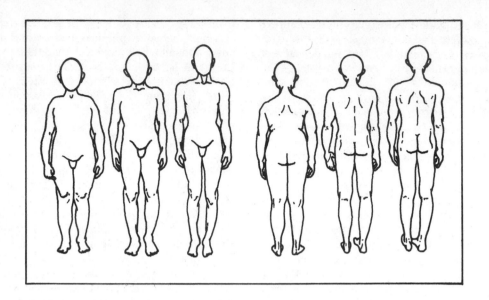

FIGURE 1. *Front and rear views, reading from the left, of an endomorph, a meso-morph, and an ectomorph boy, aged about 11½ years.* (*From F. K. Shuttleworth, "The Adolescent Period: A Pictorial Atlas,"* Monographs of the Society for Research in Child Development, 14 (1949) (Ser. No. 50). *By permission of The Society for Research in Child Development, Inc.*)

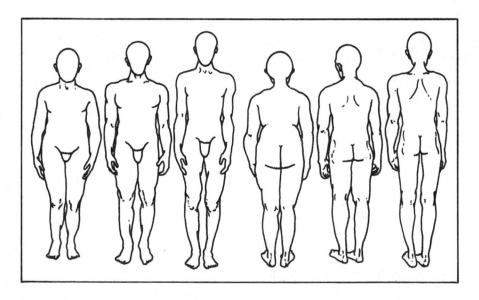

FIGURE 2. *The three boys shown in Fig. 1, in the same order from left to right, at 15 years of age.* (*From F. K. Shuttleworth, "The Adolescent Period: A Pictorial Atlas,"* Monographs of the Society for Research in Child Development, 14 (1949) (Ser. No. 50). *By permission of The Society for Research in Child Development, Inc.*)

tall and thin); (5) ectomorph (thin and tall). He also constructed a questionnaire containing such questions as the following: Which one of this group of five men is most aggressive? Which one is least aggressive?

Brodsky's research population consisted of seventy-five male college students from Howard University, all or almost all of whom would be expected to be Negro; and fifty white male college students from George Washington University. One of the things which Brodsky discovered was that there were no important differences in the way the two groups responded, which lends weight to the idea of a "cultural stereotype," or characteristic way of regarding body build.

Personality characteristics were usually assigned by the respondents in Brodsky's study to the "pure" silhouettes: the endomorph, mesomorph, and ectomorph. Those characteristics assigned to a given silhouette by a third or more of the respondents are discussed in the extracts following.

More than one third of the respondents labeled the endomorph silhouette as representing the man who probably eats the most, would make the worst soldier, the poorest athlete, would be the poorest professor of philosophy, can endure pain the least well, would make the least successful military leader, would be least likely to be chosen leader, would make the poorest university president, would be the least aggressive, would drink the most, be least preferred as a personal friend (but, ironically, would have many friends), would make the poorest doctor, and would probably put his own interests before those of others.[7]

As you can see, the picture which emerged was an almost consistently negative one. If there is any truth to the idea that a person behaves as he is expected to behave, a dismal picture of the direction of personality growth of the endomorph is presented by this study.

The *mesomorph* fared as favorably as the endomorph did unfavorably. The respondents said that he would make the best athlete, the most successful military leader, and the best soldier. They chose him as the man who would assume

[7] *Ibid.*, pp. 15–21.

leadership, as well as the man who would be elected as leader. He was judged to be nonsmoker, and to be self-sufficient, in the sense of needing friends the least. However, he was most preferred as a friend, and was judged to have many friends. Respondents also said that he would be the most aggressive, would endure pain the best, would be least likely to have a nervous breakdown, and would probably drink the least.

The stereotype of the *ectomorph* is far less socially desirable than that of the mesomorph, but in general more favorable than that of the endomorph. The ectomorph was judged to be the most likely to have a nervous breakdown before the age of thirty, to eat the least and the least often, to be a heavy smoker, to be least self-sufficient, in the sense of needing friends the most (but, unfortunately, was judged to have the fewest friends), to hold his liquor the worst, to make a poor father, and, as a military leader, to be likely to sacrifice his men with the greatest emotional distress.[8]

This study suggests that there may be characteristic stereotyped ways of reacting to different types of male physique, and that the trend of this reaction is such as to favor the mesomorph. Other studies support these findings. For example, in a study of high school senior boys and a sample of college girls, Cortés and Gatti[9] found that endomorphs rated themselves significantly more often as kind, relaxed, warm, soft-hearted; mesomorphs were also found to demonstrate a higher need for achievement than the other two body types.[10]

In an extensive study linking body build and behavior, Walker[11] had 125 preschool children rated by their teachers on sixty-four behavior items. He somatotyped the children using Sheldon's classification system. With regard to the relations between behavioral and physique data,

[8] *Ibid.*

[9] J. Cortés and F. M. Gatti, "Physique and Self-description of Temperament," *Journal of Consulting Psychology*, 29 (1965), 432–439.

[10] J. Cortés and F. M. Gatti, "Physique and Motivation," *Journal of Consulting Psychology*, 30 (1966), 408–414.

[11] R. N. Walker, "Body Build and Behavior in Young Children: I. Body Build and Nursery School Teachers' Ratings," *Monographs of the Society for Research in Child Development*, 27: No. 3 (1962).

more of the predictions were confirmed for the boys than for the girls, which suggests that physical factors may be more important in affecting the behavior of boys. Despite the popular concern about female measurements, our cultural stereotypes and expectations concerning physique and behavior do seem to be more firmly established for males. Consistent with the studies already cited, the mesomorphic body build, even among preschoolers, showed the strongest relationship to the behavioral ratings, especially for boys. Walker concluded:

> Characteristic of both boys and girls high in mesomorphy is dominative assertiveness (leader in play, competitive, self-assertive, easily angered, attacks others, etc.), high energy output, openness of expression, and fearlessness. The girls combine this assertiveness with socialness, cheerfulness, and warmth, the boys' items give more suggestion of hostility (quarrelsome, revengeful, inconsiderate) and of an impulsive, headlong quality to their activity (daring, noisy, quick, accident-prone, self-confident, etc.).[12]

In regard to the ectomorphic physique, Walker made the following observations:

> In common for both sexes are items suggesting a certain aloofness. . . . For boys, the items in general define a cautious, quiet child, not self-assertive, hesitant to give offense, looking to adults rather than to children for approval, sensitive, slow to recover from upsets. He appears lacking in energy reserves. . . . For girls, the composite picture is similar but tends more to indicate a somberness of outlook—unfriendly, tense . . . irritable.[13]

Additional support for the relationships cited above between personality and body type was obtained from mothers' ratings of these same children.[14]

The stereotypes of the jolly, plump individual, the thin bookworm, and the aggressive meso-

morph may not be very scientific descriptions, but they do establish certain expectations of behavior for both young and old with these body types. For example, a father is probably less apt to encourage a thin ectomorphic son than a muscular mesomorphic son to participate in athletics. These cultural stereotypes are adopted early by children. A case in point is the research of Staffieri,[15] who found that boys as young as six or ten years of age are already in close agreement when it comes to assigning certain personality characteristics to particular body types. For example, he found a remarkably similar tendency for the endomorphic silhouettes to be described as socially offensive and delinquent, the mesomorphic silhouettes as aggressive, outgoing, active, having leadership skills, and the ectomorphic silhouettes as retiring, nervous, shy, and introverted. He also found that ectomorphs and mesomorphs were chosen as the most popular by their peers, leading to the tentative conclusion that endomorphs are less popular, know that they are unpopular, and are inclined to reject their body image.

Body build and personality do seem to be related. These relationships are more definite for boys probably because we are clearer about what the physical criteria are for what a male should look like than we are for females. When it comes to being judged on the basis of physical appearance, the latitude allowed girls is apparently wider than is the case for boys. Be that as it may, the evidence does suggest that the broad-shouldered, muscular, narrow-hipped boy and the well-proportioned girl are more likely to win social approval and acceptance on the basis of pure physique than boys or men and girls or women who are either too heavy or too thin, too tall or too short. High self-confidence and self-esteem are personality correlates frequently associated with mesomorphic physiques in males and females. Although things like, say, leadership qualities, social approval, or high self-esteem are not *caused* by having a nice build or a well-proportioned figure, they may, in fact, be among the positive gains which *result from* a more mesomorphic appearance. Considering the feedback that a per-

---

12 *Ibid.*, p. 78.
13 *Ibid.*
14 R. N. Walker, "Body Build and Behavior in Young Children: II. Body Build and Parent's Ratings," *Child Development*, 34: 1–23 (1963).

15 J. Staffieri, "A Study of Social Stereotype of Body Image in Children," *Journal of Personality and Social Psychology*, 7 (1957), 101–104.

son both gives and receives on the basis of purely physical appearances, it is not difficult to see how an individual's physical proportions can influence his feelings about himself simply by affecting how other people react toward him. The overweight person who grows up in the face of assorted descriptive monikers like "Tubby," "Chubby," "Fatso," or "Lard," or the thin individual who is variously addressed as "Bony Ben," "Skinny Al," "Beanpole Sally," or "Hey, don't stand sideways —can't see ya" is hardly encouraged to develop self-confidence and self-esteem in the same way as is a person who is not markedly overweight, or underweight, or tall, or short. If used for a long enough period of time, the names that were originally meant to describe a person's physique can also have the effect of describing and defining, to some extent, his personality. Thus, the ectomorphic little boy who frequently hears adjectives like "delicate" and "fragile" ascribed to him may in fact grow up to be that kind of person—delicate and fragile with a low threshold for pain, stress, or frustration.

In short, one's physical appearance has a powerful potential for eliciting specific social responses. These can be positive or negative. How a person feels about himself depends, to some degree, on how he feels about the physical part of himself. How he feels about that depends, in large measure, on how others around him make him feel. Which brings us to our next topic for discussion.

BODY IMAGE AS RELATED TO SELF-CONCEPT

William James[16] was among the first psychologists to write specifically about the "physical self" as a way to underscore the fact that a person's physical features have an important place in his concept of self. The expressions "body image" or "body concept" have also been used to denote physical aspects of the self picture.

Like all other aspects of the self-concept, the image a person has of his body is subjective. A person may have a generally positive body image —he likes the way he looks, or he may have a negative body image—how he looks falls short of his expectations for himself.

The fact is, the most material and visible part of the self is our physical body. Like any other object in our physical environment, our bodies are perceived through the various senses. Occupying as it does a substantial portion of our visual and auditory fields, we see and hear a lot of ourselves. In a very important way our bodies come to occupy a central role in our perceptions.

The particular *way* a person perceives his physical body—whether distorted or not—may have important psychological consequences for him. For example, an adolescent boy may be overly concerned about his awkward coordination and refuse to attend dances; a girl may be overly sensitive to what she feels is inadequate breast development and be too embarrassed to date; a young man could have such a "narcissistic" love for his own body development that he neglects doing anything about his social or intellectual growth. Perception of the body relates intimately to perceptions of larger aspects of the self.

Body perception is so firmly established that even drastic changes in the body may not at once result in corresponding changes in body percept. A dramatic illustration of this is what psychologists have called the "phantom limb" phenomenon, which is an almost universal experience among amputation cases. For example, after a person has experienced the amputation of an arm or leg, he typically continues to feel that the limb is still there. In fact, he may feel itching in it, or feel that he can still move it, or even momentarily forget that it is gone and try to use it. Sometimes these feelings are of brief duration and sometimes they endure throughout a person's life. More often, however, they undergo gradual change in their perceived character. For example, Katz[17] has reported that a phantom hand may gradually shrink and move up into the stump so that it is eventually experienced or "felt" as a small hand embedded there. He also noted that sometimes an amputee can walk up to a wall and his hand (the amputated one) seems to go right through it.

[16] William James, *Psychology: The Briefer Course*, G. Allport, ed. (New York: Harper & Row, Publishers, 1961), Chap. 3.

[17] D. Katz, *Gestalt Psychology* (New York: The Ronald Press Company, 1950).

Ordinarily, the body is experienced as a part or aspect of the self, often constituting its outer boundary. But there are some instances in which the body and self are not mutually inclusive. For example, we have probably all had the feeling of waking up in the morning after lying on our arm in such a way as to place it sound asleep so that it seemed as if it were not even a part of us. Even amputations of parts of the body may not be perceived as resections of the self, although there are instances in which the loss of a highly valued part may really be experienced as a partial destruction of self. For example, some years ago a psychology professor friend of mine had an unfortunate power saw accident in which he lost a portion of two fingers on his left hand. He viewed it as a dumb, careless mistake on his part, but persisted in going about the business of maintaining and enhancing his self-esteem and self-regard through being a professor of psychology. Another acquaintance of mine had a similar accident not long ago involving the loss of a portion of his left forefinger and its effect on him was great depression. The difference was that he was a skilled guitarist who earned part of his livelihood by being an entertainer. My psychology friend lost but a finger; my guitar-player friend lost not only part of a finger, but also one means of self-expression and self-support. When we look at it from that point of view, it is easier to see why the loss of part of his finger should be experienced more as a partial loss of self.

If you were to ask a person to specify *where* he feels the center of self to be, he almost always locates it somewhere inside his body. Most often he points it out as somewhere "in the head" or "in back of the eyes." This is not surprising, particularly in light of the fact that we are basically "visually oriented," having our most important commerce with the world around us through our eyes.

There is also evidence to suggest that different people assume different perspectives for the self in relation to the body. In connection to this, consider the following experiment reported by Krech and Crutchfield:

In one demonstration the experimenter traced a script capital E on the subject's forehead. This symbol was deliberately chosen because

its mirror image is a 3. Logically, then, it can be identified as an E or a 3. If he "viewed" the symbol as though he were "looking out" at it from inside his head, he would have perceived it as a 3. If he "viewed" the symbol as though he were looking at his own forehead from the outside, as the experimenter was, he would have reported it to be an E. . . . [T]here are pronounced individual differences in readiness to perceive from the "inside" or the "outside" when no prior set is given. For example, in one demonstration 76 percent of a group of 202 student subjects reported the symbol as a 3 (i.e., in accord with an "inside" perspective), whereas 24 percent reported it as an E. Moreover, the tendency to see the symbol in the latter way (that is, according to an "outside" perspective) was clearly more pronounced in the male than in the female students. Perhaps here is confirmation of the common notion that females (at least in our culture) tend to be more "subjective" in their outlook than do males![18]

THE BODY AND SELF-ESTEEM

There is a considerable amount of evidence to suggest that one's *appearance* is an important determiner of self-esteem, both among men and women. For example, in a study by Secord and Jourard,[19] it was found that the feelings an individual had about his body were commensurate with the feelings that he had about himself as a person. That is, the person[s] who had negative feelings about [their bodies were] also likely to feel negatively about themselves as total persons and vice versa. In a series of studies by the same investigators,[20] [21] college students were asked to indicate the dimensions of different parts of their

[18] D. Krech and R. S. Crutchfield, *Elements of Psychology* (New York: Alfred A. Knopf, 1959), p. 203.

[19] P. F. Secord and S. M. Jourard, "The Appraisal of Body-Cathexis: Body-Cathexis and the Self," *Journal of Consulting Psychology*, 17 (1953), 343–347.

[20] S. M. Jourard and P. F. Secord, "Body-Cathexis and Personality," *British Journal of Psychology*, 46 (1955a), 130–138.

[21] S. M. Jourard and P. F. Secord, "Body-Cathexis and the Ideal Female Figure," *Journal of Abnormal and Social Psychology*, 50 (1955b), 243–246.

bodies, and to rate their feelings of satisfaction with these dimensions. In general, those who were satisfied with their bodies were also apt to be fairly secure and self-confident. In other words, persons who accepted their bodies were more likely to manifest high self-esteem than persons who disliked their bodies.

One possible reason for this relationship between self-acceptance and body-acceptance may be in the fact that the self-ideal includes attitudes related to the appearance of the body, or the so-called body-ideal. Each individual has a more or less clear idea of how he would *like* to look. If his actual body proportions come close to conforming to the dimensions and appearance of his ideal body image, he is more likely to think better of both his physical and nonphysical self. If, on the other hand, his body deviates too far from his body-ideal, then he is more likely to have lower self-esteem. It is not uncommon for a person with a poor body-image to compensate for this deficit by becoming proficient in other ways, such as, for example, developing his intellectual skill, or musical aptitude, or some other special talent or ability. In this way, the emphasis on the body-image is reduced or at least made less important through his ability to "know more" or "perform better" in specific areas than most other people. Of course another, but certainly a less healthy way of handling a poor body-image is by denying the idea that appearance or body-image is important in the first place. "Looks and appearance aren't important—how one behaves is what really counts." This is a praiseworthy attitude—one that most of us probably share to some extent. However, some persons proclaim this attitude as if it were some kind of Magna Charta releasing them from any sort of personal responsibility to themselves and use it to satisfy their needs to avoid the self-discipline involved in, say, eating less, or drinking less, or, in some instances, bathing more.

Usually, a person's body-ideal conforms more or less to the prevailing cultural standards of what a pleasant appearance is and what it is not. Margaret Mead,[22] in her studies of various cul-

tures, has observed that each society has its own idiosyncratic attitudes and standards of personal beauty. The Kalihari desert Bushman, for example, places a high premium on having over-sized hips and buttocks, while in America the desired hip-buttock measurements are much smaller. The American glamor queens of days gone by were considerably heftier than our contemporary *Playmate* foldouts. The cultural concept of an ideal body has consequences for personality hygiene, since the cultural ideal helps shape one's personal body-ideal which, in turn, influences for better or for worse an individual's overall self-esteem.

In a study of college women,[23] it was found that the ideal body proportions were five feet five inches in height, about 120 pounds in weight, and 35 inches, 24 inches and 35 inches for bust, waist, and hips respectively. As you might suspect, the girls liked their dimensions if they coincided with these ideals, but disliked them increasingly as they deviated from these ideals. Actually, the true measurements of the girls were slightly larger than their ideals, except for bust dimensions, where the average size was slightly smaller.

In a study of college males,[24] the acceptance of the body was more related to *large size*. While the women wanted to be slightly smaller in dimensions than they actually were, the men wanted to be larger, particularly in terms of being taller, with broader shoulders and chests.

Physical appearance is important to one's development of self-esteem because it plays a part in determining the nature of the responses a person receives from other people. However, we should keep in mind that it is only one of *many* determiners of self-esteem. A healthy, balanced person will build his feelings of self-regard on a variety of grounds, among which would include achievement, creativeness, social status, moral and ethical behavior, interpersonal relationships, and the like. While a certain degree of concern about one's total body-image is compatible with developing a healthy personality, too much con-

[22] Margaret Mead, *Male and Female* (New York: William Morrow & Company, Inc., 1949), pp. 138–142.

[23] Jourard and Secord (1955b).
[24] S. M. Jourard and P. F. Secord, "Body-Size and Body-Cathexis," *Journal of Consulting Psychology*, 18 (1954), 184.

cern may be a signal that the individual's self-esteem is standing on *too limited a foundation*. For example, the woman whose entire self is wrapped up in being beautiful or sexy is left with very little once the beauty and sex appeal are gone. The body-builder whose entire self rests on having large biceps and photographic muscle differentiation runs the risk of emotional bankruptcy when he gets older and discovers that there is more to life than bulging muscles and high protein diets.

SENSORY AWAKENING AND RELAXATION

Bernard Gunther

Life is change, a flowing process in which nothing is ever the same. Even in ritual or routine there is never real duplication. So-called objects, people, and events are dynamic, subtle experiences, and only seem to be static because we tend to become excessively tense, to conceptualize, to freeze existence.

"Wake up—you're dreaming!" is one of the basic themes of all the Eastern ways of liberation. Much of this so-called dream is caused by desensitization—the inhibition of emotions through chronic muscular tension, and by the categorization of life through the misuse of language and imagination.

If you carefully observe your behavior, you will find yourself seldom making direct contact with reality, and much of the time conceptualizing your existence. By verbalizing, analyzing, and imagining, you filter the unique, evolving differences of each event. Most people react to new situations in established patterns, allowing past experience to dictate or color the actual. Rather than being in contact with what is, they continually operate from a frame of reference of how things were, how things should be, how they would like them to be.

Words ultimately become hypnotic conditioning, a series of expectations, leaving little possibility for the excitement of what might be or really is.

This is not to condemn language, which is a useful communicative tool, but only to recognize the imbalance that the educational system has produced in our society. Talking and thinking have become compulsive in many instances, a defense against feeling and the world.

Desensitization of the organism is caused by excessive muscular tension. What Wilhelm Reich called "body armor" is a way of avoiding intensive excitement and overwhelming emotions. Often started in childhood, this holding against reaction may at one time have been a semi-conscious mechanism that later became automatic. No longer serving any productive function, this defense against experiencing affect limits behavior and hinders many of the spontaneous functions of the organism. Obsessive thinking is in many instances a reflection of this withholding, producing a state of chronic self-consciousness. Numbing whole areas of the body, thereby inhibiting breathing and the flow of energy, often leaves the person with a feeling of dreamlike half-aliveness, of being separate from himself and the world.

Sensory awakening is a process that leads to heightened awareness, contact, and experience. Temporarily, at least, it allows the individual to let go of some of his defenses, experience the intensity of open experience and, to some extent, the potentialities that lie within. This process consists of different experiments designed to shift attention from symbolic or verbal interpretation to the actual. Too often people *think* they feel rather than feel. Ignoring primary processes, they freeze situations and themselves so that there is no sensory contact with the richness of each event.

Sensory awakening is a method for rebalancing the nonverbal aspects of the organism with the intellect, focusing attention on simple bodily functions. Some examples are relaxation, breathing, listening, movement and touch. These, used separately or in various combinations, help bring an individual back to his senses. By distributing attention throughout the organism rather than localizing it in the head, the person is often able to make contact with his muscular tension, to learn how he creates it, and experience what it is like to gradually let go.

Derived from many sources, sensory awakening is an amalgamation of sensory awareness, yoga, Gestalt therapy, and Zen Buddhism, among others.

The first step in the reawakening process is relaxation. Though only one of the basic aspects of sensory awakening, it is primary in the facilitation of experience. Because of the fundamental nature of relaxation, it will be the focal point of all the experiments done in this chapter. Try this experiment:

Close your eyes. Become aware that you are thinking, and for a few moments observe your thoughts. Then move out of the realm of conceptualization into the area of sensation and become aware of how you feel right now. Allow whatever comes. Make no choices. Stay with this awareness for at least thirty seconds. Keep your eyes closed. Feel what your feet are resting on without looking at or moving them; experience the chair you are sitting in; bring your attention into the tip of your nose. Try doing this not with your imagination but by coming into actual contact with these sensations. Now bring your eyeballs down to the bottom of your eyes. Let them remain there for approximately thirty seconds. Spend half a minute listening to the noises in the room you are in. Become aware of the air that surrounds your body, especially in the exposed areas: your hands, neck and face. Finally, experience the results of this experiment.

The preceding experiment is one of the many ways in which you allow yourself to let go of your tensions and relax. To be at ease is one of the basic states of existence. To be unable to obtain this balance is to be in chronic tension-disease.

Relaxation is not sleep or sagginess, which are but opposite poles of hypertension. Rather, to be relaxed is a state of aliveness in which there is only the necessary expenditure of energy desirable for optimum functioning. The best example is a cat, sitting at ease, completely alive, ready in an instant to spring into action. Even in movement, there is a lack of excessive tension, allowing the organism to operate with a minimal expenditure of energy.

To be at ease facilitates functioning, enhances health, increases learning, and permits a more joyous existence. When a person is relaxed, he expends only the amount of energy necessary to perform what he is doing. This not only allows him to carry out his activities more successfully, but conserves energy, which can be used for various other tasks or enjoyments. Being at ease, the entire body operates more effectively: the flow of blood is unhindered; nerves respond with alert-

ness to each new situation. This openness makes any task easier, especially learning, and does not block or distract it by abnormal tightness. In fact, every activity is more pleasurable, because you are able to get with the experience rather than fight it.

The first step in learning how to relax is to become more aware of your tension. Tightness is a message telling you to "let go!" Yes, "telling you," for the next step is to become aware that it is you who are causing the tension. Though it may be done automatically, below the level of consciousness, it is still your own doing. The third phase of discovery is to find out how you hold and create these tensions: are you rigid in your chest? are you exerting too much pressure in your jaws? The final stage is to "let go." This is done best by not avoiding the tension but by experiencing it; moving toward and feeling it, *find out what it has to say to you*. If you really perceive and *allow*, the tightness will disappear.

This is one of the most natural and direct ways of working with tension. There are many others. It is important to know a number of different methods, since some people respond more to one approach than to another. Individual conditions, the nature and area of the "holding," are also important considerations.

When doing these experiments try not to expect certain results, even though you get them. Each time you do the experiments, the experience will be slightly different, sometimes imperceptibly so. There are no correct or incorrect experiences.

The eyes are often a source of tension, quite subtle and unsuspected, affecting the entire organism. One of the simplest ways to get rid of eyestrain is:

Lie down on your back or sit on a chair. Bring your consciousness into the area of your eyes; become aware of whatever feeling you have in this area without doing anything about it. After about thirty seconds of effortless concentration bring the palms of your hands over your eyes. The heels of your hands rest on your cheeks, your fingers over your forehead. The palms do not touch the eyelids; if you are sitting, rest your elbows on a table or on your knees. Remain in this position for a full minute, and then slowly remove your hands. Take about thirty seconds after each application to feel the result, allowing whatever may still want to develop in you as a result of this touch to manifest itself. It is desirable to repeat this process two or three times.

Seeing in our culture is too often replaced by staring: overfocusing rather than using peripheral vision, concentration on the figure to the exclusion of the background. In this manner of using our eyes we often miss more than we see. The eyes, like any other organ, operate best without unnecessary strain. To see is to allow, to be open.

Breathing is a very direct and useful method for relaxing the mind/body. When the breath is calm the organism is necessarily quiet. One of the most effective methods for the release of tension is:

Lie down and close your eyes (this experiment can be done in a seated position but is more effective lying down). Take a few moments to experience your body and its relationship to the floor. Now bring your attention to your breathing, and for a few moments become aware of how you are breathing. This is a passive process in which you make no effort to change; just watch and allow. After half a minute, place your hands on your upper chest, above the breasts, so that the palms are flat and the fingers of one hand do not touch the other. Feel the movement that goes on under your hands. After approximately one minute, take your hands away and slowly place them at your side. Take a few moments to experience the results of this touch. Then place your hands on the solar plexus, the area just above the navel. Become aware of what motion is taking place there. Again, after one minute put your hands slowly down at the side of your body and feel what is happening. Finally, place your hands on your lower belly, just inside of your frontal hip bones above the pubis. Experience what movement, if any, you feel in this area. Again, after a minute, bring your hands to the side of your body and become aware of how you feel.

Natural breathing is a function of the entire organism. It is not something that you have to do; rather, it is to be allowed. The oxygen/carbon-dioxide balance can have a great effect on how you experience the world. Minute changes can cause amazing differences in feeling and perception. As Gestalt therapy points out, holding your breath is one way of avoiding emotion and excitement, but the price is the creation of anxiety.

Focusing your awareness on the breathing process is another valuable way to relax:

Sit or lie quietly. Note your breathing. Stay with the inhalation and exhalation. After a time, become aware of the pause between letting the air out and the next breath. Bring your awareness to your nostrils and experience the air as it moves in and out. Five or ten minutes spent in this silent meditation is sure to be effective.

Moving slowly is an easy way to let go. Try this:

Close your eyes and feel your hands; now, slowly stretch your fingers out as wide as they will go, like a cat stretching its paws. Use some pressure to go as wide as you can without its being in any way painful. Stay in this position for fifteen seconds. Then, very slowly, allow your fingers and hands to settle back where they want to go. Repeat three times. After each stretch, become aware of any change that may take place in you.

Large movements of the body are even more satisfying. An example:

Close your eyes and feel your shoulders. After taking a few minutes, slowly begin to hunch them as high as you can. This must be done in slow motion. When you reach the extreme position, hold the shoulders there for a few seconds, then slowly let them down. It is important to experience each aspect of the motion. Allow your shoulders to settle where it feels right for them to go. Experience the effects, taking plenty of time. Repeat the movement two or three times.

Hunching the shoulders in this way can produce not only a release of unnecessary holding but can improve posture as well.

Bending over slowly and reaching for the floor with your fingers may be done in conjunction with the last experiment or may be done separately. The point is to do it slowly and get the feel of it. It is not an exercise to be got over as quickly as possible or a contest to see how far down you can go:

Just close your eyes and let your body communicate to you where and how it would like to stretch. Don't rush into movement until you really feel it from the inside of you. Allow yourself to stretch as long as it feels desirable, permitting any sighs, moans or yawns that want to, to come out from within. Let your feelings indicate all the areas that want to be loosened. Periodically, take time to experience the effects of your stretching.

A fine method for combining stretching, relaxing, and keeping the wrinkles out of your face is a modification of the yoga exercise called the "lion." This yoga technique can be done in front of a mirror, though this is not necessary:

Lean slightly forward with your shoulders; allow your eyes to widen as much as possible. Open your mouth wide and stick your tongue out as far as you can. Don't be inhibited. Be ferocious! Tense and tighten the neck muscles and cords, as well as those in the face. Hold this position for fifteen to sixty seconds. Then, as slowly as possible, allow your face and neck to settle. Repeat two or three times.

This experiment will increase circulation and, if done correctly, will remove fatigue that has settled in the eyes. It is important to concentrate on slowly creating the tension and slowly letting go.

As children we are taught not to stretch, as it is not good manners. However, it is good biology. Stretching is a natural method for letting go of excessive stiffness and improving muscle tone.

Still another vehicle for letting go is sound. The following method is also effective in ridding oneself of minor muscular stiffness and is suited to being done in bed before rising:

Exhale completely. Take a deep breath, and, as you let the air out, make the sound "Eeee" as highly pitched as possible. Push the sound and air out through your mouth until you have completely exhausted that breath. Concentrate on feeling the vibrations centering in your head. After letting all the air out, allow a couple of natural breaths. Then, either repeat the "Eeee" sound once or twice more, or move on to the next sound, "Aaaa" (pronounce as in "play"). Concentrate on vibrations in the throat. Follow the instructions as given for the first sound. The next sound is "Aahh." Concentrate on the chest. Now move to the belly and make the sound "Om." The sound "Om" requires a little more attention because it is divided into two syllables. The "Oohh" uses the first half of the breath while the "Mmmm" uses the second half. The final sound is

"Uuuu" (pronounce as in "true"). It is to be felt in the region of the hips.

These sound vibrations cause a massagelike effect over the entire organism. Strong exhalation cleanses the respiratory system of residual air, creating deeper breathing, and brings an entirely new supply of fresh air into the lungs.

A gentle touch is a most soothing experience. A sensitive laying on of hands will produce relaxation in the area touched and will be felt throughout the body. It is important to touch substantially, but without excessive pressure. Allow the hands to remain for some time. When removing the hands, it is essential to move away as slowly as possible. Though most parts of the body lend themselves to a gentle/firm touch, the head and shoulders are particularly well suited to this experiment:

Place your hands easily on some area of the body. For this example we will use the back. Let your hands remain on the back for about a minute. It is important not to talk during the experiment. Take your hands away as slowly as you can. Wait a few seconds for the effects of this touch to become complete. Then, make another application, making contact in the same place or some other part of the back, with another completion of this touch and a rest period. Finally, make a third touch, and sense this experience.

The preceding experiments are not just words about relaxation; they are methods. If you are willing to take the time to do them, they will help you to remember something that you already know but have forgotten: how to let yourself go and *be*—relaxed.

Comments from students about these experiments range from "I haven't been this relaxed in years," to "I feel at one with everything." Some experimenters indicate heightened feelings of warmth, brighter colors, sharper images. "I feel in the floor, rather than on it," is not an uncommon reaction. "I feel more natural, the way I would like to all the time," is another. "Nothing special," beamed a knowing Zen student after one class, understanding this open living to be his birthright.

Psychologists and patients have expressed the feeling that these experiments would facilitate the therapeutic process. Indications in both individual and group work have been most gratifying. Educators, too, have felt the possibilities of this work as an enhancement to learning. Writers and artists have found the experiments stimulating to the creative process.

The results of this work are seldom permanent. The experiments do, however, allow the individual temporarily to experience the vast possibilities of his organism, pointing out a direction in which to work. For these exercises to be ultimately rewarding, they must be done more than as experiments; they must become an integral part of daily living. At each moment, tension or relaxation reflects your basic attitude toward life and yourself—whether you are for or against, asleep or awake.

TOPIC 3

Sex-role Image

Boys have trucks, girls have dolls.
Boys are doctors, girls are nurses.
Boys are presidents, girls are 1st ladies.
Boys can eat, girls can cook.
Boys invent things, girls use what boys invent.

　　—Picture captions from child's book entitled
　　　　I'm Glad I'm a Boy! I'm Glad I'm a Girl!

Our *sex-role image* is our view or concept of ourself as a male or female. It is our sense of masculinity or femininity, of being a boy or a girl, a man or a woman. This image is based on our perception of sex-role standards, that is, culturally approved male and female behaviors, and the extent to which we value, accept, and are able to fulfill these behaviors.

The most salient feature of our self image or identity is our gender. Probably the first question asked about a new baby is, "Is it a boy or a girl?" And an early question in guessing the identity of a person in the game "Twenty Questions" is, "Is it male or female?" Once we know a person's sex, we can make some educated guesses about who the person is and also who he or she will become.

Gender is so important in society's ordering of things that there is not a neuter pronoun in the English language appropriate to describe the individual beyond his or her first few days of life. We can call a newborn baby "it," but it soon becomes a he or a she. If we write "yes" or "undecided" under sex on an IBM card, the machine is not amused. The computer, like society at large, needs to know how to classify us so we can be dealt with in proper fashion.

Each of us learns our gender very early, and the importance of this distinction is impressed on us all throughout life. Jerome Kagan, a prominent developmental psychologist, notes that "The child as young as four has dichotomized the world into male and female people and is concerned with boy–girl differences. By the time he is seven he is intensely committed to molding his behavior in concordance with cultural standards appropriate to his biological sex and he shows uneasiness, anxiety, and even anger when he is in danger of behaving in ways regarded as characteristic of the opposite sex."

All during our formative years, we are taught to behave in sex-appropriate ways. We are rewarded for doing so, and we are rejected or punished when we are less masculine or less feminine than society prefers. We also learn sex-appropriate behavior by identifying ourself with our same-sex parent or other appropriate persons and modeling ourself after them.

This process of matching behavior to biology is a more ambivalent one for girls than for boys. The male sex role is generally more privileged and more favorably regarded. Sex-role stereotypes, that is, widely shared beliefs concerning males and females in our society, favor the former at the expense of the latter. The job market, the business world, the law, and other components of our society show the same unfortunate favoritism.

If our behavior is inconsistent with sex-role standards, we may have a rough time of it. Many social critics feel that these standards are far too rigid and that we are locked into them too early (literally from the time we are dressed in blue or pink at the nursery). These critics advocate granting each sex greater freedom to engage in behaviors heretofore restricted to the other. But some observers are alarmed by the decreasing differences between the sexes and have called for new emphases on masculinity and femininity.

Becoming female

Researchers Judith Bardwick and Elizabeth Douvan note that in establishing identity girls have an easier time than boys in early childhood but a more difficult time later on. Some early patterns such as dependency are considered feminine, and boys are soon under pressure to abandon this behavior and establish their masculinity and identity. Girls grow to puberty with a bisexual identity. This identity is partly based on such feminine traits as dependency and conformity and partly on what later comes to be seen as a more masculine pattern of mastery and achievement. In adolescence and early adulthood this achievement is not so highly valued or rewarded in females as in males, and at this time young women are called upon to redefine themselves and emphasize an identity based on interpersonal relationships.

In the first article Alan Graebner presents a case study to show how the female's image of herself is subtly but persistently constricted in the socialization process. Almost from the beginning she is channeled toward her foreordained roles of wife and mother, and along the way she learns to accept a narrow definition of herself and a deprecated view of her capacities. Graebner feels that in our society men are considered to be persons or human beings first and males second—their unique potentialities are not compromised by their gender. The reverse is true for women, whose personhood is subordinated to their destiny as females.

Becoming male

Despite his privileged role, the male does not have an easy time or it. The male life span is shorter than the female's and it is filled with more physical, psychological, and social problems. For example, more males than females are brain-injured at birth and more die accidentally or by suicide. Males are more likely to have a speech, learning, or behavior disorder or to become delinquent or a school problem. There are also more males than females in mental institutions and prisons.

Males experience difficulty in defining themselves as masculine if appropriate role models and experiences are not available to them. In the second reading, Patricia Cayo Sexton accuses schools of emasculating boys. She feels that teachers are too often women and the school is too often a woman's world emphasizing feminine rather than masculine virtues. She is less worried about girls becoming too masculine than about boys becoming too feminine and advocates making schools into more active and adventurous places.

Although Sexton is alarmed by what she sees happening to males, Lester A. Kirkendall, as interviewed by James Lincoln Collier in the third article, welcomes the re-definition of masculinity. He lauds the "new masculinity" as one more in keeping with the times. The tough frontiersman, stern, strong, silent, and completely in control of himself and the situation, is giving way to the new male, who is equalitarian, cooperative, expressive, and sharing in family roles and tasks. Kirkendall feels this reordering of ideas about masculinity will benefit both sexes.

Becoming neuter

Sex-role differences are becoming less pronounced, and there is some controversy as to whether this process should be speeded up, slowed down, or reversed. Many feminists and other individuals feel that these differences in roles should be minimized. Some school officials, for example, have begun to overhaul their curricula and learning materials to eliminate sex-role stereotypes. Family life educators advocate that children be given the latitude to explore behaviors and feelings usually reserved for the opposite sex. A few critics have even proposed combining such traditionally separated activities as Girl Scouts and Boy Scouts. In fact, after much controversy the Little League in the spring of 1974 liberalized its policies to permit the participation of girls.

Other authorities disagree, and some are alarmed by the prospect of a unisex society. A number hold that the sex role is the cornerstone of identity and insist we must learn this role before we can know who we are. Such critics point out that boys and girls get support and assistance in self-definition by interacting with members of their own sex and by taking stances in relation to the opposite sex. Furthermore, they maintain that males and females are inherently different, have different needs, develop at different rates, and therefore must be treated differently in the socialization process.

In the fourth selection Carlfred B. Broderick states that sex differences will always make a difference, and he gives two reasons why each of us must learn to play our sex role well. First, he states that our sense of identity is intertwined with our sense of masculinity or femininity—we cannot be secure in our self unless we are secure in our sex roles. Second, most of us live in a thoroughly heterosexual society, and in order to participate satisfactorily we must know how to play our approved role in relation to the opposite sex.

A contrary view is taken by Lois Gould in the last reading, which is a fable concerning a child who was raised not as a boy and not as a girl, but as an X. What happened? Well, society's computers—set for cards punched M or F but not X—boggled a bit. But as for X, X did Xcellently, and so did everyone else once they got used to the notion.

FOR PERSONAL APPLICATION

1. Recall several of your own experiences with sex typing, that is, the efforts of others (or those of your own) to conform your behavior to patterns considered to be sex-appropriate.
2. Have you ever felt discriminated against because of your sex? Discuss yourself in this regard.
3. Have you ever wished or imagined or played that you were a member of the opposite sex? Discuss yourself in this regard.
4. Do you feel that you have had sufficient freedom to cross sex-role boundaries? Discuss yourself in this regard.
5. If you are a male, do you feel that your identity is primarily defined by your vocational direction? If you are a female, do you feel that your identity is primarily tied to interpersonal relationships? Discuss yourself in this regard.
6. Do you believe that current sex-role differences should be de-emphasized or re-emphasized? Discuss your answer.
7. Did you experience your elementary and secondary schools as feminine environments? Discuss your answer.
8. What changes would you advocate in family, school, and other institutions of our society to modify sex-role differences, standards, or stereotypes?
9. Describe a utopia in which men and women would have roles that you feel would be ideal.
10. What do you see to be the main ideology of the "new feminists" or "women's liberation"? Discuss your agreement or disagreement with this movement.
11. Write down a discussion item (not given above) that seems particularly relevant to this topic and you, and discuss it.

FOR SMALL GROUPS

1. *Defining sex roles.* Sit in a circle. Each member of the group in turn says the following beginning of a sentence and then completes it: "A woman is. . . ." Keep going around the circle until members run out of responses. Then each member in turn says the following beginning of a sentence and completes it: "A man is. . . ." Again, keep going around until the responses run out. Afterward, discuss the qualities associated with each sex.

2. *Criticizing sex roles.* The group is divided into male and female subgroups. Each subgroup meets separately and arrives at a list of three praiseworthy (positive, good) qualities and three changeworthy (negative, bad) qualities associated with the opposite sex. Then the entire group reassembles for a discussion of the lists.

3. *Arguing sex roles.* The members of the group arrange themselves in a line ranging from the person who is most conservative with reference to sex roles (that is, the one who believes most strongly in sharply differentiated roles for males and females) to the person who is the most liberal in this regard (that is, the one who believes most strongly in shared roles). The members discuss their views until each person feels he is in approximately the right place in line. Then the persons at each end try to convince those at the opposite end to modify their views and change their position in the line-up. What feelings and insights are aroused by this exercise?

4. *Debating sex roles.* Arrange for a debate among group members on this proposition: "Resolved that in our society males and females should be treated alike."

5. *Fantasizing sex roles.* Sit in a circle. On one card write or type this incomplete sentence: "If I were a member of the opposite sex, I would like to. . . ." On a second card write or type this incomplete sentence: "I would not like to be a member of the opposite sex because. . . ." Pass the first card around the circle, and as each member receives it, he reads the card aloud and then completes the sentence. Next, follow the same procedure with the second card. Afterward, discuss the ways that members view the privileges and restrictions of each sex role.

6. *Role playing sex roles.* Two members, one male and one female, exchange roles to enact a common situation. For example, role play a dating situation with the male taking the traditional female role and the female taking the usual male role. Or stage an argument between a feminist female and an anti-feminist male, except that the female is to take the anti-feminist position while the male enacts the feminist role. What feelings and insights are aroused by this exercise?

7. *Role playing sex roles.* Two volunteers, one conservative with reference to sex roles and the other liberal, take part. The conservative plays the part of a parent and the liberal plays the part of (1) a child who wants a "sex-inappropriate" toy (for example, a doll in the case of a boy or a football in the case of a girl), or (2) an adolescent who is electing a "sex-inappropriate" career (for example, a nurse in the case of a boy or an engineer in the case of a girl). The "parent" and "offspring"

should each try to convince the other of the rightness of his own position. What feelings and insights are aroused by this exercise?

8. *Role playing sex roles.* Proceed in the same way as in the above exercise, except that the conservative plays the part of the liberal offspring and the liberal plays the part of the conservative parent. What feelings and insights are aroused by this exercise?

9. *Seeking insights on sex roles.* Invite to your group a person with pronounced conservative views on sex roles, or one with liberal or radical views. Or invite both (but let each know who the other guest will be).

FOR FURTHER READING

Bardwick, J. M. *Psychology of Women: A Study of Bio-cultural Conflicts.* New York: Harper & Row, Publishers, 1971.

Bardwick, J. M., ed. *Readings on the Psychology of Women.* New York: Harper & Row, Publishers, 1972.

Bednarik, K. *The Male in Crisis.* New York: Alfred A. Knopf, 1970.

Boston Women's Health Book Collective. *Our Bodies, Ourselves: A Book By and For Women.* New York: Simon and Schuster, 1973.

Brenton, M. *The American Male: A Penetrating Look at the Masculinity Crisis.* New York: Coward-McCann, 1966.

Goldberg, S. *The Inevitability of Patriarchy.* New York: William Morrow, 1973.

Gornick, V., and B. K. Moran, eds. *Woman in Sexist Society.* New York: Basic Books, Inc., 1971. See esp. Judith M. Bardwick and Elizabeth Douvan, "Ambivalence: The Socialization of Women," pp. 147–159.

Graebner, A. *After Eve: The New Feminism.* Minneapolis: Augsburg Publishing House, 1972.

Maccoby, E., ed. *The Development of Sex Differences.* Stanford: Stanford University Press, 1966.

Rosenberg, B. G., and B. Sutton-Smith. *Sex and Identity.* New York: Holt, Rinehart & Winston, Inc., 1972.

Sexton, P. C. *The Feminized Male: Classrooms, White Collars and the Decline of Manliness.* New York: Random House, Inc., 1969.

Sherman, J. A. *On the Psychology of Women: A Survey of Empirical Studies.* Springfield, Ill.: Thomas, 1971.

Steinman, A., and D. Fox *The Male Dilemma: How to Survive the Sexual Revolution.* New York: Jason Aronson, 1974.

GROWING UP FEMALE

Alan Graebner

No woman, say the feminists today, escapes the penalties, the pressures, that society brings to bear on female humans nearly from the time they are born until the time they die. These pressures are both symptoms and cause of a status feminists are intent on changing. The usual term for the pressures is socialization. To understand what this means, let's take a case study of a woman we might name Nancy.

Nancy was her parent's first child. Her father then was beginning what became a successful accounting firm. Her mother was, by her own description, "just a housewife." When Nancy's father told his friends the baby had arrived, they congratulated him and then asked whether it was a boy or a girl. When he said, "a girl," they usually laughed and told him not to be disappointed; the *next* one would be a boy. His wife told him the same thing. They were right, too, for Nancy was only a year old when she had a baby brother, David. Their father complained contentedly of the expense of buying blue baby things instead of wearing out Nancy's pink paraphernalia.

The two children were so close in age they were good playmates. However, as they grew older, the toys they were given became more and more different. At Christmas and birthdays, David received cap pistols and erector sets and finally an electric train. Nancy was not overlooked by any means: play kitchen utensils, dolls, and finally a large doll house. She was not unhappy about getting a doll instead of an erector set, because she quickly learned that there are boys' toys and girls' toys. She noticed how one boy in her second-grade class was teased when he unguardedly admitted he liked dolls. And when she

once began to play with her brother's train set, he and his friends told her self-righteously it was not for girls.

Nancy's grandparents visited frequently, something Nancy liked very much, for her grandfather always told them stories and teased the two children. "What are you going to be when you grow up?" he would ask David, and they would all laugh as Dave went from fireman to race car driver to doctor. Then would come the question for Nancy: "Who are you going to marry when you grow up?" And they would all laugh when her grandfather teased her about the little boy next door.

Nancy and her brother liked to imitate their parents by "helping" in household tasks. At first they were more bother than help, but in time Nancy's mother would call her for assistance in the kitchen and in cleaning while David went to help his father when some carpentry or repairs had to be done. As each got better at these tasks, it made more sense to expect them to help.

In school Nancy was a bright child who loved to read. Almost all her books showed female characters, but not nearly as many as male figures, and somehow even mother bears wore aprons and kept house. Nancy's school books gave her many ideas for games she organized with neighbor children. One of the boys would play the man who was a doctor or a businessman or a banker while Nancy was a nurse or a secretary or a teller or stayed home to cook and sew and clean.

Much of the time, however, Nancy ran around in the neighborhood, climbing trees, wading in ditches and, if the boys would let her, playing football or double-touch tag with them. Several times she overheard her mother and grandmother discussing her exploits, worrying that she was becoming a tomboy. And gradually she learned a lady could never be a tomboy. Since she wanted very much to be grown-up—they had all the privileges, like staying up late—she tried to be a little more restrained and to act like a lady. Acting like a lady, she discerned, meant she couldn't use physical force or be too strong, but should rely on various psychological ploys to get what and where she wanted.

Being a lady came a bit easier in junior high and in high school. Nancy's mother did not encourage early dating particularly, but her girl friends spent a great deal of time talking about boys. They knew it was important for a girl to attract boys, because that was how you could tell a successful girl. That's what television shows and movies and popular songs and the magazines all said. Even their parents and ministers told the girls essentially the same thing when they warned that a promiscuous girl would suffer: she would lose her popularity with boys. If Nancy and her friends missed the point after all of this, they could still pick it up from the mental images that went with the terms for unmarried adults. Single men they knew as bachelors, and most bachelors were "eligible." Single women they heard called old maids and no one spoke of an "eligible" old maid.

Nancy and her girl friends also knew that physical appearance was important to attract boys. After all the magazines, even the billboards, they saw used women to sell things. What was significant about these women was almost always one thing—their looks. Nancy and her friends took this for granted because they had grown up seeing these images and they used these standards to judge themselves and other girls. They understood that boys did too, for the boys had also grown up seeing women this way.

Nearly everyone Nancy knew seemed to think girls did not have much aptitude for certain ways of thinking. She heard a lot of joking references to girls and mathematics, for instance. Nancy did not do badly in the math courses she took, but none of her girl friends were taking more math, so she stopped too. She did not take any physics in high school either. She heard the physics course spent a lot of time with mechanical things and she knew boys were a lot better at that than girls; her brother and father were always tinkering with things while she helped her mother in the kitchen. Besides she was not taking the math courses that would help in physics. Of course that meant when she was with a group of friends and the boys began arguing about something mechanical such as a car, she did not have much idea of what they were talking about. But she could tell them right out she was dumb; boys knew as well as the girls that girls are not very good at machinery. Anyway, she learned it made boys feel good to explain to her.

In her junior and senior years, her high school counselors began having conferences with each student, suggesting what they could do after graduation. Nancy's grades were good and everyone took for granted she would go to college. All her close friends were going. Besides, as one counselor said, she would need college to get some kind of job "just in case." She knew what that meant, of course; just in case she did not get married or was widowed early.

Nancy was not very sure what she wanted to do after college "just in case" so she and her counselor talked over a number of possibilities. Her test scores were high and she liked books, so the counselor suggested she think about being a teacher (perhaps high school English) or a librarian. But Nancy was undecided. Her best friend wanted to work with people and was talking about nursing or social work. The boys Nancy dated, who got about the same grades she did, spoke of being lawyers and doctors and architects. Nancy was impressed and was pleased and rather proud of herself to be dating boys like that. She knew her mother was too. No one suggested Nancy think of being a lawyer and the idea never came to her otherwise. She didn't even know any women lawyers; neither did her father. There was one woman doctor in town, but she was a specialist who few girls ever visited. All the other physicians were men, just as in the doctor programs on television.

Nancy still had not made up her mind when she went off to college. A year later her brother was in college too. Both of them were slow in choosing majors. This worried their father. He was hoping his son would take over the business, but Dave was hesitant. It never occurred to their father to ask Nancy if she wanted to take over the firm. And that idea never occurred to Nancy either. During Dave's sophomore year, he had long talks with their father, trying to decide on a career. Nancy was a junior by this time, but as she overheard her father tell David, "Now, your sister, that's different, because she's a woman and is going to get married and settle down with children. But how are you going to amount to anything unless you have a good job?"

In her senior year Nancy and Michael, a boy she had been dating, became serious about each other and soon announced their engagement. Nancy by then had an English major and one of her professors had been talking to her about graduate school, but once she was engaged she decided she had better be practical and get the necessary courses to teach high school so she would be able to have an income as soon as she graduated. Her fiancé was an engineer who was going to go on to business school and they both expected Nancy to support them until he finished his education.

And that is about how things turned out. They were married just after graduation, and that September Michael began graduate school while Nancy found a teaching job in a nearby high school. She found she was much better at teaching than she expected. The principal of her school was exceptionally cooperative and she was able to try out some of her own rather unorthodox and innovative ideas. They worked so well she thought of carrying them further. But when Michael finished school the best job he was offered was on the West Coast, so as a matter of course they moved there, although Nancy could not find a job at all comparable to the one she left.

Nancy did not mind too much because they planned to start a family anyway. In a few years she and Michael had two boys and a girl. The family kept Nancy busy all day long and part of the night besides. She subscribed to women's magazines or bought them at the supermarket and they always had ideas for changes around the house that Nancy felt she should try, though they took a great deal of time since they kept raising her standards. Michael was quite successful in his job and they were able to live in a very pleasant suburb with open land for the children to play in. Nancy thought occasionally about returning to teaching or even of going back to school at a nearby university, but gave up the idea after she saw a friend try it. Finding a full-time baby-sitter was nearly impossible in their suburb, and the friend's husband often grumbled that the house and meals were not the same as when she was home all day, so she had to get up early to do all the housework before she left: that made her and the children irritable for lack of sleep. Then one of the neighbors hinted that they must be in a real financial squeeze for her to endure such problems. That made her husband even unhappier and Nancy's friend finally quit. Nancy decided

the lesson was clear, at least until the children were older.

By her early 30s Nancy joked at her birthdays about not revealing her age. But she realized with some contentment that she had already achieved most of her dreams. As she ferried the children and their dog around to shopping and dentist appointments and cub scout meetings and music lessons, they made an appealing picture. In fact Michael, who left the office early one day and saw them arrive home, told Nancy they looked like an automobile ad in a woman's magazine: a pretty, well-dressed mother with three attractive children and a bouncing dog in a late model station wagon in a comfortable suburb. Michael was very proud of them and happy with himself that he had been successful enough to give his family a good life, even though it meant he was not at home as much as he should have been. And Nancy was rather pleased too. All this and a loving husband. As she reminded herself when she occasionally got restless, what more could a woman want?

What had happened to Nancy? It must be said—though some radical feminists would contest this—that a great many pleasant things had happened to her. She had grown up in a closely-knit, loving family, something she valued so highly she wanted to replicate it as an adult. She had found someone whom she could trust as an intimate companion, and who reciprocated that trust. She was able to accept and enjoy sex as a great gift. And she knew the fascinating and sometimes awesome experience of parenthood.

But that was not all that had happened to Nancy. Already as a child she had learned that girls are judged by a different standard than boys and had begun measuring her conduct by that standard. This included the recognition that girls do not do well measured on the boys' criteria. Nancy's formal education, it is true, had been much like her brother's but there was one key difference. As Bruno Bettelheim p ts it, "Boys have no doubt that their school is intended, at least, to help make them a *success* in their mature life. . . . But the girl is made to feel that she must undergo precisely the same training only because she may need it if she is a *failure*."[1]

[1] Quoted by Cynthia Fuchs Epstein, *Woman's Place: Options and Limits in Professional Careers* (Berkeley, 1970), p. 64.

Nancy had accepted the standards of success and failure presented to her. What others were available to her? Her sensitivity about her age was part of all this, for it reflected her recognition that in our society, unlike male assets such as ambition and power which are not tied to youth, the major female asset is her looks, her desirability, something that depreciates with age. (Small wonder female movie stars and Miss America contestants are usually anti-feminist; their careers are built on exploiting their sex.) As it turned out, Nancy was a "success." That success had a very high cost Nancy was virtually unaware, for she had grown up with the assumption that women define their lives in terms of others' lives, especially those of husband and children.

Another way of putting this is that much of Nancy's life was as it was because society defined her as a human female, though it defined her father and her brother and her husband as male humans. In other words, society had defined her first of all as a female, while it defined the men first of all as human. Her sex was the prime condition in her role. Their humanness was the prime condition in their roles. At this point socialization became objectification. Nancy was treated as an object, not as a full human being.

These are harsh words, and it is at this point many women who have so internalized a set of values as wives and mothers that they can see no others become so hostile they stop listening and rational discourse breaks into monologs. But in all save the most radical rhetoric, the focus of feminist attack here is not being a mother. Rather it is the "programming" society engages in as soon as the sex of the child is known. If the child is a boy, that programming is a comparatively open-ended shaping to foster choices of life patterns out of a large variety of human activity. If the child is a girl, the programming is a rigorous delimitation to female activities: sexual partner, wife, mother. As a final blow, this programming has more than its share of ironic contradictions. For example girls, who all their lives are taught that the normal goal is to marry, are forbidden to initiate proceedings to gain that end. Girls do not ordinarily ask for dates and propose; boys do.

Nancy's parents would have been quick to see the process of making objects of women in the pages of something like *Playboy* magazine;

women there, they would see, are automatically identified primarily as sexual beings. But her parents failed to recognize other manifestations of the same process when it appeared elsewhere, even in their own home, when women are automatically identified primarily as wives and mothers. Failing even to perceive what they were doing, Nancy's parents and friends and teachers and husband—in sum her whole world—identified her primarily by her sex. It is hardly surprising she responded by identifying herself primarily in the same way. It is not that being a wife and mother was necessarily wrong, but that she was given so few openings to choose anything else.

But was she really given few opportunities to choose something else? After all, no one told her explicitly she could *not* be an attorney or an airline pilot or an engineer. To put it that way is to reject the whole case study. Unlike many fathers, who according to surveys are quite antagonistic to the idea of careers for their daughters, Nancy's father had been, he thought, "neutral." He had not understood that in this context neutrality is advocacy of the status quo. Children pick up a host of non-explicit cues in the course of growing up that shape their expectations of themselves and of others. (This is the basis for the frequently-seen advice that parents not preach at their children, but be good examples to follow.)

White Americans have begun to realize this in the area of race relations. When children see television shows in which black actors appear only as domestic servants or comics; when they read school textbooks in which black people are hardly even mentioned; when they see advertisements that picture only pretty white girls; when they hear jokes that refer to blacks by uncomplimentary names and depend for humor on negative social stereotypes—when children experience all this, no one has to tell them outright that in America black people are set apart from whites and are not worth as much. White children pick this up unconsciously. And sadly enough so do black children, who may come to value themselves less because of these experiences.

Much the same process holds true for boys and girls. They grow up watching women on television whose main problems are how to get their wash whiter and floors shinier and to make themselves more beautiful and to smell better and to attract or retain a husband. Children read textbooks that hardly ever mention women, and when they do, emphasize women in a domestic capacity; after all Betsy Ross is famous for her sewing. Children see ads that use women for specific physical traits, and hear endless jokes about the ineptitude and failings of women. Boys pick up the lessons unconsciously and it shapes their attitudes toward girls.

Former senator Charles Goodell tells the story of the congressman visiting a third-grade classroom who was asked by a girl if he thought some day there could be a woman president. He replied affirmatively, pointing out there are more women than men and if they got together they could elect a woman president. And then came a little male voice from the back of the room: "Now what did you have to go and tell them that for?"[2]

On a school playground during recess a teacher watched a group of third-grade boys milling about in concentration on an active game with a kickball. One of their group ran across the field with the pack, but clear of it, shouting over and over in a shrill, worried, little voice, "but that's a girls' game; that's a girls' game." He was the voice of future attitudes for the group.

Sadly enough girls also learn these lessons, and at an early age. For example, one mother who was admitted to medical school found her four-year-old daughter heartbroken by the news, for she thought it meant her mother would have to turn into a man and not be a mother anymore.[3] The result of these lessons is a human being who from an early age is likely to be self-deprecating and fearful that in areas other than the home and family her aptitudes and chances of success are small. When asked if they "could be" governor of the state or a judge, California junior high school girls were much less likely than boys to answer yes (17 percent of the girls vs. 44 percent of the boys on the governor; 26 percent vs. 49 percent regarding the judge).[4]

The situation only worsens by college age. In one experiment, a group of college students was given a sentence and asked to complete a story from it, a common test to reveal aspirations and attitudes. The boys were asked to complete a story that began, "After first-term finals, John finds himself at the top of his medical class." The girls were given the same beginning except that the name was changed to Anne. Some remarkable differences between boys and girls were revealed. Only ten percent of the boys, but two-thirds of the girls displayed either anxiety or even rejection of the cues provided in the sentence they were given. Consider these more or less representative endings by the girls:

Anne doesn't want to be number one in her class. . . . She feels she shouldn't rank so high because of social reasons. She drops down to ninth in the class and then marries the boy who graduates number one.

Anne feels guilty. . . . She will finally have a nervous breakdown and quit medical school and marry a successful young doctor.

Anne is a code name for a nonexistent person created by a group of med. students. They take turns writing exams for Anne.[5]

Someone who even in fantasy would need such escape hatches from success, say the feminists, has been psychologically crippled. Of course, this is only one experiment with a limited group of people.* But anyone can do a bit of informal testing by using a riddle suggested by some writers. Without steering the conversation in a feminist direction, pose to a group of teenagers the following problem: A boy and his father were involved in an auto accident and both were seriously injured. They were taken to different hospitals for treatment. On approaching the boy's stretcher, the surgeon exclaimed, "I can't operate on him; he's my son." How could this be? Usually the answers will range from complicated step-

[2] *Hearings, Subcommittee on Constitutional Amendments, Committee on the Judiciary, U.S. Senate,* Ninety-First Congress (1970), p. 45.

[3] Alleen Pace Nilsen, "Women in Children's Literature," *College English,* 32 (May, 1971), 919.

[4] "Status Is the Name of the Game," *Trans-Action,* 8 (February, 1971), 10.

[5] Matina Horner, "Woman's Will to Fail," *Psychology Today,* 3 (November, 1969), 36–38, 62.

* [For a critical review of research in this area, see Thelma G. Alper, "Achievement Motivation in College Women: A Now-You-See-It-Now-You-Don't Phenomenon," *American Psychologist* (March, 1974), 194–203. See also David Tresemer, "Fear of Success: Popular, but Unproven," *Psychology Today* (March, 1974), 82–85.—Ed.]

father relationships to artificial insemination before someone may suggest that the surgeon was the boy's mother.

Behind the difficulty of this riddle is a whole system of expectations, and it is interesting to see the line of reasoning when elements of that system are endangered. A Maryland school board recently considered a proposal for coeducational tennis, and opponents produced the argument that "a high school boy, beaten at a game of tennis by a girl his own age, would feel castrated." The adolescent boy, said the opponents, learns to accept defeat from a male peer. "But if he should take a real walloping from a girl his age, why then, we very often see a true withdrawal from sports altogether. . . ."[6] Such opinions—and they are only that—ought to elicit some pointed questions. Why should a boy feel so defeated unless he has been taught all his life that girls are inferior? And who taught him that? Apparently not experience, if girls can actually beat him in a game. And why all this concern (expressed incidentally by those who do not blink at competitive, hardening sports) for the poor boy's tender psyche with not a word about the girl's feelings? Is a girl's ego so strong she can stand without damage not only defeat by a boy, but even the exclusion from competition? There is a double standard at work here, a concentration on the damage to the boy of defeat rather than on the benefits to the girl of victory. Whether defeat in tennis—or swimming or Little League baseball—would actually damage a boy is open to question. What is striking is the blatant way in which in this aspect of social conditioning male mental health gains unquestioned priority over female mental health.

Generally, when feminists speak about social conditioning, the convinced anti-feminist and the doubter feel certain they hold the trump card, and sooner or later they haul it out. Usually it goes something like this:

What the feminists cannot admit to themselves is that women really *are* different. Women have babies and men do not. Men have certain

physical and psychological (masculine) traits and women have different physical and psychological (feminine) traits. And that is what makes the world go 'round. Vive la différence!

But that line of approach is not the crushing rejoinder the anti-feminist imagines. Of course it would be ludicrous to deny that women have different reproductive equipment than men. And anyone can observe in our society that there is a series of traits we conventionally label masculine, and another series we label feminine. But are these traits innately sex-linked? Does a woman (who can bear children) differ in intellectual characteristics, aptitudes and needs from a man (who cannot)? Is anatomy destiny?

Anti-feminists are convinced it is. Blithely disregarding the enormous difficulties of separating nature and nurture (even in carefully constructed experiments), they act—and insist society act—as if they possess conclusive proof. They refuse to entertain even the possibility that we have constructed a self-fulfilling prophecy about women.

What, however, if ingenious experiments and exhaustive observation conclude there are indeed innate differences between male and female because of hormonal or nervous system differences? A carefully constructed feminist position is hardly demolished. The essence of the feminist stress on socialization is not that women are just like men. It is that society effectively closes innumerable options to women without consulting their preferences. As one psychologist (who leans toward innate differences) points out, our society, like most in recorded history, socializes children to maximize whatever original differences between the sexes exist.[7] Furthermore, even with the powerful socialization that both sexes undergo today, the range within one sex is nearly as striking as the differences between them. But those who do not fit the norms are not allowed to depart from the female status without penalty. Society has developed a whole pattern of limits for women.

[6] Quoted in *Women's Rights Law Reporter*, 1 (July/August, 1971), 39.

[7] Judith M. Bardwick, *Psychology of Women: A Study of Bio-Cultural Conflicts* (New York, 1971), p. 216.

SCHOOLS ARE EMASCULATING OUR BOYS

Patricia Cayo Sexton

Boys and the schools seem locked in a deadly and ancient conflict that may eventually inflict mortal wounds on both. In vastly disproportionate numbers, boys are the maladjusted, the low achievers, the truants, the delinquents, the inattentive, the rebellious. If teachers had only girls in their classes, they would find it easy, though dull, going, and we probably could double class size and still keep high standards of achievement and decorum. National delinquency rates are five times higher among boys than girls; in New York City 63 per cent of all dropouts are boys; more than twice as many boys as girls under fifteen are currently first admissions to public mental hospitals.

While we know many things about the boy-school conflict, our factual understanding is still too primitive to permit us to go far beyond conjecture. Boys are often raised by strong and assertive women at home (the "modern woman") and then turned over to strong and assertive women at school. Seventy-two per cent of all teachers, remember, are women. Yet a boy, if he wants to be a real boy, must free himself from the domination of these women and operate under his own power; hence, there is inevitable conflict for those who take on the painful job of struggling out of the maternal cocoon to become men, and partial or sometimes total emasculation for those who don't.

The problem is not just that teachers are too often women. It is that the school is too much a woman's world, governed by women's rules and standards. The school code is that of propriety, obedience, decorum, cleanliness, silence, physical and, too often, mental passivity. Some of this, perhaps a lot, may be good and necessary. The military establishment is able to enforce some of this code—obedience and discipline—on men without making sissies of them. But when it is not alloyed with the stronger masculine virtues, as it often is in the military but seldom is in the schools, trouble is brewed.

Unfortunately, the masculine virtues are usually diametrically opposite to the school's female ones. The masculine stress is on aggressiveness in all things, rather than passivity. It is on action and movement rather than sitting still, independence rather than obedience, speaking out rather than keeping quiet, strong group loyalty and group competition rather than individual competition—fearlessness, courage, and daring rather than timidity and surrender—conflict, struggle, and a good fight rather than perpetual peace. The female code is to make as much effort as possible in studies, the male to make the least. Basic to the problem is that boys have more energy and muscle for action and trouble; they take in more food and their output of carbon dioxide may be as much as 40 per cent more than that of girls.

Though the boy must learn to be his own authority, the school insists that he obey its authority, however arbitrary and irrational it may be. This may be reasonably good preparation for the lower rungs of a large white-collar organization or military service, but not for real manhood or free citizenship.

But the young lad's woes do not end there. Besides the school's style, there is also its content. Again, alas, this subject matter seems all too frilly and feminized. English and literature especially, the inescapable subjects, seem typically so overcast by feminine tastes as to repeatedly suggest to boys that the provinces of written language, books, imaginative expression, art are the exclusive property of women and the strange men who take interest in such flights of fancy.

If we are to stuff boys every term with English courses, surely we can find ways to convince them that "good" literature can be tough, masculine, simple, perceptive, and expressive of their own feelings and experience. Why, for example, in teaching Shakespeare, sacrifice the blood and bawdiness and the action plots, as wild as Goldfinger, to the lyricism of the language—that tends more often to be stressed?

All of this leads us back to something about which we have intermittently talked but done nothing—education that is active, exploratory, problem solving, adventurous, aggressive. Because boys want to conquer their world (and universe) rather than nest in it, they are often fascinated by machinery, technology, and the absorbing secrets of the natural world, secrets that man has, by mind, mouth, and hand, wrested from nature for use in its exploitation. These male interests are almost too apparent to mention. Yet the schools go on in their lumbering way, as though science and technology were an upstart fortune-seeker, invading the realm of the liberal arts with gadgetry and "things." The situation is often so bad and so ridiculous that a boy can come to manhood without picking up, in school, even elementary knowledge about the inner work-ings of standard parts of his intriguing environment—cars, radios, TV, space vehicles, building construction, etc.

I do not suggest that boys and girls should be segregated for instruction. The scanty evidence we have suggests that this is not preferable to coeducation. Besides, such segregation always works a hardship on someone—in this case it would be, as it used to be, the girls. But limited separation, for certain ages or subjects, might work better. We don't know. I am inclined to think, however, that the education that would best suit boys would also suit girls, at least better than what they now get, and I think we have to worry less about girls becoming more masculine than about boys becoming more feminine.

As a feminist I must admit to some selfish and ulterior motives. Only as men become at once stronger and more intellectual will it be permissible or advisable for women to do so. And, whatever improvements are made in the curriculum for the sake of boys will also profit girls.

ARE MEN REALLY MEN ANYMORE?

An Interview with
Lester A. Kirkendall
By James Lincoln Collier

What is a man supposed to be? Is there any such thing as masculinity? Are the old rules about how a man should behave, rules followed by our fathers, grandfathers, great-grandfathers, no longer valid?

Is there a "new masculinity," a new way for men to act, feel and think about themselves? One person who thinks so is Prof. Lester A. Kirkendall of Oregon State University, a warm and wise 68-year-old specialist in human relations and one of the pioneers of the sex-education movement. He sees in our society today the first gleamings of a new way for men to be, a new type of maleness. Here is what he believes:

Q. *What has it meant to be a man up until now?*

In the United States, the strong, silent man in control has been our ideal. As a father he was stern but forgiving. As a husband he dominated his wife. And it was crucial that no one see his feelings, because he believed it would undermine his authority. Boys were taught not to cry, and not to show affection, particularly for other boys. Even in his friendships, a man had to be tough. Recently I overheard a group

of college males talking. They were obviously friends, but they could express their affection only through a steady stream of pretended insults.

Q. *Have men always been like this?*

Far from it. In many former times, and even today in other places in the world, men have allowed themselves to express their tender feelings not only toward their wives or girl friends but toward other people, too. Not long ago I was speaking at a college, and I showed some slides of young men holding hands or with their arms around each other. When I ask for comments on this picture, the remarks I get usually center on homosexuality. But this time an Indonesian student in the audience said, "At home, men often put their arms around each other. Nobody thinks there's anything wrong with it. Why must it be so here?" So you see that America's strong, silent male ideal is by no means universal.

Q. *How did we develop that ideal?*

Many authorities think it had to do with the frontier beginnings of this country. Without getting into a complicated historical analysis, it has a lot to do with a man's ideas of his authority. When the pioneers were facing the rigors of an untamed land, a man had to be hard. The weakling could hardly take care of himself, much less his wife and children. Furthermore, a father had to demand that his wife and children endure hardship and toil without complaining. Thus, he couldn't give in to his feelings every time a child was cold or hungry. The ideal of the unyielding, stern male was stressed by these circumstances.

Q. *But you think this old ideal is vanishing?*

Yes. America has largely solved its problem of getting basic food and shelter. Our young people are now discovering that the old masculine ideal doesn't serve any purpose. They are searching for new ideals, and some are trying to put them into practice.

Q. *What are these new ideals?*

For one thing, young men today don't think that it is a sign of weakness to express tenderness toward people they care for. Older men still find this pretty difficult. Recently, a man in his 30s told me that he was troubled because his son still wants to kiss him on the lips. "Oh?" I said. "How old is he?" And the man replied, "Three." I felt terribly sorry for him, and even more for the boy.

Q. *Why did you feel sorry?*

Because he was denying himself and his son something vital to everybody. From the time my own children were young it was obvious that my son Karl's needs were as great as my daughter Karen's. All human beings want a sense of closeness and touching. Affection is not something only women need. It is a necessity for men, too. I think we are beginning to relearn this basic truth.

Q. *How does the "new masculinity" affect a man's relations with a woman?*

There are terrific changes in the wind here. In the past we have assumed that it was right for the husband to make final decisions, to be the boss. A man who often acceded to his wife's wishes was that figure of fun, the henpecked husband, the Caspar Milquetoast or Dagwood Bumpstead of the cartoon strips. Now more and more men are coming to realize that their masculinity is not threatened by sharing decisions or by taking on some of the so-called woman's work. A young teacher told me recently, "My wife has just as much right to develop her capacities as I have. She's taking some courses now that will enable her to teach. We have two kids, and the only way we could manage it was for me to baby-sit during her classes." A generation ago, a man who watched the children so his wife could study would have had to put up with a lot of bad jokes about who was wearing the pants. Today, most young people would take it for granted that this man is doing the right thing; they don't see that he's lost any masculinity. They believe that sharing is more important than asserting authority.

Q. *Are women growing stronger and males weaker?*

Emphatically not. It takes strength, not weakness, to compromise. The old masculinity would not bend, and often broke instead. The new male is attempting to be more flexible; like the bending reed, he may prove stronger than the storm. Take, for example, the sex act. Previously, the male assumed it was his right, indeed responsibility, to set the pace. Today many men are beginning to relinquish some control in this crucial area.

Q. *But isn't the male by nature the more easily aroused and therefore the one who initiates the sex act?*

Not necessarily. Women are quite as capable of of wanting sexual relations as men. And just as they are refusing to follow blindly the male lead in politics and work, more and more they feel it is perfectly acceptable for them to initiate the sex act on occasions—and even sometimes to be the active partner.

Q. *Are men going to accept this situation?*

The younger generation is already accepting it. I don't mean all of them by a long shot. No doubt of it, some men have trouble adapting to a sexual partner who takes the lead at times. In some cases they become impotent if pushed too hard by an assertive woman.

Q. *Some men, then, aren't going to accept "women's liberation" in bed?*

That's right. Their masculinity is too bound up with the idea of strength, and of being in control. According to the old standard, if a man "satisfied" his sex partner—that is, saw that she had an orgasm—his masculinity was confirmed.

But the "new masculinity" sees the sex act differently. Intercourse has become less merely a means to reproduce, more a matter of recreation. Sex is used less to assure a man that he is "all male," and more a means for expressing affection—of communicating, of finding closeness and intimacy. Men are going to have to learn to be more equalitarian in their sex lives or many of them are going to be defeated.

Q. *Aside from sex, how does the new freedom for women affect masculinity?*

For one thing, I think men are coming to be more willing to accept women in positions of authority. As I have said, the idea of sharing is becoming more important than who has the authority, for both men and women. A generation back the idea of a woman running for the Presidency was a subject for comedy, but it happened this year; and we know that some men are willing to vote for a woman for President. The same is true in business. I had to cope with this problem years ago. Because my courses in marriage and the family were included in the home-economics department of the university where I taught, my bosses were usually women. It rankled at first, but I got over it.

Q. *Do you think, then, that men are growing less concerned about dominance?*

The element of competition, of aggressiveness, is still there, and perhaps it always will be, but now the question is how to combine it with equality in action. Young men today seem more willing to attempt to put aside dominance, to work cooperatively.

Q. *Does all this mean, then, that we are approaching the day of "unisex"?*

No. There are some very real, deep-seated differences between the ways men and women feel, think and behave, whether you believe that they are built in by nature or by our culture. I suppose that most women, no matter how competent and self-sufficient, feel now and then that a bit of the old male paternalism would be good. My wife, for example, has always criticized her father for playing the old-fashioned dominant role in his marriage. But she definitely wants me to handle the security aspects of our marriage—insurance, mortgages and the like. So I think we will continue to see a male and female role in marriage. But the male ideal is changing. In the older day, we needed the relatively taciturn male—unyielding before the storm. Today, in a crowded, complex society, we need men who are flexible, cooperative.

But it is not just for the benefit of society that men are changing. Just as today's women are demanding the right to equal pay and more rewarding jobs, so today's young men are demanding the right to live emotionally richer lives. They don't want to spend their time controlling their feelings to meet some outmoded ideal of male strength; they want to enjoy the warmth and affection that bloom in close relationships.

What we need, in a way, is a kind of "men's lib" movement. I don't mean one that is directed against women. I mean a movement that would help us reorder our ideas of masculinity. Perhaps the women can help us in this, so that in the end we would have a "people's lib" movement, with more freedom of the heart for all.

THE IMPORTANCE OF BEING ERNEST—OR EVELYN

Carlfred B. Broderick

Being a girl isn't what it used to be and probably isn't what it's going to be, but then and now it's different from being a boy. In these days of unisex, women's lib, and gay militance I am sometimes asked whether sexual differences are becoming meaningless. My answer is that sex will always matter so long as women bear children and men father them. Some retort that it may become technically possible to bring children into the world some other way (with frozen sperm and eggs and artificial wombs). Maybe. But I personally doubt it. And so long as men and women play complementary roles in producing babies it will be important for each to be able to identify potential partners readily. It doesn't matter much what the apparent differences are— whether hair style or clothing or mannerisms or voice inflection; always there will be adequate cues.

It is fascinating to study the ways our society operates to perpetrate sex differences. From the very beginning children are named differently, handled differently, dressed differently according to their sex. Girl infants have bows scotchtaped to their hairless scalps and boys are dressed in pants long before their mobility would make it an advantage. It is true that many children wear play clothes that are identical for the sexes but rarely are "dress-up" clothes sexually ambiguous. One proof that we do an effective job in training very young children to think and act differently according to their sex comes from a special clinic at Johns Hopkins University where they work with children who, for various physical reasons, need to have their sex assignment changed. If the change can be made before age two, no serious problems are liable to arise but from two to three it gets increasingly difficult for the child and for the adults around him to adjust to the new assignment. After three the task gets so difficult that the advisability of trying must be very carefully evaluated. Somehow, by that tender age we have so indoctrinated a child that *he* is a boy or *she* is a girl that their identity as a separate individual is thoroughly tangled with his/her sexual identity.

Of course, teaching a child which of the two halves of the human race he or she belongs to is only the beginning. It is one thing to be clearly labelled "boy" in your own and everyone else's mind but it is another to learn to behave in the way that boys are supposed to behave. What constitutes "masculine" or "feminine" behavior is socially determined and varies from culture to culture and from time to time in our own culture.

One famous personality inventory which has been used to collect data on large samples of men and women over the last 30 years shows that in our culture the concept of masculinity has changed more over that time period than the concept of femininity. (This may surprise some who feel that women's liberation is pioneering the way for men's liberation.)

Thirty years ago it was more masculine to be interested in mechanics than in music, in mathematics than in literature and in things than in people. Ideas were more masculine than emotions and technical skills more than social skills. Independence was more masculine than either emotional dependence or nurturance. Only one out of six males had as "feminine" a score in the early 1940's as the average college male in the early 1970's. It is not, I think, useful to say that today's young men are more effeminate than formerly. Rather, the standard for what is masculine has changed. Business and industry and many of the professions put a higher value on emotional openness and warmth than on tough-minded competitiveness. There is more demand for interpersonal sensitivity than for unemotional rationalism. Cultural polish is more richly rewarded than mechanical adeptness.

Women, on their part, show only a slight shift toward the more independent and competitive end of the scale, although current studies are attempting to assess the impact of the burgeoning women's movement in the last two or three years. It is interesting to me to note that women's libers are not attempting to imitate men stylistically (except, perhaps, in adopting the male vernacular). They are not anxious to have women become indistinguishable from men by masking or denying their physical differences. Rather they want women, while retaining their unique qualities as women, to have equal access to economic reward and decision-making power and personal fulfillment. They have recognized what other sinned-against groups have recognized, that blind imitation of more powerful groups is a denial of one's own worth.

Despite these shifts and convergences it is still important in our society for a man to act masculinely within the limits of contemporary definition. A man who walks or talks or gestures "like a woman" is no more admired today than formerly. A girl who comes across as over-direct or too angular or who walks flat-footed is still unappreciated.

The concepts of masculinity are not only in the society, but in ourselves. This is a foundation for one of the most troublesome aspects of the highly advertised "generation gap." The parents' concepts of what is genuinely masculine or feminine were learned in another era and many are uncomfortable with their children's response to the different definitions of their own day.

But however the personal and sartorial style may have changed in the last 30 years it remains as important for a boy or girl to learn his/her sex role as ever. There are two unchanging bases for this. First, since in most cases a child's sense of self is fundamentally intertwined with its sense of being a boy or girl, great damage can be done by attacking either component. For example, in my marriage counseling practice I fairly often come across women who were clearly taught that one or the other of their parents wanted a boy. The sense of rejection this engendered lingered on into adulthood to interfere with the woman's basic feeling of worth. Similarly, there are men who as adults still live with the resentment they learned as children from their mothers who thought boys

were "not nice" and "too much trouble" compared to girls. These experiences inevitably have an impact upon one's whole self-concept as an acceptable person and not just upon his sex role.

A second reason that every child continues to need and deserve strong support in his sex role is that we live in the most thoroughly heterosexual society in the Western world. There is perhaps nothing that is voluntary that more Americans do than get married. Ninety-five percent of us get married at least once by the age of 40. That is more than watch television. Since surveys show that almost 10 percent of adult males are preferential homosexuals, this suggests that even half of our homosexuals get married heterosexually, so great is the pressure. Despite all of the talk about marriage being passé the national marriage rate is higher in this decade than it was in the 1950's and 1960's.

Clearly in a culture that places this kind of emphasis on heterosexual pairing it is vastly important to gain skills in playing the approved role vis-à-vis the opposite sex. By 5 years of age over half of the girls are sure that they want to get married eventually and by 12 over ninety percent have accepted this as their eventual goal. Boys are a bit slower to become oriented to marriage but marriage is not the only form of heterosexual pairing and the evidence is that boys are no less committed to heterosexuality than girls, albeit with a slightly different emphasis. From early grade-school onwards children have romantic fantasies and often real crushes on opposite sex classmates or adults. Success in these romantic endeavors becomes one of the chief cornerstones of self-image and peer evaluation. Indeed, much of adult fantasy and literature reveals the continuing preoccupation with these matters throughout life.

Some have been concerned that the new flexibility in role assignments between the sexes in courtship and marriage may either reflect or presage a loss of sex role identity. If men are more warmly involved with their wives and children than formerly, more open emotionally, more sensitive to others and more home-centered, does this mean [a man] has lost his sense of identity as a *man*? Similarly, does the woman who is more independent and assertive lose some essential essence of femininity? The issue will continue to be debated, but I would conclude from clinical experience that very often excessive rigidity grows out of anxiety, while flexibility in role definitions is more likely to occur among those secure in their sense of sex identity.

Differences between what is masculine and what is feminine need not be blatant to be of great importance. The point is illustrated by the tempest a few years ago when one of the Minneapolis papers ran a photograph of a pair of beautiful breasts with the caption, "Can you identify this famous movie star?" For three days they printed letters from outraged citizens who felt that the forces of rampant free sex had taken over a formerly responsible "family" newspaper. Then on the fourth day they showed the entire head and torso and it turned out to be the bust of Johnny Weissmuller of Tarzan fame (and a first class swimmer, hence the over-developed pectoral muscles). Then everyone laughed at the joke. But it was funny precisely because it *matters* whether the breasts belonged to a male or a female. If they belonged to a female they had powerful erotic significance for males, if to a male, none.

For all of these reasons I believe that sexual differences will always make a difference. No current social movement including women's lib or gay militancy is calculated to change that. In fact, both movements depend as heavily on categorizing the sexes as does traditional courtship, marriage and parenthood.

Times change and cultural definitions of what is masculine and what is feminine change. What does not change is the need in each individual to feel secure in his own identity and that includes his sexual identity. However the symbols may evolve which reassure me and others that I am a man and my mate is a woman, there will be such symbols and they will matter.

X: A FABULOUS CHILD'S STORY

Lois Gould

Once upon a time, a baby named X was born. This baby was named X so that nobody could tell whether it was a boy or a girl. Its parents could tell, of course, but they couldn't tell anybody else. They couldn't even tell Baby X, at first.

You see, it was all part of a very important Secret Scientific Xperiment, known officially as Project Baby X. The smartest scientists had set up this Xperiment at a cost of Xactly 23 billion dollars and 72 cents, which might seem like a lot for just one baby, even a very important Xperimental baby. But when you remember the prices of things like strained carrots and stuffed bunnies, and popcorn for the movies and booster shots for camp, let alone 28 shiny quarters from the tooth fairy, you begin to see how it adds up.

Also, long before Baby X was born, all those scientists had to be paid to work out the details of the Xperiment, and to write the *Official Instruction Manual* for Baby X's parents and, most important of all, to find the right set of parents to bring up Baby X. These parents had to be selected very carefully. Thousands of volunteers had to take thousands of tests and answer thousands of tricky questions. Almost everybody failed because, it turned out, almost everybody really wanted either a baby boy or a baby girl, and not Baby X at all. Also, almost everybody was afraid that a Baby X would be a lot more trouble than a boy or a girl. (They were probably right, the scientists admitted, but Baby X needed parents who wouldn't *mind* the Xtra trouble.)

There were families with grandparents named Milton and Agatha, who didn't see why the baby couldn't be named Milton or Agatha instead of X, even if it *was* an X. There were families with aunts who insisted on knitting tiny dresses and uncles who insisted on sending tiny baseball mitts. Worst of all, there were families that already had other children who couldn't be trusted to keep the secret. Certainly not if they knew the secret was worth 23 billion dollars and 72 cents—and all you had to do was take one little peek at Baby X in the bathtub to know if it was a boy or a girl.

But, finally, the scientists found the Joneses, who really wanted to raise an X more than any other kind of baby—no matter how much trouble it would be. Ms. and Mr. Jones had to promise they would take equal turns caring for X, and feeding it, and singing it lullabies. And they had to promise never to hire any baby-sitters. The government scientists knew perfectly well that a baby-sitter would probably peek at X in the bathtub, too.

The day the Joneses brought their baby home, lots of friends and relatives came over to see it. None of them knew about the secret Xperiment, though. So the first thing they asked was what kind of a baby X was. When the Joneses smiled and said, "It's an X!" nobody knew what to say. They couldn't say, "Look at her cute little dimples!" And they couldn't say, "Look at his husky little biceps!" And they couldn't even say just plain "kitchy-coo." In fact, they all thought the Joneses were playing some kind of rude joke.

But, of course, the Joneses were not joking. "It's an X" was absolutely all they would say. And that made the friends and relatives very angry. The relatives all felt embarrassed about having an X in the family. "People will think there's something wrong with it!" some of them whispered. "There *is* something wrong with it!" others whispered back.

"Nonsense!" the Joneses told them all cheerfully. "What could possibly be wrong with this perfectly adorable X?"

Nobody could answer that, except Baby X, who had just finished its bottle. Baby X's answer was a loud, satisfied burp.

Clearly, nothing at all was wrong. Nevertheless, none of the relatives felt comfortable about buying a present for a Baby X. The cousins who sent the baby a tiny football helmet would not come and visit any more. And the neighbors who sent a pink-flowered romper suit pulled their shades down when the Joneses passed their house.

The *Official Instruction Manual* had warned the new parents that this would happen, so they didn't fret about it. Besides, they were too busy with Baby X and the hundreds of different Xercises for treating it properly.

Ms. and Mr. Jones had to be Xtra careful about how they played with little X. They knew that if they kept bouncing it up in the air and saying how *strong* and *active* it was, they'd be treating it more like a boy than an X. But if all they did was cuddle it and kiss it and tell it how *sweet* and *dainty* it was, they'd be treating it more like a girl than an X.

On page 1,654 of the *Official Instruction Manual*, the scientists prescribed: "plenty of bouncing and plenty of cuddling, *both*. X ought to be strong and sweet and active. Forget about *dainty* altogether."

Meanwhile, the Joneses were worrying about other problems. Toys, for instance. And clothes. On his first shopping trip, Mr. Jones told the store clerk, "I need some clothes and toys for my new baby." The clerk smiled and said, "Well, now, is it a boy or a girl?" "It's an X," Mr. Jones said, smiling back. But the clerk got all red in the face and said huffily, "In *that* case, I'm afraid I can't help you, sir." So Mr. Jones wandered helplessly up and down the aisles trying to find what X needed. But everything in the store was piled up in sections marked "Boys" or "Girls." There were "Boys' Pajamas" and "Girls' Underwear" and "Boys' Fire Engines" and "Girls' Housekeeping Sets." Mr. Jones went home without buying anything for X. That night he and Ms. Jones consulted page 2,326 of the *Official Instruction Manual*. "Buy plenty of everything!" it said firmly.

So they bought plenty of sturdy blue pajamas in the Boys' Department and cheerful flowered underwear in the Girls' Department. And they bought all kinds of toys. A boy doll that made pee-pee and cried, "Pa-pa." And a girl doll that talked in three languages and said, "I am the Pres-i-dent of Gen-er-al Mo-tors." They also bought a storybook about a brave princess who rescued a handsome prince from his ivory tower, and another one

about a sister and brother who grew up to be a baseball star and a ballet star, and you had to guess which was which.

The head scientists of Project Baby X checked all their purchases and told them to keep up the good work. They also reminded the Joneses to see page 4,629 of the *Manual*, where it said, "Never make Baby X feel *embarrassed* or *ashamed* about what it wants to play with. And if X gets dirty climbing rocks, never say 'Nice little Xes don't get dirty climbing rocks.'"

Likewise, it said, "If X falls down and cries, never say 'Brave little Xes don't cry.' Because, of course, nice little Xes *do* get dirty, and brave little Xes *do* cry. No matter how dirty X gets, or how hard it cries, don't worry. It's all part of the Xperiment."

Whenever the Joneses pushed Baby X's stroller in the park, smiling strangers would come over and coo: "Is that a boy or a girl?" The Joneses would smile back and say, "It's an X." The strangers would stop smiling then, and often snarl something nasty—as if the Joneses had snarled at *them*.

By the time X grew big enough to play with other children, the Joneses' troubles had grown bigger, too. Once a little girl grabbed X's shovel in the sandbox, and zonked X on the head with it. "Now, now, Tracy," the little girl's mother began to scold, "little girls musn't hit little—" and she turned to ask X, "Are you a little boy or a little girl, dear?"

Mr. Jones, who was sitting near the sandbox, held his breath and crossed his fingers.

X smiled politely at the lady, even though X's head had never been zonked so hard in its life. "I'm a little X," X replied.

"You're a *what?*" the lady exclaimed angrily. "You're a little b-r-a-t, you mean!"

"But little girls mustn't hit little Xes, either!" said X, retrieving the shovel with another polite smile. "What good does hitting do, anyway?"

X's father, who was still holding his breath, finally let it out, uncrossed his fingers, and grinned back at X.

And at their next secret Project Baby X meeting, the scientists grinned, too. Baby X was doing fine.

But then it was time for X to start school. The Joneses were really worried about this, because school was even more full of rules for boys and girls, and there were no rules for Xes. The teacher would tell boys to form one line, and girls to form another line. There would be boys' games and girls' games, and boys' secrets and girls' secrets. The school library would have a list of recommended books for girls, and a different list of recommended books for boys. There would even be a bathroom marked BOYS and another one marked GIRLS. Pretty soon boys and girls would hardly talk to each other. What would happen to poor little X?

The Joneses spent weeks consulting their *Instruction Manual* (there were 249½ pages of advice under "First Day of School"), and attending urgent special conferences with the smart scientists of Project Baby X.

The scientists had to make sure that X's mother had taught X how to throw and catch a ball properly, and that X's father had been sure to teach X what to serve at a doll's tea party. X had to know how to shoot marbles and how to jump rope and, most of all, what to say when the Other Children asked whether X was a Boy or a Girl.

Finally, X was ready. The Joneses helped X button on a nice new pair of red-and-white checked overalls, and sharpened six pencils for X's nice new pencilbox, and marked X's name clearly on all the books in its nice new bookbag. X brushed its teeth and combed its hair, which just about covered its ears, and remembered to put a napkin in its lunchbox.

The Joneses had asked X's teacher if the class could line up alphabetically, instead of forming separate lines for boys and girls. And they had asked if X could use the principal's bathroom, because it wasn't marked anything except BATH-ROOM. X's teacher promised to take care of all those problems. But nobody could help X with the biggest problem of all—Other Children.

Nobody in X's class had ever known an X before. What would they think? How would X make friends?

You couldn't tell what X was by studying its clothes—overalls don't even button right-to-left, like girls' clothes, or left-to-right, like boys' clothes. And you couldn't guess whether X had a girl's short haircut or a boy's long haircut. And it was very hard to tell by the games X liked to play. Either X played ball very well for a girl, or else X played house very well for a boy.

Some of the children tried to find out by asking X tricky questions, like "Who's your favorite sports star?" That was easy. X had two favorite sports stars: a girl jockey named Robyn Smith and a boy archery champion named Robin Hood. Then they asked, "What's your favorite TV program?" And that was even easier. X's favorite TV program was "Lassie," which stars a girl dog played by a boy dog.

When X said that its favorite toy was a doll, everyone decided that X must be a girl. But then X said that the doll **was** really a robot, and that X had computerized it, and that it was programmed to bake fudge brownies and then clean up the kitchen. After X told them that, the other children gave up guessing what X was. All they knew was they'd sure like to see X's doll.

After school, X wanted to play with the other children. "How about shooting some baskets in the gym?" X asked the girls. But all they did was make faces and giggle behind X's back.

"How about weaving some baskets in the arts and crafts room?" X asked the boys. But they all made faces and giggled behind X's back, too.

That night, Ms. and Mr. Jones asked X how things had gone at school. X told them sadly that the lessons were okay, but otherwise school was a terrible place for an X. It seemed as if Other Children would never want an X for a friend.

Once more, the Joneses reached for their *Instruction Manual.* Under "Other Children," they found the following message: "What did you Xpect? *Other Children* have to obey all the silly boy-girl rules, because their parents taught them to. Lucky X—you don't have to stick to the rules at all! All you have to do is be yourself. P.S. We're not saying it'll be easy."

X liked being itself. But X cried a lot that night, partly because it felt afraid. So X's father held X tight, and cuddled it, and couldn't help crying a little, too. And X's mother cheered them both up by reading an Xciting story about an enchanted prince called Sleeping Handsome, who woke up when Princess Charming kissed him.

The next morning, they all felt much better, and little X went back to school with a brave smile and a clean pair of red-and-white checked overalls.

There was a seven-letter-word spelling bee in class that day. And a seven-lap boys' relay race in the gym. And a seven-layer-cake baking contest in the girls' kitchen corner. X won the spelling bee. X also won the relay race. And X almost won the baking contest, except it forgot to light the oven. Which only proves that nobody's perfect. Other Children noticed something else, too. He said: "Winning or losing doesn't seem to count to X. X seems to have fun being good at boys' skills *and* girls' skills."

"Come to think of it," said another one of the Other Children, "maybe X is having twice as much fun as we are!"

So after school that day, the girl who beat X at the baking contest gave X a big slice of her prize-winning cake. And the boy X beat in the relay race asked X to race him home.

From then on, some really funny things began to happen. Susie, who sat next to X in class, suddenly refused to wear pink dresses to school any more. She insisted on wearing red-and-white checked overalls—just like X's. Overalls, she told her parents, were much better for climbing monkey bars.

Then Jim, the class football nut, started wheeling his little sister's doll carriage around the football field. He'd put on his entire football uniform, except for the helmet. Then he'd put the helmet in the carriage, lovingly tucked under an old set of shoulder pads. Then he'd start jogging around the field, pushing the carriage and singing "Rockabye Baby" to his football helmet. He told his family that X did the same thing, so it must be okay. After all, X was now the team's star quarterback.

Susie's parents were horrified by her behavior, and Jim's parents were worried sick about his. But the worst came when the twins, Joe and Peggy, decided to share everything with each other. Peggy used Joe's hockey skates, and his microscope, and took half his newspaper route. Joe used Peggy's needlepoint kit, and her cook-books, and took two of her three baby-sitting jobs. Peggy started running the lawn mower, and Joe started running the vacuum cleaner.

Their parents weren't one bit pleased with Peggy's wonderful biology experiments, or with Joe's terrific needlepoint pillows. They didn't care that Peggy mowed the lawn better, and that Joe vacuumed the carpet better. In fact, they were furious. It's all that little X's fault, they agreed. Just because X doesn't know what it is, or what it's supposed to be, it wants to get everybody *else* mixed up, too!

Peggy and Joe were forbidden to play with X any more. So was Susie, and then Jim, and then *all* the Other Children. But it was too late; the Other Children stayed mixed up and happy and free, and refused to go back to the way they'd been before X.

Finally, Joe and Peggy's parents decided to call an emergency meeting of the school's Parents' Association, to discuss "The X Problem." They sent a report to the principal stating that X was a "disruptive influence." They demanded immediate action. The Joneses, they said, should be *forced* to tell whether X was a boy or a girl. And then X should be *forced* to behave like whichever it was. If the Joneses refused to tell, the Parents' Association said, then X must take an Xamination. The school psychiatrist must Xamine it physically and mentally, and issue a full report. If X's test showed it was a boy, it would have to obey all the boys' rules. If it proved to be a girl, X would have to obey all the girls' rules.

And if X turned out to be some kind of mixed-up misfit, then X should be Xpelled from the school. Immediately!

The principal was very upset. Disruptive influence? Mixed-up misfit? But X was an Xcellent student. All the teachers said it was a delight to have X in their classes. X was president of the student council. X had won first prize in the talent show, and second prize in the art show, and honorable mention in the science fair, and six athletic events on field day, including the potato race.

Nevertheless, insisted the Parents' Association, X is a Problem Child. X is the Biggest Problem Child we have ever seen!

So the principal reluctantly notified X's parents that numerous complaints about X's behavior had come to the school's attention. And that after the psychiatrist's Xamination, the school would decide what to do about X.

The Joneses reported this at once to the scientists, who referred them to page 85,759 of the *Instruction Manual*. "Sooner or later," it said, "X will have to be Xamined by a psychiatrist. This may be the only way any of us will know for sure whether X is mixed up—or whether everyone else is."

The night before X was to be Xamined, the Joneses tried not to let X see how worried they were. "What if—?" Mr. Jones would say. And Ms. Jones would reply, "No use worrying." Then a few minutes later, Ms. Jones would say, "What if—?" and Mr. Jones would reply, "No use worrying."

X just smiled at them both, and hugged them hard and didn't say much of anything. X was thinking, What if—? And then X thought: No use worrying.

At Xactly 9 o'clock the next day, X reported to the school psychiatrist's office. The principal, along with a committee from the Parents' Association, X's teacher, X's classmates, and Ms. and Mr. Jones, waited in the hall outside. Nobody knew the details of the tests X was to be given, but everybody knew they'd be *very* hard, and that they'd reveal Xactly what everyone wanted to know about X, but were afraid to ask.

It was terribly quiet in the hall. Almost spooky. Once in a while, they would hear a strange noise inside the room. There were buzzes. And a beep or two. And several bells. An occasional light would flash under the door. The Joneses thought it was a white light, but the principal thought it was blue. Two or three children swore it was either yellow or green. And the Parents' Committee missed it completely.

Through it all, you could hear the psychiatrist's low voice, asking hundreds of questions, and X's higher voice, answering hundreds of answers.

The whole thing took so long that everyone knew it must be the most complete Xamination anyone had ever had to take. Poor X, the Joneses thought. Serves X right, the Parents' Committee thought. I wouldn't like to be in X's overalls right now, the children thought.

At last, the door opened. Everyone crowded around to hear the results. X didn't look any different; in fact, X was smiling. But the psychiatrist looked terrible. He looked as if he was crying! "What happened?" everyone began shout-ing. Had X done something disgraceful? "I wouldn't be a bit surprised!" muttered Peggy and Joe's parents. "Did X flunk the *whole* test?" cried Susie's parents. "Or just the most important part?" yelled Jim's parents.

"Oh, dear," sighed Mr. Jones.

"Oh, dear," sighed Ms. Jones.

"*Sssh*," ssshed the principal. "The psychiatrist is trying to speak."

Wiping his eyes and clearing his throat, the psychiatrist began, in a hoarse whisper. "In my opinion," he whispered—you could tell he must be very upset—"in my opinion, young X here—"

"Yes? Yes?" shouted a parent impatiently.

"*Sssh!*" ssshed the principal.

"Young *Sssh* here, I mean young X," said the doctor, frowning, "is just about—"

"Just about *what*? Let's have it!" shouted another parent.

". . . just about the *least* mixed-up child I've ever Xamined!" said the psychiatrist.

"Yay for X!" yelled one of the children. And then the others began yelling, too. Clapping and cheering and jumping up and down.

"SSSH!" SSShed the principal, but nobody did.

The Parents' Committee was angry and bewildered. How *could* X have passed the whole Xamination? Didn't X have an *identity* problem? Wasn't X mixed up at *all*? Wasn't X *any* kind of a misfit? How could it *not* be, when it didn't even *know* what it was? And why was the psychiatrist crying?

Actually, he had stopped crying and was smiling politely through his tears. "Don't you see?" he said. "I'm crying because it's wonderful! X has absolutely no identity problem! X isn't one bit mixed up! As for being a misfit—ridiculous! X knows perfectly well what it is! Don't you, X?" The doctor winked. X winked back.

"But what *is* X?" shrieked Peggy and Joe's parents. "*We* still want to know what it is!"

"Ah, yes," said the doctor, winking again. "Well, don't worry. You'll all know one of these days. And you won't need me to tell you."

"What? What does he mean?" some of the parents grumbled suspiciously.

Susie and Peggy and Joe all answered at once. "He means that by the time X's sex matters, it won't be a secret any more!"

With that, the doctor began to push through

the crowd toward X's parents. "How do you do," he said, somewhat stiffly. And then he reached out to hug them both. "If I ever have an X of my own," he whispered, "I sure hope you'll lend me your instruction manual."

Needless to say, the Joneses were very happy. The Project Baby X scientists were rather pleased, too. So were Susie, Jim, Peggy, Joe, and all the Other Children. The Parents' Association wasn't, but they had promised to accept the psychiatrist's report, and not make any more trouble. They even invited Ms. and Mr. Jones to become honorary members, which they did.

Later that day, all X's friends put on their red-and-white checked overalls and went over to see X. They found X in the back yard, playing with a very tiny baby that none of them had ever seen before. The baby was wearing very tiny red-and-white checked overalls.

"How do you like our new baby?" X asked the Other Children proudly.

"It's got cute dimples," said Jim.

"It's got husky biceps, too," said Susie.

"What kind of baby is it?" asked Joe and Peggy.

X frowned at them. "Can't you tell?" Then X broke into a big, mischievous grin. *"It's a Y!"*

PART II

Behaving: Problem Motives

To live—to be alive—is to be active, and human beings appear to be in a nearly constant state of motion. We have certain needs that push and drive us. We have certain goals that pull and draw us. Pushed by our needs and pulled by our goals, we rouse ourself and eat, drink, fight, love, work, play, laugh, cry, dance, jog, and do countless other things.

Varied as our activities appear and unpredictable as we sometimes seem to be, human behavior when viewed in perspective is rather consistent or patterned. We tend to behave in somewhat the same ways, responding to the same needs and seeking out the same goals. These patterns of need-impelled and goal-directed activity are called motives.

When we describe human beings, we frequently make use of motivational concepts or ideas. For example, one person may be characterized by his strong autonomy motive, by his need to rebel and assert his freedom and independence; by contrast, another may be low in autonomy needs and constantly seeking support and help. Or an individual may have a notable drive to boss, control, and dominate others in sharp distinction to some of us who customarily defer and acquiesce.

In our society certain motives have been found to be particularly prone to lead to problems. These include patterns of behavior that are frequently frustrated, those that compete with other motives, resulting in conflict, and some that give rise to a good deal of anxiety. Part II of the book will focus on three high-problem motives: achievement, aggression, and sex.

Achievement has been a particularly bothersome pattern of behavior in this country. Ours has been an achieving society, one that has valued and emphasized excellence, status, and money. We are exhorted to try hard and do well. However, in recent years some critics have wondered whether we are under too much pressure to achieve, whether it is wise to press each individual to the limits of his ability, and whether an emphasis on achievement and competition is bringing our country to the brink of social and ecological disaster.

A second problem motive is aggression. Aggressive actions are a very popular part of our behavior repertory and prove highly satisfying, rewarding, and practical in many situations. At the same time aggression disrupts human relationships, invites retaliation, and is at the root of some important interpersonal and international problems. What can be done about aggression? Is aggression in our genes and perhaps inextricably a part of us? What should we do? Should we attempt to make ourselves over into less aggressive beings and into a less aggressive society?

A third problem motive is sex. There has been much controversy about whether or not we are undergoing a "sexual revolution," but there is no doubt that we live in an eroticized era with much more candor and permissiveness than ever before. How can each of us arrive at a philosophy of sex which is right for us? How can we relate our sexual being to the rest of who we are? These are basic questions that we should consider, and the readings which follow may help us to arrive at insights and answers.

TOPIC 4

Achievement

Let me introduce myself. I am a man who at the precocious age of thirty-five experienced an astonishing revelation: it is better to be a success than a failure. Having been penetrated by this great truth concerning the nature of things, my mind was now open for the first time to a series of corollary perceptions, each one as dizzying in its impact as the Original Revelation itself. Money, I now saw (no one, of course, had ever seen it before), was important: it was better to be rich than to be poor. Power, I now saw (moving on to higher subtleties), was desirable: it was better to give orders than to take them. Fame, I now saw (how courageous of me not to flinch), was unqualifiedly delicious: it was better to be recognized than to be anonymous.

—Norman Podhoretz

Many a father who has spent the years from 22 to 52 in a mad race to accumulate now finds himself powerless to answer his children who ask, "Why did you do it, Pop? What good did you get out of it? What have you got to show for the rat race except two cars and three picture windows?" These are terrifying questions to throw at a man in his 50s.

—James Michener

Purdue University, where I earned my B.S. degree, used to publish the names of all students who earned an "A" average during the previous semester. The first time my name was listed I was enraged, told the newspaper office "they had a nerve," and in general carried on outrageously—and the reason, which I was fully aware of, was my fear that now the girls would dislike me and the boys would be afraid of me. In other words, my academic success would shoot my social life down.

—Judith M. Bardwick

To *achieve* means to overcome obstacles, accomplish difficult things, and surpass others. The achieving person is one who shows a high degree of striving, excellence, and success. Psychological research indicates that persons who test high in this motive tend to seek out and enjoy challenges, to try hard and succeed at various tasks, and to make good grades and advance their education. Such persons also have realistic vocational goals, make progress in their careers, and are upward mobile.

In contrast with persons who are driven toward success, psychologists have identified some who are motivated by the fear of failure. What a success-seeking person finds challenging, a failure-avoiding person might regard an intimidation. Those who fear failure prefer activities where success is assured or where success is so unlikely that no one would be criticized for failing. Situations with uncertain outcomes and those that place the individual under scrutiny or evaluation are avoided. It has been hypothesized that persons who behave in this way have early histories of strong punishment for failure but only weak reward for success. Such persons seek jobs in which there is order and gradual advancement and where responsibility is shared.

A further contrast can be made between those persons who fail to achieve because they fear failure and those who fail because they fear success itself. Persons can fear success (and arrange to fail) for a number of reasons. Some women, for example, fear high achievement because they regard it as unfeminine. Achievement or success can also be feared and avoided because it makes a person (possibly one with a punitive conscience or a shrunken self image) feel unworthy of it or unable to sustain it. Or success may threaten a valued dependency on another person.

American society has been an achieving one. In fact, achievement has been one of our foremost values. The English political scientist Harold Laski has written, "The vital roots of the American spirit are either the building of a fortune or the building of a reputation which makes you held in esteem by your neighbors." To Laski the symbol of this spirit was superachiever Benjamin Franklin: statesman, diplomat, author, philosopher, scientist, inventor, businessman, and, for good measure, founder of a college.

Not everyone in our culture, of course, is driven to achieve, and scientists have been curious about the correlates and causes of this kind of motivation. Family environment appears to play an important part. High achievement motives have been found in children who have been encouraged to do well and especially to do well on their own. Parents of these children set high—but attainable—standards of performance and are warmly rewarding when these standards are met. In sum, high achievers tend to have early histories of high goals, high success, and high rewards.

Socioeconomic class is also related to achievement. As compared to middle-class persons, those in the lower class generally demonstrate less achievement motivation. (A student from a rough neighborhood took exception to this generalization. "Where I came from," he said, "simply to survive was an achievement.") Unless they are upwardly mobile, lower-class parents may not serve as achievement models for their children, and there may be little encouragement and support for achievement from other family members and peers. As a rule, lower-income children have less access to educational materials (books, newspapers, magazines, encyclopedias), less achievement-oriented schools and neighborhoods, and less opportunity to continue their education beyond a certain level.

Men demonstrate higher achievement motivation than women. In both adolescent and adult populations, males have been found to be more concerned with academic achievement and vocational success while females are more concerned with social or interpersonal matters. Socialization forces are important in this regard because girls outperform boys in elementary and secondary school. However, highly achieving girls may find themselves under considerable pressure during adolescence to redefine themselves and emphasize an identity based primarily on interpersonal relationships. And, as was indicated earlier, a young woman may fear success as much as failure if high achievement is considered to be unfeminine or otherwise unacceptable to those around her.

Some observers feel that America's strength derives in large part from its high emphasis on achievement and its consequent economic growth. One prominent psychologist holds that to help the poor in this country and to help poor and underdeveloped countries it is necessary not only to provide economic opportunities but also to undertake motivation training to increase the individual's desire to achieve. Such training has already been tried out with some success.

Other observers are less sanguine about achievement motivation at least in as far as the United States is concerned. They point out that although the rewards of achievement can be high, the costs can also be high both to the society and the individual. Concerning the society, some feel that at our present stage of development—or overdevelopment—and with our various societal ills, the present emphasis on achievement and competition might be better replaced by one on such prosocial behaviors as altruism, cooperation, and helping.

As for benefits for the individual, some authorities question the wisdom of pushing one to the limits of one's ability. For example, the academic success of a student can be purchased at great expense to the rest of his development. Persons who fight to the top of the achievement ladder not infrequently look back to wonder if it was all worth it. And some recent research indicates that the death rate from ulcers and hypertension is significantly higher in countries with high achievement motivation than in countries placing less emphasis on achievement.

The call to achievement

"If at first you don't succeed, try, try again." "Anything worth doing is worth doing well." These adages represent the many exhortations to achievement we receive throughout the socialization process. In the same spirit John W. Gardner writes in the lead article, "Our society cannot achieve greatness unless individuals at many levels of ability accept the need for high standards of performance and strive to achieve those standards within the limits possible for them." Gardner is concerned with "toning up" the society and bringing it to the "peak of performance.' In his opinion, not many people achieve excellence, but more of us could if we tried, and all of us should try.

In the drive for academic excellence, some students are forced to pay too high a price, according to Robert J. Fisher and Hannelore Wass in the second reading. They write that teachers push their students toward intellectual success at the expense of other goals. But most students do not reach the high standards set for them, and some end up with lowered opinions of themselves and a confused sense of values or a rejection of educational and societal norms.

Failures of achievement

In the third selection Harvey P. Mandel and Jim Uebner describe a non-achievement syndrome and trace it to powerful dependency needs that overwhelm impulses toward independence. As they see it, the nonachieving person is not unmotivated; rather, he is motivated to fail or to keep himself from the threat that independence poses. The article describes how, with the guidance of a counselor (the senior author), a student (the junior author) learned to take responsibility for the direction of his own life. This change is illustrated in a series of poems written by the student during the course of counseling.

Travesties of achievement

Achievement behavior may go awry and become a burlesque or caricature of itself. For some of us, no matter how well we do it's never good enough; we tell ourself we must do better. And for others, no matter how hard we labor, it's never hard enough; we give our whole life over to work.

In the fourth article, Marc H. Hollender discusses a common travesty of achievement: perfectionism. Perfectionists constantly demand a higher level of performance than is required by the situation. Such persons typically have early histories of trying—never quite successfully—to gain approval of difficult-to-please parents. In their perfectionistic behavior, these individuals attempt to prove their worth to others and to themselves. Perfectionists never achieve all they might in life because they limit themselves to what they can do perfectly, and they never obtain deep satisfaction in their achievements because no matter how well they do, it is never quite good enough.

In the last article Wayne E. Oates discusses an achievement disorder with which he is personally afflicted: "workaholism." The workaholic is addicted to work just as the alcoholic is addicted to drink, in fact, the two share a number of symptoms and remedies. As Oates sees it, the workaholic prides himself on his dedication to his occupation or profession and has no confidence in his worth in any other area of life. Workaholics need to work at working less and valuing themselves more.

FOR PERSONAL APPLICATION

1. Describe your own achievement motivation. How strong is it? How is it manifested? How satisfied are you with this aspect of yourself?
2. Would you describe yourself as an "underachiever" or an "over-achiever"? Discuss yourself in these terms.
3. Have you ever been motivated by the "fear of failure"? Discuss yourself in this regard.
4. Have you ever been motivated by the "fear of success"? Discuss yourself in this regard.
5. Discuss the familial, cultural, and other factors which have influenced the level and patterning of your achievement motivation.
6. Have your achievement needs ever conflicted with some of your other needs such as dependency and affiliation? Discuss one of these conflicts.
7. At this point in your life, what must you achieve in order to be happy or satisfied? Why? Can you be sure you will be content when you reach these goals? Why or why not?
8. Do you feel our society places too much emphasis on achievement or excellence? Why or why not?
9. Do you feel our society impedes achievement by females? Why or why not?
10. Suppose this country had not emphasized achievement during the past century or two. How different would we be as a country or people today?
11. Write down a discussion item (not given above) that seems particularly relevant to this topic and you, and discuss it.

FOR SMALL GROUPS

1. *Sharing achievement.* Each member brings something to the group or shares something with the group that represents an important achievement in his life.
2. *Sharing failure.* Each member brings something to the group or shares something with the group that represents an important failure in his life.
3. *Assessing achievement in the group.* Each member in turn discusses something he has already achieved in the group and/or something he would like to achieve in the group.
4. *Analyzing achievement in life pursuits.* Each member in turn discusses his achievement in some life pursuit or endeavor. How much is each member motivated by the need for success? How much by the fear of failure? How much by the need to avoid success? And how much by the need to fail?
5. *Plumbing achievement goals.* Members of the group divide into pairs. One partner of each pair asks the second, "What do you want?" As

soon as the other partner responds, the first partner repeats this question and keeps repeating it, pausing only for each response. When the responses are less readily forthcoming, the partners exchange roles and proceed as before. Afterwards the entire group reassembles to discuss the feelings and insights raised by this procedure.

FOR FURTHER READING

Atkinson, J. W., and N. T. Feather, eds. *A Theory of Achievement Motivation.* New York: John Wiley & Sons, Inc., 1966.

Gardner, J. W. *Excellence: Can We Be Equal and Excellent Too?* New York: Harper & Row, Publishers, 1961.

Huber, R. M. *The American Idea of Success.* New York: McGraw-Hill Book Company, 1971.

McClelland, D. C. *The Achieving Society.* Princeton, N.J.: D. Van Nostrand Co., Inc., 1961.

McClelland, D. C., and J. W. Atkinson, R. A. Clark, and E. L. Lowell. *The Achievement Motive.* New York: Appleton-Century-Crofts, Inc., 1953.

McClelland, D. C., and D. G. Winter. *Motivating Economic Achievement.* New York: The Free Press, 1969.

Milner, E. *The Failure of Success: The Middle-class Crisis,* 2nd ed. St. Louis: Warren H. Green, 1968.

Oates, W. *Confessions of a Workaholic.* New York: World, 1971.

Peter, L. J. *The Peter Prescription.* New York: William Morrow, 1972.

Peter, L. J., and R. Hull. *The Peter Principle.* New York: William Morrow, 1969.

THE IDEA OF EXCELLENCE

John W. Gardner

THE MANY KINDS OF EXCELLENCE

I have said that no society can solve its internal conflicts unless its members are lifted above the tensions of the moment by powerful shared purposes. With this in mind, let us examine certain of our own shared purposes—particularly those which bear on the problem of excellence. It will be useful to begin by reviewing our notions concerning excellence itself.

There are many varieties of excellence. This is one of those absurdly obvious truths of which we must continually remind ourselves. The Duke of Wellington, in a famous incident, revealed an enviable understanding of it. The government was considering the dispatch of an expedition to Burma to take Rangoon. The Cabinet summoned Wellington and asked him who would be the ablest general to head such an undertaking. He said, "Send Lord Combermere." The government officials protested: "But we have always understood that your Grace thought Lord Combermere a fool." The Duke's response was vigorous and to the point. "So he is a fool, and a damned fool, but he can take Rangoon."[1]

In the intellectual field alone there are many kinds of excellence. There is the kind of intellectual activity that leads to a new theory, and the kind that leads to a new machine. There is the mind that finds its most effective expression in teaching and the mind that is most at home in re-

[1] G. W. E. Russell, *Collections and Recollections* (New York: Harper & Brothers, 1903).

search. There is the mind that works best in quantitative terms, and the mind that luxuriates in poetic imagery.

And there is excellence in art, in music, in craftsmanship, in human relations, in technical work, in leadership, in parental responsibilities.

Some kinds of excellence can be fostered by the educational system, and others must be fostered outside the educational system. Some kinds—e.g., managerial—may lead to worldly success, and others—e.g., compassion—may not.

There are types of excellence that involve doing something well and types that involve being a certain kind of person. There are kinds of excellence so subjective that the world cannot even observe much less appraise them. Montaigne wrote, "It is not only for an exterior show or ostentation that our soul must play her part, but inwardly within ourselves, where no eyes shine but ours."

There is a way of measuring excellence that involves comparison between people—some are musical geniuses and some are not; and there is another that involves comparison between myself at my best and myself at my worst. It is this latter comparison which enables me to assert that I am being true to the best that is in me—or forces me to confess that I am not.

Definitions of excellence tend to be most narrow at the point where we are selecting individuals, or testing them, or training them. In the course of daily life, mature people recognize many varieties of excellence in one another. But when we are selecting, testing or training we arbitrarily narrow the range. The reasons for doing so are practical ones. Narrowing the grounds for selection is one way of making the selection process manageable. To the extent that we admit a great variety of kinds of excellence we make the task of testing virtually impossible.

Consider the relatively narrow bottleneck through which most youngsters enter a career as a scientist. What they need to a very high degree is the capacity to manipulate abstract symbols and to give the kind of intellectual response required on intelligence tests. This capacity for abstract reasoning, and for the manipulation of mathematical and verbal symbols, is useful not only on the tests but in every course they take. The capacity to understand these symbols in various combinations and to reproduce them on paper in other combinations is priceless. There are other factors which contribute to success in graduate school, but most graduate students would agree that this is the heart and soul of the matter.

On the other hand, if one looks at a group of mature scientists—in their fifties, let us say—one finds that those who are respected have gained their reputations through exercising a remarkable variety of talents. One is honored for his extraordinary gifts as a teacher: his students are his great contribution to the world. Another is respected for the penetrating ideas he puts into the stream of the science. Another is respected—though perhaps not loved—for his devastating critical faculties. And so the list goes. Some are specialists by nature, some generalists; some creative, some plodding; some gifted in action, some in expression.

Anyone who looks at the way in which the world judges his own contemporaries will recognize the varied standards of judgment which come into play. But though in daily life we recognize a good many kinds of high performance, we rarely make this variety explicit in our thinking about excellence.

And though we admit a considerable range of excellences, we are still narrower in this respect than we should be. One way to make ourselves see this is to reflect on the diverse kinds of excellence that human beings have honored at different times and places. At any given time in a particular society, the idea of what constitutes excellence tends to be limited—but the conception changes as we move from one society to another or one century to another. Baltasar Gracián said:

It is not everyone that finds the age he deserves. . . . Some men have been worthy of a better century, for every species of good does not triumph. Things have their period; even excellences are subject to fashion.[2]

Taking the whole span of history and literature, the images of excellence are amply varied: Confucius teaching the feudal lords to govern wisely

[2] Baltasar Gracián, *The Art of Worldly Wisdom* (1647), trans., Joseph Jacobs (New York: The Macmillan Company, 1892), p. 12.

. . . Leonidas defending the pass at Thermopylae . . . Saint Francis preaching to the birds at Alviano . . . Lincoln writing the second inaugural "with malice toward none" . . . Mozart composing his first oratorio at the age of eleven . . . Galileo dropping weights from the Tower of Pisa . . . Emily Dickinson jotting her "letters to the world" on scraps of paper . . . Jesus saying, "Father, forgive them; for they know not what they do." . . . Florence Nightingale nursing the wounded at Balaclava . . . Eli Whitney pioneering the manufacture of interchangeable parts . . . Ruth saying to Naomi, "Thy people shall be my people."

The list is long and the variety is great. Taken collectively, human societies have gone a long way toward exploring the full range of human excellences. But a particular society at a given moment in history is apt to honor only a portion of the full range. And wise indeed is the society that is not afraid to face hard questions about its own practices on this point. Is it honoring the excellences which are most fruitful for its own continued vitality? To what excellences is it relatively insensitive; and what does this imply for the tone and texture of its life? Is it squandering approbation on kinds of high performance which have nothing to contribute to its creativity as a society?

If any one among us can contemplate those questions without uneasiness, he has not thought very long nor very hard about excellence in the United States.

TONING UP THE WHOLE SOCIETY

A conception which embraces many kinds of excellence at many levels is the only one which fully accords with the richly varied potentialities of mankind; it is the only one which will permit high morale throughout the society.

Our society cannot achieve greatness unless individuals at many levels of ability accept the need for high standards of performance and strive to achieve those standards within the limits possible for them. We want the highest conceivable excellence, of course, in the activities crucial to our effectiveness and creativity as a society; but that isn't enough. If the man in the street says,

"Those fellows at the top have to be good, but I'm just a slob and can act like one"—then our days of greatness are behind us. We must foster a conception of excellence which may be applied to every degree of ability and to every socially acceptable activity. A missile may blow up on its launching pad because the designer was incompetent or because the mechanic who adjusted the valve was incompetent. The same is true of everything else in our society. We need excellent physicists and excellent mechanics. We need excellent cabinet members and excellent first-grade teachers. The tone and fiber of our society depend upon a pervasive and almost universal striving for good performance.

And we are not going to get that kind of striving, that kind of alert and proud attention to performance, unless we can instruct the whole society in a conception of excellence that leaves room for everybody who is willing to strive—a conception of excellence which means that whoever I am or whatever I am doing, provided that I am engaged in a socially acceptable activity, some kind of excellence is within my reach. As James B. Conant put it, "Each honest calling, each walk of life, has its own elite, its own aristocracy based upon excellence of performance."

We cannot meet the challenge facing our free society unless we can achieve and maintain a high level of morale and drive throughout the society. One might argue that in any society which has spread prosperity as widely as ours has, morale will be universally high. But prosperity and morale are not inseparable. It is possible to be prosperous and apathetic. It is possible to be fat and demoralized. Men must have goals which, in their eyes, merit effort and commitment; and they must believe that their efforts will win them self-respect and the respect of others.

This is the condition of society we must work toward. Then, unhampered by popular attitudes disparaging excellence, we can dedicate ourselves to the cultivation of distinction and a sense of quality. We can demand the best of our most gifted, most talented, most spirited youngsters. And we can render appropriate honor to that striving for excellence which has produced so many of mankind's greatest achievements.

It is important to bear in mind that we are now talking about an approach to excellence and a conception of excellence that will bring a whole society to the peak of performance. The gifted individual absorbed in his own problems of creativity and workmanship may wish to set himself much narrower and very much more severe standards of excellence. The critic concerned with a particular development in art, let us say, may wish to impose a far narrower and more specialized criterion of excellence. This is understandable. But we are concerned with the broader objective of toning up a whole society.

This broader objective is critically important, even for those who have set themselves far loftier (and narrower) personal standards of excellence. We cannot have islands of excellence in a sea of slovenly indifference to standards. In an era when the masses of people were mute and powerless it may have been possible for a tiny minority to maintain high standards regardless of their surroundings. But today the masses of people are neither mute nor powerless. As consumers, as voters, as the source of Public Opinion, they heavily influence levels of taste and performance. They can create a climate supremely inimical to standards of any sort.

I am not saying that we can expect every man to be excellent. It would please me if this were possible: I am not one of those who believe that a goal is somehow unworthy if everyone can achieve it. But those who achieve excellence will be few at best. All too many lack the qualities of mind or spirit which would allow them to conceive excellence as a goal, or to achieve it if they conceived it.

But many more can achieve it than now do. Many, many more can *try* to achieve it than now do. *And the society is bettered not only by those who achieve it but by those who are trying.*

WHAT PRICE EXCELLENCE?

Robert J. Fisher

Hannelore Wass

Ever since Terman's research on gifted children was publicized in the 1920s,[1] educators have too easily rested on the assumption that bright children who are successful in school also achieve at a high level in most other avenues of life. Because intelligent youngsters often pick up cues quickly, please teachers, gain the respect of peers, make parents proud, and enter the more renowned universities, we assume they will all become contributing well-adjusted citizens.

Terman did help to quash earlier myths, that bright children are social misfits and that potential genius is just around the corner from potential madness. But, as we take pride in the academic success of high achievers, we may gloss over some of the cost.

High achievers represent only a minority of the school population. Even if a large percentage of this favored minority turn out to be socially successful, well-rounded individuals, what about the high achievers who pay a heavy price for academic excellence? The three fictionalized cases which follow touch upon such problems.

Case No. 1. Ann's divorced mother is a waitress who has made great sacrifices for her daughter's future. Her father left home at an early age; her mother never remarried. Successful at school from the very beginning, Ann became a favorite

[1] Lewis M. Terman, *Genetic Studies of Genius* (Stanford: Stanford University Press, 1925).

of her elementary school teachers. Teachers encouraged Ann with extra help and personal interest; they responded with pleasure to her eagerness to please. Ann worked hard at school, took a part-time job, shunned social involvement with neighborhood peers She thought of herself as unattractive, was ill at ease with boys and used academic success as a compensation for low self-esteem.

As high school competition increased, her work began to suffer and her grade-point average dropped. She missed the scholarships which her counselors had hoped would ease her way at the university. Ann worried about disappointing her mother, about letting down the teachers who had shown faith in her, about meeting the increased competition in higher education.

At the university she had to work extra hours to meet expenses, refusing to accept any financial help from her mother. After attending for one semester and receiving grades which were much lower than her academic aptitude would indicate, she dropped out of school to marry the first man who had ever taken an interest in her.

Stereotyped response to case: Ann is from a broken home and has always needed the attention of her long-lost father.

Case No. 2. Marie is the daughter of a college professor and a high school French teacher. She has been surrounded with cultural influences from an early age, attending children's concerts, taking ballet lessons, practicing the piano daily. Books and television programs have been carefully screened for "suitability" by her parents.

She was expected to earn high grades and to prepare for a career in teaching. Marie took her school work seriously, prided herself on intellectual interests, snubbed the trivialities of the peer culture. High grades became the symbol of success, the means to fulfill her family's aspirations. She thrived on competition but needed to be better than anyone else.

Discovery methods of teaching or work which involved her with other students in group projects tended to upset her. After enrolling in a teaching curriculum at the university, she became extremely hostile to courses in which objectives deviated in any way from the strict acquisition of knowledge. Before graduation she decided against teaching; most students, she reasoned, were incapable of meeting her standards.

Stereotyped response to case: Marie has been made into a perfectionist, too rigidly moulded by her overly-controlling parents.

Case No. 3. Jeff is the son of a successful lawyer and a community-minded mother, both of whom are active in civic affairs. Jeff had been showered with books and toys, taken on trips across the country, provided a generous allowance, offered a new automobile for high achievement when he graduated from high school. His opinions were treated with respect by his parents; he was always made to feel that he was a contributing member of the family group. His parents have reasoned with Jeff from an early age; there were no hard and fast rules to obey without question.

At the university Jeff seemed to change his outlook. He sold his car, let his hair grow long, became a rebel against authoritarian restrictions and antiquated educational requirements. He classified his parents' liberalism as hypocrisy. He accused his upper middle-class parents' affluent generation of "selling out," of sacrificing integrity while maintaining a comfortable standard of living and keeping their consciences clear through token liberal acts. After a year and a half Jeff dropped out of school to join a commune.

Stereotyped response to case: Jeff's parents have been too permissive; they should have set limits for him at an early age.

These stereotyped explanations will not suffice. Research is identifying students whose high academic achievement is not matched by success in other areas and to call into question the educational institution's contribution to such conditions.

Research studies of academic success in school have traditionally relied on mythical means for large group data. The generalizations which were drawn from these studies have often been grossly oversimplified and misleading. We tend to have a picture of the generalized high achiever as a personally well-rounded, healthy, self-confident and socially effective youngster, while the underachiever is his sad negative counterpart.

However, a recent follow-up study of a three-year research project conducted at the University of Michigan[2] indicates that we cannot simply separate high achievers from low achievers in terms of psychological and social efficiency. This study showed that at least some high achievers have the kinds of characteristics that are commonly assigned only to low achievers.

In a computer-based analysis the computer clustered individuals in grades four through eight on the basis of similarity along a number of dimensions. Pupils were grouped on such factors as self-esteem, value orientation, perception of the teacher and the learning conditions, on mental health aspects, and peer relationships. One cluster consisted of high achievers, another of low achievers, but a third cluster was a mixture of both high and low achievers. In this mixed cluster both high and low achievers were similar on the measured dimensions. Both regarded themselves unfavorably, both lacked motivation; both placed low value on education; and both had unfavorable perceptions of the teacher, their peers, and the emotional climate in the classroom.

Similarly, in a pattern search in which the computer searched for configurations of non-intellectual factors that might characterize individual pupils, it was shown that certain patterns were descriptive of both high and low achieving pupils. Some high achievers, for example, along with a larger number of low achievers showed the pattern of low value orientation together with low self-esteem and rejection by peers. Another pattern that included high achievers was low self-esteem coupled with unfavorable perceptions of the teacher and a large amount of anxiety about school. True, a smaller number of high achievers showed the low achiever syndrome, but the study indicates that academic excellence, per se, does not preclude a pupil's need for help in the personal-social aspects of his functioning.

Teachers frequently supply stereotypes to try to explain "what went wrong" with the promising academic futures of the three cases described earlier or with other poorly integrated high achievers identified in the University of Michigan Study. A common way to avoid considering the

[2] Hannelore Wass, *Relationships of Social-Psychological Variables to School Achievement for High and Low Achievers.* Unpublished doctoral dissertation, University of Michigan, 1968.

school's contribution to the personal and cultural alienation of able students is to blame the families or to decry social values which deviate from middle class core values. We seldom question the educational institution's devotion to academic achievement at the expense of other goals. Teachers praise and reward academic success, pressure and push towards academic excellence. While offering lip-service to broader objectives, school personnel continues to over-emphasize the intellectual dimensions of learning.

Those who jump easily over the academic hurdles, who take teachers, courses, exams, and graduations in their stride, seem to justify this emphasis. We seldom consider the cost. We praise and pressure those with high measured scholastic aptitude, with little regard to any problems which we may aggravate.

A most alarming finding was reported by Ketcham and Morse.[3] They found that children's self-esteem decreases as they progress through the grades irrespective of their academic achievement. To the item "I feel pretty sure of myself" on the Coopersmith Self Esteem Inventory, they found, for example, that 12% of the third graders said "unlike me" while 34% of the eleventh graders made that response. While 84% of the third graders were proud of themselves in terms of their academic work, only 53% of the eleventh graders were. Of those children who say that they often become discouraged in school, the percentage increases with age from 22% to 43%.

Many pupils are receiving messages at school which they translate into personal failure. These increase as pupils stay longer in school, and this is true for high achievers as well as low achievers. If a lower and lower percentage of youngsters think well of themselves the longer they stay in school, can we continue to blame the homes and neighborhoods?

To counter the authority structure imposed by teachers, parents and adult power systems, the peer culture gradually takes over the allegiance of the young. A new allegiance to the youth culture contributes to the development of independence.

Child-like dependency passes into youthful rebellion to break home ties on the way to maturity. This socialization process through peer group identification is denied some youngsters, such as Marie, who need to cling to the kind of parental direction which is more appropriate for an earlier age.

On the other hand, we can hardly condemn young people when they become completely alienated from the authority structure. A young man such as Jeff may have been socialized too effectively! He has had ample opportunity to gain knowledge of parental hypocrisy and social hypocrisy. The "purer" values of a young people's commune have more attraction. Whether or not the Jeffs of the communes will have the freedom or the power to change the hypocritical values they decry is something else. Hippies and activists produce such extremely vindictive overreactions among the "straight" majority that it is difficult to be optimistic about the cleansing power of alienated groups upon the core culture.

The academic resurgence of schools has been justified through the need for greater scholarly rigor, higher standards and academic excellence. The majority of students do not reach the higher standards and they respond negatively to greater pressure by either lowered self-esteem or rejection of adult norms. Still, teachers have at least prided themselves that the success of able and ambitious youth justifies the increasing push toward intellectual goals.

Bloom[4] has cautioned that it may not be desirable to attempt to bring each individual to the highest level of development on a particular characteristic. The maximization of academic achievement may well be accomplished at some crucial personal or social cost for the individual. Such cost may be in the dimension of self-esteem, social relationships, and value orientation.

We need not raise again those earlier objectives of the 1930s and 1940s, that schools should foster democratic values and should contribute to better mental health. But it might be time to assess the products of our pressure. It is no accident that the Universities of California and Columbia have become symbols of widespread student unrest, that

---

[3] Warren A. Ketcham and William C. Morse, *Dimensions of Children's Social and Psychological Development Related to School Achievement.* Cooperative Research Project No. 1286, University of Michigan, 1965.

[4] Benjamin Bloom, *Stability and Change in Human Characteristics* (New York: John Wiley, 1964).

a large percentage of very able young people reject both the social norms of their parents and the more traditional goals of education.

If we are failing with a significant number of able, high achievers, if many exhibit lowered self-esteem, value disorientation and endure peer rejection, has all the recent emphasis been worth it? We have been raising the academic hurdles higher and higher, but we are still not winning the educational Olympic Games, even with many of those who bring natural talents with them to the race. We might begin as well to question results achieved by the middle achievers and the low achievers, those who frequently trip on the hurdles or those who do not even dare to jump.

REFERENCES

1. BLOOM, BENJAMIN. *Stability and Change in Human Characteristics*. New York: John Wiley, 1964.
2. BUSWELL, M. "Relationship between the Social Structure of the classroom and the academic success of the pupils," *Journal of Experimental Education*, **22** (1953), 37–52.
3. EDMINSTON, R. W., and B. J. RHOADES. "Predicting Achievement," *Journal of Educational Research*, **52** (1959), 177–180.
4. KETCHAM, WARREN A., and WILLIAM C. MORSE. *Dimensions of Children's Social and Psychological Development Related to School Achievement*, Cooperative Research Project No. 1286, University of Michigan.
5. PASSOW, A. H., and M. GOLDBERG. "Study of Underachieving Gifted," *Educational Leadership*, **16** (1959), 121–125.
6. ROTH, R. M., and A. MEYERSBURG. "The non-achievement syndrome," in M. Kornrich, ed., *Underachievement*. Springfield, Ill.: Charles C. Thomas, 1965, pp. 279–288.
7. SHAW, M. C., and G. T. ALVES. "The Self concept of bright academic underachievers: continued," *Personnel and Guidance Journal*, **42** (1963), 401–403.
8. SHAW, M. C., and J. GRUBB. "Hostility and able high school underachievers," *Journal of Counseling Psychology*, **5** (1958), 263–266.
9. TAYLOR, R. G. "Personality traits and discrepant achievement," *Journal of Counseling Psychology*, **11** (1964), 76–81.
10. TERMAN, LEWIS M. *Genetic Studies of Genius*. Stanford: Stanford University Press, 1925.
11. VAN EGMOND, E. "Socialization process and education," *Review of Educational Research*, **31** (1961), 89–90.
12. WASS, HANNELORE. *Relationships of Social-Psychological Variables to School Achievement for High and Low Achievers*. Unpublished doctoral dissertation, University of Michigan, 1968.

IF YOU NEVER CHANCE
FOR FEAR OF
LOSING . . .

Harvey P. Mandel and
Jim Uebner

Underachievement, whether at an elementary, high school, or college level, is of concern to a great many counselors (Roth, 1970). Among the many types of underachievers, one that has been identified as occurring rather frequently is the non-achievement syndrome pattern. It is the aim of this discussion to focus on the changes that one such underachiever experiences, as reflected in the poems which he wrote over the course of a counseling experience.

A TYPICAL PATTERN

The non-achievement syndrome pattern (NAS) has been described in detail (Roth and Meyersburg, 1963). Briefly, the pattern can first be seen around the age of eight or nine, and becomes an issue of concern, both for parents and teachers, as the child grows older. The description that follows is typical of the high school or college NAS underachiever, although the underpinnings are valid for both junior high and grammar school students with minor variations in content.

When asked about his poor performance in school the NAS underachiever produces a wide range of reasons: boring teachers, disruptive classroom situation, lack of interest generated by the subject material, poor schedule, and laziness. The common element is the underlying theme that if things were different, if he were not an innocent victim of circumstances, he would be doing much better. He further implies that he has no control over, nor can he change, his life situation.

His parents describe his life situation in the following terms: He procrastinates, seldom brings books home, and even less frequently uses them; claims that he did all his homework in study hall; convinces everyone that he'll do better next time; and crams at the last minute for final exams. Conflict inevitably arises when he brings his grades home. It is at such time that promises for projected academic excellence are made. He may actually try to carry out these promises, but only for a few short weeks. His parents tend to focus on their son's relatively few achievements, hoping that these are signs of greatness to come. Parents tend to take one of two extreme views regarding the underachievement: Either (a) they hold a nondirective approach ("Whenever my son decides to start doing well, he will, and until then, what can I do?"), or (b) they put pressure on the student to perform by begging, cajoling, forcing, or bribing. None of these tactics has the desired effect.

Underachievement in school is always paralleled by underachievement in many areas of the NAS individual's life. For example, in his social life the NAS forms tenuous relationships with females, and seldom makes a commitment or takes responsibility for major decisions within a male-female relationship. If he has no girlfriend, he provides a logical argument for the situation by claiming that he is really concentrating on school and doesn't have the time or money to devote to the opposite sex. Of course, he is really not concentrating on school at all. If he has a girlfriend, the relationship remains superficial and constant, with the ultimate aim of not rocking the boat. Thus, the kind of female that the NAS attracts in a semipermanent relationship is one who is willing to make decisions for the sake of the relationship, at least for a while. She usually becomes disillusioned when she realizes that the relationship is stagnant, and that responsibility for decisions and future commitments within the relationship are clearly hers. She is usually an achiever in many areas of her own life.

The NAS individual's male friends describe him as a nice guy. He tends to attract males of similar interests and accomplishments, and they spend many aimless hours together, a safe way of spending time and energy.

His plans for the future are vague, and by his own admission he spends little time in thinking about it. When asked about future vocational plans, the NAS individual responds with a characteristic vagueness: "I'd like to be an engineer" or "I'd like to be a mechanic" or "I'd like to be a biologist" or "All I need is to get better grades." Usually the NAS individual does not mention marriage or a family, and when it is brought up, he goes so far as to acknowledge the remote possibility, "Yeah, I guess I'll be married, someday."

A PSYCHOLOGICAL EXPLANATION

Psychologically, the NAS individual utilizes his symptoms (i.e., poor grades) to maintain dependence and reject the approaching independence-dependence conflict. He is not really lazy or unmotivated. On the contrary, he is highly motivated to do poorly or even fail. He spends many hours involved in a myriad of activities, none of which leads anywhere. He relates in terms of avoiding that which will force him to look at his choices for activity, and is excellent at game relationships.

Underlying this dynamic is the choice of the student to do poorly as an attempt at maintaining his immature relationship with his family, so that he can successfully continue his dependence and avoid taking risks of independent action and the consequent responsibilities as if he were preventing himself from being confronted by the developmental issues of adolescence [Roth, Mauksch, and Peiser, 1967, p. 395].

In essence, this dynamic serves to maintain dependence by avoiding awareness of choices for failure. The behavior is designed to prevent the completion of school, the achievement of maturity, and consequent demands that will have to be acknowledged. The NAS individual deals with the anticipation of the independence-dependence bind by electing to maintain dependence.

When an individual is unmotivated, the task is one of motivating him in some way. If, however, an individual is already motivated but in a direction leading to failure, then the task is one of exposing the underlying motivation. The approach found most effective is one in which the counselor literally intervenes in the system of logic and games that the NAS individual is using. The aim is to expose the choices that the NAS individual has made toward failure and to point out that the failure is a result of the decision, albeit unconscious, to delay the future as long as possible. A typical counselor question that is repeated many times is: "Is there anything you could have done, or can do, to change the situation?"

The following example typifies the seemingly endless excuses dealt with in counseling:

COUNSELOR: *What are your plans for the future, Fred?*

CLIENT: *Well, I plan to go into radio broadcasting.*

COUNSELOR: *What kind of things do you need to do in order to get into broadcasting?*

CLIENT: *You should have a third class engineer's license, at least.*

COUNSELOR: *Do you have it?*

CLIENT: *No, I took the test twice, but I failed it. But I plan to get it soon.*

COUNSELOR: *Why have you failed?*

CLIENT: *The last part of the test had a lot of technical things like dials and meters to read. Nobody told me about that, so I didn't study for it.*

COUNSELOR: *You mean, you didn't study for it twice?*

CLIENT: *Well, I didn't think it would be on two times in a row.*

COUNSELOR: *Was that the only reason you failed twice?*

CLIENT: *No. I didn't have much time to study for it the second time. That weekend there was a big dance I promised to take my girl to. I had to wax up my car (etc., etc., etc.).*

After many interchanges over a number of sessions the NAS logic is exposed. The excuses have been uncovered and can no longer be used as they have been before. Slowly and painfully the individual begins to realize what he has been doing. He acknowledges to himself that there are things he could have done to change many situations which he had previously contended were out of his control. He begins to confront himself with questions such as: "Who am I?" "Where am I going?" "When am I going to do it?" In effect, his self-concept is developing, and the NAS individual is experiencing the dependence-independence conflict.

In passing it may be of value to focus on the female counterpart of the NAS individual. It has been our experience that females who exhibit the same personality characteristics as the male NAS individual do not underachieve in school. Such an individual is usually sexually promiscuous, and may even become pregnant out of wedlock. We feel that this may be viewed within the context of our society. A male who wants others to make decisions for him can do so by underachieving in school. For a female, an unwanted pregnancy may serve the same function (e.g., "Things happen to me.").

CHANGE THROUGH POETRY

Much has been written about the theoretical aspects of the underachievement process, about the types of counseling approaches and the changes that are effected. Little has been written, however, which captures the essence of the experience of change. What follows is a panorama of change as evidenced in one NAS individual's poems that he wrote during and following counseling. No detailed analysis of the poetry will be attempted. To do so would in effect destroy the beauty and the nature of the process.

The poet, now 21 years old, came for counseling while he was a college student. At the beginning of counseling he exhibited many of the NAS characteristics. Gradually Jim began to show signs of discomfort, yet he continued to express the hope that change would come from the outside. The discomfort evolved into dissatisfaction, recognition of his own feelings, and an inner search for direction. Amid pain and total discomfort, Jim admitted for the first time the possibility that he created much of his life situation. He

realized that he could do something about the situation and he began to take over his own life and accept the risks involved. He called himself on some of the games he had been playing and expressed his fear of the changes and the risks that the future held. Yet at the same time, he clearly stated his decision to step into the future. Jim became clearly aware of his new-found vulnerability, yet excited about his emerging self-confidence. He stated that he no longer viewed the counselor as the helper, but more as a friend. He began to learn from the past rather than living in it, and toward the end of counseling Jim's thoughts, comments, and feelings had expanded. His focus was now on the world, social issues, and universal human concerns.

The poems were meaningful in a number of ways. When he entered counseling Jim had much difficulty in expressing any feelings directly. The implication here is that Jim viewed expression of feelings as carrying a responsibility both for revealing emotions and for the consequences of such actions. At the outset of counseling, he used the poems as an indirect way of expressing his feelings, and he revealed his poetic endeavor to the counselor toward the end of counseling. There is an obvious element of gift-giving in this presentation close to termination. But there is more —the change in the nature of the counseling relationship. The quality of the interaction shifted from one of high dependence on the counselor as the initiator of game-calling and exposing the logical games, to a mutual respect for and acceptance of an emerging peer relationship. Crucial here is the counselor's acceptance of the search that Jim had embarked upon. The process and approach involve a shift from the game relationship to one of an intensive client-centered reflective relationship. Under his own initiative, Jim's expression of an inner struggle and emerging self-concept became the focus of the counseling sessions.

The energy, originally bound up, was released in a sudden burst, and from that point onward Jim's perception of the world around him changed radically. It was a view enlarged in both its scope and focus of concern. Within he enjoyed a serene intensity of awareness that comes through to some of us once in a while.

THE POEMS IN CHRONOLOGICAL ORDER

Last night I felt I was on the edge.
A feeling of helplessness invaded me.
I wanted to stop all this wondering
and scream for an answer.
Nothing but memories were around
and I don't need to be reminded
of what I was before.

I went to bed,
thinking perhaps the morning
would erase all conflict.
This is the morning.
It is raining again.

I like music
and the songs they play on the big radio
        stations.
I can listen on the weekend
and hear the groups
and say that was Carol, or
Sandy, or
Gretchen.
We grooved on that in a park
or car or couch.
I have trouble listening to the radio now.

A song comes on
and the words hurt.
They call to my heart and say,
"Hey, don't forget your problems,
worry a while man!"
A push-button radio is nice
because in a push with a finger,
I can easily ignore my worries.

But my finger,
like my mind,
is getting tired.

I'm beginning to wonder
if I influenced the weather.
It seems when I feel really down
the heavens mourn with me.
It's raining again,
after an evening of solitude
and a night with her in my dreams.
I hate feeling alone
because now
I've got no one to warm me.
I am looking forward to the weekend.

My old friends will be surprised
to see my face on campus.
They are good people
for they like me.
Why you can never tell, but
old friends
may turn
into new lovers.

One minute
I can't make it without her,
the next minute
She's as meaningless as any blank face.
My hands don't shake any more
but my stomach compensates for it.
I can't understand her.
And more important,
I can't figure out how I work.
My mind moves back and forth
yes and no
love and then nothing
Maybe a change should be made.
A new face might make the difference.
But what about last December?
She warmed me and touched me then
so much, I couldn't help but live.
She holds something of mine
no one will ever have.
She could keep me alive.
She could hurt me.
It's my choice.
If you never chance for fear of losing,
you have already lost.
I have got to try.

Dedicated to all concerned listeners:
Floating from level
to level of uncertainty.
It seems the only constant
in my life is
inconsistency.
Maybe I have it this way
because plastic,
9 to 5,
Monday through Friday
summer home crap
makes me scared
and I want no part of it.
I'm scared, definitely,
maybe because doing

something,
would make me
somebody.
Don't anyone think I need help,
well maybe I need help,
but I don't want your hand
whether it's from your wallet
or heart.
This is my ball game.
I'm the manager.
Let me play it my way.

First
I saw the man
as a helper
and now he's a friend.
There's a difference.
I was standing
with my hands extended
knowing I couldn't make it alone.
Help me.
I felt pretty good after he
pulled me along.
Yeah, it was a lot easier that way,
and some people loved helping.
I liked being helped.
You can never have a friend
if you only ask people for help.
Being a friend is energy
in two directions.
Not only being helped
but helping just because you want to.
Sharing and enjoying,
that's what friends do.
A man helped me.
I was content with that for a while,
until I realized I am somebody.
I tried sharing and laughing with him.
I liked that better.
I liked me better too.

People,
    like roses,
always seem to come by the dozen.
When they are with you,

you might watch one,
    smell another,
        listen to one,
and perhaps,
        even touch one.
When one comes solo, it's different.
Numbers don't bother you.
You can slow down,
    take your time,
and experience all they have to share.
So I send you a single rose,
with the hope
that it might touch you also.

I watched the mountains surrounding
the park below.
It's like God put the mountains
there to guard the quiet
that affects everything in sight.
He didn't want to lose this one.
People have ravaged with bulldozers
and barbed wire before
and turned his green to gray.
I don't think he wants to live
in a penthouse
or a bi-level.
After all
he really couldn't.
Sandals
long hair and robes
just don't make it in the suburbs.

REFERENCES

ROTH, R. M. *Underachieving Students and Guidance*. Boston: Houghton Mifflin, 1970.

———, H. O. MAUKSCH, and K. PEISER. "The Non-achievement Syndrome, Group Therapy, and Achievement Change," *Personnel and Guidance Journal* (1967), 393–398.

ROTH, R. M., and H. MEYERSBURG. "The Non-achievement Syndrome," *Personnel and Guidance Journal*, 41 (1963), 535–540.

PERFECTIONISM

Marc H. Hollender

Perfectionism has been defined as "the practice of demanding of oneself or others a higher quality of performance than is required by the situation" (3). Since there might be considerable difference of opinion as to what constitutes "a higher quality of performance than is required by the situation," it seems necessary either to find a more precise definition, or to consider only those instances in which most observers would agree that the person consistently demands more than is "required by the situation." I have elected the latter course. For the purpose of the following discussion, perfectionism is said to exist when the person *himself* characterizes his mode of performing as perfectionistic and when, in all likelihood, most psychiatrists would agree with this judgment. It need only be added that not only does the perfectionist demand a certain level of performance of himself, but he cannot accept or be content with anything short of perfection.

It should be noted that I use the term perfectionism to refer to the manner in which a person *performs* or *aspires to perform,* not to the manner in which he thinks of himself or tries to see himself. In this respect I am defining the term differently than Horney(5), who used it to refer to the person who works to create an image of himself as a perfect being. She wrote: "Under inner stress . . . a person may become alienated from his real self. He will then shift the major part of his energies to the task of molding himself, by a rigid

system of inner dictates, into a being of absolute perfection. For nothing short of godlike perfection can fulfill his idealized image of himself and satisfy his pride in the exalted attributes which (so he feels) he has, could have, or should have." As I have stated, the person I shall describe does not strive to create an image of himself as a perfect being but strives to perform in a manner that is perfect. He primarily seeks acceptance from other people, not narcissistic gratification.

Although the perfectionist is not likely to be a creative person who changes the world in which we live, he *is* likely to be a painstaking worker who performs services and turns out products we value. It is little wonder then that he has rarely been singled out for psychiatric scrutiny. Like the body without pain or the mattress without bumps, he is usually taken for granted. But even though the perfectionist derives some satisfaction from his performance, he may realize that he has made a virtue out of a necessity or he may feel overburdened by the oppressive load he has heaped upon himself. Not only that, but no matter how well he does, he seldom performs to his complete satisfaction. Failing to measure up to his own standard, he periodically feels depressed. Most often the depression is fleeting, giving way to renewed hope. Occasionally, however, it is more profound and persistent and may even end in suicide.

In the psychiatric and psychoanalytic literature, perfectionism is frequently noted in case histories, but it seldom receives more than passing comment.* A well-known psychiatric dictionary (Hinsie and Campbell[4]) does not even include the term. Only one article devoted to the subject was found. In this article by Branfman and Bergler(1), entitled *Psychology of "Perfectionism,"* perfectionism was regarded as a variant of obsessive-compulsive behavior, and it was linked to oral-masochism.

Perfectionism, as a personality trait, co-exists with, blends with or is buttressed by other traits. The possible combinations are many and varied. Singling out perfectionism for detailed study is somewhat like using high magnification to examine a section of tissue on a slide. In doing so,

From *Comprehensive Psychiatry,* 6(2) (1965), 94–103. Reprinted by permission of Grune & Stratton, Inc., and the author.

* Perfectionism has been noted as a personality trait of patients suffering from migraine headaches(9).

interrelationships are obscured. It is necessary, therefore, that the reader bear in mind that some distortions may be created by the limited perspective.

In this article, I shall first present the clinical picture of perfectionism as patients describe it. Next, I shall comment on the psychodynamics or the developmental forces responsible for this trait. A clinical example will illustrate the thesis which has been presented. Finally, I shall differentiate perfectionism from compulsiveness, a fundamental distinction which is often neglected.

CLINICAL PICTURE

The perfectionist is exacting for the sake of being exacting; his approach has little to do with the requirements of the situation. He is not like the artisan or the surgeon who derives pleasure from the results of a painstaking effort and who can be less precise when the situation permits. As Missildine(7) stated: "One of the most important distinctions between the efforts of the true masters of their craft and those of the perfectionistic person is that the striving of the first group brings them solid satisfaction. They are happy with the results. Their efforts enhance their self-esteem. They rejoice in their mastery. This is not true for the perfectionistic person. His striving is accompanied by the corrosive feeling that 'I am not good enough. I must do better.' This robs him of the satisfaction which his superior performance should bring."

The perfectionist finds it difficult to sort out items in the order of their importance or to maintain a sense of proportion. A small detail that has been missed may deprive him of gratification from a job otherwise well done. He is constantly on the alert for what is wrong and seldom focuses on what is right. He looks so intently for defects or flaws that he lives his life as though he were an inspector at the end of a production line.

In the interest of achieving perfection, the perfectionist may circumscribe the range of his endeavors and thereby improve his chance of success. Sometimes he may even avoid or refuse promotions. Only occasionally does the perfectionist hold what is referred to as a "number one" position in the business world. More often he is a very reliable and useful "number two or number three man": the person who finds no job too small and who does not become bored by minutiae.

The perfectionist may be a good worker but a poor businessman, because he is unable to take an overview of an operation or engage in long-range planning. Many perfectionists must work on their own because their goading demands bring them into conflict with others. The woman who can afford household help is often without it because maids either cannot meet her stringent requirements or find her too difficult to please and quickly leave her.

Although perfectionism is generally a pervasive trait, it may be especially pronounced in certain areas while a few others may be entirely excluded. The idiosyncratic nature of the response usually reflects what was important or unimportant to the parents. For example, the element of time may or may not be a factor. One person may strive to perform a task perfectly with little or no concern about the length of time it takes; another may expect to complete the same task within a specified period of time. If there are no time limits, perfectionism may be responsible for profound work inhibitions. A person who seems to show great promise may be unable to begin a project because the design for it is never completely perfected. Or, a person who finishes a project is unable to write up the results and send them off because the presentation must be written in a manner that is so flawless that no one could possibly criticize it.

The specific form or shape of the perfectionistic pattern depends, to an extent, on the sex and circumstances of the individual. For example, a particular story is commonplace for the housewife in the middle socioeconomic strata of our society. She is the gracious hostess who is so intent that her dinner party be perfect, down to the smallest detail, that she cannot relax enough to enjoy it. For her, it is an ordeal, which she hopes and prays she will be able to endure without her tension or discomfort becoming apparent to her guests. If she is a good actress—and often she is—her charm and grace effectively conceal her misery. And her charm and grace are matched by the party she gives. Even when entertaining only a guest or two, her house is immaculate, the table is beautifully set with sterling and goblets and candles and flowers and the food is fit for a gourmet. Some women maintain that they work so hard for their guests' sake, but most of them recognize that it is also for their own sake—a personal necessity. One woman became aware of her self-deception when she spent hours preparing dinner for one old friend, knowing full well that he would hardly notice the difference between her fine place settings and the tin plates and cups in a hunting lodge.

In housekeeping and child rearing, the perfectionist woman also functions under considerable pressure. Although she realizes that she is "fussy" or exacting, she attributes her attitude to the circumstances under which she lives. She always has too much to do, and she often complains that others are not cooperative or helpful. There is a place for everything, and everything must be in its place. Behaving like a naval officer running a tight ship, she rigidly enforces discipline according to the rules she lays down. Failure to comply with these rules results in nagging or other coercive measures. If she does not demand compliance from others in the household, she spends considerable time picking up after them. She may do so without protest, or she may complain about the cross she bears. Her home is more like a show place than a place to live in. With all her concern about neatness, however, she is not usually concerned with cleanliness in the hygienic sense, since bacteria or viruses play no part in her thinking. It is only essential that the dishes and utensils look clean. The woman with a "Hausfrau neurosis" is referred to as "crazy clean" but in fact she is "crazy neat."

Because of current teachings about child rearing, the perfectionistic woman is reluctant to clamp down on her children as vigorously as she would like. She attempts to find compromises between the children's needs and her own, or she may swing from one attitude to another as the struggle wages. She may permit the children to play in a room or two and thereby separate the messy area from the neat one. Even then, the playrooms must be picked up and put in order at the end of each day or at least once or twice a week. Other mothers are like those described by Kanner(6): "These are usually mothers who have long had a tendency to obsessive perfectionism, who scrub—or have the maid scrub—the floor until it sparkles, who live by the clock and make a fetish of orderliness and regularity. The baby must be made to fit into this scheme. A multitude of books on child rearing are consulted and all but memorized. The advice of physicians is carried out far too literally. If the baby does not comply with the desired ideal of perfection, the impatient mother resorts to coercion."

The woman I have described has been encountered in practice by most psychotherapists. As would be expected, she approaches treatment much as she approaches other projects: her desire to perform perfectly and her need to please the therapist cause her to push aside many of her own wishes. Her large expenditure of energy and her ingratiating manner can be misleading. She appears to be the ideal patient when in fact she is performing like the ideal child or "teacher's pet." This pattern of behavior must be pointed out and dealt with before she will be able to seek self-knowledge for her own sake and before she will be able to seek the fulfillment of many personal aspirations.

PSYCHODYNAMICS

Discussing the psychodynamics of perfectionism is like teasing out a single thread from the intricate pattern of a fabric. A swatch must be taken to see the overall design. For the purpose of this study, I will first examine the thread—the development of perfectionism—and then turn my attention to the swatch—the relationship of this trait to related traits. The character pattern (or cluster of traits) that is formed will have a determining influence on the person's self-concept and on his interpersonal relationships.

Like other personality traits, perfectionism is learned during childhood. Although various factors may contribute to its development, I will describe only those which, in my experience, are most often implicated. The ideal subject for the development of perfectionism is a sensitive child who feels very insecure. The insecurity intensifies his need for acceptance. While struggling to gain approval, he may receive the message from his parents: "You do not do things well enough. That's why I disapprove of you and dislike you." Under these circumstances, he works harder and strives to perform better. He continues trying so long as he has hope of pleasing his parents. Partial success, which fortifies the conviction that somehow the ultimate goal is within reach, spurs him onto renewed effort. He feels: "If I try a little harder, if I do a little better, if I become perfect, my parents will love me." Success, like prosperity during the depression years, always seems to be "just around the corner."

An additional point should be noted. The parent who is difficult to please is likely to equate a poor, mediocre or even a passably good performance with badness and react by being rejecting. He is not the parent who conveys the message: "You have not done well enough and I disapprove, but I still like you." His response, which is conditional and depends on the nature of the performance, is of the black-or-white type: rejection or acceptance; there is practically no gray.

Sibling rivalry may also engender or foster the development of perfectionism. A youngster, with the "middle-child problem," may struggle for a place in the sun by doing his work better than the others. This is an effort, too, to compensate for what he feels he lacks in talent, athletic prowess or physical attractiveness. Not only does he strive to perform perfectly, but he may also become a compliant and conforming child.

With the passing of time, the need to please the parents becomes internalized and parental attitudes and requirements become part of the ego-ideal. No longer does someone else demand perfection; the person now demands it of himself. At various times when the oppressive standard becomes unbearable it may be imputed to another person (e.g., the spouse or an employer). Even if the other person does demand perfection, the struggle is still basically intrapsychic. (It is true, however, that the perfectionist is often so goaded by the pressure he places on himself that he may tolerate additional pressure poorly.)

In discussing the origins of perfectionism, Missildine(7) presented the following observations: "The adult who suffers from the results of perfectionism in his childhood is apt to be intelligent, well-educated and economically better off than most people. Belittling his own accomplishments, he drives himself with ever stiffer demands to 'do better.' . . . Our clinical work with children clearly indicates that this continual self-belittle-ment—rather than a desire to master the environment—is the real driving force behind the perfectionist's unending efforts. . . . Children need—and seek—the affectionate acceptance of themselves through their efforts to please their parents. However, perfectionistic parents tend to withhold acceptance of the child until he is striving at an upper level of performance. Even when the child does accomplish something . . . the parent subtly defers full approval and acceptance and urges the child to 'do better.' In this fashion, whatever the child has achieved is belittled. What the child gets is the promise of eventual acceptance if only he will 'do better.' . . . The perfectionistic parent keeps the child straining on tiptoe, anxious about himself and his abilities. One of the striking things about the perfectionist is that, despite all he can accomplish, he has little or no confidence whatever in himself."

Missildine's(7) thesis is interesting; I agree with it in general, but disagree with it in certain particulars. While the desire to master the environment is not the "real driving force" behind the perfectionist's unending effort, neither is it exclusively self-belittlement. The original goal of the child, it should be recalled, was to please his parents and thereby gain their acceptance. His failure led to the conclusion: "I am not good enough" or "I am unworthy." At this point the child felt belittled and began to belittle himself, but his unending effort did not stem from his need to combat the gnawing feeling of self-belittlement alone. It also continued to be, as it was in the beginning, the pursuit of acceptance. Perfectionism is motivated, therefore, both by an effort to create a better self-feeling or self-image and to obtain certain responses or supplies from other people.

The child's effort to turn in a perfect performance is a bid for approval, attention or acceptance, but it is only one ploy in an all-out campaign. Others are compliance and conformity. Personal interests or desires are pushed aside if they conflict with the parent's wishes. The need to please them, no matter what the cost, is the compelling motive. As a consequence, the child's emotional growth is stunted. He grows up to be a child-like adult needing a parental figure—an employer or a spouse—to direct much of his life.

In an effort to please his parents, the compliant

child suppresses, controls and conceals his hostility and aggression. In presenting himself as the "nice" person, he senses that he is only nice on the outside—that his appearance is like a thin veneer. As a result, he is unable to accept praise; he believes that anyone who praises him is uncritical, has been duped or is insincere. In spite of his struggle, and partly because of it, feelings of hostility and aggression are responsible for periods of anxiety, guilt and depression.

Sexuality may be handled similarly to hostility and aggression. Because of the child's preoccupation with succorance, he tends to push sexuality into the background, or at least he does not focus on it. If it becomes troublesome by threatening his relationship with his parents, he represses or inhibits its expression. Sexuality, also, reflects the general developmental level of the perfectionist: as he holds onto the child–parent stage in interpersonal relationships, he clings to the masturbatory stage in sexual relationships.

As an adult, the perfectionist struggles with haunting self-doubts and exacting demands. He sees himself as being judged by what he does, not for what he is. When he believes that he is failing, his self-critical standard becomes so intolerable that he projects it onto others and then assumes that they are frowning on his poor performance. His dread of people talking about him is his dread of self-belittlement or self-condemnation. Without a firmly-fixed, positive attitude toward himself, he is continually dependent on his performance for feelings of acceptability, adequacy and goodness. In a sense, he is like a ship without a gyroscope constantly buffeted by the sea around him.

Since perfectionism is related to the ego-ideal, failure to measure up may result in the affect of shame. In discussing the relationship of perfectionism and shame, Engel(2) stated: "From the developmental perspective, the susceptibility to shame is greatly increased when internal standards are too high, when too great perfectionism is demanded of oneself. This may come about especially when early childhood feelings of omnipotence are projected onto parental figures who also imposed unreasonable demands for performance as a condition for love. The shame then involves the feeling that one is unlovable. . . ."

As long as the perfectionist has hope of improving his performance, he continues to try. He may at times achieve limited success which brings him some satisfaction, but it does not last. He must once again try to do even better. From time to time, his demands on himself become too oppressive, and he loses hope. He then becomes moody or depressed, but usually these periods are brief. He rebounds with renewed hope that he will be able to live with his standard or that he will somehow succeed in becoming perfect. The feeling of failure and the loss of hope sometimes becomes more profound and long lasting. In itself, it can cause depression, but usually it is combined with other forces, especially with guilt about hostile or aggressive impulses.

The tendency of the perfectionist to demand perfection from others has been mentioned. Most often it is simply a matter of demanding that others perform as well as he expects himself to perform. Under certain circumstances, the perfectionist may be more tolerant of others than he is of himself. Conversely, some persons, who do not demand perfection of themselves, demand it of others. This requirement has a different psychodynamic background than that described for perfectionism. In commenting on the pattern, Branfman and Bergler(1) stated: "The impotent man seeking and never finding the 'perfect' woman, the frigid sex-shy girl who cannot find the 'perfect' husband, are well-known phenomena."

Under unusual circumstances a perfectionistic attitude can be pushed aside for a brief period. For example, during World War II one air crew member told me that as he was flying over the target he would say to himself: "Wasn't I silly to worry about whether I got 95 or 96 on an examination? Here it's life or death." Once back in the states, his old standard soon returned. He said that he again worried about how perfectly he did little things.

CLINICAL NOTE

An attractive and intelligent 22-year-old woman was admitted to a psychiatric hospital after slashing her wrists in a suicidal attempt. The attempt was a reaction to the great difficulty she experienced in being a mother to her infant son. On two previous occasions, within a period of a few months, she had tried to be the mother she expected herself to be and she had failed. Her suicidal attempt followed a last desperate effort. She stated: "I believed that I was not good enough for the baby. There were so many doubts."

The patient's pregnancy was unplanned and unwanted. Not only did she not want a child but she had not wanted to marry. She had rejected socially prominent suitors, feeling that she could not measure up to what would be expected of her. She stated: "I was afraid to get involved at all. I didn't want to become serious. My husband pretty much had to drag me down to the altar. I was willing to have an affair for years even though it made me guilty and I was afraid of becoming pregnant. I didn't want to get married but he wanted to make it legal." After two years of marriage, she "accidentally" became pregnant.

The patient was a middle daughter. Her father had abandoned the family for another woman when she was five. Her mother, who was described as a cold and vindictive person, remarried six years later and gave birth to a son when the patient was 13. The patient recalls her mother screaming at the child: "I never wanted you!" In speaking of her feelings about becoming a mother, the patient stated: "I was afraid of becoming like my own mother. I didn't want to end up yelling and screaming. I just wanted to be left alone." As a mother, she tried to be perfect. She said: "I had Spock in one hand and the baby in the other." As she struggled to be perfect and became aware that she was not succeeding, she experienced the fear that she might fail to hear her infant when he cried or that she might otherwise harm him. As a result she was unable to sleep. Finally becoming exhausted and incapacitated, she would retreat from the situation. On one occasion she wrote a note to her husband in which she said: "You deserve more than I can give."

In regard to perfectionism, the patient said: "This is something that has been with me a long time. I can forgive other people their mistakes, but I could not allow myself to make the same mistakes. No matter what I did, I had to do it perfect the first time. I was a secretary and I became a very good secretary but always there was the possibility that tomorrow there might be something that would overwhelm me. When I worked at one concern they were always trying to chide me to take a higher position, but I doubted my ability to do it. I was

afraid to take on this greater responsibility for fear of failing." When asked what she did if she made a mistake in typing a letter, she responded: "I limited myself to two mistakes. If they weren't noticeable after I corrected them I would let it go through. There are tricks: if I looked at a letter quickly and if the mistakes drew my eyes, I wouldn't let it go through."

As is typical for the perfectionist, she stated: "In my own mind I remember the negative more than the positive. If I made a mistake I would not let myself make the same mistake again." She added: "I would not tolerate intellectual slips. I would try to key myself to the people I was with. I was like a salamander to an extent. I eventually became, to a certain extent, like the person I was with." She was also perfectionistic about her personal appearance.

In regard to housekeeping she stated: "I drove my husband nuts. Anytime my husband dropped an ash in the ashtray I ran after him. Eventually I let him have one ashtray." She dreaded entertaining, because she would wear herself out with the preparations. When she had guests in for dinner she tried so hard to please them that she enjoyed herself only if she drank enough liquor so that she could relax.

When asked why she thought she was so exacting, the patient replied: "I think it goes back to wanting to be accepted—wanting to be liked. I think that basically that is what it is—not wanting to have anyone find fault with me—not giving them any reason to find fault with me. I just never seemed to be good enough no matter what I did. Everyone in the family was different, even in appearance. I was the only one who had brown eyes. I not only felt different but I looked different." She added: "I think it started out with the desire to please my mother. Instead of having her tell me what to do all the time I would just do it."

To a considerable extent she exercised control over her behavior with her husband because if she let down her guard she became "downright childish or juvenile." Her difficulty in relating generally was reflected, as might be expected, in her response to sexuality. Masturbation, but not sexual intercourse, was gratifying to her. In her relationship with her husband she derived pleasure only through manual stimulation.

The report, which has been presented, highlights a number of points made previously concerning the clinical picture and the psychodynamics of perfectionism. It is clear that the patient's perfectionism did not exist by itself but was interwoven with other problems, most notably her problem in coping with hostile impulses. Perfectionism was important in itself, however, because it had much to do with why the patient was unable to function effectively as a mother, became despondent and depressed and tried to take her own life.

PERFECTIONISM AND COMPULSIVENESS

At first glance, perfectionism and compulsiveness bear a resemblance to each other, but on closer scrutiny it is evident that they are distinctly different. Compulsiveness refers to "the tendency to repeat over and over a certain kind of behavior, despite its inappropriateness and to be unable to inhibit the behavior"(3). The following characteristics should also be noted: "Compulsive behavior is generally highly stylized or ritualistic. The person often regards his behavior as irrational, but cannot inhibit it"(3). Perfectionism, unlike compulsiveness, does not refer to repeating a certain kind of behavior over and over; it refers to the manner in which a task must be done, whatever the task. The behavior is generally appropriate, but it is carried to an extreme. Instead of being ritualistic, it is goal-directed. The perfectionist does not regard his activity as irrational even though he sometimes wishes that he could be less exacting.

In contrast to perfectionism, compulsiveness has received much attention in the psychoanalytic and psychiatric literature and has even been used in creating two well-known diagnostic designations: Obsessive-compulsive neurosis and compulsive character disorder. Compulsiveness refers to a pattern of behavior which serves to fend off unacceptable feelings or impulses; perfectionism, as previously described, is a type of performance designed to elicit commendation. Compulsiveness *protects* against disapproval; perfectionism *reaches* for approval.

Compulsiveness rarely has social value. Since it is so ritualistic, it is like running on a treadmill or even like running in the wrong direction. If com-

pulsiveness is marked, it soon attracts attention and is labelled mental illness. Perfectionism, on the other hand, is often of social value. It may even evoke admiration. Only rarely is it recognized that the perfectionist tends to be so exacting that he becomes bogged down in details. The exception would be a glaring one like the medical student who spends so much time drawing a single cell that he can never complete an assignment. The only term referring to perfectionism as a psychiatric disorder, of which I am aware, is "Hausfrau neurosis," and, significantly, it is a colloquialism and not an official designation.

In terms of psychosexual development, perfectionism is indicative of difficulty at the oral stage of development: an expression of dependency longings. Compulsiveness, in contradistinction, is indicative of difficulty at the anal stage of development: an expression of the struggle against sadistic and soiling impulses. In perfectionism, there is the need to meet the requirements of an extremely demanding and exacting ego ideal; in compulsiveness there is the need to meet the standards of an extremely stern and relentless superego. As would be expected, in clinical practice it is not uncommon to find some admixture of perfectionism and compulsiveness.

Many psychiatrists use the word compulsiveness when they actually mean perfectionism. This practice has created confusion, or at least a lack of precision, much as was created by the use of the word guilt for both guilt and shame(8). Although compulsiveness and perfectionism may coexist, it is essential to separate the two traits for theoretical and practical purposes.

SUMMARY

For the purpose of this discussion, perfectionism was defined as "demanding of oneself or others a higher quality of performance than is required by the situation." The judgment as to what constitutes a higher quality of performance than is required was made by the patient and would be in concordance with the opinion of most psychiatrists. The clinical picture of the perfectionist was presented first in general terms and then followed by a specific example. Perfectionism most commonly develops in an insecure child who needs approval, acceptance and affection from parents who are difficult to please. The child assumes that if he performs perfectly, he will receive the succorance he seeks. Later perfectionism represents an effort, also, to combat self-belittlement. A clinical note illustrated the general thesis that was developed. Finally, perfectionism was differentiated from compulsiveness: the former being a means of obtaining interpersonal supplies and of seeking a better self-image, and the latter being a mechanism for fending off unacceptable feelings and impulses. Although admixtures do occur, it is essential in clinical practice to deal with each trait separately.

REFERENCES

1. BRANFMAN, T., and E. BERGLER. "Psychology of 'Perfectionism,'" *American Imago,* 12:9 (1955).

2. ENGEL, G. L. *Psychological Development in Health and Disease.* Philadelphia: W. B. Saunders Company, 1962.

3. ENGLISH, H. B., and A. C. ENGLISH. *A Comprehensive Dictionary of Psychological and Psychoanalytical Terms.* New York: Longmans, Green and Company, 1958.

4. HINSIE, L. E., and R. J. CAMPBELL. *Psychiatric Dictionary,* third ed. New York: Oxford University Press, 1960.

5. HORNEY, K. *Neurosis and Human Growth.* New York: W. W. Norton and Company, Inc., 1950.

6. KANNER, L. *Child Psychiatry,* third ed. Springfield, Ill.: Charles C Thomas, 1957.

7. MISSILDINE, W. H. *Your Inner Child of the Past.* New York: Simon and Schuster, 1963.

8. PIERS, G., and M. SINGER. *Shame and Guilt.* Springfield, Ill.: Charles C Thomas, 1953.

9. WOLFF, H. G. "Personality Features and Reactions of Subjects with Migraine," *Arch. Neurol. and Psychiat.,* 37:895 (1937).

ON BEING A "WORKAHOLIC" (A SERIOUS JEST)

Wayne E. Oates

INTRODUCTION

Most ministers in our varied ways "work hard" trying to "help" an alcoholic when we have the opportunity to do so. Especially if we have had alcoholic persons in our near or immediate family as we grew up, we have a very hard time understanding or feeling anything in common with the alcoholic. We are likely to respond to him emotionally as if he were a "breed apart," completely different from us. I have had this experience myself. I have concluded that I myself have an addiction that is far more socially acceptable than that of the alcoholic's addiction. It is certainly more profitable. Nevertheless, when it comes to being a human being, it can be an addiction as destructive of me as a person as any other addiction. *I am addicted to work.*

When this truth dawned upon me, two things happened immediately. First, I broke into laughter. This seemed to me to be too true to be anything but painfully funny. I refuse to give up this grace of laughing at myself, because it keeps the truth from knocking me down long enough for me to begin to do something about my situation. Therefore, I want to encourage my reader to read this as a "serious jest." Second, I discovered that I have a ground of common human frailty to stand upon in fellow "admission" *with* the alcoholic. When I come right down to it, I must admit that

Reprinted from *Pastoral Psychology* (October, 1968), 16–20.

I am powerless to *do* anything about this and must ask God's help. Wrapped up in my addiction of doing is my self-sufficiency, my childish feeling of omnipotence. Admitting my helplessness is a major stride toward a salvation of "not doing," by faith and not works. Thus as the alcoholic "admits" that he is powerless and that his life has become unmanageable, I find ministers all around me echoing the same set of feelings about the "amount of work they have to do" and "can't get done." I join both the alcoholic and the minister in this type of admission. Alcoholics are amazed when I admit to them my addiction to work. Here I have a ground of real and not imagined empathy with them. Against the background of this, I have dubbed this addiction of myself and my fellow ministers as "workaholism."

THE FIRST PHASE OF WORKAHOLISM

Some men and women are addicted to alcohol. Some are addicted to drugs. Some are addicted to gambling. Others are addicted to work. Some work addicts go for years without knowing it. When I get to feeling righteous about not drinking alcohol, I tap myself on the shoulder and remember my compulsion to work! Let me tell you about what has come to me in my moment of truth!

For years I was the kind of fellow who worked on a "social" basis. I took great pride in the *amount* of work I could do. I was the talk of my community and any social gathering in which I found myself. Everybody knew that I worked hard. I boasted about being able to "hold my work," to "do more than my share," to "carry more than my end of the load." I could work any two men under the table. All men around me felt uncomfortable about the amount of work I could get done. In fact, my spiritual pride ran along the lines of feeling superior to the man who was unable to get his job done. I loved to brag—in humble and indirect ways, of course—about how much I had been able to accomplish. Fatigue to me was a sign of weakness. Sleep was necessary for ordinary people, but not for me.

Now don't get me wrong. I was as "good" as anybody else. I felt perfectly at home among my peers, for they were and still are afflicted with the same addiction. They, like me, are "workaholics." We are scheduled men looking for a scheduled God. Our God is not the bottle, women, or wild parties. We are ergodolaters—idolaters of work. Our very salvation depends upon work! In fact, the words "grace" and being "saved by grace" are very meaningful words to us *if* we can turn them into an honest day's work, use them to get ahead in the world, and outdo our neighbor. As for thinking of God as someone who loves us whether we produce or not, this is unthinkable to workaholics. Acceptance is pay for work done. In school, it was the grades we made. Now that we are out, it is the money we make that measures us, the books we write, the speeches we make, the extra jobs that the lazy, good-for-nothing "leisureholics" unloaded upon us!

THE SECOND PHASE
OF WORKAHOLISM

Up to this point, I as a workaholic am a part of my own culture. I am a workaholic and dwell among a people who are workaholics. But the second phase of workaholism is more serious. Here is where workaholism sets in. At this point, the workaholic can no longer think of himself as "one of the boys" when it comes to work. Here he becomes an addict. He is hooked. There are certain signs of it that even one's closest friend won't mention.

The first signal is when a workaholic passes out on the job. It may occur at home. He may be such an ardent do-it-yourselfer around the house that he continues to work twenty-six hours a day. He gets up two hours earlier every morning to get his work done! But nevertheless he passes out. He is out cold and his wife—and he always has one—becomes concerned as to what is wrong. She, too, had always assumed that he was indestructible. In fact, she, too, may be a workaholic.

After this blackout, thorough medical attention indicates that fatigue, dehydration, and work paralysis have set in. Rest, renewal, and diversification of interest are recommended. Here is where the trouble really starts.

After this, the social approval for overwork is gone. The patient is exhorted to "slow down," "take it easy," "avoid having a heart attack," "take more time with your family," and "get a hobby." But this just produces more isolation. He stays home more, and works and travels less. His family had gotten accustomed to his working all the time; they do not know what to do when he has an evening free "just to be with the family." Friends have gotten accustomed to the idea that he is "too busy" and have long since ceased to call, visit, or invite him on journeys, parties, etc., with them. So he is alone with nothing to do. Something has to be done. A workaholic is a man of action. So what does he do?

First, he begins to have "withdrawal symptoms." He fights a terrible battle when he leaves the office or plant. He has just *got* to take some work home with him. Usually his secretary—if for no reason other than that she doesn't want to have more work assigned her tomorrow than any one human being can do in a day—will caution him about not taking work home. If she is committed to her boss' welfare, she may even enter conspiracies with his wife to prevent this. But secretaries and wives just don't understand. They don't know what pain it is to stand outside the office building, plagued with the insatiable desire to work the way one did when he was young—all day and all night, too. He was a *man* then. Now all he is is a shadow of his former masculine invincibility. He is just a bundle of stomach distresses, heart murmurs, and jagged thorns in the flesh. It pains him to leave off work.

Second, at parties, the workaholic begins to sneak in a little work on the side. No one notices it. He is careful to conceal it. He has been told by his doctor, his wife, his friends, that he needs to have more fun. All work and no play makes Jack a dull boy. So he goes to a party, but the party is dull. He ignores the hostess, he pulls a fellow office worker aside and discusses some papers that need signing. He buttonholes a committee chairman and gets his word in about the way a certain report should be written. He pulls his immediate superior aside and tells him that the sales contract on a certain big deal is signed. The sneaking workaholic feels very pious if he thinks his boss has had one too many drinks . . . if he were only devoted to his work and on the ball!

Third, the workaholic begins to take early "slugs" of work in the morning. This is a dead ringer for a workaholic. If he has been out to a party, he has obviously wasted time. He feels guilty about this. He must, therefore, make up for lost time. He awakens early in his depression over having indulged himself the night before in the forbiddenness of play. Then he eases out of bed, gets his day's work done before it starts, and is "on the ball" ahead of his sleeping colleagues. This would not be so bad if he would have the courage to take a nap in the middle of the day. That is what the "lounge" is admirably equipped for, but it is not so used. If he is a teacher, he and his colleagues hold committee meetings, "rump sessions" of the faculty, and strategy-planning sessions for the next faculty meeting in the "lounge."

Fourth, the workaholic becomes a compulsive "moonlighter." He just *has* to take more work. He is, after all, a $20,000-a-year man. His company does not pay him enough. He must, therefore, take outside work. So he winds up working two shifts. In reality, he is not a $20,000-a-year man. He is a $10,000-a-year man who works two shifts! Or, he goes on weekend binges of work. He may even have companions who will organize a heavy weekend of effort from which it takes a full week on the regular job to recover. Such a weekend leaves a real hangover. This is the real bender pattern. You need to be careful when you try to withdraw a workaholic at this point. He is likely to go into something worse. For example, the Christmas holidays can be a terrifying experience. A man with a *month's* vacation will come tearing back to work at the end of a week begging to be allowed to work. Or, if he has to retire—he may just fold up and die, or drive his wife off her rocker with his fussing around the house all day.

In the fifth place, a workaholic uses all sorts of strategies to stay in touch with—but not too closely—the people around him. He uses alibis. He becomes defensive and bossy. He makes them feel guilty. He feels sorry for himself. He wants them to feel sorry for him. Nobody understands him. Nobody really appreciates him. And no one pays him really what he is worth. The people over him are always piling on more work. The people under him come around when they want some-thing, but he never sees them when they don't have their hand out. The people around him . . . there are none . . . he is the only one in his category!

Finally, the workaholic is likely to try different escapes. There are several of these: *The geographical escape.* The workaholic assumes that if he can change his place of work, things will be different. But when given the opportunity to do so, and having made the move, he finds himself in the same snare. In fact, the worst workaholics change jobs often, always seeking the illusory and perfect job.

The "Peck's Bad Boy" Escape. This workaholic may have worked for twenty-five years in faith-ful service to the same employer. He may have been exemplary in his morals. But one day he is caught—almost as if he had wanted to be caught—in some immoral behavior totally out of keeping with his previous behavior. He is caught as a "peeping tom," or exhibiting himself to children, or in homosexual passes at men in a washroom, or in a triangular affair with a woman much younger, or in a minor accident under the influence of alcohol while driving. He then gets some time off—not for good behavior but for bad behavior. That which his employers were not wise enough to give him for good behavior they now have to give him for bad behavior. That which they could not give him out of appreciation, they now have to give him as sick leave.

The Illness Escape. Some workaholics have a real advantage. Their bodies have better sense than either they or their employers have. A specific illness serves as a reminder of the pres-ence of the seventh day of rest in the organism and the need for relief from the demands of work. As one older man put it: "The secret of old age is to get something wrong with you that won't kill you and let it teach you how to live within your limitations."

The workaholic does not ordinarily come from the ranks of the regular "seven to three" or "nine to five" people. He comes from the self-employed —the small business man, the top executive in a large business, the professional person such as the doctor, the lawyer, the teacher, the minister, the social worker. The housewife and mother who is not employed outside the home—for pay—is particularly prone to workaholism. All of this is because these people decide *themselves* how much or how little work they are going to do.

What, then, is the cure for workaholism? The secret of the cure is in the secret of the disease. Could it be that the focus of trust in work—our own work—is the core of the disease? Is there any such thing as being accepted for our own sakes and not merely for our accomplishments? I believe there is.

More practically speaking, a man and his wife can help each other to overcome workaholism by talking with each other about their common disorder. They can make some decisions as to what their peak level of income for life should be and adjust it according to the cost of living index as time goes on. Employers can require vacation and rest time and regulate "moonlighting." This is a public health procedure. A man and woman can declare open war on credit buying so that they will not be "conned" by this equivalent of the "corner bar" in the life of the workaholic. They can establish groups of "workaholics" who will confess their helplessness and call upon a Higher Power than themselves to redeem them from self-destruction, somewhat as Alcoholics Anonymous does! They can unite in trying to convey their newfound message of hope for workaholics to other people who have not yet begun to take such fearless inventory of their lives.

TOPIC 5

Aggression

People get murdered. People kill for money, for property, or for power. They kill women because they are going to tell on them or something. It may be the girl friend of the murderer or a crook that may be murdered. Sometimes the girls do the killing: They shoot them. There is one program where the man needed pills, he had a bad heart. The girl took the pills out of his reach, and moved his phone so he couldn't call anybody, and his pen and pencil so he couldn't write anything, then he died. She killed him because she was tired of him.

> —A thirteen-year-old explains what he likes about
> television to psychiatrist Fredric Wertham

Any art mirrors society. If you're living in a violent society— and God knows we are—there's no reason we shouldn't mirror it in drama. Just look at Shakespeare. Violence is a part of drama, and drama draws from the society it reflects. . . . There's never been a film anywhere that's created violence in the world. Man's excesses in violence were around long before the movies were invented.

> —Film director Michael Winner defends violence in
> the movies

ZIP! CRASH! SOCK! SPLAT! BAM! SMASH! He's out cold!

> —Complete text for a sequence of seven frames in a
> comic book

Aggression is behavior that is designed to hurt or harm. It may be direct and simple such as a harsh word or a slap. It may be more devious such as some malicious gossip or more serious such as mayhem or murder. Or, it may be monstrous such as genocide or international warfare.

Although it is criticized and condemned, aggression remains a very popular and enduring part of human behavior. Elton B. McNeil, an expert in this area, writes, "Aggression will always be with us, since it is a form of behavior that may be satisfying, thrilling, rewarding, meaningful, and irresistible." He adds, "Push and shove wins the prize, a punch in the mouth breeds respect, a karate black-belt means 'be very polite,' and aggression is one clear-cut way to leadership. Thus, aggression is practical even when there is another choice since it is a generous contributor to your sense of personal competence and well-being."

Aggression is very much a part of our lives. The threat of aggression or punishment is a basic restraining force in the family just as it is in many other institutions of our society and in the relations of our country with other nations. Historian Arthur Schlesinger, Jr. has pointed out that although we Americans like to think of ourselves as peaceful, our country was born in bloody revolution and our history shows—among more benign strains—a continuing strain of violence.

We have been at war almost continuously for a generation. Our mass media—newspapers, magazines, books, movies, and television—are filled with images of violence. As private citizens as well as a nation, we are armed to the teeth: it has been estimated that there are more than enough guns in the homes of this country to arm every man, and our gunslaughter rates far exceed those of all comparable nations.

Man has been called the most destructive animal. Ethologists note that, as a rule, all other species settle their disputes without killing and usually without bloodshed. Man is the exception. And now, with man's great intelligence put to work to serve aggressive ends, he has the weaponry necessary to kill not only himself and others with whom he comes in contact, but all life on this planet as well. At this point in history, a program for the control of aggression is more than an ivory tower pursuit.

What can be done about aggression? There are some who believe that aggression is in our genes and there is little we can do except redirect it in some way. However, a strong case can be made that aggression is largely learned behavior that is produced by certain conditions and triggered by certain stimuli. By controlling these conditions and stimuli, we can hope to modify aggressive behavior and create more humane human beings.

The meaning of aggression

In the lead article Abe Arkoff presents an introduction to the study of aggression. He notes that the extensive human repertory of aggressive behaviors can be categorized as physical or nonphysical, direct or indirect, and focused on others or oneself. Research workers have attributed aggression to innate or physiological factors, to learning or experience, and to situational influences. If we agree that the modification of aggression is a necessary and worthy goal, each of these three sets of causes offers an avenue of approach.

The forces of aggression

Elton B. McNeil, in the second reading, rejects the notion that human beings are inherently and therefore blamelessly aggressive. He reviews the steps by which our society creates an aggressive personality ("an aggressive, hating, social monster") and the conditions in society that cause such a personality to erupt in violence. McNeil, something of a pessimist, believes aggression will always be a problem and perhaps a worsening one since we are becoming more paranoid and "more ready for violent solutions to life's problems." He calls upon us to immediately examine how we teach and reward violence.

The myths of aggression

In the third selection Suzanne K. Steinmetz and Murray A. Straus explode the myth that families are oases of serenity and good feeling. They write, "Violence seems as typical of family relationships as love; and it would be hard to find a group or institution in American society in which violence is more of an everyday occurrence than it is within the family." These authors also explore some related myths and find them to be dangerous oversimplifications. These include the "psychopathology myth" that only "sick" families are violent (violence is widespread and not limited to households with mentally-ill members), the "class myth" that violence occurs mainly in lower-class families (it is also very present in middle-class ones), the "sex myth" that violence is biologically linked to sex and therefore inherent in the family (this myth ignores important social and cultural factors), and the "catharsis myth" that family aggression is reduced if it is expressed (although some research suggests otherwise).

The benefits of fighting

There are several salient viewpoints concerning the desirability of expressing aggression. In one view, it is necessary or beneficial to express anger and act out aggressive impulses in some way. A contrary view maintains that aggression serves no useful purpose and simply leads to more aggression. There is also an intermediate view that although it is useful to let others know when we are angry, it is unwise to convert this anger into verbal or physical aggression.

Some arguments and evidence against the expression of aggression are presented by McNeil in the second article and by Steinmetz and Straus in the third, but in the last reading George R. Bach and Peter Wyden insist that fighting—if it is verbal and according to the "rules"—is not only acceptable but highly desirable. Bach and Wyden exalt and teach people the art of constructive fighting as the way to love, growth, and "game-free" living. They maintain fighting is inevitable between true intimates—that "quarreling and making up are the hallmarks of true intimacy." They slightly revise several popular sayings: "A fight a day keeps the doctor away"; and "couples who fight together are couples who stay together—provided they know how to fight properly."

FOR PERSONAL APPLICATION

1. Describe your own general level of aggression. How aggressive are you compared with other persons you know of your own age and sex? How satisfied are you with this aspect of yourself? Why?
2. Describe your own general patterning of aggression. Is your aggression typically physical or nonphysical, direct or indirect, or focused on others or yourself?
3. Describe your family and its level and pattern of aggression. Is/was your family (as myth would have it) an oasis of serenity, love, and good feeling?
4. What familial, cultural, and other forces have influenced your level and patterning of aggression?
5. What kinds of situations provoke anger or aggression in you?
6. Have you found aggression to be an effective way of coping with your personal frustrations and other problems in living? Have you found that aggression "pays"? Discuss your answers.
7. To what extent, if any, do you believe it is necessary or beneficial to express anger and/or aggression? Discuss your answer.
8. Would you agree that individuals who cannot express anger cannot express love? Discuss your own observations on this matter.
9. Would you agree that couples who fight constructively are better off than those who do not fight at all? Discuss your observations on this matter.
10. Do you believe that there is too much violence presented in our mass media or present in society generally? Why or why not?
11. In what ways, if any, do you believe that we should modify aggression in our society?
12. Write down a discussion item (not given above) that seems particularly relevant to this topic and you, and discuss it.

FOR SMALL GROUPS

1. *Distinguishing anger from aggression.* Devise a situation to demonstrate the difference between the display of anger and the expression of aggression. For example, two volunteers may role-play a situation in which one has borrowed the class notes of the other but has failed to return them in time for an examination. Or reconstruct a recent real-life situation that involved one member. Play the situation twice, once in which the frustrated party shows anger and once in which he expresses aggression. What insights are produced by this technique?
2. *Expressing aggression.* Have a volunteer (or the group in unison) beat violently on the floor or the walls of the room (if they are indestructible). Each beater is to yell or scream whatever comes to mind. What effect does this have? Could techniques of this kind provide evidence for or against the catharsis theory of aggression?
3. *Researching media violence.* Have the members bring one week's ac-

cumulation of newspaper movie advertisements with every allusion to aggression or violence circled. Or bring a television guide with each program that contains violence identified in some way. Discuss the extent to which movies and/or television contribute to the level of aggression or violence in this country.

4. *Debating media violence.* Divide into affirmative and negative teams and debate this proposition: "Resolved that physical violence should not be portrayed in children's television programs or in programs shown during children's viewing hours."

FOR FURTHER READING

Bach, G. R., and P. Wyden. *The Intimate Enemy: How to Fight Fair in Love and Marriage.* New York: William Morrow, 1969.

Bandura, A. *Aggression: A Social Learning Analysis.* Englewood Cliffs, N.J.: Prentice-Hall, Inc., 1973.

Graham, H. D., and T. R. Gurr. *Violence in America: Historical and Comparative Perspectives.* New York: Bantam Books, 1969.

Kaufmann, H. *Aggression and Altruism: A Psychological Analysis.* New York: Holt, Rinehart & Winston, Inc., 1970.

Madow, L. *Anger.* New York: Charles Scribner's Sons, 1972.

Rubin, T. I. *The Angry Book.* New York: The Macmillan Company, 1969.

Singer, J. L., ed. *The Control of Aggression and Violence.* New York: Academic Press, 1971.

Starr, A. *Human Destructiveness.* New York: Basic Books, Inc., 1973.

AN INTRODUCTION TO AGGRESSION

Abe Arkoff

*Sticks and stones may break my bones
But words can never hurt me.*
—Child's verse

Aggression, briefly defined, is behavior whose aim is harm. When they are hurled with hostile intent, words as well as sticks and stones are implements of aggression. And, by the time we reach adulthood, our aggressive repertory goes far beyond these simple measures.

Some concepts closely related to aggression are anger, hostility, and violence. Anger refers to a state of arousal that reinforces the tendency to attack. Typically, this occurs when we are thwarted in some way. However, anger may exist without aggression (we may be aroused but not strike out) just as aggression may exist without anger (for example, a murder in "cold blood").

Hostility and violence are used almost interchangeably with aggression. Hostility sometimes implies nonphysical aggression; for example, we speak of a hostile attitude or hostile criticism. Violence is more likely to connote physical aggression and perhaps of a heightened degree.

CLASSIFYING AGGRESSION

Ingenious and sophisticated as we humans are, there is almost no limit to the ways we express aggression. In attempting to sort out these ways, psychologists frequently categorize aggression as physical or nonphysical, direct or indirect, and focused on others or directed toward oneself. These categories are briefly described below.

Physical aggressions range from such relatively mild injuries as a slap or a scratch to the major crimes of rape and murder. On the nonphysical side, there are threats, taunts, insults, affronts, slights, and verbal indignities of various kinds. Of course, the nonphysical and the physical commonly appear together with the former frequently giving way to the latter as anger and tempers mount.

As indicated above, aggression may be direct or indirect. We may hit a person or insult him to his face. Or perhaps we accomplish our aims indirectly by undercutting his efforts, gossiping about him behind his back, spreading malicious tales, behaving in ways that he is certain to find annoying, purposefully doing poorly on an exam or in a game when we know he is counting on us to pass or to win, and so on.

Aggression may be directed outward or turned back toward oneself. Generally speaking, aggression is aimed toward the person or thing that is the source of our anger or frustration. But this is not always possible because the people who make us angry or frustrate us are often too powerful or important to attack. In fact, our aggressive impulses toward them can make us feel fearful or guilty. Deep feelings of depression—hopelessness and worthlessness—may result. A number of clinicians have noted that depressed individuals inhibit aggression against others and blame themselves for things which are others' fault. When aggression is again directed outward toward the original targets, the depression lifts.

THE CORRELATES OF AGGRESSION

A number of factors have been found to be related to or associated with aggression. This, of course, does not prove that these factors cause aggression although it alerts us to that possibility. One important set of factors has to do with parent–child relationships, and a number of studies have shown some tendency for "cold" or rejecting parents to have highly aggressive children. Summarizing the evidence, Norma and Seymour Feshbach (1971) conclude, "Children who are unwanted by their parents, and who are given little affection and attention, are likely to develop hostile behavior patterns."

The viewing of violence on television has been found to be correlated with aggression in children. Evidence brought together by Bandura (1973) indicates that this relationship is not of a high order but it is strikingly consistent; it shows that children who have more exposure to televised violence tend to demonstrate more interpersonal violence in their own lives. In one study particularly worth noting (Eron, Huesmann, Lefkowitz, and Walder, 1972), the viewing of violence by boys at the age of eight was found to be significantly correlated with their interpersonal aggressiveness as measured ten years later.

A correlation has also been noted between physical punishment and class membership. Greater use of physical punishment is made by lower-class families than by middle-class ones, although the difference is not great (Steinmetz and Straus, 1973). Lower-class persons also tend to be more direct and physical in their aggressive behavior. Lower-class arguments are more likely to be charged with emotion and to end in combat. Middle-class persons tend to be more restrained and sophisticated in their expression of aggression.

In our society and in most others, males are more aggressive than females, and this is true at every age, beginning with early childhood. Females are more abasive, that is, they are more likely to turn aggression back on themselves, feel guilty, criticize themselves, and accept blame. However, this difference in the way that males and females express aggression is somewhat more complex because the two sexes have different patterns of demonstrating aggression.

Evidence assembled by the Feshbachs (1971, 1973) indicates that, in comparison, boys are more likely to use direct and physical forms of aggression while girls are more apt to use indirect, nonphysical forms. For example, boys are more likely to push, hit, and punch and girls are more likely to scold or insult or to be unfriendly or unkind.

THE CAUSES OF AGGRESSION

What causes aggression? Three categories of antecedents have been identified by workers in this area: innate, learned, and situational. First, some writers have held that aggression is innate or inherent in human nature, that it is an instinct or an inherited pattern characteristic of our species. This position includes an implication that aggression or even war is inevitable or nearly so, and that the best we can do is to modulate, harness, or redirect aggression in some way.

Most social scientists reject this position. Human patterns of behavior are so heavily modified by learning that it does not seem justifiable to describe them as instinctive. However, there are certain biological or constitutional factors which may influence the acquisition or expression of aggressive behavior. For example, the males of a number of animal species appear to be more aggressive than the females, and the administration of male hormone to these females increases the latter's aggressiveness. Among human beings, newborn females appear to have greater skin and pain sensitivity than newborn males, and it has been hypothesized that this might predispose females to less physically aggressive activities. Upon reviewing the evidence, Moyer (1971) concludes "there is abundant evidence that man has innate neural and endocrine organizations which when activated result in hostile thoughts and behaviors." Further, he notes that through learning or physiological manipulation these internal conditions may be altered so that aggression does not occur.

There is also considerable evidence that aggression results from learning. Children's behavior is heavily influenced by what they see, by what they are allowed to do, and by what they are rewarded or punished for doing. Children model their behavior after others—especially prestigious others —after parents and other adults, after siblings, and after peers. The more aggression the child sees in persons who he believes are worth emulating, the more aggressive behavior he tends to initiate on his own behalf.

The child's patterning of aggression is influenced by a climate of permissiveness as well as by the rewards and punishments he encounters.

Children who are allowed to be aggressive become more aggressive. And children who are rewarded for aggressive behavior incorporate this behavior into their repertory.

Punishment of aggression has more complex effects. Punishment may inhibit aggressive tendencies without destroying them. For example, when aggression is punished in the home, it may then be transferred to a safer arena, perhaps the neighborhood outside the home or the school playground. Or it may be expressed in subtler or more indirect ways which escape punishment.

Cultural values influence the learning of aggressive patterns. For example, some cultures or subcultures place a high value on tough or assertive masculinity. Not only specific values concerning aggression but collateral values as well may be an important influence. To give an example, cultures that emphasize achievement and independence tend to have higher levels of aggression, and some authorities feel that our nearly continuous involvement in war over the last generation has heightened internal violence in this country.

While innate and learned factors in aggression relate to the person himself, the third set of factors concern situational circumstances. Frustrating situations often call forth aggression. When we are thwarted, we frequently mobilize and assert ourself as we seek for a solution. In this state of arousal, we may lash out at people who appear to be blocking our progress or who are simply nearby, safe and ready objects for assault. Not all frustration, however, leads to aggression since there are many other ways of dealing with frustrating circumstances, nor does all aggression stem from frustration since, like other patterns of behavior, aggression can be learned and become a personal strategy under varying circumstances.

Other situational factors that influence aggression include restraints and threats of retaliation which may be present. A boy is more likely to hit a younger smaller brother than an older larger one, and he is more likely to do so in his parents' absence than in their presence. And, for their part, his parents are more likely to punish his aggressiveness if there is no company present. As was indicated before, we learn aggression, and we also learn how and when and where and toward whom we may express or must inhibit aggressive impulses.

THE MERITS AND LIMITATIONS OF AGGRESSION

Growing up in American society, one learns to value aggression. As psychologist Arnold H. Buss (1971) puts it, we learn that "aggression pays." Organized crime, which is built on aggression and the threat of aggression, pays. National aggressiveness, as demonstrated in the glorification of war and war heroes, pays. The dramas we are weaned on are "shoot 'em up" rather than "talk it out." Who ever heard of a feud between cattlemen and sheepherders which was settled by compromise?

It is frequently difficult to draw the line between or separate aggression from some other qualities which may be valued by various segments of our society. We may value assertiveness, competitiveness, and "hard-hitting" masculinity. We may value drive, achievement, and self-reliance. All of these qualities seem related to or associated with aggressive behaviors, and the question arises as to whether we can have one set of qualities without the other. If not, how much of one are we willing to sacrifice or tolerate for the other?

A number of social scientists have pointed out the useful purposes served by anger and aggression. Coser (1966) notes that some violence such as racial riots serves as a signal to society that something is wrong and needs attention before even greater disruption occurs. He also indicates that violence acts as a catalyst to necessary social change when all else seems ineffective.

Some psychologists, psychoanalysts, and psychiatrists have emphasized the positive uses of anger and aggression. Rubin (1969) feels that we need to express our anger, that in attempting to inhibit it we pay a huge price in terms of physical and mental health and human relationships. Bach (1968, 1970) has advocated "constructive aggressiveness" between marriage partners. He says, "A good and fair fight a day keeps divorce lawyers away."

To look at the other side, the negative aspects

of aggression are so obvious that they need not be labored. Aggression—or at least some patterns of aggression—serves to destroy human beings and human relationships, tear apart the family, disrupt the community, and threaten the peace and even the continued existence of this planet. "Violence," writes Berkowitz (1973), one of the foremost authorities in this area, "has a way of getting out of hand and breeding still more violence."

Insofar as there exist "constructive" ways of expressing anger and aggression, we must discover and put them to use. When the control of aggression would result in the loss of other valued qualities, we must make some hard decisions about whether we are willing to pay this price. In the author's opinion, with violence at the level it is today in our country and the world, no price is too high to pay.

MODIFYING AGGRESSION

The modification of interpersonal and international aggression is such a complex and elaborate subject that it can only be mentioned briefly here. Some methods of modifying aggression are implied in what has been said about the antecedents of this behavior. Alterations can be made in a person's physiology, his learning experiences, or in the situations in which he finds himself.

It has been demonstrated that aggressive excitability, irritability, and hostility can be reduced through radical, irreversible brain surgery or through the less radical administration of hormones and drugs. However, this is an area in which much more research must be done, and we are not ready for the application of these techniques to persons beyond certain clinical groups. When Kenneth B. Clark in his presidential address to the American Psychological Association in 1971 called for research into biochemical means to prevent leaders from using power in destructive or violent ways, he caused quite a stir. The idea of a "peace pill," as his proposal was irreverently labeled, was too much for many psychologists to swallow ("Who will control the controllers?"), but Clark has adhered to his position, noting that to do nothing would lead to the destruction of all mankind.

A second approach to modifying aggression is through the alternation of learning experiences. Child-rearing techniques that teach cooperation and empathy and that minimize punishment and frustration have been advocated for reducing the level of aggressiveness. Maternal coldness has been associated with high aggression in children, and any alterations in home environments that increase the level of parental warmth and affection are likely to reduce aggression in children.

There has been considerable recent controversy concerning the effect of violence in the mass media. Does violence on television, for example, teach children to be aggressive or does it serve to absorb their aggressive energies? Further, can a high level of media aggression numb us and make us indifferent to violence? Authorities disagree, but the bulk of the evidence suggests a diminished level of media violence would have positive effects.

A number of aggression control techniques that are based on learning principles have been devised for individuals, groups, and even nations. Social scientists have had some success in applying these techniques to individuals and groups. However, establishment of international controls is still in the hands of diplomats, and their record of therapeutic success is not highly reassuring.

A third approach to modifying aggression involves situational factors. Emphasis in this area is on the reduction of frustration in the home, neighborhood, community, and in every part of society. Obviously, we must reorder our priorities and increase our efforts to modify the frustrating circumstances in which many persons and groups live. We must work from the outside in and the inside out, altering environments so that they are less frustrating to persons and improving the self images, competencies, and powers of various persons and disadvantaged groups so that they are better able to overcome their frustrations and reach their goals.

REFERENCES

BACH, G. R., and R. M. DEUTSCH. *Pairing*. New York: Peter H. Wyden, 1970.

Bach, G. R., and P. Wyden. *The Intimate Enemy*. New York: William Morrow, 1968.

Bandura, A. *Aggression: A Social Learning Analysis*. Englewood Cliffs, N.J.: Prentice-Hall, Inc., 1973.

Berkowitz, L. "The Case for Bottling Up Rage," *Psychology Today* (July, 1973), 24, 26, 28–31.

Buss, A. H. "Aggression Pays," in J. L. Singer, ed., *The Control of Aggression and Violence*. New York: Academic Press, 1971, pp. 7–18.

Coser, L. A. "Some Social Functions of Violence," *Annals of the American Academy of Political and Social Science*, 364 (1966), 8–18.

Eron, L. D., et al. "Does Television Violence Cause Aggression?" *American Psychologist* (1972), 27, 253–263.

Feshbach, N., and S. Feshbach. "Children's Aggression," *Young Children*, 26 (1971), 364–377.

Feshbach, S., and N. Feshback. "The Young Aggressors," *Psychology Today* (April, 1973), 90–95.

Moyer, K. E. "The Physiology of Aggression and the Implications for Aggression Control," in J. L. Singer, ed., *The Control of Aggression and Violence*. New York: Academic Press, 1971, pp. 61–92.

Rubin, T. I. *The Angry Book*. New York: The Macmillan Company, 1969.

Steinmetz, S. K., and M. A. Straus. "The Family as Cradle of Violence," *Society* (September/October, 1973), 50–56.

VIOLENCE TODAY

Elton B. McNeil

Thomas Rose may have said it all when he made the observation about violence that the American "people and institutions are committed to it as a logical and useful style of life. American culture . . . tolerates, approves, propagates, and rewards violence. The glamour of violent acts and the glorification of violent men create an idealization of violence in America" (Rose, 1969; p. ix).

Thus, birth control may ultimately prove to be the single trustworthy way to limit violence on this planet. It is not that we haven't tried other alternatives. Throughout history we have endeavored to reduce the human potential for violence by killing as many of our fellow men as we could. But, we have fallen behind in the task because we seem to have a limited capacity to enjoy killing people. The human condition is this: we can control violence in some of the people all of the time; we can control violence in all of the people some of the time; and we have failed throughout history to control violence in all of the people all of the time. Even if fewer are born and we kill off most of the others, we would probably be unable to manage the aggression of those remaining. We need, thus, other explanations of man's inhumanity to his fellow man.

There is another way out of this dilemma, of course. The American, tribal, love-rock musical, "Hair," has provided us with an innovative solution to the problem of man's hand turned, throughout history, against his fellow man. In song, the cast of "Hair" promises that

Reprinted from *Pastoral Psychology* (September, 1971), 21–30.

When the moon is in the seventh house,
And Jupiter aligns with Mars,
Then Peace will guide the planets,
And Love will steer the stars.

And, they have assured us that in the "Age of Aquarius" we will be visited by

Harmony and understanding,
Sympathy and trust abounding.

All we need, then, is an exceptional amount of cosmic patience.

Like Shakespeare, in *Julius Caesar*, I believe that

The fault . . . is not in our stars,
But in ourselves . . .

If we are not prepared to wait patiently for the Age of Aquarius, then we must devote our energies now to designing the means by which each of us can become effective in reducing the total amount of readiness for violence that each new generation carries into adulthood.

Man and Beast

There has been, recently, an exceptionally attractive intellectual cop-out provided Americans who can't believe the fate of violence rests with the stars. A rash of popular, semi-scientific books has taken the following position. They state, in essence, that man is an animal and animals are inherently aggressive. Man, thus, is aggressive because of the instincts he inherits as a member of his species—instincts that are similar to those of fish, chimpanzees, and other predators. These theorists conclude that man is blamelessly violent—it's in his genes. They suggest there is little we can do to change the state of planetary affairs, and even less we can accomplish by training new generations of children to a peaceful way of life.

Thus no one of us in our society needs to feel responsible since human aggression is a fixed, immutable quality that is somehow, mysteriously, built into the species. This is comfortable and also convenient, but it is, in the opinion of the most respected theorists of our time, a totally inaccurate view of man despite its satisfying emotional appeal. In moments of despair about human violence we wistfully search the animal kingdom for moral and ethical guidance. And, ever since

Rousseau, we have suspected that the human condition is one depraved by the influence of a high-rise crowding megalopolis, breakneck speed, and the unremitting clamor of a polluting industrial society. We have sought in species less complex than our own a sign that there is hope for mankind. In simplicity there may indeed be truth, but it is wildly improbable that the ant, bee, or monkey colonies have much to teach modern, interplanetary, atomic man straining to burst the bonds of time, place, and person.

We may study ants, ducks, fish, and chimps forever but we will learn little about the human condition. Studies of animals are relevant only as they apply to that very brief period in human existence when each of us is an infant without access to language. Once we learn to speak we swiftly become free of our animal cousins and enter a universe of human interaction that even the smartest chimpanzee cannot begin to comprehend. As we learn to think and speak, we truly become a distinct species; the only one in history to understand the meaning of abstractions such as liberty, freedom, equality, brotherhood, love, or democracy.

It is impossibly pessimistic to talk of aggressive "instincts" and expect that man's inhumanity to his fellow man will evaporate or fade away. Man is more than a vicious, snarling animal. The observation of Lukas (1969) is appropriate here:

This country is threatened by savagery, not violence: and this is not a play on words. The peoples of this world are governed by their characters rather than by their institutions; and there is a streak of savagery rather than violence in the American character. (p. 352)

But there is no reliable evidence that the character of our people is formed of instinctual traits passed down to us intact from our forebears.

THE AGGRESSIVE PERSONALITY

It is most probable that mankind will never eliminate aggression as a fundamental aspect of the human existence. Aggression will always be with us, since it is a form of behavior that may be satisfying, thrilling, rewarding, meaningful, and irresistible. And, the difficulty is—and always has

been—that crime pays. Push and shove wins the prize, a punch in the mouth breeds respect, a karate black-belt means "be very polite," and aggression is one clear-cut way to leadership. Thus, aggression is practical even when there is another choice since it is a generous contributor to your sense of personal competence and well-being. It is an ego-builder because successful aggression convinces you that you can tackle anything and makes you feel an admired, respected, person-to-be-reckoned-with. To understand this (if you are male) all you need do is compare the sense of satisfaction at having whipped the biggest, meanest bully in town with the satisfaction garnered from lavish praise for following an exquisitely delicate and sensitive interpretation of Anglo-Saxon tradition.

The male of the species becomes warmongering, ready to fight, and aggressive because he learns to gain pleasure and status from this social role. The female, as our society decrees, must find more subtle outlets for exactly the same feelings and impulses. It is clear that in a thousand ways we encourage aggression and reward its appearance in males, and that the process begins in early childhood.

One explanation of the psychological structure of the aggressive personality is that provided by Leonard Berkowitz (1962). He assumes that aggressiveness is learned directly by experiences with the rewards and punishments of life. The aggressive person thus learns to have a "predisposition to be readily aroused" to anger and rage and becomes remarkably quick to respond to signals in the environment that trigger this anger. Given the "habit" of anger and an appropriate "stimulus," the aggressive personality will blow up frequently and violently.

When the cues or signals to aggression are not present, however, the aggressive personality is very much like the rest of us; complaining and crabby, perhaps, but rational about non-provocative, non-controversial daily events. Since he isn't exploding *all* the time, he sees himself as a calm, rational, reasonable person except on those few occasions when he is provoked beyond all sensible human tolerance. If you ask him about his explosiveness, the aggressive person will report that most of the people in this world are too passive, spineless, and tolerant of injustice, incompetence, and insults from others. He might suggest that most of us *invite* mistreatment from others by compromising every confrontation and never standing up on our hind legs to resist or protest.

Since the aggressive person sees frustration in almost every event in life he will continuously be distressed, feel threatened, and anticipate that the future will be no different than the past. His daily brittle encounter with his fellow man will only underscore the need to be aggressive if one is to survive. When the expectation that things will always go wrong is coupled with low toleration of frustrating events and an exceptional readiness to respond to frustration with anger and violence, the aggressive personality expects trouble, searches for it, discovers it everywhere, and reacts in a predictably violent manner. Sensitized to frustration, ever ready to respond aggressively, and with few other available forms of response, he becomes the prototype of an aggressive personality and finds life a continuing hostile confrontation with others.

Growing Up Violent

How does our society fashion an aggressive, hating, social monster? It is not easily achieved since our growing youngsters rebound from even the most painful of child-rearing circumstances. Yet, if an aggressive personality is the goal, the steps that must be taken are quite straightforward.

There is one helpful preliminary condition. If you can arrange for the child to be born poor, to be one of a great number of other children, to be crowded into too little space, to be exposed to lying, cheating, stealing, and violent examples during most of his waking hours, it helps. It helps too if the child is allowed to run the streets unsupervised to acquire his primary values from peers who find themselves similarly trapped in the same hopeless, unrewarding life. In short, if the child's *real* world is a monstrous tangle of evil, injury, insecurity, and ignorance, then it will be easier to execute the few steps I am about to describe. Having such ready-made environment saves the time and trouble parents would otherwise have to spend beating, threatening, scolding, and abusing the child.

By the time the developing aggressive person-

ality is ready for school, the additional punishments he will most certainly get from his teachers are really unnecessary and will have little impact on him. The teachers will simply confirm a bitter conclusion learned earlier in life. These "children who hate" learn only that they must wait until they are big enough, strong enough, or clever enough to fight society on more even terms. But, if you can't provide such an environment for aggressive development, all is not lost. If you are dedicated and diligent there are steps you can take that will overcome the handicap of an otherwise benign environment.

STEP 1: *Have no love for the child.** Love is a mercurial element that can destroy the best of malicious intentions since love topples what hate constructs. Love undermines rejection, softens the sting of anger, and dulls the edge of rage. Love forms a protective psychological cocoon to shelter each of us from the full impact of the blows of fate, and the workings of love are invisible to the eye. Without love, the child is an object that can be used or misused as whim and anger dictate. The child not given love must go out in life and twist everyone's arm until he gets it.

STEP 2: *Shape the child's view of the world and people.* The selective reinforcement of some responses, and the punishment of others, can establish particular dimensions of personality while it eliminates others. If a combined system of deliberate and accidental reward and punishment is established early enough, continued long enough, and matched by clear examples of aggressive response to the world, the child will mature with a stable but warped view of the necessity for aggression. The helpless, dependent, uncomprehending child learns what he is taught and he learns to do as people do, not as people say ought to be done.

STEP 3: *Convince the child aggression is the only way.* The child must be taught that his hostile reactions to people and the aggressive fashion in which he treats them are necessary, natural, reasonable, correct, and not monstrous. Violence must lose its menacing aspect and be viewed as a preferred and desirable means to an essential and

* Adapted from McNeil (1966).

profitable end. The child must learn that in a jungle only savages survive, and his developing addiction to violence must be rewarded more often than it is punished. In those rare instances when punishment does occur, it must be inappropriately administered and appear to be undeserved. Once the child is convinced that violence has a rational base and is admired and rewarded, he will, in times of high anxiety, regularly become violent as a means of solving problems.

STEP 4: *Defend the child against the coercion of education, for it may produce a docile, non-aggressive, non-violent adult.* As we know, education takes advantage of the dependent nature of the growing child. It tries to inculcate peaceful values by showing him how to become an acceptable, cooperative member of the society and it praises and rewards reasonable behavior. If not thwarted by vigilant parents it can even produce the psychological reactions of guilt, fear, anxiety, a sense of loss and alienation from others, and feelings of rejection. It is from these internal emotional experiences that the child's self-image and self-esteem is formed, so he must be armored against the corrective influences that would make a decent citizen of him. This is easily done if he learns early that education is a worthless pursuit in which he will be treated unfairly.

While these steps in child-rearing are vital contributors to the final shape of adult behavior, they cannot be considered in isolation from some measure of the society to which the individual must adjust. In an organized, highly structured, stable society the "social animal" is peaceful and cooperative; in a society that is disorganized and in transition, he is capable of incredibly destructive and violent behavior. The seemingly senseless violence of humans may be one of the costs of urban living. In the neglected center of our crowded cities the young, unmarried, unemployed male product of a broken home tends to be a prime source of the purposeless assault of one human on another.

PERSONAL VIOLENCE

While it may not be perfectly accurate to say that we always kill the one we love, it is true that most of us have less to fear from crime in the streets than murder in the home. This is why it is a common observation among policemen that responding to a call of "family trouble" is an exceptionally dangerous assignment. We know that most victims have a close relationship to those who kill them and death most often occurs on home ground. Murder rarely fits the stereotype of an unsuspecting, helpless, passive victim stalked by a cold, calculating killer. Most homicides are preceded by angry quarrels in which the victim plays an active part in bringing about his own death.

In 1969, Wolfgang studied 588 homicides in Philadelphia and he concluded that:

—if you are under 16 years of age, your murderer will most likely be a parent or relative.

—if you are a woman over 16, your murderer will most likely be a husband, lover, or relative.

—women are more likely than men to kill their mates.

—when a man is killed, the killer is most likely to be his wife.

—spouse slayings are more violent than the average homicide.

—the bedroom is the most murderous room in the house.

—proportionately, more women are killed in bedrooms.

—men are in greater danger of being killed in the kitchen.

We do not really kill the ones we love. Rather, we kill those emotionally closest to us; those close enough to destroy our self-esteem. Insult, humiliation, or coercion are powerful elicitors of hostility and probably the most important source of anger and aggressive drive in humans. Laboratory studies of aggression (Berkowitz, 1962; Buss, 1961) and clinical studies of violent men (Toch, 1969) consistently point to implicit threats to self-esteem that render us impotent and diminish our status in our own eyes and in the eyes of others. Sometimes the only way to restore our personal status and demonstrate power is to injure the provoking agent (Feshbach, 1971). The relationship between personal status and violence is especially exaggerated for males weaned on a warrior definition of the male image.

The ultimate forms of aggression are perpetrated by the male of the species. Males assault their fellow humans eight times more often than do females, and murder is seven times more often a masculine act. Negroes commit a higher absolute and disproportionately higher relative rate of fatal crimes. Southern violence—black or white—is greater than in the North, and the rate of violence in the "inner city" of large metropolitan areas is uniformly high. Killing others is most frequent among members of lower socioeconomic classes, particularly the young—the years twenty to thirty-nine being the most dangerous ages. This list of "facts" of fatal encounter tells us very little since "any act, whether it is murder or abstaining from murder, is multiply determined and can be understood only as a resolution of forces both without and within the individual—a resolution of forces that produces a single act which, in the case of murder, is so dramatic that it obscures the very forces that led to it" (McNeil, 1959, p. 236).

Murderers, contrary to popular belief, may be the most docile, trustworthy, and least violent members of prison populations. Megargee (1965) examined a criminal population by dividing them into two groups, those rated *Extremely Assaultive* (manslaughter, murder, mayhem, assault with a deadly weapon, etc.) and those described as *Moderately Assaultive* (beatings). In two other categories he placed those designated *Non-Violent* (thieves, homosexuals) and *Non-Criminals* (ordinary men).

Most of us would guess that the greatest degree of violence would issue from those most hostile and least self-controlled. Yet, Megargee concluded that assaultive criminals were less aggressive and more controlled than either the non-violent criminals or the non-criminal population. Megargee suggested that assaultive persons come in two types—undercontrolled and chronically overcontrolled. Undercontrolled aggressive persons are those who are openly aggressive and possess relatively little self-control but most often express their hostility in mild or moderate fashion. In contrast, chronically overcontrolled human beings are those who have such strict control over their aggressive urges that they seldom explode. The explosion, when it comes, is fatally violent.

Thus, marriage to an undercontrolled person might mean continuous strife and turmoil but the amount of aggression released in any one of the frequent outbursts would not be excessive. Life with the chronically overcontrolled person would be peaceful and tranquil for many years, but the history of man is bloodstained by the quiet, uncomplaining husband who suddenly slaughters his wife in an unbelievably brutal fashion. These findings suggest that while murder is a highly visible measure of the violent individual, it need not reflect a lifelong pattern of assaultive behavior. Murder is often the desperate response of a normally unaggressive person who can no longer tolerate the pressures of life.

VIOLENCE AND SOCIAL PATHOLOGY

The sociologist, Lewis Coser (1966) observed that:

> While to the European thinker the fragility of the social fabric and the brittleness of social bonds seemed self-evident experiences, American social science proceeded from a world view in which social violence was at best seen as a pathological phenomenon. (p. 9)

Perhaps our history of only one massive internal conflict—the Civil War—has twisted our historical perspective until violence has come to be perceived as incidental rather than fundamental to the nature of society.

In Coser's analysis of social violence he indicates that violence is likely to be the outcome of any social structure that bars certain of its citizens from legitimate access to the ladder of personal achievement. When all such access is barred, violence may become the only reasonable alternate path. Also,:

> In the world of violence, such attributes as race, socioeconomic position, age, and the like are irrelevant; personal worth is judged on the basis of qualities that are available to all who would cultivate them. (Cloward and Ohlin, 1960, p. 175)

In this instance, the crucial factor may be the willingness to risk injury or death in moving up the ladder of life to a position of greater status. In this way, high rates of aggression among lower-class families may be a futile attempt to control the smaller world of the family when faced with failure in the larger, working world.

An important function of violence is that it is a signal of severe social dysfunction—a visible symptom of disorder in the body politic. The problem is that the American insistence on social harmony at any price leads us to deny the importance of such symptoms and to attribute them a more benign valuation. Violence is also a catalyst. Counter-aggression (e.g., of police officers in suppressing social movements) catalyzes public opinion and for all its cost in human suffering it eventually produces corrective social change. With the growth of public communications media, our citizenry can no longer remain unaware of social conditions and their "unjustified" nature.

The effect of upheaval in our society is most likely to appear in the form of a massive shaping of the life view of a multitude of individual members of our society. And a case can be made for the conclusion that we all have become more paranoid and are, thus, more ready for violent solutions to life's problems. There is validity in the assertion that an unhealthy number of us are suffering from the suspiciousness, hypersensitivity to criticism, hostility, or feelings of persecution typical of hospitalized paranoid persons. The critical issue is that for every hospitalized paranoid person there must be hundreds or thousands of us whose degree of mistrust of their fellow man is severe enough to be a constant source of painful disruption to personal, family, and community life.

Paranoia is a delusional way of thinking, a view of life that allows us to deny the existence of intolerable or unacceptable impulses by unconsciously attributing them to other persons rather than admit they are a part of the self. Many of us, of course, will react inappropriately to severe tension or personal catastrophe and become suspicious, misinterpret the motives and intentions of others, become hostile, and react aggressively or violently. Serious threats to our security or self-esteem will make us volatile, unpredictable, and ready for violence.

When paranoid thinking occurs, we not only mistrust the motives of others, but actively probe for confirmation of what we are convinced is true.

We turn all our attention to gathering credible proof of the suspected plot launched against us. That so many others would devote so much of their time and energy to making life difficult for us suggests that we must be very special persons. This delusion that we are the star of some mysterious melodrama reassures us of our importance, and this grandiose estimate of the self sows the seeds for the conclusion that these less talented but powerful and dangerous enemies are jealous and envious. Why else would they punish us, thwart us, and try to eliminate us from competition?

The person with a paranoid view of life may find others who share his elaborate delusional system (especially if it concerns loose national targets such as government, the American Medical Association, religion, race, etc.) and some paranoids may even be elevated to positions of leadership in which they can have an immeasurable impact on the course of human affairs. Or, some paranoid personalities take individual action and seek to assassinate a prominent political leader.

When we speak of the aggressive personality quick to perceive threat in an unthreatening environment and quick to respond with anger, rage, and punitive action directed against others, we are really describing a paranoid personality who is too disturbed emotionally to relate successfully to others, yet too acutely perceptive of reality to be dismissed as a "mental case." Paranoid personalities indeed have "enemies" and really are "persecuted"; it is just that they have confused cause and effect in human relationships and cannot realize that their unresolved internal fears, tensions, and low self-esteem, are producing the behavior that others view as disturbed.

If we are to control human aggression and make this a peaceful planet, it is obvious that we must find some way to correct the distorted perceptions of the many paranoid personalities that populate the ranks of each new generation.

THE WAY IT IS

Much of contemporary violence is accomplished without anger or fear. This kind of violence is sometimes called "instrumental aggression" since it is in the service of following orders or doing a job, e.g., much of modern warfare involves dropping of bombs or napalm on faceless, distant, dehumanized dots, or firing of shells at invisible enemies far beyond the visible horizon.

As Marmor (1969) noted, in horror:

We rely on the sane people of the world to preserve it from barbarism, madness, destruction. And now it begins to dawn on us that it is precisely the *sane* ones who are the most dangerous . . . who can without qualm and without nausea aim the missiles and press the buttons that will initiate the great festival of destruction that they, the *sane ones,* have prepared. (p. 340)

The most negative aspects of violence are easily obvious. It is the constructive features of violent behavior that are likely to be ignored. Riots or acts of violence are reprehensible but they unquestionably open channels of communication between the ghettos and the power structure. As costly as riotous behavior may be, it provides a release mechanism which gives a sense of power and status to people or groups who have long felt inadequate or humiliated by the existing power structure.

It is depressing but realistic to conclude with the words of Bloomberg (1969):

. . . we mislead ourselves into a fool's errand if we ask how to eliminate violence from human affairs; we can only attempt to minimize the frequency, the duration, and the intensity of its manifestations, seeking constructive expression of our capacities for aggression. But if we try solely to suppress violence once it emerges, then we can be sure that it will appear frequently, be persistent, and reach great heights of destruction. (pp. 360–61)

We have for many millenia believed that men of good will would finally prevail and excise this cancerous behavior from the body of mankind and we have failed consistently to achieve so lofty a goal. Perhaps we are better advised to look at the many ways in which we reward violence, to cease wondering why it continues unchecked, and devote our energies to realistic attempts to tame the Medusa which has for so long plagued us.

REFERENCES

BERKOWITZ, L. *Aggression: A Social Psychological Analysis.* New York: McGraw-Hill Book Company, 1962.

BLOOMBERG, W., JR. "American Violence in Perspective," in T. Rose, ed., *Violence in America.* New York: Vintage Books, 1969, pp. 359–371.

BUSS, A. H. *The Psychology of Aggression.* New York: John Wiley & Sons, Inc., 1961.

CLOWARD, R. A., and L. E. OHLIN. *Delinquency and Opportunity.* New York: The Free Press, 1960.

COSER, L. A. *The Functions of Social Conflict.* New York: The Free Press, 1956.

———. "Violence and the Social Structure," *Science and Psychoanalysis,* Vol. VI. New York: Grune and Stratton, Inc., 1963, pp. 30–42.

FESHBACH, S. "Dynamics and Morality of Violence and Aggression: Some Psychological Considerations," *American Psychologist,* 26(3) (1971), 281–292.

———. "Aggression," in P. H. Mussen, ed., *Carmichael Manual of Child Psychology,* rev. ed. New York: John Wiley & Sons, Inc., 1970.

LUKAS, J. "America's Malady Is Not Violence but Savagery," in T. Rose, ed., *Violence in America.* New York: Vintage Books, 1969, pp. 349–358.

McNEIL, E. B. "Violence and Human Development," in M. E. Wolfgang, ed., "Patterns of Violence." *The Annals,* 364 (1966), pp. 149–157.

———. "Psychology and Aggression," *The Journal of Conflict Resolution,* 3 (1959), 195–294.

MARMOR, J. "Some Psychosocial Aspects of Contemporary Urban Violence," in T. Rose, ed., *Violence in America.* New York: Vintage Books, 1969, pp. 338–348.

———. "War, Violence and Human Nature," *The Bulletin of the Atomic Scientists* (March, 1964), 19–22.

MEGARGEE, E. I. "Assault with Intent to Kill," *Transaction,* 2 (1965), 26–31.

ROSE, T., ed. *Violence in America.* New York: Vintage Books, 1969.

TOCH, H. H. *Violent Men.* Chicago: Aldine, 1969.

WOLFGANG, M. E. "Who Kills Whom?" *Psychology Today,* 3 (October, 1969), 55.

THE FAMILY AS CRADLE OF VIOLENCE

Suzanne K. Steinmetz and
Murray A. Straus

Lizzie Borden took an ax
And gave her father 40 whacks.
When the job was neatly done
She gave her mother 41.

Although intrafamily violence like that attributed to Lizzie Borden is occasionally reported, such behavior is considered totally out of the ordinary—families are supposed to be oases of serenity where love and good feeling flow from each parent and child.

Unfortunately, that lovely picture is not accurate. In fact, the grizzly tale of Lizzie Borden may not be unique. Violence seems as typical of family relationships as love; and it would be hard to find a group or institution in American society in which violence is more of an everyday occurrence than it is within the family. Family members physically abuse each other far more often than do nonrelated individuals. Starting with slaps and going on to torture and murder, the family provides a prime setting for every degree of physical violence. So universal is the phenomenon that it is probable that some form of violence will occur in almost every family.

The most universal type of physical violence is corporal punishment by parents. Studies in England and the United States show that between 84 and 97 percent of all parents use physical punishment at some point in their child's life. Moreover, such use of physical force to maintain parental authority is not confined to early childhood. Data on students in three different regions of the United States show that half of the parents sampled either used or threatened their high school seniors with physical punishment.

Of course, physical punishment differs significantly from other violence. But it is violence, nonetheless. Despite its good intentions, it has some of the same consequences as other forms of violence. Research shows that parents who use physical punishment to control the aggressiveness of their children probably increase rather than decrease their child's aggressive tendencies. Violence begets violence, however peaceful and altruistic the motivation.

The violent tendencies thus reinforced may well be turned against the parents, as in the case of Lizzie Borden. Although most intrafamily violence is less bloody than that attributed to Lizzie, some family abuse does go as far as ax murder. Examination of relationships between murderer and victim proves that the largest single category of victim is that of family member or relative.

The magnitude of family violence became particularly obvious during the summer heat wave of 1972. Page 1 of the July 22, 1972 *New York Times* carried an article describing the increase in murders during the previous few days of extreme heat in New York City and summarizing the statistics for murder in New York during the previous six months. Page 2 held an article totalling deaths in Northern Ireland during three and a half years of disturbances. About as many people were murdered by their relatives in one six-month period in New York City as had been killed in three and a half years of political upheaval in Northern Ireland.

Murder, though relatively rare, gets far more attention than less violent abuse. Even though more murders are committed on family members than any other type of person, and even though the United States has a high degree of homicide, the rate is still only four or five per 100,000 population. What about non-lethal physical violence between husband and wife? While accurate statistics are hard to find, one way of estimating the magnitude of the phenomenon is through the eyes of the police.

Just as relatives are the largest single category

of murder victim, so family fights are the largest single category of police calls. One legal researcher estimates that more police calls involve family conflict than do calls for all criminal incidents, including murders, rapes, non-family assaults, robberies and muggings. "Violence in the home" deserves at least as much public concern as "crime in the streets." The police hate and fear family conflict calls for several reasons. First, a family disturbance call lacks the glamour, prestige and public appreciation of a robbery or an accident summons. More important, such calls are extremely dangerous. Many a policeman coming to the aid of a wife who is being beaten has had a chair or a bottle thrown at him or has been stabbed or shot by a wife who suddenly becomes fearful of what is going to happen to her husband, or who abruptly turns her rage from her husband to the police. Twenty-two percent of all police fatalities come from investigating problems between husband and wife or parent and child.

One cannot tell from these data on police calls just what proportion of all husbands and wives have had physical fights, since it takes an unusual combination of events to have the police summoned. The closest published estimate is found in the research of George Levinger and John O'Brien. In studying applicants for divorce, O'Brien found that 17 percent of his cases spontaneously mentioned overt violent behavior, and Levinger found that 23 percent of the middle-class couples and 40 percent of the working-class couples gave "physical abuse" as a major complaint.

Both of these figures probably underestimate the amount of physical violence between husbands and wives because there may well have been violent incidents which were not mentioned or which were not listed as a main cause of divorce. Even doubling the figure, however, leaves us far from knowing the extent of husband-wife violence. First, there is a discrepancy between the O'Brien and the Levinger figures. Second, these figures apply only to couples who have applied for divorce. It may be that there is a lower incidence of physical violence among a cross-section of couples; or it may be, as we suspect, that the difference is not very great.

A survey conducted for the National Commission of the Causes and Prevention of Violence deals with what violence people would approve.

These data show that one out of four men and one out of six women approve of slapping a wife under certain conditions. As for a wife slapping a husband, 26 percent of the men and 19 percent of the women approve. Of course, some people who approve of slapping will never do it and some who disapprove *will* slap—or worse. Probably the latter group is larger. If that is true, we know that husband-wife violence at the minimal level of slapping occurs in at least one quarter of American families.

Our own pilot studies also give some indication of the high rate of violence in the family. Richard Gelles of the University of New Hampshire, who has done a series of in-depth case studies of a sample of 80 families, found that about 56 percent of the couples have used physical force on each other at some time.

In a second study, freshman college students responded to a series of questions about conflicts which occurred in their senior year in high school, and to further questions about how these conflicts were handled. Included in the conflict resolution section were questions on whether or not the parties to the disputes had ever hit, pushed, shoved, thrown things or kicked each other in the course of a quarrel.

The results show that during that one year 62 percent of the high school seniors had used physical force on a brother or sister and 16 percent of their parents had used physical force on each other. Since these figures are for a single year, the percentage who had *ever* used violence is probably much greater. How much greater is difficult to estimate because we cannot simply accumulate the 16 percent for one year over the total number of years married. Some couples will never have used violence and others will have used it repeatedly. Nevertheless, it seems safe to assume that it will not always be the same 16 percent. So, it is probably best to fall back on the 56 percent estimate from the 80 earlier interviews.

Since a vast amount of family violence can be documented, what accounts for the myth of family non-violence? At least one basis for the rosy, if false, view is that the family is a tremendously important social institution, which must be preserved. In Western countries one supportive device is the ideology of familial love and gentleness, an ideology which helps encourage people to marry and to stay married. It tends to maintain satisfaction with the family system despite the stresses and strains of family life. From the viewpoint of preserving the integrity of a critical social institution, such a mythology is highly useful.

Other simplifications and generalizations also block knowledge and understanding of the nature of violence in the family. The psychopathology myth, the class myth, the sex myth and the catharsis myth must be exposed and examined if the true nature of intrafamily abuse is to emerge.

THE PSYCHOPATHOLOGY MYTH

A growing number of sociologists and psychologists have suggested that a focus on conflict and violence may be a more revealing way of understanding the family than a focus on consensus and solidarity. Most members of this group, however, recognize that family conflict is legitimate, but still consider physical violence only as an abnormality—something which involves sick families. The facts do not support this *psychopathology myth*. According to Richard J. Gelles, only a tiny proportion of those using violence—even child abusers—can be considered mentally ill. Our own studies reveal that physically abusive husbands, wives and children are of overwhelmingly sound mind and body.

The fact that almost all family violence, including everyday beating, slapping, kicking and throwing things, is carried out by normal everyday Americans rather than deranged persons should not lead us to think of violence as being desirable or even acceptable. The important question is, Why is physical violence so common between members of the closest and most intimate of all human groups?

Although social scientists are still far from a full understanding of the causes of violence between family members, evidence is accumulating that family violence is learned—and learned in childhood in the home. This fact does not deny the importance of the human biological heritage. If the capacity for violence were not present in the human organism, learning and social patterning could not produce it.

If a child actually observes and experiences the effects of violence, he will learn to be violent.

Husbands, wives and parents play out models of behavior which they learned in childhood from *their* parents and from friends and relatives. Rather than being deviant, they are conforming to patterns learned in childhood. Of course, in most cases they also learned the opposite message—that family violence is wrong. However, a message learned by experience and observation, rather than the message learned Sunday-school-style, has more force, especially when social stresses become great—and family stresses are often very great. The high level of interaction and commitment which is part of the pleasure of family life also produces great tensions.

THE CLASS MYTH

Another widespread but hard-to-prove belief is the *class myth*, the idea that intrafamily violence occurs mainly in lower- and working-class families. Studying divorce applicants, George Levinger found that 40 percent of the working-class wives and 23 percent of the middle-class wives indicated "physical abuse" as a reason for seeking divorce. If almost one out of four middle-class women can report physical abuse, violence hardly seems absent from middle-class families. The nationwide sample survey conducted for the United States Commission on Violence reveals that over one-fifth of the respondents approve of slapping a spouse under certain conditions. There were no social-class differences in this *approval* of slapping, nor in reports of having ever spanked a child. At the same time, almost twice as many less educated respondents spank *frequently* (42 percent) as more educated respondents (22 percent).

Other research on physical punishment is also contradictory. Most studies report more use of physical punishment by working-class parents, but some find no difference. Howard S. Erlanger undertook a comprehensive review of studies of social-class differences in the use of physical punishment and concluded that, although the weight of the evidence supports the view of less use of this technique among the middle class, the differences are small. Sizeable differences between social classes show up only when the analysis takes into account differences within social classes of such things as race, the sex of the child and of the parent, parental ambition for the child and the specific nature of the father's occupation. Differences *within* social classes are at least as important as differences *between* classes.

Despite the mixed evidence, and despite the fact that there is a great deal of violence in middle-class families, we believe that research will eventually show that intrafamily violence is more common as one goes down the socioeconomic status ladder. Many social scientists attribute this to a lower-class "culture of violence" which encourages violent acts, and to an opposite middle-class culture which condemns violence. Although these cultural elements are well documented, we see them not as a cause, but as a response to fundamental social structural forces which affect families at all social levels but press harder and more frequently on the lower and working classes.

Willingness and ability to use physical violence may compensate for lack of other resources such as money, knowledge and respect. If the social system does not provide an individual with the resources needed to maintain his or her family position, that individual will use violence if he is capable of it. John E. O'Brien asserts that ". . . there is considerable evidence that . . . husbands who . . . displayed violent behavior were severely inadequate in work, earner, or family support roles." While lack of the occupational and economic resources needed to fulfill the position of husband in our society is more characteristic of lower-class families than others, it is by no means confined to that stratum. The 1970–72 recession, with its high rates of unemployment among middle-class occupational groups (such as aerospace engineers) provides an opportunity to test this theory. The *resource theory* of violence would predict that unemployed husbands would engage in more intrafamily violence than comparable middle-class husbands who have not lost their jobs.

Some indication that the predicted results might be found is suggested by statistics for Birmingham, England, which showed a sharp rise in wife-beating during a six-month period when unemployment also rose sharply. A 1971 *Parade* report characterized these men as "frustrated, bored, unable to find a satisfying outlet for their energy, Britishers who are reduced to life on the dole meet adversity like men: they blame it on their wives. Then, pow!!!"

In a society such as ours, in which aggression is defined as a normal response to frustration, we can expect that the more frustrating the familial and occupational roles, the greater the amount of violence. Donald McKinley found that the lower the degree of self-direction a man has in his work, the greater the degree of aggressiveness in his relationship with his son. McKinley's data also show that the lower the job satisfaction, the higher the percentage using harsh punishment of children. The same relationship was found within each social class.

Both husbands and wives suffer from frustration, but since the main avenue of achievement for women has been in the family rather than in occupational roles, we must look within the family for the circumstances that are frustrating to women. Both residential crowding and too many children have been found to be related to the use of physical punishment. As with men, frustrations of this type are more common in the lower class, since lower-class wives are unlikely to have sufficient equipment and money for efficient, convenient housekeeping.

Although intrafamily violence probably is more common among lower-class families, it is incorrect to see it as only a lower-class or working-class phenomenon. What we have called the class myth overlooks the basic structural conditions (such as lack of adequate resources and frustrating life experiences) which are major causes of intrafamily violence and are present at all social levels, though to varying degrees. Some kinds of intrafamily violence are typical of all social classes— such as hitting children—even though the rate may be lower for [the] middle class—while other kinds of intrafamily violence are typical of *neither* class—like severe wife-beating—even though the rate is probably greater for the working class and especially the lower class.

THE SEX MYTH

The *sex myth* is the idea that sexual drives are linked to violence by basic biological mechanisms developed in the course of human evolution. Violence in sex is directly related to violence in the family because the family is the main way in which sex is made legitimate. To the extent that there is an inherent connection between sex and violence, it would be part of the biological basis for violence within the family.

There is abundant evidence that sex and violence go together, at least in our society and in a number of others. At the extreme, sex and warfare have been associated in many ways, ranging from societies which view sex before a battle as a source of strength (or in some tribes, as a weakness) to the almost universally high frequency of rape by soldiers, often accompanied by subsequent genital mutilation and murder. In the fighting following the independence of the Congo in the early 1960s, rape was so common that the Catholic church is said to have given a special dispensation so that nuns could take contraceptive pills. More recently, in the Pakistan civil war, rape and mutilation were everyday occurrences. In Vietnam, scattered reports suggest that rapes and sexual tortures have been widespread. Closer to home, we have the romantic view of the aggressive he-man who "takes his woman" as portrayed in westerns and James Bond-type novels. In both cases, sex and gunfights are liberally intertwined.

Then there are the sadists and masochists—individuals who can obtain sexual pleasure only by inflicting or receiving violent acts. We could dismiss such people as pathological exceptions, but it seems better to consider sadism and masochism as simply extreme forms of widespread behavior. The sex act itself typically is accompanied at least by mild violence and often by biting and scratching.

Nevertheless, despite all of this and much other evidence which could be cited, we feel that there is little biological linkage between sex and violence. It is true that in our society and in many other societies, sex and violence are linked. But there are enough instances of societies in which this is not the case to raise doubts about the biological linkage. What social conditions produce the association between violence and sex?

The most commonly offered explanation attributes the linkage between sex and violence to rules of the culture which limit or prevent sex. Empiri-

cal evidence supporting this sexual repression theory is difficult to establish. Societies which are high in restriction of extramarital intercourse are also societies which tend to be violent—particularly in emphasizing military glory, killing, torture and mutilation of an enemy. But just how this carries over to violence in the sex act is not clear. Our interpretation hinges on the fact that sexual restriction tends to be associated with a definition of sex as intrinsically evil. This combination sets in motion two powerful forces making sex violent in societies having such a sexual code. First, since sex is normally prohibited or restricted, engaging in sexual intercourse may imply license to disregard other normally prohibited or restricted aspects of interpersonal relations. Consequently, aggressively inclined persons will tend to express their aggressiveness when they express their sexuality. Second, since sex is defined as evil and base, this cultural definition of sex may create a label or an expectancy which tends to be acted out.

By contrast, in societies such as Mangaia, which impose minimal sex restrictions and in which sex is defined as something to be enjoyed by all from the time they are first capable until death, sex is nonviolent. In Mangaia, exactly the opposite of the two violence-producing mechanisms just listed seem to operate. First, since sex is a normal everyday activity, the normal standards for control of aggression apply. Second, since sex is defined as an act expressing the best in man, it is an occasion for altruistic behavior. Thus, Donald S. Marshall says of the Mangaia: "My several informants generally agreed that the really important thing in sexual intercourse—for the married man or for his unwed fellow—was to give pleasure to his partner; that her pleasure in orgasm was what gave the male partner a special thrill, separate from his own orgasm."

Socially patterned antagonism between men and women is at the heart of a related theory which can also account for the association of sex and violence. The sex antagonism and segregation theory suggests that the higher the level of antagonism between men and women, the greater the tendency to use violence in sexual acts. Since, by itself, this statement is open to a charge of circular reasoning, the theory must be backed up by related propositions which account for the sex role antagonism.

In societies such as ours, part of the explanation for antagonism between the sexes is probably traceable to the sexual restrictions and sexual denigration mentioned above. The curse God placed on all women when Eve sinned is the earliest example in our culture of the sexually restrictive ethic, the placing of the "blame" for sex on women, and the resulting negative definition of women—all of which tend to make women culturally legitimate objects of antagonism and aggression. The New Testament reveals much more antipathy to sex than the Old and contains many derogatory (and implicitly hostile) statements about women.

The present level of antagonism between the sexes is probably at least as great as that in biblical times. In novels, biographies and everyday speech, words indicating femaleness, especially in its sexual aspect (such as "bitch"), are used by men as terms of disparagement, and terms for sexual intercourse, such as "screw" and "fuck," are used to indicate an aggressive or harmful act. On the female side, women tend to see men as exploiters and to teach their daughters that men are out to take advantage of them.

It would be a colossal example of ethnocentrism, however, to attribute antagonism between the sexes to the Western Judeo-Christian tradition. Cultural definitions of women as evil are found in many societies. Obviously, more fundamental processes are at work, of which the Christian tradition is only one manifestation.

A clue to a possibly universal process giving rise to antagonism between the sexes may be found in the cross-cultural studies which trace this hostility back to the division of labor between the sexes and other differences in the roles of men and women. This sex role segregation, gives rise to differences in child-rearing practices for boys and girls and to problems in establishing sexual identity. Beatrice Whiting, for example, concludes: "It would seem as if there were a never-ending circle. The separation of the sexes leads to a conflict of identity in the boy children, to unconscious fear of being feminine, which leads to protest masculinity, exaggeration of the differences between men and women, antagonism

against and fear of women, male solidarity, and hence back to isolation of women and very young children." This process can also be observed in the matrifocal family of the urban slum and the Caribbean, the relationships between the sexes have been labeled by Jackson Toby as "compulsive masculinity" and vividly depicted in Eldridge Cleaver's "Allegory of the Black Eunuchs." Slightly more genteel forms of the same sexual antagonism are to be found among middle-class men, as illustrated by the character of Jonathan in the movie *Carnal Knowledge*.

Obviously, the linkages between sex and violence are extremely complex, and many other factors probably operate besides the degree of restrictiveness, the cultural definition of sexuality and antagonism between the sexes. But even these indicate sufficiently that it is incorrect to assume a direct connection between sexual drives and violence, since such an assumption disregards the sociocultural framework within which sexual relations take place. These social and cultural factors, rather than sex drives *per se*, give rise to the violent aspects of sexuality in so many societies.

THE CATHARSIS MYTH

The *catharsis myth* asserts that the expression of "normal" aggression between family members should not be bottled up: if normal aggression is allowed to be expressed, tension is released, and the likelihood of severe violence is therefore reduced. This view has a long and distinguished intellectual history. Aristotle used the term "catharsis" to refer to the purging of the passions or sufferings of spectators through vicarious participation in the suffering of a tragic hero. Both Freud's idea of "the liberation of affect" to enable reexperiencing blocked or inhibited emotions, and the view of John Dollard and his associates that "the occurrence of any act of aggression is assumed to reduce the instigation of aggression" are modern versions of this tradition.

Applying this approach to the family, Bettelheim urges that children should learn about violence in order to learn how to handle it. Under the present rules (at least for the middle class), we forbid a child to hit, yell or swear at us or his playmates. The child must also refrain from destroying property or even his own toys. In teaching this type of self-control, however, Bruno Bettelheim holds that we have denied the child outlets for the instinct of human violence and have failed to teach him how to deal with his violent feelings.

Proof of the catharsis theory is overwhelmingly negative. Exposure to vicariously experienced violence has been shown to increase rather than decrease both aggressive fantasy and aggressive acts. Similarly, experiments in which children are given the opportunity to express violence and aggression show that they express more aggression after the purported cathartic experience than do controls.

Theoretical arguments against the catharsis view are equally cogent. The instinct theory assumptions which underlie the idea of catharsis have long been discarded in social science. Modern social psychological theories—including social learning theory, symbolic interaction theory and labeling theory—all predict the opposite of the catharsis theory: the more frequently an act is performed, the greater the likelihood that it will become a standard part of the behavior repertory of the individual and of the expectations of others for that individual.

In light of largely negative evidence and cogent theoretical criticism, the sheer persistence of the catharsis theory becomes an interesting phenomenon. There seem to be several factors underlying the persistence of the catharsis myth:

Prestige and Influence of Psychoanalytic Theory.
Albert Bandura and Richard Walters suggest that the persistence of the catharsis view is partly the result of the extent to which psychoanalytic ideas have become part of both social science and popular culture. Granting this, one must also ask why this particular part of Freud's vast writing is unquestioned. After all, much of what Freud wrote has been ignored, and other parts have been dropped on the basis of contrary evidence.

Whenever an element of cultural belief persists in spite of seemingly sound reasons for discarding it, one should look for ways in which the belief may be woven into a system of social behavior. Certain behavior may be least partially congruent

with the "false" belief; various social patterns may be justified by such beliefs.

Justification of Existing Patterns.
Intrafamily violence is a recurring feature of our society despite the cultural commitment to nonviolence. It is not far-fetched to assume that, under the circumstances, the catharsis theory which in effect justifies sporadic violence will be attractive to a population engaged in occasional violence.

Congruence with the Positive Value of Violence in Non-family Spheres of Life.
Although familial norms deprecate or forbid intrafamily violence, the larger value system of American society is hardly nonviolent. In fact, the overwhelming proportion of American parents consider it part of their role to train sons to be tough. The violence commission survey reveals that 70 percent of the respondents believed it is good for boys to have a few fist-fights. Thus, a social theory which justifies violence as being psychologically beneficial to the aggressor is likely to be well received.

Congruence with the Way Familial Violence Often Occurs.
Given the antiviolence norms, intrafamily physical abuse typically occurs as a climax to a repressed conflict. As Louis Coser points out:

Closely knit groups in which there exists a high frequency of interaction and high personality involvement of the members have a tendency to suppress conflict. While they provide frequent occasions for hostility (since both sentiments of love and hatred are intensified through frequency of interaction), the acting out of such feelings is sensed as a danger to such intimate relationships, and hence there is a tendency to suppress rather than to allow expression of hostile feelings. In close-knit groups, feelings of hostility tend, therefore, to accumulate and hence to intensify.

At some point the repressed conflict has to be resolved. Frequently, the mechanism which forces the conflict into the open is a violent outburst. This is one of the social functions of violence listed by Coser. In this sense, intrafamily violence does have a cathartic effect. But the catharsis which takes place comes from getting the conflict into the open and resolving it—not the releasing effects of violent incidents *per se*, but on the ability to recognize these as warning signals and to deal with the underlying conflict honestly and with empathy.

Confusion of Immediate with Long-term Effects. There can be little doubt that a sequence of violent activity is often followed by a sharp reduction of tension, an emotional release and even a feeling of quiescence. To the extent that tension release *is* produced by violence, this immediate cathartic effect is likely to powerfully reinforce the violence which preceded it. Having reduced tension in one instance, it becomes a mode of behavior likely to be repeated later in similar instances. An analogy with sexual orgasm seems plausible. Following orgasm, there is typically a sharp reduction in sexual drive, most obvious in the male's loss of erection. At the same time, however, the experience of orgasm is powerfully reinforcing and has the long-term effect of increasing the sex drive. We believe that violence and sex are similar in this respect. The short-term effect of violence is, in one sense, cathartic; but the long-term effect is a powerful force toward including violence as a standard mode of social interaction.

While the assumptions outlined in this article in some ways contribute to preserving the institution of family, they also keep us from taking a hard and realistic look at the family and taking steps to change it in ways which might correct the underlying problems. Such stereotypes contain a kernel of truth but are dangerous oversimplifications. Although there are differences between social classes in intrafamily violence, the class myth ignores the high level of family violence present in other social strata. The sex myth, although based on historically accurate observation of the link between sex and violence, tends to assume that this link is biologically determined and fails to take into account the social and cultural factors which associate sex and violence in many societies. The catharsis myth seems to have the smallest kernel of truth at its core, and its persistence, in the face of devastating evidence to the contrary, may be due to the subtle justification it gives to the violent nature of American society and to the fact that violent episodes in a family can have the positive function of forcing a repressed conflict into the open for nonviolent resolution.

WHY INTIMATES MUST FIGHT

George R. Bach and Peter Wyden

Verbal conflict between intimates is not only acceptable, especially between husbands and wives; it is constructive and highly desirable. Many people, including quite a few psychologists and psychiatrists, believe that this new scientific concept is an outrageous and even dangerous idea. We know otherwise, and we can prove it. At our Institute of Group Psychotherapy in Beverly Hills, California, we have discovered that couples who fight together are couples who stay together —provided they know how to fight properly.

The art of fighting right is exactly what we teach couples who come to us for marriage counseling. Our training methods are not simple and cannot be successfully applied by everyone. They require patience, good will, and the flexibility to adopt some challenging and unconventional ways for dealing with humanity's most personal drives. Most of all, they demand hearts and minds that are open—open to reason and to change. The great majority of our clients master the art of marital combat quickly. For them, the payoffs are warmly rewarding, and we believe that any couple with honest and deep motivation can achieve the same results.

When our trainees fight according to our flexible system of rules, they find that the natural tensions and frustrations of two people living together can be greatly reduced. Since they live with fewer lies and inhibitions and have discarded outmoded notions of etiquette, these couples are free to grow emotionally, to become more productive and more creative, as individuals in their own right and also as pairs. Their sex lives tend to improve. They are likely to do a better job raising their children. They feel less guilty about hostile emotions that they harbor against each other. Their communications improve and, as a result, they face fewer unpleasant surprises from their partners. Our graduates know how to make the here-and-now more livable for themselves, and so they worry much less about the past that cannot be changed. They are less likely to become victims of boredom or divorce. They feel less vulnerable and more loving toward each other because they are protected by an umbrella of reasonable standards for what is fair and foul in their relationship. Perhaps best of all, they are liberated to be themselves.

Some aspects of our fight training shock trainees when they first begin to work with us. We advocate that they fight in front of their friends and children. For many couples we recommend fighting before, during, or after sexual intercourse. Some people who learn about our work by way of hearsay get the impression that we encourage trainees to become expert at the sort of sick and chronic insult exchanges that proved so readily recognizable to audiences of Edward Albee's play and movie, *Who's Afraid of Virginia Woolf?* But this we never, never do. People fight in the *Virginia Woolf* style before we train them, not afterward.

The wild, low-blow flailing of *Virginia Woolf* is not an extreme example of fighting between intimate enemies; in fact, it is rather common in ordinary life. Let's listen in on a fight that we have heard, with variations, literally hundreds of times during nearly 25 years of practicing psychotherapy. We call this a "kitchen sink fight" because the kitchen plumbing is about all that isn't thrown as a weapon in such a battle.

Mr. and Mrs. Bill Miller have a dinner date with one of Bill's out-of-town business associates and the associate's wife. Mrs. Miller is coming in from the suburbs and has agreed to meet Bill in front of his office building. The Millers have been married for 12 years and have three children. They are somewhat bored with each other by now, but they rarely fight. Tonight happens to be different. Bill Miller is anxious to make a good impression on the visiting firemen from out of town. His wife arrives 20 minutes late. Bill is furious. He hails a taxi and the fun begins:

HE: *Why were you late?*

SHE: *I tried my best.*

HE: *Yeah? You and who else? Your mother is never on time either.*

SHE: *That's got nothing to do with it.*

HE: *The hell it doesn't. You're just as sloppy as she is.*

SHE (getting louder): *You don't say! Who's picking whose dirty underwear off the floor every morning?*

HE (sarcastic but controlled): *I happen to go to work. What have you got to do all day?*

SHE (shouting): *I'm trying to get along on the money you don't make, that's what.*

HE (turning away from her): *Why should I knock myself out for an ungrateful bitch like you?*

The Millers got very little out of this encounter except a thoroughly spoiled evening. Trained marital fighters, on the other hand, would be able to extract from this brief volley a great deal of useful information. They would note that while the trigger for this fight was legitimate (the lady *was* very late), it was also trivial and not indicative of what was really troubling this couple. The aggression reservoir of the hapless Millers was simply so full that even a slight jar caused it to spill over. Both partners had been keeping their grievances bottled up, and this is invariably a poor idea. We call this "gunny-sacking" because when marital complaints are toted along quietly in a gunny sack for any length of time they make a dreadful mess when the sack finally bursts.

Our graduates would also be able to point out that Bill Miller quite unfairly reached into the couple's "psychiatric museum" by dragging the totally irrelevant past (his mother-in-law's tardiness and sloppiness) into the argument; and Mrs. Miller added to the destruction when she escalated the conflict by going out of her way to attack Bill's masculinity. She did this when she castigated him as a poor provider (we call this "shaking the money tree").

Obviously, both of these fighters would benefit from the principal recommendation we make to our trainees: to do their best to keep all arguments not only fair but up-to-date so that the books on a marriage can be balanced daily, much as banks keep their debits and credits current by clearing all checks with other banks before closing down for business every evening. Couples who fight regularly and constructively need not carry gunny sacks full of grievances, and their psychiatric museums can be closed down.

By studying tens of thousands of intimate encounters like this one between the Millers, we designed a system for programming individual aggression through what we call constructive fighting. Our system is not a sport like boxing. It is more like a cooperative skill such as dancing. It is a tool, a way of life that, paradoxically, leads to greater harmony between intimates. It is a somewhat revolutionary notion, but we believe that it can serve not only to enrich the lives of husbands, wives, and lovers; it could become the first step toward controlling the violent feelings that lead to assassinations and to aggressions between entire peoples. A Utopian dream? Perhaps. But we submit that humanity cannot cope with hostilities between nations until it learns to hammer out livable settlements for hostilities between loved ones.

About eight years ago our Institute pioneered in the management of intimate aggression. We have worked successfully with more than 250 couples, and many therapists throughout the United States and abroad now use our system. But, since our methods are still widely misunderstood, we would like to emphasize that our kind of "programming" is neither as precise nor as rigid as the type achieved by computers. Anyone who tries to "program" people in a machinelike way is either kidding himself or trying to play God.

Our system amounts to a set of experimental exercises. We suggest format, but not content; the frame, but not the picture. The picture is filled in by each couple as they fight. This is known as the heuristic approach to education, a system that trains students to find out things for themselves. We train attitudes and suggest directions for further inquiry through trial and error. We formalize and civilize impulsive or repressed anger; but we preserve the spontaneity of aggressive encounters. This is vital because no fight is predictable and no two are alike.

We will describe the at-home fight exercises that we offer our clients; when, where, and how to start a fight; when and how to finish it when it has gone far enough; how couples can regulate their "closeness" to each other while they are between fights; how to score 21 kinds of results of an intimate battle. Our program does not, however, offer hard-and-fast recipes in cookbook style. It can be tried, always with due consideration for the vulnerability of the partner, by anyone without a therapist. But when a therapist is present, as is always the case at our Institute, he is no distant father figure. He participates as trainer, coach, referee, cheerleader, model, and friend.

Some readers may wonder whether all this adds up to complicated machinery constructed by psychologists who cannot bear to keep things simple. Our clinical experience suggests otherwise. Many intelligent, well-to-do trainees tell us of fights that are so abysmally crude and hurtful that it is impossible to doubt the need for fight training. But these kitchen-sink fighters are not the ones who are worst off. We have far more clients who live in a style that can be infinitely more threatening to intimate relationships. Again paradoxically, these unfortunates are the partners who fight rarely or not at all.

Although the Bill Millers, for example, sustained painful emotional injuries in their taxicab fight, they became aggressors ("hawks") under pressure. This is a point in their favor, not against them, for even this destructive encounter produced one positive result. In its way, the taxicab fight gave the Millers a rough—very rough—idea of where they stood with each other, which is the essential first step toward the improvement of any relationship. This knowledge placed them way ahead of many couples. Approximately 80% of our trainees start out as natural nonfighters or active fight-evaders ("doves"), and these people usually know much less about each other than the Millers did. After their fight the Millers knew at least how far apart they were and how far each would go to hurt the other.

In intimate relationships ignorance is rarely bliss. At best it leads to the monumental boredom of couples who are living out parallel lives in a state of loneliness à deux. The quiet that prevails in their homes isn't really peace. Actually, these people are full of anger much of the time, like everyone else on earth. After all, what is anger? It's the basic emotional and physiological reaction against interference with the pursuit of a desired goal; and an expression of strong concern when things go wrong. When partners don't fight, therefore, they are not involved in an intimate relationship; honest intimates can't ignore their hostile feelings because such feelings are inevitable.

One typical evening in the home of nonfighting pseudo-intimates began like this:

HE (yawning): *How was your day, dear?*

SHE (pleasantly): *OK, how was yours?*

HE: *Oh, you know, the usual.*

SHE: *Want your martini on the rocks?*

HE: *Whatever you want to fix, dear.*

SHE: *Anything special you want to do later?*

HE: *Oh, I don't know . . .*

In this fight-phobic home nothing more meaningful may be exchanged for the rest of the evening. Or practically any evening. For reasons to be discussed shortly, these partners won't level with each other. Their penalty is emotional divorce.

There is another group of fight-evaders who do exchange some important signals with their mates, but usually with unfortunate results. We call them the pseudo-accommodators. Here is one such husband who is about to dive into appalling hot water:

WIFE (settling down comfortably for a sensible discussion): *Mother wants to come visit from New York.*

HUSBAND (shrinking away and accommodating): *Why not?*

The dove-husband in this case was saying to himself, "Oh, my God!" He did not say it out loud because he "can't stand hassling." So his mother-in-law arrives and the fights triggered by her presence are far more terrible than the original fight with his wife which the husband managed to avoid. This husband was also practicing another technique that is popular among intimates. He expected his wife to *divine* how he really felt about the mother-in-law's visit. He was saying to himself, "If Emmy loves me she will know that I don't want her mother to come until later in the year when I'll have less pressure on my job." Too bad that most people are not talented in the extrasensory art of divining. But they're not, and many intimates therefore never really know "where they're at."

Throughout this book we will demonstrate how they can find out. Here we would only like to demonstrate the dangers of not trying.

Surprisingly few couples seem to realize how their failure to level with each other can lead to a totally unexpected, dramatic marriage crisis and perhaps even to divorce. This is what happened to another pair of doves, Mr. and Mrs. Kermit James. While making love, many husbands and wives pretend more passion than they really feel. In some marriages, both partners engage in this charade. In the case of the James family, the wife was the one who did the pretending. True intimates would confess their sex problems to each other. Pseudo-intimates, on the other hand, just go on pretending. The trouble is that unless two partners are really beyond the point of caring what happens to their union, the pretending eventually wears dangerously thin.

The Jameses had been married for eight years. One night after they had sexual intercourse Mr. James patted himself innocently on the back for his skill at love-making. Mrs. James happened to be furious at him because at dinnertime he had refused to discuss an urgent financial problem and later he had left his clothes strewn messily all over the floor. Normally she ignored such provocations just to keep things peaceful. This time, her anger at her husband got out of control. She was ready to "let him have it." She had been gunny-sacking so many additional grievances for such a very long time, however, that she reached unthinkingly for the trigger of an atomic bomb. The danger of a nuclear explosion hovers over every nonfighting marriage. Mrs. James unleashed the lethal mushroom cloud when she casually said:

"You know, I never come. I fake it."

Marriages have split up with less provocation. The Jameses gradually repaired their relationship by entering fight training at our Institute. One of the first bits of advice we gave them, incidentally, is that wise marital combatants always try to measure their weapons against the seriousness of a particular fight issue. Nuclear bombs shouldn't be triggered against pea-shooter causes; or, as we sometimes warn trainees: "Don't drop the bomb on Luxembourg!"

Fight-evading can also lead to disaster without any blow-up whatever. A somewhat extreme example are Mr. and Mrs. Harold Jacobson, a prosperous suburban couple who had been married for more than 20 years. They had raised two children and were socially popular. Everybody thought they had a fine marriage. Mr. Jacobson was a sales manager with an income of well over $20,000. His wife dressed well, played excellent bridge, and did more than her share for local causes. Both were considered well-informed conversationalists in their set, but at home Mr. Jacobson rarely said much. Peacefully, he went along with whatever his wife wanted to do.

Shortly after their younger child went off to college, Mr. Jacobson packed his clothes while his wife was out shopping and left home without leaving a note. It took Mrs. Jacobson some time to discover through her husband's lawyer that he meant to leave for good. As usual, he just hadn't felt like arguing about it. His wife was incredulous and then horrified. Their many friends were flabbergasted. None would have believed that this marriage could break up. Over a period of weeks, several of them brought sufficient pressure to bear on the Jacobsons to enter our fight-training program.

Mr. Jacobson was persuaded to start first. He joined one of our self-development groups, along with eight other individuals who were involved in marital crises but were not yet ready to work on their problems in the presence of their mates. The senior author of this book was the therapist. Together the group convinced Mr. Jacobson that the "silent treatment" which he had given his wife was not cooperation or strength but noncooperation or something worse: hostility camouflaged by phony and misleading compliance. He admitted that he had never leveled with his wife, and never clearly communicated his feelings about the way she dominated most of the family decisions; it riled him no end when she decided what they should do to "have fun," to "be creative," and all the rest. Almost invariably he went along, even though he resented it terribly in what we call the "inner dialogue" (conversations and fights which all of us keep going within ourselves). On the few occasions when Mr. Jacobson did protest mildly—always without making the true depth of his feelings clear—he found that his wife became even more assertive when she was resisted. So he became even more quiet.

At first Mr. Jacobson resisted fight training. He said that it would be "undignified" to let himself go and engage his wife in "useless" arguments. It was against his "values." It turned out that his German-born mother had taught him the virtue of the old adage, *"Reden ist Silber, aber Schweigen ist Gold"* (Talk is silver, but silence is golden). Mr. Jacobson still lived by this peasant saying, which was useful in feudal times when speaking up was indeed dangerous for serfs. He therefore believed that self-control was more virtuous than his wife's "noisy dominance."

In the course of six weekly sessions, the group thawed out this typical case of "etiquette-upmanship." We were able to convince Mr. Jacobson that speaking up in a good cause is more effective and valuable than "golden silence" that leads only to hopelessness. In his therapy group he then practiced "speaking up" and "fighting back" on a particularly domineering lady who became, in effect, a substitute for his wife. He reasoned with her. He argued. He refused to be squelched. He was elated when finally he succeeded in getting through to her, and boasted that she was "much worse than my wife."

Then Mr. Jacobson entered a second type of group. Here, four to six married and unmarried intimates work at their problems not as individuals but as couples. Having learned the value of asserting himself aggressively in the self-development group, Mr. Jacobson found that he could now face Mrs. Jacobson on a new basis. During the group sessions he noticed that the wife whom he had always considered overwhelmingly argumentative and domineering could be managed, even tamed. To his surprise, he discovered that she actually *preferred* him to speak up assertively and to share the responsibility for family decision-making. It also made him generally more attractive and stimulating to her, with pleasing sexual fringe benefits for both.

Eventually, Mr. Jacobson, like most intelligent people, came to enjoy the give-and-take of true intimacy. He dismissed his divorce lawyer and, most likely, will carry on his marriage for another 20 years, but on a fresh, realistic basis. We felt that the Jacobsons had gained a brand-new marriage without a divorce.

Like most people today, Mr. Jacobson considered "aggression" a dirty word, just as "sex" used to be. Most people feel secretive about their anger and their fights. When we first initiated fight training, we asked couples to put some of their fights on tape at home and bring us the tapes for interpretation and discussion. This system did not work too well. Some partners were too clever; they turned on the tape recorder only when it was to their supposed "advantage" and turned it off when they felt like acting as censors. Other couples resisted the tape-making at home simply because they were too embarrassed to put their anger on record and then listen to it.

The fact is that anger is considered taboo in modern society. It isn't "gentlemanly." It isn't "feminine." It isn't "nice." It isn't "mature." This is supposed to be the age of sweet reason and "togetherness." The very word "fighting" makes most people uncomfortable. They prefer to talk about "differences" or "silly arguments." And they will go to considerable lengths to maintain the quiet that isn't peace.

Partners say, "Darling, I love you too much to fight with you; you're not my enemy!" But they usually say this in their inner dialogue, not out loud to their partner. Then, when they get angrier, their next step may be a demand, also directed toward the partner but still usually unspoken: "Act nice, no matter how angry you feel!" When an intimate feels even more threatened, he may finally speak up with a plea: "Don't get angry with me!" Or he may demand to turn the partner off: "I can't take you seriously when you're angry!" In an extremity, he may link his demand to a threat: "Don't raise your voice—or else!" All this is part of the strategy of "peace at any price."

The wish to be above personal animosity is fed by many mistaken beliefs. Control of anger, rather than its expression, is considered "mature." Hostility feelings toward an intimate are not only considered the antithesis of love ("If you really love me you should tolerate me as I am"); often such "hate" emotions are considered "sick," requiring psychiatric care. If an angry partner is not seriously enough afflicted to be led away to the head doctor, he is considered at least temporarily irrational. After all, everybody "knows" that what is said in anger cannot be taken seriously; a "mature" partner discounts it as the gibberish of an emotionally upset person, much like the ranting of a drunk.

Nonfighting marital stalemates are rooted in the romantic belief that intimates should take one another as they are. Folklore and etiquette insist that one should not try to change the beloved but accept him or her, warts and all, and "live happily ever after." Once one somehow acquires the magic ability to accept the other's frailties, automatic bliss is supposed to ensue. This charming idyll is promoted not only in fiction and on the screen but even by some marriage counselors and other professionals.

The dream of romantic bliss is an anachronistic hangover from the Victorian etiquette that tried to create gentlemen and gentleladies by social pressure. But the notion that a stress- and quarrel-free emotional climate in the home will bring about authentic harmony is a preposterous myth, born in ignorance of the psychological realities of human relationships. Fighting is inevitable between mature intimates. Quarreling and making up are hallmarks of true intimacy. However earnestly a mature person tries to live in harmony with a partner, he will have to fight for his very notions of harmony itself and come to terms with competing notions—and there are always competing interests.

Everybody has his own ideas about what makes for harmonious living. Being human, one likes one's own ideas to prevail except perhaps in cases of aggression-phobic fight-evaders or excessively submissive partners who act like doormats. The mature partner may yield some of his notions, but usually not without a fight. The classic battle about where to take the family on vacation is a perfect example of such an authentic encounter.

"The mountains are most relaxing," shouts the husband.

"The beach is more fun," shouts the wife.

Such conflicting notions make it perfectly natural for everybody to be angry at his mate some of the time.

Yet many couples still consider intimate conflict revolting. "We never fight," they tell us indignantly. They are, in truth, afraid of fighting. Sometimes they fear just the stress of "hassling"; few couples know about the modern research that shows stress is valuable for keeping the nervous system toned up in the psychological sense. More likely, intimates fear that anger is a Pandora's box. They fear they "can't afford to fight" because they have so many years invested in each other. They worry that if one partner raises his voice, the other must raise his. There might be tears. The fight might escalate out of control. It could lead to rejection, even separation!

As a matter of fact, our trainees find that they tend to feel closest after a properly fought fight. Only our newest recruits wonder whether we're being facetious when we tell them, "A fight a day keeps the doctor away."

Fascinating new experiments document this paradoxical-sounding thesis. In one famous series, Dr. Harry Harlow of the University of Wisconsin reared several generations of monkeys and showed that an exchange of hostilities is *necessary* between mates before there can be an exchange of love. Harlow's calm, mechanical, totally accepting and nonfighting monkey mothers raised off-spring who grew up "normal" except that they couldn't and wouldn't make love.

Another distinguished researcher, Konrad Lorenz, made similar observations about "bonding" (loving) behavior: "Among birds, the most aggressive representatives of any group are also the staunchest friends, and the same applies to mammals. To the best of our knowledge, bond behavior does not exist except in aggressive organisms. This certainly will not be news to the students of human nature. . . . The wisdom of old proverbs as well as that of Sigmund Freud has known for a very long time how closely human aggression and human love are bound together." Indeed, one of the leading theorists on emotional maturity, Erik Erikson of Harvard University, blames the failure to achieve human intimacy on "the inability to engage in controversy and useful combat."

Oddly enough, anger can be useful just *because* it pours out with a minimum of forethought. Unless a partner hides it behind a falsely neutral or false-friendly (and ulcer-producing) façade, his anger—like spontaneous laughter or spontaneous sexual arousal—cannot be dishonest.

Making a person angry is the surest way to find out what he cares about and how deeply he cares. Since intimates keep measuring and remeasuring how much they care for one another ("Are you getting bored with me?"), they can make each other angry in normal but usually unconscious tests of the depth of their involvement.

The process starts right in the early phase of courtship when one partner tries to get the other "sore," not necessarily to "pick a fight," but just to "tease," to test the other out. How far can he go? What does she care enough about to get her "good and angry"? These fight games can be informative if they are played fairly and in a spirit that seeks not to inflict hurt but to resolve realistic conflicts. Lovers also find out by this process that affection grows deeper when it is mixed with aggression. Both feelings then become part of a natural, genuine relationship that allows for expression of the bitter as well as the sweet side of emotional involvement.

We believe, then, that there can be no mature intimate relationship without aggressive leveling; that is, "having it out," speaking up, asking the partner "what's eating" him and negotiating for realistic settlements of differences. This does cause stress, but our successful trainees learn to accept one of the realities of the human condition: the pain of conflict is the price of true and enduring love. People simply cannot release all their love feelings unless they have learned to manage their hate.

"Hate" sounds like too strong a word, but it isn't. When a partner performs according to one's expectations, one is "turned on" and feels love. When these expectations are frustrated, one is "turned off" and feels hate. This is what people recognize as the ups and downs of marriage. We call it "the state of marital swing." Unfortunately, it is usually a state viewed with vast resignation; hence the saying, "You can't live with 'em and you can't live without 'em." This hopelessness is unwarranted. At our Institute we discovered: (1) It is not a partner's sweet and loving side that shapes his bond with an intimate; it is the talent for airing aggression that counts most. And (2) aggression management not only can be learned; it can be used to *change* a partnership constructively.

Contrary to folklore, the existence of hostility and conflict is not necessarily a sign that love is waning. As often as not, an upsurge of hate may signal a deepening of true intimacy; it is when neither love nor hate can move a partner that a relationship is deteriorating. Typically, one partner then gives up the other as a "lost cause" or shrugs him off ("I couldn't care less"). Indifference to a partner's anger and hate is a surer sign of a deteriorating relationship than is indifference to love.

The problem of regulating personal aggression is rarely discussed. It hovers too uncomfortably close to home for most people. Almost everybody has a greater or lesser "hang-up" about admitting hostile feelings, even to himself. It is part of humanity's embarrassment about its inborn aggressive side. Frequently, therefore, people displace their hostilities onto others. We call this "blamesmanship" or "scapegoating," and intimates usually find the process baffling and infuriating.

Suppose it's Wednesday night. Mrs. Jones has had a trying day. She doesn't feel like making love and has decided to withhold sex from her husband. Instead of negotiating with him, she contaminates the situation with an extraneous issue and engages in blamesmanship between the sheets.

SHE: *Not tonight, dear. Besides, I can't ever feel anything anyway. Your stomach is in the way.*

HE: *That's just your excuse. It all depends on the position.*

SHE (heatedly): *You know perfectly well that I can't make it with those acrobatics. Everything would be very simple if you'd just stop stuffing yourself.*

HE (furious): *I'm comfortable the way I am and you're not going to take my gourmet tastes away from me.*

SHE (icily): *Well, something's got to give.*

HE (angry but resigned): *Oh hell, there we go again . . .*

Children are a favorite target when intimates displace their own fights onto other people. Most parental fights about children, for example, are not about children at all. The disagreement is between the parents; the child is only the battleground. Tom and Myra Robinson learned this when they conducted the following fight before one of our training groups:

SHE: *You simply must start to enforce discipline around here and make the kids toe the line.*

HE: *Why me?*

SHE: *Because I want you to be the power in this house!*

HE: *I like to be and I am.*

SHE: *No, you're not—I am! I have to be!*

HE: *No, you don't have to be, and you're not!*

SHE (getting angrier): *Don't be stupid! Who disciplines the kids? Me! Who takes all the responsibility for discipline—me!*

HE (pacing and pulling hard on cigarette): *I am glad you do, but that just makes a cop out of you . . . it doesn't really impress the kids at all.*

SHE (very red in the face): *You're driving me out of my mind! That's my point! You let me do all the dirty work. That makes me a "mean mother" in the eyes of the kids. You get all the goodies: you're their loving "super daddy." I don't like it!*

HE (flopping resignedly into an armchair): *Why shouldn't you like it when the kids and I have a terrific relationship? I don't understand you. That's one of the main attractions for coming home. I love those kids and you'll never make a "heavy" out of me!*

SHE: *OK! But I can't do it all! You have to back me up and you never do! Listen to what they just did today . . .*

HE (disgusted with her but not with his children): *Cut it out!*

SHE (totally exasperated): *Why? Don't you want to hear? Don't you want to be part of this family? Don't you want to take any responsibility?*

HE (getting up again to counterattack): *I take enough responsibility earning our living. And I don't like you when you tattle on the kids! In fact, I can't stand it . . .*

The Robinsons thought they were battling about their ideas of "parental authority," "doing a good job of raising the kids," and the role of the "man of the house." But these are only superficial cultural stereotypes. Once the therapy group began to probe what was really bothering Tom and Myra, we discovered some much deeper intimate issues which the couple did not dare confront.

It developed that Myra was jealous of Tom's love for the kids because he was not making enough passionate love to her. Tom, in turn, was not making love to Myra because since the kids came she had been a disappointment to him. She did not conform to his definition of a "good mother." What turned him off completely was her tattling because this aroused a strong memory of ugly, angry emotions from his past. His mother used to tattle to his father about his own misdeeds, and his father used to beat discipline into him every Saturday morning after his mother, behind the boy's back, had presented the father with a list of misdeeds!

Myra is also bitter because, since the kids came, the husband turned off loving her. She thinks that he thinks that she thinks: "I love my kids more than him. I only used the man to have a father for my kids, who are my joy and pride and who fulfill me." She therefore thinks: "He is jealous of my love for the kids and punishes me by withholding his love from me. He does not want to share me with anybody."

In our training group this spiral of misconceptions collapsed as the facts were exposed. By using techniques to be discussed in the next chapters, the Robinsons learned to level about their real feelings, wants, and expectations. The issue of disciplining the children never came up again. It was spontaneously handled by one partner or the other, as the situation demanded.

Another popular way to divert aggressive feelings is to repress them as "irrational" in one's personal life but to express them by directing (displacing) them onto such *symbols* as President John F. Kennedy, Senator Robert F. Kennedy, the Reverend Dr. Martin Luther King—or onto the anonymity of large, faceless groups: perhaps "kooks" or the Cosa Nostra or other criminals, or the Viet Cong and other "enemies." This displacement of hostility ultimately enables political leaders to engage in the most catastrophic form of aggression: war.

Not that politicians are the only ones who are busy manipulating human aggression. Spokesmen for the Judeo-Christian religions have urged people to pray it away. Psychiatrists have tried to analyze it or rationalize it away. The late Emily Post and other etiquette devotees would have liked to smile it away. Nothing has worked, and for the most logical reason. Anger is part of the personality, like the sex drive. It can be displaced, channeled, modified, or repressed. But it cannot go away. This is why our efforts are designed to make people face it and decontaminate it as sensibly as human fallibility permits.

We believe that the inability to manage personal conflicts is at the root of the crisis that threatens the structure of the American family. Communications between children and parents are breaking down. More and more young people are "tuning out" by escaping into the world of drugs and other short-lived emotional kicks. One out of every three marriages ends in divorce. In our largest and most "advanced" state, California, the figure is approaching an almost incredible one out of every two.

Millions of other couples continue to live together physically and legally, yet emotionally apart. Atrophy, boredom, casual infidelities, and false-front façades "for the children's sake" are no longer exceptional. No one knows how many couples are emotionally divorced. We do know that millions of husbands and wives live in card houses held together by fantasy; by social, religious, economic, or legal pressures—or by the fear of change.

The philosophers say modern man is alienated, trapped by loneliness, yet hostile to those who might come too close. They blame this sense of alienation for the anxieties of most people, for humanity's daily failures of heart and nerve. But the philosophers have stated the problem backward. It is not alienation that is becoming unbearable. It is intimacy.

We have entered a psychological ice age. Except for occasional bursts of warmth, often fueled by sex after a few cocktails, truly intimate encounter has begun to disappear from civilized Western life. Closeness has become a paradox: longed for, but increasingly intolerable. Without the sweet anesthesias of role playing, libido, or liquor many people can no longer find each other or stand each other. Sustained closeness between man and wife, parents and child, and friend with friend, is in danger of becoming extinct. We believe that this quiet private threat endangers civilization as severely as the public threats of nuclear incineration, automation, urbanization and others that are constantly talked about.

Why should this be happening today, of all times? Again, the answers are so close that it is easy to overlook them. Not so long ago, the family was not a small unit but a tribe. Tribal people rubbed shoulders constantly. Everybody used to know everybody else's business. There was less privacy but more opportunity for sharing failures and unhappiness, to get attention and help from friendly souls. The things that matter in life were more visible and understandable. Today, as everybody knows, the family is segmented. We no longer witness many happenings; we merely talk *about* them. And much of the talk has become specialist's talk that only other specialists can grasp. Who can readily share the joys and ulcers of a husband who comes home from his work as a missile expert?

These trends have turned individuals into faces within a "lonely crowd," who worship privacy and autonomy as the supposedly ideal way of coping with intimate problems. Marriage, therefore, is more of a closed-circuit affair than ever. The burden on mates and lovers is heavier; they must fulfill vital functions (reacting, sharing, etc.) that used to be the job of more than one other person. No wonder that the circuits of so many marriages are becoming overloaded, and that mates are tuning each other out and playing games with each other.

When Dr. Eric Berne's book, *Games People Play*, became a runaway bestseller, publishing experts were surprised. They shouldn't have been. America's living rooms and bedrooms are full of partners who are too weak or frightened or not sufficiently knowledgeable to tolerate authentic encounters with their supposed intimates. They recognized their own camouflaging rituals in Dr. Berne's somewhat cynical and overly flip but essentially accurate descriptions. Remember "Uproar," the pointless fight that is provoked by a husband or wife early in the evening merely to avoid sex later? It is all but a national pastime. So are such marital games as "If it weren't for you" and "Look how hard I've tried."

Dr. Berne performed a valuable service because he made game-players aware of what they are doing. However, we believe he was too pessimistic in appraising their potential capacity to drop their masks and become authentic persons capable of intimacy.

Our own clinical experience indicates that most couples would dearly like to stop playing games. They often realize that the camouflaged life is needlessly tiring and anxiety-arousing. Game-players never really know "where they're at." The more skillful they are, the less they know, because their objective is to cover up motives and try to trick their partners into doing things. The game-player's life is loaded with uncertainties, and human beings are poorly equipped to withstand uncertainty.

Unfortunately, one can't simply command game-players: "Stop Playing Games!" Something better must fill the void. People have to manage their emotions somehow, especially their aggressions. (Games are actually aggression that camouflage the desire to exploit a partner, manipulate or weaken him, do him in, etc.)

Constructive fighting makes for game-free living. It is a liberating, creative alternative that works. Since we introduced fight training, the rate of reconciliation among our Institute's problem couples has increased sharply. Follow-up studies indicate that most of our graduates are living much more satisfying (if perhaps noisier) lives than before. And for the most tragic victims of our psychological ice age, the children, the benefits are incalculable. For them, a sense of genuine family closeness is as important as food and drink. When a "nest" cools or disintegrates, children can grow only amid enormous handicaps. Young children especially thrive on intimacy and starve emotionally when they cannot share and learn it. We regard the neglect of intimacy and the absence of intimate models within many families as principally responsible for the current "generation gap." Those who are deprived of an intimate nest may never care to build or to protect one for themselves.

For intimate partners, perhaps the richest pay-off of well-managed conflict comes with yielding after a fight. Any intimate relationship implies some readiness to yield one's own self-interest when it clashes with that of the partner. Everybody knows that the give-and-take of trying to get along with someone often means bending one's own will to the wishes of the other. This is never easy because the psychological price of yielding to another is a loss (however temporary and partial) of one's own identity. Realistic intimates find that this is a small price as long as it is part of an equitable, mutual process and leads to an improved relationship.

The final benefit of yielding is the tremendous feeling of well-being that comes from making a beloved person happy. This is why it feels so delicious to make one's wife or husband laugh. It also explains why "it is better to give than to receive." In true intimacy, it really is. Which is one more reason why intimacy is worth fighting for.

TOPIC 6

Sex

Amoebas at the start
  Were not complex;
They tore themselves apart
  And started Sex.
    —Arthur Guiterman

We live in an eroticized age. There is much more sexual candor and permissiveness than ever before in our society. The present generation finds the consternation caused by the appearance of Freud's writings hard to believe. When Kinsey's *Sexual Behavior in the Human Male* appeared in 1948, *The New York Times* refused to carry advertising for it. Today's mass media are filled with sexual images.

Most articles and textbooks dealing with sex don't define it. This may be due to the assumption we all know what sex is. Or perhaps it is because sex is such a complex and encompassing subject that—once one gets beyond the amoeba—definition is nearly impossible.

Conceptualized in simplest terms, *sex* is behavior involving erotic stimulation and arousal. However, sex has a way of becoming linked or fused with other phenomena—with guilt, fear, and love, with achievement, aggression, dominance, rebellion, and so on. By the time we reach adulthood, sex is likely to have very complex meanings for us.

When psychologists write of sexual development, they frequently use the term "psychosexual"—psychological plus sexual—to indicate the intricate interweaving of our sexual being with all of our personality. We cannot understand our sexual behavior unless it is related to the rest of our personality, just as our personality picture would be seriously incomplete without the sexual component.

Sexual insight requires not only a pan-personal, but also an interpersonal perspective. Sexual relationships are interpersonal relationships. Much of the literature concerning sex has to do with statistics, and statisticians sometimes lump together acts which have very different interpersonal significance. Depending upon the circumstances, for example, an act of marital intercourse may reflect great sharing and tenderness or it may be not far removed from rape or mindless mutual masturbation.

Unfortunately, many of us lack insight into our psychosexual and socio-sexual selves. How does our sexual being relate to the rest of what we are? How does it affect our whole world of social relationships? What is the total meaning of sex in our existence?

Sex development in college

In the lead article Andrew M. Barclay chronicles the development of sex-uality in a group of college students. When they entered college, these students were heavily influenced by parental values and standards. Many were unsure of themselves and felt anxious and guilty about sex. During college, however, they gained autonomy and maturity, became persons in their own right, and achieved more meaningful sexual relationships. Still, as Barclay points out, for many students the struggle to come to terms with sex was often a more painful than pleasurable journey.

Sex casualties in college

There is vastly greater personal and sexual freedom on college campuses today than 50, 25, or even 10 years ago, and James Ring Adams inter-viewed students and staff at more than a dozen colleges to find what these changed conditions mean. He discovered no unanimity of opinion on whether this greater liberty was good, bad, or even important. However, a salient finding of his research was that a number of students have become casualties of the new freedom. These students were not ready for "libera-tion" or did not seek it, but they were nevertheless caught up in group pressures and propelled into situations with which they could not cope.

Sex education in college

How much do college students actually know about sex? Appallingly little, according to Andrew H. Malcolm, who presents his findings in the third article. Not everyone would agree, but the "information gap" is wide enough to cause some colleges to institute courses dealing with sex— catching students up on information they should have learned years be-fore. In general these courses seek to bring students out of the sexual wil-derness, give them an understanding and appreciation of their sexuality, and help them cope with changes in present-day attitudes and behavior.

A personal philosophy of sex

Each of us needs to formulate a sexual philosophy to guide our own be-havior while at the same time working for a society which—somehow—

will contain options for many kinds of people. Two prominent authorities, Albert Ellis, Executive Director of the Institute for Rational Living, and David Mace, Executive Director of the American Association of Marriage Counselors, contrast their sexual philosophies and visions of the future. Ellis, a sexual hedonist or liberal, and Mace, a sexual ascetic or conservative, differ sharply in their personal codes but both see a sexually more liberal and pluralistic society in the years ahead.

FOR PERSONAL APPLICATION

1. Trace the development of your attitudes toward sex. How have they evolved or changed?
2. Trace your sex education. What were your sources of information? How adequate were they?
3. Relate your sex attitudes or behavior to the rest of your personality.
4. Relate your sex attitudes or behavior to your pattern of interpersonal relationships.
5. From your own observations, what important changes (if any) have occurred in sex attitudes and behavior over the past few years? What is your reaction to these changes?
6. Do you see an essential difference in sex attitudes, standards, or behavior between the males and females of your acquaintance? Discuss your observations in this regard.
7. Discuss group pressures you have felt concerning your sex beliefs, attitudes, or behavior.
8. Formulate a set of sex standards that seem right for you and explain why.
9. Formulate a set of sex standards that would be appropriate for our society or a better society (utopia) and explain why.
10. Write down a discussion item (not given above) that seems particularly relevant to this topic and you, and discuss it.

FOR SMALL GROUPS

1. *Assimilating sex words.* Sex words can provoke anxiety, and we may be surprisingly unable to define, spell, or pronounce them or use them matter-of-factly in everyday conversations. See if this is so among the members of your group. Sit in a circle and have someone begin by picking a word from the list below and saying it, face-to-face, to the person on his left. This second person says the same word to the person on *his* left, and so on. Keep the word going until there is a complete round in which everyone has said the word correctly and matter-of-factly. Then start another word around. Note: the point is *not to try* to say the word in a matter-of-fact way, but to keep saying it until it *becomes* matter-of-fact. Take a break at any time to discuss the associations and reactions of group members.

vagina	scrotum	menstruation
penis	testicles	erection
vulva	sexual intercourse	orgasm
clitoris	coitus	cunnilingus
nipple	masturbation	fellatio

2. *Defining sex words.* Select a dozen or so terms from a sex encyclopedia or dictionary and write each on a card or slip of paper. (*The Sex Book* by Martin Goldstein et al. is a good resource for this exercise.) Place the cards face down in the center of the group. Each person in turn picks a card, reads the term aloud, and defines it. Then he turns to the definition in the book and reads it aloud, commenting on any differences in denotation or connotation between his and the book's definitions.
3. *Sharing reactions.* Go, as a group, to an erotic movie or arrange to have one shown to the group. Afterwards share your reactions.
4. *Seeking information.* Make arrangements and go, as a group, to a family planning clinic to learn about contraception and family planning. Afterwards share your reactions.
5. *Seeking understanding.* Invite a representative of an organization for homosexuals (perhaps Gay Liberation, Gay Feminists, or Daughters of Bilitis) to join the group for an exchange of viewpoints and insights.

FOR FURTHER READING

Comfort, A., ed. *The Joy of Sex.* New York: Simon and Schuster, 1972.

Goldstein, M., E. J. Haeberle, and W. McBride. *The Sex Book: A Modern Pictorial Encyclopedia.* New York: Herder and Herder, Inc., 1971.

Grummon, D. L., and A. M. Barclay, eds. *Sexuality: A Search for Perspective.* New York: Van Nostrand Reinhold, 1971.

Katchadourian, H. *Human Sexuality: Sense and Nonsense.* San Francisco: W. H. Freeman and Company, 1974.

Katchadourian, H., and D. T. Lunde. *Fundamentals of Human Sexuality.* New York: Holt, Rinehart and Winston, Inc., 1972.

Kirkendall, L. A., and R. N. Whitehurst, eds. *The New Sexual Revolution.* New York: Donald W. Brown, 1971.

McCary, J. L. *Human Sexuality,* 2nd ed. New York: Van Nostrand Reinhold, 1973.

McCary, J. L. *Sexual Myths and Fallacies.* New York: Van Nostrand Reinhold, 1971.

Malfetti, J. L., and E. M. Eidiltz. *Perspectives on Sexuality: A Literary Collection.* New York: Holt, Rinehart & Winston, Inc., 1972.

Otto, H. A., ed. *The New Sexuality.* Palo Alto, Calif.: Science and Behavior Books, 1971.

Student Committee on Human Sexuality, Yale University. *The Student Guide to Sex on Campus.* New York: Signet, 1971.

SEX AND PERSONAL DEVELOPMENT IN THE COLLEGE YEARS

Andrew M. Barclay

Over the past ten years, Americans have become increasingly aware of sexual behavior on the college campus. Editors of fashionable magazines, read largely by mature females, realized that the behavior of college students, specifically their sexual behavior, was an enormous potential for increasing circulation. They began publishing stories cataloguing the varied sexual activities of college-age women, and the implications were clear: Mothers, your daughters are carrying on this way. Naturally, women whose daughters were attending college rushed out to see what their children were doing, and the great myth of the campus orgy was born.

Although the so-called generation gap may not be new, it is certainly gaining popularity as an explanation for the ascribed differences between the generations. If we assume that difficulties arise when old beliefs and values are challenged, we could probably trace one of the sources of the generation gap to the rise of parental fears about what kinds of sexual activities were occurring on college campuses. Sure that their offspring were operating within the context of what is called the "new morality," parents grilled their children at every opportunity. "What do you think about those terrible people who are living together? You wouldn't do anything like that, would you?" Fathers took their sons aside to tell them, "Do anything you want, son [wink, wink], but just don't get into trouble, if you know what I mean."

These were the parents socialized according to the strict, if only public, Victorian moral code. But theirs were the children who had internalized the value of bringing home the A grades to keep their parents off their backs. They were so tied up with their studies, they were having trouble getting out for a date on a Saturday night, let alone living with anyone. Under these circumstances, "accused" by their parents' projected fears yet not really knowing "what they mean," the students probably reacted with disgust to their parents' shift in concentration. Here they were, killing themselves (they thought) for a lousy grade while their parents were trying to frame them with this new morality jazz. One way out was to say, "To hell with it," and go off in whatever direction they chose. Behind them communication with their parents broke down.

Meanwhile, back at the magazines, escalation was in progress. As one magazine reported an increase in circulation from stories about the new morality, others rushed to put their own stories into print. Of course, they had to raise the level of sexuality to keep the readers' interest. Now, according to the magazines, people were not just petting and occasionally having intercourse. "What are your daughters doing with the son of your friends and neighbors down the street? Read interviews [anonymous, naturally] with college students who tell all: the deviant sexual acts on campus, sex and drugs, STP and LSD; read all about it." It was no longer "in" for one couple to live together; now three or more lived together and shared each other's sexual favors. Parents doubled their volume of telephone calls trying to keep track of daughter's activities, while daughter wondered anxiously what her parents really wanted to know. The real beneficiaries of the new morality would seem to be Bell Telephone and the newsprint and word dealers.

In the midst of all the sensationalism—screaming headlines and overstated journalism—people seem to have lost sight of a significant fact. Many competent observers of the campus scene report that *nothing has changed over the past fifty years*.[1] College students are *behaving* in much the same way their parents did when they were in college. The conflicts students face today are

[1] See Ira Reiss, "Premarital Sex Codes: The Old and the New," Ch. 13.

those that haunted the student of the twenties: if it is all right to "make out" ("pet" in 1920), how far should you go? How does a woman know if the man she is dating is serious about her? Is intercourse really the mark of the "bad" woman that distinguishes her from the "good"? In all the excitement, few have thought to ask what college students are really feeling. The trend is starting, but only the surface has been scratched.[2]

In this chapter, sex and the college student will be presented from the students' point of view. All comments quoted here were taken from papers written by students for the interdisciplinary course, "Sexuality: A Search for Perspective," held at Michigan State University during the winter quarter of 1969. To those who would generalize from these comments, one *caveat* must be offered: Many of the students enrolled in the course were those who were lost or unsure of their own sexuality and were looking for guidance. In this respect, they are a biased sample. One has the intuitive feeling that somewhere on campus were the people who had few doubts about their own sexuality or their proper roles and who considered their present life adequate, whether it included sex or not. One might infer that we should have found a diverse population: the voluntarily chaste, those who have chosen to delay sexual activity; the neurotics, those poor souls driven to sexual excess by whatever mechanisms control these behaviors; and the "swingers," the normal, rational people who enjoy intercourse and who are sexual because they like to be. But they did not appear in the sample. In fact, despite what readers of today's magazines have been led to believe, the "swingers" constitute an extremely small percentage of the undergraduate community at Michigan State University.

ARRIVAL AT COLLEGE

Many students arrive at college bearing a set of ethics and morals learned at home and reinforced by their parents. The relationship between the student and his parents is so influenced by these

[2] P. Madison, *Personality Development in College* (Reading, Mass.: Addison-Wesley, 1969); and N. Sanford, ed., "Personality Development During the College Years," *Journal of Social Issues,* 12, No. 4 (1956), 3–70.

moral standards that many students feel that deviating from them would alienate their parents and destroy their relationship. In this respect, a female writes:

I really have only one reason for not having intercourse with the boy I am now dating. I could not live with myself knowing I had intercourse with a man I was not married to. It would kill me to have to hide that fact from my parents.

That this writer felt that she must *hide* the fact of a certain behavior from her parents in part reflects her fear of discussing the topic with them. If parents fail to talk with their children on some topics, especially sexual relations and sexual behavior, the children cannot, in fact, know what their parents actually think and are left with inferences drawn from nonverbal cues presented by their parents. Another female discusses her lack of sex education, the feelings engendered by her parents' attitude, and how it has affected her ideas.

I never even knew what the word "virgin" meant until I was seventeen years old. My ideas, however, were strong and real: Sex was dirty, unenjoyable, and only for cheap girls. My friends and I figured out all kinds of clever ways to avoid sexual encounters. I remember what a real trauma it was the first time a boy followed me into the house and I *had to* kiss him goodnight.

My poor father was very protective of me. He told me very little but he did tell me that nothing was more evil than "parking." I went parking once and felt guilty for days afterward.

It might be argued that feeling this way is perfectly normal for women in our culture. Part of the gender-role training, by necessity, has to deal with staying away from men in order to avoid rape, premature pregnancy, or both. As a result, many women internalize this training and are unable to overcome the guilt that results from even the simplest sexual acts, such as hugging and kissing.

But these guilt feelings are not restricted to females. Many males report having guilt feelings about their sexual behavior. One male wrote:

Although I have forgotten many things which appeared to be sinful before, I feel guilty for some of the things I do, and I worry about a couple of things I have done in the past. At this moment, I find it absolutely impossible to be a sexual person, perhaps because of fear. Until my fears are removed, probably through marriage, I will not be able to exhibit strong sexual behavior. I seem to be caught between what I want to do and what I think I should do.

The use of guilt as a control mechanism is so effective that we might doubt whether this student will ever be able to become the sexual person he wishes to be. It is clear that he views marriage as a magical rite that will remove his fear and allow him the freedom he wishes. Although many college students express the hope that marriage will change them by removing their fear of sex and making them more mature, it is exceptional when such changes actually do take place. For most people, the stresses of marriage intensify, rather than reduce, any existing conflicts.

The guilt control mechanism is so strong that it sometimes works to induce an avoidance of all behaviors one *thinks* might cause him to feel guilty. A person not only feels guilt for acts that he has carried out in the past, he avoids all behavior that might cause guilt. A male student wrote:

As I grew older, my enthusiasm for sexual encounters has been subdued by foresight to the guilt feelings which would follow. I'm not yet ready to commit myself to any one particular girl, and I have never been comfortable enough to want a commitment. In fact, I'm so afraid of commitment, I rarely even kiss a date good-night.

Note the manner in which this writer has begun to rationalize his avoidance of guilt. He no longer feels that he is avoiding guilt by his actions; his commitment to an individual causes the fears. Avoiding commitment is a frequent and costly consequence of utilizing guilt as the mechanism for behavioral control. Guilt is so strong a force that the individual cannot tolerate it for long and has to seek other rationales for behaving the way he does. Most individuals who use the substitution mechanism choose avoiding commitment as a means of controlling guilt. If you never become committed to an individual, nothing ever happens for which you have to feel guilty.

The consequences of avoiding commitment are that you begin to shun all individuals and avoid all commitments to any type of interpersonal relationship. Many students report feeling "dead" inside or the need to keep everyone away from them for fear of what people will find out about them. One way of interpreting this fear is as a misunderstanding; one cannot distinguish between the fear of guilt (guilt-avoidance) and the fear of disclosure. In short, the fear of guilt constricts the feelings that one person is able to hold for another.

Several students wrote that they are unwilling or unable to feel anything for anyone. For example, a male writes:

I feel it would be wrong for me to take sexual advantage of a girl without providing the compensation of marriage. It would be especially degrading to do this to a girl I loved.

In fact, I have suppressed nearly all sexual expression, mainly for lack of opportunity, but also because of a fear of what it could lead to. I fear the intimacy and knowledge that another person would have of me and I of them. I have not yet been on a date; I would not know what to do. I have no close friends; I am truly afraid of people. What else do I have except fantasy and masturbation?

Another male reports similar feelings:

My sexual being was turned upon itself. I had no way to express my sexuality except to myself. There were dates, of course, but none ever went beyond the kissing stage and my frustration only grew. Up to this point, my sexuality was deflected as a result of my fear of revealing my desires to another person as well as my belief that nice girls didn't do it.

While males are inhibiting their feelings because "nice girls don't do it" and "it would be especially degrading to do this to a girl I loved," women are thinking different thoughts. One female reports:

My father never mentioned the subject of sex in my whole life until, on the way up to Michigan State University for my freshman year, he said to be careful because boys are after only one thing.

This lack of trust is characteristic of almost all social relations between college students of either sex; and, under these conditions, it is no wonder that people have difficulty communicating with each other. In fact, it is a tribute to the flexibility of the human mind that people are able to overcome these preconceptions in order to get married at all. Sometimes, of course, people can break down the barriers between themselves and those around them when they meet someone whom they perceive as atypical of the normal stereotype. That is, a girl will meet an individual male who is able to convince her that he is not "after only one thing"; or a male will meet a female he respects and with whom he can enjoy himself without feeling guilty. But these are exceptional relationships, and they do not occur with great frequency. The average person has only one alternative other than therapy: He essentially has to outgrow the feelings learned in his parents' society.

In the meantime, many people are confused about their feelings because they have never discussed them anywhere and labeling them is difficult. To add to the confusion, these feelings become mixed with self-doubt when the student arrives at college. A male writes:

I am by nature quite aggressive, socially as well as emotionally. So if I gave vent to all my emotions toward a girl, I would be less likely to take her straight to bed than to sock her in the teeth.

A girl writes:

It's a mystery to me why I am in a muddle as far as sex goes. I guess I want everything in black and white. When I played the piano, there was no question as to whether the next note was an F♯ or a G; if I was cooking, I knew whether to add a whole cup of flour or a half. But sex was never that measured and it was very scary at first.

The student arrives at college holding his parents' status. That is, his parents' reputation and his own coincided throughout his public school years. While this experience probably offered safety and security, it also tended to fix the student in whatever role had been assigned to him. At this time in their lives, students are exceptionally sensitive to comments made about them, particularly by adults such as parents or teachers; hence, if some internal change (from shyness, for example, to a more extroverted behavior) were taking place, a corresponding external behavior might not follow. These changes usually take place just about the time that the student leaves for college, where, he discovers, he may lose even his former status. At college, the determinants of status are different from those that operated at home. Hence, the student's self-image is no longer secure, his emotions are changing without his having yet defined appropriate controls for them, and he is extremely unsure about what is or is not proper behavior.

The resulting anxiety, turbulence, and self-doubt have been summed up by one of the better writers in the course, who chose to write about her early experiences and their effect on her sexuality. The writer is a female, age twenty-two, who will be called Samantha. She normally shortens her name to "Sam" and refers to herself in the third person as such. She writes:

As a little girl I received no sexual instruction from my parents, or rather no explicit verbal instruction. My friends and I would go off to a little wooden house a short way from home and spend a great deal of time there, until my mother would notice our absence and bang violently on the door demanding: "Hey! What are you kids doing in there?" This is the earliest recollection I have of being told sex is something nice people don't talk about and only the sinful engage in with pleasure. Most of the other warnings I picked up by watching my parents together. I saw my father try to kiss my mother in front of others and have her push him away from her with a look of great disgust on her face.

There were other subtle things to remind me, too. Like all mothers mine referred to a pregnant woman as "having something wrong with her," and my mother's most agonizing fear for my sister and me was that one of us would have a child out of wedlock. Of course, no one ever told me what "out of wedlock" meant, and, most of all, how did anyone *get* pregnant anyway? All this combined into a situation which was vague and terrifying. I remember being afraid to sleep in the same room with a male cousin, fearing I would get pregnant and then what would people say about me?

After eight years in a parochial school, I went to a public high school where I was numb for four years. All I can remember is weighing 225 pounds and having greasy hair and acne. I was extremely withdrawn then; I had few friends and *no* social interaction with the opposite sex. I spent most of my time in my room listening to the radio, eating huge amounts of food, and having fantasies of how someday, somehow, THE guy was going to come along and take me away from my life of pain and desperate loneliness.

I was isolated by a wall of fear and a wall of fat. No one dared to come near me even if I would have decided to let them. I knew friends were passing me by and I wondered for hours at a time why people were having such problems growing up. I wasn't having any problems, was I? Of course I wasn't. When you stop growing at ten, you have few problems at sixteen. That is, if your defenses hold out. Mine did.

When I came up here to this campus, I told myself I would hang myself in my dorm room before I would go back to my family and town. I almost did hang myself more than once.

Weighing 225 pounds isn't the most pleasant thing in the world. Nobody, and I mean nobody, can resist laughing at a fat girl. My sense of adequacy had been killed by my parents, and the nuns ground me under the wheels of Catholicism. My appearance took care of the rest of my universe.

During my first year at school, I nearly had a breakdown but my roommate (who was crazy enough to love me) made me go to the counseling center here on campus. Once I talked to someone they got me to a counselor fast, probably because I was going to kill myself in a short period of time or, more likely, kill someone else.

I remember as a freshman seeing all the girls going out and having a good time. That never happened to me. I decided to go on a diet then and, with the help and encouragement of my roommate and suitemates, I took off about fifty pounds. I could not believe the way I looked. My sister said to me, when she saw me for the first time in three months, "Sam, I never realized it but you are really pretty." People all over were showering me with compliments, and I was bewildered by all of it. "My God," I thought, "Sam pretty." I could not believe it; I would not accept it.

I became terrified. What was happening to me? I felt absolutely dirty from head to foot. I felt like going into the shower and sitting with lye dripping over my body to take away that vulgar, disgusting feeling. I was so afraid of men, of what they might do to me, that I panicked every time one even tried to hold hands with me. Is it any wonder they rarely asked me out?

Once free from parental and family influences, most students suffer the greatest conflicts over their sexual drives. For their entire adult lives to this point, they have been told that sexual relations between consenting adults who are unmarried are wrong. At college, older and sexually more mature students seem to be behaving in ways contrary to what the student believes is correct. This difference between what the younger student feels, what he believes is correct, and what he is seeing comes at a time when his self-esteem is at its lowest. Conflict and guilt inevitably follow.

If these students are representative of the college population, it is difficult to believe the many stories in the mass media that today's college student is far more sexual than his parents were. Equally, it is difficult to be unsympathetic toward the young woman who writes:

Sexually I am a frigid person. I am trapped within; although I am trying hard to chip away at the exterior, at the first sign of a crack in the ice, I find I do not like what I see and I freeze up again. I am an iceberg. No one knows more than one-tenth of what I am or who I am. The other nine-tenths, God knows, may not even be worth knowing.

THE PERIOD OF GROWING AWAY

Learning to reach a balance between one's ethics and his drives often requires a growth in maturity, i.e., a growing away from one's parents.

During the second stage of sexual development in college the individual begins to think of himself as a person, separate from his parents and the value systems they represent. This change necessitates a sorting process: the student has to separate those ideas and values that are his from those presented by his parents and introjected during his development. In other words, he has to learn to stand up for his own ideas and to think for himself. This aspect of the growing process has been described by a sophomore female as follows:

I have discovered I am a person, separate from my parents. I have to live my own life and I cannot live it entirely for them. I have done things now that I believe are right but which they think are wrong, very wrong. I have become my own ruler now. My parents would be shocked, hurt, disgusted, and probably disappointed if they knew I have stayed overnight in a men's dorm several times. I believe nothing is wrong with it, and I have enough belief so that if they ever find out, I can stand up for myself—I hope.

My parents' views on morality and sex, I am finding, are very different from mine. Before, when I lived at home, everything my parents said was true and basically what I believed. Now, I think for myself, at least more than I did before.

I am now old enough to get married and yet my parents do not want me even to go steady. When my grandmother was told I was going steady, I got the same negative reaction from her. I dread the day I have to tell my parents I am engaged. They cannot accept the fact they do not have a little girl any more. They will never accept the fact I will want to get married.

Meaningful relationships with others or interacting with people whose beliefs about sex are different from his usually start the student on his growing process. For example, a liberal minister may aid the student in viewing sexual behavior from a different perspective. A senior female writes:

When I transferred to Michigan State, I learned that many of my friends had spent the night with their boyfriends. I accepted this for them but told myself I would never do such a thing. In the middle of my sophomore year, I heard a talk given by one of the campus ministers.

This was the first time I had ever heard anyone older than I speak about sex. It was as if a whole new world opened up to me. Here was a man telling me that sex was beautiful and even enjoyable. While the things he said stayed with me, I never even thought about them, then.

In a seminar she received additional information that led to a further change in her attitudes. She writes:

I was enrolled in a graduate seminar called "Human Sexual Behavior." I was the only virgin, the only conservative with liberal ideas. The course was extremely beneficial for me in two ways. It was the first place where so many aspects of human sexuality were discussed so openly. In addition, I was amazed to find a professor so accepting of behavior which had been termed promiscuous before. I could feel the changes occurring.

While these experiences are common, the most frequent means of growth is contact with a significant member of the opposite sex. Faculty members may start the individual thinking in a particular direction, but it is essential that the student meet someone with whom ideas and feelings can be shared. A typical description of this relationship has been written by a female:

Two years ago I met a boy I am still seeing and hope to marry someday. Through patience and tolerance, he has gradually given me new insights into love and sex as well as the relation between them. Sex seems to be related to every aspect of my personality but it is especially related to this relationship. The more love and understanding that are taking place, the more open I can be to sexual gestures.

A more complete description of this relationship has been written by a senior male:

My freshman year I met a girl named Carol to whom I immediately felt attracted. I even ventured to ask for a goodnight kiss after our first date, which was very unusual for me. Gradually, as our relationship became more complex and involved, I gathered the courage to put my hand on her breast. I still had the feeling that nice girls didn't allow such things, and

I was afraid that I would be rebuffed. To my surprise she accepted my advances and, thanks to my deep affection for her, I felt that our relationship had been enriched by this added intimacy. As time passed, our sexual relationship became more and more intense, but affection had turned to love and we accepted our relationship, for all its complexities, *sans* discussion.

The second year of our relationship was one of great anxiety for me. To me, our sexual relationship had caused tumultuous changes in attitudes about sex. It no longer had the implication "good girls don't do it." Although we had not gone very far, I was experiencing inner indecision. I wanted to go further and further, but I perceived hesitation on Carol's part and always broke off further advances whenever I felt she wanted to go no further. This second year was one of increasing sexual intimacy but no communication. That is, neither one of us was capable of discussing our relationship. We did not communicate how we felt about our sexual experiences but instead had to derive our ideas from each other's actions. It was at this stage that I experienced a great deal of frustration and Carol (as I found out later) was experiencing guilt feelings.

As our relationship continued to flourish and we discovered each could reveal his or her most personal experiences and thoughts and have them accepted by the other, we gradually began discussing sex also. Over time, we revealed more and more to each other, our anxieties, doubts, and desires. We are now able to discuss any topic, sexual or otherwise, without hesitation. Almost naturally, our sexual relationship became more free and much more satisfying because we no longer acted as two separate individuals groping for mutual satisfaction without the benefit of man's greatest gift: speech. I now feel a sense of victory in that, together, we have been able to conquer all the dragons standing between us and, in doing so, have liberated each other.

In this instance, the anxiety and guilt these people felt acted to inhibit the behavior that would have led to the reduction of these feelings, i.e., communication. Each individual involved in such a relationship feels that his emotions are somehow abnormal and thus should not be communicated. In addition, both have to feel secure enough with each other to trust one another with information not normally revealed to others. When communication leads to trust and trust to the revelation of deeper feelings, a meaningful relationship results, and the individual's sense of worth grows. Even if the relationship does not lead to marriage, it still represents a step forward by the individual involved. As a person moves through a series of similar relationships, he learns more about himself, more about the feelings of others, and, in this manner, is prepared for the relationship that leads to marriage. Before the cycle can get underway, anxiety and guilt have to be overcome so that communication can begin.

Even when the relationship between men and women is casual, the key to communication seems to be an individual's acceptance of himself and his desire to relate to others. A female writes:

I find I now have four very close male friends, and it is a beautiful experience to share a close friendship with a man. I'm not afraid to accept warmth and expressions of sexuality; in other words, I have matured enough to become involved with another person. Once I was willing to accept myself as I truly am, I could accept others in the same light.

As the process of discovery and communication develops, the individual reaches a point at which he is ready to enter into a relationship for the sheer joy of relating to another individual without anxiety and guilt. Usually, this person has been exposed to one or more liberal faculty members who can discuss sexuality rationally, and he has been involved in varying degrees with several members of the opposite sex. An additional requirement is that an individual have some insight into the nature of the relationships as well as the responses demanded by them. The outcome of all these forces is an individual who is able to understand his own feelings and, what is more important, accept them for what they are.

Individuals who have reached this point of understanding are rare on college campuses because the process leading up to understanding and self-acceptance is a long one. The individual reaches this level of maturity only after several years of interacting with others. Consider that the freshman year is often spent in confusion over values; the sophomore year is spent moving away from the values of the parents and the acceptance of a new value system. Depending upon the individual, growing into a mature acceptance of the self and others takes at least one and often two or more years. Seniors are thus the only ones who have had the time to become mature enough to accept themselves. Many, however, have not grown at all in emotional understanding, because the mere passage of time does not guarantee growth; an individual must consciously strive toward this end.

A good example of how these feelings grow has been written by a graduating senior female. She writes:

I have learned the importance of being honest and of open communication in all my interpersonal relationships. I have learned to be more spontaneous and genuine than ever before. Furthermore, I recognized that I felt controlled from doing things I wanted to do. Whether these are called fears or inhibitions, I wanted to overcome them. I have become more self-assured and better able to make decisions myself; no longer am I influenced by my friends' opinions. I was developing a truly individual self.

During the summer I began dating Bill. Here, I reacted differently than ever before. There was never any doubt in my mind that I wanted to make love with him. Our relationship was open and honest; I needed no assurance of a long-range commitment or deep love to make this decision. I cared for him and wanted to share this intimate experience with him. Also, over and above any boy I had ever dated, he handled sex so cleanly and beautifully that it was easy for me to overcome some of my hang-ups.

The whole experience was beautiful and enjoyable; it was in no way repulsive as I had earlier expected sex to be. The decision to make love with Bill was easy for me. Sexually, we have encountered several problems but working through them has made the relationship all the more rewarding for me.

In summary, the college student begins his period of growth with a feeling of independence. He becomes aware of himself as a being separate from his parents and the value system they represent. Without the support provided by parents,

the individual must rely on himself, but, in many instances, his self-esteem has been suppressed either through the actions of his parents or by the education system that trained him before his arrival at college. That is, never having experienced the feeling and responsibility of freedom, the college student is unprepared for the sudden loss of support he experiences when he tries to make decisions for himself. The individual cannot come to grips with the self-doubt he feels, nor can he deal with his newly liberated sexuality. He takes refuge in an inhibiting guilt-repression process that requires a long period of time and a great deal of work to overcome.

Freeing himself from this form of alienation often starts when the student meets a significant adult figure on campus, but he really begins to move toward establishing meaningful relationships with others when he meets a significant member of the opposite sex. Although these initial relationships may be superficial at first, they grow according as the student grows in his ability to communicate, to understand, and to trust.

The final goal of the growth process is reached when a person can become involved in relationships of some depth with members of the opposite sex and, without guilt, act in ways appropriate for the expression of feelings between them. All such relationships will not necessarily involve sexual expression, since relationships exist where sexual expression would be inappropriate. Where the feelings of the particular pair are extremely strong, however, sexual expression could be considered an appropriate response, and the mature individual is able to move in that direction without guilt, anxiety, or recriminations.

THE SEARCH FOR MEANING IN SEXUALITY

The college student views his sexuality as a significant aspect of his being, much more so than in later years when additional responsibilities claim attention. The college years are decidedly artificial in that one becomes definable according to an arbitrary scale, such as grade-point average. In the first two years of college, many students attempt to find meaning in their studies and become discouraged when they discover that their "true" persons lie elsewhere. Grades are, by far, the most shallow means of finding the self; questions such as "where am I going?" or "who am I?" or "what do I really want to stand for?" are far more meaningful, and students turn more and more to these questions as they mature.

Rejecting the grading scales, the student may turn toward people and often chooses sexual relationships as the best representation of meaningful interpersonal relationships. That is, a student will evaluate himself and the relationships he has with people in the context of sex. Although sex is important because it gratifies strong physical needs, in this instance they are only secondary. Sex here serves primarily to define one's self through the particular types of relationships an individual will seek. Dating becomes important because one's dates provide a measure of how attractive, acceptable, and worthwhile he really is in terms of the "marriage market." In some ways this definition places a burden on sexual behavior that it was never meant to carry. Sex is: physical release; a measure of how good an individual is; an index of acceptability, status, and worth; and, finally, the definitive "meaning of life." For the college student, sex becomes everything in life, an impossible situation for the student to endure. As one of the girls in the course pointed out:

> There is a lot of pressure around here in all types of relationships. You always have to contend with the social pressure; all the guys ask him what "he got" and the girls want you to tell about the absolutely marvelous relationship you have going, even if it is not sexual. The most successful relationships seem to be those in which the two people know exactly where they stand, but these are few and far between.

Before the student can become aware of the meaning of his sexual behavior, he must first begin to rationalize his behavior in the context of his original system of values. What once gave meaning to life, doing well for parents and others, may be rejected and replaced with other values providing an equal degree of meaning. This rejection involves a thoughtful examination of the original behavioral controls and a definition of new controls. In this way, the person can define himself according to the new behavior being acted out and rationalize the behavior as the surfacing of the "true self." The key word in this change in direction, however, is "thoughtful." An individual can quickly change his behavior and rationalize in any manner he pleases, but he does not automatically find meaning in his life. The change has to be well thought out and congruent with the individual's change in attitudes. Merely changing one's behavior toward greater sexual involvement and expecting that attitudes will tag along is wishful fantasy.

As an example of this type of problem, a girl writes:

> One day I realized I was free; no one would tell me what to do; there was nothing to hold me back from doing what I wanted. I had liberated myself from convention and, in this way, I could finally be myself. I didn't try to explain this feeling to myself, but I thought I felt free because I no longer held back from sex. With this liberation from hang-ups I seemed to liberate my mind from all its hang-ups. This was the beginning of life for me.
>
> I started meeting new people. It began with the friendship of one boy and led to friendships with his friends. I found a group who mean the world to me, with whom I have so many good times, with whom I can talk deeply. These are people who understand me and whom I love because of what they are.
>
> I could finally be myself and not be made fun of or laughed at. I became completely uninhibited in other aspects of my life. I have had several sexual relationships since my boyfriend left the university because I feel free. I must make the most of my life, and I am trying to do it.

This student reports that sexual behavior represents a way to demonstrate her freedom. She obviously feels that her original values were constricting her behavior, and only by changing these values can she be free. An interesting speculation is whether the change she is reporting is the outcome of "a thoughtful examination of original controls" or whether she is simply responding to the different attitudes of the new people she has met. The only way to judge whether her change of behavior is the result of shifting attitudes is to see whether her behavior persists over a long period of time or whether her original problems will reassert themselves. Another interesting area for speculation is what values will result from her search for meaning. She feels that her parents' values were constricting her behavior, but most people wind up with attitudes and values similar to those held by their parents. The question is: Will her final set of values be similar to or different from the values she held when she arrived at college?

Most students seem to use their sexual behavior as an indicator of both their own maturation and the depths to which a particular relationship has advanced. Self and other are thus simultaneously evaluated by sexual response. In addition, many individuals searching for meaning see their sexual behavior as a training ground for marriage, a provider of insight into the wishes and feelings held by members of the opposite sex. A female writes:

For me, intercourse is no longer a big problem or a source of tension. The quality of the relationship is what is important to me. I can joke about sex, laugh at it, but I really don't get anxious about it. I feel that I no longer have sexual inhibitions, only limitations in that my moral code is my own. I want to wait until it is a natural and mutually desirable decision of a relationship that I feel is founded on honesty and friendship.

I decided to take oral contraceptives so I would not become pregnant if I decided to have intercourse. I don't think I am "promiscuous" because I take the pill; I have decided to add another quality to my moral code: wait until we will be in a position to continue to have intercourse so it will develop as part of a relationship and not just a one-night experience.

I feel more responsible for my actions now, because I have the complete freedom to choose without the "built-in" excuse for saying no. I have to decide on the basis of the person and our relationship. I realize that this relationship is not easy to achieve but, having succeeded once, there is no room for compromise. This leads me to be more confident of my feminine role. I think I will approach marriage with more maturity and understanding than before.

From the opposite side, a male reports the outcome of a relationship similar to the one described above. Both parties tried to be rational about their sexual response and they found meaning in their rational approach. He reports:

We have been going together for three years and we will be married in the fall of the coming year. During the last three years, I have steadily progressed out of my hang-ups into a sort of free-flowing existence which is rarely complicated by daily occurrences commonly found to be adverse. I can attribute this to a number of factors but particularly to my relationship with Jane.

Every time we would go parking and become more aroused than our boundaries would allow, a crisis arose. Our relationship developed on the principle that, if two people get into an argument, they can always resolve their problems by reasoning them away. We overcame all our problems through the use of reason, which is not so fantastic when you think of the ridiculous things people face as problems.

Using this method, we toppled the two giants, the Church and Tradition, standing between us. In this case, the old "prove your love" line was a reality; I would not have married a girl who was not as dedicated to me as I was to her. Thus, the Church fell when we went to bed together, or maybe before that. I had spent two-and-a-half years waiting for it, and I was pleased when it finally happened. During that time, I had gone away on many vacations but had remained celibate through them all. Both of us had sacrificed something for each other; now, we have finally come to love each other and will be married.

Today, we are two very happy individuals who love each other and are sharing the same beliefs arrived at over time. We have overcome our problems concerning sex and are on even ground. Neither of us has to repress any desires arising within us; we can act out any fantasies which come into our heads. We are much happier for this loss of repression with its consequent guilt.

Common to all these papers is the idea that one has to go from a negative disposition with its guilt and repression to a positive or free type of existence. To do so, the individual has to drop earlier controls over his behavior; and usually he will thus engage in some form of sexual behavior. In order to rationalize this change in behavior, he often sees sex as a means of gaining an understanding of others or of himself. Meaning emerges from relationships with others and mirrors the degree of understanding an individual has of himself. As a person becomes more open with others, he usually becomes more open and honest with himself. Until a person is honest with himself, he cannot be honest with others. Clearly, the statements about the feelings associated with sexual freedom reflect feelings toward the self. "I was free" is a statement concerned with the sudden understanding of the self rather than a statement about a situation. In the wake of understanding the self, the individual finds new friendships based on his newly-found confidence.

All of these feelings are summed up in a paper written by a senior attempting to find meaning in her own sexuality, i.e., what it means to be a woman. Excerpts from her paper make an excellent summary of this aspect of development:

[The first part of the paper describes a Clark Gable movie seen when the writer was a young girl.] The last scene is back in that cafe—let's call it Paris; the big-shot sergeant is still laughing and he says, "What ever happened to that girl, anyway?" And Gable says, "They found her in the river three days later." You better believe that movie got me where I live. Tragedy!! She was so beautiful and she killed herself for him. For Clark Gable! If he loved her, that is what femininity had to be.

That was my first lesson in "femininity" and I have had a million others since. All these lessons taught me that being feminine is a very negative thing. A female-female is always a little confused; that's appealing. She is weak so a man can feel strong. She is dependent so she will not be able to get out of hand. He Tarzan, she Jane. To be really feminine, you have to be everything a man is not (and if he is a great guy, you are in trouble). A man can be a man all by himself but a woman is hardly a person until she *belongs* to a man.

I don't know why so many of us fall into this rut. Why do we want to *belong* to someone? Why do I have to be possessed, owned? It is similar to the way in which I used to love my dog. She was always waiting for me to come home; wagging her tail, she waited. She was ready for me to love her and always ready to lick me. But there was never any challenge nor was there any friction between us. She never disagreed with me and was always grateful for even the tiniest bit of affection. She was a pleasure to have around the house, but she was not very stimulating. She certainly did not help me grow, and we never shared anything.

This, to me, is what so many relationships turn into after marriage. The wife becomes the man's adorable little puppy. Sure, he will pet her when he wants to, comfort her when she whines, and he may even bring her a bone occasionally. He does not become a bigger man for knowing her. In fact, he often feels guilty for not wanting to pat her as often as she wants. This is fine for dogs, but we are people, people with brains. People with brains have minds of their own and opinions as well. Maybe squashing one's opinions makes for more peace but that is peace gained at an awful price: one's self-respect. Peace built on a lie.

Most of my friends have fallen into this "femininity" rut. Maybe it is because we all define "feminine" as "sexy." I do not believe this is true anymore. Sexiness is directed from the inside out; trying to be "sexy" is sexless. What is so unbelievably sexy about some people? They may have a good sense of humor or a twinkle in their eye. Show me someone who loves being alive and I will show you my idea of sexy. Energy is sexy; zest and vigor are sexy. Sexy is "What can I give?" Doggy femininity is: "What can I get?" There is a hell of a lot of difference there.

I never had much self-respect in my earlier days. I did not have a sense of my self, of who I was or just what I had to offer. How can you give to someone when you don't think you have anything to offer? You can't, and I certainly couldn't.

Self-respect is difficult to come by, however. It goes against the tide of everything we have learned since we were tiny children. Everything I ever did was for someone else's approval. I cleaned my room so my mother would like me, not because I liked a clean room. I studied in school for the grades—the ultimate score. I would cram, take the exam, and fifteen minutes later, forget everything. It had nothing to do with learning. I always tried to be everyone else's ideal something-or-other. I tried to be special because I wanted people to like me. Never did I try pleasing myself so I could hold up my head, look people in the eye, and say, "Hello! I'm me. This is who I am. Who are you?"

I think I was buying people then. If I am special enough, you will like me. I was very ambitious because I wanted some kind of title. I was all the right things for all the wrong reasons. I was polite so people would like me, not because I liked people. I didn't like people; they scared me.

I really don't think this is all my fault or the fault of any of the hundreds of girls who are so much like me. I think the system is a little at fault, too. Everything we learn is so negative. There is a great discrepancy between the reality of our lives as women and the image to which we try to conform. We are taught not to: kill, steal, lie, swear, commit adultery, not, *not*, *NOT*. If we don't do any of these uglies, we will wind up being "social creatures"; we will "fit in"; we will be "well-adjusted." If you're well-adjusted, well, man, that's just IT.

I think if we had been shown as children that there were things to DO, not just things NOT TO DO, then table manners and rules would not have had to be shoved down our throats. If we were led to feel we had some purpose, some tiny little reason for being here, then we would have been on the road to self-respect. Once you learn that, you can begin to care about other people. You finally realize you are not ugly inside; you have something to give. We have been educated to understand everything except the value of our own worth.

The fact is, I was born with two arms and two legs, eyes that see, and ears that hear in a country that taught me to read and write. I just have to wonder why. Why was I born here and not in Bombay? Why was I given a healthy body and a fine working brain? Why can I hear and taste? For my own pleasure or so I can wallow in my own enjoyment? I don't think so. I think I have to justify, to myself, the air I breathe and the space I take.

I don't think there is anyone who could tell me how to do that. No one knows what I have to offer better than I do. I have listened to all those other people in my life who knew what I "shouldn't be or should be." Believe me, I was mixed up. Now, *I* decide, and I wish others could grasp this wonderful feeling of being real so they would not become trapped in the same old rut.

My parents don't tell me what to do. No psychiatrist, no priest, no "Woman Problem" writer, no one tells me what to do. I am free, I decide. Of course, that is a little scary, because if I decide wrong, there is no one else to

blame, but I am willing to risk that. If I fail, I will try again some other way.

This is where I stand this year. Next year, I don't know where I will be. I may be all wet but I don't think so; the alternatives are all so blah. What is important is: *I* will have to see.

Here we see that much of the meaning in an immature individual's life is brought by outsiders. Rather than recognizing or discovering his own internal feelings, the person looks to others for values and goals. A large part of the early training process is designed to focus attention on others such as parents or teachers; the child learns to look to others for direction. This other-orientation has to be overcome if the shallow childhood existence is to be outgrown. All the student writers who have reported finding meaning in their lives seem to have looked within to discover meaning for their existence. As the last writer pointed out, to live entirely for another is to live no life at all.

SEXUAL ACHIEVEMENT

The final outcome of the search for meaning in sexuality is a growth in self-awareness as well as increasing joy in life. Several writers in the last section alluded to this increased joy, but it does not reach its highest point until after the person reaches a certain level of self-awareness.

The number of people who are satisfied with their sexuality is small. Out of about one hundred papers submitted for review, only four seemed to reflect their authors' growth toward a mature set of attitudes concerning sexuality. None were males, an interesting finding, but males may be too involved with the acquisition of technical skills during the college years to consider personal development. In addition, part of the female role model may involve the introspection and admission of feelings necessary to grow in this manner; such "femininity" may be too much for college-age males who have been taught to emphasize their masculine aspects.

In any case, the four females are a group who have come to grips with their past and look forward to the future. They balance the ten students quoted in the first section who knew neither their identity nor their direction. One girl writes:

I feel that I am the most stable of all my friends because I have all these positive experiences to fall back on. I know what a relationship can be, intellectually, romantically, and sexually. My method for finding these relationships is the best one for me. My decision to add sexual intercourse to my set of sexual responses is the correct one for me.

I have positive reinforcement for that decision from my own feelings, from the boys with whom I have had sexual relationships, from my peer groups, and from the psychology books I have read. One conflict does remain. I have decided not to tell my parents, although I am usually honest with them. They would be upset by my behavior and sex is a private behavior; it should remain private. My life is my own.

Perhaps this student sounds a little overly intellectual but her intent is clear. She seems to have reached an understanding with herself and can make important decisions without regret or guilt. Her last paragraph indicates her degree of control over her own life, as well as her feeling that she, rather than others, sets the direction in which she will travel.

Two others discuss their feelings about their lives after having acquired meaning in their sexuality. One writes:

Now, after having reviewed my sexual development, I again come to the question: How do I define myself sexually? I really don't. I define myself as a maturing *individual* with thoughts, goals, beliefs, and ideas that are all my own. I am open to change, yet have fairly stable ideas about most of the things I want in life. I am happy to be alive and I get a great deal of enjoyment out of just being. My relationships with others have become more fulfilling since I have become more myself. Openness in all relationships is now of major importance to me.

My sexual development has had a great influence in the determination of my individuality. In this area, I have made decisions on my own and have been proud of them. I have enjoyed the feeling of separation from those who do not believe and act in the same manner I do. We accept one another and we like each other,

yet each of us acts on her own. I used to be the type of person who did all the things that were expected of a "good" girl.

Sexually, I will probably change more in the future. As I said at the beginning, I seem to be constantly growing and my consciousness expanding. I look forward to the future, knowing it will be as exciting and as productive as the past.

This statement shows how the mature individual has gained a perspective on sexual behavior. It is no longer the most important behavior in life, but is now evaluated as growth. The writer is more interested in maintaining her individuality than proving herself through sexual behavior. Her enjoyment comes out of being alive and being open in her relationships. We may infer that, if sexual behavior is an appropriate response in a particular situation, this girl will respond in that way. She will not, however, attempt to use sex as a lever on openness, i.e., think she is communicating with someone simply because they are having intercourse. The openness has to come first, the understanding has to come first, and the awareness that sex is an appropriate behavior has to come first.

It is also overeager to assume that such individuals will always resort to sexual intercourse after gaining self-awareness. Many people may find that their pleasure in life comes from waiting for the appropriate person to come along; hence sexual behavior will take place in the context of marriage. These individuals will be able to relate to others in an open and honest way, which includes communicating their desires to remain celibate for the time being. In other words, the most important aspect of finding meaning in sexuality is gaining self-awareness, because only then can the individual make an intelligent decision about the level of sexuality appropriate for him in any particular relationship. Obviously, this level will vary from person to person and from relationship to relationship. As the previous writer has suggested, sex is not everything in life.

Another girl supports this view:

I become involved with other people on three different levels: emotionally, intellectually, and sexually. I have not yet reached the point where I have become involved with someone completely in all three ways. I know the sexual relationship will come in time and when it does, I know it will be a real relationship with no false pretenses.

I can enjoy a small degree of sex without really being involved with a person just because I can kiss a guy on our first date. It is easy for me to become involved, though; I often mistake involvement for other feelings and I have been hurt by this. It makes sense to me because I am willing to take the chance of opening up and getting involved, knowing that, the more I open up, the more I stand to get out of the relationship, one way or the other. Consequently, when I am happy, there is no one happier; if I am sad, this also seems complete. This may sound extreme, but it is great to be alive in this way.

Because I am aware of this, I am willing to give a part of myself to someone, to share that with them and trust them not to rip it apart. If it is ripped and torn apart later, I will try to share myself with someone else who will not only repair and restore me, but will restore my trust in people. I know that, even if one person can't be trusted, the whole world is not hanging on the same limb.

It is much easier to say this than to do this, but I am willing to take the risk, to be myself, and I am learning to do this more. I have a horrid fear of being stifled, and one of my major desires is to experience and feel as much as I can. I am still going through a self-questioning period, but I also think I will always be questioning myself because I can't ever conceive of getting to the point where I am completely satisfied, at least with myself as a person. On the other hand, I know I can be very content with myself as long as I try to be.

Both individuals are writing about where they are going and how they are growing. They point out that they are interested in feeling and experiencing as much as they can in order to expand and grow intellectually over time. They do not reach a particular plateau and stay there, content to review their pleasant experiences. Both report that they look forward to their experiences in the future so that they can develop an increased understanding of themselves and their environment.

In addition, the person who has achieved meaningful sexual relationships, *regardless of whether they have gone so far as sexual intercourse,* stresses the openness of communication necessary for such a relationship. A closed, protected self is unable to reach for others; when a person does not have the necessary understanding of himself, how can he possibly understand others? These two people clearly have come to an understanding of themselves and, liking what they see, are now in the process of reaching toward others.

These individuals are also distinguished by their confidence in their ability to get along; they seem to be very self-confident and have a fair degree of self-acceptance and self-love. The self-confidence gives them the security to face the possibility of being rejected in a relationship, and they enter relationships aware of this possibility. If you do not love yourself, it has been said, how can you ever learn to love others? In short, the sexually achieving individual has the desire to grow, is able to communicate effectively with others, and has a high degree of self-esteem. The rewards for this behavior seem infinitely worth the effort necessary to achieve it, especially when the passages introducing the chapter are reread. The comparison is certainly not favorable.

CONCLUSION

In the final analysis, it might well be asked: Is the whole thing worth it? Is it worth the pain of broken relationships, feelings of guilt at the outset, and the general pain that seem to accompany all rapid growth? As an answer to this question, read through the last statement in the first part of the chapter by the girl who says she is trapped within herself. Then read this statement, written by a senior girl:

At the beginning of the term I met a guy that I wanted to go to bed with. This is a new experience for me, to say the least. It frightened me, of course, but now I feel rather womanly and excited thinking about the way I felt. I am human, I am female; I do feel this way; I admit that I want to touch him; and I love it!! Listening to guys tell me I am beautiful, I smile sweetly and act as if I had heard it a hundred times before. The ugly little girl I used to be is now just a caricature in my mind, along with the terrors within my family, and the nuns.

I still have my problems. About once a month I become depressed and I feel suicidal. My feelings of inadequacy creep up on me then, and I wonder longingly if things ever will be the way I want them to be. But these times always pass, and if I do something to express the feelings like listening to loud music, talking to people who feel the same way I do, dancing hard and wild at a local night spot, or writing papers like this one, the feelings leave faster. I guess what I am saying is: I finally have some control over my life. My mother and the nuns do not.

I guess this is all I have to say about myself except that now, after twenty-two years of life, I can honestly say that I look forward to each day. I now have a very good chance of fulfilling myself; I have a very good idea of who I am and where I am going with my life; I do love people and sex **is** great with the right person. My whole life is **feeling** the excitement of a new person being born and, what is even better, this is only the beginning for me.

SEX REVOLUTION CASUALTIES

James Ring Adams

A freshman girl and her boyfriend came to a Brandeis University dorm counselor with a problem. For several months they had been sleeping in the same bed, along with the girl's roommate. Now they had a vague feeling something was wrong with their lives.

The couple, it seemed, thought they were in love, so the boy had insisted they ought to sleep together. His girlfriend found this logic hard to refute, but insisted she wanted to remain a virgin. So they had agreed to share her bed, but only for sleeping. The girl further argued that one bed was too narrow. So they moved the dorm room's other bed alongside, complete with roommate, and spent the semester sleeping three abreast on the two beds—all in perfect chastity.

The counselor remembers these students as nice, clean-cut kids caught in the dilemma of living up to the standards of "the sexual revolution." Their behavior may seem bizarre but it differs only in detail from the compromise between worldliness and innocence that thousands of students strike daily. Three in a bed is extreme, but three in a room—boyfriend, girl and roommate—is commonplace at nearly any college with increasingly popular open dorms. Even for students not involved in affairs, the ambience is likely to cause difficulty in working out not only sex but a host of other problems.

"Those kids who aren't ready," observes Dr. Tom G. Stauffer, chief psychiatrist at Sarah Lawrence College, "do have a devil of a time."

After several years of propaganda about sexual liberation on campus, many college psychiatrists and counselors are beginning to pay attention to the problems of the students who don't particularly want to be liberated. Furthermore, they are questioning the pop-Freudian assumption that an open, frank attitude about sex reduces neurotic problems. As far as campus sex is concerned, a funny thing happened on the way to the revolution.

IMPOTENCE AND INHIBITIONS

Dr. Stauffer, for one, doubts whether the new sexual openness has solved the problems of personal communication. He cites the case of a student patient who complained that he suddenly found himself impotent after a long period of personal and physical intimacy with his girlfriend. The student talked freely and openly about his sexual life. But he shied away from the heart of his problem: his girlfriend, as he casually mentioned on his third visit to the psychiatrist, had also been having affairs with several other men. Not important, thought the student, but his impotency had developed from the first time he learned about it.

"He was totally inhibited from expressing any anger," observes Dr. Stauffer, "but he was very angry with this girl." The student's sexual drives may have been liberated, but that did not preclude his suffering some very crippling problems. In short, said Dr. Stauffer, "his active, open sexual life was not any solution to his problems."

Not everyone agrees, of course, with this assessment of the effects of sexual openness. Many experts, reports Dr. Robert Michels, a Columbia psychiatrist, doubt that it has far-reaching effects. "The girl who showed her ankles 60 years ago might take off her bra and blouse today," he said summarizing this school of thought. "In effect, intercourse in our society might be what petting was 15 years ago, without any more psychological content."

Others find positive values. "Young people today have a lot of sexual problems," says Dr. Philip Sarrell, a Yale Medical School professor of gynecology. "Fortunately, they're identifying them early before they become a life-long thing."

It's difficult to get agreement, for that matter, on the extent of any sexual revolution on campus.

Statistics on sexual behavior are notoriously unreliable. Dr. Michels says, "If you ask men, they exaggerate. If you ask women, they don't tell you everything."

Some experienced sex researchers even say that the "sexual revolution" took place 50 years ago. Dr. Wardell B. Pomeroy, a close associate of the late pioneer sex researcher, Dr. Alfred C. Kinsey, says women started having premarital sex more and men started going to prostitutes less right after World War I. The rates have gradually increased he says, but the basic pattern remained the same.

Still, some things have changed on campus. The incidence of virgin brides may or may not have much changed, but behavior and attitudes are different. Students at Northeastern colleges consistently reported that casual week-end dating is dropping off and the trend is toward cohabitation, often in the college dormitory. There is even a minor academic boom in research on cohabitation. Mrs. Eleanor D. Macklin, a professor at Cornell University's Department of Human Development and Family Studies, has compiled two issues of a "Cohabitation Research Newsletter," summarizing the work of some 60 graduate students and professors across the country.

At Cornell, Professor Macklin has found a startling high rate of "Type A cohabitation"—sharing a bedroom with someone of the opposite sex four or more nights a week for three or more consecutive months. Out of 84 senior women, 54 per cent said they had tried it. Only 10 per cent of the senior women said they had never spent one night with a member of the opposite sex, compared to 33 per cent of the senior men. (This disparity may come from the fact that Cornell has roughly 2.5 men to every woman on its Ithaca, New York, campus.) Another reseacher estimated that 30 per cent of his campus had experienced some form of cohabitation.

Mrs. Macklin cautions that not every one of these cohabitors has necessarily been having sex. She has encountered several couples who have lived, and slept, together for more than three months without intercourse, because the women didn't feel ready for it.

This situation may or may not reflect "peer group pressure" to embark on an affair, but it does show that many universities are utterly unable to prevent it. Many colleges have in effect stopped enforcing any dormitory rules. Cornell, reports Mrs. Macklin, doesn't restrict parietal hours and its injunction against "continuous residence" with someone of the opposite sex is "difficult to police."

This in effect means that if there are to be any restraints on sexual conduct, they must come from within the students themselves. Often too, the surrounding atmosphere creates subtle pressures in the opposite direction. One former college administrator reports cases of students feeling themselves "forced" into sex not because either partner wanted it but because they were alone at night and somehow felt it was expected of them. Another girl, he reports, wondered what was wrong with her when she couldn't adjust to the "obviously natural" fact of her roommate having intercourse in the next bed every night.

Students say the problem is less one of ridicule from sophisticates than the fear of failing to live up to a generally accepted standard. And of course, strong individuals can resist such pressures fairly easily. "A lot of pressure about having pre-marital sex is self-imposed," said one girl. "I didn't pressure myself about it, so I didn't feel a lot of pressure."

But often the question of what to do about sex is a heavy addition to an already difficult adjustment. Joseph Katz of the State University of New York at Stony Brook writes that in studying co-residential dorms at Stanford his research team was "very much surprised when we found overwhelmingly large proportions of our students describing themselves as being severely depressed very often. Over 50 per cent described themselves as severely depressed a few times a month or more often during the past academic year." He adds, "Moreover, they give as the chief source of their depression precisely the area we were studying, namely relations with other people, including sex."

CONFUSING VIEWS

Dr. Katz finds this a step in the right direction: "In a way the present depressions are superior to the apathies of the past. The apathy came from profound discouragement. The depressions at least originate in the attempt of getting closer to other people, even if not successful."

Others are not so sanguine. "Students can't handle the lack of boundaries," says Dr. Ernest Shaw, who has just left a post as campus psychiatrist at Vassar. He thinks they're "looking for more control."

"There's a lot of self-deception," said a psychiatric counselor at a Midwestern coeducational liberal arts college. "The woman will rationalize and think she can carry the thing through. But after the affair is over, she'll feel shot down, that she's a fallen woman. What protected these girls was the idea they were in love, that this excused it."

As Sarah Lawrence's Dr. Stauffer has been finding out, some students seem afraid of the basic emotions that go with their sexual freedom. Dr. Stauffer reports he had been treating one girl, apparently successfully, for her problems completing term-papers. But his work unravelled toward the end of the spring term. He learned that her boyfriend was leaving the area at the end of school and, even though they lived together on weekends, they had no plans to keep in touch. By putting off her term papers, concluded Dr. Stauffer, the girl was mentally postponing the day of parting. But on the surface, he said, "there was not one scintilla of feeling."

Dr. Stauffer traces this confused idea of normality to the parents, who were the first generation to be exposed to the popularized idea that sexual inhibitions were harmful. Their "sexually pseudo-liberated" attempts to raise inhibition-free children grew out of "a kind of popularization of psychology with all kinds of misconceptions thrown in." But the simplistic notion that sexual frankness leads to mental health, says Dr. Stauffer, "was not what Freud was talking about."

Dr. Stauffer feels that there has been a decline recently in "the very strong sexual aggression" that has marked the campus atmosphere. Four years ago, he said, the spirit that "anything goes sexually" was "promulgated so excessively by some kids on campus that students who were offended by it were afraid to complain."

"That has changed now," he said. "It is more acceptable to say you don't want any part of that."

Dr. John Milici of Columbia University views the situation with what one could call moderate optimism. "Students are quietly and very deliberately attempting to evolve new ways of coping with the world," he said. "But how far anyone can get from the basic instinctual problems, I don't know."

SEX GOES TO COLLEGE

Andrew H. Malcolm

One rainy afternoon about five years ago, a co-ed walked trembling into Memorial Hospital at the University of North Carolina in Chapel Hill. She had a 103° fever and complained of abdominal pains.

In examination, Dr. Takey Crist, then a young resident, discovered a length of rubber tube sticking out of her uterus. The girl, it developed, had found herself pregnant; she panicked, and, fearing the future (including the school's policy of required expulsion), had been the willing but woefully ignorant, victim of a $50 abortion.

The co-ed was lucky. Although she was expelled, she recovered completely. But another girl there, also the victim of a quack abortion sought in fear, lost her uterus to the resulting infection.

It took three operations to drain the infection, and her kidneys failed briefly. After three months and $8000 in expenses, the girl left the hospital. She was sterile at age 18.

Those incidents, along with many similar ones, haunted Doctor Crist, who now is an assistant professor in the University's Department of Obstetrics and Gynecology. As a result, he has crusaded for college-level sex education and counseling at that university and has brought about some major changes. His crusade is only part of a slow, yet steadily mounting revolution on college and university campuses across the country. It might be called "a sexual revolution," for schools are seeking to close the surprisingly large information gap of their students.

The last few years and months have seen rapid development—often at student initiative—of a new type of academic courses, courses that deal explicitly with human sexuality.

Many student health clinics, once virtually confined to giving aspirin and diagnosing mononucleosis, are now counseling students on premarital sex and its ramifications, contraception, and abortion. Some also issue birth control prescriptions.

Several student newspapers publish blunt question and answer columns on sex, while sympathetic doctors or teachers oversee official seminars, informal dormitory bull sessions, and the publishing of student handbooks on sex and contraception.

The general sexual ignorance of today's college generation is appalling.

Teachers and doctors meeting with 18 to 21-year-olds have listened dumbfounded as college students asked such questions as:

- Can I get pregnant if I didn't have an orgasm? [Yes]
- Can a person get pregnant while standing up? [Yes]
- My mother told me an unmarried girl couldn't use Tampax. Is this true? [No]
- Can sperms live in bathtub water? [No]
- Is it true there are some days I can conceive and other days when I can't? [Yes]

"I thought they were joking at first," said one teacher. At Chapel Hill, Doctor Crist questioned 600 co-eds on their sexual habits and tested their knowledge of the pelvic anatomy. The test involved matching questions and answers. Of those who were sexually active, over a quarter could not answer any of the questions. No one got 100 percent right and only 59 percent answered half the questions correctly.

Of those girls less sexually active about 80 percent answered half the questions correctly and 9 percent scored 100. From this, Doctor Crist concluded, "The more you knew about physiology the more responsible you were."

Doctor Crist found that the girls learned about sex and their own anatomy from friends, books, and parents—in that order. Many said they learned of menstruation and sex not from parents but from books that mysteriously appeared on their beds at home one day.

Dr. Ronald J. Pion, of the University of Hawaii's School of Public Health, blames sexual ignorance on embarrassed parents who pass "their problems on to their children."

It's part of our heritage, he said, "of protecting 'childhood innocence' by keeping kids away from death, birth, and sex."

"College," adds 31-year-old Doctor Crist, "is just not the place for young people to learn where babies come from. They have more important things to do. Unfortunately, the information gap is so wide now that the college has to take some responsibility."

The result has been a rapid growth in the last few years of what are, in effect, remedial sex education courses for college students.

The publishers of *Human Sexuality*, believed to be the first college textbook on the subject, report that it is now being used by 210 colleges across the nation. It was published in 1967.

When the author, James Leslie McCary, first offered his course on human sexuality at the University of Houston in 1964, he had 185 students.

Nowadays, 1200 students pack Cullen Auditorium twice a week for a 60-minute lecture and 30-minute question and answer period.

"It's a shame," says Professor McCary, "that a semester of a college student's life is devoted to material he should have started learning in the first grade.

"But this generation of freer thinkers seems to be the one that will stop the cycle, that will quit taking the runaround and misguiding behavior of the older generation. They want to make their own decisions on what is right."

There are indications he is correct. Several studies in recent years have shown these physically mature youths tend to take a liberal attitude on premarital sexual relations.

Moral issues aside, the problem is that largely due to young people's basic ignorance of sex, contraception, and own anatomies, a number of serious social problems have emerged.

These include hundreds of thousands of illegitimate babies born each year. Nationwide, more than 300,000 are born annually, almost 250,000 of them to mothers between the age of 15 and 24. "It is good girls who get pregnant," remarked one doctor recently. "Genuinely promiscuous girls know better."

To an apparently dwindling number of its opponents, college sex education programs threaten only to compound these problems, giving immature young people just the information they need to run wild sexually.

Yet, as Professor McCary notes: "We've always had sex education in the schools, you know. It's just a matter of whether it's accurately in a class or inaccurately in the school yard."

He also points to a Yale study of unmarried pregnant girls. At the hospital where they gave birth, some of the girls got instruction in human reproduction and birth control methods; the other girls didn't. Within 12 months, researchers found, 57 percent of those who received no instruction were back at the hospital pregnant and unmarried. Of the others, only 7 percent returned in that condition.

So a number of colleges have assumed a new role—sex educator. Schools such as Michigan State, Southern Connecticut State, Yale, Brown, Mt. Holyoke, and the Universities of Chicago, Seattle, Pittsburgh, and Houston offer credit and noncredit academic courses on human sexuality.

Even where formal courses are not available, students have organized their own symposiums, typically lasting for three or four days. Students at Smith and Amherst colleges, though, jointly planned their own 10-week noncredit course last year with the help of sympathetic doctors and faculty members. It attracted 390 students—of them 310 were women.

In an attempt to broaden their basic science curriculum to cover social issues related to their future work, three medical students at the University of South Dakota last December staged a four-day seminar on sexuality, which drew crowds every session.

With $800 contributed by local doctors and $500 from the school, they rented films, bought pamphlets, and hired lecturers, who covered a range of topics from techniques of sexual intercourse, contraception, and abortion to homosexuality, population control, and the physical and psychological effects of wanted and unwanted pregnancies.

"I don't want to become a doctor just to push pills," said 23-year-old Don Rollins, one of the organizers. "I want to be in there helping with the real problems of society."

A number of student health services have also added sex education counselors and/or obstetrician-gynecologists to their staffs. At the University of Chicago, for instance, two such counselors, three doctors, and two nurses operate a clinic open to any registered student older than 18.

There, a student can obtain without cost a wide range of information on sexual matters, including advice on contraception and abortion. The director, Dr. James L. Burks, estimates that about 80 percent of those seeking sexual advice ask about contraception. And that advice, many doctors agree, must be given frankly and without moralistic lectures.

"As physicians," says Doctor Crist, "it is not our job to establish what is good and bad, but what is necessary."

And apparently more campus doctors believe it is necessary to prescribe birth control devices or pills, as is done on a limited scale at Chicago, Doctor Burks said.

A study by the American College Health Association in 1966 found that 96 percent of 323 colleges surveyed would not prescribe birth control pills for unmarried students.

According to the association, a similar survey made last year but not yet fully tabulated, is expected to reveal some significant shifts, including a large number of schools that have changed their minds.

The 12,000 students at the University of Chicago also have access to a new course titled "Human Reproduction." Far more students than are formally registered attend the three weekly class meetings. And the clinic staff is frequently asked to appear at informal evening discussions in various school dormitories.

Another interesting outgrowth of the campus sex education movement is the development of pamphlets dealing in the frankest terms with sexual questions and fears of students.

Last month students registering at the University of Rhode Island were given a pamphlet describing various methods of birth control.

Last fall a 64-page booklet titled "Sex and the Yale Student" was distributed to students at that school in New Haven, Connecticut. Although it was a student publication, Yale officials praised coverage of such topics as abortion, venereal disease, and birth control methods, and characterized the booklet as "desperately needed."

Similar pamphlets have appeared at McGill University in Montreal, Duke, Boston University, and the University of Pennsylvania. At the Universities of South Dakota and Chicago, among others, such publications are being written.

Penn's 58-page pamphlet, conservatively titled "A Guide for University of Pennsylvania Students—1970–71," is distributed by the university and was written by Dr. Elaine C. Pierson. Doctor Pierson had authored a column on the same subject in the school newspaper, *The Daily Pennsylvanian*.

The publication notes in a foreword: "Raising an unplanned child, without a father might be kind of fun for the first nine months; then children cease being toys."

It proceeds to discuss contraception methods, abortions, venereal disease, orgasms, premature ejaculation, frequent coitus, and relative size of penis and vagina. It also lists local sources for further information.

Penn also has "Talking Point," an unofficial counseling service for students by 60 volunteer medical students. That effort includes a 24-hour answering service to put worried students instantly in touch with informed peers. There is also a family planning clinic and a sex counseling center for further aid.

Probably the newest student sex handbook is "Elephants and Butterflies . . . and Contraceptives," which owes its title to an E. E. Cummings poem entitled "The Elephant and the Butterfly." The 24-page illustrated guide grew out of Doctor Crist's distress on that rainy afternoon in Chapel Hill in 1966. After the incident with the scared co-ed who had undergone a quack abortion, Doctor Crist became increasingly concerned over the students' sex problems. Word soon spread on campus that he had a sympathetic ear for student difficulties and fears.

Then he was being asked to speak to ever-larger campus gatherings, and, later, to student groups throughout the state.

"Sex to many," he says, "is a dirty three-letter word that can only be described with four-letter words. I say, yes, that's right, four-letter words like love, give, and take."

The school newspaper, *The Daily Tar Heel*, began a weekly column by Lana Starnes, a student, in collaboration with Doctor Crist, answering student queries such as "How do I know when to start taking my pills?" and "What is cunnilingus?"

"These kids are really in a sexual wilderness," Doctor Crist says. "Every day they're faced with profound changes in sexual attitudes on television, in literature, and in movies.

"Basically, they are a very honest generation. They want to bring things out in the open and talk about them. This comes as quite a shock to an older generation that has invested in a whole lot of sexual shame. But to these students, hypocrisy is a much more serious evil than being concerned with a lot of sexual morality pushed by an adult society."

Last summer with Doctor Crist's help a group of medical students went through five drafts of "Butterflies . . ." before they felt they had the right one. "We wanted the kids to carry the book out in the open and to look up their answers without fear. In short, we didn't want them to be ashamed of knowing about their own sexuality," Doctor Crist said.

Within four days after the booklet was published, all 10,000 copies were gone. And, soon after, requests for copies began pouring in from 23 states and Canada.

Dedicated to "the prevention of the tragedy of unwanted pregnancies and venereal disease," the booklet uses plain language and colored diagrams to explain the male and female anatomies. "Effective contraceptive practices are reliant upon a healthy appreciation and a solid understanding of male and female physiology," the first section notes.

Most of the booklet is devoted to discussing all means of contraception and their various effectiveness. "Let's be realistic," one paragraph states. "The inconvenience of contraception is a small price to pay to prevent the tragedy of an unwanted pregnancy."

Other sections describe the symptoms of pregnancy and venereal disease and provide names and addresses, both locally and nationally, for help.

Doctor Crist, in a note in the booklet, explains that "It was written not to promote promiscuity, but in recognition of the fact that many young people are in fact risking pregnancy, and in hopes of increasing their individual and social responsibility."

The same theme runs through a new course, "Topics of Human Sexuality," which Doctor Crist and six other doctors and a retired state legislator began at the University of North Carolina this term. Originally, the class was designed for 30, but the demand pushed it up to 200. And another 400 students were turned away, although many kept telephoning Doctor Crist at all hours of the day and night, seeking a place in the class.

"We're really just at the very beginning of this revolution," says the young doctor, although, he adds, at least the university no longer expels an unmarried girl who is found to be pregnant.

"We've got to teach these young people to understand the functions of normal, healthy human bodies, to regard sex as more than a physical thing, to get them to quit thinking that using a contraceptive is unromantic, to learn of the meaningful relationships that can come from human sex and the responsibilities that go with it, and so much more," he said.

Higher education, he maintains, must take seriously this very important part of education that will equip the whole man and woman for his and her responsible participation in society.

Other educators agree, but say that the colleges alone cannot shoulder the entire responsibility, especially since an estimated 40 percent of the co-eds have had intercourse before they enter college. Basic, healthful sex education should begin when elementary school does, they say, if not before.

The University of Hawaii's Doctor Pion suggests, for example, that a few minutes a day on the popular television show for preschoolers, "Sesame Street," be devoted to introducing the very basic concepts of medicine and health.

"Just like arithmetic progresses to calculus," he said, "family education can begin with the simplest forms in kindergarten and follow a sequential development."

This, he and others argue, would enable colleges eventually to shift their role from the remedial to what they regard as higher education's proper role in the area—the advanced study of the more profound and meaningful aspects of human relationships.

Meanwhile, however, at least some progress has been made. In Houston, Professor McCary recently said, "I don't think my class will necessarily help my students today. But it will make a difference to their children."

THE USE OF SEX IN HUMAN LIFE

A Dialogue between Albert Ellis and David Mace

D.M. *The subject we are to discuss is sex.*

Isadore Rubin, with shrewd insight, has examined my sexual philosophy as it is revealed in various writings, and has called me an "enlightened ascetic." One of my friends tried to commiserate with me about this label; but I hastened to reply, "No, no. Isadore is quite right. I accept the description."

"Asceticism" is, of course, a bad word in our present hedonistic culture. And since this makes me something of an anachronism, I must explain myself. It goes back to my religious philosophy. I believe the true goal of life is the upward struggle, the relentless pursuit of our aspirations. Hedonism, the quest of pleasure for its own sake, would be for me a self-defeating goal. So for me, sex, as a source of sensual pleasure, must always take a secondary place. Secondary to what? To the development, in the fullest possible range of depth and breadth, of a creative relationship with a person of the opposite sex. I do not see sex and love as the same thing. They can even be opposites. I see the development of the capacity to love as the only worthwhile goal in life. Sexual needs can contribute enormously to the achievement of this goal. They can also contribute enormously to making it unattainable. So for me, sex must be offered up, dedicated if you like, on the altar of love. This means that the first human task in dealing with sex is to make it an obedient servant and not to let it become a tyrannical master. The second task is to channel its vast creative energy so that it becomes a source of enrichment to the personalities of the partners and to their relationship.

This view of sex is not just a theory. I have tried to put it into practice; and the result, for me, has been highly gratifying. This puts me broadly in favour of the conventional pattern of sex morality; though not necessarily for the conventional reasons. I suppose I could easily be viewed (and by some people I probably am viewed) as the complete, dumb conformist . . . a slave to tradition. Yet I don't happen to have been much of a conformist in other areas. I have been a restless wanderer on the face of the earth. I have changed my profession several times. I have changed my views and opinions drastically on a multitude of questions. Yet I have remained a convinced advocate of permanent, exclusive, monogamous marriage! How can I do other than be in favour of it, when it has brought me such profound and lasting satisfaction? So my philosophy of sex, and my experience of life, go along together. They are in complete accord.

A.E. David calls himself an enlightened ascetic and says that he is opposed to hedonism. What he actually seems to mean is that he is a long-range rather than a short-range hedonist; that is, one who goes for pleasures, enjoyment, and happiness, but who is willing to forego many present pleasures, such as momentary sex sensations, for certain future or greater gains, such as love, or absorption in some vital interest. I quite go along with this view and have heartily espoused it in my writings on rational-emotive psycho-therapy. Rational therapy, in fact, stems philosophically largely from some of the views of Epictetus, who was a famous Stoic; and it teaches that we must often tolerate frustrations and annoyances in order to achieve fewer irritations and greater pleasures in the future.

I, too, have often sacrificed sensual and sexual pleasures for love; including love of my work and some of the sexual and therapeutic ideals to which I am devoted. Ironically enough, as I have often pointed out to my friends, the more I write about sex and defend sexual liberty, the less time do I have available to take advantage of some of the luscious sexual opportunities that come my way. That is too bad; but just as David sees the development of the capacity to love as the only worthwhile goal in life, I see the devotion to a larger and more enduring cause as more valuable to me than promiscuous and unfortunately time-consuming copulation.

Where I seriously part company with many other Stoics, though not necessarily with David, is in my belief that others need not be as long-range hedonistic as I am, and that they have a perfect right to go for any kind of immediate, highly hedonistic goal they prefer; whether it be sex, drinking, smoking, or any of the other so-called vices. Nor do I think that marital love, for all its satisfactions, is the greatest possible thing for all people at all times. Whatever my own sex-love life may be, therefore, I strongly espouse and vigorously fight for the expression, on the part of the millions of individuals who inhabit this earth, of their *particular* sexual bents . . . as long as they do not needlessly harm or exert coercive pressure on others in the process. I feel, in other words, that David and his wife Vera's personal achievement of a fine, monogamous relationship is great for them, and that it probably more than compensates them for any sacrificing of immediate sexual pleasures that they may well have made in the course of achieving *their* kind of a relationship. But I am most sceptical that this kind of love-oriented monogamy is best for all the many kinds of humans who inhabit the earth; and I am rather sure that it would actually be anathema to many of them.

Consequently, I fight for a general sexual freedom or permissiveness that would allow David and Vera to be the way they are, that would allow me to be the kind of long-range hedonist that I am . . . and that would also permit the rest of humanity to be, sexually and amatively, pretty much the way it is or would like to be. Even if people pick what is indubitably the wrong mode of sex or love relationship, and thereby defeat their own ends, I think that they have an inalienable right to be wrong *and that they should never be condemned for being so.*

D.M. Now let me, against the background of my personal philosophy, try to indicate how I see what is happening to sex in our contemporary world. This discussion we are having today is part of an "agonizing reappraisal" that is going on in human culture today, as a result of the vast changes that are taking place in our world.

In the course of this upheaval, the conventional pattern of sex morality has been taking a beating. As an advocate of that pattern, I ought to be feeling pretty glum. But I don't feel that way at all; because, although I still find the conventional morality worth defending, I altogether deplore the way it has been imposed on people in the past. I have no wish to impose my views on others. I hate fanatical dogmatism . . . not just because it is unpleasant, but because it is totally ineffective. I insist on my right to commend to others what I believe to be the best way to use sex. But I equally insist on your right to commend to others what you believe.

I realize that for long centuries my philosophy of sex . . . often, alas, in distorted forms that I would repudiate . . . was the only one that got a hearing. You know well, Albert, that if you had lived a few hundred years ago, and spoken your mind as freely as you do today, you would be pining in some dark, dismal dungeon! Instead of that, you're on the crest of the wave. Everyone wants to hear your daring, avant-garde philosophy. Nobody wants to listen to me, because what I have to say is considered to be "old hat"! Does this enrage me? Not at all. I count it real progress that the world has become an open forum on this question and other questions.

I think what we are doing in the world today is to look for criteria that we can agree on . . . criteria that will enable us to judge when sex is being ethically used. I have worked out some criteria which seem to me to be valid, and I'd like to put them along-side any that you have, to see how far we can agree.

My first principle is that sex should not be used as a means of exploiting another person. I'm pretty sure you would accept this; although we'd probably disagree about just what exploitation means in a variety of human situations. My second criterion is that any pattern of sex behavior, if practiced universally, should be good for children. This may seem an unexpected approach. But I argue that, since the primary biological purpose of sex is to produce children, no use of sex in human relationships can be valid that makes it thwart the implications of its biological ends. So I believe that, so long as marriage and the family provide the best setting for child development, the use of sex in ways that threaten the effective functioning of the family becomes unethical.

A third criterion, which many people would put first, is that any use of sex should contribute to, and not hinder, the highest development of the person concerned. I would put it last because I think it is really subsumed within the other two.

A.E. I certainly would agree, first, that sex should not be used as a means of exploiting another person. And I also agree with your third point; namely that any use of sex should contribute to, and not hinder, the highest development of the person concerned. I paraphrase these two points in my own words in my book, "Sex Without Guilt": "Every human being should certainly refrain from sex participations which needlessly, forcefully, or unfairly harm others. And each of us, if we are to remain rational and non-neurotic, should cease and desist from all sex behavior which is clearly self-defeating."

On your point about the necessity that any pattern of sex behavior, if practiced universally, must be good for children, I agree less completely. I do not think that the primary biological purpose of sex is to produce children, but to produce physical pleasure which may or may not lead to procreation. Today, especially, we know perfectly well how to have this pleasure without its usually resulting in offspring; and sex and procreation are becoming increasingly separated. This is all to the good, since there is no reason why the two must be related, just because they unfortunately have been in the past. Although, therefore, I would agree that sex should not be used against children (as, for example, when a husband and wife engage so intensively in either monogamous or non-monogamous sex relations that they actually neglect the welfare of their offspring), I think that sex and childraising can be today, and largely should be, kept pretty much apart. This is one case where biology has, fortunately, been pre-empted by technology.

I also doubt very much whether marriage and the family, as we today know these institutions, do provide the best setting for child development; and in many ways I think they probably provide the worst child-rearing milieu. Eventually, I suspect that we shall have much more effective methods than this one. While, however, family rearing prevails, I would agree that sexual patterns of behavior should preferably be arranged so that they will minimally disrupt child-raising activities. With a little imaginative planning, this can easily be done, whether sex is participated in on a monogamous or a non-monogamous basis.

D.M. I think we should get down to cases. Let's start with the simplest and least complicated form of sexual activity, masturbation. I think I know your view about this . . . you not only accept it, but positively give it your blessing.

As it happens, I am in substantial agreement with you on this subject. And since this may seem to be inconsistent with my religious position, I ought to offer a word of explanation.

Religious people have gone through agonies of guilt about masturbation. In my view their guilt feelings have had little sound foundation. They have been rooted in two ideas, both of which I reject. The first is the Jewish idea that the waste of semen is a great evil. This was based on the mistaken view that the male ejaculate was a po-

tential human life . . . the substance out of which a child could grow. To waste this was, therefore, to destroy a potential life . . . something very close to procuring an abortion. Of course, now that we know that a prodigal waste of reproductive material takes place anyway, this argument collapses.

The other idea is the Catholic one that concupiscence, or sexual desire, is of itself evil. I know this is an oversimplification, but it's near enough to the truth. And it is a view that is being more and more rejected by enlightened religious people today.

So I see no ethical wrong in masturbation. It is, of course, an incomplete sexual experience; and it is often used, ineffectively, in an attempt to escape from non-sexual conflicts. But for the most of us, at one time or another in life, it provides a useful safety-valve that relieves biological tension where no other means of sexual fulfillment are ethically available. I shudder to think of the sexual exploitation that might occur, both in and out of marriage, if masturbation were not available as a harmless means of relief.

A.E. I am happy to hear that David is taking such an enlightened view on masturbation, and cannot conceive of any sane and educated person taking a radically different view today. As he has noted, my position for the last 20 years has been that masturbation is not only unharmful but is actually a good thing, particularly in view of the fact that other sex outlets are still highly limited in our culture and that therefore, many of us would have to be entirely abstinent for long periods of our lives if we did not resort to auto-erotic practices. As I note in the latest edition of my book, "The Art and Science of Love": "The fact is that the vast majority of Americans engage in a considerable amount of masturbation for some period during their lives. In view of our other restrictions on sexual activity, they would be abnormal if they did not."

D.M. Suppose we now turn to homosexuality. Here I think the attitudes codified in our laws have been severe to the point of brutality.

In counseling with homosexuals, I have been made vividly aware of their predicament, and I have felt deep compassion for many of them. I am inclined to take the view that is rapidly gaining ground today, that private homosexual acts between consenting adults should be outside the concern of the community. Where there is exploitation of minors, I would treat homosexuality on the same basis as heterosexual exploitation.

A.E. I am entirely in agreement with David that private homosexual acts between consenting adults should be outside the concern of the community. My own widespread contacts with homosexuals, many of whom I see as patients and others of whom I know socially, has convinced me that fixed or exclusive deviants are almost invariably severely disturbed individuals . . . not because they engage in homoerotic acts, but because they are incapable of also enjoying heterosexuality. Nonetheless, however neurotic or psychotic these people may be, they should be treated with compassion, and should not be castigated or persecuted for being disturbed.

D.M. And now it's surely time we got to heterosexuality, which happily is the condition of the overwhelming majority of us! For me, the focus obviously is on marriage as the relationship in which the sex relationship between a man and a woman comes to full flower, with all its rich overtones. I have devoted most of my life to efforts to increase the number of successful marriages in the world. I, therefore, tend to see all heterosexual relationships against the background of marriage.

I favor premarital chastity . . . not as a standard ruthlessly imposed on young people, as in the past; but as a freely accepted act of self-discipline. I have elaborated my views on this subject in the "Encyclopaedia of Sexual Behavior," which Albert Ellis edited. However, I am well aware that the chances that this pattern will be freely accepted by many young people in our modern world, now or in the future, are not promising. It has been said that the point of suspense in the modern novel is no longer focussed on whether she will or she won't, but on whether he can or he can't!

I do not sit in judgment on those who choose a pattern other than the one I commend. But I have not yet been persuaded that I am wrong in holding to this ideal; and I shall continue to do so, even if I find myself in a tiny minority, until otherwise convinced.

Of course, I expect you to be in complete disagreement with me on this point.

A.E. Yes, you are quite right about my disagreeing with you in regard to premarital chastity. I have stated for years, and still vehemently hold, that premarital heterosexual relations are good, damn good, and that they should be encouraged rather than discouraged. They are a natural prelude to marriage; enhance sex competence and confidence, provide adventure; lead to more loving relationships; permit harmless variety and pleasure. Neither in our own society nor in many other world cultures are they incompatible with good marriage; and my own view is that they increase rather than decrease the chances of a subsequent fine marital involvement. They are only dangerous when engaged in by individuals who are too immature or unwise; and even these kinds of persons can usually harmlessly benefit by restricting their premarital relations to petting to orgasm instead of to penile–vaginal intercourse. Although I fully agree with David on the values of self-discipline, I see little value to arbitrary or needless restraint, such as that entailed in maintaining premarital chastity. Among enlightened and educated young people today, I would call the preservation of virginity before marriage an overt display of arrant masochism.

D.M. Needless to say, my philosophy of sex included also a belief in marital fidelity as the desired pattern of behavior. Are we also in total disagreement on this question?

A.E. My view on marital infidelity has long been that for the average married couple it is impractical, in that it tends to result in more harm than good. Since few couples today can take the insecurity and jealousy that accompany adultery, and it is, therefore, practiced in a surreptitious, trust-destroying manner it is inimical to marriage. I recently, however, have run across many couples who are quite comfortable when they honestly and openly engage in mate-swapping or other forms of what I call civilized adultery. For these individuals, I see no reason why they cannot beneficially engage in marital infidelity; and as far as I can tell, in many instances (though of course not in all), their marriages are actually improved thereby. Although David's concept of marriage may indeed be ideal for him and millions of others in today's world, there is no reason to believe that it is ideal for all, or that we shall not evolve better forms of marriage in the future that will encompass radically different views of adultery than are comfortably included under our existing marital concepts.

D.M. To sum up, I would like to give you my view of what is going to happen about sex in our culture. I believe we shall see a more and more widespread acceptance of a state of affairs that has always in fact existed, despite every attempt to control people's sexual behaviour. Society will become a three-layered cake. First, there will be a group of people who will practice sexual freedom completely, and will choose not to marry at all. They will be allowed to do so, with appropriate safeguards against exploitation. Second, there will be a group that will choose marriage, with some degree of sexual freedom before and during it. Some of them may in a life-time have several marriages. Third, there will be a group who will adhere to the traditional ideal and will choose life-long monogamy, preceded in at least some cases by premarital chastity.

These three patterns will, I think, settle down to a flexible co-existence in our society, and will achieve their own pattern of equilibrium. This will give us all an opportunity to see the various patterns at work, unimpeded by harsh judgments and acrimonious controversy. In that kind of atmosphere, I believe that what is best will have a chance to justify itself. "By their fruits ye shall know them."

A.E. I heartily agree that the future of sex in our culture, as in most other cultures of the world, will tend to be much less monolithic and more pluralistic than it has been, or at least has theo-retically been, up to the present time. The three patterns of sex behavior that David outlines will in all probability exist coexterminously; and perhaps a few additional major patterns as well. I have no doubt that lifelong monogamy will be one of the main modes of sexuality for a good many decades to come; but I think that it will be increasingly preceded by premarital varietism. I also believe that marital infidelity, with the full consent of both parties, will probably increase significantly.

I finally agree entirely with David Mace that a flexible co-existence in our society of several different patterns of sex-marital behavior will be a good thing, as long as we view them objectively and dispassionately. Perhaps this kind of experiment will show, as David implies that it will, which system of behavior is, in the long run, best. Or perhaps it will show, as I think it will, that no one pattern of sexuality is utterly good for all people at all times, and that the first principle of human physiology and psychology—namely, the fact that we are all individually different as well as in some respects similar—should light the way to our sexual, as well as to most of our non-sexual, pathways.

PART III

Feeling: Problem Emotions

Humans are emotional beings. We feel love and hate. We feel delight and sorrow. We feel shame, guilt, and pride. We feel anger, rage, and jealousy. Sometimes we even feel calm and at peace.

Emotion can be defined as a feeling state of the individual that stems from and influences his behavior. Our behavior affects our feelings. When our goal-seeking behavior is going well, our emotional tone is generally positive; we are in good spirits and may feel cheerful or elated. When goals are blocked and needs go unmet, our tone is negative, and we may feel angry or depressed.

Our behavior affects our feelings, and our feelings affect our behavior. Research has shown that when we are happy, we tend to be more generous and benevolent. When we are angry, we may be tempted to strike out, and when we are fearful, we may tend to withdraw. When we are very relaxed or content or sometimes when we are very anxious or depressed, we may be nearly immobilized, and it may be difficult for anyone to get us to do anything.

Strong and persistent emotions can make us ill. We may refer to a trying situation as "sickening" and mean this both in a figurative sense and literally. In strong feeling states the body is mobilized for action and changes take place in the internal organs. With unremitting mobilization certain physiological dysfunctions or psychosomatic illnesses may occur.

Emotions can make us ill, but emotions can also make or keep us well. In recent years psychotherapists have increasingly encouraged their clients to reveal and express their emotions. Some therapists teach relaxation and tranquil feeling states to counteract fear and tension. Still others encourage persons to focus on, augment, and make the most of their peak experiences—those high but transient states of happiness we all have upon occasion.

Many different states of emotion have been described by psychologists, writers, poets, and others who have been interested in human feelings. Interestingly, surveys of textbooks and professional journals indicate that psychologists have for many years been preoccupied with the study of unpleasant emotions. By contrast, a survey of literary sources shows a greater emphasis on pleasant states of feeling.

In Part III of the book, the focus will be on two exceedingly important emotions: happiness and anxiety. Happiness has been subjected to little scientific study until recently. For example, many psychology textbooks do not index a single listing for happiness. Yet the pursuit of happiness has been a persistent quest even though not everyone agrees that happiness is a very worthy or even an achievable emotion. How important is happiness? What causes it? How may it be enhanced? These are some of the questions the readings on this topic raise and attempt to answer.

Anxiety, by contrast, has been one of the most studied of all emotions by psychologists. Our times have been lamented as the "age of anxiety," but not everyone agrees that we human beings are too anxious. It has been pointed out, for example, that our society requires anxiety to make it work just as each individual requires a certain amount to act as a signal, rouser, and moving force. Anxiety can be either a positive or a negative force in our life. The readings on anxiety have been chosen to highlight both the positive and the negative aspects of anxiety and to show how we can make a start toward accepting the positive and minimizing the negative.

TOPIC 7

Happiness

We hold these truths to be self-evident, that all men are created equal, that they are endowed by their Creator with certain unalienable Rights, that among these are Life, Liberty and the pursuit of Happiness.

—from the Declaration of Independence

In the Declaration of Independence the founding fathers of this country proclaimed our right to pursue happiness, and it is this pursuit that is one of the most important human quests or goals. Whether it is possible to obtain happiness by pursuing it is quite another matter. There is an old saying that goes, "Those who search for happiness never find it." And in describing happiness, Philosopher Alan Watts wrote, "Like your shadow, the more you chase it, the more it runs away." However, some workers concerned with human potentiality believe we can increase happiness by specifically attending and learning to elaborate our peak moments.

Whether one can find happiness by pursuing it is an open question. But certainly it is impossible to understand happiness without studying it, and American psychologists and other social scientists have not been very occupied with the latter pursuit. Lin Yutang, a Chinese philosopher who gave happiness considerable thought (he wrote that for him happiness was largely a matter of digestion), called this "the West's most studiously avoided subject."

One reason for the nonpursuit of happiness—by psychologists at least —is this subject has not been considered within their realm of endeavors. Over the years the question of happiness has been approached as an ethical problem (Is happiness a worthy goal?), a theological problem (Should happiness be sought here and now or ensured in the world to come?), or a political problem (Can the happiness of the individual be subordinated to the general good?). But only recently has happiness come to be considered a suitable subject for psychological study.

A second reason for the lag in the study of happiness is that clinical attention has been preempted by the more compelling negative affects such as depression, anxiety, and fear. Happy people don't call attention to themselves or seek help. Unhappy people do, and they fill the offices, schedules, thoughts, and writings of psychiatrists, psychoanalysts, psychologists, social workers, counselors, and other professionals in this area.

A third reason for the scientific neglect of this subject concerns the difficulties researchers have found in dealing with happiness and other emotions both theoretically and in the laboratory. Happiness is conceptually complex and does not lend itself well to study under controlled conditions. In the name of science, investigators have been almost fiendishly ingenious about producing anxiety in research subjects. However, positive affects and mind states have received little laboratory attention until recently.

An introduction to happiness

In the first article Abe Arkoff reports on the state of happiness. Although most of us are busily occupied in the pursuit of happiness, not all philosophers or scientists agree that this is a worthy, important, or even achievable emotion. Even so, when people are surveyed the great majority are—or at least report themselves to be—reasonably happy. Some things which have been found to be positively associated with happiness are wealth, health, education, social involvement, and personal competence. People who are happy in marriage and vocation appear to be particularly high in general satisfaction or contentment.

An introduction to superhappiness

In the second reading, Abraham H. Maslow calls attention to moments of awesome or intense happiness, which he labels "peak experiences," and explains what he has learned about them. For one thing, such peaks are natural—not supernatural—experiences, and they are common in all kinds of persons from the most actualized to those who are quite ill. Peaks are precipitated by many things, some of which are quite mundane, but individuals' subjective experiences tend to be quite similar. One must be open to such experiences, but some of us are not and instead work against them because we fear emotion or the loss of control. Maslow notes that peaks can be highly therapeutic and can even change our life.

An introduction to a happy man

In the last selection, David F. Ricks and Alden E. Wessman present the case of "Winn," who was the happiest of twenty men involved in their study of personality and mood. The roots of Winn's happiness were his warm and supportive family, his fortunate intellectual and physical endowments, and his successful experiences and relationships. Winn's one apparent flaw was that he was seemingly overcontrolled and oversocialized. This raised the intriguing possibility that the processes of civilization—which are held by some to be the source of human discontent—may make a considerable contribution to personal happiness.

FOR PERSONAL APPLICATION

1. How happy are you? Very happy? Rather happy? Or not too happy? What accounts for your general level of happiness or unhappiness?
2. Compare your present general level of happiness with the levels that were characteristic of your earlier stages of life and the levels you anticipate in the stages to come. (If it would be helpful for illustrative purposes, draw a graph showing your levels of happiness, realized or anticipated, during the various stages or periods of your life: early childhood, middle childhood, later childhood, adolescence, early adulthood, middle adulthood, later adulthood, or use a broader, narrower, or different classification that fits your own case.)
3. How variable is your happiness? Discuss and account for your changes in mood over the past several weeks or months.
4. Discuss a recent "peak experience" you had.
5. Discuss a recent "nadir experience" you had.
6. Are you considerably occupied or preoccupied with the pursuit of happiness? Why or why not?
7. Do you consider happiness an important, possible, or worthy goal? Why or why not?
8. Describe the happiest or unhappiest person you know. What appears to account for this person's happiness or unhappiness?
9. Do you interpret the socialization processes you have experienced as maximizing, minimizing, or as having little effect on your potential for happiness? Discuss your answer.
10. Write down a discussion item (not given above) that seems particularly relevant to this topic and you, and discuss it.

FOR SMALL GROUPS

1. *Sharing peak stimuli.* Some of our peak or minipeak experiences occur in connection with certain things that make a strong appeal to our senses. Possible examples are the sight of an orchid or a Van Gogh, the taste of chocolate or licorice, the smell of mint or lavender, the touch of velvet or satin, the sound of a favorite singer or band, or our inner response during a moment of meditation or relaxation. Each member brings or conveys to the group something that elevates his own moods. The group is encouraged to feel or empathize with the person in his experience. (Specifically prohibited are all stimuli and activities that are illegal or that are likely to result in loss of employment or other nadir experiences for the instructor.)

2. *Sharing peaks and nadirs.* Each member keeps a log or diary of peak and nadir experiences for a one-week period (the week before happiness is discussed in the group). When the group meets, the members share these experiences and discuss their overall meaning.
3. *Sharing peak ages and stages.* Certain periods of our life may be traumatic and have far-reaching effects, and certain periods may be particularly happy and important to us in this respect. Each member shares the recollection of a period of his life that was particularly happy and discusses the meaning this period had for his overall development.
4. *Maximizing group happiness.* Each member tells the others what aspects of the group make him happy and also what aspects of the group make him unhappy. Afterwards the group considers ways in which it can maximize the happiness and minimize the unhappiness of its members.

FOR FURTHER READING

Bradburn, N. M. *The Structure of Psychological Well-being.* Chicago: Aldine, 1969.

Jones, H. M. *The Pursuit of Happiness.* Cambridge, Mass.: Harvard University Press, 1953.

Lowen, A. *Pleasure.* New York: Coward-McCann, 1970.

Russell, B. *The Conquest of Happiness.* New York: Liveright, 1930.

Schutz, W. C. *Joy.* New York: Grove Press, 1967.

Watts, A. W. *The Meaning of Happiness* (Perennial Library ed.). New York: Harper & Row, Publishers, 1970.

Wessman, A. E., and D. F. Ricks. *Mood and Personality.* New York: Holt, Rinehart & Winston, Inc., 1966.

THE STATE OF HAPPINESS*

Abe Arkoff

Happiness is a warm puppy.
　　　　　　　—Charles M. Schulz

Happiness is a stock that doubles in a year.
　　　　　　　—Ira U. Cobleigh

Happiness is an imaginary condition, formerly often attributed by the living to the dead, now usually attributed by adults to children, and by children to adults.

　　　　　　　—Thomas S. Szasz

THE MEANING OF HAPPINESS

What is happiness? There are many definitions of happiness and each of us may have our own. There are even some definitions of what happiness is not. For example, Archbishop Whately once remarked that happiness was no laughing matter.

Although the Declaration of Independence proclaims our right to pursue happiness, it has no glossary of terms, and Noah Webster didn't produce his dictionary until 30 years later. However,

* The author deeply appreciates the help of his colleagues Samuel I. Shapiro, Bruce M. Stillians, and Herbert B. Weaver on this paper.

the most recently revised form of his work, *Webster's Third International Dictionary,* defines happiness as "a state of well-being characterized by relative permanence, by dominantly agreeable emotion ranging in value from mere contentment to deep and intense joy in living and by a natural desire for its continuation." *The Random House Dictionary of the English Language* defines happiness more simply as "good fortune; pleasure; contentment; joy."

How do we define or describe our own happiness? Psychologist Joel R. Davitz (1970), who was interested in devising a dictionary and grammar of emotions, asked his psychology colleagues what they meant when they described themselves as happy or as in any other emotional state. Davitz eventually abandoned this approach as unprofitable. He writes, "Apparently a psychologist talking to another psychologist about his emotions is not a situation likely to elicit clarity of communication, and I found myself even more confused by my sampling of current jargon of American psychology."

A persistent man and no snob, Davitz then began to talk to nonpsychologists, whereupon he notes, "The conversations changed dramatically. For the most part, people were quite clear about what they meant by various emotional labels, and while they did not always communicate with the verbal grace and precision of my fellow psychologists, they frequently gave rather rich and dramatic definitions of the emotional words they used" (p. 251). Examples of the ways these nonlexicographers and nonpsychologists define their own happiness can be seen in Table 1.

TABLE 1

How do people describe their own happiness? Joel R. Davitz, a psychologist interested in devising a dictionary and grammar of emotion, gathered together some of the ways:

"There is an inner warm glow, a radiant sensation; I feel like smiling; there is a sense of well being, a sense of harmony and peace within, everything is going right for me; I'm optimistic and cheerful; the world seems basically good and beautiful; men are essentially kind; life is worth living; there is a renewed appreciation of life; I'm optimistic about the future; the future seems bright; I'm loose,

---

relaxed, in tune with the world; there's a feeling of warmth all over; I think about beautiful things; I feel safe and secure, I'm at peace with the world; there is a mellow comfort, a sense of being very integrated and at ease with myself, in harmony with myself; there is a sense of fullness, a sense of smiling at myself; I am free of conflict; there is a sense of 'rightness' with oneself and the world; nothing can go wrong; my movements are graceful and easy, I feel especially well coordinated; there is a general release, a lessening of tension, I am peaceful, tranquil, quiet, completely free from worry; I am really functioning as a unit."

"There is a sense of being more alive, I am excited in a calm way; there is an inner buoyancy, a warm excitement, a sense of vitality, aliveness, vibrancy, an extra spurt of energy or drive, a special lift in everything I do and say; I feel bouncy, springy, effervescent, bubbly, wide awake, with a sense of lightness, buoyancy and upsurge of the body, more alert; there is a particularly acute awareness of pleasurable things, their sounds, their colors, and textures—everything seems more beautiful, natural, and desirable; there is an intense awareness of everything; I seem to experience things with greater clarity; colors seem brighter, sounds clearer, movements more vivid; I seem to be immediately in touch with the world; a sense of being very open, receptive, with no separation between me and the world; a sense that I'm experiencing everything fully, completely, thoroughly; that I'm feeling all the way, all my senses seem to be completely open; there is a strong sense of interest and involvement in things around me."

"I keep thinking how lucky I am; I have a sense of sureness, I feel strong inside, taller, stronger, bigger; there is a sense of being important and worthwhile, a sense of more confidence in myself; a feeling that I can do anything; I feel clean, as if I look especially good; there is a sense of being more substantial, of existing, of being real."

"I feel outgoing, I want to make others happy; there is an intense, positive relationship with another person or with other people; a communion, a unity, a closeness, friendliness and freedom, mutual respect and interdependence; I want others (or the other person) to feel the same as I do; there is a sense of trust and appreciation of another person; a sense of loving everyone, everything."

"I seem to nurture the feeling within myself; I want the feeling to continue, to keep going; I feel like singing, like laughing; there is a sense of accomplishment, fulfillment; there is an excitement, a sense of being keyed up, overstimulated, supercharged."

"It's a very personal feeling; a simple, pure feeling; it's more an 'inner' than an 'outer' feeling; the feeling flows from the inside outwards; the feeling seems to be all over, nowhere special, just not localized" (1970, pp. 254–255).

THE IMPORTANCE OF HAPPINESS

Is happiness important? This question may seem like a needless one since so many of us are committed to its pursuit. Happiness achieved a rank of fifth in a list of 18 values or end-goals that were appraised for importance by a national cross-section of adult Americans in 1968 (Rokeach, 1973). However, in a similar appraisal with midwestern college students as subjects, happiness was found to rank second (Rokeach, 1973), and students from three community colleges in California ranked happiness first (Brawer, 1971). "Becoming happy and content" was also among the highest rated life goals in a nationwide survey of freshmen some years ago (Richards, 1966).

Happiness or elation was found to be a key emotion by Wessman and Ricks (1966), who studied mood and personality in college men and women at Harvard and Radcliffe, respectively. These investigators analyzed daily mood records of elation versus depression and 15 other affects such as energy versus fatigue, tranquility versus anxiety, and harmony versus anger (see Table 2). A close relationship was found between relative standing on elation versus depression and almost all the other scales. "Thus," they write, "if a subject was generally elated he tended to stand toward the positive end on most of the other affects measured. Overall comparison of individuals on their relative level on elation-depression would, then, give general indication of the general 'goodness' or 'badness' of their moods" (p. 244).

Is happiness important? Although a strong case can be made for the affirmative side of this question, many vigorous (although perhaps unhappy) individuals would vigorously disagree. Some feel that happiness is a trifling and insignificant emotion, others that it is unworthy, and still others that its pursuit may be incompatible with the attainment of more meritorious goals.

Political scientist John H. Schaar, critic George Jean Nathan, and physicist Albert Einstein are representative of those who have taken a dim view of happiness. In an essay on happiness, Schaar observes that happiness may be a goal "unworthy of a great nation or a great man." Some supportive testimony is provided by Nathan, who held that "no happy man ever produced a first rate piece of painting, sculpture, music, or literature." And Einstein seemingly dismissed the whole subject when he wrote, "Well-being and happiness are such trivial goals in life that I can imagine them being entertained only by pigs."

Schaar's essay (1970) is thoughtful and compelling. He notes that the persons we admire most are not the happiest ones. "Admirable men have sought nobility, or beauty, or magnanimity, or purity of heart—all treasures of the spirit, and not conditions of the external world." He adds that many of the things we do are not to make our lives happy but rather, to make them "worthwhile, demanding, difficult, challenging, even painful. Willingness to sacrifice happiness and pleasure for other things seems at least as basic to human life as happiness (pp. 25–26)."

Many of us have a certain ambivalence toward happiness and pleasure. Happiness can make us feel guilty if we think we are unworthy and don't deserve it. Some equate pleasure with sin or consider it to be a temptation to abandon duty and obligation. The great lawyer and lecturer Clarence Darrow wrote, "If a man is happy in America, it is considered that he is doing something wrong."

Is there some happy compromise concerning the importance or value of happiness? Wessman and Ricks arrive at what appears to be an appropriate perspective when, in reviewing their research, they write, "We think it desirable that people be happy—we hold happiness generally superior to misery. But happiness is not everything. We found much to admire and respect in the lives of some of our emotionally complicated and less happy men. In short, while we do not depreciate—and in fact rather admire—happiness in many of its features, we also hold that it is not the sole criterion for judging the worth of human life" (pp. 248–249).

THE POSSIBILITY OF HAPPINESS

Is it possible to achieve happiness? Some philosophers have concluded that unhappiness is the natural state of man. Nietzsche wrote, "I fear we are not born to be happy." In the same vein, but with a lighter spirit, psychoanalyst Thomas S. Szasz aphorized, "Happiness is an imaginary condition, formerly often attributed by the living to the dead, now usually attributed by adults to children, and by children to adults."

In his essay on happiness Schaar (1970) arrives at the thought that "it is man's lot to be always a beggar at the gates of the kingdom of happiness, and that he is in the greatest danger when he thinks he has found the key to the gate." Schaar concludes that a "temporary and qualified unhappiness" is the most we can achieve in this indifferent world. The same conclusion was reached by George Bernard Shaw, and he was immensely relieved by it. He wrote, "A lifetime of happiness! No man alive could bear it; it would be hell on earth."

A number of psychologists have cautioned us not to seek—as some of us apparently do—perfect happiness or almost perfect happiness. Ellis and Harper (1961) write, "Anyone who tries to give you a rule by which you can always be happy is either a fool or a knave." Robert Peck (1959) studied a group of fairly typical adults and concluded that for most people life is never "brilliantly happy." He writes, "Unalloyed joy is an unknown or forgotten sensation." The most we can ask for is "good health, mental and physical, with which to meet each day."

By contrast, voices mostly within humanistic psychology and especially in the human growth or human potential movement have been raised to affirm the individual's great capacity for happiness. Herbert A. Otto (1970) writes, "Perhaps the natural state of the human organism is one of joyful communion with others, with itself, and with the universe." Other representatives of this more optimistic group include William C. Schutz (1967) and Alexander Lowen (1970); their respective (and aptly titled) books *Joy* and *Pleasure* present their prescriptions for maximizing happiness and well-being, mostly through awakening and enlivening the body.

Abraham Maslow (1962, 1971) was one of the chief optimists concerning the possibility of happiness. He lamented psychologists' obsession with negative emotions and pointed out that there are more moments of happiness in our lives than we generally acknowledge. Maslow held that we can come to know the conditions that make these "little moments of ecstasy" or "peak experiences" happen and then facilitate these conditions to make for greater happiness.

THE ASSESSMENT OF HAPPINESS

How can happiness be assessed? One of the pioneer measures of happiness was called the *Euphorimeter,* which calls to mind an interesting gadget of some kind (possibly to be hooked up to the funny bone). However, the Euphorimeter was merely a psychometrically unsophisticated questionnaire that was little used.

Two major measures of happiness that are employed in current research are mood scales and questionnaire items. Mood scales have been used to gauge fluctuations in happiness or elation and other affects. Through averaging, data from such scales can also provide global or general estimates of happiness. An example of this kind of instrument is the elation versus depression scale presented in Table 2, above.

Questionnaire items have been used to appraise happiness in a number of national surveys. These items are relatively simple measures that may be worded to provide general assessments of happiness as well as estimates of mood variability. A general item used in one set of surveys (Bradburn, 1969; Bradburn and Caplovitz, 1965) was: "Taken all together, how would you say things are these days—would you say that you are *very happy, pretty happy,* or *not too happy?*"

In the same set of surveys a measure of mood variability was constructed by having respondents indicate their positive and negative affect experiences during the several weeks preceding the interview. They were also asked to compare their current level of happiness with the level that they had experienced a few years earlier. The questionnaire item used here was: "Compared with your life today, how were things four or five years ago? Were things *happier* for you then or *not quite as happy* as now or *about the same?*"

Despite the obvious limitations of these simple measures, a review of the relevant happiness literature by Robinson and Shaver (1969) shows a relatively consistent set of findings from study to study over a period of years. First, the level of happiness in various nationwide samples has remained quite constant over the years. Second, the kinds of subgroups that tend to be happy or unhappy have remained constant from sample to sample. And, third, upon reassessment, individuals tend to express the same level of happiness or satisfaction as they had done previously. (More information concerning some of these findings is presented in the material which follows.)

THE AMOUNT OF HAPPINESS

How happy are we? Thoreau wrote that most men lead lives of quiet desperation, but the majority of us appear to be either quite happy or tolerably so. At least, that is what we report when we are surveyed. In a series of four nationwide studies conducted between 1957 and 1965 (Bradburn, 1969), the percentage of respondents who indicated that they were "very happy" or "pretty happy" ranged from 83 percent to 91 percent. The remainder, 9 to 17 percent, reported themselves to be "not too happy."

In a second series of nationwide studies carried out in 1965 and repeated in 1968 (Robinson and Shaver, 1969), respondents were asked to indicate how satisfying their lives were. The results of the two surveys were in close agreement and showed the respondents to be generally satisfied. About nine out of ten indicated that their lives were "completely satisfying" or "pretty satisfying." Only one in ten reported a "not very satisfying" existence.

Two assessments of happiness in college students produced results consistent with the above investigations. Wessman and Ricks' small groups of Harvard men and Radcliffe women achieved a mean rating of about 6 on the ten-point elation-depression scale. This rating is slightly toward the elation end and described as "Feeling pretty good, 'O.K.'" Constantinople (1965) used the same scale with large groups of University of Rochester undergraduates and found about the same average rating.

THE VARIABILITY OF HAPPINESS

Considerable information concerning variability of mood is presented by Bradburn and by Wessman and Ricks. People differ in their overall level of happiness; some are generally happier than others. People also differ in the variability of their moods from day to day and within a particular day; some individuals are steady and stable while others are moody and have many ups and downs. Research indicates that those of us whose moods fluctuate considerably from day to day are also the ones who tend to show considerable spread between the best and the worst mood of a particular day.

It might be assumed that individuals with sharply varying moods are generally unhappy, but research has not shown this to be true. There appears to be no relationship between mood level and mood variability. Writing about the college students they studied, Wessman and Ricks conclude, "Thus there were happy and stable individuals, happy and variable individuals, unhappy and stable individuals, unhappy and variable individuals, with most people, of course, in intermediate positions on the two independent aspects (p. 244)."

It might also be assumed that persons who experience many positive moods are relatively free of negative ones while those with many negative moods would experience few positive ones. Again, research does not support this assumption. The amounts of these two kinds of moods appear to be uncorrelated. We may have many positive and many negative moods or very few strong states of either, although most of us arrive at a somewhat positive balance. Investigators note considerable differences in the amounts of feelings that different people report, with quantity being unrelated to quality: people who report relatively more feelings are not necessarily happier or unhappier than those who report relatively less.

Wessman and Ricks found their college subjects to be either generally stable or generally variable in mood. Some interesting personality differences were found between the stable and variable men (there were little data concerning college women in this regard). Stable men described themselves as independent, serious, quiet, and reserved, and they had pride in their own standards and character. Variable men saw themselves as open, outgoing and productive, and they placed more value on originality and inventiveness. The steady men criticized themselves for being too cautious and isolated and insufficiently warm, friendly, free, and spontaneous. The variable men faulted themselves for being spread too thin, for not fulfilling their ambitions, and for lacking composure and the ability to absorb frustrations. The steady men were tightly organized and well controlled; they had conquered their inner turmoil but were not very spontaneous or lively. By comparison, the variable men were more unrestrained and vulnerable but they were also more responsive and original.

THE PEAKS AND NADIRS
OF HAPPINESS

We all have our ups and downs. Sometimes we have a particularly up up—which Maslow called a "peak experience"—when we feel great happiness. And we also have some downmost downs—which Thorne (1963) labeled "nadir experiences" —when we feel devastatingly unhappy.

A study of peak and nadir experiences among college students and hospitalized mentally ill patients showed, as common sense would suggest, that the former reported a greater proportion of peaks while the latter reported more nadirs (Margoshes and Litt, 1966). However, nadirs need not be completely negative experiences. In one investigation of peak and nadir experiences in college students it was found that nadirs had more powerful and enduring effects than peaks. And a substantial portion of the nadir effects were eventually positive or beneficial, providing some support for the old sayings that suffering makes one wise and adversity introduces a person to himself. Some students of this study reported that their nadirs had brought them closer to others or had given them greater confidence in themselves. One student, whose nadir was caused by a breakup with his girlfriend, reported the following.

> The nadir experience definitely had a more lasting after-effect than the peak experience. The nadir experience influenced me to experiment with drugs, start drinking, smoking, seek out promiscuous relationships, etc. These changes were accompanied by a self-evaluation period that is still in operation. Now, more than ever before, I am self-critical and self-analyzing. I am trying to improve my personality in all respects and at all times. Before my nadir experience, I didn't pay much attention to my faults.

I am open to criticism much more now than before the nadir experience. The desperate changes such as with drugs, smoking, etc. were only temporary; but the attitudes and values I have about them have changed considerably. I am much more tolerant and understanding concerning such behavior today. I try not to condemn or make evaluations about things which I haven't experienced [Ebersole, 1970, p. 208].

Peak experiences have attracted scientific attention largely through the influence of Maslow. He noted that moments of great happiness could have various effects. For example, during peaks we may become excited, alert, and feel fully alive. Or we may feel delight, rapture, even ecstasy. Or, by contrast, we may find ourselves quiet, serene, and deeply content.

From his observations Maslow concluded that peak experiences are more common than is usually supposed and, in fact, occur in almost everyone although they are frequently not recognized as such. Some of us deny these experiences or reject them or dismiss them as trivial. We may value toughness and tight control and attempt to shut out emotion. Or we may be afraid of our emotions, especially the flood of feeling that peaks can bring.

Consistent with Maslow's observations, a number of researchers have found that some subjects are completely unfamiliar with peak experiences. For example, Thorne conducted some pilot studies on peak and nadir experiences and reported that "many young adults seem to have difficulty in differentiating what a peak experience is, and somewhat pitifully inquire when they can expect to have one." Approximately 12 percent of the 133 college students studied by Whittaker (1970) reported no peak experiences; some of their comments were: "I can think of no circumstances in which this may have happened to me." "Am I retarded? I don't think I've ever felt like that." "I'm not sure I even understand this feeling. Maybe I haven't looked for it. Sounds great, though. I've missed out (p. 4)."

What kind of people report more peak experiences? What kind report fewer or none at all? Some partial answers to these questions are provided by McClain and Andrews (1969), who studied a group of upper division and graduate students at the University of Tennessee. Using various personality measures, they found some interesting differences between students who tend to have peak experiences ("peakers") and those who do not ("nonpeakers"). As compared to nonpeakers, peakers were more intelligent, intellectual, and imaginative. Peakers were also more forthright, assertive, and autonomous. Some other qualities more common in peakers than nonpeakers were subjectivity, sensitivity, openmindedness, and experimental-mindedness.

Maslow felt that peak experiences stemmed from many sources and were not necessarily arcane, esoteric, or restricted to "far-out" people. Peaks might be produced by a moment of love or sex or by a deep insight or burst of creativity. A peak (or at least a minipeak) might even be brought on by seemingly mundane experiences such as a good dinner with good friends.

Whittaker's research, which involved 66 male and 67 female college juniors from five diverse campuses, provided data concerning the sources of peak experiences in this group. Each student was asked to indicate the occasions on which he or she had felt deeply, intensely, and exhilaratingly alive. The students' responses appeared to be largely sortable into nine broad categories and the small remainder were subsumed in a tenth and miscellaneous classification.

The first general category was *academic* and was composed of four subcategories including academic achievement (exhilaration on completing or doing well in a project, lab, paper, exam, or some accomplishment via solving or discovering), an academic course (a stimulating course, seminar, or discussion group), academic study (excitement during reading or studying material for a course, independent research, or extracurricular intellectual reading), and an academic person (a stimulating professor or visiting speaker). Some excerpts from the written responses of the students illustrate these kinds of academic peaks:

Often I get the feeling of aliveness in class discussion or when I feel that I am growing, learning. However, most often it is when I realize that all my learning will be, and is, meaningful and it can be useful [female, literature].

When reading and discussing material for a class in non-western religion I felt very free in my reactions to the material and felt no compulsion to restrain myself in expressing them. . . . During science comprehension examinations and was asked about the possibilities for uses of the moon in the future and allowing my imagination to roam [female, pharmacy].

When I first got into a computer book this year. . . . Studying math in my second year. . . . After one of our high table guest speakers during my freshman year. I really felt a love of learning for its own sake [male, computer science].

Sometimes in an academic situation when I know I am doing very well I feel this way—very competent and able—as when taking a test and I am aware that I am doing an excellent job [female, psychology].

Mostly when attached to the study of history when I felt I really understood the significance of a given historical event [male, history].

Introductory sociology. Fantastic professor who exhibited real understanding of the people and their actions and needs. Exciting reading list. I was incredibly motivated in doing all my papers. The only time I've ever identified with the expression "the joy of learning" [female, sociology].

The second category was *social*, which included making new friends, being with close friends, and relating to friends through discussions. (Interpersonal relationships of a romantic nature were placed in a different category.) The social category was a more important source of peaks in females than males. Some excerpts from student accounts concerning this kind of peak experience follow:

I felt this type of mood when everything was going right for me or when I was with a group of friends having a good time and feeling like I belonged. . . . This year when I moved into a sorority house and made new friendships and learned what it is like to live with other people besides my family [female, anthropology].

In interpersonal relationships. Usually when with another person, when discussing problems, theirs or mine [male, mathematics].

This mood has sometimes arrived to find me just sitting at my desk while leaning back in my chair and connecting my finger tips. Of course, I most enjoy this mood when it is shared with others. . . . Our group shares a close, sensual perception [male, sociology].

One time last year when a whole group of us got stoned and spent a very enjoyable evening exchanging observations [male, economics].

I felt this way during a trip to L.A. with some of my buddies. We were all sitting in the sun, on the beach, shooting the bull, drinking beer. As I was sitting there, all sorts of wonderful feelings just kept running through my head. I felt good towards everybody [male, criminology].

The third category was *artistic* and involved both formal and informal creative endeavors such as visual arts, music, literature, or drama. Artistic peaks were not reserved for students majoring in these areas. The majority of students mentioning such experiences had primary commitments to other pursuits.

When I have had the occasion to compose music and write lyrical poetry . . . and having experienced the sense of having expressed some of the beauty I have touched by merely existing. Music blows my mind. It always has [male, pharmacy].

I feel "most alive" during sketching . . . the "exhilarating mood" can only be experienced alone. After several hours of deep, intense concentrated effort, I like to think I have given life and expression to a blank paper surface. The art form might become a source of reaction for another individual and this in itself is a source of immense satisfaction to me. I have rarely, if ever, experienced this mood in direct connection with an academic course. What you yourself deem very valuable may be looked upon in a disparaging way by academicians. As a result, I save my 110% efforts for such out-of-class projects [male, economics].

The fourth category, *athletic*, generally involved deep participation in some sport. However, a few of the peak experiences were more vicarious spectator experiences, and these were more likely to be reported by women. Overall, many more athletic peaks were reported by males than females.

I find myself on occasion in the mental high you describe when participating in athletic competition—which is very important to me. I have never been that enthused on any academic matters here [male, government].

I think I felt this way while taking ski lessons. I was learning different techniques from an instructor who motivated me. I learned quicker and progressed more rapidly from his teaching than anyone else. I became more aware of how I could control my body and its actions and at the same time, mentally, I was concentrating hard in order to devote myself really completely to master my body [male, criminology].

In any situation of this type "success" would have to be the catchword. It can involve success in the form of victory as in athletics. Intramural victories—an excellent "high"—reinstate your faith in self [male, political science].

The fifth category, *nature*, included significant experiences involving the out-of-doors. Some of the students' peaks were in direct response to the natural environment as such or to activities which occurred in natural settings. Included were experiences involving the ocean, woods, mountains, open spaces, seasons, or weather.

When I have stood overlooking the sea. I was totally at ease and exhilarated by the calm and beauty. I experienced a beautiful feeling of happiness and awareness of life around me [male, business administration].

I remember such a time from natural energies while climbing out of meadow country by trail under a full summer moon [male, philosophy].

During times of awareness of nature around this campus as on bright clear spring days when walking alone and I have felt a great closeness, a great feeling of common brotherhood with nature and humanity of all times past and present [male, history].

The sixth classification was *altruistic* and included helping or serving others. Included in this category were tutoring others and assisting children or adults in community programs. This category was a greater source of peaks for women than for men.

When I am teaching someone it is for me a very important way of feeling involvement. I find when I am truly giving of myself to someone else, then I am most alive [female, English literature].

This past summer I was employed as a secretary for the Head Start program in my hometown. Although the majority of my work was at a desk, the contact, physical contact, with the pre-schoolers, and the challenge itself, was enough to make any person feel needed and useful to others [female, accounting].

My work in a soup kitchen in NY's lower East Side this last summer during which the demand for activity and service allowed me no time for wallowing in introspection. During this time I became aware of the existence and need for social revolution [female, English].

In this case, I would have to say my experiences coaching basketball in an underdeveloped portion of the city. I found it very challenging and rewarding to say the least. It was both physically and intellectually stimulating [male, pre-medical].

The seventh category was *sexual* and included both romantic and more specifically sexual experiences. Peak experiences of these kinds were not very much elaborated by the students, perhaps because of their very personal or seemingly obvious nature.

When things were going good for me with my girl last fall [male, physical education].

During emotional, intellectual and/or physical intercourse with lovers [female, history].

I feel that particular way, in a manner of speaking, whenever I truly accomplish some goal I set out to achieve. I feel this way quite regularly, one could say, after a good relationship with my girl in whatever we may do [male, journalism].

In my freshman year when I was first falling in love; being more sure of myself and knowing he was becoming more sure of us [female, sociology].

During the past 3 months with my closest friend of the opposite sex who I will probably marry [male, history].

The eighth category was *drugs*. This source of peaks was more common for male than for female students. Although drug experiences were mentioned by a relatively small minority of students, they seemed particularly significant for some of these students.

The first semester of my junior year I had a white exchange student as my roommate. He brought "something" with him that turned me on. Dig it? It gave me a feeling that was indescribable [male, business administration].

Talking with people who I have gotten stoned with about my ideas of the universe, the relationship of different realities, consciousness and astrology—usually with taking LSD or mescaline or hashish.

When stoned, in the mountains or during and after a seminar with Alan Watts [male, philosophy].

Drugs have been a most enlightening experience for me. I found Dexadrine stimulating, allowing me high mental capacity and efficiency over about ten hours. After prolonged usage, I have discovered that I can direct the effects of marijuana into constructive, insightful and creative outlets. Much of it is unorganized and what I call "gapped reasoning," that is, I leave gaps between ideas. LSD helped me pick up the "cues" much easier. With drugs, I can understand myself and others and the dynamics involved much better. It is my interest. I have experienced few, if any, other significantly "alert" periods [male, psychology].

The ninth classification, *political,* included involvement in a campaign, movement, or demonstration of some kind. This category of peak experience was more common for males than for females. As with drug experiences, political experiences seemed to be a particularly significant source of stimulation for a small group of students.

During the last political campaign, when I felt like I might be able to change something even though slightly. There was a great sense of commitment which I generally lack and feel that I need [male, economics].

I felt most alive when I was helping with the cause of black advancement. It was during this time that Martin L. King was killed and it became even more necessary to help with our cause [male, sociology].

This feeling comes over me when I'm involved in political activities whether at school or out of school as when I ran a teach-in following the demonstration at the October regents' meeting [male, government].

This year in our work to get three fired professors rehired—seeing the dedication and creativity of the group and knowing that it was connected not only with the specific campus issue but with the larger social revolution as well—was an exhilarating experience. There was a sense of self-sacrifice for future generations which added meaning [female, English].

All of the remaining responses were subsumed in a *miscellaneous* classification. These included such infrequently mentioned peak experiences as self-discovery (via introspection or meditation), performance (extemporizing or participating in a practiced way before an appreciative audience), travel (touring or encountering new places), and leisure (free time and pressure-free activities).

Maslow concluded that one cannot make peak experiences happen, but must allow them to happen by putting oneself in the proper mood to receive them. However, he also concluded that from past experience we can know the conditions under which peaks have occurred; by manipulating or arranging these conditions we can increase the likelihood of having peak experiences.

Some therapists and educators feel that we should focus more on our peaks. We can maximize these experiences when they do occur by recognizing them, welcoming them, and making the most of them. We can determine the activities that produce peaks and pursue these activities. People who have achieved deep relaxation in hypnotic states sometimes are able to recreate these feelings without hypnosis. And in the same way, we may be able to capture the experiences we have in peak moments and re-live these feelings on later occasions.

THE CORRELATES OF HAPPINESS

Many things have been thought to be correlated with happiness. Some are so commonly mentioned and so completely unproven that they qualify as myths. There is, for example, the myth of happy childhood (research does not substantiate that this is a notably happy time), the myth of the happy savage (anthropologists have not located many blissful primitives), the myth of the happy ignorant (the educated report themselves to be happier), and the myth of the happy poor (which few poor believe and few rich wish to verify).

The "correlates" of happiness refer to the phenomena that are related to or associated with this state. However, the *causes* of happiness may be quite another matter, since the mere correlation of two things does not necessarily mean that one causes the other. For example, both phenomena may be products of yet another phenomenon. Still, as will be seen in the section to follow, some of these correlates are believed to be important influences on happiness.

Reviewing the research reports in this area (many of which are brought together by Bradburn, 1969; Fellows, 1966; Robinson and Shaver, 1969; and Wilson, 1967), one can compile a fairly long list of happiness correlates. To generalize, happiness and the good things of life (or at least the things that most people value) tend to go together. Happy people tend to have a lot to be happy about or, to put it the other way around, people who have a lot to be happy about tend to be happy.

To start with a common finding, wealth is related to happiness. There are unhappy rich and happy poor (the myth is not 100 percent wrong), but people who have high incomes tend to report themselves as happier than those with low ones. Individuals whose incomes are extremely modest appear to be particularly unhappy. However, beyond the attainment of a certain comfortable level, increments in income are not accompanied by fully commensurate increments in happiness. (A not-so-old saying goes, "A man with ten million dollars is not necessarily happier than one with nine million.")

Health, as well as wealth, is associated with happiness. However, some research suggests that the relationship between health and happiness is less pronounced than that between illness and unhappiness. When we are healthy, we commonly take our physical well-being for granted, and it may not be a source of pleasure. By contrast, illness obtrudes itself on our life and can become a matter of considerable unhappiness.

Education has been shown to be related to happiness in a number of studies. In general, the higher our education, the greater our happiness. College graduates report greater happiness than adults who have not gone beyond high school, and high school graduates in turn report more happiness than adults whose formal education ended in grade school.

Vocational status is strongly related to happiness. Employed persons are generally happier than those who are unemployed or retired. Among the employed, persons with higher status positions report greater happiness than those with less prestigious jobs. One's vocational happiness is an important aspect of one's general well-being; if we are happy in our work, we are likely to be happy in other areas of living, although this generalization has notable exceptions and reversals.

Marital status shows some interesting relationships with happiness. Married persons, in general, report greater happiness than those who are single, and happily married persons are particularly satisfied with their lives. Single persons, in turn, report more happiness than those who are divorced or widowed. Comparing married and single males and females, married men appear to be happiest, followed by married women, then single women, and finally—lagging at some distance—single men. (This calls to mind Artemus Ward's controversial assertion that old bachelors don't die, they just rot away like a pollywog's tail.)

Although large-scale data are generally lacking, there appear to be some important racial differences in happiness. In several national studies, blacks reported themselves to be less happy or less satisfied than whites. There are apparently no comparable data for American Indians, but various assessments suggest that members of this group are considerably less happy than the general population.

One can apparently be happy or unhappy at almost any age or stage of life. Research between age and happiness does not show any large or consistent relationship between these two variables. One possible exception is that happiness in the oldest groups under investigation (age 50 or 55 or 60 and above, depending upon the study)

appears to be somewhat less than for younger groups. It has been suggested that the decrease of happiness in this oldest category may be primarily due to disruption of marriage through divorce or death of the spouse, but health and economic factors may also be involved.

A number of other social and personal factors have been found to be associated with happiness. Individuals who are more involved with social and leisure-time activities are happier than those who are not engaged in these pursuits. Those individuals who esteem themselves and feel personally competent are more likely to be happy. Anxiety, worry, and psychosomatic symptoms tend to be associated with unhappiness.

THE CAUSES OF HAPPINESS

Many of us may feel from our own experience, from our observations, and from just plain common sense that some of the correlates mentioned above are also important causes of happiness. When people are surveyed, they make prominent mention of three of these correlates as important sources of their happiness or unhappiness and of their satisfaction or dissatisfaction, and as the basis of their hopes and fears for the future. These three correlates are their economic or material situation (including their jobs), their families, and their health and that of their loved ones. These findings should come as no surprise since economic, familial, and physical well-being are fundamental to human existence.

Some investigators have been interested in relating childhood conditions to adult happiness. Does a happy childhood produce a happy adult? Wessman and Ricks found that the happier men in their study did not show a single pattern of development. However, in general they did have happier childhoods. These men were generally from warm and supportive homes, had appropriate role models with whom they established positive ties, and were able to develop a solid sense of their own identity.

Happiness in childhood augurs well for happiness later on but it does not guarantee it. Child psychologist Elizabeth B. Hurlock (1973) reviewed studies of happiness throughout the lifespan and concluded, "Many happy children become unhappy, neurotic, maladjusted adolescents, adults, or elderly citizens. Many whose childhood was unhappy, on the other hand, become happier as life progresses" (p. 342).

Hurlock feels that three things are a prerequisite to a happy existence: acceptance, affection, and achievement. She called these the "three A's of happiness." Sigmund Freud said something similar when he was asked what people should be able to do well. He replied simply, "Lieben und arbeiten." They should be able to love and work.

This discussion has focused on the roots of happiness in the general population, but for any individual there may be a number of special sources. To look at it from the negative side, a person's unhappiness may relate to his special frustrations and conflicts, his anxieties, fears, and worries, and the particular conditions in which he finds himself. A beginning of a sentence from an incomplete sentence test reads, "What makes me unhappy . . . " If we reflected on this sentence fragment and responded as candidly as we could, probably no two of us would answer in exactly the same way. This might also be true of our response to the sentence beginning, "What makes me happy . . ."

THE ENHANCEMENT OF HAPPINESS

"Well, why *not* a technology of joy, of happiness?" This is Maslow's (1971) exuberant question and challenge. All things done in the name of human welfare have some implication for happiness, and it would be impossible to note every strategy here. However, it may be helpful to identify certain broad and dichotomous philosophies that encompass these many strategies. Such strategic dichotomies include amelioration versus enhancement, direct versus indirect approaches, and environmental versus personal emphases.

Amelioration strategies include attempts to lessen unhappiness and reduce anxiety while enhancement strategies are those aimed at making us happy or even happier than happy. Underlying amelioration is the philosophy that great happiness is not possible or, at least, not probable and we do well to "get along" or "get by." By contrast, enhancement strategies stem

from the more optimistic philosophy that human beings have greater, even far greater, capacity for positive emotion than is generally realized.

Conventional psychotherapies have been largely ameliorative. This is well represented by Freud's oft quoted statement, "Much has been accomplished if we can change neurotic misery into common unhappiness." This orientation has in part been due to the use of a medical model and a focus on illness rather than wellness. And in part it stems from an occupation with grossly unhappy and anxiety-laden client populations who urgently require some measure of help.

Some innovative therapies also have taken ameliorative stands on happiness. For example, Janov (1970) has stated that happiness is neither the aim nor the result of his approach. He writes, "Let me make clear that the finished patient is not ecstatic or even 'HAPPY.' Happiness is not a goal of Primal Therapy. Finished patients may still have many more hurts to feel because they have a lifetime of unfelt hurts behind them. So they will have their moments of misery after therapy, but as one patient put it, 'At least it is *real* misery with some kind of end to it'" (pp. 101–102).

In their rational-emotive therapy, Ellis and Harper (1961) do not promise happiness or even complete freedom from unhappiness but hold that people can learn the art of almost never being desperately unhappy or miserable. Referring to unhappy individuals, this pair writes, "They can teach themselves to be fairly consistently mature, thinking, reflective. If they do, they will never reach the state, in all probability, in which they are completely, consistently happy; nor even the state where they are never in any way unhappy. They can, nonetheless, finally, with much work and effort, train themselves to be never—well, practically never—intensely miserable for any sustained period of time. What more can one reasonably ask?" (pp. 77–78).

By contrast, some therapies (and especially some very recent ones) have explicitly taken on the task of enhancement. In the preface to their book *Gestalt Therapy Now*, Fagan and Shepherd (1970) set their therapeutical goal as *joy*—not simply freedom from unhappiness; they explain, "Now we use words such as enhancement, intimacy, actualization, creativity, ecstasy, and transcendence to describe what we wish for ourselves and others." Other examples are Otto's Peak-Joy Method (1970) and Bindrim's Peak-Oriented Psychotherapy (1968), both of which relate to Maslow's work on peak experiences (1962; 1971). A further example of this approach is provided by Lewis and Streitfeld's *Growth Games* (1971).

The second dichotomy concerns direct versus nondirect approaches to happiness. The latter deny that happiness can be effectively obtained by pursuing it; in fact, they maintain that that is the way to make oneself unhappy. They believe we find happiness when we stop looking for it or that happiness comes secondarily or incidentally as we occupy ourself in other pursuits. In his book *The Meaning of Happiness* (1970), Alan Watts wrote that "happiness cannot be had by any form of direct striving. Like your shadow, the more you chase it, the more it runs away." And fellow philosopher Aldous Huxley compared happiness to coke (he meant a form of coal, not cola) and said it was "something you get as a by-product in the process of making something else."

By contrast, there are those who advocate pursuing happiness head-on. Implicit in some oblique notions is that happiness has to be earned somehow, and you get it for doing good or doing well. The direct approach holds that happiness need not be earned so much as it must be willed or practiced, which requires us to focus on it in a straightforward and even business-like way.

There are oblique elements in many therapies and religions, which aim to create a stronger or better person and perhaps on this account a happier one. The two enhancement therapies noted earlier, the Peak-Joy Method and Peak-Oriented Psychotherapy, could be used as illustrations of nonoblique or head-on approaches. To these could be added a number of other approaches, including those described in Schutz's *Joy* and Lowen's *Pleasure*.

The final dichotomy contrasts environmental with personal approaches to happiness. The utopians and Skinnerians are examples of environmentalists who advocate the creation of better societies to produce happier people. Bertrand Russell, in his book *The Conquest of Happiness*, wrote that in judging the society of the future, "the question is whether those who

have grown up in it will be happier than those who have grown up in our society or those of the past." In Skinner's utopian novel *Walden Two*, society's master planner Frazier announced that in addition to making a science of human nature possible, his goals were to "make men happy" and "to assure the continuation of that happiness."

Unlike the environmentalists, the personalists believe that the wellspring of happiness (or joy or tranquility) is within the individual. Each of us can create his own happiness independent—or somewhat so—of environmental conditions. The personalists include a varied assortment of bedfellows, including some philosophers, religionists, human potentialists, Zen masters, yogis, biofeedbackers, and positive thinkers.

The rational-emotive school of psychotherapy noted earlier as ameliorative is also personalist in philosophy. Its founder Albert Ellis (1957) writes, "Most human unhappiness is caused or sustained by the view one takes of people and events rather than by the people and events themselves. One has enormous control over one's emotions if one chooses to work at controlling them by saying logical and unself-defeating sentences to oneself" (p. 348).

Social critic Joseph Wood Krutch was perhaps the most insistent of all personalists. Like Ellis, Krutch was an ameliorater, and he rejected utopian thinking since it implied "that man not only *can* be almost perfectly happy but also that he can be *made* so—whereas nothing in human experience justifies any such assumption." According to Krutch, man has been able to invent a variety of hells but never a utopia where one could be perfectly happy and perfectly content or even where one would want to live for very long.

Happiness, said Krutch (1966), for the most part does not depend upon what is provided to us. Rather, in our society we each make our own happiness. Krutch then quotes the four lines which Samuel Johnson added to the end of Goldsmith's *The Traveler:*

How small of all that human hearts endure,
That part which laws or kings can cause or
    cure!
Still to ourselves in every place consigned,
Our own felicity we make or find.

RETROSPECT, LAMENT, AND PROSPECT

In summary, the psychological study of happiness shows most of us consider happiness to be an important and achievable emotion and, when asked, most of us profess to be tolerably happy. Our degree of happiness is not related to general moodiness or fullness of feeling but has positive relationships with self-esteem, wealth, health, education, and involvement in social and leisure-time activity and also with familial history and vocational and marital well-being. Enhancement of happiness depends upon one's philosophy and strategy. We must consider how high we set our goal (nonmisery or peak-joy?), whether to pursue this goal directly or indirectly, and whether by personal or by environmental means.

It is obvious that the psychological literature on happiness does not deal adequately with the questions raised by philosophers. And certainly the concern shown by psychologists for this subject does not match that shown by poets, songwriters, or people in general. Surveys substantiate Maslow's claim that psychologists have been more occupied with the study of negative and dysphoric states than with more positive and pleasant ones (Carlson, 1966; Lindauer, 1968).

A number of writers on happiness have begun their papers by lamenting the lack of psychological information on this important state. To begin a paper on happiness with a lament seems inappropriate, but it may be no better to save it for the end. At present the more positive aspects of human being are gaining research attention, and happiness—although not bursting out all over—now appears more frequently in the literature. If this trend continues, some not-too-distant writer on happiness will be able to omit the customary lament and start off on a note of pleasure or even joy.

REFERENCES

BINDRIM, P. "Facilitating Peak Experiences," in H. A. Otto and J. Mann, eds., *Ways of Growth*. New York: Grossman, 1968, pp. 115–127.

BRADBURN, N. M. *The Structure of Psychological Well-Being*. Chicago: Aldine, 1969.

———, and D. CAPLOVITZ. *Reports on Happiness*. Chicago: Aldine, 1965.

BRAWER, F. B. *Values and the Generation Gap*. Washington, D.C.: ERIC Clearinghouse for Junior Colleges and American Association of Junior Colleges, 1971.

CARLSON, E. R. "The Affective Tone of Psychology," *Journal of General Psychology*, 75 (1966), 65–78.

CONSTANTINOPLE, A. P. "Some Correlates of Happiness and Unhappiness in College Students." Unpublished doctoral dissertation, University of Rochester, 1965.

DAVITZ, J. R. "A Dictionary and Grammar of Emotion," in M. B. Arnold, ed., *Feelings and Emotions*. New York: Academic Press, 1970, pp. 251–258.

EBERSOLE, P. "Effects of Nadir Experiences," *Psychological Reports*, 27(1) (1970), 207–209.

ELLIS, A. "Outcome of Employing Three Techniques of Psychotherapy," *Journal of Clinical Psychology*, 13(4) (1957), 344–350.

———, and R. A. HARPER. *A Guide to Rational Living*. Englewood Cliffs, N.J.: Prentice-Hall, Inc., 1961.

FAGAN, J., and I. L. SHEPHERD, eds. *Gestalt Therapy Now*. Palo Alto, Calif.: Science and Behavior Books, 1970.

FELLOWS, E. W. "Happiness: A Survey of Research," *Journal of Humanistic Psychology*, 6(1) (1966), 17–30.

HURLOCK, E. B. *Adolescent Development*, 2nd ed. New York: McGraw-Hill Book Company, 1973.

JANOV, A. *The Primal Scream*. New York: G. P. Putnam's Sons, 1970.

KRUTCH, J. W. "Danger: Utopia Ahead," *Saturday Review*, 49(32) (1968), 17–18, 46.

LEWIS, H. R., and H. S. STREITFELD. *Growth Games*. New York: Harcourt Brace Jovanovich, 1971.

LINDAUER, M. S. "Pleasant and Unpleasant Emotions in Literature: A Comparison with the Affective Tone of Psychology," *Journal of Psychology*, 70 (1968), 55–67.

LOWEN, A. *Pleasure*. New York: Coward-McCann, 1970.

McCLAIN, E. W., and H. B. ANDREWS. "Some Personality Correlates of Peak Experiences: A Study in Self-actualization," *Journal of Clinical Psychology*, 25(1) (1969), 36–38.

MARGOSHES, A., and S. LITT. "Vivid Experiences: Peak and Nadir," *Journal of Clinical Psychology*, 22(2) (1966), 175.

MASLOW, A. H. "Lessons from the Peak-experiences," *Journal of Humanistic Psychology*, 2(1) (1962), 9–18.

———. "Education and Peak Experiences," *The Farther Reaches of Human Nature*. New York: Viking, 1971.

OTTO, H. A. *Group Methods to Actualize Human Potential: A Handbook*. Beverly Hills, Calif.: Holistic Press, 1970.

PECK, R. F. "Measuring the Mental Health of Normal Adults," *Genetic Psychology Monographs*, 60 (1959), 197–255.

RICHARDS, J. M., JR. "Life Goals of American College Freshmen," *Journal of Counseling Psychology*, 13(1) (1966), 12–20.

RICKS, D. F., and A. E. WESSMAN. "Winn: A Case Study of a Happy Man," *Journal of Humanistic Psychology*, 6(1) (1966), 2–16.

ROBINSON, J. P., and P. R. SHAVER. *Measures of Social Psychological Attitudes*. Ann Arbor, Mich.: Institute for Social Research, University of Michigan, 1969.

ROKEACH, M. *The Nature of Human Values*. New York: The Free Press, 1973.

RUSSELL, B. *The Conquest of Happiness*. New York: Liveright, 1930.

SCHAAR, J. H. ". . . and the Pursuit of Happiness," *Virginia Quarterly Review*, 46(1) (1970), 1–26.

SCHUTZ, W. C. *Joy*. New York: Grove Press, 1967.

SKINNER, B. F. *Walden Two*. New York: The Macmillan Company, 1948.

THORNE, F. C. "The Clinical Use of Peak and Nadir Experience Reports," *Journal of Clinical Psychology*, 19(2) (1963), 248–250.

WATTS, A. W. *The Meaning of Happiness*. New York: Harper & Row, Publishers, 1970. (Perennial Library ed.)

WESSMAN, A. E., and D. F. RICKS. *Mood and Personality*. New York: Holt, Rinehart & Winston, Inc., 1966.

WHITTAKER, D. "College Student Needs and Identity as Indicated by Their Self-reported Peak Experiences." Paper presented at the meeting of the American Orthopsychiatric Association, San Francisco, March, 1970.

WILSON, W. "Correlates of Avowed Happiness," *Psychological Bulletin*, 67(4) (1967), 294–306.

LESSONS FROM THE PEAK-EXPERIENCES

Abraham H. Maslow

What I'm going to talk about tonight is an excursion into the psychology of health, or of the human being at his best. It's a report from the road, of a job not yet done—a kind of commando raid into the unknown in which I have left my scientific flanks very much exposed. This is a warning to those of you who like neatly finished tasks. This is far from finished.

When I started to explore the psychology of health, I picked out the finest, healthiest people, the best specimens of mankind I could find, and studied them to see what they were like. They were *very* different, startlingly different in some ways from the average. The biologist was right who announced that he had found the missing link between the anthropoid apes and civilized man. "It's *us!*"

I learned many lessons from these people. But one in particular is our concern now. I found that these individuals tended to report having had something like mystic experiences, moments of great awe, moments of the most intense happiness or even rapture, ecstasy or bliss (because the word happiness can be too weak to describe this experience).

These moments were of pure, positive happiness when all doubts, all fears, all inhibitions, all tensions, all weaknesses, were left behind. Now self consciousness was lost. All separateness and distance from the world disappeared as they felt *one* with the world, fused with it, really belonging in it and to it, instead of being outside looking in. (One subject said, for instance, "I felt like a member of a family, not like an orphan.")

Perhaps most important of all, however, was the report in these experiences of the feeling that they had really seen the ultimate truth, the essence of things, the secret of life, as if veils had been pulled aside. Alan Watts has described this feeling as, "This is *it!*", as if you had finally gotten there, as if ordinary life was a striving and a straining to get someplace and this was the arrival, this was *Being There!*; the end of straining and of striving, the achievement of the desire and the hope, the fulfillment of the longing and the yearning. Everyone knows how it feels to want something and not know what. These mystic experiences feel like the ultimate satisfaction of vague, unsatisfied yearnings. They are like a sudden stepping into heaven; like the miracle achieved, like perfection finally attained.[1]

But here I had already learned something new. The little that I had ever read about mystic experiences tied them in with religion, with visions of the supernatural. And, like most scientists, I had sniffed at them in disbelief and considered it all nonsense, maybe hallucinations, maybe hysteria—almost surely pathological.

But the people telling me or writing about these experiences were not such people—they were the healthiest people! That was one thing learned! And I may add that it taught me something about the limitations of the small (not the big) orthodox scientist who won't recognize as knowledge, or as reality, any information that doesn't fit into the already existent science. ("I am the master of this college; what I know not is not knowledge.")

These experiences mostly had nothing to do with religion—at least in the ordinary supernaturalistic sense. They came from the great moments of love and sex, from the great esthetic moments (particularly of music), from the bursts of creativeness and the creative furore (the great inspiration), from great moments of insight and of discovery, from women giving natural birth to babies—or just from loving them, from moments of fusion with nature (in a forest, on a seashore,

[1] "If a man could pass through paradise in a dream, and have a flower presented to him as a pledge that his soul had really been there, and if he found that flower in his hand when he awoke, ay, what then!" Coleridge.

mountains, etc.), from certain athletic experiences, e.g., skindiving, from dancing, etc.

The second big lesson learned was that this was a *natural*, not a *supernatural* experience; and I gave up the name "mystic" experience and started calling them peak-experiences. They can be studied scientifically. (I have started to do this.) They are within reach of human knowledge, not eternal mysteries. They are in the world, not *out* of the world. They belong not only to priests but to all mankind. They are no longer questions of faith but are wide open to human inquisitiveness and to human knowledge. Observe also the implication of naturalistic usages for the words "revelation," "heaven," "salvation," etc. The history of the sciences has been of one science after another carving a chunk for itself out of the jurisdiction of religion. It seems to be happening again here. Or to put this all another way, peak-experiences can be considered to be *truly* religious experiences in the best and most profound, most universal, and most humanistic sense of that word. It may turn out that pulling religion into the realm of science will have been the most important consequence of this line of work.

The next big lesson learned was that peak-experiences are far more common than I had ever expected: they were *not* confined to healthy people. These peak-experiences occurred also in average and even in psychologically sick people. As a matter of fact, I now suspect they occur in practically everybody although without being recognized or accepted for what they are.

Think for a minute how crazy this is in its implications. It's taken a long time for it to soak in on me. *Practically everybody reports peak-experiences if approached and questioned and encouraged in the right way. Also I've learned that just talking about it, as I'm doing now, seems to release from the depths all sorts of secret memories of peaks never revealed to anyone before, not even to oneself perhaps.* Why are we so shy about them? If something wonderful happens to us, why do we conceal it? Someone pointed out once, "Some people are scared to die; but some are scared to live." Maybe this is it.

There is considerable overlap between the characteristics of peak-experiences and the characteristics of psychological health (more integrated, more alive, more individual, less inhibited, less anxious, etc.) so I have been tempted to call the peak-experience a transient or temporary episode of self-actualization or health. If this *guess* turns out to be correct, it is like saying almost everyone, even the sickest people, can be psychologically healthy part of the time.

Still another lesson that by now I'm very sure of: peak-experiences come from *many, many* sources and to every kind of person. My list of sources seems to keep on getting longer and longer as I go on with these explorations. Sometimes I am tempted to think that almost any situation where perfection can be attained, or hope fulfilled, or perfect gratification reached, or where everything has gone smoothly, can produce in some people, at some times, a peak-experience. These can be very humble areas of life or of the workaday world; or the situation may have been repeated a thousand times before without producing a peak-experience.

"If your everyday life seems poor to you," wrote Rilke in his *Letters to a Young Poet*, "do not accuse it; accuse yourself, tell yourself you are not poet enough to summon up its riches, since for the creator there is no poverty and no poor or unimportant place."

For instance, a young mother scurrying around her kitchen and getting breakfast for her husband and young children. The sun was streaming in, the children clean and nicely dressed, were chattering as they ate. The husband was casually playing with the children; but as she looked at them she was suddenly so overwhelmed with their beauty and her great love for them, and her feeling of good fortune, that she went into a peak-experience. (This reminds me of my surprise at getting such reports from women. The surprise taught me how much we had masculinized all this.)

A young man working his way through medical school by drumming in a jazz band reported years later, that in all his drumming he had three peaks when he suddenly felt like a great drummer and his performance was perfect.

A hostess after a dinner party where everything had gone perfectly and it had been a fine evening, said good-bye to her last guest, sat down in a chair, looked around at the mess, and went into a peak of great happiness and exhilaration.

Milder peaks have come after a good dinner with good friends as a man sat smoking a fine cigar, or in a woman after she had done a really good cleaning up in her kitchen and it shone and sparkled and looked perfect.

Thus it is clear that there are many paths to these experiences of rapture. They are not necessarily fancy or occult or arcane or esoteric. They don't necessarily take years of training or study. They are not restricted to far-out people, i.e., to monks, saints, or yogis, Zen Buddhists, orientals, or people in any special state of grace. It is not something that happens in the Far East, in special places, or to specially trained or chosen people. It's available in the midst of life to everyday people in everyday occupations. This is a clear support for the writers on Zen and their concept of "nothing special."

Now another generalization which I'm fairly sure of by now. No matter what the source of the peak-experience, all peak-experiences seem to overlap, to tend to be alike. I can't say they're identical—they're not. But they're much *closer* to being identical than I had ever dreamed. It was a startling thing for me to hear a mother describing her ecstatic feelings during the birth of her one child and using some of the same words and phrases that I had read in the writings of St. Theresa of Avila, or Meister Eckhardt, or in Japanese or Hindu descriptions of *satori* or *samadhi* experiences. (Aldous Huxley makes this same point in his "Perennial Philosophy.")

I haven't done this very carefully yet—these are so far only pilot or preliminary explorations— but I do feel safe in generalizing all peak-experiences to some extent. *The stimuli are very different: the subjective experience tends to be similar.* Or to say it in another way: our *kicks* are the same; we just get them from different paths, perhaps even from rock and roll, drug addiction and alcohol in less strong people. I feel more sure of this after reading in the literatures of mystic experiences, cosmic consciousness, oceanic experiences, esthetic experiences, creative experiences, love experiences, parental experiences, sexual experiences, and insight experiences. They all overlap; they approach similarity and even identity.

One main benefit I've gotten from this discovery, and that we all may get, is that it will help us to understand each other better. If a mathematician and a poet use similar words in describing their peak-experiences from a successful poem and a successful mathematical proof, maybe they're more alike subjectively than we have thought. I can make such parallels between a high school athlete running to a touchdown, a business man describing his feelings over plans for a perfect fig canning factory, a college student catching on to the Adagio movements of Beethoven's Ninth Symphony. I feel men can learn more about women's inner life (and vice versa) if they learn about the things that give them their highest satisfaction and feelings of creativeness. For instance, college girls significantly more often than college boys report their high moments to come from *being* loved. The boys significantly more often get their happiest moments from success, conquest, achievement, winning. This finding conforms both to common sense knowledge and to clinical experience.

If our inner experiences of happiness are very similar no matter what stimulates them and no matter how different the people these experiences happen to (that is, if our insides are more like each other than our outside) then this may furnish us a way of being more sympathetic and understanding with people who are very different from ourselves; athletes and intellectuals, women and men, adults and children, etc. An artist and a housewife are not 1000 miles apart. In some moments they speak a common language, have common experiences, and live in the same world.

Can you bring about these experiences at will? No! Or almost entirely no! In general we are "Surprised by Joy," to use the title of C. S. Lewis's book on just this question. Peaks come unexpectedly, suddenly they *happen* to us. You can't count on them. And, hunting them is a little like hunting happiness. It's best not done directly. It comes as a by-product—an epiphenomenon, for instance, of doing a fine job at a worthy task you can identify with.

Of course we can make it more likely, or less likely, out of our experiences in the past. Some fortunate people can almost always have a peak-experience in sex. Some can count on certain pieces of music, or certain favorite activities like dancing or skindiving. But none of these is ever *guaranteed* to bring on a peak-experience. The most propitious frame of mind for "receiving" them is one of receptivity, almost a kind of passivity, or trust, or surrender, a Taoistic attitude of letting things happen without interfering or butting in. You have to be able to give up pride, will, dominance, being at the wheel, being in charge. You have to be able to relax and let it happen.

I think this will do for you what it did for me—renew my interest in Taoism and the lessons it has to teach. So also for Zen. (On the whole, I can say that my findings conform more with the Zen and Tao philosophies than with any of the religious mysticisms.)

I'm very sure now that the ineffability of such experiences has been overstated. It *is* possible to talk about them, to describe them, and to communicate them. I do it all the time now that I've learned how. "Ineffable" really means "not communicable by rational, logical, abstract, verbal, analytic, sensible language." The peak-experience can be described and communicated fairly well if: (1) you both have had such experiences yourselves, and (2) if you are able to talk in poetic or rhapsodic language, to let yourself be archaic in Jung's sense, to think-feel in a metaphorical or primary process way—or what Heinz Werner has called physiognomical language.

It's true the psyche *is* alone, encapsulated—cut off from all else—and for two such isolated psyches to communicate across the great chasm between them seems like a miracle. Well, the miracle happens.

What is the relation between the peak and the peaker? is my next question. Already it seems evident to me that there is some kind of dynamic isomorphism at work, some kind of mutual and parallel feedback or reverberation between the characteristics of the perceiver and of the perceived world so that they tend to influence each other. To put it very briefly, the perceiver has to be worthy of the percept. Or better said, they must deserve each other like well-married or badly-married couples. Kindness can *really* be perceived only by a kind man. A psychopathic personality will never be able to understand kindness, conscience, morality, or guilt since he himself lacks them entirely. But the person who is

good, true, and beautiful is more able to perceive these in the world outside—or the more unified and integrated we are, the more capable we are of perceiving unity in the world.

But there is also an effect in the other direction. The more integrated the world, or the more beautiful or just, the more the world tends to make the perceiver more integrated, or beautiful or just, etc. Seeking out the highest values in the world to look at helps to produce or strengthen them in us. For instance, an experiment we did at Brandeis University proved that in a beautiful room, people's faces look more alive and alert and higher in well-being, than they do in an ugly room. Or to put it another way, peak-experiences are more apt to come to nicer people, and they are more likely to happen to a particular person the better world conditions are.

This position needs many more examples to make it clear. I intend to write about this at greater length. It's a very important point.

In the peak-experiences, the "is" and the "ought" merge with each other instead of being different or contradictory. The perception is that what *is, ought* to be just that way. What *is* is just fine. This raises so many difficult questions that I don't want to make too much of it at this point, beyond recording that it *does* happen.

Finally, one finding that contradicts some of the mystics, especially of the East: I found all peak-experiences to be transient experiences—temporary not permanent. Some of the effects or after-effects may be permanent but the high moment itself is not.

PROBLEMS AND PUZZLES

Peak-experiences have been highly therapeutic for some people; and for others, a whole outlook on life has been changed forever by some great moment of insight or inspiration or conversion. This is easy to understand. It's like having been in Heaven for a moment and then remembering it in the dull moments of ordinary life. One person said characteristically, "I know life *can* be beautiful and good, and that life can be worth living; and I try to remember that when I need it during the grim days." One woman after natural childbirth, still breathless with the wonder of it said to her husband, "This has never happened to anyone before!" Another one, recalling the same experience said, "Once I was a queen, the most perfect queen of the earth." A man recalled his experience of awe from being in a wartime convoy at night with no lights. He melted into the whole vast universe and was not separate from all its beauty. A man recalled a burst of exuberance going over into sheer crazy, childish joy as he cavorted in the water like a fish, all alone so that he could yell out his great happiness at being so perfectly physical. And, of course, good and beautiful sex under the right circumstances is *often* reported to have this sort of effect.

It is easy to understand how such beautiful experiences should leave therapeutic effects, ennobling and beautifying effects, on the character, on the life outlook, on the way the world looks, on the way that the husband looks, or the baby. What is difficult to understand is why so often this does *not* happen. Practically everyone can be brought to realize he has been through such experiences. Why is it, then, that human beings are such a feeble lot, so full of jealousy, of fear, of hostility, of sheer misery? *This* is what I can't figure out.

One clue may come from a current investigation some of us are making on "Peakers" and "Non-Peakers"; i.e., the ones who reject or deny or suppress their peak-experiences, or who are afraid of them. It is our hunch that the peaks will do no good when they are rejected in this way.

At first it was our thought that some people simply didn't have peaks. But, as I said above, we found out later that it's much more probable that the non-peakers have them but repress or misinterpret them, or—for whatever reason—reject them and therefore don't use them.

Some of the reasons for such rejection so far found are: (1) a strict Marxian attitude, as with Simone de Beauvoir, who was persuaded that this was a weakness, a sickness (also Arthur Koestler). A Marxist should be "tough." Why Freud rejected his is anybody's guess; perhaps (2) his 19th century mechanistic-scientific attitude, perhaps (3) his pessimistic character. Among my various subjects I have found both causes at work sometimes. In others I have found (4) a narrowly rationalistic attitude which I considered a defense against being flooded by emotion, by irrationality, by loss of control, by illogical tenderness, by dangerous femininity, or by the fear of insanity. One sees such attitudes more often in engineers, in mathematicians, in analytic philosophers, in bookkeepers and accountants, and generally in obsessional people.

The effects of refusing to recognize peak-experiences must be many. We are now trying to work them out.

One thing I have already learned is that authoritative approval lifts the lid off these experiences for many people. For instance, whenever I lecture to my classes or other groups about these peaks, obviously in an approving way, it always happens that many peak-experiences come into consciousness in my audience, or are "remembered" for the first time; or—as I prefer to think today—emerge out of chaotic, unorganized preconscious experience to be given a name, to be paid attention to, to stand out as figures against the background. In a word, people then "realize" or "understand" what's been happening to them. Many of you who are now listening to me will find this to be so. It's a very close parallel to the emergence of sexual feelings at puberty. But this time, Daddy says it's all right.

A recent subject has taught me something else that may be relevant here; namely that it is possible to have a peak experience as the woman did in childbirth, without recognizing that this is like other peak-experiences—that they all have the same structure. Perhaps this is a reason for lack of therapeutic transfer of peaks, a reason why sometimes they have no generalized effects. For instance, the woman finally realized that her feelings when her husband had once made her feel needed and important to him were very much like her feelings while giving birth, and also like the great gush of motherliness and love when confronted by an orphaned child. Now she can generalize the experiences and use them throughout life, not just in one isolated corner of it.

This work is also beginning to shed some light on an old puzzle noted by many religious writers —especially by those who have written about conversion, like William James or Begbie, as well as many of the old mystics. They implied often that it was *necessary* to go through a "dark night of the soul," to hit bottom—to experience despair as a prerequisite to the mystic ecstasy. I get the feeling from some of this writing that it is as if human will, pride, and arrogance first have to express themselves to the fullest. After will and pride have been proven to yield only total misery, the person in the depths may *then* be able to surrender, to yield, to become humble, to bow his head and bend his knee; to offer himself on the altar; and to say "not my will, but thine be done." I should stress that this is not *only* a religious phenomenon; something of the same sort can happen to the alcoholic, to the psychotic, to the female in her struggle with the male, or to the youngster in his struggle with his parent.

The trouble with this problem has been, I now think, that it can take *either* a healthy *or* a sick form. For instance, this whole scheme works not only for religious conversion or mystic experience, but also for sexuality. It's very easy to pick out sexual elements in mystical literature and you can see how a sex-denying religious would have to reject anything of the sort, and how a debunker like H. L. Mencken would snicker out loud at the whole business. For *all* people for whom sex and religion (in the "higher" life) didn't mix, this was a dilemma they got hung up on. Well, *this* part of the problem is certainly no problem any longer, at least not for those who think sex (or love-sex at least) is a wonderful and beautiful thing, and who are perfectly willing to think of it as one of the gates to Heaven.

But there are other problems. Pride can easily be a sick thing, but so also can the *lack* of pride be, i.e., masochism. It looks as if human beings must be able *both* to affirm themselves (to be stubborn, stiff necked, vigilant, alert, dominant, aggressive, self-confident, etc.) and *also* to be able to trust, to relax and be receptive and Taoistic, to let things happen without interfering, to be humble and surrender. For instance, we now know that *both* in proper sequence are necessary for creativeness, for good thinking and theorizing, for interpersonal relations, and certainly for sexual relationships. It seems true that females have to be extra good at trusting and yielding and males at asserting and affirming, but both must be able to do both.

We have seen that so far as the peaks are concerned, apparently most of them are *receptive* phenomena. They invade the person and he must

be able to *let* them. He can't force them, grasp them, or command them. Will power is useless; so is striving and straining. What's necessary is to be able to let go, to let things happen. I can give you some very homely examples to show what I mean. It was Angyal who told me that, in his experience, really obsessional people couldn't "float" in the water. They just couldn't let go, or be *non*-controlling. To float you must trust the water. Fight it and down you go. The same is true for urination, defecation, going to sleep, relaxing, etc. All these involve an ability to let go, to let things happen. Will power only interferes. In this same sense it begins to look as if the intrusion of will power may inhibit peak-experiences.

A final word on this point. "Letting go," "trusting," and the like does *not* necessarily mean a "dark night of the soul," or "black despair," or breaking down of pride or being forced to one's knees. Healthy pride goes very nicely with healthy receptivity. It is *un*-healthy pride only that has to be "broken."

This, by the way, is another point of difference between mystic experience and these peak-experiences.

I have elsewhere pointed out an unsolved problem, that peak-experiences make some people more alert, excited, "high," while others relax, grow quiet, and more serene. I don't know what this difference means, or where it comes from. Perhaps the latter means more complete gratification than the former. Perhaps it doesn't. I have run across at least one subject who gets tension headaches from peak-experiences, especially esthetic ones. She reports stiffness, tension, and great excitement in which she gets very talkative. The headache is not unpleasant and she doesn't avoid it but rather goes looking for more. This headache goes together with other more usual reports. For instance, I quote, "the world looks nice and I feel friendlier. I have a feeling of hopefulness (which is not usual for me). These are the moments when I *know* what I want—sure, less doubt; I'm more efficient and make faster decisions, less confusion. I know better what I want—what I like. I feel not only more hopeful but more understanding and compassionate," etc., etc.

The questions I asked were about the moments of rapture, of greater happiness. They, therefore, observed the well-known fact that tragedy, pain, and confrontation with death all may produce the same cognitive or therapeutic effects in people with sufficient courage and strength. So also the fusion of happiness with sadness—of laughter's closeness to tears—have to be investigated. I was told often enough of the tears that came with tremendous happiness (e.g., weeping at the happy wedding) or with the triumph of justice (e.g., tears at the happy ending), or the lump rising in the throat (e.g., at the peak of an especially beautiful dance performance), or the chills, goose flesh, shivering—and in one case—even incipient nausea, at musical peaks. These questions call for intensive and extensive investigation.

The study of peak-experiences inevitably brings up a very difficult problem that must occupy psychology for the next century. This is what some of the old mystics and some theologians called the "Unitive Consciousness" and by other names as well. The problem as the religionists phrased it was how to live a godly life in an ungodly world, how to live under the aspect of eternity, how to keep the vision of perfection in an imperfect world, how to remember truth, goodness, and beauty in the midst of falsehood, evil, and ugliness. In the past, all sorts of people left the world behind in order to achieve this vision, e.g., immured themselves in monasteries, or lived ascetic lives, etc. And many have tried to subdue the flesh, the body, the appetites out of the mistaken belief that these contradicted the eternal, the perfect, the divine, the realm of Being.

But think! Peak-experiences can very meaningfully be assimilated to—or even replace—the immature concepts in which Heaven is like a country club in some specific place, perhaps above the clouds. In peaks, the nature of Being itself is often perceived nakedly and the eternal values then seem to be attributes of reality itself, or to say it another way, Heaven is all around us, always available in principle, ready to step into for a few minutes. It's anywhere—in the kitchen or the factory, or on a basketball court—*any*place where perfection can happen, where means become ends or where a job is done right. The Unitive Life is more possible than was ever dreamed of, and one thing is very clear—research will bring it closer and make it more available.

One last word. It must by now be obvious to those who are familiar with the literature of mystical experiences that these peak-experiences are very much like them, and overlap them but are not identical with them. What their true relationship is, I do not know. My best guess is that they are different in degree but not in kind. The total mystical experience, as classically described, is more or less approached by greater or lesser peak-experiences.

WINN: A CASE STUDY OF A HAPPY MAN

David F. Ricks

Alden E. Wessman

Conditions favorable to happiness and the characteristics of the happy man have always interested thoughtful people. But happiness is not a favored topic in psychology, nor are case studies of even moderately happy men frequent in our literature. Most psychologists with whom we have discussed Winn have been skeptical, cautious, or even pessimistic and cynical about the possibility that we have been able to study a really happy man. But is this pessimism justified? With Aristotle, we might ask if we have to wait until an exemplary man is dead before we can say that he was happy, and whether, while he is still alive, we cannot try to speak the truth about him.

"Winn" was studied for three of his undergraduate years by a team of psychologists directed by Henry A. Murray. Consistent with Murray's belief in consensual validation, Winn was studied by many people using their own special methods, all ultimately related into a consistent case formulation. Winn wrote an autobiography, took over a dozen tests, confronted himself on film, and opened his memory, moods, and fantasies to psychological scrutiny. This report draws on everything we know of Winn, with particular emphasis on a six-week study into the variations and levels of his moods.*

Winn was originally picked for study after his self report indicated a higher general level of happiness than other students. His happiness was

* A. E. Wessman, and D. F. Ricks, *Mood and Personality*. New York: Holt, Rinehart & Winston, 1966.

confirmed by an exceptionally low score on the MMPI Depression scale and by consistently high hedonic levels during the intensive study of moods. Independent observers of his behavior ranked him at the top of the group on current happiness, while those who studied his life history considered it the happiest of the twenty we investigated. It might be possible to find more happy men, but these data seem sufficient to show that Winn can serve as a model of happiness until they are discovered.

WINN'S BELIEFS AND CHARACTER

The language of psychology, like the language of everyday discourse, provides many words for misery and few for happiness. Our description of Winn suffers from this poverty, and we will have to resort too often to words that common use has so weakened and vulgarized that we distrust their communicative power. When we say that Winn had always had the admiration and love of a fine family; that he was satisfied with his background and his accomplishments; that he enjoyed life and expected to go to Heaven; we know that these words fail to convey the full meaning they had for Winn. Some readers will ask themselves, "What was he trying to hide?" We believe that he hid very little, and that what he did hide from himself was partly revealed in our tests and observations.

When we first met him in the fall of his sophomore year Winn impressed us as tall, lean, handsome, and a good natural athlete. Busy with his own activities, he was cooperative with our research project but not overly involved with it. Although he was always friendly, an intrusive question could bring a quick flush of anger to his face and a good-natured but sharp retort. He had the manly ability to know his ground and stand on it.

If Winn created any negative reaction, it was a feeling that he was too good to be true, too assured of his own superiority, or too limited in his perspectives. He was generally tolerant and he detested dogmatism, but he had apparently not given much consideration to ways of others or seriously doubted that his current track in life was the best possible.

Winn had noticed his impact on girls and

female teachers since early adolescence, and he was equally confident about his other qualities:

> I would regard my customary attitude as genial and confident. I am sure most people like and respect me. I am likewise sure some people feel me conceited and self-centered, especially if they know me only slightly. My good friends find me understanding and interested in them. Many people have me marked for success.

Well aware of his own good fortune, he felt that "fortunate people should use some energy in making others happy," and hoped to help solve some of the world's problems of hunger, despotism, and poverty. "I would like to make some truly great contribution in the field of science, believing that this will, in the long run, help almost everyone." He esteemed "people engaged in the search for truth and also people who make life happy and good for others." He had tasted strong draughts of success but felt that American society over-stressed competition, since "some people cannot stand the strain." For himself, though, competition was a stimulus: "I have always found that as soon as I attained something I had hoped for something else always attracted my ambition. . . . I have the potentialities to do something really worthwhile." His anticipated future included raising a good family, contributing to knowledge, helping people, and a substantial income.

Success was important to Winn, as was the innate satisfaction of work, but these were not exclusive goals. Although he occasionally felt that he should be more conscientious, he contented himself with a high but not spectacular grade record and reserved time for music, talk with friends, dating, and social life.

Winn had thus far been able to get and to do almost everything he wanted. Like most of the other happy people, he had a strong bent toward sociability, enjoyed his work but was not immersed in it, and was able to relax and enjoy both active play and the passive pleasures of food and rest.

Personal Philosophy

Winn's beliefs, although apparently strongly felt products of personal experience, sounded closer to the well-trodden utilitarian ways of J. S. Mill than to contemporary philosophies of anxiety and despair:

> Central to my philosophy of life is happiness. I think I have the right to be happy and I want to make other people happy. . . . Often the two aspects are concomitant—I am happy when I have made someone else happy. . . . To be fully happy, I need to be loved, and thus I feel marriage is essential to my complete happiness. I want to be loved for what I do, to be sure, but mostly I want to be loved for what I am.
>
> Gratification of the senses, when not immoderate, brings happiness. I do not mean only sexual gratification; pleasant and beautiful sights and sounds are included.
>
> My religion is essentially personal; I need not be a devout member of any religious sect to live a good life. . . . My concept of the afterlife does not include a hell . . . because I feel everyone has the same right to heaven. . . . If one has lived a bad, unhappy life on earth, there are too many contributing factors to say he is bad and should be punished. In my afterlife I will be happy and I will be with all those I loved while alive.
>
> Also in my after-life, infinite wisdom and knowledge will be available. I love knowledge, or truth; I find it beautiful. . . .
>
> I think the criterion for action is this: do what you will, just so long as you retain your self-respect. . . . This self-respect ties in with my happiness and with the happiness of loved ones, for to respect myself I cannot make them unhappy.
>
> I have the right to my own philosophy and every person has the right to live his own life according to his own philosophy, so long as he does not interfere with my happiness. . . . My philosophy is not one that everyone can live by; it is not a universal one, it is mine. This is important; some people would not live good lives according to my philosophy, I imagine.

Winn was deeply aware that he was "society's child." Since "society has laid down some good rules for the protection of the human race," he did not care to oppose society. The tinge of rebellion in his philosophy, and his assertion of individuality, were mild compared to the philosophies of his peers. Winn was essentially in harmony with his family, his community, and his religion.

The only *passion* Winn strongly expressed was a "thirst" for knowledge. Pure thought provided some of his most intense experiences. He compared mathematics to music, in that each time he worked with a familiar set of equations it was like listening to a symphony that he knew well but in which new things appeared on each new hearing.

Winn's philosophical emphasis on happiness, the possibility that any admission of unhappiness would be an admission of shortcoming, raises a question as to the validity of his conscious descriptions. We believe that his desire to be good may have slightly biased the report of his moods, but careful examination of his life history, and of the deeper levels of his personality, show that Winn's happiness had a solid foundation.

Life History

Until he came to Harvard, Winn lived in "the middle of a middle-class area" in a small Middle Western city. According to his autobiography, his parents were both white, Protestant, and valedictorians. Winn's father worked his way through college during the depression, then taught school, served as Sunday School Superintendent, and took an active part in community affairs. When Winn was about ten years old his father, with a growing family, left teaching for more lucrative work in industry, and the family moved into an upper-middle-class social position. Winn's early life was bounded by his neighborhood and the farm of his mother's parents, but in this little territory Winn was top dog: the boss of younger brothers at home, the most talented student in schools, a leader in every activity. At college he continued near the top, no longer the most brilliant student, but still bright enough to major in physics, graduate with honors, compete for major fellowships, and enjoy college social life and the Harvard band. He might have realized that there were larger worlds to conquer—but except for science, in which he knew he was a novice, he was not troubled by ambitions beyond his present reach. Like his father, he had "done excellent jobs on all projects he entered," and that was enough.

Winn's family life was conventional—the middle-class home, summer trips to Grandpa's farm, and the relatives' pride in his accomplishments could come out of stock fiction—but it was unusual in its happiness. His parents' harmony and affection reflected their continuing affectionate ties with their own families. Both were highly respected in their community. Neither parent had disappointed Winn and both had been "wonderful, kind, and understanding." "Perhaps they do a little too much to see that I have the best in life, but they are firm with me when needs be." In Winn's training "all of the vices and virtues were stressed, truth perhaps more than the others." Winn was punished by a spanking, by either parent, if he "got too far out of line." He attended Sunday School regularly.

Winn began his own life story with his uneventful birth, bottle feeding, and the foods he liked as a child. He was not an exceptionally happy baby—"I did cry a great deal, or so I am told"—but he was soon a self-confident child, "I was not retarded in learning to walk, and I was in general confident on my feet." A dislike for being alone began early and persisted, "solitariness was my one important fear." He did not want to "leave my Mommy" in the first two grades and frequently missed school. He still felt that he was not so adventurous as Billy, his next younger brother, nor so independent as Carl, the youngest. The combination of an exceptional interest in food and a marked dependence on adults, particularly his mother, indicated a lasting theme in Winn's life. Winn was still his family's and his society's child, with a philosophy of life that was "pretty much of a family philosophy" and "not independent of the way my society looks at things." Luckily for Winn's oral optimism, the world was still his oyster, and, as we will see when we reach his Rorschach, his breast of chicken, ice cream, and lemon meringue pie as well.

Another theme began with his first memory, the birth of his brother Billy when he was two and a half years old:

I was playing outside with a ball and a stick. It was a rather dark, cloudy, November day, and my father came out of the house (Billy was born at home) and told me I had a little brother. This did not "shake me up" at all, and I went inside to see my new brother. I was not impressed and went back outside to play ball.

Given Winn's close tie to his mother, it is likely that he was impressed by this intruder. In Winn's loving but controlled family it is probable that open anger about Billy and his claims on their mother was not encouraged. Minor "accidental" injuries to Billy punctuated the next several years of Winn's history and continued to find reflections in Winn's projective tests.

Winn's tie with his mother might have made trouble later, but the birth of Billy, and later of Carl, seemed to shake him up, in spite of his negation, and to force him to work free. His dependency was overcome and his self-control established early in life. He became quite adept in dealing comfortably with peers and potential rivals. This pattern was long established and by the time he was in high school "I quarreled seldom (usually my word was *law!*) and was not too moody."

An element of over-control, however, ran through Winn's history. His steady girl, for example, accused him of never acting on impulse. His brother Billy, unlike Winn, was a "wild" boy, often hurt in accidents, and his example may have pushed Winn to caution. Also, Winn recalled that he had acted on impulse and hurt himself. Once he fell down stairs and bent his nose. Once he ran into a fence and cut his jaw. Neither of these defects was apparent to the observer, but to Winn, who had few, any defect made a difference.

From childhood on Winn had a varied but not exceptionally intense fantasy life. He was troubled by the quick vividness of his fantasies, so unlike the restrained quality of his everyday thought. For a while he played with a fantasy of being a kind of turtle, possibly in response to feelings of holding himself in check. Until the age of sixteen he occasionally had a dream of being carried off his feet by a tornado, probably a fear of what would happen if his impulses were allowed expression. This dream was always the same, and eventually he feared it enough to permanently refuse sulfa drugs, which seemed to cause it.

Winn's school history was filled with steady achievement, prizes, adulation, and affection from teachers. He was "president of everything," and his best friend was a boy who "usually ran against me for office, and was always very gracious when he lost." Winn had many playmates when he was little. When he entered high school he limited himself to a few intimate friendships, though his activities produced many casual ones. An early admiration for athletes had given way, by junior high school, to a desire to be a professional musician. Although Winn was regarded as a "near-prodigy," he disliked his music teacher and decided by ninth grade to be a scientist, a career that embodied the qualities he most admired— beauty, truth, dignity, and intelligence. A theme in his fantasies became, and continued to be throughout college, somehow combining these goals with making money. At the end of high school these fantasies reached preliminary fruition when Winn won a large Harvard scholarship.

Winn's sexual activities were not unusual— some mutual fondling in pre-adolescence, a bit of sexual display with other boys, spin-the-bottle and post-office in early adolescence, quickly settling to steady dates with a girl whose background was like his own. He received sex instruction from his parents, beginning with his mother's explanation of pregnancy when he was eight and ending with his father's discussion of masturbation when he was thirteen. His sexual fantasies were about girls he knew and involved ordinary sexual play. He had not engaged in intercourse at the time we knew him, and he had never picked up girls. It would be hard to regard either Winn's behavior or his fantasies as wild, yet he reported:

I've got a pretty good imagination and will run hog-wild and crazy sometimes, so that what I do isn't—never is it—well, almost never—a reflection of some of the wild things that go on within.

In his behavior, on the other hand, he felt:

I have been pretty conventional. The first son . . . always make your parents proud of you. . . . Very little rebellion at all really.

His sexual fantasies from thirteen to sixteen concerned romantic conquests and erotic adventures. But from sixteen on he had even stronger, more frequent fantasies of a satisfying, harmonious, and enduring marriage that would produce a large, happy family. His fantasies were almost as monogamous, faithful, and mature as his behavior.

The marriage Winn fantasied for himself was very close to the one that nurtured him. Winn's innocent narcissism might have played some part in this—he was not critical of the family that produced his own character—but more important was love for his parents and identification with his admired father. Winn, as a little boy, listened in wonder to his father's series of bedtime stories about an original mock-heroic character. Later he watched his father become a community leader while remaining a loving parent. In school he was given special attention by teachers who liked his father. The fact that his college age fantasies had already moved beyond adolescent identity turmoil and on to intimacy and family life was probably due to the model provided by his father's exemplary role in his family and community.

Rorschach Test

Four seconds after Winn was handed the first card he reported "Looks like Cupid with wings." His performance throughout followed as quickly, without apparent effort. Within a few minutes he was through, yet his last response, "Looks like some X-rays I've seen of kidney and urinary tracts," suggests that the Rorschach shook Winn. Comparison of the anxiety implicit in his last response with the almost vapid Cupid might suggest that Winn's depths were not completely in harmony with his surface. Though neither the Rorschach nor any other evidence indicted Winn for conscious bad faith, the Rorschach did show a repressive trend that was less definite in other material. Like the TAT, it indicated a need to take flight from strongly emotional situations, to resort to distancing and intellectualization—and so to form and maintain a barrier between the deeper springs of his personality and its calm surface.

Most of the thirty-seven responses Winn produced in his orderly way were unoriginal interpretations of the obvious details of the cards, and many were only revisions and refinements of his first responses. Most of Winn's percepts were mainly determined by form, with other determinants subdued. Winn's intellect was clearly in the

saddle, but the effort of keeping it there was apparent in the unimaginative use of his fine mind.

Winn had an unusually sensitive response to those elements of the cards that suggest texture, to "shaggy," "furry," "bushy" dogs, rabbits, and furs. He was open and undefensive about the tenderness these percepts suggested: his dogs were touching noses, the furry mink stole would "go around your neck." He was less at ease with more powerful feelings: "The red parts don't seem to help. I can't seem to get them into anything." Later, in the inquiry, he said that "just their shape" suggested "gun holsters" and "cowboy boots with spurs," both indicative of a "cowboys and Indians" kind of aggression, not enough to frighten most people but enough to make Winn anxious. He saw in Card VI "maybe something nasty to bash someone over the head with—jagged and sharp—those whiskers are what do the damage when you swipe."

Winn's need to abstract himself from angry feelings was indicated by the response that followed this "nasty" percept: "That looks to me like looking down on an atoll in the South Pacific, a coral reef formation." Distance (looking down), intellectualization (an atoll), and rigidification (coral reef formation) are all suggested in this percept. The progressive fading out of a lively response was even more apparent in the sequence of responses to Card III, with "people playing the piano," an activity in which he himself took part, giving way to "native types dancing," followed by the dehumanization of the dancers into two birds facing each other, "a kind of abstract painting that doesn't really look like birds." Certainly Winn did not have a pathological degree of inhibition, yet even this paragon had his problems, and his defensive ways of handling them.

Winn's oral optimism was mentioned earlier. In addition to lemon meringue pie and banana splits, his Rorschach was filled with lavishly described drumsticks, chicken breasts, a bowl of ice cream, a shrimp cocktail, and a smoking pipe. Though Winn would blush at the association, these percepts might be related to the girls he preferred: "My female partner is usually of the voluptuous type with pleasantly large, well-formed breasts—small petite girls do not appeal to me."

Thematic Aperception Test

Winn's stories dealt with the perils that beset the ways of "nice, average" boys and girls who live in a world of temptations. Johnny struggles between the violin his parents gave him and his love of football; Nancy, who is "just a common girl," is "very sensitive to the wants and needs of other people." Two "level-headed, intelligent, sensible" young people wait for each other, marry, and have nice children. As if to defend a world in which Pandora's box is still unopened, he told one story in which innocence was confronted with suspicion and emerged triumphant. Sin was only allowed around the edges of his fantasy, a warning against the unwary impulse and its potential for destruction: in Card 4 an "average guy" in "a nice neighborhood" began to run around with boys his parents didn't like and then to smoke and drink and keep late hours. In spite of his wife's efforts to reform him he killed a man and ended life in prison. Another man, who was "never much good" because he "didn't care to work," became a hobo and ended as a cadaver on the table of an "up-and-coming" medical student.

In Winn's early stories good was rewarded and evildoing led to grief. The community was omnipresent—even more than parents, the agency through which rewards and punishments were channeled to the hero. The only disturbing element was, not too surprisingly for Winn, injury to someone near to him. Winn's active, self-assertive, confident drive must have involved him often in situations which verged on aggression toward others. In the stories he told, as in the Rorschach, the most usual fate of an aggressive thought was modulated expression, followed by attempts at undoing or minimizing consequences, by attempts to achieve distance, or by active mastery through skill and control. Virtue and community always triumphed over the aggressive individual—a state that changed, however, as Winn moved on to the more "fantastic" last ten pictures in the TAT.

In Winn's story to Card 11 impulse finally won a round. In this story, an apparent symbolic battle over masturbation was concluded when "Beelzebub" knocked the hero "down into a deep gorge, where the fiery river flowed." In another long, involved story a mysterious woman "expressed an interest" in the hero and "seemed to be able to defy the law of gravity" because she "could take an object and make it float around," a situation which fascinated the hero but made him feel in mortal danger. Against powers such as these—sexual impulses, particularly toward fascinating women—Winn fantasied having a "magic charm" which would "stand firm" and protect him against their pagan charms. But the charm failed him (being secretly in league with the enemy power), and he could concede without distress "so Beelzebub won again." If Winn had been less able to relax controls he might have had serious neurotic inhibitions—but while he did keep a firm grip on aggression, he could enjoy his sexual fantasies. Yet sexual activity was dangerous. Sexual misdeeds might be reported home and make everybody "terribly ashamed of what kind of man" one was. And if one relaxed controls too much, got too excited, it might be hard to control *both* sex and aggression. Thus a story of extra-marital flirtation ended in rape, murder, and execution. In another story a young man turned out to be a vampire who preyed on young girls and had to be eliminated to protect the community. Where sex alone was concerned Winn's private morality did not seem so strong as his fear of damaging his public image. But when sexuality was fused with aggression, or when aggression alone was concerned, he drew back with horror.

The other act punished by drastic retributions was discovering forbidden knowledge. The impulse that frightened him seemed to reflect concern over the origins of his little brothers, a curiousity not completely satisfied by his mother's explanation of pregnancy. One of his stories dealt with an archaeologist who wondered about a "dark, terrible secret" in a pyramid, found a papyrus that told him "the rules of how to get into this room," and made his way in, only to find that the "mummy cases" opened up and held tight to him. As he died he realized that he "had violated a curse and was going to be done away with by supernatural powers."

We have speculated that Winn's mild narcissism and exhibitionism originated in the situation of being displaced by his little brothers and at the same time prohibited from being either too outraged or too curious. Forced to stand on his own two feet, he could still outshine his brothers, and all rivals, by the glory of his achievements. When he gave his fantasy free rein, as he did in a story about the world's fastest rope climber, his fantasied exhibitionistic pleasure was intense:

> He got terrific feelings of power in this, because all of those people would stand there and look at him, and marvel at him, and nobody felt that anybody else in the world could be able to do things like that.

This desire for favorable attention and admiration seemed to be successfully diverted and socialized in his school successes and thirst for knowledge, though the story above suggests that secret knowledge, even science, could be dangerous.

The most original of Winn's productions, in any test or situation, was the image he created for the blank TAT card (16):

> This scene is on the planet Alpha Centuri . . . sort of half desert and half jungle. And the desert part is very rocky and, strangely, the rocks seem to be sculptured into architectural forms. They're square rocks and rectangular rocks and spherical rocks, and then there's a piece of sand stretching as far as the eye can see. . . .
>
> Then, over on the jungle side, there's this lush red-jungle red because chlorophyll is red on this planet. And there are . . . plants there that are kind of like animals. They are able to move in a certain way, and they can fight each other, and if you get near one it'll grab you and eat you up. These plants are grouped together to form a community, and they fight against each other all of the time. The wars of these plants are really something terrible and they have darts that they can shoot off, and secretions that come out of them. And they strangle each other by vines and roots, and dam up water supplies. . . . The way they kill one another is to drag the person, or the plant, to the edge of the jungle and throw him out into the desert. So that, sprinkled along the desert I've described, occasionally you'll see a little ashy crust. . . .

We might speculate that this vivid image portrayed an unconscious feeling of inner division, half dry, abstract, static intellect; the other half an infant jungle of fantasy. Winn had half renounced the capacity to tame fantasy by subjecting it to reality, and to give vitality to conscious thought by feeding it with imagination. Too often, his impulses died in the full light of conscious thought.

Winn's TAT, like his Rorschach, suggested depths at which he was not completely integrated, nor entirely the conventional All-American success story that he appeared on the surface. Was he then not really as happy as he seemed? We believe that at college he was truly happy, though at some later time he might find himself less satisfied with his work, less content with his successes, and more in need of inner refreshment than public adulation. Then even Winn might become unhappy. Yet these hints in his projective tests should not be overemphasized: to deny Winn any weaknesses at all would be to deny him humanity, and he certainly had more than enough strengths to counterbalance his weaknesses.

Data from Mood Study

A. *Mood levels:* In a study specifically designed to study characteristic levels and degrees of variability in happiness, anxiety, anger, and other moods, Winn's average hedonic level over a period of forty-two days was at the 7th level of a 10 point scale, "Feeling very good and cheerful." This level placed Winn at the top of the set of college students we studied, with only one other man near him. Only twice did his daily average drop below "Feeling pretty good, O.K.," and then it slid only to "Feeling a little bit low, just so-so." On six of the forty-two days his average mood for the day was "Elated and in high spirits." Only once, during a sudden painful illness, did his lowest mood drop to a really low point—and the next day he was able to report "Still in infirmary but feeling well and in good spirits. Only slight pain and discomfort."

Winn's high hedonic level was matched by equally high means on several other scales. According to these long-term reports, he was consistently confident that people thought well of him, felt that his abilities were sufficient and his prospects good, that he was accepted and liked, and that his life was ample and satisfying. He generally felt that he was open and responsive, pretty close to his own best self, and free within wide limits to act as he wanted. Thus, in the broad area of human interaction and social and moral judgment Winn felt that he was living a highly satisfying life. Winn did not feel quite as well off regarding work, nor was he regularly as energetic or secure as he might have been had his impulse expression been more free. But, taken together, Winn's day-to-day reports indicated that he was a very contented and happy person in the major aspects of his life and remarkably free from emotional distress.

B. *Mood changes and their relationships:* Besides studying characteristic *levels* of happiness and unhappiness, we investigated the ways in which men *varied* in their moods of happiness and unhappiness, anxiety and ease, openness to the world or withdrawal from it, and so on. The ways in which feelings varied in concert or in opposition were studied by factor analysis of individual patterns of change over six weeks. Winn was slightly toward the stable end of the group. But unlike most of the stable men, who had differentiated kinds of mood perturbations, Winn experienced his ups and downs as general mood swings. One large factor accounted for about two-thirds of the common variance in Winn's emotional changes. Four smaller factors reflected subsidiary feeling variations, each partially independent from Winn's fluctuations in hedonic level.

The major contrast in Winn's emotional life contrasted zestful, extremely happy days with somewhat less happy ones. Although all feelings were related to this major axis of happiness, they differed in the degree to which they were related. Energy, harmony and sociability with others, receptivity toward the world, and loving tenderness, together with feelings of approval by the community, were the main components of Winn's happiest moods. His best times came when he was involved with others, three of his happiest days coming in a series of parties over a football weekend, another set coming during a period of easy work and much socializing around the Thanksgiving weekend. Winn was exhilarated by social events of all kinds, reporting with equal excitement "The Yale weekend has started! Party in room!" and "Thanksgiving Dinner at Professor B's. What a good day!" In every report of happy times the food and liquor consumed played a large part. When Winn was in danger of being put on a restrictive diet to control an illness he discovered during the course of the study he reported in his daily diary, "I'll *die* if I have to give up frappes," and later he wrote, "Thank God! (for ice cream)." Unlike sadder men who had found the world less to their liking, Winn nourished an ardent openness to people, food, and fun. Unlike the more strictly work-oriented men, Winn could have a happy social time without guilt and could get along without over-concern for getting ahead.

The second factor described a contrast between calm, steady days and more excited, adventurous days with high peaks and low troughs. The first, and main, element in Winn's mood changes might be called American Epicureanism, the second Protestant Stoicism. On his less stoic, more excited days Winn hit his worst *troughs* of anxiety and anger, but also achieved his highest *peaks* of impulse expression, work, and thought. These seemed to be the days when some exceptionally powerful inner drive worked its way toward expression and powered both work and thought to new levels. At the end of one week when impulses, work, and thought had all hit high peaks, Winn reported "Have had very vivid dreams all week. Sex and violence."

The other idiosyncratic factors, describing variations on these general themes, will not be described here.

C. *Self- and ideal descriptions in depression and elation:* Each subject in our mood study twice filled out Q-sorts describing his self and his ideal concepts, once when elated and another time when depressed. The consistency of Winn's Q-sort self-descriptions in the two moods was about average for this group, his self-description in depression correlating .59 with his self-description in elation.

Winn chose two items as "most characteristic" of himself in both of his extreme moods:

Comfortable in intimate relationships. Sexually aware.

In elation the other items he selected as "most characteristic" were:

Adventuresome. Warm and friendly. Excels in his work. Placid and untroubled. Dynamic. Ambitious. Inventive, delights in finding new solutions to new problems. Accomplishes much, truly productive.

When Winn felt depressed this self-description was replaced by a less lively set of "most characteristic" qualities:

Doesn't apply himself fully. Able to take things as they come. Stands on his own two feet. Preoccupied with himself. Attempts to appear at ease. Quietly goes his own way. Good judge of when to comply and when to assert himself. Tactful in personal relationships.

Study of all the changes suggests that Winn, in his more elated moods, conceived of himself as warm, outgoing, and successful. When his mood lowered he retreated to a cautious position in which autonomy became more important than social participation and self-preoccupation threatened to replace both human relationships and intellectual productivity. But the changes were not great, and Winn remained oriented toward others and satisfied with himself even at his lowest.

Winn's self-description was rather close to his ideal in elation ($r = .75$) and only moderately different in depression ($r = .40$). Both of these figures were well within the top third of the group. The slight differences between his self-conception and his ideal in elation need not be reported here. The somewhat larger gaps in his depressed moods between the self and what Winn would have liked it to be were mainly concerned with work. Winn's super-ego was apparently a standard Protestant Ethic conscience, emphasizing work as temporal salvation. His slight deviations from this conscience carried him toward a more playful, resilient, responsive, and less driven character. We do not want to minimize the healthy significance of Winn's close approximation to his ideals, but it is also clear that Winn as he was had more life than he would have had if he came closer to his ideal.

CASE SUMMARY

Every source of data seems to confirm Winn's happiness and to show consistent themes in his character. Other men we studied surpassed Winn in depth and extent of social awareness, in richness of personality, in dedication to particular goals, or in other valued characteristics. But none equalled him in genuine, consistent zest and happiness.

What generated and sustained Winn's happiness? Part of the explanation seems rooted in his background and his gifts. Favored with a loving family that was respected in its community, fostered growth, and provided worthy and approachable models, possessed of sufficient means and opportunities, and gifted in face, form, intellect, health, and talent, Winn was consistently successful in his enterprises and his relationships. To the degree that the future is his responsibility this success seems likely to continue.

But Winn can also be seen as more than the sum of his background and his talents. His current personality showed a steadfast optimism, supported by a lively, active orientation toward the world, love of human contact, and balanced, mature judgment. We found only minor flaws in his general well-being, the main ones being an overly strong barrier between rationality and impulse and too much fear of community disapproval. But Winn's successes were not crass or calculating, and one of the sources of his happiness was reasonable willingness to accept limitations, to curb any inclinations toward narcissistic insatiability he may have had, and to tread the middle road between excess and deprivation with caution, intelligence, and due regard for his fellow man.

General Characteristics of Happy and Unhappy Men

We noted that Winn was studied as part of a general investigation of mood and personality. The contrasts between the happy and unhappy men suggest some general characteristics of happiness. The happy men possessed self-esteem and confidence. They were successful and satisfied in interpersonal relations. They showed ego-strength and a gratifying sense of identity. Their lives had organization, purpose, and the necessary mastery of themselves to attain their goals. The less happy men were pessimistic in their expectations and lower in self-esteem and self-confidence. More unsuccessful with their interpersonal relations, with evidence of isolation, anxiety, and guilt, they showed little sense of satisfying ego-identity. They felt inferior in their academic performance and their lives lacked continuity and purpose.

No single developmental success or trauma seems to account for happiness or unhappiness. Rather, multiple sources are found in the cumulative series of an individual's long-term life experiences. Important bases for self-esteem had been impaired in the lives of the unhappy men. Their damaged identities hampered their potential for intimacy and satisfying commitment. Unfavorable outcomes of several developmental crises had left the unhappy men prone to self-limitation frustration, and disappointment. Nor could one source account for the success of the well-adjusted, social extroverts such as Winn. These men were not of a single pattern, but did generally come from warm, supportive home environments that were conducive to growth and responsibility. Though there were exceptions, developmental transitions were generally smooth and residual conflicts subdued. Important needs had not become overly checked by disturbing affect. They were able to make positive identifications with respected, approachable role models and these had in turn favored the establishment of a worthwhile sense of self.

Lest our readers conclude that this is a simple and unqualified paean to happiness, let us make our position clear. We hold that it is desirable that people be happy—it is generally superior to misery. But happiness can also be constricting. There was much to admire and respect in the lives of some of the more complicated and less happy men.

Is Psychology Ready for Happiness?

Can we move on from these empirical descriptions to a systematic formulation of the character of the happy man and of the conditions for happiness? Can psychology add anything not yet said in the long history of the problem? The classic Socratic formula, that the happy man is temperate, just, brave, and pious, seems a remarkably apt summary of Winn's main characteristics. If we add to this Aristotle's comment that happiness requires, in addition to excellence, the possession of good birth, personal gifts, and external fortune, we have summarized most of Winn's outstanding virtues.

Modern psychology has emphasized other qualities possessed by Winn—pro-action, adjustment, ego-strength, competence, and identity. But these seem, while necessary, not yet sufficient. Since Freud and Abraham, psychoanalysts have also emphasized the oral qualities of the optimistic person. Winn typified these, together with the qualities of good conscience and self-acceptance psychoanalysis posits for the man free from depression. The skeptical analyst might also note that denial might contribute to happiness, or even be necessary if one is to be happy. Identification with suffering can upset complacency. Winn, in the bright sunshine of successful youth, did seem lacking in shadows, perspective, and awareness of tragedy. His happiness perhaps rested on his limitations as well as on his gifts.

We can only note here that Winn's adjustment, while beautifully articulated with current American society, does not offer a trans-societal formula for happiness. Winn, society's child, had both the assets and the limitations of his particular segment of American culture. But a full treatment of this aspect of Winn would take us far afield.

The most tantalizing puzzle offered by Winn arises from his inhibitions and the limited degree to which his personality can be considered spontaneous, self-actualizing, or internally congruent. If a controlled, well-socialized man such as Winn can stand as a model for happiness, then we must consider that civilization must have inherent satisfactions as well as inherent discontents, and that due regard for maturation and refinement of impulses must temper our enthusiasm for the simpler prescriptions of psychological hedonism. The formula that happiness equals the sum of satisfactions minus the sum of dissatisfactions, which is the logical derivative of hedonistic theories, must be tempered by consideration of the quality, age appropriateness, and lasting value of the satisfactions being considered. We often hope that the study of psychology can increase human insight and awareness, and so increase the range of alternatives available to the lives of its students. To do this psychology must deal with human lives on a scale that boldly comes to grips with problems of quality and value. The study of happy men and women can perhaps be a step in this direction.

TOPIC 8

Anxiety

It is clear that we have developed a society which depends on having the right amount of anxiety to make it work.

—Margaret Mead

I think I've got a secret. It's keep your bloody eyes open, all your senses open. You never know what might be useful. It's like a disease with me. Learning to fly in the navy during the war, you had to develop a technique, a certain feeling, a poise— it was fatal to be too relaxed, fatal to be too tense.

—Laurence Olivier

Anxiety is a state of arousal caused by a threat to well-being. When we are anxious, we feel endangered or challenged in some way, and we are tense or uneasy and ready to act or respond. To be anxious is, of course, a common human experience. For some of us, feelings of this kind may be more salient than any other emotion.

Anthropologist Margaret Mead writes that our society needs a certain amount of anxiety to function properly, and psychological research suggests that stress, up to a certain point, is helpful in learning and performing certain tasks. Too much anxiety can disorganize our efforts or even paralyze us. With too little anxiety, we may not rouse ourself and do the things that need to be done.

Although our era has been called "the age of anxiety," Mead finds modern stress preferable to the terror, fright, and hunger of simpler societies. Still, in these turbulent and rapidly changing times, we can be under considerable and sometimes scarcely tolerable strain. And there is little prospect that we will be able to relax in the years ahead. Futurists such as Alvin Toffler in his widely read *Future Shock* have written of the stressful and explosive changes to come.

Our era might also be called "the age of the tranquilizer." Enormous quantities of pills have been consumed by individuals who are seeking relief from their anxieties, fears, and worries. And in very recent years many people have sought other ways of combatting anxiety or finding peace of mind through relaxation techniques, meditation, individual and group therapies, and related experiences of various kinds.

Although we tend to think of anxiety as bad and try to avoid or reduce it, or defend ourself against it, anxiety actually plays a useful role as a signal, rouser, and moving force. If we permit ourself to experience anxiety, it warns and directs us, stirs and excites us, and drives us on. Personal growth is frequently accompanied by anxiety since we feel threatened whenever we leave safe and familiar ruts.

Many persons believe that somehow they should be free of anxiety. They consider anxiety a sign of abnormality for to be normal means (they think) that one is relaxed, happy, and has peace of mind. But meaningful living necessarily involves anxiety—a small amount much of the time, and perhaps great bursts or waves upon occasion. A moderation of anxiety, a tolerance for it, and an understanding of it—not a completely stress-free life—is as much as we should want and aspire to achieve.

The impact of anxiety

In the first article, Abe Arkoff sums up the evidence concerning the effects of anxiety on behavior. Psychological research supports the idea that stress, up to a certain point, facilitates the learning and performance of various tasks. This research also suggests that in considering the impact of stress, one must take into consideration the characteristic anxiety level of the individual. People who have generally elevated levels tend to fare poorly in stressful situations. Furthermore, research evidence indicates that the performance of more complex tasks is more impaired by stress than is the performance of simpler tasks.

The positive impact of anxiety

In the second selection Daniel A. Sugarman and Lucy Freeman focus on the merits of anxiety. Anxiety alerts us, rouses us, and prompts us to do what we should do. Anxiety is both a sign and a price of growth: we become anxious when we leave comfortable plateaus and begin the ascent to higher reaches. Some of us so fear fear—become so anxious about being anxious—that we become worse off than before. Anxiety, these writers point out, is not necessarily the enemy; it can be a good—though sometimes painful—friend and helper.

Conquering anxiety through rational–emotive therapy

Rational–emotive therapists hold that human unhappiness stems in large measure from irrational ideas which govern our emotional life. By identifying these irrational ideas, replacing them with rational substitutes, and acting upon the replacements, we can greatly improve. Albert Ellis and

Robert A. Harper feel that anxiety consists largely of the irrational idea that "if something is or may be dangerous or fearsome, one should be terribly occupied with and upset about it." In the third reading they present 11 tactics for a counterattack on anxiety within a larger strategy which tells us to track our worries to the irrational sentences we recite to ourselves, and then challenge, contradict, and act against these irrational ideas.

Conquering anxiety through reactive inhibition therapy

In the fourth article G. Donald MacLean and Robert W. Graff present "a simple home remedy for fears" which has been found to be effective with some college students. Called "reactive inhibition therapy," this procedure encourages the subject to experience a particular fear as deliberately and fully as possible. By focusing on a feared situation, either actual or imagined, and by reacting vigorously to it, one can ultimately reduce or eliminate the fear. The technique has been found to work best with specific fears and in the presence of a sympathetic person to whom one can verbalize or act out one's feelings.

Conquering anxiety through systematic desensitization

In the last selection Martin Katahn describes a Vanderbilt University program for alleviating the anxiety of students. One element is a systematic desensitization procedure in which the student describes and arranges anxiety-provoking situations in a hierarchy ranging from the most to the least upsetting; then, in order to desensitize these situations, the student is taught deep relaxation and in this state he visualizes these situations beginning with the least anxiety-provoking and proceeding in time to the top of the hierarchy. The second element in the program is a series of group counseling sessions that relate to five common anxiety-producing problems: scheduling, study habits, student–instructor relations, misconceptions about academic demands, and confusion concerning academic goals.

FOR PERSONAL APPLICATION

1. How anxious are you? Do you think you have too much anxiety, too little, or just the right amount? Discuss your answer.
2. Is anxiety a positive or a negative factor in your life? Why?
3. What situations tend to make you anxious? Why?
4. Discuss a non-objective anxiety or fear you have—that is, one that seems "childish," inappropriate, or not commensurate with the threat involved in a particular situation.
5. Discuss a growth situation—a time when you were taking on a challenging task, assuming a new role, or starting off on a new life direction

—that was accompanied by considerable anxiety. How did you respond to this anxiety?

6. Discuss one or more ways that you have used to control or manage your anxieties.
7. Do you think there is too high a level of anxiety or stress in our society today? Why or why not?
8. Do you think that people in this country today are generally more anxious or under greater stress than a century ago? Why or why not?
9. Write down a discussion item (not given above) which seems particularly relevant to this topic and you, and discuss it.

FOR SMALL GROUPS

1. *Sharing fears.* One member begins by telling the group about a personal fear, what he thinks has caused it or what it means, how it affects his life, and how he has tried to deal with it. Other members of the group respond to this person, relating his fear to fears they have or have had and making suggestions from their own experience as to how this fear can be understood and dealt with. Then a second person tells the group of one of his fears and the process continues as before.
2. *Sharing fears about the group.* Each member in turn discusses something about the group that makes him (or has made him) worried, fearful, or anxious. After everyone has had a chance to speak, the group discusses how it can alleviate or deal with the fears of its members in the group situation.
3. *Contrasting the positive and negative faces of anxiety.* Anxiety can be a negative or positive force, but we more commonly think of it as the former than as the latter. In this exercise each group member presents from his own life two examples of anxiety-laden experiences, one in which anxiety was negative or debilitating and the other in which it was positive or facilitating.

FOR FURTHER READING

Gray, J. *The Psychology of Fear and Stress.* New York: McGraw-Hill Book Company, 1971.

Klausner, S. Z., ed. *Why Man Takes Chances: Studies in Stress-seeking.* Garden City, N.Y.: Doubleday Anchor Books, 1968.

Marks, I. M. *Fears and Phobias.* New York: Academic Press, 1969.

Martin, B. *Anxiety and Neurotic Disorders.* New York: John Wiley & Sons, Inc., 1971.

Rachman, S. *The Meanings of Fear.* Baltimore: Penguin Books, 1974.

Sugarman, D. A., and L. Freeman. *The Search for Serenity.* New York: The Macmillan Company, 1970.

Toffler, A. *Future Shock.* New York: Random House, Inc., 1970.

STUDYING ANXIETY

Abe Arkoff

Anxiety is one of the most important problems in psychology, and it is becoming one of the most studied and written about. The material which follows describes some approaches to the study of anxiety and presents some of the findings these approaches have revealed.

SOME APPROACHES

Some of the earliest information about anxiety was gathered by professionals who treated adjustment problems and described the individuals who came to them for help. More recently, knowledge about anxiety has been acquired through the use of specially devised tests and experimental situations.

Descriptive Approaches

One way to learn about anxiety is to observe and describe people who say they feel anxious or who are designated as anxious on some other basis. Since none of us is free of anxiety and most of us have some very anxious moments, information about anxiety can come from simply noting our own behavior in threatening situations.

People who have adjustment problems and seek help generally have a heightened level of anxiety, and the therapist is in a good position to study this phenomenon. There are many descriptions of anxious people in the psychological literature. Here is a case history of an anxiety reaction presented by a psychiatrist who describes the patient's anxiety, traces its cause and course, and shows its treatment and outcome.

A twenty-two-year-old married woman was referred to the psychiatrist by a friend of hers. She was an attractive, intelligent young woman who, although very anxious, was quite sincere in her efforts to find a solution to her problems. She had for some time recognized that her difficulties were on an emotional basis. She said that she feared insanity and that she had become increasingly nervous and disturbed about a multitude of things for the previous six months. Her final decision to seek psychiatric consultation had been precipitated by an anxiety attack which had lasted for about five days. She had been forced to quit her work because of this anxiety and had become increasingly fearful about everything which she had to do. She was apprehensive about such simple things as leaving her home, meeting people, going to bed, greeting her husband, or even answering the doorbell.

She was accompanied to her initial interview by her husband, a merchant. Because of her anxiety, she had been unable to come to this interview alone. Her repeated anxiety attacks during the previous week had frequently necessitated her calling her husband from his work. She had been able to achieve some measure of comfort only when he was sitting near her. She had often awakened him during the night when she had been unable to sleep and on numerous occasions had called the family physician at all hours of both day and night.

This patient's history, which she herself gave, revealed that she had been married for about six months and felt that her marriage was a successful [and] proper one. Her husband was the head of a thriving business and was obviously quite attached to her and interested in her well-being. She had been a laboratory technician prior to marriage and had graduated some two years previously. She said that she had always performed her work adequately and had left her job only because of the gradual increase in her apprehensiveness. Her family history revealed that she had one sister, three years her senior, who apparently had no emotional problems of consequence. Her parents were living and, as she stated in the initial interview, were happy and well-adjusted people.

The patient spontaneously went on to say that she had always been a moody person who had either been "way up or way down." She said that she had also been inhibited and made friends rather slowly, but got along with them quite well after she established good relationships. She had always been timid in her initial contacts with people for fear of possible resentment or rejection. She was unable to say why they might resent or reject her, but she always refrained from thoroughly accepting others until she had convinced herself that they were truly friendly toward her and that there was no chance that she might be snubbed or ignored.

As the patient described her childhood and adolescence, it soon became evident that in addition to being the youngest child she had also been the favorite, particularly of her father. He had showered many gifts upon her and had never hesitated to show his preference for her. Her mother had been more of the disciplinarian in the family, and in spite of the patient's occasional attempts to be friendly with the mother, the relationship had always been distant and cool. Further elucidation of this area showed that the mother had never been excessively demanding, but had certainly been less permissive than the father. The patient had been able, in the majority of situations, to obtain whatever she wanted and had rarely denied herself anything. If she was unable to obtain whatever she wanted from her mother, it was usually possible for her to get it from her father. As a result, whenever she had run into frustration, she had always turned to her father. He had constantly praised her and had frequently been her ally against her mother.

This patient said that the majority of her complaints had begun soon after her marriage. As she talked, it became evident that she felt that her husband was not as understanding as she had hoped that he would be. She had discovered, soon after marriage, that their financial status, though adequate, was certainly not unlimited. At times it became necessary for her to deny herself things and such a deprivation had rarely occurred to her prior to marriage. She had also begun to discover that there were many responsibilities which fell to her after marriage that were of a type she had never experienced or expected. Actually these responsibilities stemmed from her husband's normal tendency to expect her to share their marital responsibilities. There had been numerous occasions when the patient had become extremely angry at her husband, stamped her feet, and screamed at him, as she had previously done at

her own parents. However, she soon found that her husband did not respond to this in the same "understanding" way as her parents had.

As succeeding interviews passed, it became increasingly evident that she was an extremely narcissistic, selfish, and immature woman, who had never been given the opportunity to learn to carry responsibilities herself. From childhood onward, she had always been able to turn toward her father in times of difficulty and he, in turn, had always provided her with an easy solution, often removing the difficulties of the situation in which she was involved. She had expected the same sort of treatment from her husband, and when it was not forthcoming, had found him wanting in good qualities. She had become increasingly angry at him and, at the same time, entertained some doubts as to the wisdom of choosing him as her marital partner. She had always assumed, unrealistically, that marriage would be a utopian type of existence, and she had fantasied that there would be few responsibilities. Actually, without realizing it, she had expected to get the same kind of treatment from her husband as she had from her father. When reality was presented to her in the form of her husband's reasonable demands, she had become extremely hostile. Much of this hostility remained within her, with only portions of it being expressed in occasional temper outbursts and the remainder of it remaining within her on an unconscious level. It gradually came into conflict with her conscience's demands, and thus she began to feel guilty. The result was that instead of feeling the resentment itself, she began to suffer acute anxiety attacks which, without psychotherapy, might have merged into a true chronic anxiety reaction.

After approximately a dozen interviews, the patient began to recognize her immature strivings and to improve her adjustment in marriage. She could accept her husband's demands more and was willing to attempt to fulfill at least some of them. As her understanding of her own immaturities and unrealistic expectations increased, her anxiety symptoms diminished. She ceased hating and began to use her aggression constructively and to receive the strengthening benefits of love and approval which a healthy environment always gives to maturely behaving people.

In summary, then, this patient had reached adult life and marriage with an immature and unrealistic outlook. Because of her childishness she made excessive demands upon her environment. These had always been sufficiently satisfied in the past, particularly by her father, so that there had been no great reason for the weaknesses of her personality to reveal themselves in the form of anxiety. However, when she married and had to face additional responsibilities, she became chronically dissatisfied and frustrated. This stirred up a great deal of inner resentment, some of which appeared in explosive outbursts, but much of which remained within her, stirring up considerable guilt. Her anxiety appeared as a warning signal to keep the true extent of her inner resentment from becoming evident to her. As is true of many neurotic conflicts her anxiety gradually spread to involve new areas of her life until she became almost totally immobilized. However, and this is also typical in many such cases, as her understanding of her own personality and her relationships increased, her anxiety diminished. Her symptoms disappeared and her own desire to mature became more prominent as well as more gratifying.[1]

Relational Approaches

Another way that anxiety has been studied is by relating it to other phenomena. For example, we might be interested in the relationship between anxiety and age. (Are children more anxious than adults?) Or we might be curious about the relationship between anxiety and occupation. (Are artists more anxious than policemen?) Or we could pursue the relationship between anxiety and culture. (Are Americans more anxious than Frenchmen?)

Some modest information concerning these several questions has been provided by anxiety questionnaires which have been administered to large groups of people. For the relationship between anxiety and age, results indicate that anxiety fluctuates in early childhood. It rises consistently in adolescence and declines through early and middle adulthood. After age sixty or sixty-five, it rises again.

Concerning the relationship between anxiety

and occupation, the results do not support Gilbert and Sullivan's operatic claim that "a policeman's lot is not a happy one!" Policemen, engineers, and clerical workers were among those with lower anxiety scores. Occupational groups with higher levels of anxiety included artists, newspaper editors, and air cadets in training.

Concerning the relationship between anxiety and culture, the results did not indicate that Americans were anxiety ridden. . . . When compared with the subjects of five other countries, Americans proved to have the lowest anxiety scores. The investigator notes, "National comparisons are invidious and notoriously tricky, but these results may possibly fit a theory that low anxiety is associated with better economic level and closer political integration" (Cattell, 1963, p. 104).

Experimental Approaches

In descriptive and relational approaches, people are observed, described, and measured, but no attempt is made to manipulate them or change their behavior. In the experimental approach, subjects are observed under certain controlled conditions to see the effect of these conditions. Such conditions may be created in the laboratory or they may exist in real life.

In the laboratory it is not easy to devise meaningful situations in which anxiety can be elicited and its effects studied. For one thing, there is a limit to the amount of stress to which human subjects can be exposed. Furthermore, as was noted, subjects react differently to stress; a situation which will prove stressful for one person may scarcely affect another.

Many methods have been used to induce stress or anxiety in laboratory situations; just a few examples will be presented here. Some experimenters have devised generally frustrating environments. In one experiment subjects were forced to remain awake all night while they were exposed to a number of other irritating circumstances (Sears, Hovland, and Miller, 1940). Another investigator surreptitiously locked groups of subjects in a room into which smoke was allowed to seep to give theappearance of an outbreak of fire (French, 1944). In a study involving children, the subjects were placed in a room with some very attractive toys which, how-

[1] Reprinted from *Introduction to Psychiatry* by O. Spurgeon English and Stuart M. Finch. By permission of W. W. Norton & Company, Inc., Copyright © 1954, 1957, 1964 by W. W. Norton & Company, Inc. Pp. 155–157 (1957 ed.).

ever, were inaccessible (Barker, Dembo, and Lewin, 1943).

Sometimes subjects are aroused by being told that they are taking an important personality or intelligence test on which they would want to do well, and their performance is compared with that of control subjects given neutral instructions (Sarason and Palola, 1960). After they have been aroused, they may be given very difficult tasks, and they may be arbitrarily failed and criticized (Sarason, 1957).

Some investigators have used the threat of physical pain to induce stress. In one experiment, electrodes were attached to the arm of the subject and he was led to anticipate a series of painful electrical shocks (Sarnoff and Zimbardo, 1961). In another, the subjects were led to believe that the apparatus to which they were affixed was faulty and that they were liable to receive a dangerous charge of electricity (Ax, 1960).

Motion pictures have also been used as sources of threat. In one study, "Wages of Fear," a film depicting the perilous journey of men driving trucks loaded with nitroglycerin, was used to produce stress (Alexander, Flagg, Foster, Clemens, and Blahd, 1961). Another group of experimenters has made wise use of an anthropological film showing painful puberty rites in the Arunta, a Stone Age culture of Australia (Lazarus and Opton, 1966).

The situations described above are not real life, of course. Furthermore, there are some problems inherent in the laboratory use of deception and stress. Psychologists conducting research are expected to follow the code of ethical standards set forth by the American Psychological Association. This code puts restrictions on the experimental use of stress and requires that harmful aftereffects be avoided or removed as soon as possible (Ethical Standards of Psychologists, 1963).

Many stress situations can be observed in real life, but they are usually more difficult to study than those in the laboratory. One set of investigators studied young men who were experiencing the real stress of paratroop training (Basowitz, Persky, Korchin, and Grinker, 1955). Another made an intensive study of the behavior of patients who were undergoing major surgery (Janis, 1958). A third investigated the effect of stress on learning and conditioning by using people (undergraduates, graduates, and staff members of the University of Illinois) who were undergoing real-life events which might be considered anxiety provoking; these included giving oral reports which were part of course requirements, taking preliminary examinations for the doctoral degree, and appearing in a drama before a large audience on opening night (Beam, 1955).

SOME FINDINGS

What effect does anxiety have on behavior? Anxiety has been defined as a state of arousal, and the discussion will first consider the effects of arousal in general. We know that in order to get anything done we must rouse ourselves or be aroused to some extent. In such situations we probably would not use the word "arousal," but we might talk about being motivated or getting a move on.

How aroused we need to be depends on the task which confronts us. If we seem too little activated or energized for what is in store, we may give ourselves a pep talk, or somebody else with an interest in the matter may prod us a bit. Sometimes, however, we get so highly aroused that we are unable to act effectively in a particular situation, and we may need to stop racing our motor, simmer down, and cool it.

The idea that there is an optimal level of arousal for a particular task situation has been explored by a number of psychologists. In this connection Woodworth and Schlosberg write:

In a sense, *all* behavior is organized or patterned; when we say it is disorganized, we are evaluating it in terms of its efficiency in attaining some specific objective that confronts the organism. It is a safe bet that there is an optimum level of activation for each task; it would be low for reading a light novel, higher for working a math problem, and still higher for playing football. Below the optimum level the organism lacks energy, persistence, and concentration, but above this level his performance lacks precision; it is disorganized as far as the task is concerned [1954, p. 111].

A similar idea has been developed by Malmo (1962), who theorizes that there may be an optimal level of activation for a specific individual on a specific task (but this level is not necessarily optimal for another person or on another task). Relatively more or less than this optimal amount leads to a poorer performance. Malmo schematizes his idea in this way:

Activation level	Low	Moderate	High
Expected performance level	Low	Optimal	Low

In an analogous fashion, a number of psychologists have written about the usefulness, even the necessity and attractiveness, of mild or moderate levels of anxiety. Hebb (1955) calls attention to the "positive attraction of risk taking." He says, "When you stop to think of it, it is nothing short of extraordinary what trouble people will go to in order to get into more trouble at the bridge table, or on the golf course. . . ." Mowrer (1953) puts the matter in even stronger terms; he writes that "normal anxiety is the force that keeps driving the personality toward wholeness, toward unity, and toward maximal effectiveness. It is the force which helps the personality achieve ever higher levels of synthesis, new integrations, and a more stable and durable organization."

Margaret Mead develops the idea that there is an optimal ("right") amount of anxiety for our society as well as for the individuals that make it up. She writes:

It is clear that we have developed a society which depends on having the right amount of anxiety to make it work. Psychiatrists have been heard to say, "He didn't have enough anxiety to get well," indicating that, while we agree that too much anxiety is inimical to mental health, we have come to rely on anxiety to push and prod us into seeing a doctor about a symptom which may indicate cancer, into checking up on that old life insurance policy which may have out-of-date clauses in it, into having a conference with Billy's teacher even though his report card looks all right.

People who are anxious enough keep their car insurance up, have the brakes checked, don't take a second drink when they have to drive, are careful where they go and with whom they drive on holidays. People who are too anxious either refuse to go into cars at all —and so complicate the ordinary course of life—

or drive so tensely and overcautiously that they help cause accidents. People who aren't anxious enough take chance after chance, which increases the terrible death toll of the roads [1956, pp. 13, 56].

What does the experimental evidence indicate? First, it tends to support the idea that stress, up to a point, may be helpful in learning and performing certain tasks. Martin (1961) reviews the evidence on this point which has come out of the psychological laboratory. Comparing the results of many investigators, he notes that the findings are not clear-cut but that they tend to support the generalization that "increasing stress results in improved performance up to a point and impairment thereafter."

Second, the evidence suggests that the characteristic or general anxiety level of the individual must be considered. Reviewing the evidence, Sarason (1960) concludes that, more often than not, subjects with high scores on anxiety scales do more poorly under laboratory stress conditions than subjects with lower scores. Sarason also notes that, compared with low anxious subjects, high anxious ones "have been found to be more self-deprecatory, more self-preoccupied, and generally less content with themselves."

Third, the evidence indicates that the complexity of the task or situation must be considered; performance of more complex tasks is more likely to be impaired by high anxiety than the performance of simpler ones. In situations, for example, where there is only one response, anxious subjects may perform at higher levels than less anxious ones, but in complex situations involving a number of strong, competing responses low anxious subjects may be at an advantage (Martin, 1961; Sarason, 1960).

In this connection it has been observed that individuals of certain characteristic anxiety levels may be at an advantage in a number of situations and at a disadvantage in others. One set of investigators devised a test to measure anxiety specific to testing situations. Using it in a study involving college students, they found that subjects with high anxiety levels did better on course examinations than did less anxious students. In this type of situation the instructor and his demands were known to the class, and the anxious students in particular could alleviate stress by making the necessary preparation. However, in novel test situations, those for which no preparation was possible, the less anxious students did better than the more anxious ones (Sarason and Mandler, 1952).

REFERENCES

ALEXANDER, F., G. W. FLAGG, S. FOSTER, T. CLEMENS, and W. BLAHD. "Experimental Studies of Emotional Stress. I. Hyperthyroidism," *Psychosomatic Medicine*, 23 (1961), 104–114.

AX, A. F. "Psychophysiology of fear and anger," *Psychiatric Research Reports*, 12 (1960), 167–175.

BARKER, R. G., T. DEMBO, and K. LEWIN. "Frustration and Regression," in R. G. Barker, J. S. Kounin, and H. F. Wright, eds., *Child Behavior and Development*. New York: McGraw-Hill Book Company, 1943, pp. 441–458.

BASOWITZ, H., H. PERSKY, S. J. KORCHIN, and R. R. GRINKER. *Anxiety and Stress*. New York: McGraw-Hill Book Company, 1955.

BEAM, J. C. "Serial Learning and Conditioning Under Real-life Stress," *Journal of Abnormal and Social Psychology*, 51 (1955), 543–551.

CATTELL, R. B. "The Nature and Measurement of Anxiety," *Scientific American*, 208(3) (1963), 96–104.

ENGLISH, O. S., and S. M. FINCH. *Introduction to Psychiatry*, 2nd ed. New York: W. W. Norton & Co., Inc., 1957.

"Ethical standards of psychologists," *American Psychologist*, 18 (1963), 56–60.

FRENCH, J. R. P. "Authority and Frustration. Studies in Topological and Vector Psychology. III. Organized and Unorganized Groups Under Fear and Frustration," *University of Iowa Studies in Child Welfare*, 20 (1944), 231–308.

HEBB, D. O. "Drives and the C.N.S. (Conceptual Nervous System)," *Psychological Review*, 62 (1955), 243–254.

JANIS, I. L. *Psychological Stress*. New York: John Wiley & Sons, Inc., 1958.

LAZARUS, R. S., and E. M. OPTON, JR. "The Study of Psychological Stress: A Summary of Theoretical Formulations and Experimental Findings," in C. D. Spielberger, ed., *Anxiety and Behavior*. New York: Academic Press, 1966, pp. 225–262.

MALMO, R. B. "Activation," in A. J. Bachrach, ed., *Experimental Foundations of Clinical Psychology*. New York: Basic Books, Inc., 1962, pp. 386–422.

MARTIN, B. "The Assessment of Anxiety by Physiological Behavioral Measures," *Psychological Bulletin*, 58 (1961), 234–255.

MEAD, M. "One Vote for This Age of Anxiety," *New York Times Magazine* (May 20, 1956), pp. 13f.

MOWRER, O. H. "Neurosis and Psychotherapy as Interpersonal Process: A Synopsis," in O. H. Mowrer, ed., *Psychotherapy: Theory and Research*. New York: Ronald Press, 1953.

SARASON, I. G. "The Effect of Anxiety and Two Kinds of Failure on Serial Learning," *Journal of Personality*, 25 (1957), 383–392.

———. "Empirical Findings and Theoretical Problems in the Use of Anxiety Scales," *Psychological Bulletin*, 57 (1960), 403–415.

———, and E. G. PALOLA. "The Relationship of Test and General Anxiety, Difficulty of Task, and Experimental Instructions to Performance," *Journal of Experimental Psychology*, 59 (1960), 185–191.

SARASON, S. B., and G. MANDELER. "Some Correlates of Test Anxiety," *Journal of Abnormal and Social Psychology*, 47 (1952), 810–817.

SARNOFF, I., and P. G. ZIMBARDO. "Anxiety, Fear, and Social Affiliation," *Journal of Abnormal and Social Psychology*, 62 (1961), 356–363.

SEARS, R. R., C. I. HOVLAND, and N. E. MILLER. "Minor Studies of Aggression. I. Measurement of Aggressive Behavior," *Journal of Psychology*, 9 (1940), 275–295.

WOODWORTH, R. S., and H. SCHLOSBERG. *Experimental Psychology*, 2nd ed. New York: Holt, Rinehart & Winston, Inc., 1954.

THE POSITIVE FACE OF ANXIETY

Daniel A. Sugarman and
Lucy Freeman

Your pain is the breaking of the shell that
enclosed your understanding.
Even as the stone of the fruit must break.
That heart may stand in the sun, so must you
know pain . . .

—Kahlil Gibran, *The Prophet*

Anxiety is thus the most painful of all emotions, and many people will do anything to avoid direct confrontation with it. Like a child terrified of going to the dentist, they permit anxiety to fester and cause psychic decay. They refuse to submit to the direct confrontation which removes the decay and the chronic pain. Some use so much energy defending themselves against anxiety that there is little left for the enjoyment of living.

We are learning that it is not anxiety itself, but the way we handle anxiety, that makes the difference between emotional sickness and health. Anxiety, as we have seen, may cause us to fall physically ill. Most important, a refusal to acknowledge the anxiety within us prevents the possibility of greater personality growth.

The widespread use of tranquilizers has helped —and hindered. On one hand, millions have obtained sufficient relief from anxiety to cope with daily difficulties; but the indiscriminate use of these powerful medications has prevented many from coming to terms with their conflicts. If

they were just a little more desperate, they might seek psychological help and get at the source of the anxiety.

THE GIFT OF ANXIETY

In our hedonistic society, it is difficult for many to believe that anything which stings a bit can be of value. Nevertheless, in spite of our love of the sun, rainy days are important in the total scheme of things. Without any anxiety, we would become like vegetables, unable to sense the passing danger that threatens us from every side. The hypervigilance anxiety brings makes it easier for us to detect danger and take appropriate measures against it.

One mother described to me how, in putting her eight-month-old baby to bed one night, she felt suddenly anxious about his health. It seemed he did not look healthy, as though he were coming down with a cold; nor did she like the way he sounded when he cried. With these thoughts in mind, when she went to bed, she had difficulty sleeping. About two in the morning, she became aware of wheezing noises from the child's bedroom. Dashing to his side, she found him in the midst of a severe attack of the croup. Hardly breathing, the child was rushed to the emergency room of a hospital where his life was saved. In this case, as in others, without anxiety on the part of the mother, there might have been a tragedy.

A patient of mine, made anxious one evening by a television program warning against breast cancer, decided to examine her breasts. To her horror, she noted a small lump. Prompt biopsy, performed forty-eight hours later, revealed the lump to be malignant. Although she lost a breast, she is now, five years later, very much alive and well. Without her anxiety, the outcome probably would have been different.

Too often we are ashamed to admit anxiety. Nourished by an emotional diet of heroes, we inflict unreasonable expectations upon ourselves. A deer or rabbit, unencumbered by the pretense of courage, will take to its heels at the first sign of danger and, by doing so, ensure its survival.

An adolescent patient told me that several other teen-agers had tried to tempt him into a drag race on a busy highway. When he refused to take part because he felt that to race on that particular highway was too dangerous, the others called him chicken. He replied, "I'd rather be a chicken than a dead duck."

Often those willing to acknowledge their anxiety turn out to be stronger than those who equate anxiety with cowardice. I have seen patients delay treatment because they were "going to work it out by myself," only to crack under the burden of unbearable anxiety.

One woman developed a severe anxiety condition during the early 1940s. Sent to a state mental hospital, she was given shock treatments, insulin therapy, and medication. In spite of all attempts to help her, her anxiety remained at a painfully high level. After five years of unsuccessful attempts to cure her, her family signed a permission form for a lobotomy (an experimental operation in which certain sections of the brain are destroyed, causing the person to become unable to experience anxiety in any depth).

After the lobotomy, she seemed considerably improved. She began to sleep and gained over fifty pounds. She no longer was agitated or anxious, and it was decided she could be sent home. Once home, however, she had to be cared for almost constantly by her family because she had lost all sense of possible danger. She could not emotionally comprehend that cars traveling at a rapid speed could pose a threat, and she would cross the street on a red light. One day, while no one was watching, she blindly walked into a speeding car. Although she survived the accident, she paid a terrible price for her lack of fear.

The more psychologists learn about the child, the more they learn about the role anxiety plays in helping us to grow into human beings. Some feel that without anxiety the child would never learn the social skills required to live among other people. It is probably the anxiety over losing the approval and love of parents that propels us to higher marks in school and control of our aggressive and sexual impulses.

Anxiety is the force behind much learning. A student under the pressure of a final examination in physics may be motivated to pick up the book, burn the midnight oil, and cram. As a result, he may find that, not only has he passed the test, but

learned a bit of physics. His more carefree classmate, not anxious enough to study, may find his academic career prematurely terminated as a result of flunking the exam.

In many ways, anxiety can force us to learn something that will increase our security. Psychoanalysts point out that one of the greatest motivations for a child to learn to walk is that once he learns, he can overcome to some extent the anxiety he feels when separated from his mother. Being able to walk permits him to reach his mother more readily, and he no longer feels so helpless.

Anxiety can also be a sign that we have violated some moral code. One woman, although in love with her husband, started an affair in a childish attempt to get revenge because she felt he had neglected her. As the affair progressed, she developed many symptoms of anxiety. She felt shaky and light-headed and very depressed. During the course of psychotherapy, she became aware of the underlying motives for her affair and gave up the destructive relationship with her lover. She was able to tell her husband how she felt about him. Although there was a period of strife, their problems were out in the open, and her anxiety diminished. In this case, as in others, anxiety had mounted to the point that the person finally did something about an unhappy life.

Anxiety may also prepare us for a stressful future situation. A man who has to give an important speech can be goaded by anxiety to rehearse not only his speech but the fear he may feel on the podium. As he faces this fear in anticipation of the event, there is a better chance that on the day of the speech he will be less afraid.

Dr. Irving Janis, a psychologist, studied the relationship between anxiety in patients about to undergo surgery and their recovery. He reported that those patients completely without anxiety before an impending major surgical operation had a more difficult postoperative period. He concluded that patients who expressed reasonable anxiety before surgery had fewer reactions of fear and anger after surgery.[1]

---

[1] I. L. Janis, *Psychological Stress* (New York: John Wiley & Sons, Inc., 1958).

THE SIGN OF GROWTH

One young man in his middle twenties came to me for psychological consultation and testing. He drank excessively and was separated from his wife, whom he had beaten rather cruelly on several occasions. He had a severe psychosomatic skin condition which had persisted for seven years. Repeated consultations with dermatologists produced little change, and every dermatologist he saw suggested that he receive psychotherapy. Although not painful, the skin condition was disfiguring and marred what otherwise would have been a handsome appearance.

After looking over his psychological test and the interview material, I felt the prognosis for change in this man was dim. In both his interview and the projective testing, it seemed that he rarely experienced even a twinge of overt anxiety. It was evident his symptom was bound up with whatever anxiety he felt and that he had little conscious awareness of being anxious.

The appearance of anxiety in psychological testing or clinical interview is a favorable prognostic sign. Psychotherapists know that when a patient complains of anxiety and tension and anxiety-related symptoms, his chances of recovery are usually good; but when a patient has all his anxiety bound up in a particular symptom and feels little overt discomfort, the path of therapy is likely to be extremely difficult. The more anxious a patient, the greater his motivation to change and to explore his unconscious conflicts. As he becomes more comfortable, this motivation may diminish, so that he loses interest in further exploration.

When I was interning in clinical psychology, I worked at a large Veterans Administration neuropsychiatric hospital, which held several thousand patients. At that time, the hospital was divided into two units. One was an acute intensive treatment unit for recent admissions and patients readmitted after having made a good adjustment for a time outside the hospital. In general, the treatment facilities were aimed at this particular group, thought to have the best prognosis for recovery and discharge. The second unit was for continued care. On this service were placed patients who had either been hospitalized for many years or whose prognosis was poor.

I was impressed with the fact that, for the most part, those patients in the second unit made the best hospital adjustment and were relatively free from anxiety. Many, having lived in the hospital for years, were allowed grounds privileges, went home weekends, and in general were model patients. They slept well, ate well, and required little tranquilizing. The staff referred to them as burnt out. This meant there was little evidence of anxiety or conflict, that they had adjusted to a marginal level of existence.

On the acute intensive treatment unit, however, the situation was very different. These patients were agitated, anxious, fearful, and confused. When you walked into one of these wards you could sense the suffering and turmoil, signs that the patients were still fighting to resolve their conflicts rather than giving in to regressive illness.

THE PRICE OF GROWTH

As we move through life, the stability of our personality is not always the same. There are times our defenses work well and life proceeds with little anxiety; but there are other times when defenses fail and we feel less stable or more anxious. Sometimes we experience anxiety when underlying growth is taking place. There has been little awareness that hardly any personality growth occurs without some anxiety.

Even the ancients recognized that anxiety and growth were associated. In the Bible a state of fear and anxiety is closely connected with impending revelation. When Moses came down from the mountain after his encounter with God, he frightened the people of Israel—it is written that, "When Aaron and all the people of Israel saw Moses, behold, the skin of his face shone, and they were afraid to come near him."[2]

The study of history and social psychology suggests that, in many situations, a state of national panic is the prelude to increased awareness of national goals and to legislation that may create a period of greater calm and stability.

Many positive steps in our life are accompanied by anxiety. Each time we extend ourselves further, accept new responsibility, or affirm our

[2] Exod. 34:30.

independence, we may also feel a measure of anxiety.

Once while traveling on a train in September, I sat next to a young girl who, pale and tense, sat with her teeth clenched, obviously very anxious. We began to talk; she told me she was on her way to college and that this was the first time she had ever been away from her family. As she spoke of leaving home, she plainly revealed both the anxiety she felt and her determination to become independent.

She described how she had always been over-protected by her mother and three older brothers and said that although it was hard for her to do, she had decided it would be the best thing for her to go to college in a distant city.

After she got off at her destination, I thought about her and the fact that she would have been relatively free of anxiety had she decided to remain at home. She was not going to let a little anxiety stop her from developing into an indepen-dent young woman. Some others, afraid of the anxiety of separation, have remained home, tied to mother and hearth forever.

In children the relationship between anxiety and growth is emphasized. I observed my son at the local swimming pool. Barely knowing how to swim at the beginning of the summer, he made tremendous advances under the tutelage of a good instructor. Towards the middle of the sum-mer, he was able to navigate anyplace in the pool. Not content with this, he began to eye the diving board. With some trepidation, he first dived from the side of the pool. He then tried the low board. After a time, he looked up at the high board. After some encouragement, he mounted to the top of the high board, a pathetic sight to see. He was pale, tense, and very anxious. Finally, he jumped. When he emerged from the depths, he had on his face that smile of pure joy that comes from having conquered anxiety.

Observation of children shows that they will attack again and again a fearful situation until it no longer causes anxiety. Once they have mas-tered it, they are ready to move on to the next fearful situation. Almost every sign of growth and independence contains some seeds of anxiety. The first day at kindergarten, the first night of sleep-ing at a friend's house, the first time on a bi-cycle—all produce anxiety. The child who has

learned early not to shrink in the face of anxiety, but to move through it, will have that sense of increasing mastery which sets the foundation for a healthy personality.

Adults, too, may experience anxiety when they are about to grow or undertake some new respon-sibility. One man described the anxiety he felt at his house-closing. He had always had difficulty in accepting responsibility or long-term commit-ments. He had been living in a small, over-crowded apartment with his wife and two children. Although wanting to own a house, he had previously rejected this idea as bearing with it too much responsibility. Intellectually, he knew that living in a house was the only sensible thing to do, but his emotional difficulties prevented him from taking the step. After some therapy which helped him gain confidence in himself, he bought a house. His anxiety at the closing could be seen only as a prelude to growth and a rejection of his old neurotic patterns of behavior. After a short spell of discomfort, he began to feel good about what he had done.

Often we feel anxiety when we violate some childish, no longer appropriate, taboo. I worked with a young lady who was in acute conflict over her wish to remain home with her aged father and her love for a young man who wanted to marry her. She had been raised in a home where she had been controlled by a guilt-inducing father. After her mother had died, five years prior to treatment, her father in subtle, and not-so-subtle, ways had made it clear that he "probably couldn't live if she left him." After work, she would come home to care for this tyrant. She felt chronically de-pressed, but did not realize the cause of this depression.

The situation came to a crisis when she fell in love. When the young man proposed, she was thrown into acute anxiety, and sought help. After a short period of treatment, she decided she would accept the proposal of marriage, but still became anxious each time her father made her feel guilty for leaving him. Shortly after the wed-ding, however, she felt happier than she had been in her entire life. Her father, now thrown on his own, became more active socially and even re-sumed working. She reported he was faring better than at any time since his wife had died.

Almost every milestone in our life may be a

source of anxiety—the first day of school, graduation, the first job, marriage, the birth of a child, the sending of a child to camp. Sometimes, too, anxiety will arise when we assert ourselves to others, going against the dreams they may have for us. A young adolescent I saw was rather introverted, preferring to spend time either by herself or with one or two close friends. She had literary ability and in one afternoon might produce a poem or short story, many of which were published by the school magazine. Her English teacher, recognizing her talent, encouraged her to send her work to other magazines. When writing, or with one or two of her friends, she felt at peace with herself and the world.

Her mother, however, had different ideas about the proper activities for her daughter. When she sat down to write, her mother would disparage her efforts, asking why she was not out with the group.

After a period of therapy, armed with a greater sense of self-respect and self-understanding, this girl was able to take a stronger stand against her mother's demands. As she did so, she began to experience anxiety. Although more uncomfortable, she was now accepting a sense of her own identity.

Sometimes anxiety will flash to warn us that something is amiss. One man, a patient of mine, for several years had held a particular job that was well below his potential. This man was bright, sensitive, and alert, but because he had a low sense of self-esteem, his level of aspiration was far below his ability. In treatment, it became evident he was bored by his job—the boredom that comes from doing something for which one is highly unsuited. After a while, he resolved to give up the job and go back to school. Not unexpectedly, his anxiety decreased. Boredom is a way of denying anxious feelings.

In essence, anxiety warns us that our relationship with ourselves is not all it should be. Seen in this light, anxiety no longer is a frightening enemy which must be tranquilized out of sight.

AT TIMES OF CRISIS

At the time of a psychic crisis, anxiety mounts just the way our temperature rises as our body defenses rally to fight an infection.

Anxiety, viewed correctly, can be seen as an indicator of a possible threat to our integrity and personality. If we can affirm ourselves by moving through rather than fleeing from anxiety, healthy growth can be the result.

Once I served as head counselor in a girls' camp situated in a rural, secluded area. The counselors were young and insecure, hardly much older than the girls they were hired to supervise. Most of the young lady counselors felt homesick during the week of orientation that preceded the arrival of the campers. Observation of two preceding years in this camp had taught me that if the counselors could endure the first week of indoctrination, their homesickness would end as soon as they became busy with responsibilities. Life in camp would then settle down into pleasant routine.

One morning, about three days before the girls were to arrive, two tearful seventeen-year-old junior counselors came to see me and said they were so homesick that they wanted to leave. I allowed them to express their feelings, gave them Kleenex to wipe away the tears, and pointed out that for them to remain in camp and follow through on a commitment they had made would be a sign of growth. I suggested that before they made any decision about leaving, they wait and see how they felt when camp swung into full operation in a few days.

One of the young ladies, unable to tolerate her separation anxiety for one more day, decided she wanted to leave immediately, and arrangements were made for her to depart the next morning. The other one clenched her teeth and said she would give it a try for one week more. When the campers arrived and a full program went into operation, she became involved in camp activities and was visibly more content. There was no more talk of going home. One day towards the end of the summer, she spontaneously came over to me and said, "I want to thank you! I feel more grown-up than ever before."

Although hardly a controlled experiment, this illustrates the point that whenever we feel in conflict, with heightened anxiety, the way is open either to growth or regression. If we can learn to use anxiety as a mandate to growth, we will be far happier.

It is precisely at times of crisis and acute anxiety that old patterns begin to break down and there comes the chance to build new ones. During heightened anxiety, we become inordinately suggestible and seek new solutions to problems. This is why someone in a crisis very often needs prompt, understanding, professional help.

For many years, those experiencing severe anxiety who attempted to get help from outside sources found themselves pitted against a formidable array of secretaries, social workers, and other clinic personnel who would interview them, then report that there would be a "seven month wait for therapy." An increasing awareness of how much someone in the midst of an acute anxiety-producing crisis needs help has led to such innovations as walk-in clinics or 24-hour psychological services.

Once it was believed wise, when a person was in a state of crisis, to send him away on an ocean voyage, a cross country trip, or a stay at a rest home out in the country where there was peace and quiet, so that he could regain his perspective. But now most psychiatrists and psychologists agree that the best therapy is to give someone assistance while he is in the crisis, not to remove him from the possible resolution of it. Even when hospitalization is required because someone is so out of contact with reality that he might be harmful to himself or others, the hospital should be near the patient's family.

One of President Kennedy's most important acts of mental health legislation provided federal aid to *local* treatment centers. In advocating this, one report stated:

The idea simply stated, is that if you remove a troubled person from his home, family, and town, you take away from him all of his loves, likes, and accustomed surroundings. That would be very hard on the majority of us who live happily enough—though with troubles and problems. Take a really troubled person away from his natural environment and give him nothing but the sterile isolation of a lackadaisically run hospital and you deprive him of all chance to get out of the pit of fantasy and back to the real world. On the other hand, if you enable a person to use the best parts of his accustomed way of life, and help him to solve his problems at the same time, you may have

activated the most important ingredient in his cure, which is himself.[3]

Study after study indicates that when a person receives prompt, intensive treatment after a crisis, long-term hospitalization may be avoided.

There are some psychologists and psychiatrists, albeit a minority, who view a serious mental disorder, such as schizophrenia, not as sickness, but as one sign of a life-crisis which, if handled properly, can result in new growth. Two psychiatrists, observing the recovery of severely ill individuals, suggested that schizophrenia may be "a transitional episode in the process of emancipation from an old method of adjustment and 'learning' a new one."[4]

A psychiatrist, Dr. Kazimierz Dabrowski, in *Positive Disintegration,* maintained that crisis and anxiety may be the beginning of the individual's climb to higher levels of development. He wrote:

In relating disintegration to the field of disorder and mental disease, the author feels that the functional mental disorders are in many cases positive phenomena. That is, they contribute to personality, to social, and very often to biological development. . . . The symptoms of anxiety, nervousness, and psychoneurosis as well as many cases of psychosis, are often an expression of the developmental continuity. They are processes of positive disintegration.[5]

Every psychotherapist has seen persons who, after suffering deep anxiety in which they go through an episode of severe emotional disorder, emerge much stronger than before.

In *The Vital Balance,* Dr. Karl Menninger cites well-known persons who did not begin to gain fame until they endured a period of emotional turmoil, which we term mental disorder. Dr. Menninger mentions, among others, Abraham Lincoln, John Stuart Mill, and William James. Of James, he wrote: "This is a man who thereafter

[3] Roche Laboratories, *Careers in Psychiatry* (New York: The Macmillan Company, 1968), p. 172.

[4] Thomas French and J. Kasonin, "A Psychoanalytic Study of the Recovery of Two Schizophrenics," *Psychoana. Quarterly,* 10 (1941), 1–22.

[5] Kazimierz Dabrowski, "A Theory of Positive Disintegration," *Int. J. of Psychiat.,* 2(2) (March, 1966).

became one of the greatest scientists who has ever lived, certainly the greatest psychologist and perhaps the greatest philosopher that America has produced. He transcended his illness to become 'weller than well.' "[6]

When a patient is in therapy, one often sees an increase in his anxiety as the herald of improvement. Sometimes a patient finds this alarming. At such times, it is necessary for him to be aware that the anxiety indicates something within is stirring and does not necessarily mean he is getting worse.

Dr. Karen Horney wrote: "Any anxiety that does arise during analytic therapy is usually alarming to the patient because he tends to regard it as impairment. But more often than not this is not so . . . emerging anxiety may also have an eminently positive meaning. For it may indicate that the patient now feels strong enough to take the risk of facing his problems more squarely. . . ."[7]

When a patient begins to *feel* his suffering for the first time in his life, anxiety may result. I worked with a young, unmarried, professional woman who, at the beginning of therapy, had many symptoms of, although she experienced little, overt anxiety. As she began to get more in touch with her feelings, her anxiety increased, for she confronted her own emptiness, yearnings, and unfulfilled desires.

During this difficult time in her therapy, I received a letter in which she said that she could not sleep, that she had a million conflicting thoughts, that she felt depressed and lonely, and that anything could start her crying. She said that she was ashamed of her feelings and almost wished she had never gone into therapy because before it, she had felt that she could never love anyone or anything and could accept not getting married or having anybody, but that now she felt capable of loving deeply and wanted a family.

In many ways she *was* more comfortable before therapy. Although she had symptoms, she was protected behind the barricade of not feeling. As

her feelings were released, she felt at first as if she would be swept away by their intensity. But after a short while, she was able to live more comfortably with herself in a manner she never before believed possible.

Sometimes patients avoid anxiety in the early stages of therapy by blaming all their difficulties upon their mother or father or society. After a while, if therapy is successful, the patient realizes that while all these may have contributed to his emotional distress, his own strong desires and imagination were partially responsible. He also knows that what he does about his life now is solely up to him. This may create new anxiety for a time.

Dr. Thayer A. Greene wrote:

How much easier and less anxiety-producing it is to perceive the problem as social and collective rather than individual and personal. Yet whatever social forces operate upon our lives, it is we who must make an individual response. No single lesson makes itself more clear to those who have gone through extensive psychotherapy than that to blame it all on God, society, mother and father, rarely if ever brings healing and change. When all the accounts have been added up, the individual must still pay the bill if he is to be freed from the negative and confining power of the past—not only his own but that of his family and culture. Whether or not the particular dilemma in which an individual finds himself is his "fault" is usually quite beside the point. The handicap, the crippling anxiety, the behavioral compulsion, may not be his fault at all and yet be his *fact*, i.e., the reality of his life situation. He must engage himself personally with this fact in order to grow.[8]

With patients who do well in psychotherapy, I have noted that although in the early part of treatment, they handle severe anxiety by saying, "Isn't it awful?" Or "Aren't I terrible?" they gradually accept anxiety as an *opportunity* to learn more about themselves. When anxiety can be regarded as a teacher, the patient often becomes an apt pupil. To use anxiety constructively,

[6] Karl Menninger et al., *The Vital Balance* (New York: The Viking Press, Inc., 1963), p. 408.

[7] Karen Horney, *Neurosis and Human Growth* (New York: W. W. Norton & Company, Inc., 1950), p. 340.

[8] Thayer Greene, *Modern Man in Search of Manhood* (New York: Association Press, 1967), p. 12.

as a valuable tool in learning about ourselves and what threatens us, is not an easy task. But if we can learn to do this, we will be rewarded with the prize of increased self-knowledge.

In *Advice from a Failure*, Jo Coudert describes how an episode of anxiety can be used to enhance self-understanding.

And it seems to me that this is how we come to know ourselves, not by asking: What am I like? but by asking: What do I do? This is not to imply that the question of why is unimportant but to suggest that the way to get at *why* is to start with what. When I started with: Why did I have an anxiety attack? all I got from myself were rationalizations. When I asked: What was I doing? I could reply that I was about to be critical and then I could think back to other times when it was appropriate to be critical and remember what my reaction had been. . . .[9]

Sometimes psychotherapy allows a patient to become *too* comfortable; his anxiety has been tranquilized. Then the job of the therapist is to mobilize a bit of anxiety so that the healing process may once again take place.

THE WILLINGNESS TO BE HUMAN

To some extent I have stressed the anxiety that results from conflict and from crisis. There is, however, the anxiety that comes from being alive, for, to be human is to be finite and limited, and to be finite and limited is to be anxious.

In some dark, deep recess of our minds, in spite of the din of music and noise and friends and work and travel and sports and food, we never lose the awareness that some day we will die. When we feel alive, we are using our full potential and the thought of death drifts into the shadows.

The knowledge of our finiteness can help us to savor the moments we live, to help us use our limited time in a useful, enjoyable manner. That knowledge can also help keep us appropriately humble in the face of the forces of nature, can

[9] Jo Coudert, *Advice from a Failure* (New York: Dell Publishing Co., Inc., 1966), p. 64.

make us give pause and consider our little vanities. The knowledge that we are temporary visitors on this planet can put petty quarrels into proper perspective. Temporary frustrations can be seen as part of reality. We can live more in the present and stop pursuing a vain, relentless search for security. Once we accept a certain basic anxiety, we can begin to live more fully.

The willingness to recognize the reality of anxiety indicates an ability to recognize all of reality. Most of us are all too eager to deny that we are anxious. When we do, we gain momentary relief, but pay a high price. We keep out of touch with our real feelings. Our chances of facing our conflicts and easing our anxiety are lessened. We find that we are more alienated than ever, both from our feelings and other people.

If one is able to acknowledge anxiety and battle it, healing forces are frequently set in motion. Dr. Paul Tillich once spoke of the necessity of having the "courage to be," which includes the acceptance and facing of anxiety.

Paradoxically, true courage seems to begin with the admission of anxiety, just as the possibility of true living begins when we do not deny the possibility of death.

THE FEAR OF FEAR

In our society which, sometimes subtly, sometimes not so subtly, suggests that we should be happy all the time, anxiety is too often hidden; unhappiness, uncertainty, conflict, and doubt are all denied. I have seen a large number of patients who practically considered it un-American to be anxious. They feel guilty because they have moments of panic in spite of having accumulated all the necessary material possessions they wish. Often the first step with such patients is to help them feel less guilty about the fact that they *are* anxious.

That many Americans become guilty when they experience anxiety has been noted by psychotherapists. Dr. Robert Nixon writes:

The work of Freud taught us how to begin to free sexuality and anger from control of guilt, and now we must take the next step and free our anxiety from control by guilt, and still more, from control by fear. Franklin Roosevelt said our greatest fear is of fear itself, and a more appropriate comment could hardly be voiced. To free our anxiety it is necessary, first, to stop fearing it; we need to learn to stop fearing what we have been taught to fear.[10]

Anxiety is as normal a part of the life process as teething. Like teething, it can be unpleasant and, if severe, cause pain. Too often, the fear of anxiety makes the anxious person avoid anything that might possibly cause it. Then a growing fear of anxiety results which may create more discomfort than the original fear.

[10] Robert Nixon, *The Act of Growing* (New York: Random House, Inc., 1962), p. 134.

If you ski, you know that the ability to ski increases by taking the risk of feeling frightened on the new high slope that looks possible but difficult. As soon as you master this slope, skiing down it without anxiety, you are ready to move to the next mountain, one that offers still more challenge.

If someone looks on anxiety as an enemy, a "disease," the therapeutic way is likely to be rougher and longer. But if he views anxiety as an opportunity to look within, as a mandate for further development, not only will the psychic way be easier, but his anxiety will also lessen that more swiftly. Anxiety is a feeling to become aware of, to be faced, to be understood, and then, almost automatically, it is present only when we realistically need it.

CONQUERING ANXIETY

Albert Ellis and Robert A. Harper

Our patients and our associates often try to confound us on one special point, where they feel that our technique of rational-emotive therapy comes a cropper and sadly begins to bog down. "You may be quite right," they say, "in insisting that most human difficulties are caused by the illogical sentences we tell ourselves and that we can overcome our difficulties by changing these sentences. But what about anxiety? How can we possibly control or change that by challenging and questioning our own assumptions? That's one human trait you'll never be able to change very much, no matter how rationally you approach it."

But these critics are wrong. Anxiety *is* approachable and controllable by straight thinking. For anxiety, basically, consists of Irrational Idea No. 6: *The idea that if something is or may be dangerous or fearsome, one should be terribly occupied with and upset about it.*°

This is not to say that real or rational fears do not exist. They certainly do. When you are about to cross a busy intersection, you would be insane not to fear the possibility of getting hit by a moving vehicle; and you would be equally crazy if you were not to some extent *concerned* about your safety. Fear of this sort is not only a natural and somewhat instinctive human tendency, but also a necessity for self-preservation. Without

Reprinted from Albert Ellis and Robert A. Harper, *A Guide to Rational Living.* (Englewood Cliffs, N.J.: Prentice-Hall, Inc., 1961), pp. 132–143. © 1961 by Institute for Rational Living, Inc.

° [This irrational idea is one of ten that Ellis and Harper believe can cause us to lead anxious and hostility-laden lives. Consult their book for information concerning the other nine irrational ideas—Ed.]

your being, in any circumstance whatever, duly fearful or concerned about your safety, it is unlikely that your days on this earth would long continue.

Nonetheless: fear is not anxiety. Anxiety consists of *over*-concern, of *exaggerated* or *needless* fear. And it most frequently, in this society, is not related to physical injury or illness but to mental "injury" or "harm." In fact, probably 98 percent of what we call anxiety in modern life is little more than *over-concern for what someone thinks about you*. And this kind of anxiety, as well as exaggerated fear of bodily injury, is quite illogical on several counts:

1. If there is a possibility that something truly is or may be dangerous or fearsome, there are only two intelligent approaches you may take: (a) determine whether this thing actually *is* dangerous to your well-being; and (b) if it is, then either do something practical to alleviate the existing danger or (if absolutely nothing can be done) resign yourself to the fact of its existence. Bellyaching about it or continually reiterating to yourself the holy horror of a potentially or actually fearsome situation will not in any way change it or better prepare you to cope with it. On the contrary, the more you upset yourself about the existence of this dangerous situation, the less able you will be, in almost all instances, to assess it accurately and to cope with it.

2. Although it is perfectly true that certain accidents and illnesses (such as airplane accidents or the onset of cancer) *may* befall you one day, and that it will be quite unfortunate if one of these misfortunes *does* occur, once you have taken reasonable precautions to ward off such a possible mishap there is simply nothing else that you can usually do about it. Worry, believe it or not, has no magical quality of staving off bad luck. On the contrary, it frequently increases the probability of disease or accident by unnerving the vulnerable individual. Thus, the more you worry about getting into an automobile crackup the more likely you are, if you are driving the car (from either the front or the back seat!), to get yourself into just such a crackup.

3. The assumed catastrophic quality of most potentially unpleasant events is almost invariably highly exaggerated. The worst thing that can happen to you in life is usually death—and

sooner or later you will have to die anyway. If you are truly in dire physical pain for a long period of time (as when you have an incurable cancerous condition and cannot find relief in drugs), you can always commit suicide. Virtually all misfortunes other than these which people continually worry about—such as loss of a loved one, missing a boat, or having a tooth pulled—turn out to be, when they actually occur, far less dreadful than one may have worriedly dreamed them up to be for a long time before their occurrence. The worst thing about almost any "disaster" is usually your exaggerated *belief* in its horror rather than anything intrinsically terrible about it. Life holds innumerable pains in the neck for all of us; but terrors, horrors, and catastrophes are almost entirely figments of our worried imaginations.

4. Worry itself is probably the most dreadful condition with which a human being can exist; and most of us would probably be literally better off dead than "living" in its continual throes. If you are ever faced with the real danger of blackmail, injury, or death, and there is no possible way to avoid the issues involved, then you would better frankly and fearlessly face up to your problems, and accept whatever penalties (such as possible legal consequences) may accrue from facing them, rather than continue to live in fear. A life in jail or even no life whatever may well be preferable to spending the rest of your days running, hiding, and panting with fear.

5. Aside from the possibility of physical harm, what is there *really* ever to be afraid of? So people may disapprove of or dislike you. So some of them may boycott you or say nasty things about you. So your reputation may be besmirched, your name be considered mud. Tough; disadvantageous; rough. As long as you do not *literally* starve, or go to jail, or be harmed bodily by their censure, why give yourself a super-hard time about the wheels that turn in their heads? If you stop worrying and *do* something about their possible disapproval, the chances are that you will sooner or later counteract it. If there is nothing that can be done: tough again. That's the way the cards fall. Why make the game of life so much more difficult by fretting and stewing about its existing inequities?

6. Although many things seem terribly fearful

to a young child, who has little or no control over his destiny, an adult is usually *not* in this precarious position and can either change the truly fearful circumstances of his life, or, if these are not changeable, can philosophically learn to live under such conditions without making himself panicky about them. Human adults do not *have* to keep reactivating fears that may have been fairly realistic in some earlier period of their lives but that are no longer valid.

Mrs. J. T. Borengrad provides us with an illustration of the foolish perpetuation of fears that were once realistic but that, at the time she came for psychotherapy, had no objective validity. As a child, she had learned to take whatever was said or done with hardly a word of protest because she had a sadistic father who would severely punish her for the slightest questioning of his authority. Then (quite likely because she believed she deserved no better) she married an equally sadistic man and remained with him for ten years until he became openly psychotic and had to be committed to a mental hospital, leaving her the full responsibility of rearing their two young daughters.

During both her childhood and her first marriage, then, Mrs. Borengrad lived under truly fearful circumstances. But not so during her second marriage. For a meeker man than Mr. Borengrad could scarcely be found; and he hardly ever lifted his eyebrow at her. Nonetheless, she became exceptionally disturbed and came to therapy in a veritable state of panic. Having majored in psychology in college, she stated her symptoms in somewhat sophisticated terms:

"It looks like I'm behaving exactly like Pavlov's dogs. I apparently got conditioned to react to anyone close to me with fear and trembling, with submission and underlying resentment, and I am going through the old conditioned response business over and over. Even though my husband is the kindest man in the world, and my teenage daughters are almost like lovely little dolls, I live in constant generalized fear. Ring the bell just before presenting the steak, and pretty soon the dog slobbers for the food he knows he's going to get. Well, ring the bell with me, and I immediately cringe with terror—even though the sadistic treatment I used to receive from my father and my first husband no longer follows its ringing.

Just being present with any member of my family, bell or no bell, I quickly start cringing."

"Maybe it looks like conditioning to you," the therapist said, "but my own feeling is that the very word conditioning is so vague and general that it actually masks the detailed processes that are going on. Now let's look much more closely at these so-called conditioning processes. First, let's see what used to go on with your father and your first husband."

"They would get angry at some little thing that I did or didn't do, I noticed their anger, then I also saw how they followed it up—by punishing me severely in some manner. Then, naturally, whenever I began to see that they were growing angry, I immediately became very fearful of the punishment that would follow. And I either ran away or went into a panic state or asked them to beat me quickly and get the horrible thing over with."

"All right; that's a good description. But you left out a very important part of the process."

"What's that?"

"Well, you said that they got angry; and you knew you would be punished; and then you went into a panic state. But the second part of the process—the part where you knew that you would be punished—is being glossed over too easily. What you really mean, don't you, is that you perceived their anger and then, in a split-second, you told yourself something like: 'Oh, my heavens! There he goes again, getting angry at me for practically nothing. And now he's going to punish me for doing practically nothing. Oh, how terrible! Oh, how unfair! What a poor miserable, helpless creature I am to have an unfair father (or husband, as the case might be) who takes advantage of me like this and against whom I am too weak to protect myself!' Isn't this, or something much like this, what you said to yourself once you perceived your father's or your first husband's anger?"

"Yes, I'm sure you're right about that. Particularly with my father, I would tell myself how awful it was that I had a father like that, while Minerva Scanlan, my best friend, had such a nice, easy-going father who never even yelled at her and certainly never hit her or punished her in any other way. I was so *ashamed* to have a father like mine. And I thought I came from such a terrible

family—so bad, in fact, that I wouldn't even want Minerva or anyone else to know just *how* bad they were and how badly they treated me."

"And with your first husband?"

"There, too. Only this time I wasn't so ashamed of him but of my *marrying* him. I kept saying, whenever he got angry and I knew he was about to pounce on me, 'Oh, how could I ever have been so stupid as to marry anyone like him. After I saw so much of this kind of thing at home, too! And then I went right out and repeated this horrible mistake, voluntarily. And now I'm staying with him, when I should have the guts to leave, even if I have to work my hands to the bone to take care of the children myself. How could I have been so stupid!' "

"All right, then. Note how we not only have the stimulus, the anger of your father and your first husband, and the conditioned response, your great fear of punishment, but we also and more importantly have your self-blaming *interpretations* of the horror of the stimulus. Thus, whereas you theoretically could have told yourself, 'There goes crazy old dad getting angry again, and he's probably going to punish me unjustly. Well, too bad; but I can survive his punishment and eventually, as I grow up, get away from him and live in a non-punishing environment.' You actually largely said to yourself, 'I'm to blame for coming from such a crazy family and for being so weak as to let the old buzzard take advantage of me.' And, with your first husband, whereas you could have said to yourself, 'Too bad: I made a mistake in marrying this sadistic individual; but I'm strong enough to get away from him and leave him to his own sick ways.' You again said: 'I'm to blame for making this terrible mistake of marrying this bastard; and now I'm too weak and idiotic to get away from him.' "

"What you seem to be saying, then, is that it wasn't necessarily the actions of my father and my husband—their anger followed by their punishment—that conditioned me to be so upset when I was with either of them, but really my own unjustified interpretations of their actions."

"Yes, your own *partly* unjustified interpretations. For you were, of course, especially when you lived with your father, a little girl who appropriately *should* have been scared of your father's physical assaults; and no matter what you might have philosophically told yourself at the time, you were in some *real* danger, and it would have been inappropriate for you *not* to be frightened at all."

"But that was not exactly the case when I was married to my first husband."

"You're quite right: it wasn't. Again, with him, you might have had a little reason for fear, since he was psychotic and he could have literally killed you when he got angry. But as you yourself pointed out before, you also could have easily, or with some but not too much difficulty, left him—which was not true when you were a girl living in your father's home. So much of the so-called 'conditioned' fear with your husband was distinctly your own doing: the result of your falsely telling yourself that you couldn't cope with the situation, were a dunce for having married him in the first place, and were a slob for staying with him. If you had told yourself other and more sensible things than this, you would soon have left him—or might even have stayed and been very unafraid of him."

" 'Conditioning,' then, is something of a cover-up word for what we largely do to ourselves?"

"Yes, very often. In Pavlov's case, don't forget that *he*, Pavlov, conditioned the dogs from the outside: he completely controlled the event of whether they would or would not get their piece of steak when the bell rang. And in the case of your father, since he was much bigger and stronger than you, he also largely controlled the event of whether or not you would be severely beaten once he got angry. But not entirely! For had you had a better and different philosophy of living when you were with your father—which not very many but some few young girls of your age do somehow manage to acquire—you could have (unlike Pavlov's dogs) changed the situation considerably. Thus, you could have somehow influenced your father and induced him to punish one of your brothers or sisters, rather than you; or you could have managed literally to run out of the house most of the times you knew he was about to punish you; or you could have accepted your punishment more stoically and not been too bothered by it; or you could have tried many other gambits to change or ameliorate the effects of your father's behavior. But because of your poor philosophy of life at the time—which, to be

sure, your father among others helped you acquire—you passively submitted to his blows—and also blamed yourself for having such a father and for having to submit. So although your situation was indeed fearful, you helped make it positively *terrifying*."

"I can see what you mean. And with my first husband, I guess, I did even worse. There, I didn't have to submit at all; but I just about forced myself—with what you again would call my poor philosophy of life—to do so, and again to be absolutely terrified."

"Exactly. Although only some of your so-called 'conditioning' was self-effected in your relations with your father, probably the far greater part of it was self-wrought in your relations with your first husband. Where you could have nicely *un*conditioned yourself with him—by telling yourself how ridiculous it was for you to stay with and suffer the punishments of such a palpably disturbed man—you did the reverse and worked very hard to condition yourself still more."

"And what about my present state, with my second husband?"

"Your present state is an even better proof of the thesis we have been discussing than anything else. For you will remember, again, that in the case of Pavlov's dogs, when he kept presenting the bell without the steak, the dogs soon became unconditioned and stopped salivating, since they soon realized, or somehow signaled themselves, that the steak and the bell did not go together any longer. Accordingly, therefore, if you had been classically conditioned by the experiences with your father and first husband, both of whom were tyrants, you should have gradually got quite unconditioned by your several years of experience with your second husband, who is practically an angel when compared with the first two."

"He actually is. Unbelievably nice and unpunishing."

"But your merely being in his or your daughters' presence, you say, causes you to go into a state of panic?"

"Yes, I can't understand it. But that's just what happens."

"I am sure that you really *can* understand it, if you look a little more closely, and stop convincing yourself that you are 'automatically' conditioned by your past experiences. For if your husband's behavior is obviously not reinforcing your previously learned fear, and this fear still actively persists, then *you* must be doing something to reinforce it, to keep it alive, yourself."

"You really think I am?"

"You must be—unless we believe in some kind of magic. If you, as we just noted, were at least partly instrumental in setting up the original terrible fear of your father and your husband, even though they certainly also contributed mightily to the situational context of the fear, and if your present husband is not contributing to that context to any serious degree, who else but you *is* keeping the fear alive?"

"Hmm. I see what you mean. And what do you think that I'm telling myself to keep my fear alive?"

"What do *you* think? I am sure that if you start asking yourself you will soon start to see."

"What occurs to me, first of all, is that I am probably telling myself, or still telling myself, what you pointed out before: that I always was too weak and inadequate to do anything about myself and that I still am. And that therefore I *do* have something to be afraid of—my own weakness."

"That's a good point. These things usually become circular, just as you indicated. First, your father abuses you, then you tell yourself you can't do anything to stop his abuse, then you get terribly fearful. But, once you get fearful, and you only half-heartedly try to overcome your fear, you start telling yourself that you can't do anything about *that*. So you get fearful of becoming, and of not being able to do anything about becoming, fearful. Quite a pickle!"

"You know, I think that's exactly it. I used to be fearful of my father and my first husband—though really, as you're pointing out, of myself, of my weakness. And now I'm fearful of *remaining* fearful—of remaining weak. And even though my present husband and daughters are *not* abusing me, I'm afraid that I couldn't handle the situation if they *did* abuse me. I'm so afraid of being inadequate—and so afraid of being afraid—that I make myself panicky most of the time."

"Precisely. Then, probably, to take it one step further, you actually do get so frightened, and act so badly because you're frightened, that you then become convinced of your original hypothesis—

that because you're so weak and inadequate, no one could ever possibly love you, including, especially, your own present husband and daughters."

"So I really start with a great need to be loved and a fear that, because I'm so worthless, I won't get this need fulfilled. Then because of my fear I behave badly. Then I note that I behave badly and say to myself: 'That proves how worthless I am!' Then, because I have doubly proved my 'worthlessness,' I get even more afraid that I won't be loved the next time. And so on, and on."

"Right. And then, going one step further, you hate yourself for being so weak and for having such a dire need for love; and you resent your present husband and daughters for not fulfilling your dire need to the exact extent you demand that they fill it—and for not making up for all the anger and punishment that your father and your first husband foisted on you. So that, mixed in with your terror, is a goodly degree of resentment—which only tends to make you still more upset."

"As you said before: Quite a pickle! But what do I do now to get out of it?"

"What do you think you do? If you're telling yourself sentences 1, 2, 3, and 4 to get result Number 5, and result Number 5 is highly undesirable, how do you manage not to get it again?"

"By *un*telling myself sentences 1, 2, 3, and 4!"

"Yes—or by challenging and questioning their validity."

"I have to ask myself, then, *why* I am so weak and worthless and *why* I can't stand anyone's anger."

"Yes. And also 'Why *don't* I deserve, now, to have a mild and cooperative husband and daughters?' And: 'Why, if I do happen to get frightened because I remind myself of some past threat that really doesn't exist any more, can't I then *see* what I am doing, and calm myself down pretty quickly?' "

"And if I try this kind of questioning and challenging and persist at it, then there's no reason why I have to continue to live in this kind of panic state I've been forcing myself into for such a long time?"

"No, no reason at all. Try it and see. And if it works, as I'm sure it will, that will be great. And if it doesn't then we'll quickly discover what *other* nonsense you are telling yourself to stop it from working."

"The main thing, if I understand you correctly, is that no matter what upsets me or what I am frightened at, it is now my *own* doing. It may not have been in the past. But it now is."

"In the main, yes. Occasionally, you may have a truly fearful circumstance in your life—as when you are on a sinking boat or in a car that is about to have a head-on collision with another car. But these kinds of realistic fears are rather rare in modern life; and the great majority of the things we now get panicked about are self-created 'dangers' that exist almost entirely in our own imaginations. *These* are your own doing; and these may invariably be undone by looking at your crooked thinking and straightening it out."

"O.K. What you say sounds reasonable. Let me do a little trying."

Mrs. Borengrad did try. Within the next several weeks she not only ceased being terrified when in the presence of her daughters and her present husband, but was able to do several other things, including making a public speech at her community center, a thing which she had never been able to do before in her life. She learned, and as the years go by she still continues to learn, that unlike Pavlov's dogs she can recondition or uncondition her feelings and her responses *from the inside* and that she does not *have* to respond to someone else's actual or possible anger with woeful feelings of fright.

In general, the most effective kinds of counterattacks against any needless and inappropriate fears that you may have may be taken along the following lines:

1. Track your worries and anxieties back to the specific sentences of which they consist. Invariably, you will find that you are telling yourself: "Isn't it terrible that—" or "Wouldn't it be awful if—." Forcefully ask yourself: "*Why* would it be so terrible that—?" and "*Would* it really be so awful if—?" Certainly, if this or that happened it might well be inconvenient, annoying, or unfortunate. But would it *really* be catastrophic?

2. When a situation actually is fearful—as when you are about to take a trip in a rickety old airplane—then the only sensible things to do are (a) change the situation (for example, don't take the trip) or (b) accept the danger as one of the unfortunate facts of life (thus, accept the fact that you may be killed in the rickety plane; that this is too bad if you are; but that life, to be reasonably lived, must be replete with considerable risk-taking). If a danger can be minimized, act to reduce it. If it cannot be minimized, or it would be more disadvantageous for you to avoid it than to risk it, then you have little or no choice and you'd *just better* accept it. No matter how you slice it, the inevitable is still inevitable; and no amount of worrying will make it less so.

3. If a dire event may occur, and you can do no more than you have already done to ward it off, then *realistically* weigh the chances of its occurring and *realistically* assess the calamity that will befall you if it actually does occur. Although another world war *may* occur tomorrow, what are the chances that it *will*? If it does occur, what is the likelihood that you *will* be maimed or killed? If you are killed, will it *really* be much more catastrophic than your peacefully dying in bed ten or twenty years later?

4. To overcome a specific anxiety, verbal *and* active depropagandization are usually essential. You must first realize that *you* created the anxiety by *your* internalized sentences, and you must vigorously and persistently ferret out these sentences and challenge and contradict them. Then you must *also* push yourself to *do* the thing you are senselessly afraid of and *act* against your fear.

Thus, if you are afraid to ride on busses, you must realize that your overconcern is rooted in your own negative propaganda: in your telling yourself that busses are dangerous, that horrible things can happen to you in a bus, that if anything dreadful did happen on a bus you would not be able to stand it, and so on. And you must contradict this nonsense by showing yourself that busses are not very dangerous; that very few people are injured while riding on them; that if an unpleasant event occurs on a bus, you can handle it; and so forth. Finally, however, you must force yourself, over and over again, to keep riding on busses and to keep telling yourself, while riding, rational counterpropaganda to eradicate your irrational self-sentences. The more you do the things you are afraid of *while* logically parsing and contradicting your self-imposed fearfulness, the quicker and more thoroughly your needless anxieties will vanish.

5. Most modern anxieties are intimately related to the underlying or overt dread of making public mistakes, of antagonizing others, of losing love. You should always suspect that some dire fear of disapproval lies behind your seemingly more objective fears and should continually and powerfully challenge and fight this basic anxiety of our time.

6. It is best to convince yourself—since this is invariably true—that worrying about many situations will definitely aggravate rather than improve them. If, instead of telling yourself how awful it would be if something happened, you tell yourself how silly, senseless, and self-defeating it will be if you *keep worrying* about this "awful" thing, you will have a much better chance of short-circuiting your irrational anxieties.

7. Try not to exaggerate the importance or significance of things. Your favorite cup, as Epictetus noted many centuries ago, is merely a cup of which you are fond and your wife and children, however delightful, are mortal human beings. You need not take a negativistic, defensive so-what attitude and falsely tell yourself: "So what if I break my cup or my wife and children die? Who cares?" For you *should* care for your cup and your wife and children and will lead a more zestful and absorbing life if you do. But if you exaggeratedly convince yourself that this is the *only* cup in the world or that your life would be completely useless and worthless without your wife and children, you will only be falsely overestimating the value of undeniably good things and making yourself needlessly vulnerable to their possible loss.

It is good to remember, in this connection, that to enjoy a positive event wholeheartedly does *not* mean that you must catastrophize its absence. You may enjoy your cup, your wife, and your children wholeheartedly and truly care for them. But their sudden removal, although certainly a distinct loss and something that you should considerably *regret*, need not be *calamitous*. This loss, however difficult, merely removes *something* that you ardently desire and love—it does not remove *you*. Unless, of course, you *insist* on identifying your*self* with the people and things you love; and that kind of identification is emotional sickness.

8. Distraction, as we noted in the last chapter,

may be a good temporary dissipator of groundless fear. If you are worrying about your plane's falling, forcing yourself to concentrate on a magazine or a book may give you some respite. If you are afraid that you are not making a good public speech, vigorous focusing on the content of your talk rather than on the reactions of your audience will often calm your fears. For deeper and more lasting removal of anxieties, however, a thoroughgoing philosophic approach, along the lines previously noted in this chapter, will be much more effective.

9. Tracking your present fears to their earlier origins, and seeing how though they were *once* fairly appropriate they *no longer* hold water, is often a useful anxiety-reducing technique. When you were a child, you normally feared many things, such as being in the dark or arguing with an adult. But you are now no longer a child. Keep showing yourself this and demonstrating that you can easily take certain chances now that it might have been foolhardy for you to take some years ago.

10. Don't be ashamed of still existing anxieties, no matter how senseless they may seem. Certainly it is wrong, meaning *mistaken*, for a grown person like you to retain childish fears. But *wrong* or *mistaken* does not mean *criminal* or *blameworthy*. And if people dislike you because you are anxious, that is largely their problem and is again nothing to worry about. Admit, by all means, that you are needlessly fearful; forthrightly tackle your silly worries; but don't waste a minute beating yourself over the head for being, for the nonce, afraid. You have much better things to do with your time and energies!

11. No matter how effectively at times you combat your anxieties, and temporarily eradicate them, do not be surprised if they return from time to time. It is the nature of almost all human beings to fear again, at least from time to time, what they have once feared in the past, even though in general they are no longer afraid of this thing (Solomon and Wynne). If you once had a fear of high places and you conquered it by deliberately frequenting such places, you may still, on occassion, become afraid when looking down from heights. This is perfectly usual and expectable. In these circumstances, merely accept the returned fear, thinkingly and actively go to

work on it again as you have done in the past, and you will quickly see, in most instances, that it returns to limbo.

Always remember, in this connection, that you are a mortal being; that humans have innate limitations; that they never *completely* overcome groundless fears and anxieties; and that life is a ceaseless battle against irrational worries. If you fight this battle intelligently and unremittingly, however, you can *almost* always be free from *almost* all your needless concerns. What more can you ask of a good life?

BEHAVIORAL BIBLIOTHERAPY: A SIMPLE HOME REMEDY FOR FEARS

G. Donald MacLean and
Robert W. Graff

The present paper briefly describes an anxiety reduction technique which is effective with a college population.

Reactive inhibition therapy, a very simple and seemingly effective extinction technique, was described a few years ago in a brief case report by Malleson (1959). The technique has been used by the authors with apparent success in several cases. A recent empirical investigation provides initial objective evidence that the technique is as effective as desensitization in a controlled laboratory situation (Calef and MacLean, 1970).

Because of the apparent simplicity of the reactive inhibition technique, a set of instructions based on Malleson's paper was made available to clients as a handout. The handout is typically given to a client, if it seems appropriate, during an initial interview, with very cursory instructions, e.g., "Here's a paper you might find helpful. Read it, try it, and let me know what happens when you come back next week." In some cases, the results have been very gratifying.

Although it is not entirely clear in such cases that the handout led to the improvement, it is the opinion of the therapists and the clients that it did. In other cases, the handout has not been as successful.[1]

[1] A copy of the handout may be obtained from the authors.

A SIMPLE HOME REMEDY FOR FEARS[2]

In many cases, when you have a specific kind of fear or anxiety, such as test anxiety or speech anxiety, a crucially important part of the fear is a wish to avoid or escape from the feared situation. As long as the wish persists, reciprocally the fear will persist. If you can persuade yourself to experience the fear without trying to avoid it, the vicious circle of fear leading to the escape urge leading to more fear can be unwound. (The footsteps that follow you past a cemetery in the dark become louder and more menacing the more you hurry. Only when you stop and permit them to approach do they disappear.)

The home remedy for fear is simply to experience the fear, deliberately and as fully as possible. The technique is probably most efficient if you have a sympathetic friend present so you can verbalize and act out the fear. Think about the feared situation or object. Imagine that you are in the feared situation, or actually put yourself in the feared situation. In some cases it may be easiest to do this in progressive stages. As you do so, do not attend primarily, to the feared situation or to the wish to escape the situation. Concentrate on the fear itself. Attend as actively as you can and experience as fully as you can the unpleasant emotions and all the concomitant bodily sensations that are aroused. If it's appropriate, go on to imagine all the undesirable consequences of being in the feared situation, the failure and loss of self-esteem that will result, and the ensuing scorn, ridicule, and rejection by friends, parents, and others.

Take for example an agoraphobic person, say one who cannot walk from home to his place of work alone. He might begin by going to the foot of his front door steps, where he experiences all the fear possible there. When he has tried and tried to feel all the fear possible, and becomes so bored by it that he cannot feel more, then he advances, say, 25 yards or so down the sidewalk, or until the fear is rekindled. There again he is to stand still and experience his emotions, and so on.

It is very important for you to understand that the aim of the exercises is to experience the

[2] Based on a paper by Nicholas Malleson, entitled "Panic and Phobia," which appeared in *Lancet* in 1959.

fears and all the bodily sensations that always accompany them, and not simply to achieve such-and-such a distance, or such-and-such a contact. One often meets people, particularly people with phobias of situations rather than objects (situations are less easily avoided) who say they *can* do so-and-so if they have to; but the mere doing of it does not at all reduce the phobic abhorrence the next time. Facing a feared situation by sheer will power is possible in many cases, but this does nothing to reduce the fear. For successful fear reduction, full attention to and experience of the internal unpleasantness is essential.

In some cases where it is more convenient to imagine the feared situation, it may be necessary to repeat the treatment a number of times. Say you are suffering from test anxiety and you use this method to reduce the fear. You may do so at a time when you are not faced with a test. As the date of an actual examination approaches, you may begin to experience some fear. Do two things. First, every time you feel a little wave of spontaneous alarm, *do not* push it aside; *do* enhance it, augment it, try to ex-

perience it more profoundly and more vividly. Second, if you do not spontaneously feel fear, make a special, deliberate effort to try to do so two or three or six times a day, no matter how difficult or ludicrous this might seem.

This technique works best with specific fears —the more specific the fear, the more effective the technique. It works best if there is a sympathetic friend present, to whom you can describe your sensations as you experience your fear. Like most good home remedies, it sometimes doesn't work at all, but it can cause little harm, and sometimes it works amazingly well.

REFERENCES

CALEF, RUTH ANN and G. D. MACLEAN. "A Comparison of Reciprocal Inhibition and Reactive Inhibition Therapies in the Treatment of Speech Anxiety," *Behavior Therapy* (1970).

MALLESON, N. "Panic and phobia: a possible method of treatment," *Lancet* (1959), #7066, 225–227.

ALLEVIATING THE COLLEGE STUDENT'S ANXIETY

Martin Katahn

While anxiety over examinations and other aspects of academic life seems fairly widespread from grade school through college, the lack of clear-cut therapeutic measures, as well as lack of funds and personnel, has discouraged the development of regular programs for its alleviation.

Since 1964, Vanderbilt University has used a test-anxiety program (funded by a research grant from HEW's National Institutes of Health) with groups and individuals to determine the effectiveness of personal counseling combined with systematic desensitization. The desensitizing process involves deep breathing and the relaxing of select muscle groups while visualizing anxiety-arousing situations. Our approach has proven valuable even when anxiety is so extreme that it is accompanied by such symptoms as nausea, insomnia, and skin rashes. Although we have dealt almost exclusively with college students, we completed some encouraging pilot work at the seventh grade level this past spring.

Except for the desensitization, our approach to increasing student efficiency may be in many ways similar to general academic counseling; it does, however, differ from traditional counseling or therapy in that we do not attempt to determine the individual's personal dynamics or the origin of his anxiety.

Groups are composed of a leader, a graduate student who serves as assistant leader, and six to eight students who report that they feel extreme anxiety while preparing for and taking tests. In the first two of eight scheduled meetings they learn an abbreviated version of deep muscle relaxation as described in the book *Behaviour Therapy Techniques* by Wolpe and Lazarus. In addition, the students construct an anxiety hierarchy: a list of anxiety-causing experiences ranked in ascending order. In the ensuing meetings, as they imagine these scenes, they practice relaxation responses. Subsequently, almost all students involved report reduced anxiety in real-life situations, and about 75 percent of them show significant academic improvement.

Systematic desensitization occupies the last 15 to 20 minutes of our group meetings. During the first 40 minutes we give some advice on academic matters; the students discuss their attitudes toward education and actually practice studying more efficiently.

We suggest that members of the group purchase a book, *How To Study in College*, by Walter Pauk, but we do not refer to anything specific in it unless students bring up various topics that are of interest to them.

The problems or issues students typically discuss in our group program appear to fall into five categories.

First, anxious students have great difficulty in starting to study and in organizing their daily activities, often because their anxiety about academic matters makes studying an uncomfortable business. Just picking up a notebook or a textbook triggers enough anxiety to make them postpone studying in favor of doing something—*anything*—else.

To help with this problem, we teach the students how to approach studying with a relaxed attitude and suggest things to do that might relieve any tension built up during study. Within a few weeks, students simply make a relaxation response to the slightest feeling of tension—in much the same way that a basketball player relaxes all his muscles when he exhales just before making a free throw from the foul line.

We also help each student set up a study schedule which suits his personal needs, using our own study and work habits and those of others in our department as examples of how to balance work and play. While some students like to set up a weekly plan, we usually find that a daily schedule with a modest goal seems to work best. We rehearse with students what they should say to friends who try to interrupt their study periods.

Second, anxious students have a poor approach to studying itself, and the problem is usually compounded by poor reading habits. They begin their assignments by inching along, sentence by sentence, trying to understand every single point the first time through, and often giving up if the material becomes too difficult. We suggest that students first skim their assignments completely, giving in-depth attention only to summaries that occur at the end of sections or chapters. We advise them, in doing detailed reading, to adopt the instructor's frame of mind: that is, to imagine that they will have to convey the meaning of what they have read and discuss it with others.

At first, we practice on newspaper editorials and magazine articles that deal with contemporary issues. We show the students how glancing down the columns of the editorial page or quickly scanning the pages of a magazine article will orient them to the major issues and opinions. Before we read the articles in detail, we suggest to the students that when they come to the natural end of any section or to the end of the article itself, they review for at least a minute what they have read. Finally, as a group, we discuss the article.

Following this practice, students bring in their own assignments and spend a portion of the time reading and presenting ideas to the group. We find that as they become more comfortable studying and as they develop better study habits, they begin to enjoy studying and they are motivated to succeed. Grade point averages increase, and I am sure these factors contribute.

Third, anxious students are more sensitive to threatening instructors. Instructors who make a habit of calling on individuals to answer questions in class without warning are particularly alarming. The anxious student is so afraid he will be called upon that he cannot concentrate on the lecture. To combat this, we have students prepare questions for the professor in advance of the class. This tends to forestall his calling upon them, thus enabling them to pay better attention to the class proceedings. The students practice voicing their questions in the group.

Tension rises when anxiety-prone students have difficulty understanding the instructor. Either with or without reason, such students tend to feel it is their own fault. We tell them that since they are paying so much for their education they ought to speak up and ask the instructor to repeat himself or to explain more carefully—especially considering that, after class, they often find that their friends were also confused. As a result of the urging and practice in our group meetings, some students speak up in their courses for the first time in their lives.

Fourth, anxious students often have misconceptions about the effort required for academic success. They feel that a single reading of an assignment or a single attempt at a problem in mathematics or physics is all that it *ought* to take to understand the material. We use ourselves as examples to illustrate that meaningful and difficult material takes many readings and much thought.

Fifth, anxious students often lack clear-cut academic goals. This does not mean that anxious students have no professional aspirations but that they find little meaning or significance in the academic endeavor.

Many of our most stimulating group meetings occur when the discussion contrasts the motivations and goals of professors with those of students. Here my assistant leaders and I use ourselves as examples: I tell them I am doing teaching and research in the area of anxiety and learning because to me this is the most satisfying and exciting thing I could do with my time each day. My reward occurs when a few students in my classes become interested in the subject matter that intrigues me—especially when they express ideas that stimulate me in novel ways about my work. I give several good illustrations of how the ideas of students in my courses have modified my thinking and contributed to my research.

The students' motivations and rewards contrast sharply with mine. They are often in a course because of some university requirement, or because it is needed for graduate school. Interest in subject matter is quite secondary in importance to the need for obtaining a good grade. Education cannot be meaningful in its richest sense in this context.

At the end of our test-anxiety program, in an effort to determine just which of its aspects (systematic desensitization, group discussion, or identification with the leaders as models) is most important, we give the students a questionnaire. Systematic desensitization seems important to them, but they usually feel that the most significant aspects of the program are just being able to talk about their problems with other students, discovering that others have similar experiences, and learning to reorganize their study habits. They say getting to know a professor better and understanding the teacher's point of view are also helpful.

The students' appraisal may be correct. But we feel that without the rather quick relief from anxiety symptoms that desensitization gives, the other aspects of the counseling program might in time lose their effectiveness. In brief, we feel that systematic desensitization works directly to take the pain out of test-taking, studying, and other classroom activities, while our discussion and behavioral rehearsals serve to make learning more meaningful and enjoyable.

PART IV

Becoming: Problems in Actualization

In the beginning—at the moment of conception—we are a single cell. By the time we reach adulthood we have grown into approximately one million million (1,000,000,000,000) cells and become a very complicated being.

Our genes carry the blueprints for our growth, and we develop in accordance with these inherited potentialities. But development is not, of course, a simple matter of unfolding. We are also shaped and molded— sometimes even kneaded and pummeled—by environmental forces and pressures. What we are (and are becoming) results from a complex interaction of inborn and external forces.

Development is a continuous process, but for purposes of study it is traditionally divided into a number of stages. We are infants, then children, then adolescents, then adults. Finally we grow old and die. Each stage has distinguishing characteristics and each presents us with some tasks to accomplish before we move on to the next.

Our development tends to be orderly. But in the process there are spurts and slowdowns. Sometimes we seem to leap ahead, and sometimes we creep along. Occasionally we rest or stay put or even reverse, giving up some perhaps hard-won gains.

Scientists and humanists have always been intrigued by human potentiality, and some of us may wonder what we could become if we realized all of our promise—if we actualized ourself completely. What would we be if we were everything we could be? This is, of course, a question that can never be fully answered, but it is almost impossible not to pose it. In Part IV of this book, three concepts which touch on this question and the actualization process will be pursued: defense, growth, and death.

Defense refers to the behavior we employ to protect ourself from threat or anxiety. Many things we perceive in our environment and also in ourself arouse anxiety and trigger defensive behavior. The process of growth and change itself is sometimes threatening and puts us on the defensive. And, for whatever reason, when we divert substantial energies to defense, our development and actualization suffer.

Growth, in the somewhat special sense it is used in this book, refers to personal development in a desired direction. Since values differ, we will not always agree on what is desirable change or even how desirable it is to change. Some of us may be ambivalent about growth; our urge to explore and try new things may be in strong competition with the desire to maintain what we have (and who we are) and play it safe.

Death refers to the cessation or end of life, but all of life is influenced by the inexorability of death, by the certainty that each of us will die, and the necessity of making the most of the years we have allotted to us. Some of us try to shut out all thought of dying to preserve an illusion of never-endingness, but others believe that until we accept the prospect of death, we cannot sense the wonder and preciousness of life and the urgent necessity for making the most of it and ourself.

TOPIC 9

Defense

Subject was a pretty university freshman, but one who did not pay much attention to her appearance. She was shy, inhibited, and quite tense and anxious throughout the interview. She denied the existence of any emotional problems or conflicts.

This student seemed capable of structuring the world only in intellectual terms. She seemed totally out of touch with her feelings and went to great lengths to repress or deny them. What came across was a marked affective barrenness, almost like that in cases of severe emotional deprivation.

She could not handle the expression of anger and had to deny and repress her rage. At times she turned her rage in on herself, and she described crying occasionally in response to feeling hurt. She also tended to project her rage and felt people were out to hurt her.

She led a constricted and inhibited life with very few friends or acquaintances, most of her time being devoted to academic work. "I don't make friends easily. I'm usually backward and shy." She did not confide in friends or her parents. "I don't feel I should burden others—not that I have very many burdens."

She had no relationships with young men and had had only one date in her life. "I am pretty young to go out too much. I see downfalls in it. Some kids go steady and it breaks up and they are usually lost. They have lost the art of making friends and it's difficult for them."

She had a long-time interest in becoming a research chemist. She seemed to be doing well academically and was making progress toward this occupational goal; in fact, she seemed wrapped up in this to the exclusion of all else.

—Condensed case study from an investigation of college students by William A. Westley and Nathan B. Epstein.

Many situations pose a threat to our well-being and cause anxiety. And some of us carry a heavy load of anxiety with us into many situations. How do we deal with our anxiety? Can we get on with the tasks of everyday living? Can we even risk growing and become different and more than we are? Or must we turn our energies to controlling our anxiety or defending ourself against it?

Defense refers to behavior that is employed for protection against threat or anxiety. It is helpful to consider a distinction that is sometimes made between defense behavior and task behavior. *Task behavior* is that involved in the achievement of the work at hand, such as taking a test, giving a speech, or running a race. *Defense behavior* bolsters our self-esteem when our task behavior is unsuccessful. For example, if we study hard and apply ourself to an important test (task behavior), upon learning that we have failed the test we can either prepare to take it again (more task behavior) or try to shore up our self-esteem by depreciating the test or denying that it was important or that we really cared or tried to do well on it (defense behavior).

Human behavior is complex, and a particular action which appears to be task behavior may upon closer analysis seem to be a defensive maneuver or at least partly so. The test we take and pass may move us along in our career (task behavior), but our motivation in taking it may also be to allay anxiety and reassure ourself that we are worthy and able to compete and get ahead in this world. However, some of our actions are so patently defensive (although perhaps not to us), that others see through us right away and perhaps accuse us of trying to cover up.

In a somewhat broader perspective, it is helpful to contrast defense and growth behavior. *Growth behavior* involves movement toward patterns which are more highly valued; for example, when a person becomes more independent, we may say he has grown. In contrast, *defense behavior* (or *safety behavior* as it is sometimes referred to in this context) involves adherence to present, familiar, and less valued patterns of response.

To illustrate, a comparison might be made between a person who stays put in a secure, routine job with one who undertakes a new career that involves risk and challenge. Or compare a person who tries to live life by certain minimum essentials and avoids adding new dimensions (the college woman in the above case study is an example) with one who is not so concerned with the tried and true, the safe and familiar, or the easily manageable. In each instance, the contrast is between the defense- or safety-oriented person versus one who is oriented toward growth.

How much of our life is devoted to defense and safety? How much is concentrated on task accomplishment and growth? We may have defended ourself so subtly and so well that it is impossible to distinguish one aspect from another. But some of us will sense that our life is more constricted and less rich than it could be and that we have been more occupied with defense and safety than with growth.

Defense and everyday life

Human ingenuity being what it is, we devise many ways to defend ourself against anxiety. Psychologists have described dozens of defense mechanisms, and one has written that the number of defenses a psychology student knows "depends upon who his teacher is and which textbook he reads." The first reading on this topic, an excerpt from a textbook written by the editor, describes 13 common and important defense mechanisms. All of us have probably made some use of each of these defenses in dealing with everyday threats and anxieties.

Defense and rationalization

"Man likes to think of himself as a rational animal," writes Elliot Aronson in the second selection. "However, it is more true that man is a rationalizing animal, that he attempts to appear reasonable to himself and to others." Aronson points out that we frequently feel called upon to defend ourself against dissonant cognitions, that is, several conflicting ideas, beliefs, or opinions. This defense is especially necessary when the image we have or want to have of ourself is inconsistent with our impulses and behavior, and we must somehow rationalize this discrepancy to preserve our self-esteem. Rationalization permits us momentary peace but prevents us from growing or forming useful insights into our personal inconsistencies and absurdities.

Defense and disclosure

Self-disclosure is both a sign of a healthy personality and a means of achieving a healthy personality, writes Sidney M. Jourard in the last article. Until we open ourself to others, they cannot know us or love us, and neither can we know ourself nor grow. It is not easy to let down our defenses, but it can be even more difficult to keep them up. Jourard writes, "Every maladjusted person is a person who has not made himself known to another human being, and in consequence does not know himself. Nor can he find himself. More than that, he struggles actively to avoid becoming known by another human being. He works at it ceaselessly, 24 hours daily, and it is work!"

FOR PERSONAL APPLICATION

1. How defensive are you? Discuss this aspect of your behavior.
2. Observe yourself during one full day and note each instance in which you felt called upon to defend yourself.
3. Describe several anxiety-laden situations in which you (or a person you observed) demonstrated task behavior and/or defense behavior.
4. Discuss the defense and growth forces at work in your own life or in the life of a person you know.
5. Describe your use of a particular defense mechanism.
6. To what extent are you a "rationalizing animal" rather than a rational one? Describe your rationalizing behavior.
7. To what extent do you know yourself? Describe this aspect of your self-disclosing behavior.
8. To what extent have you made yourself known to another person? Describe this aspect of your self-disclosing behavior.
9. Write down a discussion item (not given above) that seems particularly relevant to this topic and you, and discuss it.

FOR SMALL GROUPS

1. *Defending oneself.* Each member writes something about which ne feels defensive or which he has disclosed to very few people (perhaps no one) on an index card without signing his name. The cards are gathered, shuffled, and read in turn by the leader or one member who invites the reactions of the group.
2. *Defending oneself in the group.* Each member in turn tells one thing about the group that has made him feel defensive. After everyone has had a chance to speak, the group discusses how it can deal constructively with the information it has received.
3. *Describing defenses.* Each member describes or acts out a defense mechanism he has used without identifying it by name. Other members of the group are then asked to identify the mechanism and also to relate their own experience in using that mechanism.
4. *Portraying defenses.* A set of cards, each with the name of a defense mechanism, is placed face down in the center of the group. Each member in turn picks a card and without showing it to the group presents an example of the mechanism to the group. Other members of the group are then asked to identify the mechanism and also to relate their own experience in using this particular defense. (In a variation of this exercise, the group is divided into teams or pairs. Each team draws a card and is given five minutes in private to prepare a skit that portrays the defense. When the group reassembles, each team presents its skit, and the observers are asked to identify and discuss the defense mechanism that has been portrayed.)
5. *Disclosing oneself to the group.* Each member in turn tells the group one important thing about himself which the group does not know.
6. *Trusting others.* One obstacle to disclosure is lack of trust; as we learn to trust others, we open ourself more to them. In this exercise, the group is divided into pairs. One member of each pair is blindfolded and led on a walk by the other for a 15- to 30-minute period. Then the partners exchange roles for a similar length of time. (In a more difficult variation of this exercise, the blindfolded member is not permitted to talk.) Afterwards the group reassembles and the members share reactions to their "trust walk."

FOR FURTHER READING

Arkoff, A. *Adjustment and Mental Health.* New York: McGraw-Hill Book Company, 1968.

Aronson, E. *The Social Animal.* San Francisco: W. H. Freeman, 1972.

Jourard, S. M. *The Transparent Self.* Princeton, N.J.: D. Van Nostrand Co., Inc., 1964.

Jourard, S. M. *Self-disclosure.* New York: Wiley-Interscience, 1971.

Luft, J. *Of Human Interaction.* Palo Alto, Calif.: National Press Books, 1969.

SOME COMMON
DEFENSES

Abe Arkoff

We are constantly flooded by stimuli arising in our environment and from within ourselves. Of course, we cannot respond to every stimulus. We cannot express every impulse.

We find some of the stimuli in the environment unpleasant, painful, and threatening. If these stimuli are too threatening, we may attempt to defend ourselves against them. Perhaps we avoid them or ignore them or reinterpret them so that we no longer find them so bothersome.

Impulses arising in ourselves also can prove threatening. We may have worrisome thoughts and distressing feelings that we seek to inhibit or modify. We may seek to get a grip on ourselves so that we will not do something we are tempted to do.

Or perhaps we have already done something which has filled us with guilt and remorse. We may seek to atone for it or make some restitution. Or we may attempt to alter the memory of it in some way and see it differently so that we can live with ourselves.

Certain patterns of behavior that are employed for protection against threat or anxiety are called *defenses*. These patterns are sometimes called "defense mechanisms" or "adjustment mechanisms," and they do tend to operate in a machine-like or automatic way (Kroeber, 1963; Murphy et al., 1962). Sometimes they are referred to as "ego defense mechanisms" since they serve to defend the ego or the self from threat.

Patterns which have been identified as defenses are sometimes very simple. For example, Menninger and his colleagues (1963) include such simple expedients as laughing it off and crying it out as "coping devices of everyday living." However, many defenses are much more complicated.

As individuals, we vary in the patterns of defense that we show. Fairly early in life each of us develops a repertoire of defenses that characterizes our own individual adjustment (Murphy et al., 1962). Still we may show a preference for certain defenses in certain situations or at certain times (Swanson, 1961).

Following are some defenses or defensive aspects of behavior that seem particularly common or particularly important in the adjustment process.

SUPPRESSION

We cannot respond to every stimulus or express every impulse to which we are subject. For one thing, we do not have enough time or energy to do so. For another, some of our impulses may be unacceptable to us or threatening to our general well-being.

One of the ways that we have of dealing with threatening impulses is to make a deliberate effort to inhibit them. We may, for example, be occupied with a bothersome thought or obsessed with some worry, and we attempt to put it out of mind. We may feel that we are about to break down and cry, but we struggle to hold back our tears because we don't want to give the appearance of weakness. Or, perhaps, we are about to lash out at someone but we count to ten to give ourselves time to cool off.

Behaving in this way, that is, effortfully inhibiting the expression of a threatening impulse, is called *suppression*. As the definition implies, suppression is a relatively conscious or voluntary process. The person is aware of the threatening impulse and makes an effort to control or suppress it.

Suppressive efforts, of course, are not always successful. Despite attempts to achieve peace of mind, we find ourselves occupied with threatening thoughts and feelings. Despite the struggle for self-control, we indulge in actions which cause us trouble and regret.

Sometimes suppression works or continues to work only if it is combined with other efforts. We may be able to suppress a particularly bothersome thought only if we keep ourself busily occupied with other thoughts and activities. And we may be able to suppress a particular action only if we avoid environments which seem to stimulate it; for example, we get along with some people only by keeping out of their way and seeing them as little as possible.

We use suppression a great deal in everyday life. We close our eyes to unpleasant sights. We deafen our ears to criticism. In conversations, we sometimes deliberately choose pleasant topics, and when we hit upon material which provokes anxiety, we change the subject by tacit or explicit agreement. For example, at a party the conversation may get around to the subject of cancer, or heart attacks, or nuclear destruction, and somebody will ask that the subject be changed to something more pleasant (Dollard and Miller, 1950).

Suppression is a useful and necessary mechanism. Every society requires its individuals to inhibit or modify their impulses in some way. Some people run into difficulty because they lack the ability to make certain suppressions.

All of us have had troublesome thoughts or worries which have kept us from working effectively. It has been suggested that suppression is a defense that can be perfected and used to give us "mental freedom" (Dollard and Miller, 1950). Through practice we can learn to remove our attention from one thing and focus it on something else. Appropriate use of suppression occurs when there is a task that must be done and when other matters competing for attention are insoluble or may be postponed. Freed, at least for a while from other problems, we can become absorbed in the more urgent activity.

Of course, not all uses of suppression are beneficial. Some people seem overly inhibited or overly suppressed in one or more areas of living. Suppressions can be detrimental when their effect is to push away a problem that should be faced. Constantly shunted aside, many adjustment problems grow less manageable, and the momentary relief that suppression brings can be purchased at considerable cost to future happiness.

REPRESSION

The process of inhibition is not always conscious and deliberate. Sometimes it appears to occur automatically, without the individual's awareness. The automatic inhibition of a threatening impulse is called *repression*.

Although automatic, noninsightful inhibitions are classified as repressions while deliberate, insightful ones are called suppressions, actual behavior is seldom so neatly dichotomous. Frequently, there is partial insight or semiawareness of defense processes. Sometimes, too, an impulse which is usually well repressed becomes bothersome, and one needs to take more deliberate actions to contain it.

Suppression is easily understood, but the concept of repression is more difficult to grasp and accept; indeed, many psychologists have challenged the usefulness or validity of this idea (MacKinnon and Dukes, 1962). Dollard and Miller have suggested that repression can be understood as a process in which the person prevents himself from *thinking* about something which would be painful or threatening just as in some instances he prevents himself from *doing* something which might cause pain or embarrassment. They state:

Repression is somewhat harder to understand than other symptoms because we are not used to considering the stopping of thinking as a response. We cannot point to it and study it in the same way that we can examine overt responses.

Yet to stop talking is obviously a response. Everyone has had the experience of catching himself just in time before blurting out something he would have regretted saying. It is possible to learn either to stop talking about certain limited subjects or to stop talking altogether in some situations. According to our hypothesis, stopping thinking is a similar response [1950, p. 203].

A pattern of behavior may have been so heavily punished in the past or so associated with unhappy experience that the person prevents himself from expressing it in any way. Aggressive behavior, for example, is frequently severely disciplined and, as a consequence, can be severely repressed. In a similar way, early sex behavior may have been the occasion of considerable unhappiness and punishment, with considerable subsequent repression.

Like attempts at suppression, repressive efforts are not always successful. Heightened anxiety levels and bursts of anxiety are commonly interpreted by clinicians as evidence of failing repressions. In the same way, some individuals who suffer from chronically elevated anxiety are thought to have considerable but precarious repressions.

Some sudden changes in behavior are also interpreted as failures in repression (and, as will be seen later, as failing reaction formations). For example, a generally meek individual may show a sudden and violent outburst of anger that may surprise others and himself as well. Or a relatively kind and gentle person may do something that seems very cruel and very much out of character.

Slips of the tongue and pen, lapses in memory, and certain mishaps or accidents have also been attributed to the workings of (and weakenings in) repression. Such occurrences have been held by Freud (1904) and others to be evidence of incomplete repressions. Brenner writes:

A slip of the tongue or a slip of the pen is often the consequence of a failure to repress completely some unconscious thought or wish. In such cases the speaker or writer expresses what he would have unconsciously liked to say or write, despite his attempt to keep it hidden. Sometimes the hidden meaning is openly expressed in the slip, that is to say, it is clearly intelligible to the listener or reader. On other occasions the result of the lapse is not intelligible and the hidden meaning can only be discovered from the associations of the person who made the slip [1955, p. 146].

Everyone has probably caught himself saying something he did not consciously mean to say. A student who flunked a course wrote to his teacher as follows: "I could register for the *curse* in Summer School if I had to" (Vaughan, 1952). Perhaps we "forget" to check essential materials out of the library, thereby neatly resolving the conflict between studying or not studying over the week-end. Or maybe we do something "accidentally" which somebody else may claim was accidentally on purpose.

Like suppression, repression serves us by defending us from threatening impulses. It prevents us from thinking distressing thoughts, from feeling distressing feelings, and from engaging in certain actions which might prove dangerous or painful. It helps us hide out thoughts and feelings and actions from ourselves just as we sometimes more consciously attempt to conceal certain things from others.

Repression can prove detrimental in the long run for a number of reasons. Problems that are kept out of awareness cannot be faced and solved. In addition to the use of this mechanism, we may have to restrict our lives in various ways and use other defenses to prevent the inhibited impulses from finding expression. Energy consumed in the process might otherwise be available for the activities of everyday living. Repression brings some relief from anxiety, but it can also restrict, impoverish, and distort behavior (Cameron and Magaret, 1951).

Whether repression is good or bad depends upon the uses that are made of it. Hall notes what happens when there is a considerable reliance on this defense:

Although repression is necessary for normal personality development and is used to some extent by everyone, there are people who depend upon it to the exclusion of other ways of adjusting to threats. These people are said to be repressed. Their contacts with the world are limited and they give the impression of being withdrawn, tense, rigid, and guarded. Their lips are set and their movements are wooden. They use so much of their energy in maintaining their far-flung repressions that they do not have very much left over for pleasurable and productive interactions with the environment and with other people [1954, p. 88].

LYING

Throughout life we constantly struggle to understand ourselves. The reasons for our behavior are often unknown or unclear. For a particular bit of behavior there may be a dozen plausible reasons.

At the same time we are constantly called upon to explain our actions to others: Why did you do that? How could you do such a thing? Why do you feel that way? Where did you ever get such an idea?

How much of the truth do we know? How much of the truth do we tell others? How much of the truth do we tell ourselves? And how much do we need to lie?

Lying, as a defense, refers to the deliberate use of falsehood to prevent threat to one's well-being. The liar attempts to bring about a false belief which would be to his own benefit. Like suppression, lying is generally thought of as a conscious process; the liar knows that he is lying; although he attempts to deceive another person, he himself is not deceived.

The very young child does not make a sharp distinction between reality and fantasy, between truth and untruth. Stone and Church write:

It is because the preschool child's world is a mélange of what to the adult are fact and fiction, shot through with magical potentialities, that the child may seem to adults uninstructed in his ways to be playing free and easy with the truth. During most of this period, however, the very notion of an untruth is inconceivable to the child. A preschool child will have a very hard time complying with an adult's request that he repeat a statement such as "the snow is black," although he could enjoy *pretending* that snow is black. When, however, the child's own wishes conflict with reality, reality is likely to yield. If the child can make things so merely by thinking or saying them, then his claim that he has performed an assigned task or his denial that he has committed a misdeed is sufficient to do or undo the action in question. The young child can create past history—not to mention a present and a future—by waving the wand of his tongue. But he is not lying, in the sense of thinking one thing and saying another [1957, pp. 158–159].

As the child grows older he becomes better able to tell the difference between what is true and what is not. Demands are placed upon him to always tell the truth and never lie. But, paradoxically enough, demands are also placed upon him to recognize situations in which he should not tell the truth since certain sorts of lies are a promi-

nent part of our life. Woolf (1949) writes, "What education really demands and teaches the child is to know when not to lie, when not to tell the truth and when a lie is necessary." He presents the following example:

A mother told me the following story of her four-year-old son. The family were expecting a young girl and her fiancé to call. The child overheard the comment that while the fiancé was nice, he had an ugly long nose which spoiled his looks. In the evening, when the couple was sitting in the drawing room with the family, the child approached the fiancé with a stick in his hand and said as he touched the young man's nose with it: "This has to be cut off." The little boy behaved with calm and assurance and without the slightest awareness of the embarrassment caused by his unsuitable veracity. He was later enlightened, in rather an awkward manner, about the possible negative consequences of truthfulness in real life. His veracity was described to him as insolence and terrible rudeness, and this new point of view was confirmed by suitable "educational measures" [1949, p. 266].

George Washington is reputed to have never told a lie. Probably nobody (except a liar) would claim to have equaled that record. Many of us have never stopped to consider what part falsehood plays in our general adjustment. If we do think about it, we will probably admit to having made some use of lying as a defense against threat.

Even those of us who pride ourselves on our honesty may confess to an occasional benign or white lie, that is, one which we feel is trivial, not harmful, or even for someone else's benefit. Even so, we might have to admit that such a lie was for our own benefit as well, that it served our purposes to tell it.

Much of our lying is accomplished by omission rather than by commission. We may justify omitting the truth by saying that what people don't know won't hurt them. Karpman calls this "implied lying." He writes:

This is a form of lying which consists of merely maintaining silence, of refraining from telling the truth rather than the actual telling of an untruth. It is more correctly called dissembling or dissimulation. A person may say, "I didn't tell you about this before, but—" and then proceed to confess some past action, the absence of your knowledge of which had led you to form an entirely different impression of his behavior than that which is now disclosed by his retarded admission of this or that reprehensible action [1949, p. 147].

A similar way of lying is by telling a half-truth. This is usually a statement that is not really false in itself, but which is designed to be interpreted or misinterpreted in a way that will be beneficial to the teller. For example, suppose there is an important book which we should be conversant with; we did buy a copy, but we have never opened it. A colleague asks us if we have read it, and we answer that we have a copy of it at home. We hope that he will assume that we have read it and let the matter rest there.

Telling the truth, the whole truth, and nothing but the truth is not easy. Honesty is valued by our culture, but so are other qualities with which honesty sometimes conflicts. So, for example, is politeness, and it is sometimes impossible to be both polite and completely honest.

From the standpoint of adjustment it is useful to try to understand the push behind a lie. To what extent is it simply a polite convention? To what extent is it benevolent and designed to help another? To what extent is it defensive and used to get oneself out of a difficult or threatening situation?

RATIONALIZATION

Not all misrepresentations can be considered conscious and deliberate. The reason for a particular bit of behavior may be unknown or unclear. Or there may be a number of possible explanations. In such situations it is perhaps only natural that the person leans toward explanations which are socially and personally acceptable.

Interpreting behavior in an acceptable way in order to prevent a threat to one's sense of well-being is called *rationalization*. Unlike lying, which is a conscious process, rationalization is usually considered to operate without the individual's full insight or awareness. The liar attempts to deceive others, but he himself is not

deceived. By contrast, the rationalizer deceives others and himself as well.

It is frequently difficult to classify a bit of behavior as either a lie or a rationalization. Sometimes we seem to half deceive ourselves. We may not be completely satisfied with the way we have explained things. Are we fooling ourselves? Maybe we are. But, then again, maybe we're not.

How do we know if we are rationalizing? If there are two or four or eight possible reasons, how can we know whether a particular one is real or rationalized. Jourard (1963) suggests that a person may be rationalizing if his announced aim and the consequences of his behavior do not agree, if there are other possible explanations for his behavior, and if he refuses to consider them. For example, a parent may steadfastly maintain that his severe and arbitrary disciplinary policies are for his child's own good even though there is considerable evidence that the child is suffering because of them.

Consider the numerous opportunities that you have to employ rationalization in the course of a single day. Although you have vaguely decided to go on a diet, you sit down to a large breakfast of fried ham and hot cakes dripping with syrup and melted butter because, as you tell yourslf, everyone needs a good breakfast to start the day right. In your first class you decide not to take notes because you never seem to get very much out of them anyway. Between classes you go to the snack bar rather than the reserve room because the book you need will probably be checked out already. The waitress forgets to add the price of dessert to your lunch check, but you decide not to call this to her attention because it wasn't very good anyway.

In the afternoon you get into a bridge game with some other students, and when your partner criticizes you for making a couple of stupid mistakes, you announce that you're glad that you don't take the game as seriously as all that. In the evening you sit down to study for a test on the following day, but you can't concentrate. Well, you tell yourself, it's too late to cram now. If you don't know it now, you never will. Besides it would be better to take it easy this evening, relax, and go into the test with a clear head. So off you go to a movie.

MALINGERING

All or almost all of us have been sick, but our experience with illness has doubtless varied. It would appear to go without saying that a person would rather be well than sick. On reflection, though, such a preference would seem to depend in part on how ill we're treated when we're well and how well we're treated when we're ill. For some individuals, sicknesses are not a completely unrewarding state of affairs.

One of the ways that we have of adjusting to difficult situations and protecting ourselves from threat is by pretending to be ill. Removal of a threat or anxiety by feigning illness is called *malingering*. Like suppression and lying, this defense is usually thought of as a conscious one; the person is not deceived himself, but he attempts to deceive others.

Samuel Clemens (Mark Twain) clearly and vividly describes this defense in Tom Sawyer:

Monday morning found Tom Sawyer miserable. Monday morning always found him so—because it began another week's slow suffering in school. He generally began that day with wishing he had had no intervening holiday, it made the going into captivity and fetters again so much more odious.

Tom lay thinking. Presently it occurred to him that he wished he was sick; then he could stay home from school. Here was a vague possibility. He canvassed his system. No ailment was found, and he investigated again. This time he thought he could detect colicky symptoms, and he began to encourage them with considerable hope. But they soon grew feeble, and presently died wholly away. He reflected further. Suddenly he discovered something. One of his upper front teeth was loose. This was lucky; he was about to begin to groan, as a "starter," as he called it, when it occurred to him that if he came into court with that argument, his aunt would pull it out, and that would hurt. So he thought he would hold the tooth in reserve for the present, and seek further. Nothing offered for some little time, and then he remembered hearing the doctor tell about a certain thing that laid up a patient for two or three weeks and threatened to make him lose a finger. So the boy eagerly drew his sore toe from under the sheet and held it up for in-

spection. But now he did not know the necessary symptoms. However, it seemed well worth while to chance it, so he fell to groaning with considerable spirit.

But Sid slept on unconscious.

Tom groaned louder, and fancied that he began to feel pain in the toe.

No result from Sid.

Tom was panting with his exertions by this time. He took a rest and then swelled himself up and fetched a succession of admirable groans.

Sid snored on.

Tom was aggravated. He said, "Sid, Sid!" and shook him. This course worked well, and Tom began to groan again. Sid yawned, stretched, then brought himself up on his elbow with a snort, and began to stare at Tom. Tom went on groaning. Sid said:

"Tom! Say, Tom!" [No response.] "Here, Tom! *Tom!* What is the matter, Tom?" And he shook him and looked in his face anxiously.

Tom moaned out:

"Oh, don't, Sid. Don't joggle me."

"Why, what's the matter, Tom? I must call auntie."

"No—never mind. It'll be over by and by, maybe. Don't call anybody."

"But I must! *Don't* groan so, Tom, it's awful. How long you been this way?"

"Hours. Ouch! Oh, don't stir so, Sid, you'll kill me."

"Tom, why didn't you wake me sooner? Oh, Tom, *don't!* It makes my flesh crawl to hear you. Tom, what *is* the matter?"

"I forgive you everything, Sid. [Groan.] Everything you've ever done to me. When I'm gone—"

"Oh, Tom, you ain't dying, are you? Don't, Tom—oh, don't. Maybe—"

"I forgive everybody, Sid. [Groan.] Tell 'em so, Sid. And Sid, you give my winder-sash and my cat with one eye to that new girl that's come to town, and tell her—"

But Sid had snatched his clothes and gone. Tom was suffering in reality, now, so handsomely was his imagination working, and so his groans had gathered quite a genuine tone.

Sid flew down-stairs and said:

"Oh, Aunt Polly, come! Tom's dying!"

"Dying!"

"Yes'm. Don't wait—come quick!"

"Rubbage! I don't believe it!"

But she fled up-stairs, nevertheless, with Sid

and Mary at her heels. And her face grew white, too, and her lip trembled. When she reached the bedside she gasped out:

"You, Tom! Tom, what's the matter with you?"

"Oh, auntie, I'm—"

"What's the matter with you—what is the matter with you, child?"

"Oh, auntie, my sore toe's mortified!"

The old lady sank down into a chair and laughed a little, then cried a little, then did both together. This restored her and she said:

"Tom, what a turn you did give me. Now you shut up that nonsense and climb out of this."

The groans ceased and the pain vanished from the toe. The boy felt a little foolish, and he said:

"Aunt Polly, it *seemed* mortified, and it hurt so I never minded my tooth at all."

"Your tooth, indeed! What's the matter with your tooth?"

"One of them's loose, and it aches perfectly awful."

"There, there, now, don't begin that groaning again. Open your mouth. Well—your tooth *is* loose, but you're not going to die about that. Mary, get me a silk thread, and a chunk of fire out of the kitchen."

Tom said:

"Oh, please auntie, don't pull it out. It don't hurt any more. I wish I may never stir if it does. Please don't, auntie. *I* don't want to stay home from school" [1929, pp. 50–53].

In the same way, many of us have pretended to have a headache in order to avoid a situation that may be boring or threatening, or, once we are in the situation, the "headache" conveniently furnishes us with an excuse to leave. A "backache" has been used by more than one soldier (but not always successfully) as an excuse to get out of a hike or a run through the obstacle course.

Pretending to be ill may serve to get us the attention, sympathy, or nurturance that we might not otherwise receive. Like Tom Sawyer, we can overdo this defense and tax the patience and credulity of those who are exposed to it, but it is difficult to disprove an ache or pain or some other such vaguely defined malady. In fact, the malingerer himself may become half convinced of the validity of his complaints.

ADJUSTMENT BY AILMENT

Sometimes, without any conscious pretense, we may feel ill even though the doctor can find nothing physically wrong. Or perhaps we feel more ill or more incapacitated than we should from a particular ailment. Or we get well more slowly than we should.

The relatively noninsightful use of illness, imaginary or real, as a way of averting anxiety is called *adjustment by ailment*. Unlike malingered conditions which are deliberate pretenses, adjustments by ailment imply no conscious deceit. In this latter defense the individual is unaware of the psychological implications of his behavior.

In actual practice, however, it may be difficult to distinguish between malingering and adjustment by ailment. Some situations appear to contain elements of both, and an act of malingering may gradually shade into adjustment by ailment as we slowly convince ourselves that we are indeed as ill as we were pretending to be. For example, we may be searching for an excuse to avoid attending a trying social or professional function. If we were ill, we tell ourselves, we wouldn't have to go. Well, we already feel a little upset. The more we think about it, the more upset we become. Finally, we decide that we really are sick; we thus spare ourselves the pain of going to the function as well as the pain of admitting that we didn't want to go.

In anxious states the body's functioning is upset, and it is easy to imagine illness. An upset cardiovascular system may convince us that we have heart disease or at least a severe headache. An upset digestive tract may lead us to believe that we have a stomachache or indigestion. Overwhelmed by problems, we indeed feel tired, worn out, and sick. Describing a trying experience, we may say, "I was just sick about it," and mean it both figuratively and literally.

This defense protects us from threat in various ways. We may use an imaginary ailment to take our attention away from an anxiety-provoking problem. We may use the "ailment" as an excuse to avoid an unpleasant situation or once in the situation, to get out of it with no loss of face. Sometimes an imaginary ailment serves to attract the attention and sympathy of others. And occasionally we employ it to punish ourselves and rid ourselves of feelings of guilt.

Simulated ailments may help us to handle difficult situations but, to the extent that they are successful in doing so, they make it unnecessary for us to face our real problems and attempt to solve them. With extensive reliance on this defense, we may become a chronic "psychological" invalid. Not only psychological problems but real medical problems as well may go unattended because of the masking effect of imaginary ones.

FIXATION

In the process of growing up we move through a number of stages: infancy, childhood, adolescence, and adulthood. Each succeeding stage offers new opportunities and carries additional responsibilities. Some individuals move continually forward, enjoying the opportunities and accepting the responsibilities afforded by each stage. Others, caught up in frustrations, conflicts, and anxieties, become arrested at a particular stage. And a few, under the pressure of problems, may move backward into earlier, more manageable stages.

Fixation refers to the continuation of a pattern of behavior which has become immature or inappropriate. A person who uses fixation as a defense responds to threat by adhering to old ways of doing things rather than trying out those which would be more suited to the situation at hand. In the face of threat the fixated person is unable or unwilling to vary his behavior, and the greater the threat the more fixated he may appear.

People vary in the extent and duration of their fixations. Some appear to be fixated in many ways or in a number of areas of adjustment, while others show a very few fixated patterns. Furthermore, fixations may be relatively enduring, or they may be quite temporary and transient.

If a person has made extensive use of fixation, he will appear to be generally immature. You may know someone who is chronologically an adult, but who acts more like an adolescent. Or someone who, although not immature in his behavior, rigidly adheres to the same habits of living and is relatively closed to new experience. As one grows older, he tends to get more fixed or set in his ways.

Fixations can occur at any level of development. Those which date from early development, of course, will appear less age appropriate than those which take place later on. Some of us may have been told: Grow up and act your age! But the charge (or insult) is more serious if we're accused of acting like a baby than if we are said to be behaving like a child.

Most fixations are relatively limited and affect only part of one's life. For example, consider the situation of a young man who has completed college, has a responsible and well-paid position, and participates widely in community activities. But he lives at home, has quite a close relationship with his mother, shows very little interest in young women of his own age, and on the few occasions on which he does date, he feels awkward and uncomfortable. Although he is immature in his heterosexual relationships, he is able to function adequately in a number of other areas of daily life.

An instructor who defined fixation as "arrested development" received the following test response from a student: "Fixation is a rest in development" (Vaughan, 1952). And this is a positive value of fixation. One cannot always make steady progress in every area of adjustment. Sometimes there is a need to combine partial progress with partial fixation. Sappenfield sums this up very nicely:

> Continued fixation at a particular level of adjustment in some areas of behavior may provide the feeling of security that is required as a basis for the individual's progression to a higher level of adjustment in some other area of behavior. The individual may progress in certain respects while remaining fixated in other respects; after a particular progressive adjustment has been "consolidated," so that he feels secure in this adjustment, he may then progress in other respects [1954, p. 265].

Of course, fixations are a serious matter if they are relatively widespread and enduring or if they affect important areas of functioning. Persons fixated at immature levels do not become adults in the complete psychological sense of this word. They may be unable to fully accept the responsibilities of adult status and unable to fully participate in its rewards.

REGRESSION

Sometimes we progress but find ourselves threatened by our new experiences. When we encounter frustration, conflict, and anxiety, perhaps we tend to withdraw or retreat. Since present patterns of behavior seem inadequate, responses which were rewarding in the past may be renewed and relied on.

Regression refers to the recovery of a pattern of behavior which was characteristic of an earlier level of development. Used as a defense, regression implies that the individual finds his present behavior threatening and reinstates responses which had seemingly been outgrown. The regressed person appears, then, to be functioning in an age-inappropriate way. . . .

It is not uncommon for a child to show some regression upon the birth of a sibling. A considerable amount of the parents' attention may be given over to the new baby, leaving the older child with feelings of deprivation. Although he has been walking for several years, suddenly he may insist that he is unable to do so, that he is too little and must be carried. Baby talk which has been largely outgrown crops up again, and toilet habits may be abandoned. Such regressions may be interpreted as attempts to regain lost attention or status.

Fixation and regression are somewhat similar; both imply the use of behavior which is relatively immature or inappropriate. In fixation, however, the individual has not progressed beyond a certain level, while in regression he has advanced beyond the level but then retreats. The young man who never formed age-appropriate relations with young women was said to be fixated. Contrast this example with that of a young woman who tries but finds it impossible to meet the demands of marriage and regresses by returning home to her parents.

Regression is encouraged by the human tendency to selectively repress unpleasant memories while allowing pleasant ones free expression. People frequently long for the good old days. Old graduates at class reunions grow nostalgic for their college days. They talk about the football games, parties, and the night of the raid on the girl's dormitory, but fail to recall the examinations, term papers, and financial privation.

Like fixations, regressions may be relatively permanent and widespread or considerably more momentary and limited in their effects. All of us make some use of temporary, partial, or limited regressions. In recreation we retreat from the responsibilities and cares of everyday living and regress to play activities, to games and sports and hobbies. At a convention or party we may let down our hair and engage in unadult antics. And almost anyone in extreme provocation may indulge in a childish display of anger, tears, or other feelings.

It has been suggested that the healthy, mature, and creative adult has the ability to be childlike when he wants to be; that is, he has the ability to voluntarily regress and recapture the qualities of childhood (Kris, 1952; Maslow, 1958; Schafer, 1958). He can be completely spontaneous, vigorously emotional, and uncritically enthusiastic; he can engage in great nonsense and wild fantasy. Then he can become controlled, rational, critical, sensical, and realistic again (in short, grown-up) (Maslow, 1958).

When regressions are involuntary, they are of more dangerous consequence. Regression may become relatively permanent. It may encompass a number of areas of adjustment. It may involve a retreat to very early patterns of behavior. Adjustments have been noted in which there is a general regression to childish or even infantile levels of functioning. In extreme cases, the regressed individual may be completely unable to take care of himself.

IDENTIFICATION

Our lives are bound up with the lives of others. We share in the lives of the people close to us and these people, in turn, share in our lives. To some extent, their successes are our successes, their failures are our failures, and our successes and failures are theirs.

Identification is a general term which refers to the various ways in which we establish a oneness with another person, group, or object. We are said to "identify" with another person when we model our behavior after him and become like him. We also identify when we regard another person as an extension of ourselves so that, in a sense, what happens to this person also happens to us.

Used as a defense, identification implies that we feel threatened and respond by drawing upon the valued qualities of others. We may copy their patterns in order to enhance ourselves. Or we may establish or emphasize a mutual identity which in some way leads to our own enhancement.

Just as we grow physically by ingesting food, our personality grows by taking in or introjecting the forms of behavior that we are exposed to (Szasz, 1957). Small children model their behavior after their parents, their siblings, and other people with whom they come in contact. Behavior that is seen as having successful consequences and models who are highly rewarding and highly regarded are especially apt to be copied (Bandura and Walters, 1963).

Probably all of us have seen some little girl enacting the identity of her mother. She makes up with her mother's lipstick, dresses in her mother's clothes, and totters about in her mother's high heels. She cares for her dolls as her mother cares for her, addressing them with the same words and in the same tones. She sets the table, pours the "tea," and even gossips with the imaginary guests (perhaps in a way that mother may find a little too identical).

Boys frequently express the desire to be like their fathers. They wish to be as big as their fathers and have their fathers' strength or privileges or material possessions. Boys copy, share in, and draw on their fathers' accomplishments. ("*My* dad can lick *your* dad!" "Oh yeah, my dad can lick the whole world with one finger!")

Parents identify with their children and share in their children's accomplishments. The father who was unable to complete school may pride himself on his children's education. Their diplomas can mean more to him than his own ever could. A mother whose own career or marriage has been a failure may identify closely with her daughter; the mother may direct her daughter's progress and share in her success.

We identify with groups as well as with other people. We may identify with our neighborhood or school, our gang or club, our race or religious designation, and our state or country. Sometimes such identifications are painful or embarrassing for us, and we struggle to disidentify ourselves and form new, more acceptable identifications.

Identification can be a very open and conscious process or it can be a very subtle one into which we have only a limited insight. And we may identify with someone or something only in part or seemingly completely. For example, the enthusiastic fan at a football game is more than a spectator; with ten seconds left and goal to go, he is as poised and ready as any man on the field to get that ball over the goal line.

We pattern ourselves after prestigious and accomplished models, those who are successful in reaching the goals that we may be struggling for. In effecting a model's behavior, we may be able to attain his successes. Or, at least, he may reward us for our efforts (or punish us less) or love us more (or hate us less).

In establishing a common identity with another person, we participate in this person's life. We vicariously share in his status or achievement and feel more worthy and fulfilled ourselves. Identifying with a prestigious group of people or a powerful or successful organization may bring similar feelings of worth and satisfaction.

Difficulty occurs when models for identification are absent, inadequate, or harmful. A boy whose father is bumbling and ineffectual may take over these qualities for himself. Or, at least, he may be very threatened by his identity with his father. A girl whose mother is antagonistic toward males may introject her mother's unfortunate attitudes. When the parent of the same sex is missing, unsympathetic, or hostile, the child may pattern himself after the parent of the opposite sex and develop behavior inappropriate to his own sex role.

Sometimes damage is done when a number of important models have conflicting patterns of behavior. A husband and wife, for example, may have important differences in standards and values; their children through identification with both parents can take over these incompatible systems and experience considerable conflict. Or an adolescent or young adult may find that his parents, his teachers, and his age-mates, all of whom he is identified with to some extent, present very different examples.

PROJECTION

A feature of some identifications is the taking in or introjection of something from the external environment. Not everything that we take in or everything that we become will serve us well or be valued by us. Just as we strive to acquire and accentuate prized patterns of behavior, we struggle to avoid, inhibit, or disassociate ourselves from those which we hold in low esteem.

Projection refers to our tendency to attribute our own thoughts, feelings, and actions to others. We tend to regard other people as somewhat like ourselves. If, for example, we feel bored in a particular situation, we imagine that others are bored too. If we hold a particular belief very strongly, it may be difficult for us to understand how anyone else could not feel as we do.

Both positive and negative qualities can be projected. It has been suggested that we project acceptable and positively valued characteristics to people whom we like and identify with. Unacceptable, negatively valued qualities are projected to people whom we dislike, to people whom we feel we could not possibly be like (but, of course, are) (Zimmer, 1955).

If we sense good in ourselves, we may tend to see good in others. To the pure, all things are pure, goes an old saying. If we sense bad, we may see other people in the same unfavorable light; for example, we may see ourselves and others too as hostile and self-seeking: "It's all dog-eat-dog," we say, "so I better get in the first bite."

Used as a defense, projection implies that a person has certain thoughts or feelings or actions which are threatening to him, which he then denies are his, and instead attributes to others. As is indicated, three steps are involved: (1) a sense of some unacceptable motive operating in oneself; (2) a repression of this motive; and (3) an attribution of this motive to others.

Those of us who use projection as a defense may be especially hostile to other people who seem to share our unacceptable impulses (Cohen,

1956). "That's like the pot calling the kettle black," we sometimes say when one person criticizes another for a fault he has himself. Sometimes the projector has some insight into what he is doing, and occasionally an individual suggests that maybe the reason he cannot get along with another person is that this person is too like himself.

In our own culture aggressive impulses frequently undergo repression and projection. Those of us who sense unacceptable feelings of hostility in ourselves may attribute these feelings to others, most commonly to the person for whom the hostility was originally felt. We may start off with the thought: I hate you, and I'd like to hurt you. Through projection, we wind up with the thought: You hate me, and you'd like to hurt me.

Sexual urges are also frequently repressed and projected. A young woman who senses a strong but unacceptable sexual motivation in herself may deny this and instead see others as overly interested in sex. A man who is tempted to be unfaithful to his wife may be considerably concerned about his wife's "flirtations." An individual who has homosexual impulses may react against them and accuse others of making indecent advances.

Most frequently people are the objects of projection, but in some cases animals, natural and supernatural forces, or even inanimate articles may serve as objects. Primitives project human motives onto their gods, sometimes perceiving them as angry and at other times content. Sometimes a tennis player will conduct an ostentatious investigation of his racket after he has completely missed the ball—as if there were a hole in it big enough for the ball to go through. The person who stumbles on a chair may go back and kick the chair for tripping him.

Jourard (1963) suggests a number of guideposts for establishing whether or not a person is using projection as a defense. He says that we may suspect such is the case if bad things are imputed to others with little justification, while these same things are denied in oneself but with some evidence to the contrary.

In projecting threatening qualities we are able to accomplish a number of things. First, we can disclaim responsibility for these qualities. (*I* don't have dirty thoughts, but *they* do.) Second, we can attack these qualities, thereby establishing distance from them. (I can't stand people who have dirty thoughts.) Third, we may feel that we are not so blameworthy since these qualities are widely shared. (So what if I have a dirty thought now and then? Everybody does.) And, fourth, we may gain some vicarious satisfaction from seeing these qualities indulged in by others. (I'd better keep my eye on these people and see what sort of dirty things they're up to.)

Insofar as we project positive qualities, our relationships with others may be facilitated. For example, a person who is genuinely friendly may project this feeling and expect that other people are friendly too. Whether the people he comes in contact with are friendly or not, his attitudes and behavior increase the possibility of their being so. To some extent people respond in kind, and just as aggression is frequently met with aggression, one friendly overture may prompt another.

In projecting negative qualities we protect ourselves from seeing ourselves in an unfavorable light. In the long run, however, this negative projection can be seriously detrimental to adjustment. It prevents us from facing problems and dealing with them effectively. Furthermore, as we project negative qualities onto others and then act in accordance with this projection, relationships with others will suffer. The projection mechanism carried to an extreme is seen in certain paranoid processes.

DISPLACEMENT

Some of our behavior is threatening because of the people that it is directed toward or because of the particular form that it takes. Assuming that we express an impulse only in certain ways and only toward certain people, we may escape anxiety.

In *displacement* there is a shift of thought, feeling, or action from one person or situation to another. Displacement occurs because the original impulse causes or would cause considerable anxiety. Consequently, there is a shift to a neutral object or to one that is more vulnerable or less dangerous than the original. . . .

Sometimes the new object is similar to the original; the two may stand for each other or be identified with each other in some way, and the new object symbolizes the old one. For example, the little boy who is angry with his mother may trample her flower bed instead of attacking her directly. Or he may take his feelings out on his teacher if she in some way reminds him of his mother and is more vulnerable to attack.

Sometimes, however, the similarity between the new object and the old one is quite subtle and can be understood only by a person with a good deal of psychological training. Occasionally, on the surface at least, there appears to be no relationship. Occasionally, too, displacement seems to be a diffuse process in which the troublesome impulse is channeled to many new objects with little apparent rhyme or reason.

It has already been noted that the aggressive impulse is one that is frequently diverted or displaced. Other processes that commonly undergo displacement are fear, love, and attention.

Fears may be displaced in the same way that aggressive impulses are. People who are constantly worried about little things which appear to constitute no danger may actually be concerned about something more important which has been repressed. A child who fears his father, a person with whom he must be in constant association, may displace this fear to animals. A woman who hates her husband and fears that she may do him violence may instead express a fear of knives and other sharp instruments.

The people whom we wish to love and be loved by do not always respond. In this event, we may displace our love and affection to someone else. For example, a boy who is unable to establish a satisfactory relationship with his father may turn his affection to a teacher, a scoutmaster, or some other adult male. Sometimes a person who has been jilted by a lover finds and quickly marries someone else on the rebound. Some forms of self-love appear to be displacements: constantly rebuffed by others, a person may remove all of his affection to himself (Symonds, 1946).

Sometimes we make doubly sure that upsetting problems stay out of the focus of attention by keeping ourselves busy with other activities. A man who is having difficulty with his homelife may displace his attention to his work; in fact, he may throw himself into his job with such vigor that his friends mistakenly attribute his adjustment difficulties to overwork. In the same way, a woman who is having trouble with her roles of wife and mother may busy herself in social or professional activities. Many people look forward to their vacation as the time when attention can be diverted from the bothersome problems of the everyday environment.

Through the use of displacement we are able to discharge our feelings in acceptable directions. Positive and negative feelings may be separated and applied to separate objects. Positive feelings may be displaced to objects that will accept and respond to these feelings. Negative feelings may be diverted from important and dangerous objects onto those which are unimportant and vulnerable. In this way, we may love some things, hate others, and not be torn by ambivalence (Isaacs, 1937; Symonds, 1946).

Unfortunately, insofar as displacement involves negative feelings, one relationship may be improved at the cost of another. Although the second object is more vulnerable than the first, it may be an important one nevertheless. For example, the employee who displaces feelings of hostility from his office to the home environment ensures the safety of his job at the expense of vital family relationships (Sappenfield, 1954).

REACTION FORMATION

When we sense things in ourselves that are threatening to our self-esteem and general welfare, we may attempt to convince ourselves and others that these things are not so. One way that we can accomplish this is by accentuating opposite qualities. We strive to feel, think, and act in ways that are sharply in contrast to the ways that we tend to feel, think, and act.

Reaction formation refers to efforts to inhibit, mask, or overcome certain impulses by emphasizing opposite ones. Using such behavior as a defense against threat is very common. Sensing fear, we may attempt to act very brave. Sensing weakness, we may attempt to be tough and hard-boiled. Sensing unacceptable dependence, we may make a great show of rebellion. Sensing anxiety-provoking affectionate feelings, we may react by being very cynical and take a cool and jaundiced view of human beings (Sarnoff, 1960).

A person who is strongly tempted by unacceptable sex needs can react against them by being extremely puritanical. He may prevent any sexual expression in himself and avoid almost all association with the opposite sex. Furthermore, he may criticize others who engage in any sexual activity no matter how mild; sometimes he may even attempt to prevent them from doing so. Whether his activities are ostensibly on his own behalf or seemingly on the behalf of others, they are designed to help him keep his own forbidden impulses in check.

Sensing unacceptable aggressive urges in himself, a person can react against them by being very kind. Such a person will appear to be extremely polite, deferent, and solicitous about the welfare of others. He may be unable to be aggressive even when aggressive actions appear to be quite appropriate. His behavior is dedicated to keeping his hostile impulses under control.

A reaction formation toward selfish tendencies may be manifested in extreme generosity. Stinginess and avarice may be repressed and replaced by magnanimous actions. In this patterning the person will feel compelled to give and be generous; he must constantly demonstrate to himself and others that he is not the self-seeking person he inwardly suspects himself to be.

Reaction formations are characterized by their extreme and compelling strength. As was noted, reaction formations to sex may be manifested in very puritanical behavior, those to aggression may produce excessively mild and gentle actions, and those counteracting selfishness may compel great generosity. In each case the individual will be unwilling and unable to modify his position. The force of the reaction is necessary to prevent the original impulse from breaking out of control into open expression.

Reaction formations may show inconsistencies and imperfections. Sometimes the forbidden behavior and the reaction behavior exist side by side. For example, a person who has reacted strongly against a tendency to be dirty and disorderly may still engage in certain activities or have certain places in which he is very messy.

Sometimes, too, a reaction formation will break down, allowing the original impulse free expression. A child who has always been extremely polite and well behaved may be caught in acts of extreme cruelty toward animals. A man who has always seemed extremely mild in his actions may suddenly lash out in some verbal or physical aggression. A woman who has spent a good deal of her life attacking certain patterns of behavior may suddenly be found to be engaging in this very behavior.

Reaction formation plays an important part in the socialization process. Generosity, kindliness, orderliness, and many other personal qualities that are valued in our society are not natural expressions of the child; they are partly formed in reaction to earlier, diametrically opposite patterns of behavior. The small child, for example, has little concept of cleanliness; it is through constant training that he develops a dislike for dirt, a disgust for filth, and a loathing for his bodily wastes.

It is interesting to observe reaction formations in the process of development. One might note, for example, a sudden shift in a child from attraction to dirt to aversion to dirt. A little girl who formerly played in her dress until it was filthy suddenly becomes sensitive to the smallest spot. Any garment that is the slightest bit dirty must be immediately removed. Little by little, her actions may become modulated so that she learns to be clean but not excessively so.

Severe, unmodulated reaction formations distort our lives. We need to be clean, of course, but we should not need to be always immaculate. We should be generous, but we should not feel compelled to give. We need to be kind, but we should be able to express hostility when the occasion seems to warrant it. In general, we should not be strangers to any of our impulses; instead of attempting to seal them off, we should learn to know them and express them in the ways we value. . . .

FANTASY

The world we live in, reality, leaves much to be desired. Our efforts may help to change it. Or we may change our perceptions of it and somehow see it as a more desirable place. Or we may be able to escape it for a while by constructing a private and more satisfying world.

Fantasy refers to imaginary constructions. It includes make-believe play, reveries, and day-dreams. Novels, movies, plays, and similar literary and dramatic works might be considered to provide the individual with ready-made fantasy experiences.

As a defense, our fantasy life provides us with an escape from the dangers, threats, and boredom of the real world. In our fantasies we can meet our unmet needs and reach our unreached goals. We can picture ourselves as a different sort of person and the world as a different sort of world.

Freud (1900) and others have pointed out the strong element of wish fulfillment in fantasies. Holt notes a number of reasons why, in daydreams, wishes may be expressed in very direct, crude, and primitive ways. He writes:

The fact that the daydream is private and uncommunicated, that it is a regressive and often not recalled kind of thinking, makes it possible for the fulfillment of wishes to be relatively direct and for the wishes themselves to be unsublimated and close to the hypothetical state of original drives. If someone has annoyed us, we can easily imagine killing him or inflicting on him tortures we would not even consider witnessing in reality, much less carrying them out ourselves [1961, p. 29].

Fantasy is a very common pursuit at every age. The child acts out his fantasies. His play is filled with make-believe. He pretends that he is the person he would like to be, living in a world he would like to live in. He becomes his father, a cowboy, a spaceman, or a ferocious animal. He finds himself on the Western plains, high above the earth, or deep in the jungle. In his play he escapes the limitations of being young and weak and small and under the domination of adults.

As we grow older we increasingly daydream our fantasies rather than act them out. We not only create new experiences, we also relive old ones that have been enjoyable. Sometimes our fantasies are previews of events which are to occur in the future; certainly part of the pleasure of a vacation, a trip, or a party is in its anticipation.

In later maturity, many daydreams tend to be re-creative ones. In his fantasies the elderly person may live again happy experiences out of his past. Even these daydreams have elements of creativeness; in memory some old experiences become more satisfying than they were in actuality.

"Conquering hero" and "suffering hero" are two common types of fantasies. In conquering-hero fantasies the individual imagines that he is the master of some situation. He is a famous athlete, a brilliant student, a great lover, or a fascinating conversationalist. He is applauded, acclaimed, and sought after. In fantasy he may reenact an old experience but this time he says and does all the things that he failed to say and do during the actual experience.

In conquering-hero fantasies a person may have the experiences that are not forthcoming in real life. For example, a youth who is hungry for heterosexual experience may imagine a relationship with some girl who has caught his eye. He may daydream about asking her for a date and then conjure up the conversations they would have, the dances and parties they would attend, and the affection they would share. In the same fashion, a single woman may daydream that she is married, has a handsome and considerate husband, attractive children, and a nice home.

In suffering-hero fantasies the individual imagines himself to be the victim of some situation. He sees himself as undergoing great hardship or suffering adversity. He is cold and hungry, unloved and unwanted, or destitute and outcast. He may be wounded, dying, or dead.

In fantasying oneself in such pitiful circumstances, a person becomes a figure who is deserving of the sympathy and commiseration of others. At the same time he is worthy of their admiration for carrying on so well in the face of such circumstances. Elements of revenge may also be present since now certain people will be very sorry that they did not treat the person better in the past. Suffering-hero daydreams are common in children who are having difficulties with their parents.

When life is uninteresting and frustrating, fantasy permits us to escape into a dream world where exciting things occur and difficult goals are reached. In fantasy we can relive the pleasant experiences of the past (sometimes making them even more pleasant than they really were), and we can live in advance the anticipated pleasures of the future. Creative thinking and fantasy are closely related; representing our needs, activities, and goals in fantasy may be the first step to insti-tuting them in reality (Hartmann, 1958; Varendonck, 1921).

Fantasy becomes detrimental when it becomes a substitute for reality achievements. Compared with the ideal goals available in fantasy, the small rewards possible in the real world may seem hardly worth the effort. Fantasy can rob a person of large amounts of time which otherwise might be applied to real-life pursuits. In some serious adjustments the individual tends to be unable to distinguish completely between the worlds of fantasy and reality.

REFERENCES

BANDURA, A., and R. H. WALTERS. *Social Learning and Personality Development.* New York: Holt, Rinehart & Winston, Inc., 1963.

BRENNER, C. *An Elementary Textbook of Psychoanalysis.* New York: International Universities Press, 1957.

CAMERON, N., and A. MARGARET. *Behavior Pathology.* Boston: Houghton Mifflin Co., 1951.

COHEN, A. R. "Experimental Effects of Ego-defense Preference on Interpersonal Relations," *Journal of Abnormal and Social Psychology,* 52 (1956), 19–27.

DOLLARD, J., and N. E. MILLER. *Personality and Psychotherapy.* New York: McGraw-Hill Book Company, 1950.

FREUD, S. *The Interpretation of Dreams* (1900). London: Hogarth, 1953.

———. *The Psychopathology of Everyday Life* (1904), in *Basic Writings of Sigmund Freud.* New York: Vintage Books, Random House, 1938.

HALL, C. S. *A Primer of Freudian Psychology.* Cleveland: World Publishing, 1954.

HARTMANN, H. *Ego Psychology and the Problem of Adaptation.* New York: International Universities Press, 1958.

HOLT, R. R. "The Nature of TAT Stories as Cognitive Products: A Psychoanalytic Approach," in J. Kagan, ed., *Contemporary Issues in Thematic Apperceptive Methods.* Springfield, Ill.: Charles C Thomas, 1961, pp. 3–43.

ISAACS, S. *Social Development in Young Children.* New York: Harcourt, Brace, 1937.

JOURARD, S. M. *Personal Adjustment*, 2nd ed. New York: Macmillan Company, 1963.

KARPMAN, B. "Lying: A Minor Inquiry into the Ethics of Neurotic and Psychopathic Behavior," *Journal of Criminal Law and Criminology*, 40 (1949), 135–157.

KRIS, E. *Psychoanalytic Explorations in Art*. New York: International Universities Press, 1952.

KROEBER, T. C. "The Coping Functions of the Ego Mechanisms," in R. W. White, ed., *The Study of Lives*. New York: Atherton Press, 1963, pp. 178–198.

MACKINNON, D. W., and W. F. DUKES. "Repression," in L. Postman, ed., *Psychology in the Making*. New York: Alfred A. Knopf, 1962, pp. 662–744.

MASLOW, A. H. "Emotional Blocks to Creativity," *Journal of Individual Psychology*, 14 (1958), 51–56.

MENNINGER, K., M. MAYMAN, and P. PRUYSER. *The Vital Balance*. New York: Viking Press, 1963.

MURPHY, L. B., et al. *The Widening World of Childhood*. New York: Basic Books, Inc., 1962.

SAPPENFIELD, B. R. *Personality Dynamics*. New York: Alfred A. Knopf, 1954.

SARNOFF, I. "Reaction Formation and Cynicism," *Journal of Personality*, 28 (1960), 129–143.

SCHAFER, R. "Regression in the Service of the Ego: The Relevance of a Psychoanalytic Concept for Personality Assessment," in G. Lind-zey, ed., *Assessment of Human Motives*. New York: Holt, Rinehart & Winston, Inc., 1958, pp. 119–148.

STONE, L. J., and J. CHURCH. *Childhood and Adolescence*. New York: Random House, Inc., 1957.

SWANSON, G. E. "Determinants of the Individual's Defenses Against Inner Conflict: Review and Reformation," in J. C. Glidewell, ed., *Parental Attitudes and Child Behavior*. Springfield, Ill.: Charles C Thomas, 1961, pp. 5–41.

SYMONDS, P. M. *The Dynamics of Human Adjustment*. New York: Appleton-Century-Crofts, 1946.

SZASZ, T. S. "A Contribution to the Psychology of Schizophrenia," *A.M.A. Archives of Neurology and Psychiatry*, 77 (1957), 420–436.

TWAIN, MARK (Samuel L. Clemens). *The Adventures of Tom Sawyer* (1875). New York: Harper, 1929.

VARENDONCK, J. *The Psychology of Daydreams*. New York: The Macmillan Company, 1921.

VAUGHAN, W. F. *Personal and Social Adjustment*. New York: Odyssey Press, 1952.

WOOLF, M. "The Child's Moral Development," in K. R. Eissler, ed., *Searchlights on Delinquency*. New York: International Universities Press, 1949, pp. 263–272.

ZIMMER, H. "The Roles of Conflict and Internalized Demands in Projection," *Journal of Abnormal and Social Psychology*, 50 (1955), 188–192.

THE RATIONALIZING ANIMAL

Elliot Aronson

Man likes to think of himself as a rational animal. However, it is more true that man is a *rationalizing* animal, that he attempts to appear reasonable to himself and to others. Albert Camus even said that man is a creature who spends his entire life in an attempt to convince himself that he is not absurd.

Some years ago a woman reported that she was receiving messages from outer space. Word came to her from the planet Clarion that her city would be destroyed by a great flood on December 21. Soon a considerable number of believers shared her deep commitment to the prophecy. Some of them quit their jobs and spent their savings freely in anticipation of the end.

On the evening of December 20, the prophet and her followers met to prepare for the event. They believed that flying saucers would pick them up, thereby sparing them from disaster. Midnight arrived, but no flying saucers. December 21 dawned, but no flood.

What happens when prophecy fails? Social psychologists Leon Festinger, Henry Riecken, and Stanley Schachter infiltrated the little band of believers to see how they would react. They predicted that persons who had expected the disaster, but awaited it alone in their homes, would simply lose faith in the prophecy. But those who awaited the outcome in a group, who had thus admitted their belief publicly, would come to believe even more strongly in the prophecy and turn into active proselytizers.

This is exactly what happened. At first the faithful felt despair and shame because all their predictions had been for nought. Then, after waiting nearly five hours for the saucers, the prophet had a new vision. The city had been spared, she said, because of the trust and faith of her devoted group. This revelation was elegant in its simplicity, and the believers accepted it enthusiastically. They now sought the press that they had previously avoided. They turned from believers into zealots.

LIVING ON THE FAULT

In 1957 Leon Festinger proposed his theory of *cognitive dissonance*, which describes and predicts man's rationalizing behavior. Dissonance occurs whenever a person simultaneously holds two inconsistent cognitions (ideas, beliefs, opinions). For example, the belief that the world will end on a certain day is dissonant with the awareness, when the day breaks, that the world has not ended. Festinger maintained that this state of inconsistency is so uncomfortable that people strive to reduce the conflict in the easiest way possible. They will change one or both cognitions so that they will "fit together" better.

Consider what happens when a smoker is confronted with evidence that smoking causes cancer. He will become motivated to change either his attitudes about smoking or his behavior. And as anyone who has tried to quit knows, the former alternative is easier.

The smoker may decide that the studies are lousy. He may point to friends ("If Sam, Jack and Harry smoke, cigarettes can't be all that dangerous"). He may conclude that filters trap all the cancer-producing materials. Or he may argue that he would rather live a short and happy life with cigarettes than a long and miserable life without them.

The more a person is committed to a course of action, the more resistant he will be to information that threatens that course. Psychologists have reported that the people who are least likely to believe the dangers of smoking are those who tried to quite—and failed. They have become more committed to smoking. Similarly, a person who builds a $100,000 house astride the San Andreas Fault will be less receptive to arguments about imminent earthquakes than would a person who is renting the house for a few months. The new homeowner is committed; he doesn't want to believe that he did an absurd thing.

When a person reduces his dissonance, he defends his ego, and keeps a positive self-image. But self-justification can reach startling extremes; people will ignore danger in order to avoid dissonance, even when that ignorance can cause their deaths. I mean that literally.

Suppose you are Jewish in a country occupied by Hitler's forces. What should you do? You could try to leave the country; you could try to pass as "Aryan"; you could do nothing and hope for the best. The first two choices are dangerous; if you are caught you will be executed. If you decide to sit tight, you will try to convince yourself that you made the best decision. You may reason that while Jews are indeed being treated unfairly, they are not being killed unless they break the law.

Now suppose that a respected man from your town announces that he has seen Jews being butchered mercilessly, including everyone who had recently been deported from your village. If you believe him, you might have a chance to escape. If you don't believe him, you and your family will be slaughtered.

Dissonance theory would predict that you will not listen to the witness, because to do so would be to admit that your judgment and decisions were wrong. You will dismiss his information as untrue, and decide that he was lying or hallucinating. Indeed, Elie Wiesel reported that this happened to the Jews in Sighet, a small town in Hungary, in 1944. Thus people are not passive receptacles for the deposit of information. The manner in which they view and distort the objective world in order to avoid and reduce dissonance is entirely predictable. But one cannot divide the world into rational people on one side and dissonance reducers on the other. While people vary in their ability to tolerate dissonance, we are all capable of rational or irrational behavior, depending on the circumstances—some of which follow.

DISSONANCE BECAUSE OF EFFORT

Judson Mills and I found that if people go through a lot of trouble to gain admission to a group, and the group turns out to be dull and dreary, they will experience dissonance. It is a rare person who will accept this situation with an "Oh, pshaw. I worked hard for nothing. Too bad." One way to resolve the dissonance is to decide that the group is worth the effort it took to get admitted.

We told a number of college women that they would have to undergo an initiation to join a group that would discuss the psychology of sex. One third of them had severe initiation: they had to recite a list of obscene words and read some lurid sexual passages from novels in the presence of a male experimenter (in 1959, this really was a "severe" and embarrassing task). One third went through a mild initiation in which they read words that were sexual but not obscene (such as "virgin" and "petting"); and the last third had no initiation at all. Then all of the women listened to an extremely boring taped discussion of the group they had presumably joined. The women in the severe initiation group rated the discussion and its drab participants much more favorably than those in the other groups.

I am not asserting that people enjoy painful experiences, or that they enjoy things that are associated with painful experiences. If you got hit on the head by a brick on the way to a fraternity initiation, you would not like that group any better. But if you volunteered to get hit with a brick *in order to join* the fraternity, you definitely would like the group more than if you had been admitted without fuss.

After a decision—especially a difficult one that involves much time, money, or effort—people almost always experience dissonance. Awareness of defects in the preferred object is dissonant with having chosen it; awareness of positive aspects of the unchosen object is dissonant with having rejected it.

Accordingly, researchers have found that *before* making a decision, people seek as much information as possible about the alternatives. Afterwards, however, they seek reassurance that they did the right thing, and do so by seeking information in support of their choice or by simply changing the information that is already in their heads. In one of the earliest experiments on dissonance theory, Jack Brehm gave a group of women their choice between two appliances, such as a toaster or a blender, that they had previously rated for desirability. When the subjects reevaluated the appliances after choosing one of them, they increased their liking for the one they had chosen and downgraded their evaluation of the rejected appliance. Similarly, Danuta Ehrlich and her associates found that a person about to buy a new car does so carefully, reading all ads and accepting facts openly on various makes and models. But after he buys his Volvo, for instance, he will read advertisements more selectively, and he will tend to avoid ads for Volkswagens, Chevrolets, and so on.

THE DECISION TO BEHAVE IMMORALLY

Your conscience, let us suppose, tells you that it is wrong to cheat, lie, steal, seduce your neighbor's husband or wife, or whatever. Let us suppose further that you are in a situation in which you are sorely tempted to ignore your conscience. If you give in to temptation, the cognition "I am a decent, moral person" will be dissonant with the cognition "I have committed an immoral act." If you resist, the cognition "I want to get a good grade (have that money, seduce that person)" is dissonant with the cognition "I could have acted so as to get that grade, but I chose not to."

The easiest way to reduce dissonance in either case is to minimize the negative aspects of the action one has chosen, and to change one's attitude about its immorality. If Mr. C. decides to cheat, he will probably decide that cheating isn't really so bad. It hurts no one; everyone does it; it's part of human nature. If Mr. D. decides not to cheat, he will no doubt come to believe that cheating is a sin, and deserves severe punishment.

The point here is that the initial attitudes of these men is virtually the same. Moreover, their decisions could be a hair's breadth apart. But once the action is taken, their attitudes diverge sharply.

Judson Mills confirmed these speculations in an experiment with sixth-grade children. First he measured their attitudes toward cheating, and then put them in a competitive situation. He arranged the test so that it was impossible to win without cheating, and so it was easy for the children to cheat, thinking they would be unwatched.

The next day, he asked the children again how they felt about cheating. Those who had cheated on the test had become more lenient in their attitudes; those who had resisted the temptation adopted harsher attitudes.

These data are provocative. They suggest that the most zealous crusaders are not those who are removed from the problem they oppose. I would hazard to say that the people who are most angry about "the sexual promiscuity of the young" are *not* those who have never dreamed of being promiscuous. On the contrary, they would be persons who had been seriously tempted by illicit sex, who came very close to giving in to their desires, but who finally resisted. People who almost live in glass houses are the ones who are most likely to throw stones.

INSUFFICIENT JUSTIFICATION

If I offer George $20 to do a boring task, and offer Richard $1 to do the same thing, which one will decide that the assignment was mildly interesting? If I threaten one child with harsh punishment if he does something forbidden, and threaten another child with mild punishment, which one will transgress?

Dissonance theory predicts that when people find themselves doing something and they have neither been rewarded adequately for doing it nor threatened with dire consequences for not doing it, they will find *internal* reasons for their behavior.

Suppose you dislike Woodrow Wilson and I want you to make a speech in his favor. The most efficient thing I can do is to pay you a lot of money for making the speech, or threaten to kill you if you don't. In either case, you will probably comply with my wish, but you won't change your attitude toward Wilson. If that were my goal, I would have to give you a *minimal* reward or threat. Then, in order not to appear absurd, you would have to seek additional reasons for your speech—this could lead you to find good things about Wilson and hence, to conclude that you really do like Wilson after all. Lying produces great attitude change only when the liar is undercompensated.

Festinger and J. Merrill Carlsmith asked college students to work on boring and repetitive tasks. Then the experimenters persuaded the students to lie about the work, to tell a fellow student that the task would be interesting and enjoyable. They offered half of their subjects $20 for telling the lie, and they offered the others only $1. Later they asked all subjects how much they had really liked the tasks.

The students who earned $20 for their lies rated the work as deadly dull, which it was. They experienced no dissonance: they lied, but they were well paid for that behavior. By contrast, students who got $1 decided that the tasks were rather enjoyable. The dollar was apparently enough to get them to tell the lie, but not enough to keep them from feeling that lying for so paltry a sum was foolish. To reduce dissonance, they decided that they hadn't lied after all; the task was fun.

Similarly, Carlsmith and I found that mild threats are more effective than harsh threats in changing a child's attitude about a forbidden object, in this case a delightful toy. In the severe-threat condition, children refrained from playing with the toys and had a good reason for refraining—the very severity of the threat provided ample justification for not playing with the toy. In the mild-threat condition, however, the children refrained from playing with the toy but when they asked themselves, "How come I'm not playing with the toy?" they did not have a superabundant justification (because the threat was not terribly severe). Accordingly, they provided additional justification in the form of convincing themselves that the attractive toy was really not very attractive and that they didn't really want to play with it very much in the first place. Jonathan Freedman extended our findings, and showed that severe threats do not have a lasting effect on a child's behavior. Mild threats, by contrast, can change behavior for many months.

Perhaps the most extraordinary example of insufficient justification occurred in India, where Jamuna Prasad analyzed the rumors that were circulated after a terrible earthquake in 1950. Prasad found that people in towns that were *not* in immediate danger were spreading rumors of impending doom from floods, cyclones, or unforeseeable calamities. Certainly the rumors could not help people feel more secure; why then perpetrate them? I believe that dissonance helps explain this phenomenon. The people were terribly frightened—after all, the neighboring villages had been destroyed—but they did not have ample excuse for their fear, since the earthquake had missed them. So they invented their own excuse; if a cyclone is on the way, it is reasonable to be afraid. Later, Durganand Sinha studied rumors in a town that had actually been destroyed. The people were scared, but they had good reason to be; they didn't need to seek additional justification for their terror. And their rumors showed no predictions of impending disaster and no serious exaggerations.

THE DECISION TO BE CRUEL

The need for people to believe that they are kind and decent can lead them to say and do unkind and indecent things. After the National Guard killed four students at Kent State, several rumors quickly spread: the slain girls were pregnant, so their deaths spared their families from shame; the students were filthy and had lice on them. These rumors were totally untrue, but the townspeople were eager to believe them. Why? The local people were conservative, and infuriated at the radical behavior of some of the students. Many had hoped that the students would get their comeuppance. But death is an awfully severe penalty. The severity of this penalty outweighs and is dissonant with the "crimes" of the students. In these circumstances, any information that put the victims in a bad light reduces dissonance by implying, in effect, that it was good that the young people died. One high-school teacher even avowed that anyone with "long hair, dirty clothes, or [who goes] barefooted deserves to be shot."

Keith Davis and Edward Jones demonstrated the need to justify cruelty. They persuaded students to help them with an experiment, in the course of which the volunteers had to tell another student that he was a shallow, untrustworthy, and dull person. Volunteers managed to convince themselves that they didn't like the victim of their cruel analysis. They found him less attractive than they did before they had to criticize him.

Similarly, David Glass persuaded a group of subjects to deliver electric shocks to others. The subjects, again, decided that the victim must deserve the cruelty; they rated him as stupid, mean, etc. Then Glass went a step further. He found that a subject with high self-esteem was most likely to derogate the victim. This led Glass to conclude, ironically, that it is precisely because a person thinks he is nice that he decides that the person he has hurt is a rat. "Since nice guys like me don't go around hurting innocent people," Glass's subjects seemed to say, "you must have deserved it." But individuals who have *low* self-esteem do not feel the need to justify their behavior and derogate their victims; it is *consonant* for such persons to believe they have behaved badly. "Worthless people like me do unkind things."

Ellen Berscheid and her colleagues found another factor that limits the need to derogate one's victim: the victim's capacity to retaliate. If the person doing harm feels that the situation is balanced, that his victim will pay him back in coin, he has no need to justify his behavior. In Berscheid's experiment, which involved electric shocks, college students did not derogate or dislike the persons they shocked if they believed the victims could retaliate. Students who were led to believe that the victims would not be able to retaliate *did* derogate them. Her work suggests that soldiers may have a greater need to disparage civilian victims (because they can't retaliate) then military victims. Lt. William L. Calley, who considered the "gooks" at My Lai to be something less than human, would be a case in point.

DISSONANCE AND THE SELF-CONCEPT

On the basis of recent experiments, I have reformulated Festinger's original theory in terms of the self concept. That is, dissonance is most powerful when self-esteem is threatened. Thus the important aspect of dissonance is not "I said one thing and I believe another," but "I have misled people—and I am a truthful, nice person." Conversely, the cognitions, "I believe the task is dull," and "I told someone the task was interesting," are not dissonant for a psychopathic liar.

David Mettee and I predicted in a recent experiment that persons who had low opinions of themselves would be more likely to cheat than persons with high self-esteem. We assumed that if an average person gets a temporary blow to his self-esteem (by being jilted, say, or not getting a promotion), he will temporarily feel stupid and worthless, and hence do any number of stupid and worthless things—cheat at cards, bungle an assignment, break a valuable vase.

Mettee and I temporarily changed 45 female students' self-esteem. We gave one third of them positive feedback about a personality test they had taken (we said that they were interesting, mature, deep, etc.); we gave one third negative feedback (we said that they were relatively immature, shallow, etc.); and one third of the students got no information at all. Then all the students went on to participate in what they thought was an unrelated experiment, in which they gambled in a competitive game of cards. We arranged the situation so that the students could cheat and thereby win a considerable sum of money, or not cheat, in which case they were sure to lose.

The results showed that the students who had received blows to their self-esteem cheated far more than those who had gotten positive feedback about themselves. It may well be that low self-esteem is a critical antecedent of criminal or cruel behavior.

The theory of cognitive dissonance has proved useful in generating research; it has uncovered a wide range of data. In formal terms, however, it is a very sloppy theory. Its very simplicity provides both its greatest strength and its most serious weakness. That is, while the theory has generated a great deal of data, it has not been easy to define the limits of the theoretical statement, to determine the specific predictions that can be made. All too often researchers have had to resort to the very unscientific rule of thumb, "If you want to be sure, ask Leon."

LOGIC AND PSYCHOLOGIC

Part of the problem is that the theory does not deal with *logical* inconsistency, but *psychological* inconsistency. Festinger maintains that two cognitions are inconsistent if the opposite of one follows from the other. Strictly speaking, the information that smoking causes cancer does not make it illogical to smoke. But these cognitions produce dissonance because they do not make sense psychologically, assuming that the smoker does not want cancer.

One cannot always predict dissonance with accuracy. A man may admire Franklin Roosevelt enormously and discover that throughout his marriage FDR carried out a clandestine affair. If he places a high value on fidelity and he believes that great men are not exempt from this value, then he will experience dissonance. Then I can predict that he will either change his attitudes about Roosevelt or soften his attitudes about fidelity. But, he may believe that marital infidelity and political greatness are totally unrelated; if this were the case, he might simply shrug off these data without modifying his opinions either about Roosevelt or about fidelity.

Because of the sloppiness in the theory, several commentators have criticized a great many of the findings first uncovered by dissonance theory. These criticisms have served a useful purpose. Often, they have goaded us to perform more precise research, which in turn has led to a clarification of some of the findings which, ironically enough, has eliminated the alternative explanations proposed by the critics themselves.

For example, Alphonse and Natalia Chapanis argued that the "severe initiation" experiment could have completely different causes. It might be that the young women were not embarrassed at having to read sexual words, but rather were aroused, and their arousal in turn led them to rate the dull discussion group as interesting. Or, to the contrary, the women in the severe-initiation condition could have felt much sexual anxiety, followed by relief that the discussion was so banal. They associated relief with the group, and so rated it favorably.

So Harold Gerard and Grover Mathewson replicated our experiment, using electric shocks in the initiation procedure. Our original findings were supported—subjects who underwent severe shocks in order to join a discussion group rated that group more favorably than subjects who had undergone mild shocks. Moreover, Gerard and Mathewson went on to show that merely linking an electric shock with the group discussion (as in a simple conditioning experiment) did not produce greater liking for the group. The increase in liking for the group occurred only when subjects volunteered for the shock *in order* to gain membership in the group—just as dissonance theory would predict.

ROUTES TO CONSONANCE

In the real world there is usually more than one way to squirm out of inconsistency. Laboratory experiments carefully control a person's alternatives, and the conclusions drawn may be misleading if applied to everyday situations. For example, suppose a prestigious university rejects a young Ph.D. for its one available teaching position. If she feels that she is a good scholar, she will experience dissonance. She can then decide that members of that department are narrow-minded and senile, sexist, and wouldn't recognize talent if it sat on their laps. Or she could decide that if they could reject someone as fine and intelligent as she, they must be extraordinarily brilliant. Both techniques will reduce dissonance, but note that they leave this woman with totally opposite opinions about professors at the university.

This is a serious conceptual problem. One solution is to specify the conditions under which a person will take one route to consonance over another. For example if a person struggles to reach a goal and fails, he may decide that the goal wasn't worth it (as Aesop's fox did) or that the effort was justified anyway (the fox got a lot of exercise in jumping for the grapes). My own research suggests that a person will take the first means when he has expended relatively little effort. But when he has put in a great deal of effort, dissonance will take the form of justifying the energy.

This line of work is encouraging. I do not think that it is very fruitful to demand to know what *the* mode of dissonance reduction is; it is more instructive to isolate the various modes that occur, and determine the optimum conditions for each.

IGNORANCE OF ABSURDITY

No dissonance theorist takes issue with the fact that people frequently work to get rewards. In our experiments, however, small rewards tend to be associated with greater attraction and greater attitude change. Is the reverse ever true?

Jonathan Freedman told college students to work on a dull task after first telling them (a) their results would be of no use to him, since his experiment was basically over, or (b) their results would be of great value to him. Subjects in the first condition were in a state of dissonance, for they had unknowingly agreed to work on a boring chore that apparently had no purpose. They reduced their dissonance by deciding that the task was enjoyable.

Then Freedman ran the same experiment with one change. He waited until the subjects finished the task to tell them whether their work would be important. In this study he found incentive effects: students told that the task was valuable enjoyed it more than those who were told that their work was useless. In short, dissonance theory does not apply when an individual performs an action in good faith without having any way of knowing it was absurd. When we agree to participate in an experiment we naturally assume that it is for a purpose. If we are informed afterward that it *had* no purpose, how were we to have known? In this instance we like the task better if it had an important purpose. But if we agreed to perform it *knowing* that it had no purpose, we try to convince ourselves that it is an attractive task in order to avoid looking absurd.

MAN CANNOT LIVE BY CONSONANCE ALONE

Dissonance reduction is only one of several motives, and other powerful drives can counteract it. If human beings had a pervasive, all-encompassing need to reduce all forms of dissonance, we would not grow, mature, or admit to our mistakes. We would sweep mistakes under the rug or, worse, turn the mistakes into virtues; in neither case would we profit from error.

But obviously people do learn from experience. They often do tolerate dissonance because the dissonant information has great utility. A person cannot ignore forever a leaky roof, even if that flaw is inconsistent with having spent a fortune on the house. As utility increases, individuals will come to prefer dissonance-arousing but useful information. But as dissonance increases, or when commitment is high, future utility and information tend to be ignored.

It is clear that people will go to extraordinary lengths to justify their actions. They will lie, cheat, live on the San Andreas Fault, accuse innocent bystanders of being vicious provocateurs, ignore information that might save their lives, and generally engage in all manner of absurd postures. Before we write off such behavior as bizarre, crazy, or evil, we would be wise to examine the situations that set up the need to reduce dissonance. Perhaps our awareness of the mechanism that makes us so often irrational will help turn Camus' observation on absurdity into a philosophic curiosity.

HEALTHY PERSONALITY AND SELF-DISCLOSURE

Sidney M. Jourard

For a long time, health and well-being have been taken for granted as "givens," and disease has been viewed as the problem for man to solve. Today, however, increasing numbers of scientists have begun to adopt a reverse point of view, regarding disease and trouble as the givens, with specification of positive health and its conditions as the problem to solve. Physical, mental and social health are values representing restrictions on the total variance of being. The scientific problem here consists in arriving at a definition of health, determining its relevant dimensions and then identifying the independent variables of which these are a function.

Scientists, however, are supposed to be hardboiled, and they insist that phenomena, to be counted "real," must be public. Hence, many behavioral scientists ignore man's self, or soul, since it is essentially a private phenomenon. Others, however, are not so quick to allocate man's self to the limbo of the unimportant, and they insist that we cannot understand man and his lot until we take his self into account.

I probably fall into the camp of those investigators who want to explore health as a positive problem in its own right, and who, further, take man's self seriously—as a reality to be explained and as a variable which produces consequences for weal or woe. This paper gives me an opportunity to explore the connection between positive health and the disclosure of self. Let me commence with some sociological truisms.

Social systems require their members to play certain roles. Unless the roles are adequately played, the social systems will not produce the results for which they have been organized. This flat statement applies to social systems as simple as that provided by an engaged couple and to those as complex as a total nation among nations. Societies have socialization "factories" and "mills" —families and schools—which serve the function of training people to play the age, sex and occupational roles which they shall be obliged to play throughout their life in the social system. Broadly speaking, if a person plays his roles suitably, he can be regarded as a more or less normal personality. Normal personalities, however, are not healthy personalities (Jourard, 1958, 16–18).

Healthy personalities are people who play their roles satisfactorily, and at the same time derive personal satisfaction from role enactment; more, they keep growing and they maintain high-level physical wellness (Dunn, 1958). It is probably enough, speaking from the standpoint of a stable social system, for people to be normal personalities. But it is possible to be a normal personality and be absolutely miserable. We would count such a normal personality unhealthy. In fact, normality in some social systems—successful acculturation to them—reliably produces ulcers, paranoia, piles or compulsiveness. We also have to regard as unhealthy personalities those people who have never been able to enact the roles that legitimately can be expected from them.

Counselors, guidance workers and psychotherapists are obliged to treat with both patterns of unhealthy personality—those people who have been unable to learn their roles and those who play their roles quite well but suffer the agonies of boredom, frustration, anxiety or stultification. If our clients are to be helped they must change, and change in valued directions. A change in a valued direction may arbitrarily be called growth. We have yet to give explicit statement to these valued directions for growth, though a beginning has been made (Fromm, 1947; Jahoda, 1958; Jourard, 1958; Maslow, 1954; Rogers, 1954). We who are professionally concerned with the happiness, growth and well-being of our clients may be regarded as professional lovers, not unlike the Cyprian sisterhood. It would be fascinating to pursue this parallel further, but let it suffice for us to be reminded that we do in fact share membership in the oldest profession in the world. Our branches of this oldest profession probably began at the same time that our sisters' branch began, and all branches will continue to flourish so long as they meet the needs of society. We are all concerned with promoting personality health in the people who consult with us.

Now what has all this to do with self-disclosure?

To answer this question, let's tune in on an imaginary interview between a client and his counselor. The client says, "I have never told this to a soul, doctor, but I can't stand my wife, my mother is a nag, my father is a bore, and my boss is an absolutely hateful and despicable tyrant. I have been carrying on an affair for the last ten years with the lady next door and at the same time I am a deacon in the church." The counselor says, showing great understanding and empathy, "Mm-humm!"

If we listened for a long enough period of time we would find that the client talks and talks about himself to this highly sympathetic and empathic listener. At some later time the client may eventually say, "Gosh, you have helped me a lot. I see what I must do and I will go ahead and do it."

Now this talking about oneself to another person is what I call self-disclosure. It would appear, without assuming anything, that self-disclosure is a factor in the process of effective counseling or psychotherapy. Would it be too arbitrary an assumption to propose that people become clients because they have not disclosed themselves in some optimum degree to the people in their life?

An historical digression: Toward the end of the 19th century Joseph Breuer, a Viennese physician, discovered (probably accidentally) that when his hysterical patients talked about themselves, disclosing not only the verbal content of their memories but also the feelings that they had suppressed at the time of assorted "traumatic" experiences, their hysterical symptoms disappeared. Somewhere along the line Breuer withdrew from a situation which would have made his name identical with that of Freud in history's hall of fame. When Breuer permitted his patients "to be," it scared him, one gathers, because some of

his female patients disclosed themselves to be quite sexy, and what was probably worse, they felt quite sexy toward him.

Freud, however, did not flinch. He made the momentous discovery that the neurotic people of his time were struggling like mad to avoid "being," to avoid being known, and in Allport's (1955) terms, to avoid "becoming." He learned that his patients, when they were given the opportunity to "be"—which free association on a couch is nicely designed to do—they would disclose that they had all manner of horrendous thoughts and feelings which they did not even dare disclose to themselves, much less express in the presence of another person. Freud learned to permit his patients to be, through permitting them to disclose themselves utterly to another human. He evidently didn't trust anyone enough to be willing to disclose *himself vis-à-vis*, so he disclosed himself to himself on paper (Freud 1955) and learned the extent to which he himself was self-alienated.

Roles for people in Victorian days were even more restrictive than they are today, and Freud discovered that when people struggled to avoid being and knowing themselves they got sick. They could only become well, and stay relatively well, when they came to know themselves through self-disclosure to another person. This makes me think of George Groddeck's magnificent *Book of the It* (*Id*) in which, in the guise of letters to a naive young woman, Groddeck shows the contrast between the public self—pretentious role-playing—and the warded off but highly dynamic *id*—which I here very loosely translate as "real self."

Let me at this point draw a distinction between role relationships and interpersonal relationships —a distinction which is often overlooked in the current spate of literature that has to do with human relations. Roles are inescapable. They must be played or else the social system will not work. A role by definition is a repertoire of behavior patterns which must be rattled off in appropriate contexts, and all behavior which is irrelevant to the role must be suppressed. But what we often forget is the fact that it is a person *who* is playing the role. This person has a self—or, I should say, he *is* a self. All too often the roles that a person plays do not do justice to all of his self. In fact, there may be nowhere that he may just *be* himself. Even more, the person may not *know* his self. He may, in Horney's (1950) terms, be self-alienated.

This fascinating term "self-alienation" means that an individual is estranged from his real self. His real self becomes a stranger, a feared and distrusted stranger. Estrangement—alienation from one's real self—is at the root of the "neurotic personality of our time" so eloquently described by Horney (1936). Fromm (1957) referred to the same phenomenon as a socially patterned defect.

Self-alienation is a sickness which is so widely shared that no one recognizes it. We may take it for granted that all the clients we encounter are self-alienated to a greater or lesser extent. If you ask anyone—a client, a patient, or one of the people here—to answer the question, "Who are you?" the answer will generally be, "I am a psychologist, a guidance worker, teacher or what have you." The respondent will probably tell you the name of the role with which he feels most closely identified. As a matter of fact, the respondent spends a greater part of his life trying to discover who he is, and once he has made some such discovery, he spends the rest of his life trying to play the part. Of course, some of the roles—age, sex, family or occupational roles—may be so restrictive that they fit a person in a manner not too different from the girdle of a 200-pound lady who is struggling to look like Brigitte Bardot. There is Faustian drama all about us in this world of role-playing. Everywhere we see people who have sold their souls—their real self, if you wish—in order to be a psychologist, a guidance worker, a nurse, a physician, a this or a that.

Now I have suggested that no social system can exist unless the members play their roles and play them with precision and elegance. But here is an odd observation, and yet one which you can all corroborate just by thinking back over your own experience. It's possible to be involved in a social group, such as a family or a work setting, for years and years, playing one's roles nicely with the other members—and never getting to know the *persons* who are playing the other roles. Roles can be played personally and impersonally, as we

are beginning to discover in nursing. A husband can be married to his wife for fifteen years and never come to know her. He knows her as "the wife." This is the paradox of the "lonely crowd" (Riesman 1950). It is the loneliness which people try to counter with "togetherness." But much of today's "togetherness" is like the "parallel play" of 2-year-old children, or like the professors in Stringfellow Barr's novel (1958) who, when together socially, lecture past one another alternately and sometimes simultaneously. There is no real self-to-self or person-to-person meeting in such transactions.

Now what does it mean to know a person, or, more accurately, a person's self? I don't mean anything mysterious by "self." All I mean is the person's subjective side—what he thinks, feels, believes, wants, worries about, his past and so forth—the kind of thing one could never know unless one were told. We get to know the other person's self when he discloses it to us.

Self-disclosure, letting another person know what you think, feel or want, is the most direct means (though not the only means) by which an individual can make himself known to another person. Personality hygienists place great emphasis upon the importance for mental health of what they call "real self being," "self-realization," "discovering oneself" and so on. An operational analysis of what goes on in counseling and therapy shows that the patients and clients discover themselves through self-disclosure to the counselor. They talk, and to their shock and amazement the counselor listens.

I venture to say that there is probably no experience more horrifying and terrifying than that of self-disclosure to "significant others" whose probable reactions are assumed but not known. Hence the phenomenon of "resistance." This is what makes psychotherapy so difficult to take and so difficult to administer. If there is any skill to be learned in the art of counseling and psychotherapy, it is the art of coping with the terrors which attend self-disclosure, and the art of decoding the language—verbal and non-verbal—in which a person speaks about his inner experience.

Now, what is the connection between self-disclosure and healthy personality? Self-disclosure, or should I say "real" self-disclosure, is both a symptom of personality health (Jourard, 1958,

218–221) and at the same time a means of ultimately achieving healthy personality. The dis-
closer of self is an animated "real self be-er." This,
of course, takes courage—the "courage to be"
(Tillich 1954). I have known people who would
rather die than become known, and in fact some
did die when it appeared that the chances were
great that they would become known. When I say
that self-disclosure is a symptom of personality
health, what I mean really is that a person who
displays many of the other characteristics that
betoken healthy personality (Jourard, 1958;
Maslow, 1954) will also display the ability to
make himself fully known to at least one other
significant human being. When I say that self-
disclosure is a means by which one achieves personality health, I mean something like the following: It is not until I *am* my real self and I *act* my
real self that my real self is in a position to grow.
One's self grows from the consequence of being.
People's selves stop growing when they repress
them. This growth-arrest in the self is what helps
to account for the surprising paradox of finding
an infant inside the skin of someone who is playing the role of an adult.

In a fascinating analysis of mental distress,
Jurgen Ruesch (1957) describes assorted neurotics, psychotics and psychosomatic patients as
persons with selective atrophy and overspeciali-
zation in the aspects of communication. I have
come to believe that it is not communication *per
se* which is fouled up in the mentally ill. Rather,
it is a foul-up in the processes of knowing others
and of becoming known to others. Neurotic and
psychotic symptoms might be viewed as smoke-
screens interposed between the patient's real self
and the gaze of the onlooker. We might call the
symptoms devices to avoid becoming known. A
new theory of schizophrenia has been proposed
by an anonymous former patient (1958) who
"was there" and he makes such a point.

Alienation from one's real self not only arrests
one's growth as a person; it also tends to make a
farce out of one's relationships with people. As
the ex-patient mentioned above observed, the
crucial break in schizophrenia is with sincerity,
not reality (Anonymous, 1958). A self-alienated
person—one who does not disclose himself truth-
fully and fully—can never love another person
nor can he be loved by the other person. Effective

loving calls for knowledge of the object (Fromm,
1957; Jourard, 1958). How can I love a person
whom I do not know? How can the other person
love me if he does not know me?

Hans Selye (1946) proposed and documented
the hypothesis that illness as we know it arises in
consequence of stress applied to the organism.
Now I rather think that unhealthy personality has
a similar root cause, and one which is related to
Selye's concept of stress. It is this: Every maladjusted person is a person who has not made
himself known to another human being, and in
consequence does not know himself. Nor can he
find himself. More than that, he struggles actively
to avoid becoming known by another human
being. He works at it ceaselessly, 24 hours daily,
and it is work! The fact that resisting becoming
known is work offers us a research opening, incidentally (Dittes, 1958; Davis and Malmo, 1951).
I believe that in the effort to avoid becoming
known a person provides for himself a cancerous
kind of stress which is subtle and unrecognized
but nonetheless effective in producing not only
the assorted patterns of unhealthy personality
that psychiatry talks about but also the wide
array of physical ills that have come to be recognized as the stock in trade of psychosomatic
medicine. Stated another way, I believe that other
people come to be stressors to an individual in
direct proportion to his degree of self-alienation.

If I am struggling to avoid becoming known by
other persons then of course I must construct a
false public self (Jourard, 1958, 301–302). The
greater the discrepancy between my unexpur-
gated real self and the version of myself that I
present to others, the more dangerous will other
people be for me. If becoming known by another
person is a source of danger, then it follows that
merely the presence of the other person can serve
as a stimulus to evoke anxiety, heightened muscle
tension and all the assorted visceral changes
which occur when a person is under stress. A
beginning already has been made in demonstrating the tension-evoking powers of the other person through the use of such instruments as are
employed in the lie detector, the measurement of
muscle tensions with electromyographic apparatus and so on (Davis and Malmo, 1958; Dittes,
1958).

Students of psychosomatic medicine have been

intimating something of what I have just finished saying explicitly. They say (Alexander, 1950) that ulcer patients, asthmatic patients, patients suffering from colitis, migraine and the like, are chronic repressors of certain needs and emotions, especially hostility and dependency. Now when you repress something, you are not only withholding awareness of this something from yourself; you are also withholding it from the scrutiny of the other person. In fact, the means by which repressions are overcome in the therapeutic situation is through relentless disclosure of self to the therapist. When a patient is finally able to follow the fundamental rule in psychoanalysis and disclose everything which passes through his mind, he is generally shocked and dismayed to observe the breadth, depth, range and diversity of thoughts, memories and emotions which pass out of his "unconscious" into overt disclosure. Incidentally, by the time a person is that free to disclose in the presence of another human being, he has doubtless completed much of his therapeutic sequence.

Self-disclosure, then, appears to be one of the means by which a person engages in that elegant activity that we call real-self-being. But is real-self-being synonymous with healthy personality? Not in and of itself. I would say that real-self-being is a necessary but not a sufficient condition for healthy personality. It is in fact possible for a person to be much "nicer" socially when he is not being his real self than when he is his real self. But an individual's obnoxious and immoral real self can never grow in the direction of greater maturity until the person has become acquainted with it and begins to be it. Real-self-being produces consequences, which in accordance with well-known principles of behavior (Skinner, 1953) produce changes in the real self. Thus, there can be no real growth of the self without real-self-being. Full disclosure of the self to at least one other significant human being appears to be one means by which a person discovers not only the breadth and depth of his needs and feelings but also the nature of his own self-affirmed values. There is no conflict between real-self-being and being an ethical or nice person, because for the average member of our society self-owned ethics are generally acquired during the process of growing up. All too often, however, the self-owned ethics are buried under authoritarian morals (Fromm, 1947).

If self-disclosure is one of the means by which healthy personality is both achieved and maintained, we can also note that such activities as loving, psychotherapy, counseling, teaching and nursing all are impossible of achievement without the disclosure of the client. It is through self-disclosure that an individual reveals to himself and to the other party just exactly who, what and where he is. Just as thermometers, sphygmomanometers, etc., disclose information about the real state of the body, self-disclosure reveals the real nature of the soul or self. Such information is vital in order to conduct intelligent evaluations. All I mean by evaluation is comparing how a person is with some concept of optimum. You never really discover how truly sick your psychotherapy patient is until he discloses himself utterly to you. You cannot help your client in vocational guidance until he has disclosed to you something of the impasse in which he finds himself. You cannot love your spouse or your child or your friend unless he has permitted you to know him and to know what he needs to move toward greater health and well-being. Nurses cannot nurse patients in any meaningful way unless they have permitted the patients to disclose their needs, wants, worries, anxieties and doubts. Teachers cannot be very helpful to their students until they have permitted the students to disclose how utterly ignorant and misinformed they are. Teachers cannot even provide helpful information to the students until they have permitted the students to disclose exactly what they are interested in.

I believe we should reserve the term interpersonal relationships to refer to transactions between "I and thou" (Buber, 1937), between person and person, not role and role. A truly personal relationship between two people involves disclosure of self, one to the other, in full and spontaneous honesty. The data that we have collected up to the present time (using very primitive data-collecting methods) have showed us some rather interesting phenomena. We found (Jourard and Lasakow, 1958), for example, that women consistently are higher self-disclosers than men; they seem to have a greater capacity for establishing person-to-person relationships—interpersonal relationships—than men. This characteristic of women seems to be a socially-patterned phenomenon, which sociologists (Parsons and Bales, 1955) refer to as the expressive role of women, in contradistinction to the instrumental role which men universally are obliged to adopt.

Men seem to be much more skilled at impersonal, instrumental role-playing. But public health officials, very concerned about the sex differential in mortality rates, have been wondering what it is about being a man, which makes males die younger than females. Here in Florida, Dr. Sowder, chief of the state health department, has been carrying on a long-term, multifaceted research program which he has termed "Project Fragile Male." Do you suppose that there is any connection whatsoever between the disclosure patterns of men and women and their differential death rates? I have already intimated that withholding self-disclosure seems to impose a certain stress on people. Maybe "being manly," whatever that means, is slow suicide!

I think there is a very general way of stating the relationship between self-disclosure and assorted values such as healthy personality, physical health, group effectiveness, successful marriage, effective teaching, effective nursing, etc. It is this: A person's self is known to be the immediate determiner of his overt behavior. This is a paraphrase of the phenomenological point of view in psychology (Snygg and Combs, 1949). Now if we want to understand anything, explain it, control it or predict it, it is helpful if we have available as much pertinent information as we possibly can. Self-disclosure provides a source of information which is relevant. This information has often been overlooked. Where it has not been overlooked it has often been misinterpreted by observers and practitioners through such devices as projection or attribution. It seems to be difficult for people to accept the fact that they do not know the very person whom they are confronting at any given moment. We all seem to assume that we are expert psychologists and that we know the other person, when in fact we have only constructed a more or less autistic concept of him in our mind.

If we are to learn more about man's self, then we must learn more about self-disclosure—its conditions, dimensions and consequences. Beginning evidence (Rogers, 1958) shows that actively accepting, empathic, loving, non-punitive responses—in short, love—provides the optimum conditions under which man will disclose, or expose, his naked, quivering self to our gaze. It follows that if we would be helpful (or should I say human?) that we must grow to loving stature and learn, in Buber's terms, to confirm our fellow man in his very being. Probably this presumes that we must first confirm our own being.

REFERENCES

ALEXANDER, FRANZ. *Psychosomatic Medicine*. New York: W. W. Norton & Co., Inc., 1950.

ALLPORT, GORDON. *Becoming: Basic Considerations for a Psychology of Personality*. New Haven: Yale University Press, 1955.

ANONYMOUS, "A New Theory of Schizophrenia," *Journal of Abnormal Social Psychology*, 57 (1958), 226–236.

BARR, STRINGFELLOW. *Purely Academic*. New York: Simon and Schuster, 1958.

BUBER, MARTIN. *I and Thou*. New York: Charles Scribner's Sons, 1937.

DAVIS, F. H., and R. B. MALMO. "Electromyographic Recording during Interview," *American Journal of Psychiatry*, 107 (1951), 908–916.

DITTES, J. E. "Extinction during Psychotherapy of GSR Accompanying 'Embarrassing' Sexual Statements," *Journal of Abnormal and Social Psychology*, 54 (1957), 187–191.

DUNN, H. L. "High-level Wellness for Man and Society," *American Journal of Public Health*, 49 (1959), 786–792.

FREUD, SIGMUND. *The Interpretation of Dreams*. New York: Basic Books, Inc., 1955.

FROMM, ERIC. *Man for Himself*. New York: Holt, Rinehart & Winston, Inc., 1947.

———. *The Sane Society*. New York: Holt, Rinehart & Winston, Inc., 1957.

GRODDECK, G. *The Book of It*. New York and Washington: Nervous and Mental Diseases Publishing Co., 1928.

HORNEY, KAREN. *The Neurotic Personality of Our Time*. New York: W. W. Norton & Co., Inc., 1936.

————. *Neurosis and Human Growth*. New York: W. W. Norton & Co., Inc., 1950.

JAHODA, MARIE. *Current Concepts of Positive Mental Health*. New York: Basic Books, Inc., 1958.

JOURARD, S. M. *Personality Adjustment: An Approach through the Study of Healthy Personality*. New York: The Macmillan Company, 1958.

————, and P. LASAKOW. "Some Factors in Self-Disclosure," *Journal of Abnormal and Social Psychology*, 56 (1958), 91–98.

MASLOW, A. H. *Motivation and Personality*. New York: Harper & Row, Publishers, 1954.

PARSONS, TALCOTT, and R. F. BALES. *Family, Socialization and Interaction Process*. New York: The Free Press, 1955.

RIESMAN, DAVID. *The Lonely Crowd*. New Haven. Yale University Press, 1950.

ROGERS, CARL R. *The Concept of the Fully-Functioning Person*, Mimeographed manuscript, privately circulated, 1954.

————. "The Characteristics of a Helping Relationship," *Personnel and Guidance Journal*, 37 (1958), 6–16.

RUESCH, JURGEN. *Disturbed Communication*. New York: W. W. Norton & Co., Inc., 1957.

SELVE, HANS. "General Adaptation Syndrome and Diseases of Adaptation," *Journal of Clinical Endocrinology*, 6 (1946), 117–128.

SKINNER, B. F. *Science and Human Behavior*. New York: The Macmillan Company, 1953.

SNYGG, D., and A. W. COMBS. *Individual Behavior*. New York: Harper & Row, Publishers, 1949.

TOPIC 10

Growth

You are almost certainly much better than you think you are. More than you now permit yourself, you can be happier, stronger, braver. You can be more loving and giving; warmer, more open and honest; more responsible and responsive. You can perceive worlds richer and fuller than any you now experience. You have it in you to be more creative, more zestful, more joyous. All these prospects are within you. They are your potential.

      —from *Growth Games* by H. R. Lewis and H. S. Streitfeld

Upon meeting a friend who has been away for some time, we may be startled by how different he is. Or perhaps someone we see every day suddenly appears to be changed in some way. Or maybe it is ourself who seems somehow to have a new dimension. People change. When these changes are for the better, we say that they represent growth.

Growth, in the sense used here, refers to personal development in a desired direction. Of course, people's values differ and we may not agree as to what constitutes desirable change. Generally, an individual is said to show growth when he becomes more capable and competent, more productive and creative, more perceptive, insightful, and understanding, or more knowledgeable, prudent, and discerning.

What we consider to be growth for one person may not be the same as growth for another. For example, we may feel a particular individual shows growth when he settles down and becomes more conscientious about his undertakings. We may conclude that another person has grown when he loosens up, becomes more spontaneous, and stops worrying so much.

Some writers have described growth as a process of self actualization. In growing, we realize our potentiality. We become more fulfilled, completed, or perfected. Each of us possesses a set of capacities—a promise of what we can become—and as we grow we develop these capacities and make good on this promise.

It can be both bothersome and intriguing to consider this notion of potentiality. It is bothersome because we can never really know our own growth capacities until we realize them. A set of test scores may provide a rough estimate of our limits in a certain area, and sometimes in a burst or spurt of development we get some inkling of the person we might be, but generally this notion is a rather mysterious one.

Still it is intriguing to consider the ramifications of this concept. Various thinkers in this area suggest that human beings generally develop only a small fraction of their potentiality. One researcher has estimated that if the human brain were to function at only half of its capacity, we would find it easy to master 40 languages. What could we accomplish if we somehow developed the unrealized part of ourself? Who would we be if we were everything we could be?

Actualizing oneself

In the first article Herbert A. Otto states the human potentiality hypothesis that human beings have capacities or powers far beyond those which are realized. (Otto himself estimates that we operate at about 4 percent of capacity.) Evidence for this hypothesis is found in the extraordinary powers shown by special groups of persons or by ordinary individuals in special circumstances. Otto describes the human potential movement which makes use of growth centers and group methods to enhance individual growth, and he also advocates changes in society and the family to create growth through more open communication, loving, caring, and trust.

Unfreezing oneself

We strive to construct a stable world, writes Sidney M. Jourard in the second article, but we need to "unfreeze" our self image in order to grow. This image must be constantly restructured to accommodate what we have become, what we are becoming, and what we can become. Jourard feels that we grow when we suspend our fixed ideas about ourself and become open to new experience through observation, reflection, and meditation. Other people help us grow by confirming our progress and by encouraging and even challenging us to be more than we are or think we can be.

Becoming oneself

Drawing upon his experience as a psychotherapist, Carl R. Rogers, in the last reading, explains the process of becoming a person whether with the aid of therapy or without it. Each person appears to be asking two questions: "Who am I?" and "How may I become myself?" When the psychological climate is favorable, a process of becoming takes place in which the individual drops his defenses, experiences the hidden aspects of himself, and discovers who he is. As a result, he becomes more open to experience, more trusting of himself, more responsible for himself, and more willing to accept himself as involved in a continual stream of becoming rather than as a fixed entity.

FOR PERSONAL APPLICATION

1. To what extent have you actualized or realized your potentialities? Discuss your answer.
2. Recall and interpret a time of your life—a month, a week, a day—when you felt wonderfully creative or productive or growing.
3. How have you changed in the past few years? Is this change "growth"? Why or why not?
4. Do you feel that your concept of yourself or others' concept of you is "frozen" or in some way prevents you from growing? Discuss your answer.
5. Describe a situation in which you surprised yourself by what you could do or in some way obtained some insight into the person you could become.
6. What kinds of future personal growth would you consider desirable in yourself?
7. If you continue developing as you have, who do you expect to be 10 or 20 or 30 years from now? Are you satisfied with this prospect? Why or why not?
8. Who would you be 10 or 20 or 30 years from now if you quite fully actualized or realized your potentialities? What might keep you from becoming this person?
9. What early socialization experiences have facilitated or impeded your personal growth?
10. In what ways have your high school and/or college experiences facilitated or impeded your personal growth?
11. What kinds of changes would you advocate in the socialization process or in society generally to assist people in the realization of their potentialities?
12. Write down a discussion item (not given above) that seems particularly relevant to this topic and you, and discuss it.

FOR SMALL GROUPS

1. *Planning growth.* Each member in turn becomes the focus of the group's attention. He enumerates his personal strengths as he sees them and also tells what prevents him from fully developing these strengths. The members of the group respond to what the focal person has said, adding any further strengths they detect in the person and suggesting ways he may overcome developmental barriers. Then together the focal person and the group construct a picture of the person as he could be in five or ten years if he makes the most of his strengths and realizes his potential.
2. *Growing in the group.* The members discuss each person in turn by indicating the growth he has shown so far within the group and suggesting directions for his further growth in the group situation.
3. *Confronting growth conflicts.* Within each person there may be impulses to grow that conflict with impulses to stand pat or stay put. Let the

members silently reflect for a few minutes on the growth and antigrowth forces in themselves and also the reasons behind each set of forces. Then a volunteer or each member enacts this conflict before the group by taking both roles (growth/antigrowth) in turn and moving between them. The person should vigorously throw himself into each role, bringing it to life with appropriate words, gestures, stances, and movements, continuing until he gains some insight or arrives at a possible resolution of the conflict. Afterwards other members may contribute their observations, insights, and suggestions.

4. *Sharing growth experiences.* Each member recalls and shares with the group his recollection of a personal growth spurt—a time of his life when he made rapid progress in some area of development or endeavor.

FOR FURTHER READING

Chickering, A. W. *Education and Identity.* San Francisco: Jossey-Bass, 1969.

Heath, D. H. *Growing Up in College.* San Francisco: Jossey-Bass, 1968.

Katz, J., et al. *No Time for Youth: Growth and Constraint in College Students.* San Francisco: Jossey-Bass, 1968.

Lewis, H. R., and H. S. Streitfeld. *Growth Games.* New York: Harcourt Brace Jovanovich, 1971.

Madison, P. *Personal Development in College.* Reading, Mass.: Addison-Wesley, 1969.

Otto, H. A. *Guide to Developing Your Potential.* New York: Charles Scribner's Sons, 1967.

Otto, H. A., ed. *Explorations in Human Potentialities.* Springfield, Ill.: Charles C Thomas, 1966.

Otto, H. A., ed. *Human Potentialities: The Challenge and the Promise.* St. Louis, Mo.: Warren H. Green, 1968.

Otto, H. A., and J. Mann, eds. *Ways of Growth.* New York: The Viking Press, 1968.

Rogers, C. R. *On Becoming a Person.* Boston: Houghton Mifflin Co., 1961.

and Carl Rogers. I could name many more, and of course, colleagues in foreign countries.

NEW LIGHT ON HUMAN POTENTIAL

Herbert A. Otto

What is the human potentiality concept? Briefly the concept is that the average healthy human being is functioning at a very small fraction of his potential. American psychologist James, at the turn of the century, hypothesized that the average healthy human being is functioning at 10 percent of capacity. Margaret Mead, in an essay which she contributed to my book, *Explorations in Human Potentialities*, published in 1964, estimated that the average healthy human being is functioning at 6 percent of capacity (Otto, 1964). My estimate currently is that we are operating at 4 percent of capacity. Why has this estimated percentage been decreasing? Because we are discovering that every human being has more powers, resources, and abilities than we suspected ten years ago, five years ago. And I will make this point clearer subsequently.

Who are some of the people that believe in the human potentiality's hypothesis? The late Abraham Maslow, and, of course, Gardner Murphy, the well-known psychologist who, I believe, needs to be called "the Father of Human Potentiality's Movement." Murphy published his book, *Human Potentialities,* in 1954. He was virulently attacked by members of various professions for writing this book. In 1964 I asked him to contribute an essay to *Explorations in Human Potentialities*. Since that time, he has been even more active in many of the areas of human potentialities. In addition to the foregoing behavior scientists there are also the outstanding late Gordon Alport, Margaret Mead whom I have mentioned, Dr. J. L. Moreno,

INDICATORS OF HUMAN POTENTIALITY

Now, what are some of the indicators of human potential? Remember in childhood when you stepped outside how great it smelled, how all the colors seemed to be so much brighter? Remember when your parents stepped into the room you sometimes sensed without their saying a single word what they were going to say? What is going on here? Well, we have various sensory capacities which successively diminish during adulthood. During childhood we are much more open to nonverbal cues that parents give out. Of course, this type of sensory capacity can be regained.

Clinical psychologists are trained in interpreting the nonverbal cues given by people, so that by the time a person has walked into the office and sat down in the chair the psychologist, if his training was good, has already learned a great deal about him. Through sensory awareness training which is available in many of the growth centers, these capacities can be reawakened, restimulated so that once more the individual will be in touch with the environment and with people in a way that he is not now.

Another indicator of the human potential is subliminal cues which we are continually picking up. When listening to a speaker, we are picking up noises in the background, humming and so on. We are taking in a tremendous amount of information and we are conscious of only a very small fragment of the information that we take in. You may remember the Coconut Grove fire in Boston where many people were killed. A psychiatrist at the Harvard School of Public Health studied this fire. He found about a dozen people had walked in and walked right out before the fire because they felt uneasy about the whole situation. They could not put their finger on why they felt uneasy, they just felt strange and something told them to get out of there. This occurred from an hour to fifteen minutes before the fire actually broke out. The hypothesis is that these people somehow smelled the fire smoldering somewhere. Their unconscious or their brain computer mechanism told them, *Get out of here before those flashy hangings there catch fire and kill all those people.* The computer put two and two together and gave them danger signals which they followed. The lesson from that is, begin to follow your intuition more.

We can look at the brain as a computer mechanism, but vastly more powerful than any computer ever built. As a matter of fact, some researchers with the brain research laboratory at the University of California at Los Angeles believe that the capacity of the human brain is infinite, whatever that means. I like to use a computer analogy because we can say that the human brain has absorbed a tremendous amount of information during its lifetime, even during the twenties, thirties, and before that. And we have not yet learned to program ourselves for problem-solving purposes. One of the fascinating questions is, What is keeping us from using this tremendous storehouse of information in a way to solve problems?

We have another indicator of the human potential from primitive tribes. Here you have tremendous sensory acuity so that many members of Indian tribes can look at the print of a deer and say, "This animal passed an hour and a half ago—it is so high, it weighs so many pounds." There are innumerable instances of medicine men who can look at the bright, beautiful skies with the sun shining and say to the anthropologist who is visiting, "In an hour we are going to have a very bad thunderstorm." The anthropologist cannot tell, but the medicine man has great sensory acuity and perceives certain clues which the anthropologist does not recognize. There are many primitive tribes which have an extraordinarily well-developed sense of smell. We have closed this off because we are living in an environment redolent with carbon monoxide and poisonous industrial fumes.

Another indicator of the human potential comes from studies particularly of Australian bushmen who have been found repeatedly by a diverse number of scientists to have extrasensory perception, that is, the ability to communicate over long distances by "non-physical" means under extremely rigorous and prescribed conditions. This brings us to the question of extrasensory perception and the whole area of parapsychology which has been a black sheep for several decades. Many scientists still do not accept that extrasensory perception is a fact—it still remains a controversial area despite innumerable studies, despite the work of Dr. Joseph B. Rhine, one of the pioneers and founders of this work in the United States. Even after he was attacked on the basis of his statistical handling of data and was cleared by the highest professional association in the United States, the attacks persisted. I only want to point out to you that if people were to accept the extrasensory perception hypothesis it would shake them to their very roots. This involves them in change, this involves them in *change of what they have been taught, i.e., their beliefs system.* I propose that this is why we have this tremendous opposition to the type of factual knowledge offered by parapsychology.

The USSR has over twenty government-supported laboratories and research centers in this area. The specific phenomenon, mental telepathy, is called *radio brain wave communication.* The Russian scientists believe that the human brain somehow "broadcasts." Their approach is different from ours; they accept the phenomenon as given. They utilize the average man in their research and put him through training. Their total research approach is geared in that direction. Our research approach has been to select the highly gifted person who has these extrasensory capacities and then to test and to try to study and understand this phenomenon and to prove that it exists. I could speak at length about this area but all I want to say is that I see this as an indicator of human potential. United States industry has invested large sums in research in extrasensory perception and those of you who are interested will find more about this in *Guide to Developing Your Potential* (Otto, 1967).

Creative capacity is another indicator of human potential. All of us have fantastic creative capacity. Going all up and down the United States I am struck over and over again by the tremendous creative ferment, the creative capacities that surround me. Data suggest that if you go through a creativity training course your creative potential will have a greater flowering than it has ever had before. Again, there are a number of studies by American industries in this area. General Electric is one of the outstanding ones.

Another indicator of the human potential is our new understanding of the autonomic nervous system. My generation has been taught that you cannot control the autonomic nervous system. We have found out recently (through bio feedback research) that heartbeat, blood pressure, motility of the digestive system, and brain waves (alpha rhythms, etc., and now beginning work with beta rhythms) can be brought under human control. The implications are fantastic. You will find more and more statements by scientists (and these are hard-core scientists, who are in the biological field) who believe that we will discover that the human body has the capacity to regenerate itself. I believe this will happen within this generation if we invest more research in these areas rather than in trips to the moon. The inner universe of man is what we need to explore. This current preoccupation with furnishing man with more and more artificial organs is a dehumanizing type of research. Put an artificial kidney in man, put an artificial heart in man, put an artificial stomach in man, you make him more and more like a robot. That energy, those resources should go into studying why we have deathbed remissions, why we have people who are terminal with incurable diseases, but who, all of a sudden seem to make an unconscious decision toward health and regenerate themselves. Or using faith and their belief in God as their medium for self-generation, they then do seem to bring about organismic regeneration. There are enough cases on record all over the world to show that the human body has this capacity. This is what we need to study. Year after year I talk to physicians throughout this nation and I mention this. "Oh, yes," they say, "I can give you three or four cases right off the top of my head of things that should not have happened medically but happened right in front of my eyes." That is where the research money should go—not into artificial hearts, artificial kidneys. That is putting the cart in front of the horse.

The people who are obsessed with making man more mechanical and more dehumanized enjoy playing around with gadgets, that is their thing. I think that is great, but I am talking about social policy, where research should go in the best interest of the largest number. I think everybody should do his thing, as the young people say

today. But I am interested in research policy for the best of the nation—for all of us. It is not in dehumanizing man by inventing more gadgets to put into him. I venture to say that there is no research going on in the area of studying self regeneration of man on the deathbed and similar cases considered medically hopeless, and where these demonstrated remissions have taken place and are taking place even now. This is happening. I would like to hear of such work, if it is going on.

Mentation is another indicator of the human potential—our capacity for using our mental equipment. In this field, our colleagues in the USSR are miles ahead. They have been investing some of their best brainpower in this area. In 1964 in a barber shop, I happened to run across an article in *Soviet Life Today*, their journal for consumption in English-speaking countries. This statement was made about man's capacity to use his mental equipment:

The latest findings in anthropology, psychology, logic and physiology show that the potential of the human mind is very great indeed. As soon as modern science gave us some understanding of the structure and work of the human brain, we were struck with this enormous reserve capacity.

Man under average conditions of work and life uses only a small part of his thinking equipment. If we were able to force our brain to work at only half of its capacity, we could, without any difficulty whatever, learn 40 languages, memorize the large Soviet encyclopedia from cover to cover, and complete the required courses of dozens of colleges.

This statement is hardly an exaggeration. It is the generally accepted theoretical construct of man's mental potentialities. How can we tap this gigantic potential? It is a big and very complex problem with many ramifications.

I spoke to former Vice-President Humphrey and various other individuals in our government in an effort to obtain massive support for research in human potentialities. I even painted the Russian bear on the wall, saying, however, that I did not want to see this as competition but as both nations making a joint contribution to mankind, exchanging scientific information. I got verbal assurances of support from Humphrey and it ended there.

Another indicator of the human potential is the spiritual potential which every human being has, which I believe our churches are not helping us to tap. It is my belief that our churches encourage devitalized, low-level spiritual experiencing and that every human being who so wishes can have the deep mystical experience of Jacob Boehme, Dean Inge, and other mystics. Every man can certainly have a deeper sense of communion and union than is currently available through church rituals. It is understandable that churches are not too interested in fostering this because people who have this type of communion often turn into heretics and start to oppose the church structure. I believe that every man has a great potential for spiritual experiencing and that this is a relatively neglected area.

Finally, there is the Grandma Moses effect. Many people on reaching advanced age discover that they have capacities, abilities, and powers that they have never used but which they now, finally, get around to using. They are better off than those people who take these capacities and latent powers to the grave with them. When I visit the so-called retirement villages I find all sorts of people with all sorts of talents that they are finally utilizing. Grandma Moses, who discovered in her later years that she had this fantastic painting talent, is just an example of this phenomenon, so we called it the Grandma Moses effect.

Along with this we have what we call "the short-circuit theory." It goes as follows: If we do not utilize our energies in the actualizing of our potential (the latent capacities represent energy sources or reservoirs), these same energies are turned into self-destructive channels. In other words, if we are not actualizing our potential and investing ourselves in actualizing our potential throughout our life, this energy is directed to self-destructive channels. This is my opinion at this point. There is an analogy here in athletics which goes like this, "If you don't use it, you lose it." If you do not use your muscular system it deteriorates. It deteriorates to the point where it is harmful to you. We say, therefore, that developing your potential can be your most exciting lifelong adventure.

If I say something about the human potential hypothesis and the 10 percent hypothesis, people often say, "Gee, here comes someone who is putting us under even more pressure, when I am already doing the very best I can." My answer to that is, "Do you remember a day in your life when things were going tremendously well, when you were creatively, fantastically productive and you were happy, your heart was singing inside you and things were just going beautifully?" All of us have had days like that. That is how it feels when you are actualizing more of your potential. It is basically a joyous experience. Yes, what leads up to that point may be turmoil because it involves change. Growth involves change, but the realization of the growth, the step forward, is basically joyous for most of us. It is a tremendous feeling of satisfaction and joy.

THE HUMAN POTENTIAL MOVEMENT

Now we come to the human potential movement. About four years ago there were only three growth centers: the Esalen Institute, Kairos, and Oasis in Chicago. Today we have over 175. Growth centers subscribe to the human potential hypothesis and they use the small-group approach to actualize human potential. In 1960 I started at the University of Utah and organized the Human Potentialities Research Project. We experimented, and found that it is exceedingly difficult for people to actualize their potential by themselves. We utilized the small-group laboratory approach and developed a multiplicity of methods which have been published in the book, *Group Methods to Actualize Human Potential*.[1] The emphasis in the growth centers is on a small-group approach under the leadership of professionals, who work 95 percent with nonpatient groups, that is, with healthy human beings who are functioning well and wish to actualize more of their potential. Why do we have so many people going back again and again and again to have these group experiences? (When I conduct a group, about 50 percent are repeaters.) Because it works; because

[1] Holistic Press, 160 South Robertson Blvd., Beverly Hills, Calif., 1971.

it helps people to actualize more of their capacity to be more creative. It helps people to work out problems; it helps people to get a more positive self-image. Often it also changes their family life in a positive direction.

Essentially the human potentiality hypothesis that every human being is functioning at a very small fraction of his capacity is a message of hope, because even the Bowery bum, even the mentally retarded child or adult—everyone has fantastic capacities which we have not yet learned how to tap, but which can be tapped. My methods are used in ghettos; they are used in old-age homes; they are used with people who are out of work. We have just conducted a program working with the Human Resources Development Organization in San Diego with excellent results. We are saying this human potentialities approach has something to offer to everyone. Unfortunately, the human potentiality hypothesis is not known by the general population in the United States, only by a small percentage of the intellectual elite. It should be a popular notion: it should be known abroad and worldwide; it should be the hope of all nations.

We are participants in a profound period of change. I think Alvin Toffler's book (*Future Shock*), the rise of communes, women's lib, the ecology movement, and so on, are all signs that point in the direction of change. I would like to quote from Dr. Richard E. Farson's article, "The Education of Jeremy Farson," a report prepared for the State of California State Committee on Public Education, March 1967:

In the future even more than today, change will not be an episode in our life, but life itself. Life will be seen, not as being, but as becoming, as process. And only those who can live in process and enjoy change for its own sake will be happy. Change, then, is the one thing of which we can be certain. . . . We will have to become flexible enough to enjoy the transitory quality of life. We will derive pleasure and meaning from temporary relationships and fleeting encounters. Our personal adjustments to life have been anchored in familiarity, stability, the reliable sameness of things, the permanence of values, places, relationships. In the future our adjustment to life will be based on our ability to cope with the process of change.

That is putting it right on the table. If you are past-oriented, you are giving yourself continually negative inputs, because wherever you go there is change. You can come back to a campus in five years or three years, and there is change. If your heart is in the past, you are breaking your heart.

PERSONALITY AND ENVIRONMENT

The influence of the environment on the personality has been consistently underplayed, understressed, underestimated by behavioral scientists —first for the reason that the complexity of intrapsychic processes has been so overwhelming and is still so overwhelming. Second, if we begin to say that the personality is to a very large extent dependent upon the environment for it functioning, we have to take responsibility for the environment. I propose this is another reason behavioral scientists have "copped out" from acknowledging the close connection between personality and environment. Why do I make such a strong statement? Because many years ago sensory deprivation experiments showed conclusively that if you deprive a man of all inputs by putting him into a tank of water, submerging him with an oxygen apparatus in a completely darkened room where all sounds are excluded, in three to four hours he starts to hallucinate. Why? Because personality is fantastically dependent upon the inputs of the environment which include the entire personal environment and the total environment to sustain it.

The worst punishment that can be inflicted by our penal system is to put a man in solitude. If he stays in solitude long enough, he goes "stir-crazy," which means he becomes psychotic. That is the way he is punished, and that is the most frequently used mode of punishment. In the more sophisticated forms of this punishment, the punishment cells are so designed that the man never even hears when he gets the food shoved in through a system of double doors. He is in complete darkness, he cannot hear any sound, and eventually he goes "stir-crazy," unless he has a strong personality or resources to cope with this. Even these people suffer tremendously. Both the physical and interpersonal environment have a great deal to do with the process we call personality. That we have been unwilling to face this is one of the tragedies of our times.

The media in this respect have a fantastic impact on us. I would like to quote to you from an article in the *Saturday Review* which I wrote some time ago on the subject of human potentialities: "As a result of a *steady diet of violence* in the media a slow erosion in man's self-system takes place; this erosion affects what I call the trust factor. If we have been given a certain amount of affection, love and understanding in our formative years, we are able to place a certain amount of trust in our fellow man.

"Trust is one of the most important elements in today's society, although we tend to minimize its importance. We basically trust people. For example, we place an enormous amount of trust in our fellow man when driving on a freeway or an expressway. We trust those with whom we are associated to fulfill their obligations and responsibilities. The element of trust is a basic tool in human relations. People we distrust usually sense our attitude and reciprocate in kind. The consistent emphasis in the news on criminal violence, burglarizing, and assault makes slow but pervasive inroads into our reservoir of trust. As we hear and read more and more about the acts of violence and injury men perpetrate upon one another year after year, with so little emphasis placed on the loving, caring, humanitarian acts of man, we begin to trust our fellow man less, and we thereby diminish ourselves. It is my conclusion the media's successive emphasis on violence, like the drop of water on the stone, erodes and wears away the trust factor in man. By undermining the trust factor in man, the media contribute to man's estrangement from man and prevent the full flourishing and deeper development of communion and community with all men."

Even more destructive, or perhaps as destructive in wearing down the trust factor, is the continual display of violence on television and movies which conditions us to accept violence as it is continually shown—that the way to solve a problem is to become violent, to beat somebody up, to murder him, even to torture him. This is in effect a way of showing people how to solve personal and social problems. The current fantastic rise in crime rate is largely due to this conditioning or programming of the American population in ways to solve problems through violence. That is what is taking place in this country, and we are sitting on our haunches and letting it happen.

THE FAMILY CLUSTER

People in the current commune movement are seeking a truly loving and caring interpersonal environment—one which the family, from their perspective, is not providing sufficiently.

The family obviously is in trouble. One of the ways out of the dilemma is the family cluster. The family is so stuck or frozen in the status quo that it will be very difficult for it to pull itself up by the boot straps. The only way the family can develop into a unit which has more open communication, more loving, more caring is by getting together with other families and forming an extended family—a family cluster. The family cluster is based on Dr. Frederick Stoller's concept of the family network described in *The Family in Search of a Future* (Otto, 1970a). A multi-base alternative is a partial solution to the critical problem of anomie, man's estrangement from himself and from his fellow man.

The family cluster consists of three to five families who maintain their separate abodes and who meet regularly. They begin by first establishing a loving and caring relationship distinguished by open communication. Then, after a certain series of experiences which we have carefully spelled out in my monograph and which create a loving environment, the families involved begin to talk about goals and objectives, that is, What do we want to do as an extended family? What functions, if any, do we want to share jointly? The whole thrust of the family cluster is to help family members develop and actualize their potential— to enrich, improve, and strengthen the quality of family life. I firmly believe that the family will be with us for a long period of time but that more and more alternatives will arise with a slow but steadily increasing percentile of the population becoming interested in sampling such alternatives. We need to be tolerant toward alternative structures and accept them, because we may end up in one. How do we know? I found a quote by Hemingway many years ago that astounded me. He said that he had given up saying "I'll never do that!" because he found himself years later doing the very same things he said he would never do.

STRENGTHENING THE FAMILY

I feel very strongly that we need to strengthen the family. We need a network of federally supported marriage counseling clinics for marital and premarital counseling services available in every state in the nation, to everyone who wants and needs these services. This could help reduce marital unhappiness and divorce. We need federally-supported as well as state-supported marriage counseling clinics. I would like to quote from my article, "Has Monogamy Failed?":

Presently medical science widely recommends that we have an annual physical checkup as a means of prevention of disease. In a similar manner, annual assessment and evaluation should be available to couples interested in developing and improving their marriage. The goal would be to identify, to strengthen, and to develop family potential before crises arise, with the main focus on helping a family achieve an even more loving, enjoyable, creative, and satisfying marriage relationship. I propose that we have Marriage and Family Potential Centers all over the nation to which a family could go once a year for a checkup and perhaps, even more important, to have more positive joyous inputs for their marriage. By "inputs" I mean to pick up suggestions, hints, research on how to make marriage even more satisfying.

The plan for the Marriage and Family Potential Center was developed in 1968 by a colleague, Dr. Lacey Hall, and me during my stay in Chicago. The project was supported by the Stone Foundation, but owing to a number of complex reasons it was never fully implemented. This is certainly a tragedy, for a great need exists for a Marriage and Family Potential Center to train professionals for work in the family potential area.

There is a great apathy in this country about the family. It is difficult to obtain any support. For example, I know of no one doing any research in the area of family strengths.

In my opinion the family still remains our most satisfying unit for human relations. Let us support it. Let us strengthen it. Let us develop the potential of the family.

DEVELOPING INDIVIDUAL POTENTIAL

Most people are "stuck" or "frozen" in very deeply established habit systems. In developing individual potential the idea is now to throw out all habit systems, but to begin by becoming aware of how habits stifle us. The ruts of habit wear deeper and deeper until finally they are six feet deep and there you have a grave with the ends knocked out. We need to become aware of how habit systems impinge on us, how they keep us from new experiences. People eat the same breakfast food, use the same stuff to brush their teeth, use the same motions to wash themselves, use the same mode of recreation, go to the same three or four restaurants, order the same drinks. If you want to develop yourself—actualize processes and tap more of your potential—start rooting out some of these restrictive habit systems and reach out for new experiences and inputs. Risk for yourself new experiences. Go to types of movies you would not normally go to. If you like the *Sound of Music* maybe you should go see *Mash*.

In our educational system we kill intellectual curiosity. Statistics show that the average graduate from our college reads one book a year. That, I think, is the greatest indictment of our educational system. The handwriting on the wall cannot be clearer. The information-input and information-output approach—the "if you repeat what I said exactly in my words you get an A" sort of thing—all too often is what education is in our colleges and universities. We need to get our intellectual curiosity aroused. We need new experiencing, risking, getting into human potentialities groups, getting into growth centers, risking of ourselves in growth.

I would like to share with you one method I use that I have found extremely valuable: the self-acknowledgment method. When we complete what we consider to be a good piece of work in our vocation, nine times out of ten we get very little acknowledgment. Hardly ever does a superior say, "That was a good show," or a colleague say, "Gee, that is a good piece of work!" or whatever, but we know that we have done a good job. Therefore, I give acknowledgment to myself every time I complete something that I know is of superior quality and that I really like. In these instances I give myself a very handsome present. Something that really "turns me on." Consequently, I look forward to the present that I am going to give myself whenever I complete a good creative piece of work. By this process I assure that high quality performance and creativity will both recur. That is a way of self-acknowledgment. It really works.

Finally I would like to talk about our Developing Personal Potential groups now used in many colleges. I go all over the United States training members of counseling departments or of psychology departments, whoever is interested in the use of these methods designed to actualize human potential. The developing-personal-potential leaders use these group methods. Our whole emphasis is on building a loving and caring environment in which open communication is practiced and in which there is real concern for each other. This is in many ways different from the "encounter" and "sensitivity" environment where so often anger and hostility pervade the whole group experience. We do not force people to participate in any of our methods. Participation is voluntary, and the amount of change and personal growth we see in people during a weekend is often truly amazing.

Each one of you is operating at a small, very small, fraction of your potential. My wish and my hope for you is that you make actualizing your potential your most exciting lifelong adventure.

REFERENCES

Murphy, Gardner. *Human Potentialities*. New York: Basic Books, Inc., 1958.

Otto, Herbert A. *Explorations in Human Potentialities*. Springfield, Ill.: Charles C Thomas, 1964.

———. *Guide to Developing Your Potential*. New York: Charles Scribner's Sons, 1967.

———, ed. *The Family in Search of a Future*. New York: Appleton-Century-Crofts, 1970a.

———. "Has Monogamy Failed?" *Saturday Rev.* (April 25, 1970b).

———. *The Family Cluster: A Multi-base Alternative*. Beverly Hills: Holistic Press, 1971.

GROWING EXPERIENCE AND THE EXPERIENCE OF GROWTH

Sidney M. Jourard

Growth has always fascinated man, but he has studied it only from its "outside." None of the scientific accounts of growth and development are informed by the experience of the one growing. Instead, we have accounts of physical and behavioral development, as these appear to the scientist's eyes, or as they leave traces on his recording apparatus, to show up as "growth curves" in a scientific treatise. The other side of growth needs to be shown, if for no other reason than to round out the story. The present chapter offers an essay toward a "phenomenology of personal growth."

Everything looks different when I visit the neighborhood where I grew up. The stores and houses look smaller, decayed, less imposing than I remember them to have been. My old school chums are balder, fatter; some look defeated and resigned, and others are smug, more self-satisfied than they were when I knew them years ago. Their change appears to me as a kind of fall, a failure to realize many of the dreams which I knew animated them in their younger days. My own change (which I become acutely conscious of at times like these) feels to me like growth. I feel that I have grown, while they have just grown older.

What is growth? What is my growth? How does it appear from the outside, from the point of view of another? Do I experience my growing? Or do I only see a difference, say, between old and more recent pictures of myself and conclude that I have changed. Indeed, I have heard tape recordings of my speech and seen moving pictures of myself taken several years ago; and seeing how I looked and sounded makes me almost nauseous. I don't recognize myself as the source of those impressions. I experience myself from the outside, and can't recapture the "feel" of the person I was. Yet at times I have undergone some engrossing experience and, in a flash, realize that I am changed. I experience myself and the world in new dimensions, as if a veil has been suddenly lifted.

What is the essence of this change? Is it growth? What brings it about? Can I help it along, or hinder its occurrence? Can another person bring it on? Prevent it? In this chapter, I am going to speak of growth from an "inside" point of view, of the growth of experience and the changed experiencing that is growth. There are many accounts available about growth as it appears on the outside, as recorded by instruments or by scientific observers, but few about growing awareness. Since I *am* my awareness, an account of growing, changing awareness must at the same time be an account of my growth.

Growth is the disintegration of one way of experiencing the world, followed by a reorganization of this experience, a reorganization that includes the new disclosure of the world. The disorganization, or even shattering of one way to experience the world, is brought on by new disclosures from the changing being of the world —disclosures that were always being transmitted, but which were usually ignored.

BEING IS CHANGE

Change is in the world. The being of the world is always changing. My body is in the world, and it changes from instant to instant. Things and other people are in the world; and they metamorphose, swiftly or ever so slowly. I may not be aware of the change that *is* the world. The world-for-me may not appear to change; but rather it may seem congealed, constant, fixed. I may also experience my own being as unchanging.

In fact, people *strive to construct* a stable

world, a world they can control and get their bearings in. A view of the world exclusively as constant is an achievement—a *praxis,* not a "given." A naive view of the world sees it as *both* a "buzzing, blooming, confusion" and as stable and "structured." We simply cannot navigate in a world that changes swiftly. And so we "freeze" it by pledging not to notice change until it has reached some critical degree, until it has gone so far it can no longer be ignored. Then, we might acknowledge it. If everything changed during the night, and you awakened to a new experience of yourself and the world, you might be terrified. But if suddenly, the world froze, so that as everything now is, it would remain for eternity, you would be horrified. It would be hell—a hell of perfect predictability and boredom.

The disclosure of change is going on all the time. Change is *experienced,* however, only at moments. The awareness of change is frequently the experience of *surprise*: the "unexpected" has just been presented to us.° The world, or my own bodily being, is not as I had believed it to be. My expectations about being, my concepts and beliefs about the world, have just been disconfirmed. The awareness that things are different is not growth, though it is a necessary condition of growth. A growth *cycle* calls for (a) an acknowledgment that the world has changed, (b) a shattering of the present experienced "world-structure," and (c) a restructuring, retotalization, of the world-structure which encompasses the new disclosure of changed reality.

° Psychologists will note the relation of the present phenomenological theory of growth to Festinger's (1957) considerations of "cognitive dissonance." "Balance" theories, as well, as in Heider (1958) or Secord and Backman (1965), also bear upon this question. Shaw's (1966) concept of "upended expectations" is a cognate term, and Kelly's (1955) dialectic of "construing" and reconstruing of experience is likewise related. Murphy's (1947) and Werner's (1948) formulations of the stages in perception, from the global and undifferentiated, through the differentiated, to the integrated or unified stage, is a relevant theoretical formulation of growth, taken over from biological views of physical growth. Finally, the dialectic as formulated by Hegel and Marx, and reformulated by Sartre in phenomenological terms (1960, 1963), and expounded by Laing and Cooper (1964), provides a framework within which the present chapter may be viewed.

The retotalization of experience which consummates a growth cycle happens when a person sets goals and projects for himself, when he envisions a possibility and sets about trying to bring it to fruition. In fact, the growth cycle is often tripped off by a *failure* in goal-seeking. As one sets about trying to make or do something, he finds that his initial concepts and beliefs about what and how things *are,* are false. They do not ground accurate predictions about the world and oneself (Kelly, 1955; Shaw, 1966). Faced with failure, he must then suspend his present beliefs and let the world disclose itself to him as it *now* is. If he does this, he can revise his concepts and get on with his project.

A growth cycle can also be triggered when goals and projects turn stale; when money can no longer buy anything that the person wants; when the fame that was once the person's glory has turned to ashes; and when the love of that woman, long-pursued, is now experienced as cloying, suffocating possessiveness. The lack of fulfillment when long-enjoyed goals are achieved signifies, however indirectly, that *our personal being* has changed, unnoticed by us. Our *concept of ourselves,* as the person who would be fulfilled by this pleasure or be made happier by that "success," *has gotten out of touch with the reality of our being.* We are in for some surprises. The boredom signifies the imminence of growth. The time is ripe for the experience of new goals, and new unfoldings of our being. It is time to let the world and ourselves disclose their being to our experience. We may undergo this new experience (if we let it happen) in delight, or in the terrifying realization that we are going out of our minds.

The world is full of Being, of many beings—some human, some animal, some inanimate. Being has many forms. Every being in the world can be likened to a kind of broadcasting station, transmitting signals of its being to other beings in the world. This transmission is ceaseless. As people and things and animals exist, they change; and they broadcast the fact of this change into the world. You and I are both beings, but beings of a special kind. We have (or are) awareness. We are embodied consciousnesses. We experience the transmissions that originate in our bodies; and through our bodies, we experience some of the transmissions of being that originate elsewhere.

As human beings, we originate transmissions of our being, and we receive transmissions from other beings. My being discloses itself to me—I experience my own being—and it is disclosed to you through my appearance and behavior. *My* experience of *my* being is different from *your* experience of *my* being. And my experience of the being you disclose to me differs from your experience of your own being.

OUR CONCEPTS "FREEZE" THE WORLD AND BLIND US

Man is a *concept-maker*. He forms *concepts* of the being of the world, and of his own self-being. A concept is an abstraction from what *is*. From a phenomenological and existential perspective, *a concept is a commitment to stop noticing the changing disclosures* (*disclosures of change*) *incessantly being transmitted by the beings in the world.** When I identify something as a cow, I rubricize it. I let it disclose enough of its being for me to classify it into the category *cow*. Then, I stop receiving, though the cow hasn't stopped sending. It is a cow. It is this very cow, Bossie. Bossie is that cow which presents itself to me as black and white, of the kind "Holstein," with a big chip flaked off her left front hoof. I "know" Bossie. I can anticipate what she will do, on the basis of her past disclosures to me and my awareness of these disclosures. I can get milk from Bossie. She will kick me if I approach her from the right side. And so on. But Bossie is continually changing, and these changes are continually revealed to the world. So long as I think of Bossie as I always have, I ignore these disclosures. I address Bossie as if she has not changed. Indeed, for the purposes I pursue in my transactions with Bossie, these changes may not make any difference, until enough change has occurred that my predictions about Bossie are not borne out, and my purposes are thwarted. I start milking Bossie, and no milk comes. I say, "Something's wrong. Bossie is different. She has changed. She is not the Bossie I knew." Of course

* Gendlin's (1962, 1964) formulations have strongly influenced the present exposition. His analysis of personality change is of the most far-reaching theoretical and practical significance, in my opinion.

she isn't. She never was. No sooner did I form a *concept* of Bossie (stop perceiving her disclosures) than it was out of date. When I say, "Bossie has changed," all I am doing is belatedly acknowledging a change that has been inexorable and continuous. For my purposes (getting milk out of her), she did not change. When my purposes were thwarted, I was forced to expand my awareness of Bossie, to suspend my concept of her being, and to let her being address me. My concept of Bossie (which terminated my perception of the multiple disclosures of her changing being) enabled me to fulfill my milking project. When the project was stymied, my concept became perceptibly incongruent, out of date with the actuality of Bossie's being. In fact, if I propose some new projects that involve Bossie, I may find that my concept of her being requires revision. I may wish to enter her in a race. I believe she is a fast runner and can win me a prize. I test her—I put her in a situation where she can disclose her running ability. I find her slow. My concept of Bossie's being must now include the assertion that "she is slow."

GROWING, SUSPENDED CONCEPTS, AND THE WORLD'S DISCLOSURE-TO-ME

Enough of cows, and enough of Bossie. I am going to contend that when my concepts—of myself, of you, of cars, of cows, of trees, and of refrigerators—are shattered, and I again face the world with a questioning attitude; when I face the being in question and *let it disclose itself to me* (it always was disclosing, but I paid it no attention after I conceptualized it); and when I re-form my concept on the basis of this newly received disclosure—then, *I have grown*. I will suspend my concepts when my projects in life (which depend on accurate concepts of reality for their fulfillment) are thwarted, when my predictions about how things will act or react prove wrong. Then, if I adopt the attitude of "let the world disclose itself to me," I will receive this disclosure and change my concepts; and I will have grown.

My concepts of being can change under more pleasant circumstances than failure. In those rare moments when I have gratified all of my urgent needs—I have done my work, I feel good and fulfilled, and I want nothing out of the world just now—then the world will disclose all kinds of new faces to me. I am letting the world "be itself, for itself." I may then notice all kinds of things about my friends, trees, the sky, animals, whatever is there; things that call upon me to enlarge my previous concepts of those same beings. Thus, success and gratification can be psychedelic (consciousness-expanding). They can open up my world for me and let me experience it in new dimensions.

You may notice that I appear different from the last time you saw me. My behavior and my verbal disclosures will show a change to you. You will say of me, "He has changed, he has grown." You will have to modify your concept of me at that time. *If you do, then you will have grown.* Your action toward me will reflect your changed concept of me, your changed experience of me. And I shall then say to you, "You have changed; you have grown." You will feel confirmed in your being. You will feel understood; you will feel that the disclosure of your changed being—in words and actions—has been received and acknowledged by me.

I have a certain concept of my being, of myself. This is my *self-concept.* It is my belief about my own being. My being discloses itself to me in the form of my intentional experience of myself. I experience the feel of my body's existence. I experience my own action from the inside. I form a concept of myself—what I am like, how I react, what I am capable of and what I cannot do—on the basis of this self-experience. You may also tell me what and who you think I am, on the basis of your experience of the outside of my being; and I take your belief into account. We may agree that I am thus and such a kind of person—a man, a psychologist, kind, strong, able to play a fair game of handball, unable to sing in key, etc. Once I have formed this concept of who and what I am, I proceed to behave in the world as if that is all and everything I am or can be. My behavior, my self-disclosure, endlessly confirms my self-concept. It is as if I have taken a pledge to present this and only this as my being (Goffman, 1959).

In fact, my being, like all Being, *is change.* This change discloses itself to me through my experience and to others through my behavior. But if you and I have formed a concept of my being, neither of us pays attention to the ceaseless transmission of my changing being. It is transmitted, but no receiver is tuned in to acknowledge the change. Things can get more complicated. I may notice the changes, and change my concept of myself accordingly. You may not notice the changes. You treat me as if I were the same person. I do not recognize myself as the one you believe I am. I feel you are talking to somebody else, not me.

Or, you may notice the changes before I do, and change your concept of me accordingly. Again, I may not recognize the "me" that you seem to be addressing. Your concept of me is disjunctive from my self-concept.

Or, I may display and disclose the newly experienced facets of my being to you. You may say, "I don't recognize you. You are not yourself today. I don't like the person you seem to be. I'll come see you when you have gotten back into your 'right mind.'" If you thus disconfirm my newly experienced and tentatively disclosed being, and if I am unsure of myself, I may try to suppress and repress my newly emerged being and seek to appear to you and to me as the person I *was.* If I do this chronically, and successfully, I enter an untenable situation; and I may become mad (Laing, 1960).

GROWING AND THE MODES OF EXPERIENCING

There is also another way in which I might grow through a relationship with you. I may have a fixed concept of you and hence behave toward you in a habitual, stereotyped way. My action toward you is predictable. I always become aggressive in your presence. I experience you as a source of harm to me; and I attack first, to protect myself. My concept of you is that you are menacing, that you harbor ill will toward me. *When I experience you, I may not be undergoing a perceptual experience, but rather an imaginative experience of your being.* I tune out your disclosed being, and I replace it by an imaginative experience (Sarte, 1961). Or a fantasy (Laing, 1960) experience. Imagination veils perception. In fact, much of our experience of the people in our lives, even when they are face-to-face with us, is *not* perceptual, but *imaginative*, or fantastical.*

The perceptual mode of experiencing entails the readiness to receive inputs of disclosure from the other, such that one's awareness of the other is a changing awareness. But the imaginative and fantasy modes of experiencing "tune out" fresh disclosures. My image of you remains fixed, unchanged by your disclosures, because I do not pay them any attention. Now, if you can break through my imaginative experience, or my fantasy image, of you; if you can catch my attention, by a shout, a blow, a scream of pain or joy—I may, as it were, "wake up" from my daydream-like experience of your being and undergo a fresh perceptual experience of you. You will surprise me. If you do this, if you get me "un-hung" from fixation on these modes of experiencing you—the imaginative and the fantasy modes—so that I can now perceive you, I shall have grown. My consciousness of you will have expanded. My awareness will have grown; and where I had previously been aware of you only as an image or a concept (though I wasn't *reflectively* aware that this was an image), now I can experience you preceptually. If my consciousness expands so that I can experience you or the world in many more modes than I could hitherto—imaginatively, perceptually, recollectively, in the mode of fantasy—then I have grown. I *am* my awareness; and if my awareness expands, *I* have grown.

My world of awareness may not only be fixed in one *mode* of experiencing, e.g., the abstracting, conceptual mode or the imaginative mode; my world may also be confined to some one or two sensory "channels" of awareness. For example, I may limit my clear awareness only to visual and auditory impressions and exclude the worlds of smelling, tasting, or the feel of my own body. If you can turn me on to my feelings, to smells, to

---

* Laing's (1961) analysis of fantasy as a mode of experience is a contribution to phenomenology of high importance. He shows what Freud's "unconscious" is like as it is embodied in our conscious experience of the world.

tastes; if you can wake up my imagination; if you can get me to experience the feel of my body—you will have expanded my awareness and helped me to grow. You could caress me (cf. Sartre, 1956, pp. 389–391) out of my "mind" and into my experience of my body. . . .

GROWTH, THROUGH SUSPENSION OF SELF-CONCEPT AND SELF-CONSCIOUSNESS

If I, from time to time, suspend my concept of myself and "tune in" on my being, if I meditate or reflect on my experience, then I must re-form my self-concept. I shall believe myself to be different. I shall act differently. I *am* different. Moments of meditation are the times (rare in our culture) when we try to let the changing flux of our being disclose itself to us (Kretschmer, 1951; Maupin, 1965). If we learn how to do it or let it happen, meditation can give us the *experience* of transition in our being and can yield transitional experiences (Shaw, 1966). In meditation, too, we let the world disclose more of its changing being to us; and we may find ourselves experiencing more of the variety in the world.

But meditation is not the only occasion when our self-concepts are put into question and temporarily suspended. Whenever we are unselfconscious, whenever our attention is fully focused upon some task or some project, our being changes; and our changing experience of our changed being goes on spontaneously. We let our personal being *happen*. We do not try to monitor and control it so that it conforms to a concept, yours or mine, of my being. Fascinated engagement at *anything* can let change happen and be experienced such that the next time I reflect upon myself, I find my experience of myself different from how I remember it the last time I reflected. And my concept of myself will have to change to encompass the new experiencing I have undergone. Challenge, fascination, total involvement in some task or project such that self-consciousness and self-conceptualizing is *not* the mode of experience, will permit the changed self-being to be experienced.

GROWTH THROUGH DIALOGUE

If I engage in conversation with you, in dialogue; and if you disclose your experience of yourself and of me to me in truth; and if I receive your continuing disclosure; and if I disclose my experience of myself and of your disclosures to you in truth—*then I must be letting change happen* and be disclosed to us both. If I reflect upon my experience of the dialogue, I must notice that I am different from the way I was when we began the dialogue. But if I have (as it were) pledged myself to appear before you and to myself as *this* kind of man and no other, then my intentional disclosures to you will be very selective. Perhaps I will lie to you, to preserve your present concept of me, or at least *my* concept of *your* concept of me. Indeed, if my pledge of sameness is made to myself, then every time my *actually* changed being discloses itself to me, I will become threatened and repress it. I will pretend to myself I did not have the experience of hatred, or of anxiety, or of lust. And I will believe my own pretense to myself. Then, I shall not grow. My concept of myself will become increasingly estranged from the ongoing change of my being. If my self-concept is too discrepant from actuality, the disclosure to me of my changed being will become more insistent. I will then have to pretend and repress much harder. If the change is too great, the experience of change will no longer be repressible. It will declare itself in my experience and perhaps in my behavior; I may become terrified and feel I have "gone out of my mind." Actually, I have, if by "mind" we mean "self-concept." If still I insist on trying to appear to you as the same person I was, I may develop neurotic symptoms. Or if I am terrified enough, I may become psychotic.

GROWTH AND YOUR EXPERIENCE OF ME

You can help me grow, or you can obstruct my growth. If you have a *fixed* idea of who I am and what my traits are, and what my possibilities of change are, then anything that comes out of me beyond your concept, you will disconfirm. In fact,

you may be terrified of any surprises, any changes in my behavior, because these changes may threaten your concept of me; my changes may, if disclosed to you, shatter your concept of me and challenge you to grow. You may be afraid to. In your fear, you may do everything in your power to get me to un-change and to reappear to you as the person you once knew.

But if you suspend any preconceptions you may have of me and my being, and invite me simply to be and to disclose this being to you, you create an ambience, an area of "low pressure" where I can let my being happen and be disclosed, to you and to me simultaneously—to me from the inside, and to you who receive the outside layer of my being.

If your concept of my being is one that encompasses more possibilities in my behavior than I have myself acknowledged; if your concept of my being is more inclusive and indeed more accurate than my concept of my being, and if you let me know how you think of me; if you let me know from moment to moment how you experience me; if you say, "Now I like you. Now I think you are being ingratiating. Now I think you can succeed at this, if you try"; if you tell me *truly* how you experience me, I can compare this with my experience of myself, and with my own self-concept. You may thus insert the thin edge of doubt into the crust of my self-concept, helping to bring about its collapse, so that I might re-form it. In fact, this is what a loving friend, or a good psychotherapist, does.

There is another way you can help me grow and that is through challenging me and encouraging me to attempt new projects. We actually construe and conceptualize the world and ourselves in the light of the projects we live for. It is our commitment to these which structures our worlds. The beings in the world, including our own being, reveal different faces of themselves to us, depending upon the projects we are pursuing at the moment. The trees in the forest reveal their timber footage to the lumber merchant, the bugs in their trunks to the insect-collector, and their colors to the painter. My muscular strength or weakness reveals itself to me as I try to chop the forest down, and I form a concept of my muscular strength. I may never come to question or doubt this estimate I made. My self-concept gets frozen if my projects are frozen, and if I become too adept and skilled at fulfilling them.

Suppose, when I find my existence dull and boring, I decide to try some new project—to write a book, climb a mountain, change jobs. I tell you of this, at first, faint resolve. I am afraid to try, because, as I presently think of myself, I don't believe I have the capacity to succeed. If you encourage me to try and encourage me and support me when the going gets rough, so that I stick with the project with more and more single-mindedness, I discover in myself transcendent powers I never experienced before and never imagined I had. I do not and cannot transcend my *possibilities;* I don't know what these are and won't know until I stop living. I only transcend my *concept* of what my possibilities might be. You can help me transcend my self-concept by challenging and supporting me in new projects that I undertake.

Even the decision to *attempt* something new results in a new experience of myself and the world, *before* I actually get going. If I decide to start a new book, I begin to experience friends as interferences in this project; movies and television, formerly very inviting, become dull and boring. The whole world and my experience of myself change with the change in projects. If you help me give up old projects that are no longer satisfying, delightful, or fulfilling and encourage me to dare new ones, you are helping me to grow.

CONTEMPLATION, MEDITATION AND GROWTH

You can help yourself grow if you will engage in aimless contemplation and meditation. To contemplate the world before you, in its visual, auditory, olfactory, and tactual dimensions means simply to let the world present itself to you. You are not searching for anything when you contemplate. Rather, you are letting the world disclose itself to you as it is *in itself.* You can do this only when you suspend your work, your striving, your goals and projects. When you suspend your projects in this way, you open the "doors of perception," and let birds, trees, other people, in fact

everything disclose itself to you. All these beings always were, but you didn't notice so long as you were involved in some task or mission. Such contemplation yields a different experience of the world, which must change your concepts of the world, and it thus fosters growth. Maslow (1962, pp. 109–118) has described such contemplation as "B-cognition," and has pointed out that it has dangers as well as delights. The dangers, of course, are that one might simply revel in the sheer beauty of evil rather than do something about it. But it cannot be gainsaid that contemplation of the world in this aimless way enriches experience.

Instead of gazing upon the world and letting it disclose itself to you through your eyes, ears, nose, and hands, you can meditate upon your own experience of your bodily being. Perhaps close your eyes, or seek a tranquil setting with no sudden distractions. Let your experience happen without direction. Engage in free reverie. You may find yourself now recalling something of the past, now vividly imagining—in playful ways—all kinds of possibilities. You may find yourself experiencing anger for somebody, love for somebody else, you may find you have aches and pains you hadn't noticed before. Some of your self-experiencing may be frightening. It may help you to meditate if, instead of closing your eyes, you gaze with or without fixed focus at a mandala, or a flower. If you gaze long enough, your experiencing may turn on fully and freely. Instead of being frozen into some one mode of experiencing—say, perceiving, or imagining, or remembering—which may be customary for you, you may find that you become "unglued" and then integrated. You experience perceptions fused with memories fused with imagination fused with conceptualizing fused with fantasy fused with emotion. This richness may truly shatter your self-concept, so that when you "pull yourself together," you are truly a different person from the person you thought you were.

As I said before, your being and mine are always in process of change, in consequence of the way we live, the passage of time, and sheer past experience. But living as we do mostly at a conceptual level and for definite projects—dealing, not with concrete things, but with *concepts* of things and people and of ourselves—we reflect quietly upon our awareness of ourselves, we suspend the concepts, and we let our being disclose itself to us. And thus we grow.

GROWING OUT OF OUR MINDS

Growing entails going out of our minds and into our raw experience. Our experience is always of the disclosure of the world and of our own embodied being. When we function, smoothly, habitually, and effectively in the world, our concepts are confirmed; and we do not receive new disclosure. When we meet impasses and failure in the pursuit of our projects, then our habits, concepts (a habit can be seen as the "outside" of a concept), and expectations are challenged, or upended (Shaw, 1966). Failure of our projects gives us a whiff of the stink of chaos, and this can be terrifying. Our concepts get cracks in them when we fail. Through these cracks, the encapsulated experience "contained" by the concept might leak or explode; or through the crack there may occur an implosion of more being. When there are no concepts, there is nothing—no-thing we can grapple with, get leverage on, in order to get on with the projects of living. There is the threat of pure chaos and situationlessness. If we experience the pure nothingness, we become panicked, and seek quickly to shore up the collapsing world, to daub clay into the cracks in our concepts. If we do this, we don't grow. If we let the concepts explode or implode and do not reform them veridically, we appear mad, and are mad. If we re-form them, to incorporate new experience, we grow.

Once again, we must consider projects, this time in relation to *integration,* a vital and crucial phase of growth. When our projects are obstructed, because our concepts are out of phase with being, the concepts must explode, or become fractionated, differentiated into parts. We experience chaos. Our commitment to the old projects, or recommitment to new projects, serves as the field of force which organizes the fractionated experience of being into meaningful wholes, concepts, gestalten. Growth is our experience of our concepts and percepts being detotalized and then retotalized into newly meaningful unities.

I know I am ready to grow when I experience surprise—a dissonance between my beliefs and concepts and expectations of the world and my perception of the world (Festinger, 1957). I am also ready to grow when I experience boredom, despair, depression, anxiety, or guilt. These emotions inform me that my goals and projects have lost meaning for me; that my being has gotten too big, too out of phase with my concepts of my being. I have a choice at these moments, if indeed I can experience them. I may have become so unaccustomed to and maladept at reflection and meditation that I simply don't notice these all-is-not-well signals. And I continue to pursue my projects and to believe my beliefs as if experience were confirming them.

But if I do acknowledge the signals, my choice is either to meditate, suspend my concept and preconception of self, and let my changed being disclose itself to me, even when it hurts (it frequently does); or to decide to affirm the project of being the same (an impossible project, but one that many people try to live). If I decide to try to be the same, then I will repress my experience of change, of all-is-not-well signals. I have resolved, really, to stop perceiving myself.

The invitation to suspend preconceptions and concepts, to let being disclose itself, is actually an invitation to go out of one's mind. To be out of one's mind can be terrifying; because when projects are suspended, and experiencing is just happening, myself and the world are experienced as infinite possibility: anything might be possible. Since nothing *definite* is possible, purposeful action is *im*possible. Yet, if a person can endure this voyage within his own experience—his Odyssey within—he can emerge from it with a new concept of his being and with new projects; the new concept of being will include more of his being in it. But this new integration will last only so long, and then the entire process must be repeated again. A sentient life is an endless series of getting out of one's mind and concepts, only to reenter and to depart again.

SURPRISE AND GROWING

The experience of surprise is a sign of one's readiness to grow. Amazement and wonder signify that one's concepts of self and of the world and of other people are "loose," ready to be re-formed. The "know-it-all," the "cool" one, has pledged himself never to be surprised. Everything that the world discloses is no more than an unfolding of what he has expected and predicted, or so he tries to convey to others. But when a man can be dumbfounded and surprised at what comes out of him or at what his friend or spouse is capable of doing and disclosing, he is a growing person.

In fact, if I intentionally adopt the "set" that all of my concepts are tentative and provisional, I invite others, myself, and the world to reveal surprisingly new facets of their being to me, so that even my daily life can be an unfolding of newness, where simply perceiving the world or the self is a source of endless variety and surprise.

If I am with you, and I have willfully adopted the set that I do not know and cannot ever fully know all your possibilities, my very presence embodies an invitation to you to surprise me, to show off, to transcend your (and my) previous concepts of your being. I can tell when I am in the presence of a person with a closed mind. I feel constrained to shut off most of my possibilities. But in the presence of a wonder-er, I feel an absence of prejudgment, a permissive acceptance; and my terror and self-consciousness about revealing surprises is diminished.

In short, if you and I retain our capacity for surprise, we aid and confirm one another's growth.

REFERENCES

FESTINGER, L. *A Theory of Cognitive Dissonance*. New York: Harper & Row, Publishers, 1957.

GENDLIN, E. T. *Experiencing and the Creation of Meaning*. New York: The Free Press, 1962.

———. "A Theory of Personality Change," in P. Worchel and D. Byrne, *Personality Change*. New York: John Wiley & Sons, Inc., 1964.

GOFFMAN, E. *The Presentation of Self in Everyday Life*. Garden City, N.Y.: Doubleday & Co., Inc., 1959.

HEIDER, F. *The Psychology of Interpersonal Relations*. New York: John Wiley & Sons, Inc., 1958.

KELLY, G. *The Psychology of Personal Constructs*. New York: W. W. Norton & Sons, Inc., 1955.

KRETSCHMER, W. "Die meditativen Verfahren in der Psychotherapie," *Zeit. f. Psychother. u. Med. Psychol.*, 1(3) (1951).

LAING, R. D. *The "Divided" Self*. London: Tavistock, 1960.

———. *The Self and Others*. London: Tavistock, 1962.

———, and D. COOPER. *Reason and Violence*. London: Tavistock, 1964.

MASLOW, A. H. *Toward a Psychology of Being*. Princeton, N.J.: D. Van Nostrand & Co., 1962.

MAUPIN, E. "Individual Differences in Response to a Zen Meditation Exercise," *J. Consult. Psychol.* (1965).

MURPHY, G. *Personality: A Biosocial Approach to Origins and Structure*. New York: Harper & Row, Publishers, 1947.

SARTRE, J. P. *Being and Nothingness: An Essay on Phenomenological Ontology*. London: Methuen, 1956.

———. *La Critique de la Raison Dialectique*. Paris: Librairie Gallimard, 1960.

———. *The Psychology of Imagination*. New York: Citadel Press, 1961.

———. *The Problem of Method*. London: Methuen, 1963.

SECORD, P. F., and C. BACKMAN. *Social Psychology*. New York: McGraw-Hill Book Company, 1965.

SHAW, F. J. *Reconciliation: A Theory of Man Transcending*, S. M. Jourard and D. C. Overlade, eds. Princeton, N.J.: D. Van Nostrand & Co., 1966.

WERNER, H. *The Comparative Psychology of Mental Development*. Chicago: Follett, 1948.

WHAT IT MEANS TO BECOME A PERSON

Carl R. Rogers

A frequently-raised question is: "What problems do people bring to you and other counselors at the Counseling Center?" I always feel baffled by this question. One reply is that they bring every kind of problem one can imagine, and quite a number that I believe no one would imagine. There is the student concerned about failing in college; the housewife disturbed about her marriage; the individual who feels he is teetering on the edge of a complete breakdown or psychosis; the responsible professional man who spends much of his time in sexual fantasies and functions inefficiently in his work; the brilliant student, at the top of his class, who is paralyzed by the conviction that he is hopelessly and helplessly inadequate; the parent who is distressed by his child's behavior; the popular girl who finds herself unaccountably overtaken by sharp spells of black depression; the woman who fears that life and love are passing her by, and that her good graduate record is a poor recompense; the man who has become convinced that powerful and sinister forces are plotting against him;—I could go on and on with the many different and unique problems which people bring to us. They run the gamut of life's experiences. Yet there is no satisfaction in giving this type of catalog, for, as counselor, I know that the problem as stated in the first interview will not be the problem as seen in the second or third hour, and by the tenth interview it will be a still different problem or series of problems. You can see why I feel baffled as to how to answer this simple question.

I have however come to believe that in spite of this bewildering horizontal multiplicity, and the layer upon layer of vertical complexity, there is a simple answer. As I follow the experience of many clients in the therapeutic relationship which we endeavor to create for them, it seems to me that each one has the same problem. Below the level of the problem situation about which the individual is complaining—behind the trouble with studies, or wife, or employer, or with his own uncontrollable or bizarre behavior, or with his frightening feelings, lies one central search. It seems to me that at bottom each person is asking: "Who am I, *really?* How can I get in touch with this real self, underlying all my surface behavior? How can I become myself?"

THE PROCESS OF BECOMING

Getting Behind the Mask

Let me try to explain what I mean when I say that it appears that the goal the individual most wishes to achieve, the end which he knowingly and unknowingly pursues, is to become himself.

When a person comes to me, troubled by his unique combination of difficulties, I have found it most worth while to try to create a relationship with him in which he is safe and free. It is my purpose to understand the way he feels in his own inner world, to accept him as he is, to create an atmosphere of freedom in which he can move in his thinking and feeling and being, in any direction he desires. How does he use this freedom?

It is my experience that he uses it to become more and more himself. He begins to drop the false fronts, or the masks, or the roles, with which he has faced life. He appears to be trying to discover something more basic, something more truly himself. At first he lays aside masks which he is to some degree aware of using. One young woman describes in a counseling interview one of the masks she has been using, and how uncertain she is whether underneath this appeasing, ingratiating front there is any real self with convictions.

I was thinking about this business of standards. I somehow developed a sort of knack, I guess, of—well—a habit—of trying to make people feel at ease around me, or to make things go along smoothly. There always had to be some appeaser around, being sorta the oil that soothed the waters. At a small meeting, or a little party, or something—I could help things go along nicely and appear to be having a good time. And sometimes I'd surprise myself by arguing against what I really thought when I saw that the person in charge would be quite unhappy about it if I didn't. In other words I just wasn't ever—I mean, I didn't find myself ever being set and definite about things. Now the reason why I did it probably was I'd been doing it around home so much. I just didn't stand up for my own convictions, until I don't know whether I have any convictions to stand up for. I haven't been really honestly being myself, or actually knowing what my real self is, and I've been just playing a sort of false role.

You can, in this excerpt, see her examining the mask she has been using, recognizing her dissatisfaction with it, and wondering how to get to the real self underneath, if such a self exists.

In this attempt to discover his own self, the client typically uses the therapeutic relationship to explore, to examine the various aspects of his own experience, to recognize and face up to the deep contradictions which he often discovers. He learns how much of his behavior, even how much of the feeling he experiences, is not real, is not something which flows from the genuine reactions of his organism, but is a façade, a front, behind which he has been hiding. He discovers how much of his life is guided by what he thinks he *should* be, not by what he is. Often he discovers that he exists only in response to the demands of others, that he seems to have no self of his own, that he is only trying to think, and feel, and behave in the way that others believe he *ought* to think, and feel, and behave.

In this connection I have been astonished to find how accurately the Danish philosopher, Soren Kierkegaard, pictured the dilemma of the individual more than a century ago, with keen psychological insight. He points out that the most common despair is to be in despair at not choosing, or willing, to be one's self; but that the deepest form of despair is to choose "to be another than himself." On the other hand "to will to be that self which one truly is, is indeed the opposite of despair," and this choice is the deepest responsibility of man. As I read some of his writings I almost feel that he must have

listened in on the statements made by our clients as they search and explore for the reality of self—often a painful and troubling search.

This exploration becomes even more disturbing when they find themselves involved in removing the false faces which they had not known were false faces. They begin to engage in the frightening task of exploring the turbulent and sometimes violent feelings within themselves. To remove a mask which you had thought was part of your real self can be a deeply disturbing experience, yet when there is freedom to think and feel and be, the individual moves toward such a goal. A few statements from a person who had completed a series of psychotherapeutic interviews, will illustrate this. She uses many metaphors as she tells how she struggled to get to the core of herself.

As I look at it now, I was peeling off layer after layer of defenses, I'd build them up, try them, and then discard them when you remained the same. I didn't know what was at the bottom and I was very much afraid to find out, but I *had* to keep on trying. At first I felt there was *nothing* within me—just a great emptiness where I needed and wanted a solid core. Then I began to feel that I was facing a solid brick wall, too high to get over and too thick to go through. One day the wall became translucent, rather than solid. After this, the wall seemed to disappear, but beyond it I discovered a dam holding back violent, churning waters. I felt as if I were holding back the force of these waters and if I opened even a tiny hole I and all about me would be destroyed in the ensuing torrent of feelings represented by the water. Finally I could stand the strain no longer and I let go. All I did, actually, was to succumb to complete and utter self-pity, then hate, then love. After this experience, I felt as if I had leaped a brink and was safely on the other side, though still tottering a bit on the edge. I don't know what I was searching for or where I was going, but I felt then, as I have always felt whenever I really lived, that I was moving forward.

I believe this represents rather well the feelings of many an individual that if the false front, the wall, the dam, is not maintained, then everything will be swept away in the violence of the feelings that he discovers pent-up in his private world. Yet it also illustrates the compelling necessity which the individual feels to search for and become himself. It also begins to indicate the way in which the individual determines the reality in himself—that when he fully experiences the feelings which at an organic level he *is*, as this client experienced her self-pity, hatred, and love, then he feels an assurance that he is being a part of his real self.

The Experiencing of Feeling

I would like to say something more about this experiencing of feeling. It is really the discovery of unknown elements of self. The phenomenon I am trying to describe is something which I think is quite difficult to get across in any meaningful way. In our daily lives there are a thousand and one reasons for not letting ourselves experience our attitudes fully, reasons from our past and from the present, reasons that reside within the social situation. It seems too dangerous, too potentially damaging, to experience them freely and fully. But in the safety and freedom of the therapeutic relationship, they can be experienced fully, clear to the limit of what they are. They can be and are experienced in a fashion that I like to think of as a "pure culture," so that for the moment the person *is* his fear, or he *is* his anger, or he *is* his tenderness, or whatever.

Perhaps again I can indicate that somewhat better by giving an example from a client that will indicate and convey something of what I mean. This comes from the recording of the thirty-first interview with this woman. She has talked several times of a recurrent feeling which troubles her and which she can't quite pin down and define. Is it a feeling that developed because she practically had no relationship with her parents? Is it a guilty feeling? She is not quite sure, and she ends this kind of talk with this statement:

Client: And I have the feeling that it isn't guilt. (Pause: she weeps) So . . . course I mean, I can't verbalize it yet. It's just being *terribly hurt!*

Therapist: M-hum. It isn't guilt except in the sense of being very much wounded somehow.

C: (Weeping) It's . . . you know, often I've been guilty of it myself, but in later years, when I've heard parents . . . say to their children, "stop crying," I've had a feeling, as though, well, why should they tell them to stop crying? They feel sorry for themselves, and

who can feel more adequately sorry for himself than a child. Well, that is sort of what . . . I mean, as-as though I thought that they should let him cry. And . . . feel sorry for him too, maybe. In a . . . rather objective kind of way. Well, that's . . . that's something of the kind of thing I've been experiencing. I mean, now . . . just right now.

T: That catches a little more of the flavor of the feeling, that it's almost as if you're really weeping for yourself. . . .

C: And then of course, I've come to . . . to see and to feel that over this . . . see, I've covered it up. (Weeps) I've covered it up with so much *bitterness*, which in turn I've had to cover up. (Weeps) *That's* what I want to get rid of! I almost don't *care* if I hurt.

T: (Gently) You feel that here at the basis of it as you experienced it, is a feeling of real tears for yourself. But that you *can't* show, mustn't show, so that's been covered by bitterness that you don't like, that you'd like to be rid of. You almost feel you'd rather absorb the hurt than to . . . than to feel the bitterness. (Pause) And what you seem to be saying quite strongly is, I do *hurt*, and I've tried to cover it up.

C: I didn't *know* it.

T: M-hm. Like a new discovery really.

C: (Speaking at the same time) I never really did know. It's almost a physical thing. It's . . . it's sort of as though I were looking within myself at all kinds of . . . nerve endings and-and bits of-of . . . things that have been sort of mashed. (Weeping)

T: As though some of the most delicate aspects of you—physically almost—have been crushed or hurt.

C: Yes. And you know, I do get the feeling, oh, you poor thing. (Pause)

T: Just can't help but feel very deeply sorry for the person that is you.

I hope that perhaps this excerpt conveys a little bit of the thing I have been talking about, the experiencing of a feeling all the way to the limit. She was feeling herself as though she were nothing but hurt at that moment, nothing but sorrow for her crushed self. It is not only hurt and sorrow that are experienced in this all-out kind of fashion. It may be jealousy, or destructive anger, or deep desire, or confidence and pride, or sensitive tenderness, or shuddering fear, or outgoing love.

It may be any of the emotions of which man is capable.

What I have gradually learned from experiences such as this is that the individual in such a moment is coming to *be* what he *is*. When a person has, throughout therapy, experienced in this fashion all the emotions which organismically arise in him, and has experienced them in this knowing and open manner, then he has experienced *himself*, in all the richness that exists within himself. He has become what he is.

The Discovery of Self in Experience

Let us pursue a bit further this question of what it means to become one's self. It is a most perplexing question and again I will try to take from a statement by a client, written between interviews, a suggestion of an answer. She tells how the various facades by which she has been living have somehow crumpled and collapsed, bringing a feeling of confusion, but also a feeling of relief. She continues:

You know, it seems as if all the energy that went into holding the arbitrary pattern together was quite unnecessary—a waste. You think you have to make the pattern yourself; but there are so many pieces, and it's so hard to see where they fit. Sometimes you put them in the wrong place, and the more pieces not fitted, the more effort it takes to hold them in place, until at last you are so tired that even that awful confusion is better than holding on any longer. Then you discover that left to themselves the jumbled pieces fall quite naturally into their own places, and a living pattern emerges without any effort at all on your part. Your job is just to discover it, and in the course of that, you will find yourself. You must even let your own experience tell you its own meaning; the minute *you* tell it what it means, you are at war with yourself.

Let me see if I can take her poetic expression and translate it into the meaning it has for me. I believe she is saying that to be herself means to find the pattern, the underlying order, which exists in the ceaselessly changing flow of her experience. Rather than to try to hold her experience into the form of a mask, or to make it be a form or structure that it is not, being herself means to discover the unity and harmony which exists in

her own actual feelings and reactions. It means that the real self is something which is comfortably discovered *in* one's experience, not something imposed *upon* it.

Through giving excerpts from the statements of these clients, I have been trying to suggest what happens in the warmth and understanding of a facilitating relationship with a therapist. It seems that gradually, painfully, the individual explores what is behind the masks he presents to the world, and even behind the masks with which he has been deceiving himself. Deeply and often vividly he experiences the various elements of himself which have been hidden within. Thus to an increasing degree he becomes himself—not a facade of conformity to others, nor a cynical denial of all feeling, nor a front of intellectual rationality, but a living, breathing, feeling, fluctuating process—in short, he becomes a person.

THE PERSON WHO EMERGES

I imagine that some of you are asking: "But what *kind* of a person does he become? It isn't enough to say that he drops the facades. What kind of person lies underneath?" Since one of the most obvious facts is that each individual tends to become a separate and distinct and unique person, the answer is not easy. However I would like to point out some of the characteristic trends which I see. No one person would fully exemplify these characteristics, no one person fully achieves the description I will give, but I do see certain generalizations which can be drawn, based upon living a therapeutic relationship with many clients.

Openness to Experience

First of all I would say that in this process the individual becomes more open to his experience. This is a phrase which has come to have a great deal of meaning to me. It is the opposite of defensiveness. Psychological research has shown the way in which sensory evidence, if it runs contrary to the pattern of organization of the self, tends to be distorted in awareness. In other words we cannot see all that our senses report, but only the things which fit the picture we have.

Now in a safe relationship of the sort I have

described, this defensiveness, or rigidity, tends to be replaced by an increasing openness to experience. The individual becomes more openly aware of his own feelings and attitudes as they exist in him at an organic level. He also becomes more aware of reality as it exists outside of himself, instead of perceiving it in preconceived categories. He sees that not all trees are green, not all men are stern fathers, not all women are rejecting, not all failure experiences prove that he is no good, and the like. He is able to take in the evidence in a new situation, *as it is,* rather than distorting it to fit a pattern which he already holds. As you might expect, this increasing ability to be open to experience makes him far more realistic in dealing with new people, new situations, new problems. It means that his beliefs are not rigid, that he can tolerate ambiguity. He can receive much conflicting evidence without forcing closure upon the situation. This openness of awareness to what exists at *this moment* in *this situation* is, I believe, an important element in the description of the person who emerges from therapy.

Perhaps I can give this concept a more vivid meaning if I illustrate it from a recorded interview. A young professional man reports in the forty-eighth interview the way in which he has become more open to some of his bodily sensations, as well as other feelings.

Client: It doesn't seem to me that it would be possible for anybody to relate all the changes that I feel. But I certainly have felt recently that I have more respect for, more objectivity toward, my physical makeup. I mean I don't expect too much of myself. This is how it works out. It feels to me that in the past I used to fight a certain tiredness that I felt after supper. Well, now I feel pretty sure that I really *am tired*—that I am not making myself tired—that I am just physiologically lower. It seemed that I was just constantly criticizing my tiredness.

Therapist: So you can let yourself *be* tired, instead of feeling along with it a kind of criticism of it.

C: Yes, that I shouldn't be tired or something. And it seems in a way to be pretty profound that I can just not fight this tiredness, and along with it goes a real feeling that being tired isn't such an awful thing. I think I can

also kind of pick up a thread here of why I should be that way in the way my father is and the way he looks at some of these things. For instance, say that I was sick, and I would report this, and it would seem that overtly he would want to do something about it but he would also communicate, "Oh, my gosh, more trouble." You know, something like that.

T: As though there were something quite annoying really about being physically ill.

C: Yeah, I am sure that my father has the same disrespect for his own physiology that I have had. Now last summer I twisted my back, I wrenched it, I heard it snap and everything. There was real pain there all the time at first, real sharp. And I had the doctor look at it and he said it wasn't serious, it should heal by itself as long as I didn't bend too much. Well this was months ago—and I have been noticing recently that—hell, this is real pain and it's still there—and it's not my fault.

T: It doesn't prove something bad about you—

C: No—and one of the reasons I seem to get more tired than I should maybe is because of this constant strain and so—I have alredy made an appointment with one of the doctors at the hospital that he would look at it and take an X-ray or something. In a way I guess you could say that I am just more accurately sensitive—or objectively sensitive to this kind of thing. I can say with certainty that this has also spread to what I eat and how much I eat. And this is really a profound change, and of course my relationship with my wife and the two children is —well, you just wouldn't recognize it if you could see me inside—as you have—I mean —there just doesn't seem to be anything more wonderful than really and *genuinely*—really *feeling* love for your own children and at the same time receiving it. I don't know how to put this. We have such an increased respect— both of us—for Judy and we've noticed just— as we participated in this—we have noticed such a tremendous change in her—it seems to be a pretty deep kind of thing.

T: It seems to me you were saying that you can listen more accurately to yourself. If your body says its tired, you listen to it and believe it, instead of criticizing it; if it's in pain, you can listen to that; if the feeling is really loving your wife or children, you can *feel* that, and it seems to show up in the differences in them too.

Here, in a relatively minor but symbolically important excerpt, can be seen much of what I have been trying to say about openness to experience. Formerly he could not freely feel pain or illness, because being ill meant being unacceptable. Neither could he feel tenderness and love for his child, because such feelings meant being weak, and he had to maintain his facade of being strong and masculine. But now he can be genuinely open to the experiences of his organism—he can be tired when he is tired, he can feel pain when his organism is in pain, he can freely experience the love he feels for his daughter, and he can also feel and express annoyance toward her, as he goes on to say in the next portion of the interview. He can fully live the experiences of his total organism, rather than shutting them out of awareness.

Trust in One's Organism

A second characteristic of the persons who emerge from therapy is that the person increasingly discovers that his own organism is trustworthy, that it is a suitable instrument for discovering the most satisfying behavior in each immediate situation.

If this seems strange, let me try to state it more fully. Perhaps it will help to understand my description if you think of the individual as faced with some existential choice: "Shall I go home to my family during vacation, or strike out on my own?" "Shall I drink this third cocktail which is being offered?" "Is this the person whom I would like to have as my partner in love and in life?" Thinking of such situations, what seems to be true of the person who emerges from the therapeutic process? To the extent that this person is open to all of his experience, he has access to all of the available data in the situation on which to base his behavior. He has knowledge of his own feelings and impulses, which are often complex and contradictory. He is freely able to sense the social demands, from the relatively rigid social "laws" to the desires of friends and family. He has access to his memories of similar situations, and the consequences of different behaviors in those situations. He has a relatively accurate perception of this existential situation in all of its complexity. He is better able to permit his total organism, his conscious thought participating, to consider, weigh, and balance each stimulus, need, and demand, and its relative weight and intensity. Out of this complex weighing and balancing he is able to discover that course of action which seems to come closest to satisfying all his needs in the situation, long-range as well as immediate needs.

In such a weighing and balancing of all of the components of a given life choice, his organism would not by any means be infallible. Mistaken choices might be made. But because he tends to be open to his experience, there is a greater and more immediate awareness of unsatisfying consequences, a quicker correction of choices which are in error.

It may help to realize that in most of us the defects which interfere with this weighing and balancing are that we include things which are not a part of our experience, and exclude elements which are. Thus an individual may persist in the concept that "I can handle liquor," when openness to his past experience would indicate that this is scarcely correct. Or a young woman may see only the good qualities of her prospective mate, where an openness to experience would indicate that he possesses faults as well.

In general, then, it appears to be true that when a client is open to his experience, he comes to find his organism more trustworthy. He feels less fear of the emotional reactions which he has. There is a gradual growth of trust in, and even affection for, the complex, rich, varied assortment of feelings and tendencies which exist in him at the organic level. Consciousness, instead of being the watchman over a dangerous and unpredictable lot of impulses, of which few can be permitted to see the light of day, becomes the comfortable inhabitant of a society of impulses and feelings and thoughts, which are discovered to be very satisfactorily self-governing when not fearfully guarded.

An Internal Locus of Evaluation

Another trend which is evident in this process of becoming a person relates to the source or locus of choices and decisions, of evaluative judgments. The individual increasingly comes to feel that this locus of evaluation lies within himself. Less and less does he look to others for approval or disapproval; for standards to live by; for decisions and choices. He recognizes that it rests within himself to choose; that the only question which matters is: "Am I living in a way which is deeply satisfying to me, and which truly expresses me?" This I think is perhaps *the* most important question for the creative individual.

Perhaps it will help if I give an illustration. I would like to give a brief portion of a recorded interview with a young woman, a graduate student, who had come for counseling help. She was initially very much disturbed about many problems, and had been contemplating suicide. During the interviews one of the feelings she discovered was her great desire to be dependent, just to let someone else take over the direction of her life. She was very critical of those who had not given her enough guidance. She talked about one after another of her professors, feeling bitterly that none of them had taught her anything with deep meaning. Gradually she began to realize that part of the difficulty was the fact that she had taken no initiative in *participating* in these classes. Then comes the portion I wish to quote.

I think you will find that this excerpt gives you some indication of what it means in experience to accept the locus of evaluation as being within oneself. Here then is the quotation from one of the later interviews with this young woman as she has begun to realize that perhaps she is partly responsible for the deficiencies in her own education.

Client: Well now, I wonder if I've been going around doing that, getting smatterings of things, and not getting hold, not really getting down to things.

Therapist: Maybe you've been getting just spoonfuls here and there rather than really digging in somewhere rather deeply.

C: M-hm. That's why I say—(slowly and very thoughtfully) well, with that sort of a foundation, well, it's really up to *me*. I mean, it seems to be really apparent to me that I *can't depend on someone else* to give me an education. (very softly) I'll really have to get it myself.

T: It really begins to come home—there's only one person that can educate you—a realization that perhaps nobody else *can give* you an education.

C: M-hm. (long pause—while she sits thinking) I have all the symptoms of fright. (laughs softly).

T: Fright? That this is a scary thing, is that what you mean?

C: M-hm (very long pause—obviously struggling with feelings in herself).

T: Do you want to say any more about what you mean by that? That it really does give you the symptoms of fright?

C: (laughs) I, uh—I don't know whether I quite know. I mean—well, it really seems like I'm cut loose (pause), and it seems that I'm very—I don't know—in a vulnerable position, but I, uh, I brought this up and it, uh, somehow it almost came out without my saying it. It seems to be—it's something I let out.

T: Hardly a part of you.

C: Well, I felt surprised.

T: As though: "Well for goodness sake, did I say that?" (both chuckle).

C: Really, I don't think I've had that feeling before. I've—uh, well, this really feels like I'm saying something that, uh, *is* a part of me really. (pause) Or, uh, (quite perplexed) it feels like I sort of have, uh, I don't know. I have a feeling of *strength*, and yet, I have a feeling of—realizing it's so sort of fearful, of fright.

T: That is, do you mean that saying something of that sort gives you at the same time a feeling of, of strength in saying it, and yet at the same time a frightened feeling of *what* you have said, is that it?

C: M-hm. I am feeling that. For instance, I'm feeling it internally now—a sort of surging up, or force. As if that's something really big and strong. And yet, uh, well at first it was almost a physical feeling of just being out alone, and sort of cut off from a—support I had been carrying around.

T: You feel that it's something deep and strong, and surging forth, and at the same time, you just feel as though you'd cut yourself loose from any support when you say it.

C: M-hm. Maybe that's—I don't know—it's a disturbance of a kind of pattern I've been carrying around, I think.

T: It sort of shakes a rather significant pattern, jars it loose.

C: M-hm. (pause, then cautiously, but with conviction) I, I think—I don't know, but I have the feeling that then I am going to begin to *do* more things that I know I should do. . . . There are so many things that I need to do. It seems in so many avenues of my living I have to work out new ways of behaving, but—

maybe—I can see myself doing a little better in some things.

I hope that this illustration gives some sense of the strength which is experienced in being a unique person, responsible for oneself, and also the uneasiness that accompanies this assumption of responsibility.

Willingness to Be a Process

I should like to point out one final characteristic of these individuals as they strive to discover and become themselves. It is that the individual seems to become more content to be a process than a product. When he enters the therapeutic relationship, the client is likely to wish to achieve some fixed state; he wants to reach the point where his problems are solved, or where he is effective in his work, or where his marriage is satisfactory. He tends, in the freedom of the therapeutic relationship, to drop such fixed goals, and to accept a more satisfying realization that he is not a fixed entity, but a process of becoming.

One client, at the conclusion of therapy, says in rather puzzled fashion: "I haven't finished the job of integrating and reorganizing myself, but that's only confusing, not discouraging, now that I realize this is a continuing process. . . . It is exciting, sometimes upsetting, but deeply encouraging to feel yourself in action, apparently knowing where you are going even though you don't always consciously know what that is." One can see here both the expression of trust in the organism, which I have mentioned, and also the realization of self as a process.

Here is another statement of this same element of fluidity of existential living. "This whole train of experiencing, and the meanings that I have thus far discovered in it, seem to have launched me on a process which is both fascinating and at times a little frightening. It seems to mean letting my experience carry me on, in a direction which appears to be forward, toward goals that I can but dimly define, as I try to understand at least the current meaning of that experience. The sensation is that of floating with a complex stream of experience, with the fascinating possibility of trying to comprehend its ever-changing complexity." Here again is a personal description of what it seems like to accept oneself as a stream of becoming, not a finished product. It means that a person is a fluid process, not a fixed and static entity; a flowing river of change, not a block of solid material; a continually changing constellation of potentialities, not a fixed quantity of traits.

CONCLUSION

I have tried to tell you what has seemed to occur in the lives of people with whom I have had the privilege of being in a relationship as they struggled toward becoming themselves. I have endeavored to describe, as accurately as I can, the meanings which seem to be involved in this process of becoming a person. I am sure that I do not see it clearly or completely, since I keep changing in my comprehension and understanding of it. I hope you will accept it as a current and tentative picture, not as something final.

One reason for stressing the tentative nature of what I have said is that I wish to make it clear that I am *not* saying: "This is what you should become; here is the goal for you." Rather, I am saying that these are some of the meanings I see in the experiences that my clients and I have shared. Perhaps this picture of the experience of others may illuminate or give more meaning to some of your own experiences.

I have pointed out that the individual appears to have a strong desire to become himself; that given a favorable psychological climate he drops the defensive masks with which he has faced life, and begins to discover and to experience the stranger who lives behind these masks—the hidden parts of himself. I have pictured some of the attributes of the person who emerges—the tendency to be more open to all elements of his organic experience; the growth of trust in one's organism as an instrument of sensitive living; the acceptance of the fearsome responsibility of being a unique person; and finally the sense of living in one's life as a participant in a fluid, ongoing process, continually discovering new aspects of one's self in the flow of experience. These are some of the things which seem to me to be involved in becoming a person.

TOPIC 11

Death

*The confrontation with death—and the reprieve from it—makes
everything look so precious, so sacred, so beautiful that I feel
more strongly than ever the impulse to love it, to embrace it,
and to let myself be overwhelmed by it. My river never looked
so beautiful. . . . Death and its ever present possibility makes
love, passionate love, more possible. I wonder if we could love
passionately, if ecstasy would be possible at all, if we knew
we'd never die.*

—Abraham Maslow, in a letter written while he
was recuperating from a heart attack

Death can be defined as the cessation or end of life. And some observers
say that birth is the beginning of death, that each moment we live we
die a little, or at least each moment brings death a little nearer. There
are also some who believe that until we face the fact that we will die—
until we get a real sense of our own mortality and the preciousness of life
—we cannot truly begin to live.

It is difficult for many of us to think or talk about death or be in its
presence. Our language reflects this difficulty. For example, we speak of
someone as "nearing the end" instead of "dying," and as "passed away,"
"gone," or "departed" rather than "dead." We maintain the illusion that
somehow a fatally ill member of our family will get better. We resist going
to see a friend who is hospitalized and dying. We try to keep some distance from death.

The prospect of our own death is particularly hard to deal with. We
human beings are bound up in ourselves. How can we understand that we
will one day stop, come to an end, and cease to be? We relish experience.
How can we conceive of a time when we will never think or feel or act
again? And we are social beings. How can we comprehend being separated from the ones we love—alone, apart, even abandoned?

Some investigators who are interested in **the** study of dying and death
have encountered considerable resistance to **their** work. They have found
that to some extent death is a taboo subject in our society. Psychiatrist
Elisabeth Kübler-Ross, for example, had a hard time locating dying sub-

jects because hospital personnel denied they had any such patients. In fact, some staff members accused her of having a morbid interest in death, implying that this topic were somehow not suitable for scientific investigation.

Very recently there has been increasing interest and candor about death. One reason for the change in attitude has been that in this nuclear age many of us do not feel much more than a button-push away from destruction. A second reason has been that science and technology, in which we have placed so much faith and hope, seem to produce as many threats to well-being as they eliminate. And a third reason is the increased coverage of violence and destruction by mass media; we see death on our television screen every evening with the six o'clock news.

Our rate of mortality is 100 percent. Each of us will die, and death will touch our lives in many ways before our own time comes. The more we bring this subject out into the open, the more we will be able to understand it and accept our own finitude. And the more we will be able to change death as a personal and social event by investing it with meaning and dignity.

On death

The author of the first article, my,* lamenting the way we avoid serious discussion of death, went out to converse with a dozen people who live with death every day. These people included a psychiatrist who had an interest in geriatrics, an obituary writer, a survivor of Auschwitz, a monument dealer, a pathologist, a spiritual medium, two funeral directors, a cemetery director, a rabbi, a priest, and a woman kept alive by a kidney machine. Some had come to terms with death, some were still groping for answers, and their questions and insights are passed along to those of us who are still wrestling with our own mortality.

On death and dying

In the second selection, research psychiatrist Elisabeth Kübler-Ross notes that we live in a death-denying society. We cannot conceive of our own death; we have the illusion that because we have mastered so many other things we will somehow conquer death as well. Then how do we finally come to terms with death and perhaps even die with dignity? Dr. Ross studied 400 terminally ill patients over a four-year period and found that a number of these patients passed through five stages of adaptation: (1) denial ("No, not me."), (2) anger ("Why me?"), (3) bargaining ("Yes me, but . . ."), (4) depression ("Yes me."), and (5) acceptance ("My time comes very close now and it is all right.").

* "my" is the pen name of the author of a one-person journal, *Observations from the Treadmill*.

On living forever

According to Gary Fisher in the last reading, death is a problem in identity; the more constricted an identity is, the more susceptible it will be to destruction. "When we identify ourselves with our 'skin encapsulated ego,'" Fisher writes, "we naturally face annihilation." By contrast, when we create, we broaden our identity, flow out into the world, and blend with things beyond ourself, and then physical death is not our ending.

FOR PERSONAL APPLICATION

1. Beginning with your earliest childhood recollection, trace the development of your ideas and attitudes concerning death.
2. Discuss your present ideas and attitudes concerning death.
3. When and how would you prefer to die? Why?
4. If your physician knew you had a terminal disease, would you want to be told? Why or why not?
5. How would you want to spend your remaining time if you found that you were terminally ill? How would you want others to treat or regard you? Why?
6. Discuss your ideas and attitudes concerning funerals. What kind of funeral would you want for yourself? Why?
7. Discuss your ideas and attitudes toward disposing of bodies after death. What would you want done with your body when you die? Why?
8. Discuss your ideas or beliefs concerning life after death.
9. Discuss your ideas or attitudes concerning suicide.
10. Discuss your ideas or attitudes concerning euthanasia.
11. Discuss a time when death touched your life; for example, a time when you were critically ill, when you seriously considered suicide, or when a close relative or friend died.
12. Write down a discussion item (not given above) that seems particularly relevant to this topic and you, and discuss it.

FOR GROUP ACTIVITY

1. *Write your own eulogy.* The members write their own eulogies and bring these to the group. Each member, in turn, lies down in the middle of the room (possibly closing his eyes and being covered with a sheet) while his eulogy is read over him. After all members have been eulogized, share your feelings and reactions.
2. *Fill out your own death certificate.* In the group situation each member is handed a blank death certificate and asked to complete it as it may be completed upon his death. After all have done this, share your feelings and reactions.
3. *Symbolize your life and death.* Darken the room as much as possible

and give one member a wooden kitchen match. He is to use this match in some way to represent himself and his existence. First, he responds to the match before lighting it. Then he lights the match and responds as it burns. Finally he responds to it after it goes out. This procedure is followed until every member has had a turn; then the group shares its feelings and reactions.

4. *Seeking insights on death.* Make arrangements and go as a group to visit a funeral director at a mortuary or funeral home, or visit a cemetery director at a cemetery or memorial park. Or invite a physician, psychiatrist, nurse, nursing home attendant, minister, or someone else who has had close association with the terminally ill to visit and talk with your group.

5. *Debate euthanasia.* Have your group argue or debate the issue of euthanasia (sometimes called "mercy killing"). If you decide to have a debate, divide into affirmative and negative teams and address yourselves to this proposition: "Resolved that upon his request (or with the permission of next of kin if he is incompetent) it would be lawful to put painlessly to death a person suffering from a painful, debilitating, and incurable disease or condition."

FOR FURTHER READING

Fiefel, H., ed. *The Meaning of Death.* New York: McGraw-Hill Book Company, 1959.

Gordon, D. C. *Overcoming the Fear of Death.* Baltimore: Penguin Books Inc., 1972.

Gunther, J. *Death Be Not Proud: A Memoir.* New York: Harper & Row, Publishers, 1949.

Kastenbaum, R., and R. Aisenberg. *The Psychology of Death.* New York: Springer, 1972.

Kavanaugh, R. E. *Facing Death.* Baltimore: Penguin Books Inc., 1974.

Kübler-Ross, E. *On Death and Dying.* New York: The Macmillan Company, 1969.

Kübler-Ross, E. *Questions and Answers on Death and Dying.* New York: The Macmillan Company, 1974.

Kübler-Ross, E. *Coping with Death and Dying.* (Cassette tapes.) Flossmoor, Ill.: Ross Medical Association.

Kutscher, A. H., ed. *Death and Bereavement.* Springfield. Ill.: Charles C Thomas, 1969.

Kutscher, A. H., and M. Goldberg. *Caring for the Dying Patient and His Family.* New York: H. S. Publishing Corporation, 1973.

Mitford, J. *The American Way of Death.* New York: Simon and Schuster, 1963. Also New York: Fawcett World, 1969 (paperback edition).

Shneidman, E. S., ed. *Death and the College Student.* New York: Behavioral Publications, 1972.

DIALOGUES ON DEATH

my

It is said that man cannot be free in life unless he is free from the fear of Death. We laugh at macabre undertaker jokes, sigh at romantic poems about lost lovers, thrill to films with titles like "Diabolic" and "Psycho," and are mildly titillated by the newspaper accounts of plane crashes and grisly murders. Yet all the while, we avoid serious discussion. Too morbid. Serious talk brings it too close to home—the deaths of our loved ones, of the most loved one of all . . . Ourself. Shudder and turn away. Change the subject. Give a nervous little laugh and say oh yes I'll think about that later. And when later comes, it is too late and we make others think about it for us and in their grief (or guilt) arrange for us what we should have arranged for ourselves.

Clouded by myth and superstition. Hidden behind euphemisms. Passed away. Departed. Eternal sleep. Just reward. Not buried, interred. Not a grave, a final resting place. Not undertakers, funeral directors. Not gravestones, monuments. Not a body, mortal remains. Not ashes, cremains. And we've made the whole thing become so commercial with our "grief therapy" and our "final memory picture" that we not only have to keep up with the Joneses in Life, we have to keep down with them in Death. Well, now we grow older and live longer and we're still scared of dying. There is a death every 16½ seconds in this country. We just don't want it to be us. Transplants and artificial organs are having a race with the Bomb. Science vs Science. What Is Death. The Ethics of Death. The Morals of Death. Abortion and Transplants. Euthanasia and Cryogenics. Genetic Manipulation and Is God

Dead. The lawyers, doctors and clergy argue on these intellectual matters, but what about us? We're still afraid! What about that, Buddha? What about that, Confucius? What about that, Muhammad? Moses? Jesus?

If you fear Death, you must find your own answers. These Dialogues On Death are with people who live with it every day. They are interesting, often fascinating people. Most of them are groping for the answers too. One or two have found them. Perhaps they may be of help. Don't turn away because the subject is distasteful. It needn't be. That's the point.

1

"I don't fear Death, but I certainly don't want to hurry it along."

Dr. Maurice Linden is a 55-year-old psychiatrist with a more than passing background in Geriatric Psychiatry. He looks like Broderick Crawford. Strong round face, deeply tanned, partially bald, burly with big square shoulders, a bull neck, short muscular arms and a too big belly. His office is on the second floor of the Jefferson Unit of Philadelphia State Hospital at Byberry. We sit in semi-darkness, a whirring fan behind me competes with his rapid low voice. His left hand toys continuously with the hornrimmed glasses on his desk. Between us, there is a large cheap ceramic ashtray with two green snakes coiled around the edge and meeting head to head. Each has one red eye. He apologizes for keeping me waiting.

"I just had to close my eyes for a few minutes. It's too busy, my schedule. I don't get enough rest. Days, nights, weekends. Too much. And I have my own private practice. But that's what makes medicine worthwhile. I recall a patient of mine. She was a dear and beautiful person. She had been in analysis for some time when she developed cancer of the uterus. It was inoperable. She was aware of the mass inside her and that her chances were not good. We talked a good deal about Death. They were no longer analytical sessions, they became philosophical discussions about a wide range of subjects.

"I told her that I felt that life had been good to me, that I had had many rich and rewarding experiences. That I realized that Death comes to everyone and that if I should have to die, I was quite ready. In that way I introduced the idea to her. I tried to keep her hopes up. I told her that there was still a chance, that I had heard of cases where the cancer was sloughed off.

"Later, I met with my patient's family. I explained that she was anxious that they not be dependent upon her, that they be able to care for themselves. I said that I interpreted that to mean just the opposite, that she wanted them to be with her and to care for her and love her. I was very close to her. I think I loved her as much as anyone in the family. I even talked to her doctor. I was quite put out because he was withholding certain drugs that could alleviate some of the pain on the basis that she would become addicted. My God, if you can't make an addict out of a dying patient!

"Aging is depressing. One begins to lose things —youth with all of its vitalities. Youth is a possession, Old Age is not. They begin to think it would be better to die. It's a passive suicidal wish. Others manage not to be depressed. There are compensations for Old Age. Wisdom, for example. I can always tell. If I ask a patient where he expects to be in ten years, what plans he is making, and he answers—well I have this cottage at the shore I'm going to fix up and I'll probably be living there—then I know he's still pretty vital and has adjusted to some degree. But if he answers—Oh, I don't know—or, I may not even be here by then—well, I know he's depressed.

"There is also the aspect of guilt which plays a very strong role. Guilt about how they have treated other people, guilt about leaving loved ones behind. But one thing about Old Age I learned many years ago. There is no such thing as Old Age. No one ever admits that they are old. I have this group at the Naval Hospital—all old men. They're really decrepit, in bad shape, some so far gone they can't even hold their heads up. A real bunch of Old Geezers. I say, if there's an old man in the room, hold up your hand. Nobody holds up his hand. Most of them are in their 70's or 80's, but if I ask them how old they feel, they usually say 50 or 55. You see, you look at yourself in the mirror and you can see you're aging, but you're not growing older inside. It's just the physical you, not the you that's inside. As you grow older, there is this coming apart of the Psyche and the Soma.

"Now I've grown older. I'm fifty-five. And I can appreciate many of the aspects of Old Age. I'm slowing down, I tire more easily, I have less vigor. But my Ego is essentially unchanged. I still have the same values to a degree, the same desires. We develop this strong love of self, this self adulation is Narcissism. A little bit, of course, is important. I think it was Rabbi Akiba who said: 'If I don't love me, who will?' But this Narcissism makes us believe that the world simply cannot continue without us. After all, Reality is when we're here. If we are not here, where is Reality?

"I witnessed my father's death. He developed cancer from stomach ulcers. He was in the hospital on the Coast. I went out to see him. We joked a lot. That was the way in my family, to kid around and joke back and forth. They wanted him to stay in the hospital longer, but he insisted that we take him home. He said get me a hospital bed at home. He wanted to be able to look out the window at his lawn and his car. So we got him the hospital bed and he stayed in the back room—it was once my room—looking out the window at the lawn and the garden he cared for. And his car. He had a Packard and he loved it even though he couldn't drive it any more.

"Nobody told him what was wrong, not even the doctor. Finally, I had to leave to go back East. He was still fairly strong and I had to leave. I thought I'd be strong and just go in and say goodbye, but when I went in I just collapsed. I fell across the bed, crying. He patted my head and he said, 'Don't worry. Everybody has to die, sooner or later. It's as simple as that.' He was consoling me! After he died, we found he had been reading all of my medical books. Every section on cancer had been worn. He knew all the time.

"There is really not a great deal of preoccupation with Death among old people. They don't seem to have the fear we would expect. Many grow tired and look forward to it. I'm growing older and more tired. I have depressions. I don't fear Death, but I certainly don't want to hurry it along. But I'm not afraid of it. I don't think I believe in a Life After Death, but I've never met anyone, not even an avowed atheist, that didn't hold at least some small prospect of the existence of God. The nearest thing to soul of which I can conceive is this Life Force that's deep inside us. Freud called it the Id. But I don't believe in soul in the traditional sense. Yet matter cannot be destroyed. We are created from matter and after Death, we return to matter in a different form. I don't know."

2

"I wouldn't go to a funeral if my life depended on it."

Alden Whitman is the Chief obituary writer for the New York Times. He looks more like the owner of a bookstore in Princeton than an obituary writer, but then what should an obituary writer look like? In six years he has written the obituaries of T. S. Eliot, Martin Buber, Adlai Stevenson, Helen Keller, John Steinbeck, Ho Chi Minh, Bertrand Russell and many more which you can read in his "The Obituary Book" published earlier this year. Fifty-eight. Small. Twinkling blue eyes peering over half-glasses perched on his nose, the lower half of his face covered with a squarely trimmed beard which barely reveals an impish grin. A pipe and a bow tie.

"I don't deal with Death. I write about people's lives for the breakfast table set. I do forty or so obits a year—about one a week. I write them in advance, sometimes years in advance. I write mostly about men over seventy, except the President, the Vice President and other officials. The toughest obits to write are scientists or philosophers, because there is so much to their lives. These are more like biographies that I do.

"I often visit with important people before I write about them. I'll be leaving soon for a 'ghoul tour' in Europe. It's not for historical material. That's all available in files. You try to get anecdotes, of course, but mostly you try to get a feel, a sense of the man. I've written about many people that I've known, some that I've known intimately. I'm not really affected, it's my profession. But if it's someone whom you dislike—like Franco who did so much harm to the people of Spain, who was such a dreadful man, or Hess—well, you can't help getting a little subjective and some hatred may come out in the writing. Or, if it was someone whom you liked, who you had a high regard for, then some of that warmth may also come out. If it's a House Obit—someone you've worked with and know well, it may be too tough so you let someone else do it.

"You don't like to do an obit after the fact. You end up doing a job in a day or two that should have taken weeks. You try to avoid that. Some people write in with their own obits. I like that. We file them until they may be needed. We have a pretty extensive file, oh there must be a couple thousand or so accumulated over a period of time. I sat at a copy desk for twenty-five years. I got bored. The position opened up and I took it. I've been doing it ever since. You try not to make them all alike. That's the challenge of the job, to come up with ways to make them different.

"I don't think much about Death. I don't go to funerals, they're barbaric. I wouldn't go to a funeral if my life depended on it. It's been a life-long policy. I think the Jewish funeral is a much better way to deal with grief. A quick burial and sit Shiva with the family to take their mind off the grief. Or the old Irish Wake is a good idea. I'm an Athiest and I hold no brief for the After-Life. In my will I direct that I should be cremated as quickly as possible. Cryonics? I think Cryonics is a farce.

"I haven't written my own obit. I've never even thought of it. That would be the absolute height of Narcissism."

3

"We were 1200 that arrived together at Auschwitz. Four survived."

Her name is now Marie Schwartzman. In November of 1941, it was Marie Zausznica. Three months later, it was 35056. She was sixteen years old in Paris, the second oldest of seven children. Her father and mother had come from Poland after the First World War. He was a clothing designer working for the French Government to redesign the Army's uniforms. When the war came, he joined the Foreign Legion to avoid the Polish Draft since he was still a Polish citizen. He was in the South of France when Paris was taken by the Germans.

"Nobody thought it would happen. We had the Maginot Line. It would protect us. And the French Government—we were French—it would protect us. Refugees from Germany used to tell us what they were doing to Jews in Germany, but no one wanted to believe them. The Maginot Line lasted two days. And half the French Government was selling out to the Germans. When they took Paris, it was already too late. My mother was under forty, but she was alone. My father was away. She didn't know what to do. At first it was all right, but soon they started to round up the Jews.

"We lived across from a church. My mother used to get shots—hay fever, I guess—the nuns used to come to give them to her. They said, let us take the children. Then when you come back, we'll return them. She said no, if we were to die, we would die together. There were always rumors before a round-up—don't sleep at home for a few nights, there's going to be trouble. Sometimes the French police would tell us when they knew. My father came home. Even though he was still in Unoccupied France, he wanted to be with us.

"I adored my father. I would wash his feet for him, anything. My mother and I weren't getting along too well at the time. He opened a small business. One day he was leaving for work. Outside, two Germans and a French policeman stopped him and asked if he knew Monsieur Zansznica. He was too honest. He said, I am Monsieur Zansznica. They told him to get a blanket and some things for a few days. When he came in, he told me what to do, who owed him money, things like that. Then he left. We never saw him again.

"One day, a friend told us they were coming for three of us, the three oldest. My older sister was about nineteen and worked in a hospital as a nurse. After me, the next youngest was another sister, about thirteen. The youngest was my little brother. He was two and a half. We had a house in the country. We went there for awhile, but it started to get rough there too and we were running out of money. By this time, the French were becoming Anti-Semitic. It was the result of the propaganda—The Jews have caused all your problems. The Jews are the reason you are hungry. The Jews. The Jews. If you know of Jews still free, it is your duty to turn them in. You will be rewarded.

"We went back to Paris. I was playing the piano. My mother told me to stop, that there was no sense in telling everyone we had returned. I said, it's only two o'clock in the afternoon, no one will hear. At two-thirty the Germans came. They only wanted the same three. We hid my younger sister behind a closet. It was very frightening. We spent the night in the police station. Then they said come and meet the rest of the family. They had gone back for everyone else.

"We were taken to a camp outside of Paris where we stayed until February 1942. Then we were taken by train to Auschwitz. We were separated in the train. We had the baby, but my mother was in the other car with the milk. It was very bad. At Auschwitz we were separated into files of five. My mother and brothers and sisters were in front of me. My oldest sister was carrying my baby brother. They were loaded into the trucks. It was very frightening. There was so much noise. The SS were shouting and they had dogs and clubs and they were hitting everybody. We were all so tired. They asked my sister if my brother was her baby. She answered wrong. She said yes. So they put her on the truck too. I never saw them again. I learned later that the trucks were for the crematory. For many years after, I refused to believe it. I blacked it out. Then, one day, I believed it.

"I was at Auschwitz from February '42 until May '45. I was very lucky and I had a lot of help from people I often didn't even know. I hated it. Inside me I would get so mad when I would see one human being degrade another that way. One time I got so mad, I started to the fence to throw mud or something at the guard. He pressed the button and I saw sparks as my fingers touched the fence, so I stepped back. Then he shot me. It wasn't bad—in the foot—but it got infected and I had a bad time.

"The facilities were very bad. The food was terrible. There was no water. The Germans were not organized at first. Everything was very confusing. We did work, but it was foolish kind of work. I was on a road. Pick up one stone here, put it there. Later, pick the same stone up and put it back. There was typhus and we were quarantined. There [were] two kinds of typhus. The one [which] came from lice and the one [which] came from water. We had both. There was no medicine for the Jews, no hospital. The inmate doctors would help you if you paid some bread, some rations. Otherwise, they would do nothing.

"Finally, I was selected for the crematory. Tauber was the head of the camp. At the formation, I kept telling him—I won't let you kill me. You won't kill me. I'm not going to die. I'm not!—We had to take our clothes off and get in the trucks. I moved to the front of the truck. Tauber got in next to the driver. I kept shouting to him, over and over—I'm not going to die! You're not going to kill me! I won't die!—As we walked into the gas chamber, he threw a blanket over me and motioned me out." *Marie testified at Tauber's trial at Nuremberg.*

"I was assigned to Block 25. That's where they put you when you're sick. In three days, if you're not better, you go to the crematory. I was one of the . . . like maids . . . to clean the Block. The dirtiest work. I got typhus and I was very sick. But I had help. When Tauber came in the daytime, the others said I was sleeping because I worked all night. If he came at night, they said I was sleeping because I worked all day. Finally he said he didn't believe it. Tomorrow, she goes. The next day, I crawled to the door. I couldn't walk. But I stood at the door and opened it to let him in. He looked at me and said nothing.

"I had a very strong will to live. The ones who wanted to survive, did. The others gave up. The Germans had . . . well, not respect, but perhaps understanding for the ones who felt like that. It was easy to die if you wanted to. Some committed suicide on the wire fences. Or if you got really tired, you could just stop. On Sundays, we used to have exercise they called it. Running up and down the road, only nobody could run. If you wanted to die, you could just sit down and refuse to go further. Then they would shoot you.

"We had the famous Dr. Mengala. You've probably heard of him. He was replaced by Dr. Rhode. He was a wonderful, wonderful man. He closed down the crematoria. He opened a Jewish

hospital. He died, I think, and Mengala came back. I was in a potato kommando. It was a very bad kommando. It was cold and underground. I think I would have died in that kommando. But a friend said she would put me down for the hospital and I became a nurse. I was sick, but the doctor made believe he didn't know. Once I was under the bed and I made believe I was cleaning. I couldn't get up.

"Sometimes I was ready to die, but most of the time I had a very strong will to live. The first few weeks were the worst. Sometimes they made the women strip and go up and down in front of the men who they lined up to watch. At first, I was very upset. I was only sixteen. But afterwards I even walked over to talk to them. It didn't make any difference, they didn't care. Everyone was in bad shape. Was I pretty? I don't know. How could you be pretty there, with your hair cut off?

"Toward the end, they brought in the Hungarian Jews. For some reason they left them alone until late in the war. Half a million of them. The three crematoria were working day and night. The crematory kommando revolted. They refused to work. They were replaced and then they went to the gas chambers. I was in Briginka, the little camp between two of the crematoria. The job of my kommando was to sort the packages of the people who went to the gas chambers. They used to tell everyone—take your jewelry, take all of your belongings—then they would take it away anyway. It bothered me the work. I used to faint. Or I used to sleep a lot. Anything to blank out what was happening. Afterwhile, they put up a fence so we couldn't watch.

"We were evacuated. The Germans were afraid to be taken by the Russians. We were packed into railroad cars. It was very bad. People were dropping right and left. There was no water. We slept on dead bodies. When our food was gone, we took the food of the dead. The worst was no water. We were in those cars for three weeks. Finally, we arrived at Ravensbrueck. I was very frightened. Ravensbrueck was where they conducted the experiments. I would have drawn the line on two things . . . the prostitution and the experiments. I would have died first. We arrived on February 11. I know, because it was a coincidence—the same day I arrived at Auschwitz.

There was much confusion. The attitude of the Germans changed. Now we heard about their orders and duty. But we left and started walking. I wanted to run away, but a soldier said where would you go? I was liberated on May 6 in Lux.

"What I have told you is nothing. There were things that happened that no one would believe. They would say it couldn't happen. I can't even wear a low cut dress in the back from the marks of the dogs. We were 1200 that arrived together at Auschwitz. Four survived. After I was liberated, it was very difficult. I had no one. I had no money. No job. I was sick for eighteen months with tuberculosis. At first I stayed only with others from Auschwitz. All they talked about was hate and revenge. They would always say to others, oh what do you know, you weren't there. But I did not feel that way. I knew I must break away from them or go mad. So I made new friends and I stopped talking about it.

"I was not afraid of Death. It was just that I wanted so to live. I thought I was too young to die. Now, sometimes, I am very tired. I see things happening like before. Vietnam and all the killings. Drug addicts. It's such a senseless waste of life. I think if I had to go through it now, again, at my age, I would not make it. I don't have the strength. So many people then just gave up. Especially the young. I was very lucky.

"I have no fear. Except in my sleep. I used to have such nightmares. I would wake up screaming horribly and literally tear my hair out. Then I would not sleep for two or three days. It's not so bad now. I am not afraid. What could possibly happen? So many things happened to me then, nothing could be worse. Over and over, I asked why. Still I have no answer. You cannot blame just the people who did it, yet how can you blame everyone? I do not believe in God. How could anyone after that? And I do not believe in Life After Death.

"When I am dead, I want to be cremated and throw the ashes away, maybe somewhere to help flowers grow. I do not think of the crematoria then and cremation now in the same way. They are separate. I am not afraid of dying. Even if it was cancer or some other painful death. I have known so much pain that a little more now would not bother me. I could take it. Then I would sleep and never wake up."

4

"You could make a million dollars if you wrote an exposé on the cemeteries. They make Capone look like an amateur."

I'm no coward, but I'm not independently wealthy either. If you use my name they'll make trouble. They can do it, too. Let them try to guess who it is, if they want to. If the things I have to say make some of them sweat . . . good. They deserve it. Maybe some of them will stop charging for foundations when there are none. Maybe some of them will give the Perpetual Care they're getting paid for, and put the money in a trust fund like they're supposed to. Pennsylvania needs a Cemetery Commission like some of the other states to watch over the interests of the individual lot owner. He's getting taken! I could tell you plenty."

So said this monument dealer, who for obvious reasons wishes to remain anonymous. And though it is a sad commentary, we shall honor his request. He is neither [a] small dealer nor is he new to the business. It has been in his family for several generations. He says that only some of the cemeteries with which he deals are guilty of the unethical and often unlawful practices of which he speaks.

"Most of the people in this business are terrible businessmen. You can make good money in it, but most of them were just stonecutters and they didn't know about business. They would take an order for a stone from somebody in his forties, charge him what it was and forget about it. Now the guy lives another twenty years before he dies. The price of the stone has doubled or tripled, but the stonecutter didn't figure the increase when he originally charged."

(This business does 1500–2000 monuments a year in a range of $200 to $2000, with the average about $400. There is an additional charge of as much as $120 by the cemetery which usually insists on providing the foundation for the stone. Granite is usual. Marble wears poorly, especially in cold climates.)

"Mitford's book attacked the wrong people. You could make a million dollars if you wrote an exposé on the cemeteries. They make Capone look like an amateur. The old days of the small, family cemetery is gone. Now it's the big boys and the promoters. A fast buck, that's all they want. Some of the things they pull are outrageous. But they get away with it because they've got a captive audience. The undertakers can't do anything. I talked to one undertaker who was having a disagreement with a cemetery. So the cemetery called and said, that funeral you got lined up for Tuesday? We can't handle it. You'll have to make it Wednesday. He said, I can't do that! Well there wouldn't be a grave on Tuesday. So he sweated. He really sweated. In the end, he gave in. He had no choice.

"They sell bronze markers for a hundred-fifty bucks on Pre-Need. They're sports. They give two-three years to pay. So what? They get the use of the money for twenty years before the marker's needed. The cost increase in ten years doesn't even match the first year's interest on the money. They charge a hundred-fifty for a dis-interment. It's a racket. They use machines now, not hourly laborers. I talked to an operator who told me it takes one-fourth the time it used to. Or the Gardens, that's a joke. The father's already buried in a site, now the mother dies. 'Mrs. Goldman, have you seen our Shalom Gardens? It's so quiet and peaceful. It's surrounded with shrubbery and has genuine rocks from King Solomon's Mines in Israel and no monuments for vandals to turn over. We won't even charge to move your father to the Garden.' Before they're through, they've sold a $1500 deal and freed up a gravesite that originally cost $50 or so and now sells for plenty more. For what? The ground cost them twenty dollars or so based on their acreage and the lousy bushes cost a couple hundred dollars.

"The crematory, that's a racket too. You can make a fortune with those urns on a shelf. And don't believe they burn those caskets. I wouldn't swear to it because I've never seen it with my own eyes, but some of those guys are supposed to be my friends and they wink at me. I know they lower the body down in the casket, but when it gets below the floor they remove the body and give the undertaker back the casket. They don't burn those caskets.

"I don't see many tears in my business. Usually it's a year or so after and they're over the shock. I like to deal with the Middle Class. Some people in this business deal with one kind of trade— Italians or Jews or Colored—but I deal with them all. The Italians and Poles go for the most elaborate. Lately, I've been getting a big Colored trade. I like them. They spend well and there's no fuss. I get along well with the Jews because they know I'm no bigot. People don't have many arguments over monuments. They usually know what they want. But the young people lose respect for the old people. I've learned one thing in this business: don't rely on your children. Don't grow old and expect them to be understanding.

"Some people make fun of the monuments I have on display. They laugh or joke or lay down in front of them to make fun. But let somebody die and they're here the next day or so, buying the biggest they can afford. I don't know why people go in for so much show. I think it's guilt and remorse. A guy can't dig his wife up and talk to her. Maybe he treated her rotten. Maybe he beat her, cheated on her. So he feels guilty and buys a big monument.

"I had a guy once, a machinist. His wife died and left him $5000. So he wanted to have a tomb he could visit. I said that was possible. But he said he wanted to see her and touch her. I said, but the thing is sealed . . . you can't do that. He said he'd written to Russia to the Communists to see how they did it with Lenin. I told him that must cost thousands and thousands for pumps and to keep that stuff circulating and they can't touch him anyway. So next he decided he wanted a sculptured angel on a base over the grave with her wings spread like so. Well, we do that. But he said he wanted the face to be that of his wife. Then he wanted to run a wire from the cemetery office to the gravesite so he could have an illuminated halo that would go on over the angel at night. People get whacky sometimes, after a death! Fifteen years later that guy hasn't even put up a wooden cross at his wife's grave. I don't know what happened to the $5000. He used to play the horses a lot.

We were interrupted by an old man and his son. They wished to purchase a stone, but there was considerable discussion over the inscription. The old man was Jewish and spoke with a thick accent. First there was a problem over his wife's Hebrew name. He said in English it was Sophie, in Hebrew it was Sheva. But he couldn't spell it. They looked it up in a book of Hebrew names. Was he pronouncing it correctly? Was he a Litvak or a Galitz? Was it S or Ch? Finally, they found it. It meant Life. "She lived, all right," said the old man. "Look, my name is Swartz. S—W. That's the way the Guvment said, that's good enough for me. But she spelled it Schwartz. S—C—H. People asked why. Whatsa matter, ain't you married? I told 'em . . . we was married. But this is a double marker. If you spell her S—C—H and you spell me S—W, people will ask wasn't they married? It's not right. So her name got to be Swartz with a S—W. Ok?"

"I don't think much about Death. I'm not very religious. In my business Sunday is the busiest day, so I never went to church. I have a Will, but I don't specify what I want. My wife and I have an understanding. No viewing. We don't believe in that nonsense. A simple casket and burial under ground. I don't see cremation. It's like burning a dead cat or burning the garbage. I just can't see that. But I don't think too much about it. Except I'm starting to see a lot of friends dropping by the wayside. I don't believe in a Life After Death. You know what they say. Nobody's ever come back to tell about it."

5

"The first autopsy I did as a Resident was the girl I took to my high school prom. . . . It was quite a shock."

Dr. Marvin Aronson is Philadelphia's Chief Medical Examiner. Medium height, balding, a faint red mustache on a round face, an old pipe clenched between his teeth. He is very heavy. His hands are constantly busy as he talks, tamping his pipe or cleaning it or lighting it or clipping his nails. He is a great fan of Sherlock Holmes and plans to write mysteries based on the many plots that he has already outlined. Dr. Aronson is a forensic pathologist, certified by three Boards.

"I came here thirteen years ago. I finally decided to go to work at thirty-four after spending a lot of time learning medicine. I only intended to stay a year or so, but I liked it so much I stayed. With my experience, I could go on to a job on the outside that would pay forty or fifty thousand more than I make here, but I like this too much. We investigate deaths that are known or suspected to have been unnatural. We have a staff of sixty-five, five of which are professional. We're caught in a budget squeeze, but no worse I guess than others in the city. Our budget for next year is about $220,000 which means a salary cut of fifteen percent.

"We were promised to go on computer, but it never happened. No money. In the basement there are literally a billion facts and pieces of valuable information. There's no one to correlate it. Give me three million dollars and two years and I'd have it all on computer. If they'd have done it when I suggested, it would have only cost a million. There are tremendously important clues there to the solving of diseases and the social violence of Man. But I'm the only one who believes it.

"We examine about 4500 bodies a year here. About 1800–2000 of them are autopsied. Most of the autopsies we do are intended to confirm our opinion on the cause of death. Attorneys around here have gotten pretty sophisticated. They know a gunshot wound may not be sufficient to cause death. Many times the autopsy exonerates the accused. Once we've taken jurisdiction of a body, the decision to autopsy is ours. We do not need the family's approval. However, where there are borderline cases and the family requests through the funeral director that there be no autopsy, we try to cooperate.

"At one time, many of the bodies that came through here were unclaimed and had to be buried at city expense. I think the cost for that is now around seventy dollars, but we have very few—maybe five or ten a year—and I would guess that whoever gets the contract next year will want more. Seventy dollars doesn't go very far today. A lot of our work is investigative and by tracking down families, we've saved the city a lot of money. Easily the cost of the investigator.

"I keep my own statistics. As of the first of the year, I have done 3,719 autopsies. It doesn't change my attitude if I know the dead person. Of course I wouldn't want to autopsy my father or my wife or my children. I've got a whole lot of cousins, some of whom I wouldn't mind autopsying, but if it was somebody who I knew really well, I'd have somebody else do it. I'm the Chief and I have a staff to do things like that. You see, you arrive at certain conclusions at an autopsy, and I wouldn't want someone to think that my conclusions were influenced by my former relationship with the person. That would be the reason, not the emotional impact.

"I autopsied two people that I actually knew pretty well. One was the first autopsy I did as a Resident, but I didn't know at the time who it was. It was the girl I took to my high school prom. She committed suicide. The job had already been begun, so that when I got there her face was covered. And she had married, so I didn't recognize her name. When I finished up and saw her face, it was quite a shock. The other one was a fellow student in medical school. He had committed suicide much later and of course I hadn't seen him in long time. Funny, one thing I realized at the time of the autopsy was that he was a fairy. I was surprised that I hadn't known he was a fairy in med school. Of course, he may not have been a practicing homosexual when I knew him.

"One thing that really affects you is kids. I don't care how much experience you have, whenever it's a kid it's as if you're just starting. It gets worse when you have your own kids. That's why I tell my kids—yes, your father is different and that's why there are rules in this house that are different from anybody else's down the street. I'm sorry, but that's it.—My kids aren't allowed to have a balloon in their mouth. They're not allowed to have cap pistols. They're not allowed to swim alone. I've made them have a great deal of confidence in the water. It wasn't easy, it had to be subtle so I didn't instill fear instead. But I wanted them to know that if they were ever in a situation, they could remain afloat for a long, long time.

"When I was about six, my grandfather died and I was very close to that situation. About a year later, I had reason to see that these old people with their payyes and yarmulkes were a bunch of hypocritical old bastards. That was when I became a seven and a half year old Atheist. Now, I've come around again to believing in a Supreme Being. I'm not formally religious, but I think I've developed a sense of Life . . . that we all play a part in the Medium of Life, like a bacterium relates to a culture medium. There are two unique circumstances in Death. The first is that it is universal. We all die. The second is

that no other animal but Man knows this and makes plans for, or at least contemplates, his own death.

"I think about my death from time to time. I don't think my work has in any way influenced my views. My wife knows, I've talked about it many times, that I would want my body turned over to The Anatomical Board for dissection by medical students. If for some reason my body is unsuitable, then I would wish it cremated and thrown to the wind or somewhere where it won't cause pollution."

6

"Whoever tell you he can talk with the Dead is a liar!"

My long search for a Spiritual Medium led me finally to a dingy store front in a run-down section of town. The sign out front read: Spiritual Advisor—Palms Read. The door was open and I walked in. I was in a small darkened room about eight feet by ten. My eyes grew accustomed to the darkness and I saw an old Gypsy woman seated at one end of a low sofa. At the other end of the sofa, a small child was sprawled in sleep. There were two more children sleeping on another old sofa across the room. Through a partially curtained doorway, I could see into another much larger room at the end of which a young woman stood cooking at a stove. The smell of herbs and cooking oil permeated the whole place.

The old Gypsy gave me a toothless grin and patted the sofa next to her. I handed her my card.

"I'm looking for a Medium," I said. "Someone who can be in touch with the Other World."

She answered, but I had difficulty understanding her. She became exasperated, finally yelling over her shoulder in a broken voice to the woman in the other room. The language was unfamiliar. The daughter came out and asked what I wanted. I told her. She shrugged.

"Nobody around here can do that. Mostly, they read palms. My mother here knows about Spirits." She walked back to the kitchen. I tried again.

"I'm looking for someone who talks to the Spirits."

She pointed to her ear and said, "I can't hear so good." Then her hand fluttered to her chest. "I just got back from the hospital."

"Are you feeling all right?"

"Are you a doctor?"

"No."

"Are you a newspaper writer?"

"Yes."

The old Gypsy took a deep breath. Then she surprised me with a loud clear voice that I had no difficulty understanding. "Whoever tell you he can talk with the Dead is a liar! Some people would die just to be able to talk to the Dead. When God take them, they don't talk no more. Whether to Heaven or whether to Hell, the Dead Man don't talk. Whoever tell you he can hear him is crazy in the head."

She sank back weakly on the sofa. As I left, she was still patting the sofa next to her and showing her gums in another toothless grin. One of three children whimpered in his sleep.

7

"We have a joke around here. When someone says that doesn't look like so and so when she was alive, we say yeah but you ain't never seen her dead before."

The Baker Funeral Home is one of Philadelphia's better known black funeral homes. I waited in a dimly lit entrance hall. It was early in the morning. The doors to Chapel A were open and I looked into the large high ceilinged room. There were three sections of metal folding chairs, about twenty rows of ten to a section. Up front, surrounded by a great many flowers, was an open casket in which I could just make out the figure of a black man. The face was covered with a white cloth. In the hall a table held a stack of white mimeographed papers, programs from the memorial service of the night before. It included several hymns and the announcement of the interment scheduled for that morning. Wendell Baker arrived and we went into a small office adjacent to Chapel A. On the way he turned on the air conditioning in the chapel. A tall man, good-looking with his hair cut short but worn in a natural, mustache and goatee. He is thirty-six and cool.

"We're very busy here all the time. We have about six hundred cases a year, eighteen this week. Everybody wants the weekend. We just can't do everybody for the weekend. We get very few cremations, I don't think ten in the last ten years. This business is built on customs and traditions and social mores. The black people are very emotional about their funerals. The Italians are too. They probably spend the most. But the black people and the Italians and the Jews, they don't believe in cremation.

"About 50% of our cases have been autopsied. It's not true that undertakers charge a hundred dollars more to embalm after an autopsy, but sometimes we have to charge more. What they didn't tell you and what they don't tell the family is what goes on sometimes. It makes it harder to do the job of embalming. Also, they don't tell the family why they do autopsies. Every doctor wants an autopsy to confirm his diagnosis. Hospitals need them to authenticate their records. I can see an autopsy sometimes, for science, but not on an old person. Most of the old people die of heart trouble. Why do an autopsy on an eighty year old? Sure we try to talk the family out of an autopsy.

"Embalming is for sanitary purposes. You wouldn't want an unembalmed body around in the summer, no sir. Why, we have air conditioning and a big exhaust fan that operates from the roof—that's the hum you hear—but even with all that, you can smell it when you pass my Preparation Room. Wow, you wouldn't want to have unembalmed bodies in the summer! We have a joke around here. When someone says that doesn't look like so and so when she was alive, we say yeah but you ain't never seen her dead before.

"I went to Morgan State in Baltimore where I studied Economics, and I went to Eckles Embalming School here in Philadelphia. They closed. Nobody new going into the business. Couldn't make a go. I didn't want to join the business as a kid, because my Daddy's pretty strict and he wouldn't pay much. Now I see him from a different perspective. He's got a fine reputation. He started this business in 1928. My mother said he was crazy—people was jumpin' out of windows and blowin' holes in their heads, gettin' out of business. He saved three hundred dollars in the Depression and came home and said, I'm goin' into business. Once he accused me of not workin' hard enough. On the way home, I told my mother and she said, son, in the old days your Daddy had three jobs. Many a night he'd come home, plop down in a chair and sleep for two hours, then go back to work. So I guess he had a right to tell me I wasn't workin' hard enough.

"There's no trouble anymore with racism in the cemeteries. Again, there are traditions. Most black people want to be buried with the rest of their family. I don't think there'd be any trouble from a cemetery if an established firm like ours wanted ground for a black person. But the white and black firms work pretty well together. We're all in the same business. There's no 'Block Bustin' in cemeteries. We're workin' together to try to hold down the outsiders comin' in and drivin' prices down. You can't get a corporate charter in Pennsylvania anymore, so a big outfit like this Texas oil company comes in and buys someone to get the charter. Then they go into the finance business and they go into the cemetery business and they start lowering the prices.

"One of those outfits bought an established place in a black community and they want a black man to front it. It's white owned, but they get a black man to front. That's the way it was mostly in the South. There was a few black millionaires in the business down South, but mostly it was white owned with a black front. My conception's changed since I've traveled down South. You might have to work hard for Mister Charlie, but one thing was you always knew where you stood. There's no BS, Mister Charlie calls a spade a spade. If you're doin' somethin' he don't like, he tells you. Not like up North.

"When Death is business, I don't have any trouble. I'm cool and I handle it. But if it's my own family or someone I know well, I get as emotional as anybody. I'm very religious, but in a philosophical way. I had polio when I was eighteen months old and I had rheumatic fever when I was four. I had something like St. Vitus Dance at the same time and the doctors didn't hold no hope for me. I've been shot and stabbed. I been run over by a bus, a truck and a car. I've had every childhood disease you can think of. I think about Death, all right. I think about the Man up there watchin' over me.

"Some people say they don't see me at church.

I'm a Trustee. Well, I'm there. I don't have no Day of Rest, just a piece of one. I go over, check the money and do the books, then run back for a quick lunch, see my kids and get back to work. I do a lot more churchin' than those hypocrite deacons who get up there and pray for five minutes, then go chasin' after some woman.

"I think more about dyin' than Death, I guess. I have a Will, but there's nothin' in it about what to do with me. I haven't thought much about it. I'd want to be buried above ground, though. I know too much about what goes on underneath the cemeteries. Maybe in a mausoleum. But I don't personally go for all the Pomp and Circumstance. That's what people want and it's my business, but I wouldn't want it for my family."

8

"I could sit down next to a casket and eat my lunch and it wouldn't bother me. Unless it was someone near and dear, and then my attitude hasn't changed in forty years."

Charles Clark is the Director of West Laurel Hill Cemetery, one of Philadelphia's finest. He is also a director of the Pennsylvania Cemetery Association and the American Cemetery Association. He was extremely suspicious and the interview began badly. He seemed certain that I was intent on an exposé a la Jessica Mitford, and I had difficulty convincing him otherwise. He said that her book was unfair and did not give a representative cross-section of either the cemetery business or the undertaker business, that West Laurel Hill was a very ethical place and had never cheated anyone. West Laurel Hill was founded as a private non-profit corporation in 1869. It consists of 187 acres in which 95,000 have already been interred. Burial sites begin at $55 for charity cases and go up to $5000. When I suggested that perhaps under the circumstances we should conclude the interview, his attitude changed and we had a nice chat. Clark, in his sixties, was conservatively dressed in slacks, a sports jacket and a bow tie. Balding, glasses, a faint pencil-thin mustache.

"I came here in '31. I was in the insurance business, but I hadn't weathered the Depression. I told the Director here that I had no money and if he wanted me to be able to maintain payments on my plot here, he'd have to give me a job. He said he'd never heard that given as a reason for a job before, so he hired me. The first week I didn't have enough money to buy coveralls, so I cut grass in a bowler and a Chesterfield coat.

"I don't think we ever had an application for a grave made by a Colored family before the Civil Rights legislation was passed. We still have only ten or twenty Colored here. But we were always nonsectarian. As early as '38, our attorneys said if you have an application from a Colored person, you better sell him.

"Some cemeteries are definitely unethical. We don't let them into our association. We have a reputation to protect. These promoters—they offer free dishes if you purchase a site—or they offer a free grave to a Veteran, then charge twice the going rate for a site next to it for his wife. These are the ones that make a bad name for the rest of us. It's bad publicity. But I think we have the best relationship with the undertakers of anyone in the business.

"Our crematorium was started in '38. The first in Philadelphia was about the turn of the Century. The first in the country was built much earlier in Washington, Pennsylvania. Anyone can be cremated in our crematorium. We do have certain requirements. The body must be delivered in an acceptable container. One delivered a body in a pouch. We wouldn't accept it. Our men have to handle the body then. But it doesn't have to be an expensive casket. One manufacturer makes an acceptable container out of rigid cardboard. As for embalming, that's a legal question. The law says you must embalm after 48 hours.

"People have a mistaken idea on what cremains look like. It's not a fine powder. Within the ashes are bone fragments sometimes six inches long. Bones are calcium and that's not combustible." *In her book, [Jessica] Mitford claimed that the heat was kept deliberately low enough to insure that these fragments would be present, so as to dissuade people from scattering ashes.* "They have the idea that they can just spread the powder around, but they can't. The law says that cremation is not the ultimate disposition of the body. If the ashes are unclaimed or the family has signed the release authorizing us to dispose of the cremains, they are consigned to under the ground

burial. We wait until we have two or three hundred, then we put them under ground with no marker. Or they can be interred in a regular site or an urn garden. We also operate a Columbarium where we will sell shelf space. We do not provide an urn, but we do sell them. Otherwise, the cremains are placed in a cardboard box and mailed to the family."

Later, on visiting the crematorium:

"These two caskets are awaiting cremation. The wooden one will of course be consumed, but not the metal one. We can't have a high enough temperature to melt down the metal. We use 1700 degrees Fahrenheit. We'll remove the lid of the metal casket and lean it on one side. Afterwards, it has to be cooled and removed, then carted away. It's really more work, but some people seem to need that elaborate a show."

In the "shipping room," several boxes were ready to be mailed. Certified parcel post or, occasionally by air or truck. About twelve inches cubed, the boxes were wrapped in white paper with a red seal on the top. I picked one up. It weighed about five or six pounds. Clark brought me an open box yet to be wrapped. It was filled with grayish ashes with little bits and pieces of off-white bone.

"Cryogenics? It's very expensive. How long are you going to have to keep the body frozen? Even when we set up trust funds for Perpetual Care, we have trouble. Costs go up, interest fluctuates. Then there's the problem of space. Where will you put all of the bodies? And how about damage from the freezing process? Even if there was no damage, say you have a nineteen year old you freeze just before the last breath or just after the last breath, and you bring him back even twenty years later. What's going to happen to him? Everybody is twenty years older, but he's still the same. No, I think it's just a fad. If Forest Lawn isn't in it—and they're out for the buck—then I don't think it's got much demand. I was out at Forest Lawn two or three times. I don't see that sort of thing. This latest is even worse than their Last Supper area. Now they've got the Crucifixion, a whole panorama. Then they open up a gift shop connected with it. That kind of commercialism is a desecration.

"When I first came here, I had to turn my back when a funeral passed, I was that emotional.

Now, I could sit down next to a casket and eat my lunch and it wouldn't bother me. Unless it was someone near and dear, and then my attitude hasn't changed in forty years. But I'm here to serve people who need me, regardless of how I feel. My wife and I both believe in cremation. And no funeral. I think it's a desecration. Rows of mourners lined up looking in the casket—doesn't he look nice, he almost looks alive—nobody looks nice when they're dead.

"I studied as a boy for the Ministry and I was a Sunday School teacher, but I don't go to church anymore. My wife was Episcopalian and I was divorced, so when she married me, she was thrown out of her church. I believe in God, a Supreme Being, but I don't think some native in the far Pacific, who hasn't discovered Christ, is damned. He has a God—maybe the Sun or the Wind or something. I'm not certain I believe in a Life After Death . . . but I'm not certain there isn't one either."

9

"When I die, I want the full treatment. After all, I'm in the business. I can get it wholesale."

A large pink stucco building, fronted with tinted glass. The huge raised letters over the door spell Goldsteins' in script. Inside, elegant draperies, thick carpets, plush sofas and paneled walls. It could be the lobby of a small resort hotel, except for the small prayer books tastefully placed on a corner table. The first page reads: Goldsteins'—A Family Staff for Sympathetic Family Service. There follows, in addition to the prayers, the pictures of eleven members of the "Family" and several pages of copy concerning the impressive facilities including modern lighting, engineered air conditioning, hi-fidelity sound systems and special humidity and temperature controls. Bennett Goldstein, 39, was modishly dressed. Sculptured hair and tinted glasses. We talked in his large paneled office on the walls of which hung framed diplomas of various members of the family.

"Goldsteins' was started by my father and my cousin in 1944. She was a figurehead. It was actually my father and my uncle. They worked for other funeral directors before that. My father

worked for an Italian. They did livery work. I started in '49. I always wanted to be an undertaker, even when I was a kid. I went to Central High, then to Eckles Mortician School. It's closed now. Eckles ran off with his secretary. My uncle and my father are still active, but it's my show now. This place was my idea. I wanted to be the top banana. We are the largest Jewish funeral director in the city, probably the state. We handle about eleven hundred funerals a year. They go all the way from no cost for indigents to as high as $8000. The average is $1200. Our 'season' is from November to March. From the first frost, that's the busiest time for us.

"We're different from the others. We're a family operation. We give family service. We know most of the people we service. Probably ninety-five percent know one or another of us. Many of the other funeral directors are family owned too, but usually they are neighborhood funeral homes. It would be hard to get into a business like this, with an operation this size. You'd have to have a half a million dollars or three quarters of a million to invest before you'd even begin to make anything.

"About ninety percent are embalmed. Only the real Orthodox Jews don't get embalmed. We don't charge extra if someone's been posted [autopsied], but some do. The problem is that when we embalm, we need the neck veins and arteries. But they often cut them and it makes it very difficult. Also, it's usually a young first year Resident. Sometimes, he postpones [the autopsy] until the next day. In the Jewish religion, burial is supposed to be the next day.

"We don't have too many cremations. The trend is to immediate-family viewing, then a closed casket funeral. I think they realize that these open casket viewings for the general public are barbaric. I've had some strange requests. One wanted cremation and the ashes scattered over Valley Forge. Another wanted ashes scattered in the Bahamas. I was going there on a fishing trip, so I took the ashes along. I took care of the Valley Forge request also. The most unusual request came from a woman who refused to attend her father's funeral. Then, a week after the burial, she had the body disinterred, re-embalmed with a special fluid—I don't even know how they did that, I've never heard of a complete embalming—then the body was shipped to the Cryonics Society in Long Island. She had to buy a special capsule for about six or seven thousand dollars. The capsule was placed in liquid nitrogen about 270 degrees below zero. The Perpetual Care was about nine thousand dollars. The whole thing is ridiculous. I don't think there are more than about six or seven frozen bodies in the country.

"You get pretty used to Death in this business. You handle it pretty matter-of-factly unless it's someone you know. My cousin was murdered by her boyfriend last New Year's Eve. That was pretty rough. It's always rough when you're close, no matter how long you're in the business. But you go away every five or six weeks for a few days. Get the place out of your system. Then you come back and you can work.

"I'm scared of Death. I don't think I'm afraid of dying. I always tell my doctor, if there's something the matter with me, don't tell my family, tell me so I have time to put my affairs in order. When I die, I want the full treatment . . . a bronze casket, a sealed vault in the family plot, but only the religious service. After all, I'm in the business. I can get it wholesale. I want to go in style. I'm not very, very religious, but I go to synagogue on the High Holidays and maybe eight or nine Friday nights. I believe in God. And I believe in a Life After Death. Sort of. Well . . . it's a nice thing to believe in."

10

"There are even caterers now who cater the meal at Shiva. And there's laughing and joking. It all lacks dignity."

Rabbi Sheldon Freedman at 33 has been an Orthodox Jewish rabbi for nine years. He is the spiritual leader of Philadelphia's Adath Zion Congregation, a Conservative synagogue. He is also chairman of the Funeral Standards Committee of the Philadelphia Board of Rabbis. Stocky. Modishly long sideburns, conservatively cut hair. A plain dark suit. Coming in from the outside, he replaces his gray straw hat with the traditional black yarmulke. His cluttered study is lined with books.

"Death was always a hang-up with me, perhaps because I lost my father very suddenly when I was eighteen. He was not yet thirty-nine. I've always felt that what a rabbi says is terribly important at the time of a funeral. He can give some sense of meaning to the person's life for those who are still living. But it is a time which is not repeated, so the things which the rabbi does not say, he will not have the opportunity to say again. Often the rabbi did not even know the deceased. He may try to talk to the family, to see what he was like. Or he may just have the basic information—he was sixty-five, he was a father, his children's names and so forth—and he makes up the rest. And then there are burying rabbis who may do six or seven funerals a week. They do a splendid job, but it's usually canned.

"For the first five years or more, I wrote everything down, word for word. Now I don't do that. The eulogy or Hesped is very important in the Jewish tradition. The Jewish funeral is really for the dead not the living, and the Hesped is his right. In fact if the children should request no eulogy, they are to be ignored. Only if the deceased requested no eulogy can there be none. The purpose of the Hesped was to glorify the deceased, but also to make the assembled mourners cry—I don't do that—not to cry too much, but to cry. There were even professional criers—Kononim—hired to mingle with the mourners and to cry during the Hesped. The eulogizer was to be the first to be paid from the estate, before debts, taxes or inheritances.

"The traditional Jewish funeral is a very simple affair. As chairman of the Funeral Standards Committee, I have had to do battle many times with funeral directors. They are very kind, very considerate, very solicitous . . . but very commercial. They are in business to make money. If they embalm, then they can have an open casket, use a cosmetologist, sell an expensive casket. I had one case where the family was told that the law insisted on embalming after twenty-four hours. That's not true. It is required only if the family does not object on religious grounds. In this case the death was on a Tuesday and the funeral could not be for several days and the weather was very warm. But they did it. They can do it when they want to.

"Years ago people would sell their household possessions in order to dress the body in the most magnificent clothes possible, far above what they could afford. Then they would go without food. In fact, that's where the tradition began of having neighbors prepare the food for the mourners. Finally the rabbis decreed that no matter whether a poor man or a king, all should be dressed in a shroud. And the casket should be a plain one. We don't still use a bier which was used in Biblical days. Cremation is not allowed because the Bible says that you shall return to dust in the Earth. Jewish cemeteries are consecrated ground, but there was provision for a Gentile member of a mixed marriage to be buried near the fence.

"The Jewish religion definitely believes in A Life After Death. Some say it is not covered in the Bible, only in the Midrash, but it is alluded to in the Bible, definitely in David's Psalms. The Soul in Jewish tradition—it's not in the Law—rises in stages. The first day, the third, seven days, a month and a year. And it is judged along the way. In fact each day in our prayers, three times a day, there is mention of the Hereafter.

"I've had different people relate unusual experiences. One was an old man in his seventies with a diseased spleen that had to be removed. He was not a well man anyway and the doctors told him he had only a ten percent chance, but the spleen had to be removed. He said all right. Well he survived and when I went to see him he said, Rabbi I've been to the Other Side. I said, what do you mean? And he said, there were some people who kept pulling me and telling me I must go with them, but I refused and said I was not ready to go, that I wanted to live yet awhile, and they let me. He swore that it happened, that he didn't make it up. That was his story.

"Another man, young yet in his forties, had a serious heart attack. He almost didn't make it. He told me that he talked to God and that he told God he was not ready, that he still had much to do, and that God gave him a number of years more. That was his story. He had a complete transformation. Sold his business, grew a beard, moved to Baltimore to a Yashiva. His wife cooks for the Yashiva. His children go to school at the Yashiva. A complete transformation.

"The traditional Jewish funeral is a continuity with the past and is prescribed by Jewish Law. But the commercial aspects have begun to turn it into a party, and I'm against that. There is such guilt on the part of people—why didn't I tell him how much I loved him? Why did I argue with him? Maybe I hastened his death.—So now they decide he will have nothing but the best. An expensive casket, a vault, a huge monument, flowers. Then someone who has attended this funeral has to arrange one for [his] father and naturally they have to show that they loved their father as much as the other people loved theirs. It becomes competitive. There are even caterers now who cater the meal at Shiva. [*Week of mourning in which the family is visited at home by friends and relatives.*] And there's laughing and joking. It all lacks dignity.

"I don't think much about Death. I'm a fatalist. I don't believe I'll live a long life. Perhaps because my father died early, and his father. I am a great believer in an Ethical Will. I have two children—twenty months and five years. From time to time I write them letters and deposit them in sealed envelopes. I want them to know their father, what I believe in, what I would hope of them. It may be that this is a way of extending our lives a little, but I think it means more than that. If I should die now, what would my children know of their father?

"Certainly it's a natural thing, but Death is a tragedy, a calamitous event. I cannot minimize Death. You can adjust to the death of a loved one. You can adapt to the loss of an arm, to the killing of people in a war, to the Hydrogen Bomb . . . but it is no less a tragedy. It is said that scar tissue is the strongest type of skin. Perhaps the scars of Death make us stronger that live."

11

"I believe God gives us a moment of choice . . . to go willingly or unwillingly and when it is my time, I hope to go willingly."

Twelve years ago, when The Right Reverend Monsignor Charles Mynaugh was appointed Director of Radio and Television for the Philadelphia Diocese, the Church of Saint Stephen had a congregation of over 3000 families. Today, in spite of the population increase in the parish, the congregation is down to 800 families and he is their priest. The parish is predominantly black, but the congregation is about half white. Msgr.

Mynaugh is fifty-five. Thin gray hair, aluminum framed glasses, a friendly if not robust face. We chatted at the Rectory on a warm summer afternoon.

"There are really very few prerequisites in a Catholic funeral. We make no great demands. People think of us as stern dictators, scowling and saying you must do this, you must do that. We are in opposition to cremation because it flaunts the Concept of Resurrection. It says: I do not believe in the Resurrection and to prove it I will have my body cremated and scatter the ashes. Well that's wrong. But I'm sure that there are other areas of the world where Catholics are cremated. In Europe in some places, there is no more room. As for suicide, there's no problem to be buried in a Catholic cemetery. We just don't make a public thing of it, a public ceremony. I've had some over the years and the families are quite thankful not to have a public ceremony. We cannot grant a Christian burial to someone who has been in public scandal. If I should run off with someone, that would be a scandal, and we would not wish to appear to sanction such an act. As for autopsy, embalming, viewings, wakes . . . this is all custom. The Church has nothing particular to say about these things.

"I was fortunate to have been chaplain at an Old Age Home for three and a half years—Sacred Heart—and there were 180 people from about sixty to a hundred years old. Most were well and lived happily. Some were senile and some were sick. I helped many to face Death. I would say it was split down the middle between those who looked forward to Death and those who feared it. I would tell them that the end of their life on this Earth was nearly at hand, but that it was God's Will. I told them to think of the many good things they had accomplished in their lives. Not to dwell on the weaknesses and the mistakes. We all have them, and God had already forgiven them since we had administered the Sacraments. That God was a loving and merciful God. It was almost always of help.

"We service Temple University Hospital and do the same thing. Of course there are so many more—about half the patients are Catholic—and we don't get to know them in the same way. We try not to make it mechanical, although sometimes it turns out that way. Sometimes the family requests that we come. It's funny though, they always tell me to just make believe I dropped in, so the patient won't be upset. I tell them that's ridiculous. If I'm to deliver the Sacraments, I can't have just dropped in, after all. Most of the patients are glad to see me. Damn glad!

"This business of Last Rites. We used to call it Extreme Unction. Then it was called Last Rites. I don't know where that came from. Now we call it the Sacrament of the Sick. Yet the prayers have always been the same, they've never changed. We ask for forgiveness, but we ask for the patient to be cured. We annoint the Oil of the Sick to the five senses—eyes, ears, nose, mouth, hands and feet if possible—to help them get better! But you still have nurses who ask if you've delivered Last Rites.

"Once I had a patient I had seen several times. Finally the family asked me to come to deliver the Sacraments. When I entered the room there must have been a dozen people around the bed. The doctor asked me to wait a little bit, so I stood against the wall. A head nurse came in and, seeing me, said that they didn't want the patient to be disturbed or to worry. I pointed to the crowd and said if that didn't disturb the patient, I certainly wouldn't. I think people who are dying are receptive to me, but I wouldn't describe their participation as active. It's a wonderful thing to be able to help in such a time. It's a very Christian thing.

"We say that as long as there is organic life, the Sacraments should be given. But if I deliver the Sacraments to someone [who] has been dead for an hour or so, I have a hang-up on the part about praying for cure and annointing with oil. I skip it and shorten the prayers. It's mostly for the peace of mind of the survivors anyway. I pray for the soul of course, but the rest is of no help to the person who is dead. Some people wait to be baptized until they know they are ready to die. They know about the innocence of one who has just been baptized, so they're afraid to [be] baptized too early. They don't use it as license, of course.

"Most of the concepts and laws come from the Judaic Laws. Especially the hygienic ones—the quick Jewish burial—it gets hot in the Middle East, you know. As for the eulogy, that's a regional thing. There was a statute in this diocese against eulogizing. I guess one could get carried away and practically canonize someone. The Homily is supposed to use the themes from the readings of the Scriptures and to apply them to everyday life. The Homily is like a eulogy and is a definite part of the service, but if someone asked me to omit it, I would.

"I find the whole idea of Cryonics, of freezing and preserving bodies, abhorrent. But I do sympathize with the idea of Death with dignity. I think that once there is no longer hope, life should not be prolonged. I've had arguments with doctors over this keeping of patients 'alive.' They keep the body going, but what about the person? I've seen some of the apparatus in the Intensive Care Unit—pumps to pump blood, pumps to pump air—these contraptions. For what? I tell them if there's no hope, to stop. I see no ethical or moral difference between not connecting the plug and disconnecting the plug. No difference.

"I come from a large family. There were nine of us. I'm the youngest. I was present when my mother died. She was ninety-seven. And when my brother died. He was next to youngest. I did not feel differently about helping them than anyone else, because I feel so strongly. I would like to think that a Catholic is better prepared to accept Death. The security the Church offers, the special relationship that a priest has with his parishioners. It's a wonderful and Christian thing.

"I think a lot about Death, not just since my brother died, but for the last five to seven years. I wouldn't say I'm totally without fear. It still is a mystery, you know. I have this concept of the Spirit of Choice. I believe God gives us a moment of choice . . . to go willingly or unwillingly. And when it is my time, I hope to go willingly. As long as I try to make the right choices day by day, then I hope to make the right choice when it's time to die. If I still have work to do here, that's God's problem isn't it? He makes the decision."

12

"He said: Do you believe in Me? And I said: No. I don't know how many times He said that to me. . . . Finally on the tenth day He said: Do you believe in Me? And I said: Yes, I believe in You.

And I woke up. They hadn't expected me to pull through, but I did."

Charlotte Jasper is an attractive forty, deeply tanned with blue eyes and a shag haircut with blond streaks. With the exception of her right arm which is somewhat distorted with lumps from the wrist to the elbow, it would be difficult to know that she was sick. Upstairs in the front bedroom of the Jasper home, a nicely furnished half-a-double in a neat residential area, is a kidney machine that keeps her alive. Charlotte has been very near Death twice during her ten year bout with an incurable kidney disease. On both occasions, she saw God. And God saved her.

"It started with a strep throat and the infection went to my kidneys. It doesn't always do that, sometimes it goes to the heart. Or it can just clear up. I was pretty bad. I didn't even know what Nephritis was, never heard of it. The kidneys can't get rid of the poisons. The kidney functions like a filter, only mine didn't work and my body filled up with fluids. My blood was full of poison.

"My husband went everywhere trying to get me on a machine. He went to anybody and everybody. I felt even worse for him than I did for myself. He tried so hard. The machine was very expensive. At that time, there were only two in the city. They cost as much as twenty or thirty thousand dollars. Everywhere he went, he struck out. Meanwhile I was really sick. They tried different things. Put a hole in my stomach to drain it that way, but that was no good. How many holes can you put in your stomach? Then they put—a loop it was called—a loop in my stomach. I felt awful with that, itchy and wet where the pads were on my stomach, like I was a baby in diapers. Every night I had to mix this solution and have it enter my stomach through one tube and come out the other. I was up half the night . . . all night, actually. I think if I'd of had to have that loop my whole life, I couldn't have taken it.

"Well I was really bad. The doctor told my husband I had about a month to live. He works for Food Fair, so he went to them for help. That was strange too. He says it wasn't his words that came out of his mouth. He didn't know where they came from, it was like a record. The big executives there had to decide. Then one day, for no reason, he was transferred to manage another store. Next door was a bowling alley owned by one of the Friedlands. They own Food Fair. He didn't have anything to do with Food Fair directly, though. He came into the store one day and Marty told him about me. What a marvelous, marvelous man! He called Lou Stein who was president. Mr. Stein told him they were considering the matter and Morris Friedland said: Who do you think you are? God? So they did it. I still don't know how much was involved, but it was a wonderful thing. Like a miracle.

"I was so bad, I went into a coma. I was in the coma for ten days. That was when it happened the first time. I saw God. His face was like the sun. You know how they draw the sun with the points around it to denote the rays? Well His face was the sun. I don't know about the body. It may have been a woman's body, like a nurse. But it didn't make any difference about the body. And the face didn't matter much either. I always thought God didn't want you to see His face anyway. But I remember His voice vividly. It was a nice, clear, man's voice. Not a booming one like in the movies. He said: Do you believe in Me? And I said: No. I don't know how many times he said that to me. Each time I said no. For a long time before I went into coma, I kept saying: What did I ever do that You should do this to me? I guess that's why I kept saying no.

"Finally on the tenth day He said: Do you believe in Me? And I said: Yes, I believe in You. And I woke up. They hadn't expected me to pull through, but I did. It was very vivid at the time. I remember I was very awed that I had spoken with Him and He had helped me. Now as time goes by, I'm less sure because I ask myself what did I ever do to deserve such treatment? Why should God treat me like I'm special. I haven't done anything for anybody. People all do things for me! Yet I know it was Him and I know He did it all for me. But I don't know why.

"Then last year, I had pneumonia and I was pretty sick. No, that was two years ago. I didn't go into coma, but I was pretty bad. A man on the machine in the hospital also had pneumonia. I may have caught it from him because we were on the machine together, side by side. Well he died and I didn't. I was so sick I didn't care if I lived or died, but I lived. And he died. Why?

"Last year I developed Bronchitis. They gave me codeine to stop the cough. We didn't know at the time, but my body couldn't get rid of the drug and it was building up in me. I was always groggy. When they couldn't give it to me orally, I got a needle. Then I went into coma again for three days. That's when I had the second dream. I felt I was already dead. In fact, I could look up and see the lid of the coffin. Then . . . it had to do with the sun . . . I was behind it but it wasn't hot. You know how you're supposed to burn up if you get near the sun. But it was cool.

"God was talking to some people there. He was dressed in white like a doctor. He was discussing me. I couldn't hear everything. This was less vivid than the first time. He was saying: What shall we do with her? Shall we send her back? Then He said: I think we'll send her back. And I came back, real fast-like. And I woke up. And I was better. I was still pretty sick, but I got better and here I am. I talk about it, but not to just anyone. You have to be interested. I mean it was a very real experience, and I don't want people poking fun at me.

"My parents came over from the Old Country —Russia. My father was learned in the Talmud. He was like a mayor in his little village in Russia, because of his learning and all. But he didn't go to synagogue much. My mother bought kosher food, but we didn't keep two sets of dishes. My husband is more religious. He has a lot of Faith. His father wanted me to keep kosher, so I do, but we don't go to synagogue often. I get fidgity now if I sit for a long time.

"I was always afraid of Death. I believed in God because I was afraid not to believe in God. But I always felt you could only be special to God if you had a lot of Faith and I never did. That's why it's all so strange. I mean, first I said what did I ever do to deserve this sickness. Then I said what did I ever do to deserve this special treatment. I'm no longer afraid of God. I love God. When I light the candles on Friday nights and I say all the prayers, then I tell God that I hope that He has a good week. I mean, He does so much for us, that's the least we can do for Him. I know there is a God. There must be. Look around you. If we were built like a rock, then maybe you could say different. But when I look at someone and see how their eyes work and their hands and their bodies . . . it's such a miracle. It has to be God's work.

"I have these five girls who come in. They're terrific! You ought to interview them, they're a scream. Five psychiatrists. I go on the machine every third day. We get up at five in the morning and my husband puts me on before he goes to work. There are two tubes with needles that have to go in my arm. One carries the blood to the machine to be cleaned and the other carries it back. That's another thing, I have such big veins. I'm lucky. Some people have a lot of trouble, but I don't. They made a fistula here under the skin. Tied the vein and artery together. It takes six hours and the girls sit with me and joke. Afterwards, I'm really drained and tired. I like to be alone then, because I haven't the strength to do anything. I lose five or six pounds in that six hours. It knocks you out. The next day, though, I'm completely different. I feel terrific!"

Charlotte showed me the machine. "We don't have normal vacations. We can only go away for a day or two, then I have to go back to the machine. There's a real story there, about the trouble people have had to get a machine. Now they have production lines, so it's a little easier. This one costs about $5000, but there are smaller ones now that are more portable. In the beginning it was really terrible. We spent everything we had, even borrowed on the house. Finally I had to go to my neighbor. We didn't want to, but we were down to the bottom. She was wonderful. She said don't worry about a thing. They started a Charlotte Jasper Fund to pay some of the bills. We still owe the hospital about $6000. The Fund has a little bit left in it and they're paying off the hospital slowly. It's an expensive proposition. Without money, people just have to die.

"That machine keeps me alive, I would die without it so I have nothing against it. But that's because I have a family to take care of. If I was young and single, I don't think my attitude would be the same. Some say they'd rather die. I've seen kids on the machine. It's terrible. What have they to look forward to? The longest anyone has been on the machine is eleven and a half years, but that's because that's how old the kidney machine is.

"Lately I've been thinking about transplants. The kidney seems to be the easiest to transplant, but the rejection is the problem. My husband says that when the time is right, we'll know it. He has so much Faith. I'm still afraid of Death. I mean, you don't know what it's like. I mean, can you see when you're in the coffin or what? But I'm not afraid of God. I just don't know why I was so special. I never did anything for anybody."

ON DEATH AND DYING*

Elisabeth Kübler-Ross

I was asked this morning why this topic on death and dying has taken such a long time to come into public awareness. Dying and dignity have been with us for as long as there has been mankind. Why is it now that we have to give seminars and workshops on death and dying? Has it taken us all these decades to begin to be aware that we are finite and that we have to treat dying patients?

PSYCHIATRIC BASIS

I believe I shall talk like a psychiatrist for about five minutes and try to explain what death means and what the fear of death really represents. In terms of the unconscious, we cannot conceive of our own death. This is very important to understand. I believe that it shall happen to everybody in this room, but not to me. If I am forced to conceive of my own death, then I can only conceive of it as a malignant intervention from the outside. I cannot possibly conceive of dying of old age at home in my own bed. If I have to die, in my unconscious, I can only conceive of it as being killed. I am not afraid of death per se, but rather the destructive catastrophic death that hits me from the outside when I am not prepared. Perhaps the most complicated thing to understand is that I cannot differentiate between the wish and the deed. In the Bible it says somewhere that to lust after your neighbor's wife is as bad as actually doing it. In terms of my reality, testing

* Edited from a presentation made to a group of physicians.

this is actually absurd. I can have all sorts of fantasies of what I would like to do, but as long as I don't do it, that is satisfactory. In terms of my unconscious that is not acceptable. If you understand this, then you can see what is relevant and what is important to understand, especially in the death of a parent of a young child.

Little children have a peculiar concept of death. They regard death not as a permanent happening, but as a temporary happening. Every normal 4- or 5-year-old child who is angry at mommy wishes mommy to drop dead. That is very normal behavior. Children think of it when they are angry, when they feel small and impotent and helpless, and they wish mommy would drop dead only to make her get up again when they are hungry and they want a peanut butter-and-jelly sandwich. The trouble is that the little 4- or 5-year-old boy may really lose his mother by death, separation, or divorce. He then feels that he has actually contributed to her death. This thinking shows that he cannot yet differentiate between his wish to kill mommy and whether he has actually done it. If we understand this, then we appreciate many of the complications of dying patients who sometimes, decades later in their old age, moan and groan and cry and have a lot of somatic complaints which we cannot understand medically. When we talk to these people, we see that they have a peculiar sense of guilt; they feel that they have committed a crime and they have to be punished before they die. These patients suffer far beyond our medical understanding.

OUR DEATH-DENYING SOCIETY

Why is dying different now? People have the same kind of unconscious thoughts and fantasies that they had years ago. What has changed, I think, is our society, which has become increasingly a death-denying society. Half of our patients now die in hospitals, as compared to 50 years ago when people died at home in a familiar environment with a little bit of chicken soup instead of transfusions, with their families around them instead of interns, residents, and laboratory technicians. People who are dying in a hospital are attached to several pieces of monitoring equipment and we, as physicians, pay a lot of attention to these gadgets. Sometimes we feel very uncomfortable when a dying patient looks at us and would like to ask a question in regard to dying or to some unfinished business or to fears and fantasies. In Switzerland, where I am originally from, there is no embalming. They do not have drive-in funeral homes such as we are beginning to have in the United States where you drive up in your sports car, look through a glass window, sign a guest book, and take off. All of this is an attempt to deny that people die. We have a society where we deep freeze people and promise at high cost to defrost them in 50 or 100 years. We have had questions from widows about whether they are eligible for social security, or if they are allowed to get married again. In this sense, people use denial that their next of kin are really dead.

Joseph Matthews has provided a beautiful description of the death-denying society and if you will bear with me I will read just one page to give you an even better description of what I mean by a death-denying society:

To symbolize the dignity of the father's death the family decided to clothe the father in a pine box and rest him in the raw earth. Having been told that caskets ranged from one hundred to several thousand dollars, they asked for the one hundred-dollar coffin.
"What $100.00 coffin?" replied the astonished undertaker.
"Why, the one you mentioned."
"Oh no, caskets begin at $275.00."
"Did you not mention a $100.00 coffin?"

The persistent wishes of the family were met and the pine box was selected. Later Matthews describes his experience after his father had been prepared by the undertaker:

My father was 92. In his last few years he had wonderfully put chiseled wrinkles. I had helped to put them there. His cheeks were deeply sunken, his lips pale: he was an old man. There is a kind of glory in the face of an old man, but not so with the stranger lying there. They had my papa looking like he was 52. They had put cotton in his cheeks and had erased the best wrinkles. His lips were painted. He looked ready to step before the footlights of a matinee performance. I fiercely wanted to pluck out the

cotton, but was afraid. At least the make-up could come off. I called for alcohol and linens and a very reluctant mortician brought them to me. I began the restoration. As the make-up disappeared, the stranger grew older. He never recovered the looks of his 92 years, but in the end the man in the coffin became my papa.

Later he describes his experience at the cemetery:

I say I smelled that fresh earth, but there was none to be seen. What I did see was difficult to believe. I mean that green stuff. Someone had come before us and covered that good raw earth, every part of it, with green stuff. Every scar of the grave was concealed under simulated grass just as if nothing had been disturbed here—just as if nothing was going on here, just as if nothing were happening. What an offense against nature, against history, against papa, against us, against God.

It goes on, but I shall stop here. You have to ask yourself why we have to conceal the grave, why we have to cover up that good earth with artificial greens, why we have to pretend that nothing is happening. You must understand that the fear of death is the fear of a catastrophic happening, a catastrophic destructive force that destroys us from the outside.

Then we also have to look at death in the past and death in the present. In the old days death also came as a catastrophic happening in the form of epidemics. It erased populations of whole villages, but it was not man-made. In times of war you faced your enemy face-to-face and had a chance to kill rather than to be killed. These things have changed. In the past, epidemic disease was the killer; now we have developed antibiotics, vaccines, all sorts of things that can master the old types of death. In our fear of death we have also created weapons of mass destruction. We now have weapons that you cannot defend yourself against physically. We cannot see, smell, or hear an enemy and I am thinking of chemical warfare, bacteriological warfare, and means of mass destruction, all of which are man-made. We are afraid, we are guilty, and still hope "it shall happen to thee and to thee but not to me!" I think this is the reason why this society, especially at this time, is using such a mass denial. We live in the illusion that, since we have mastered so many things, we shall be able to master death too.

PHYSICIANS' REACTIONS TO DYING PATIENTS

How does this affect you as physicians? How does this affect our patients? I had a glimpse of this 4½ years ago through a chance happening. Some theology students knocked at my door and asked me if I would help them to write a paper on a crisis in human life. Several had chosen dying as the biggest crisis man had to face, but they were stuck. They did not know how to do research on dying. You cannot experience it, you cannot verify it. I suggested that one way that you could really collect some data and understand it was by getting close to dying patients and asking them to be our teachers. I had a similar experience some years earlier when I tried to understand what it is like to be schizophrenic. I spent two years in the state hospital where I sat with schizophrenic patients and asked them what is it like, how did it start, what are the changes, what does it feel like, until I had the feeling that I really knew what it was like to be a schizophrenic from the patient's point of view. Because I had this good learning experience, I recommended the same kind of methods to my theology students.

I promised them that I would interview dying patients, and that as they would become more comfortable during the interviews, I would drop out and let them continue the dialogue until they had enough data. A week later, after asking numerous people, there was not a single dying patient in that 600-bed hospital! There was just nobody dying. When I pushed, I was given all sorts of rationalizations. These patients were too sick, too weak, too tired, or "they don't feel like talking." Occasionally I was told that if I talked to patients about dying they would jump out the window. It was extremely difficult during the first year. It took an average of ten hours a week to get permission to see a single terminally ill patient. In all fairness I must say that I was new at the University of Chicago, and so the physicians had no assurance that I would not cause trauma or that I would be tactful. But this same kind of resistance I have also seen in Colorado; it was not associated with the University of Chicago alone. When we finally obtained permission to see a patient, he was an old man who was ready to talk. He put his arms out and said please sit down *now*. I told him, "No, not now," because my students were not with me. My needs as a teacher prevented me from seeing his needs. I described to the students the next day his outstretched arms, his pleading eyes, how he emphasized the *now*. The next day when I came with the students he was in oxygen, he could hardly talk, and the only thing he was able to say was, "thank you for trying anyway." He died about half an hour later. This was our first and most difficult patient, because of our own feelings, which prevented us from really listening to his needs.

We decided we would meet in my office and talk to each other about what we called our "gut reaction"—how we really felt about this type of work, about seeing these kinds of patients, and about the reception we would get from the patients. One of the students, who was as white as a bed sheet, said, "Oh, I'm not afraid of death," and the other students questioned him as to why he was so pale. They wanted to know why he was the only one who denied his fear. He said that he had been the hospital student chaplain in a state hospital the year before and that he had been assigned to a ward where a patient was dying. He had walked into the ward and said (I am quoting him almost verbatim now): "I yelled at the peak of my voice, 'God is love, God is love' until the patient dropped dead." This was his proof that he was not afraid! I told him that when I was a little girl in Switzerland, I had to go down to the wine cellar to get a bottle of wine and the darker the cellar became, the louder I yodelled. That experience reminded me of him.

What I am trying to say is that after each patient interview, we tried not only to listen to the patient, but also to ourselves, to our own reactions; we tried to get to know ourselves better. In these after-interview discussions, we analyzed how we really reacted—when we had some tender thoughts, and when we had some difficulties. We also learned to become more sensitive, not only to the patients, but to ourselves and to our own needs. Dr. Wall described beautifully in his book on the dying patient how a social worker was faced for the first time with a dying patient and what her reactions were. He said every time she entered the patient's room, she felt strong feelings of guilt.

She was going to live, while he, of her own age, was going to die. She knew he wanted to talk to her, but she always turned the talk into a little joke or into some evasive reassurance, which had to fail. The patient knew and she knew because he saw her desperate attempts to escape; he took pity on her and kept to himself what he wanted to share with another human being. So he died and did not bother her.

We have interviewed more than 400 patients during the last four years. We have seen many times that patients want to talk and that they would very much like to share their thoughts with another human being. It is very difficult sometimes to try to do that. When we come in, we tell them that we would like them to be our teacher, that we would like to know what it is like to be very sick, and sometimes we use the word dying. Many of our patients respond like we are opening flood gates. They share with us things that we were never aware of.

I think the most important thing that we have learned, and I am summarizing a bit now, is that all our patients know when they are terminally ill, whether they have been told or not. To me this is a very consoling thought. They not only know when they are seriously ill, but patients can even tell you the approximate day of their death, right up to their actual demise. They will tell you goodbye and you know this is the last time you will see them. This is also true for children. We asked our patients the question that we are most often asked, and that is, would the patient have liked to be told. Two-fifths of our patients had never been told, although they knew it anyway after a while. Our patients usually told us that they would like to be told if it is serious, but not without hope. Hope for the healthy and the living is a very different thing. We tend to forget that sometimes. Hope for the living is always associated with cure, treatment, and, if that is not possible, a prolongation of life and perhaps relief of pain and suffering. When a patient says to you, "I hope the research laboratories work on a new

drug and I am the first one to get it and by some miracle I am going to walk out of this hospital," that is hope prior to the final stage. When the same patient then, suddenly, a few days later, looks at you and says, "I hope my children are going to make it," then you know that this patient has changed to the kind of hopes that dying patients express, which are very reasonable, very appropriate, and not unrealistic. It is not wise at this point to tell them, "Oh, come on now, you are going to make it, you are going to get well." I think at this point we should support them, encourage them, and reinforce the hope that the patient expresses.

STAGES BETWEEN AWARENESS OF SERIOUS ILLNESS AND DEATH

Patients go through five stages between their awareness of serious illness and their death, if they have a minimal amount of time available.

Stage 1 (Denial)
Most patients respond with shock and denial when they are told that they have a serious illness. This may last from a few seconds to a few months. Most of the patients we interviewed had dropped their denial; only three, less than 1% maintained it to the very end. Patients begin to see, when they are seriously ill, that the family comes in and does not know what to talk about and becomes estranged. Someone may come in with a red face and smile. Others may change their conversation a bit; they may talk more about a triviality because of their discomfort. Patients accept quickly that things are not at all perfect.

Stage 2 (Anger)
When the patient cannot maintain his denial anymore, he will become difficult, nasty, demanding, criticizing; that is the common stage of anger. How do you respond to one who complains and criticizes everything you do? You may tend to withdraw and not deal with him anymore. What else can you do? You can avoid him, you can stick the needle in a bit farther—not consciously—but when you are angry you touch patients differently. We can measure some of these responses.

In California some investigators measured the response time between patients ringing for the nurse and the nurse actually coming into the room. They showed that patients beyond medical help, terminally ill patients, had to wait twice as long as other patients for the nurse to respond. This behavior should not be judged; it should be understood. It is very difficult to remember that members of the helping professions, who work hard all day, may have a difficult job coming into the dying patient's room. In the first place, the professional is uncomfortable; second, she is worried that the patient may ask how long he has to live or all sorts of unpleasant questions, and then, if the nurse does something for the patient, he may begin to criticize her. The nurse comes in and shakes the pillow, and the patient says, "I just wanted to take a nap, can't you leave me alone." When you don't shake the pillow, the patient remarks, "Why can't you ever straighten up my bed?" Whatever you do is criticized. Such patients are very difficult to manage and the families suffer tremendously because, when they come in and visit, they are always too early, too late, or there are not enough people, or too many people. Someone has to do something for these patients, to facilitate life for everybody concerned. It is important to understand that these patients are not angry with the nurse or the family. The more vibrant the nurse is when she comes into the patient's room, the more energetic she is, the more she is going to get through to the dying patient. In a way she should be able to accept the anger as a compliment, because what the nurse reminds the patient of is functioning health, ability to go to work, to go for a coffee break, all those things that the patient is about to lose. Because the nurse reminds the patient of all these things, and because he is desperately attempting to deny that he is dying, he becomes angry and says in effect, "Why me?" But he is also asking, "Why couldn't this happen to Joe Blow or somebody else?" If the nurse can put fuel into the fire, if she can help him to express this anger, if she can permit him to ask the question, "Why me?" without the need to answer it, then she will have a much more comfortable patient almost immediately. We interviewed a young patient who was dying. She was in my office and

looked completely numb and I asked her if she felt like screaming. She looked as if she were on the verge of an explosion. She asked if we had screaming rooms in hospitals. I said no, we had chapels. "No, this is wrong," she said, "because in chapels we have to pray and be quiet and I need just to do the opposite. I was sitting out in the car yelling at God and asking him, 'Why did you let this happen to me?'" I encouraged her to express this in my office and to cry on my shoulders. They never scream as loud as they think they will.

If you can help patients express the question, "Why me?" you can help them express their rage and anger; then your patients become more comfortable and ring for the nurse less often and stop nagging and complaining. Sometimes they even quickly become much more comfortable patients and we wonder what has happened to them.

Stage 3 (Bargaining)

That is often when they reach the stage of bargaining. In the bargaining they may pray for another year to live; they would donate their kidneys or their eyes, or they may become very good people and go to church every Sunday. They usually promise something in exchange for extension of life. Some of the promises are not made to God, but to someone on the hospital staff. We had a woman who asked to be relieved of some of her tremendous pain for one day so that she would not be dependent on injections around the clock. She said she would just love to go home one more day and the reason for this was that her favorite son was getting married. We tried everything, and finally we were able to teach her self-hypnosis to relieve her pain. She left the hospital and looked like a million dollars. She attended her son's wedding. I was curious about patients who only ask for one single day; how do they react when their bargaining time is up? It must be extremely difficult. I waited for her, she saw me in the hallway and she was not happy to see me at all. Before I could ask her a question, she said, "Dr. Ross, don't forget, I have another son." This is the most typical part of bargaining. Promises are never kept; patients say, "If I could live just long enough for my children to go through high school," and then they add college, and then they add I just want a son-in-law, and then they would like to have a grandchild, and it goes on and on.

Stage 4 (Depression)

If, in the denial stage, they say "No, not me," then in the anger stage they say, "Why me," and in the bargaining stage they say, "Yes me, but." When they drop the "but," it is, "Yes me." Then the patient becomes very depressed.

There are two kinds of depression and it is important to understand the two different kinds. The first type is a reactive depression in which the patient cries when he talks about it, and mourns the losses which he has experienced. Later on he becomes quiet and depressed. When you enter his room, you see a man crying and he doesn't say what he is crying about. It is very difficult to accept such behavior over a long period of time. What does the physician do when he enters the room of a patient who is crying, especially if it is a man? This is one area in which men have a much more difficult time than women. The physician may be quiet. Many physicians go into the room and give the patient a pat on the back and say, "Come on, it is not so bad." We try to cheer them up because, as physicians, we cannot tolerate crying patients very well. The reason our tolerance is low is not because of the patient; it is rather because of our own inability to tolerate depressed patients over a long time. Sometimes we request a psychiatric consultant, which is not appreciated by most patients. It is an inappropriate request because the patient's response represents normal, not abnormal behavior.

If I were to lose one beloved person, I would be allowed to mourn and everyone here would respect that as being socially acceptable. But who has the courage to face not only the loss of one person, but the loss of everybody he has ever loved? It is a thousand times more sad, and takes much more courage to face. What we should be trying to do is to tell our patients that it takes a man to cry and that we mean it completely and willfully. We should help them express their grief, which, in fact, is a preparatory grief. It is not mourning and grieving over things lost; rather, it is a grieving and mourning over impending loss. The patient is beginning to separate himself from the people that he has to leave in the near future. This is what we call preparatory grief.

Stage 5 (Acceptance)

If the physician can help his patient through a preparatory grief, the patients will ask once more to see the relatives, then the children, and at the very end, only one beloved person, who is usually husband or wife and, in the case of children, naturally, the parents. This is what we call . . . decathexis, when the patient begins to separate; when he begins to feel no longer like talking; when he has finished all his unfinished business; when he just wants the companionship of a person who is comfortable, who can sit and hold his hand. It is much more important than words in this final stage. If the physician can help the patient express his rage and his depression and assist him sincerely through the stage of bargaining, then most patients will be able to reach the stage of acceptance. It is not resignation—there is a big difference. Resignation, I think, is a bit like giving up. It is almost a defeat. A stage of acceptance is almost beyond any affect. It is the patient who has said, "My time comes very close now and it is all right."

A woman who was always hoping for a miracle drug that would cure her suddenly looked with an almost beaming face and said, "You know, Dr. Ross, a miracle has happened." I said, "What miracle?" and she replied, "The miracle that I am ready to go now and it is not any longer frightening." This is the stage of acceptance. It is not happy; the time is rarely ever right. People almost always want to live, but they can be ready for death and they are not petrified anymore. They have been able to finish their business.

Even children, depending on age, can show these stages, but to much less of an extent than adults. Very small children are only afraid of separation. They have no real concept of death yet. When they are a bit older, the added fear is one of mutilation. Later on they see death as a man whom they run from at night—a bad man; they want the lights on at night, as they are afraid of darkness. Later on they realize that death is not a temporary but a permanent happening. They begin to see it after the age of 9 years or so as a biological force, almost like grown ups. Sometimes children talk about death and dying, too—not in words, but in pictures. A little boy tried to paint what he felt like. He drew a huge tank and in front of the barrel was a tiny, little figure with a stop sign in his hand. This to me represents the fear of death, the fear of the catastrophic, destructive force that comes upon you and you cannot do anything about it. If you can respond to him by saying it must be terrible to feel so tiny and this thing is so big, he may be able to verbally express a sense of smallness or impotence or rage. The next picture he drew was a beautiful bird flying up in the sky. A little bit of its upper wing was painted gold. When he was asked what this was, the boy said it was the peace bird flying up in the sky with a little bit of sunshine on its wing. It was the last picture he painted before he died. I think these are picture expressions of a stage of anger and the final stage of acceptance.

COMMENT

A PHYSICIAN: *I wonder if I could urge you to tell a story that you told yesterday afternoon concerning the reaction of the nurse in encouraging patients to achieve a state of acceptance of death.*

DR. ROSS: *Many people wonder whether all patients should die in a state of acceptance. Somebody once asked me that, and I said you try to elicit the patient's needs. One nurse in the audience arose very angrily. "I have been angry and a rebel all my life and I hope I can die that way." My answer to her was, "I hope they let you die that way and not sedated to keep you 'nice, quiet, and peaceful.'" It is very important to remember that the patients who have used denial all their lives may want denial and may die in a stage of denial. We should not project our own values onto the patient. The "stages of dying" affect not only terminally ill patients. You can apply these lessons to everyday living.*

If a man loses a girlfriend, he may deny it at first; then he becomes angry at the other suitor. Then he sends her some flowers to bargain, and if he cannot get what he wants, he becomes depressed. Eventually, he reaches the stage of acceptance, when he finds another girlfriend.

A PHYSICIAN: *Were there any differences between the patients who were told by their physi-cians about their fatal illnesses as opposed to those who were not? What guidelines would you recommend to physicians in determining whether the patient should be told or not?*

DR. ROSS: *I could tell after a while whose physician the patient was by the degree of comfort experienced by the patient. I did not even have to ask anymore. I do not believe the variable is whether or not they have been told. The variable is how comfortable the physician is in facing the dying patient. We had, at our institution, one surgeon who was particularly effective in this area. I think that he conveyed to them verbally or nonverbally the belief that he would stay with them until the end. The patients were able to pick this up. It is something that is more important than anything else. It is a conviction that the doctor is going to stick it out no matter what. He always did that. The patients knew that, even though there was no more possible surgery or medical treatment, he would still come to see them and care for them. Those patients had it much easier. In fact, we hardly ever got referrals. We sometimes went to see them because we needed some "good patients" who were not troubled all the time. I am in favor of telling patients that they have a serious illness because patients accept that almost without exception, as long as you always allow for some hope.*

A PHYSICIAN: *What advice do you have for the families of patients who are dying?*

DR. ROSS: *That is only difficult if the patient or the family lags behind in the stages. We have patients who have already separated themselves from their relatives. In fact, we have a patient now at the hospital who is waiting to die. His family has stopped visiting him. The nurses are terribly upset because the wife called up and said that if her husband died, they should not bother calling during the night. She would call in the morning to check. This family has already separated itself and yet the husband is still alive and very lonely. When I went to see him, he expressed a lot of grief and asked if I would pray that it would soon be over. There is nothing much that he wants to do. It is more often true that the patient has reached a stage of acceptance and the family has not. That is the time when the family begins to run around and beg you for life-prolonging procedures. We have had one difficult case where a woman was ready to die. She had accepted it and was only concerned that her hus-*

band could not accept it. The husband was busy arranging for additional surgery, which was scheduled for the following Monday. The patient could not tolerate the thought of an additional procedure. She became very anxious and uncomfortable prior to surgery. She demanded twice as much medication for pain and finally, in the room outside of the operating room where she was prepared, she had an acute psychotic episode and became paranoid and screamed, "They are going to kill me, they are going to kill me." In her psychotic state she kept saying, "Talk to that man, talk to that man." When I talked with her husband and tried to explain what had happened, he said that he would rather have as a last memory his beautiful, dignified, wonderful wife than know that she was dying a psychotic woman. When he was able to convey to her that he had accepted and acknowledged the fact that she was terminally ill and the surgery was permanently cancelled, she soon became nonpsychotic. She lived for about one week and she even went home one more time to help her husband turn the clock back a little bit.

We have had three instances so far where patients used psychotic defenses against artificial and extraordinary life-prolonging procedures. We have had some very traumatic cases where husband and wife could not reach the same stage at the same time. I think a golden rule for us as physicians is to know enough to stop the extraordinary measures when a patient has reached the stage of acceptance. When the patient has come that far, then I think many of us know that such interference is no longer therapeutic, and may only gratify our own needs.

A PHYSICIAN: *Do you ever tell a patient he is dying?*

DR. ROSS: *You never tell a patient he is dying; never. You don't have to—you just tell him that he has a serious illness. You say, "It looks pretty grim," or "It looks pretty bad." Then you wait for and answer his next questions. He may ask you, "Is it going to be painful?" "Am I going to be alone?" "How long is this going to last?" You say you dont know, because the worst thing that we have experienced is people who tell time, for example, people who figure on six months, which is not correct anyway.*

A PHYSICIAN: *Have you noticed whether or not the patient's religious orientation has affected his view toward resignation in the end?*

DR. ROSS: *Not resignation but acceptance! I have a peculiar patient population, or at least I*
tend to think so. I have very few really religious people. The few I have—and I mean those with a deep intrinsic faith—have it much easier, but they are extremely few. I have an even smaller number of real atheists who believe nothing, and they have it rather easy too. About 95% are somewhere in between. They are struggling at the end very desperately, but they would like to have the rock of Gibraltar and they only have a straw; they would like to enlarge that and get more faith, but it is somewhat too late. Many patients become more religious in the end, but it is not really effective.

SUMMARY

Psychiatrically it is extremely important to appreciate that, in terms of the unconscious, we cannot conceive of our own death and that, in addition, we cannot differentiate between the wish and the deed. Although people today have the same kind of unconscious thoughts and fantasies about death that other persons had years ago, our society has changed and has become increasingly a death-denying society. We live today in the illusion that, since we have mastered so many things, we shall be able to master death too.

Certain generalizations based on interviewing more than 400 dying patients in the past four years can be stated. All patients know when they are terminally ill, whether they have been told or not. Patients usually state that they would like to be told if it is serious, but not without hope.

Most, but not all, patients pass through five stages (denial, anger, bargaining, depression, and acceptance) between their awareness of serious illness and their death, when they are faced with a potentially fatal illness. The knowledgeable physician, particularly one who is himself comfortable in facing the dying patient, can help these patients pass through one or all of these stages by appropriate verbal and nonverbal support—particularly the support engendered by the patient's realization that his physician will stay with him until the end.

REFERENCE

KÜBLER-ROSS, E. *On Death and Dying*. New York: The Macmillan Company, 1969.

DEATH, IDENTITY, AND CREATIVITY

Gary Fisher

The interrelationship among death, identity, and creativity is probably a simple one when fully understood. I do not pretend to that understanding. However, I would like to make some statements concerning glimpses of the interrelationship which I have caught.

In thinking about death, its seeming opposite, life, is the first phenomenon to appear. Gibran expresses the contradiction poetically and meaningfully, "If you would indeed behold the spirit of death, open your heart wide unto the body of life. For life and death are one, even as the river and the sea are one" (Gibran, 1946). That life and death are one and that life and death are a process, what does this mean to us as individuals? Are we not dead when we are dead? We are dead when we are what we think being dead is. This statement may look like utter nonsense. Try this statement: We are alive when we are what we think being alive is. Does that make any better sense? Let us specify what it is to die. Death is a point in a process, a point of change in a process of experience. Death is change and change is death. Putting this very concretely, whenever a part of us changes, that part dies, dies in the sense that it no longer holds a position of the strength (in psychological terms, the motivating force) in ourself or our existence as it previously did. When we change, part of the self dies and this is death. As a result, a new constellation or configuration of the "personality" or being obtains. This new configuration may contain new elements or it may contain fewer elements with a redistribution or new "weighting" of the elements in the configuration. Elements previously existing may perhaps now have greater opportunity for expression since other inhibiting elements have disappeared. (Parenthetically, I must observe that I am always amazed to see how infrequently people die. I have the same experience that all of you have had in meeting people after a period of years and finding "They haven't changed [died] a bit.")

It seems obvious that the problem of the death of our physical self is a problem insofar as we identify the self with our physical body. When we do this and we see a person's dead body then we assume that he is dead because we have identified "him" with his body and its actions, its appearance, its smell, its sound, its color, and so on. Thus, when we see that these things are gone, we assume that he, too, is gone. Identifying ourselves with our bodies and others with their bodies then makes physical death a cessation of individuality and awareness. In one of the Buddhist sects, the novice must sit and watch the decomposition of the body of someone he has known well. This practice is to help cast some doubt on the assumption that body and individual being are one and the same thing. I imagine that it would be difficult to continue to believe that one's friend, after a couple of weeks of decomposing, was just that mess of magots, worms and bone before one's eyes. The emphasis in Zen, of making an experience, of concretizing an abstraction, so that it becomes a felt reality, is meaningful and leads to knowing. Rather than abstractly thinking that man is more than his body, and rather than having an intellectualized concept of this possibility, as is more Western man's inclination, the Zen approach has us experience it.

The problem of physical death then has something to do with our identity and what is considered to be "me." When we identify ourselves with our "skin encapsulated ego" (to borrow Alan Watt's phrase), we naturally face annihilation. When we can identify with something beyond our skin-self, then death has a different face. The problem, of course, is a process of coming to know parts of ourselves that we do not already know. Or said differently, identifying with things that we do not now know and therefore have no identity with. The solution is to identify with the life process—to experience, for instance, our cellular consciousness (awareness of that fantastic neuro-physiological activity) and to experience an-other's cellular consciousness, and on the other extreme, to experience (in Eastern religious terms) the "void," the unmanifested energy (the absence of any thing), the source of all life.

How does one begin this new identity? I think this broader identity occurs by our being willing to permit ourselves to experience—by learning to let go and coming to know our feelings, attitudes, perceptions, moods, relationships, forms and the senses we heretofore did not know exist. This occurs by leaving ourselves and by becoming other experiences that have been unknown. Man, of course, has eternally searched for vehicles for such travel, and Aldous Huxley describes with vividness these methods in *Heaven and Hell* (Huxley, 1955). The goal is to leave that usual, known and familiar experiential referent, the self, and to move the awareness or energy to an un-known experiential referent, e.g., another human being, a rose, a note from a violin string, or an amoeba. Giving up one's ego and its fringe bene-fit, "reality" (a tautological phenomenon), one is able to *become* what was previously defined as "other" and not-self and to experience the existen-tial nature of differing referent points or energy manifestations. Example: It is experiencing "rose-ness" and not "me experiencing rose-ness"—the elimination of the subject-object relationship.

There is a very practical aspect to all this ethereal experience, because these experiences give us an identity which is considerably more than our previous body-in-skin one. As we learn to let ourselves experience we find an ever widen-ing identity. This of course is most important in our human relationships. When we can come to know that others are just as we are, we can stop being afraid of them, and stop being afraid we are different from them—better or worse—as all comparison ends the same way—separateness, loneliness and anxiety.

Perhaps crucial to the present discussion is some statement of the experience of timelessness of one's existence or one's knowing. There cease to be concepts of "beginning" and "end," but rather points of experience. What is described as "being at one" is known. I have heard described somewhere that time is an endless series of verti-cal lines and space is an endless series of hori-zontal lines and that at every point where two lines intersect, an individual consciousness exists. Besides being delightful poetry, the picture por-trayed is analogous to the experience where an individual is apprehended as an experiencing node in time and space. Timelessness of one's existence is known when one experiences what is—the here and now, not the past and future, but the "is-ness" of the "now-ness."

Death then is a problem in identity: The more constricted the identity, the more vulnerable it is to destruction; whereas identity with being, with life process, increases the resistance to its destruc-tion. Taking this to concrete examples, we can understand why a multimillionaire commits sui-cide because he has financial difficulties. His identity was so constricted that when he "lost" his money, he "lost" his identity and was no longer an individual nor an identity. When a physically attractive woman who has identified herself with her physical beauty "loses" this beauty, she "loses" herself and catastrophe results. When the identity is narrow and constrictive it is more vulnerable, because events and time can change the covering or irrelevant attributes of an indi-vidual and adjustment problems are inevitable.

Death then is a problem in identity just as any living change is a problem in identity. The resis-tance in psychotherapy is partly a resistance to change, to dying, to becoming someone or some-thing one previously has not been. And this always necessitates giving up part of the self. In the transcendental experience, giving up the old basic assumptions about self is literally experi-enced as dying. Often these experiences are accompanied by the complete sense modalities where one sees the world as one saw it being visually destroyed, where one hears the world come thundering and crashing down, and where one feels the fire as it consumes the old world.

Now I think creativity enters this proess be-cause creativity has something to [do] with the malleable interaction of attributes. In the creative relationship there are attributes of both the creator and that out of which is created, and part of the creative process is the mingling or fusion of those attributes so that something unique is pro-duced. Creativity has something to do with the creator going out into other forms and making manifest a "reality" which proceeds from this fusion. Michelangelo could not have created the David without marble and the attributes of that marble. Attributes of the creator and that from which is created intermingle, out of which is produced a manifest "original," which is a product of those particular attributes of the creator and that out of which is created. So a creation is a particular combination of attributes of both the creator and his material. This process can only occur by the human being allowing himself to go out of self, to go into other forms, other energy modalities, and permitting himself to fuse with this material so that what is produced manifests both himself and his material. The yang in the process is man and the yin is his material. The active merges with the passive and the creator's identity includes his partner, the material. The creator is thus not "I creating some thing" but rather "transcended self and material becoming some new experience-thing."

Creativity occurs when man can permit himself to flow into the world about him and identify and participate in it. Creativity is seen as a life force which is able to merge with other aspects of being to produce new realities which are idiosyncratic to the creator and his material. Creativity has to do with this release of energy into the outside world. This often comes as a culmination of, or as a solution to, inner turmoil. The creative expression bursts out of the organism into the world. Perhaps this occurs when man sees his solution as a merging with the world and his solution to inner threat as a merging with something outside of him, that is, reducing the distance between self and what is considered "not self." I wonder if part of what we call creativity comes when man makes

a desperate attempt to communicate with the world about him and goes out into his material (the world) to reduce anxiety that results from his separateness from it. In this respect, creativity is most beneficial to the creator. He again achieves a union with part of, or the whole of, the cosmos. He again becomes "one" through being able to break through his skin-encapsulated ego and to becoming part of that world about him.

I have attempted to outline some of the interrelationships between death, identity and creativity. Death is seen as a point of change in a continuous experiential knowing. Physical death becomes a problem for a constricted identity, an identity with a skin-encapsulated ego. When one's identity becomes broadened so that he experiences himself as a manifestation of the life and death process (change), then physical death is seen as a point in this process. Creativity is released when an individual permits himself to experience, and creativity is seen as a blending of man with the world around him to produce a "reality" which has a particular combination of the attributes of self and the material. Creativity is seen as a process of a union with the world, a solution to the experienced loneliness, separateness, and anxiety, so that man again becomes part of the cosmos.

REFERENCES

Gibran, Kahlil. *The Prophet*. New York: Alfred A. Knopf, 1946.

Huxley, Aldous. *Heaven and Hell*. New York: Harper & Row, Publishers, 1955.

PART V

Belonging: Problems in Commitment

Human beings form commitments, and the commitments we form give pattern to our existence. We are attracted to others, and join our life to other lives. We become interested in various pursuits and follow them as careers or avocations. The persons and pursuits we join, pledge, and dedicate ourself to, give us a sense of direction and belonging.

Of course we vary greatly in the extent and kinds of our commitments. Some of us follow convention, and in a usual way complete our education, find a job, fall in love, marry, obtain a home, establish a family, and form ties with a community. Others reject or greatly alter this pattern, moving in our own way and at our own speed to evolve our own unique life style.

Many aspects of human life have to do with commitment and belonging. Some of the most central of these aspects are noted above and include love, marriage, family, and vocation. In Part V of this book, each of these aspects will be considered and some attention will be given to the impact of new patterns and styles on them as well as the implication of these new patterns and styles for the future.

Love, a keystone of commitment, has been given little attention by scientists until very recently. Some, who have noted the critically short supply of love, have advocated cultivating love as a sorely needed crop or skill. Certainly the need to love and the ability to love vary widely from one person to another. Some of us are lucky in love or skillful at loving, but many lives include little that could be called love.

Almost all of us marry, but ideas about marriage are changing. For one thing, modern marriage is less likely to be a lifetime commitment; currently about one in every three marriages ends in divorce. (But most divorced persons remarry, a phenomenon which indicates a commitment to the institution of marriage if not to one's spouse.) Second, the kind of commitment people now make in marriage is changing; the old patriarchal form of monogamy is on its way out, and the number of equalitarian and shared-roles (and even reversed-roles) marriages is rapidly increasing.

Human beings generally live in families. We grow up in one family, and grow out of it to form a family of our own. Our living is family living. But families—like marriage itself—are changing. Students of the family have noted some considerable changes in parent and children's roles, and futurists have predicted some quite novel changes to be expected in the family of the future.

When Freud, the founder of psychoanalysis, was asked what a person needed to do well, he answered, "Lieben und arbeiten." To love and to work. Work is an important part of our life. We work to live, and if we are caught up in our pursuits, we live to work. Our work may help us grow or keep us from growing. The readings on this topic throw some light on this important matter.

TOPIC 12

Love

What is this thing called love?
—Song popular in the 1930s

Love is a many-splendored thing
—Song popular in the 1950s

What the world needs now is love
—Song popular in the 1960s

What is this thing called love? Perhaps a psychologist is one of the last persons we should ask to define love. Many psychology texts scarcely mention the word. Their indexes reveal a number of related concepts with which researchers are more comfortable: interpersonal attraction, secondary positive reinforcers, complementary needs, and so on. Poets and writers are more likely to call love love and to accept it as it is.

At its simplest, *love* is affection that one individual expresses for another. Or, if that seems overly simple or too nonchalant, *love* can be defined as a warm, tender, or passionate attachment for someone or something. However, some authorities equate love with the qualities that they consider to be desirable in an interpersonal relationship—qualities such as acceptance, respect, and sharing.

Love is a many-splendored thing, and many different kinds of love have been described and written about. Harry F. Harlow, a psychologist who takes love seriously, finds it useful to identify five affectional systems, including the love of the mother for the child, the love of the child for the mother, peer-mate or age-mate love, heterosexual love, and paternal love. Other writers have expounded romantic love, passionate love, erotic love, neurotic love, brotherly love, self love, open love, multiple love, and even "real" love.

The ability to form loving relationships is a skill that evolves through a number of developmental systems or stages. As Harlow points out, each stage prepares us for the more complex one to follow. If our love experience in one stage is deficient or defective, we do not develop the proper foundation for the next step. For example, successful heterosexual love evolves from successful peer-mate relationships, just as peer-mate relationships build on the mother-child bond. When this early bond has been largely absent or overly intense, the individual may be seriously handicapped in forming later peer-mate and heterosexual love ties.

What the world needs now is love. On this point social scientists are in harmony with songwriters. A number of observers have noted that contemporary human beings are poor at the art of loving, poor even in attaching the proper value to love, and this may ultimately be the undoing of the human race.

Recently some influential scientists have issued an urgent call for a renaissance of love. In an address anthropologist Ashley Montagu announced, "As a result of our misunderstanding of what we are on this earth for, we have brought ourselves very near to the edge of doom. I regard most people as dead, simply as creatures wandering around, having no realization of why they are on this earth. They have no idea that the only reason for being on this earth is to live to love." And human potentialist Herbert Otto recently wrote, "We are at a point in our development where a massive nourishing and flourishing of love has become a necessity if we are to survive as a species."

A loving relationship

What is a loving relationship? In the lead article, Donald L. Taylor, focusing primarily on marriage, answers that question in three ways: First, he describes what love is not—what people frequently give instead of love. Second, he presents a traditional conception of love as an emotion. And third, Taylor provides a sociopsychological definition in which love is identified as acceptance, esteem, understanding, and sharing.

Self love

Many of us have been taught that we should not love ourselves, but Erich Fromm believes that love is all of a piece and that self love is therefore inseparably connected with love for others. In the second selection he writes, "If an individual is able to love productively, he loves himself too; if he can love *only* others, he cannot love at all." Fromm contrasts self love with selfishness, which he sees as an opposite. Selfish people are incapable of loving others or themselves, and their selfishness is an attempt to compensate for their failure to care for and respect themselves.

Unromantic love

In the third reading, Margaret Horton rejects romantic love as too demanding, illusion-ridden, and power-based. She reviews other models of love and combines their best features into what she calls "epigenetic love"—a love that continually grows and changes with time and experience. Epigenetic love is realistic, equalitarian, and nonpossessive. It is not a love we *fall into* that somehow lasts forever, but rather a love we *grow into* that lasts as long as the parties work at it and find it right for them (this may be longer than for the forever kind of love).

Multiple love

In the last reading Herbert A. Otto maintains that monogamic love is for most persons unsatisfactory or impossible. He holds that at various times of life we may need a loving and sexual relationship with more than one person, and such relationships may result in personal growth. More than this, if our society fostered all possible love relationships, we would be less destructive and more human. Otto presents a credo based on the maxim "commitment without chains" that offers, he says, "the freedom which we as lovers must have, to continue to grow in our love throughout the years."

FOR PERSONAL APPLICATION

1. Present a definition of love (original or not) that you think is a good one and explain why.
2. Are you a loving person? Discuss your answer.
3. Describe a loving relationship that you have had and indicate its effect on you.
4. Contrast two persons you know (one may be yourself) who are quite different in their ability to love or show love. What accounts for the difference?
5. Would you accept Taylor's definition of love as acceptance, esteem, understanding, and sharing? Why or why not?
6. Do you love yourself enough? How does your love (or lack of love) for yourself relate to your love for others?
7. Have you ever been "in love"? How realistic or romantic was this experience? Was it hurtful or helpful? Why?
8. A distinction has been made between couples who "fall in love" and those who "grow in love." Discuss this difference and from your observations or experience give an example of each kind of love relationship.
9. A distinction has been made between love relationships that are contracted "forever" and those that run "until further notice." Discuss this difference and give your reactions to both kinds of contracts.
10. Do you agree that there are times in life when it is possible or desirable to have more than one sexual and loving relationship? Why or why not?
11. What changes in marriage, the family, or in society generally would make us more loving?

12. We sometimes hear of children who get "too much" love or people who love "too much" or "too well." What does this mean? Is too much love possible?
13. Discuss a poem, short story, novel, autobiography, biography, movie, play, or other creative work that gave you some insight into love.
14. Write down a discussion item (not given above) that seems particularly relevant to this topic and you, and discuss it.

FOR SMALL GROUPS

1. *Defining love.* Each member writes his definition of love on a card. The cards are gathered, shuffled, and placed face down in the middle of the group. Then the members in turn pick cards and comment on the definitions. Finally, the group attempts to arrive at one definition that is acceptable to all its members.
2. *Loving others.* For a three-minute period each member silently considers two questions: "How loving am I?" "How can I be more loving?" When the three minutes are up, the members share their answers with the group.
3. *Loving oneself.* For a three-minute period each member silently considers two questions: "How much do I love myself?" "How can I give myself more love?" When the three minutes are up, the members share their answers with the group.
4. *Relating to others.* Put a book or some object on the floor to indicate the center of the group. Then, a volunteer (or several in turn) stations everyone including himself in a particular place in the room to indicate how close he (the volunteer) feels (1) to the center of the group, and (2) to each member. Have the volunteer and all the group members discuss their placements.

FOR FURTHER READING

Berscheid, E., and E. H. Walster. *Interpersonal Attraction.* Reading, Mass.: Addison-Wesley, 1969.

Curtin, M. E., ed. *Symposium on Love.* New York: Behavioral Publications, 1973.

Fromm, E. *The Art of Loving.* New York: Harper & Row, Publishers, 1956.

Fromme, A. *The Ability to Love.* New York: Farrar, Straus & Giroux, 1965.

Harlow, H. F. *Learning to Love.* San Francisco: Albion, 1971.

Haughton, R. *Love.* Baltimore: Penguin Books Inc., 1971.

May, R. *Love and Will.* New York: W. W. Norton & Co., Inc., 1970.

Miller, H. L., and P. S. Siegel. *Loving: A Psychological Approach.* New York: John Wiley & Sons, Inc., 1972.

Otto, H. A., ed. *Love Today: A New Exploration.* New York: Association Press, 1972.

WHAT IS A LOVING RELATIONSHIP?

Donald L. Taylor

In spite of the strong cultural emphasis on the need for love, its importance has not been overemphasized. This is dramatically demonstrated by case histories of individuals who did not or have felt they did not receive love during their childhood. Their lives are handicapped by their inability to form intimate relationships. Many of them are cold and impersonal. Others selfishly seek what they have missed or, as a protective gesture, reject any expression of love from others. In extreme cases infants suffer from marasmus because of the lack of love.

Case histories not only dramatize the need for love; they also reinforce the proposition that many people do not know how to give and get love. The severely handicapped need psychiatric help. The less handicapped can profit from marriage counseling by: (1) Learning how to effectively express love; (2) becoming able to recognize requests for love; (3) developing the ability to distinguish between love and love substitutes; and (4) developing an understanding for the nature of a loving relationship.

RECOGNIZING REQUESTS FOR LOVE

The drive for love manifests itself in many different ways. So diverse are these efforts that both clients and counselor need to watch for them with particular care. The negative approach is a fairly typical one, and one that can be easily misunderstood. For example, one client made the following statement, "I'm not worth much. I'm lazy, inde-

cisive, and very much an opportunist. I don't see how anyone could like me." What he didn't say but did imply (as he later confirmed) was, "Maybe nobody likes me, but I surely need some liking. I am really rather helpless in the matter, so I hope someone is going to love me regardless of what I am."

This implication is often overlooked. Instead, the focus of the response is on whether the person is what he says he is. A typical answer to such an evaluation is, "You're really not as bad as you say." Such a response not only ignores the client's search for love, but it can discourage him from making further requests. It may cause an individual to ask himself, "If I'm not as bad as I think, why doesn't someone love me?" His rationalization may have been destroyed and his defense against the cruel thought of being unloved without reason been shattered. The result can be further retreat from the possibility of a loving relationship.

The response could also create a different type of dilemma. A basic need of everyone is to be loved for what he is—good or bad. An individual may challenge another person's ability to love him by presenting to that person his worst possible features. If the other person cannot recognize these traits and still show love, the individual is left wondering whether he is really loved or not.

The validity of any self-appraisal is not particularly important when it is seen as an effort to find love or to test someone's ability to love. When a counselor responds that what a client is, or thinks he is, is not decisive in the search for love, he makes it possible for the individual to continue his search and to express his need more directly.

The opposite approach to obtaining love is to attempt to discover other people's expectations and try to conform to them, the implication being, "If you can't love me for what I am, perhaps you'll love me for what I can do to please you." If the response sustains the assumptions of this approach, it ultimately leads to the use of a variety of virtues as substitutes for love. The problems which result are the subject of the next section.

Some clients will not seek an expression of love in any manner. They appear solidly independent and even indifferent. However, such a posture is likely to indicate a need for love. It will disappear as a person gains confidence that the possibility of getting love really exists. Such a person is also likely to be concerned about sudden and unexpected withdrawals of acceptance. As confidence builds within him, his ability to take them in his stride will grow.

The skill of recognizing the need for love in individuals should be related to the realization that offering love is not enough. The idea that a love-starved individual will always be appreciative of an offer is unrealistic. It can be anticipated that such offers may be rejected many times before they are accepted. Reactions may vary from further retreat to obnoxious behavior. They should not be interpreted as failure on the part of the person who offers love nor as an indication that the recipient really does not want to be loved. The situation may be similar to the problem of getting the body of a dehydrated child to retain water.

SUBSTITUTES FOR LOVE

To avoid developing the capacity to love or to express love, many people substitute other values and virtues for it. One common substitute in marriage is service. In essence, some people operate on the assumption, "Since I can't really love you, I'll take good care of you. I'll fix you good meals, I'll care for your clothes, and the house will be as neat and clean as you require." The services are not offered merely as services, however, but as proof of love.

Other virtues are also offered and sometimes imposed on a spouse. Some of the more common substitute currencies are kindness, loyalty, obedience, consideration, praise, and hard work. Substitutes for love are not always so specific. Often they are channeled into a neurotic need to be good. If one is good, love is not so important. This disposition easily leads a person into the position of living according to a variety of proverbs which describe the good wife and good husband. Two common examples are: "Marriage is a fifty-fifty proposition, but, if necessary, go ninety per cent of the way." "Behind every successful man is a woman."

Slavish acceptance of a proverb as an indication or proof of love creates a variety of problems.

For example, take, "Do all you can to make your partner happy." There are three implications in this statement which create trouble in marriage. First is the assumption that the partner needs to be made happy. This, of course, is an insult to a person who is already happy or one who feels capable of satisfying his own needs. One husband, in response to his wife's almost constant effort to care for him, angrily asked, "Why are you so concerned about me? I'm not helpless. I know what I want, and I know how to get it." This type of response is unexpected. The spouse may easily interpret it as rejection, or at least as a questioning of his good intentions. One woman made this complaint, "It seems he is not really interested in me. After dinner, I ask him if I can bring him anything. He says, 'No thanks.' When I try to comfort him after a hard day's work, he tells me to leave him alone. All I'm trying to do is help him and let him know I care."

The reactions to this feeling of rejection follow response patterns common to many failures. Often the neurotic responds with even more concern for his partner's happiness. It almost seems as if he unconsciously says, "I'm going to make her happy even if it destroys our marriage." The recipient of this happiness can only more strongly defend her capabilities or capitulate. Neither makes her happy.

Another reaction is to become self-righteous. If such feelings are put into words, they sound like this, "OK, I've done everything I can do to make this marriage work. I'll sulk and be the silent partner until he comes to his senses. Let him go ahead and do things wrong. Someday he'll learn to appreciate me."

Still another is disillusionment. The person is hurt and even confused. He may have the urge to withdraw from the marriage. He may blame both marriage itself and his partner for the trouble.

A fourth reaction is to be overwhelmed. This is more likely if the person's efforts to make his spouse happy have been carried out over a period of years. The wife of a graduate student was near this condition. The world she had been building was about to crumble, and it was almost more than she could endure. She complained bitterly after seven years of marriage, "This love, honor, and obey stuff has almost ruined me. If anyone needs a sabbatical, I'm the one. I've cooked meals, raised kids, and been research assistant, footnoter, typist, and giver of consolation for my husband. I really believed his success would make me happy. To get to the point, though, let me tell you he still doesn't have his degree. When he flunked his German exam, I almost had a fit. I yelled at him, and I called him dumb and lazy. I am truly sorry for the way I acted. He was so stunned he didn't say a word. I know I hurt him. This makes me feel worse. He has really tried. It's not easy for him to support us and go to school, too. He accepted my apology. He acts as if nothing happened and has signed up to take his German exam again. The only trouble is I can't be the good wife and mother any longer. Encouragement from the folks has no effect."

This sense of being overwhelmed may be accompanied by self-blame. The person asks himself, "What did I do wrong?" instead of the more reasonable question, "What's wrong with the way we are living?"

At the opposite extreme, the response to overeagerness to help is a continued acceptance of the services. The dependent type of person is likely to accept and ask for more. One alcoholic had nothing but genuine praise for the attention his wife gave him. "She's a good wife and deserves a lot more than she gets." The uselessness of the relationship was that the neurotic needs of both partners were consuming the major part of the marriage. The wife's goodness only added to the husband's fear that he was a weakling. Why else was she so anxious to help? The wife, on the other hand, was partially satisfied, but had no real sense of accomplishment. All the time a feeling of hostility was growing within her. She began to wonder why it was her lot to have such a never-ending task.

If a person accepts the assumption, "I am supposed to make my spouse happy," he usually proceeds to do so. The problem at this point is whose definition of happiness is going to be used. The loving husband who is determined to make his wife happy doesn't always ask her what happiness means to her. It is not likely to occur to the neurotic that there are other definitions of happiness than the one he learned in childhood. One man bitterly complained, "I can't understand my wife. For over ten years now I've tried to give her what she wanted. I don't argue with her. I am

patient when she's upset. I compliment her. No one can say I am not kind." The wife, without realizing it, diagnosed the problem. "You would think he was living with his mother. He does everything to please me. But it becomes sickening. I have hoped and hoped he would once stand up for himself—yell at me or even push me around. I can't respect him this way."

Sometimes a person has formulae for happiness which he wants his spouse to follow. Every time one particular husband complained about his work or his friends, his wife told him he could expect no more. "You're not going to be happy until you learn how to be polite. Sit down now and we'll figure out what went wrong."

This woman explained to the counselor that her husband was too frank and aggressive around people. "If you want to get ahead in the world, you have to be considerate. I tell my husband this every day. Whenever he practices it, he is liked by everybody. When he tells people what he really thinks, he gets into trouble." Without a pause to apply her own advice to herself, she continued, "Now he is losing his considerateness at home. He's going to ruin our marriage if he's not careful. Maybe you can help me. There's no reason in the world why we can't be happy if he'll just listen."

The motives of this woman were sincere—she wanted to help her husband. She knew what had made her happy as a child: she had obeyed her parents, had been pleasant to them, and had given them the right answers. The formula she now used was somewhat similar but more sophisticated and was spotted with many of her own projections, such as fear of peoples' opinions and fear of making mistakes. Her recipe for happiness was accompanied by a large amount of generosity. She didn't mind her husband coming late for dinner if he found it difficult to break away from his friends. Handsome gifts to friends and relatives pleased her even if they involved some self-sacrifice. Anything was acceptable if it fit her particular formula.

Sometimes both partners accept the principle of making each other happy. Since they do not come for counseling, one can only speculate about them. However, there are couples who have reported that such an arrangement was not particularly satisfactory. They compared making each other happy to two people who insist on feeding each other at mealtime. It works, but it is a slow and tedious way to eat. A better way is for each individual to take what he wants when he wants it, just as he does at the dinner table.

The third problem is the personal neglect which develops when an individual devotes most of his time to making someone else happy. Everyone has desires which need to be satisfied. Often, when they are not satisfied, the result is a feeling of lack within the individual. As clients introspect after becoming aware of this situation, they talk about a feeling of always being short-changed after sacrifice. Even a so-called full repayment by the spouse fails to give them satisfaction.

Sometimes they raise the question of whether or not it is possible to attain genuine satisfaction or self-fulfillment by living through other people. When they realize that such a philosophy is basically unsound, many of them find themselves releasing long repressed feelings. One wife talked about it this way, "I guess I have been storing resentment inside me for a long time. When the cork popped the other night, I resented everything he said. I resented him when he stood up and I resented him when he sat down. I followed him to his room and resented it when he tried to escape. I recalled things from years back and yelled at him about those things." Resentment is not the only feeling related to this pattern of living. Catharsis also brings expressions of hostility, anger, and sadness. Accompanying these feelings toward other people is a rather typical reaction toward one's self which was expressed by one person this way, "Boy, what a sucker I've been." Unless these feelings are expressed, they stay inside a person. Under such circumstances, the individual must suffer from the wear and tear of containing them. There is also the possibility that he will project these feelings onto his partner.

When a counselor recognizes such syndromes, what does he do? The following general suggestions are offered. He can: (1) Confirm the unreality of the situation; (2) support the partner who is rebelling against the neurotic pattern; (3) interpret to both partners what is happening; (4) explain the possibilities of different kinds of relationships; and (5) help clients face disillusion-

ment and other consequences of realizing the futility of being good for goodness' sake.

The realization that the neurotic use of goodness isn't working comes at almost any time in counseling. During an interview, a man may say, "I'm tired of pleasing my wife. No matter what I do, she expects more." A counselor can respond in this way, "It really doesn't pay to try to please your wife." Or if there is less certainty that a client has faced the reality of the situation, the reflection can be, "You seem to be wondering if the efforts to make your wife happy are really worth-while." On occasion a client will ask a pointed question, "What do you think about it?" The counselor's answer should confirm the fact that neurotic goodness creates problems in marriage. Or the answer can be direct: "Pleasing doesn't pay off."

When a client does not recognize the nature of his problem, a counselor is sometimes tempted to confront him with it. This is not likely to be effective in helping a client realize his difficulties. Instead, he may become defensive. He will then retreat to his habitual way of living and the problems of the neuroticism will continue.

There are times when a counselor, through support, unwittingly encourages the neuroticism of goodness. The dangers are obvious. Such action prevents the client from realizing the problem; and in some instances, the added effort to be good, encouraged by the counselor, may be the precipitating factor in bringing on a psychotic episode. It might also present the person with such a burden that he will decide to withdraw from the responsibilities of marriage. He may ask for a divorce, simply walk out, or remain in the marriage but take no active part.

There are cases in which one partner realizes the futility of being good for goodness' sake and the other partner does not want a change. The result may be rebellion and conflict. The counselor doesn't take sides in this, but can support the rebelling partner by agreeing that his point of view is realistic and needs consideration. At the same time, if he is counseling the other partner, he can help interpret to that partner why his spouse is rebelling. For example, the woman who has been substituting kindness and consideration for sexual relationships with her husband may be confused and angry when her husband refuses to accept the substitutes. The counselor should help her see that this is the difficulty rather than let her define the problem as one of an ungrateful husband.

TRADITIONAL MEANING OF LOVE

If goodness is not love, what, then, is love? The traditional answer is that love is an emotion. From this point of view, it is explained in terms of physiological–psychological factors. Love is sometimes described as a feeling focused in the pit of the stomach: "My stomach is all knotted up." This conception stems from more scientific statements which declare love to be a stimulation of the visceral parts of the body.

The psychological definition is geared more to introspective analysis of a state of feeling within the individual. A person in love may be "light hearted," "moved by deep exhilaration," "light headed," or "bubbling with joy." The marriage counselor with this orientation may ask a person to declare himself to be or not to be in love. He may try to identify or confirm love through the use of questionnaires which have responses that he considers indices of love.

Another traditional meaning of love focuses on feelings of concern or responsibility. Individuals with these qualities in mind speak of motherly love, Christian love, and love for mankind. Sometimes this interpretation is ascribed to married love after the more physical and more intense psychological symptoms of romantic love recede.

There are two reasons why the traditional concepts are of limited use to the marriage counselor. First, it is difficult to identify love by physical symptoms or by introspection. Second, the focus on relationship in marriage counseling requires a relationship definition of love. The measurement of visceral reactions is not a practical approach for the marriage counselor. Even observable reactions such as heart palpitation or activity of the sweat glands may indicate love, anger, or fear. Introspection is also unreliable, because under pressure a person may say he loves when, in reality, he is rationalizing to cover other feelings. An example is the mother who rejects her child but portrays herself as a loving mother through overconcern and overprotection. Other observations are needed to verify personal judgment, not only for the sake of the individual professing love, but also for the person loved.

The second difficulty with the traditional approaches is that they are centered on the individual. In marriage, when a man tells his wife he loves her, she wants to know what this means in terms of their relationship. Does it mean extra kisses, extra consideration? Thus a counselor needs to define love in terms of attitudes and behavior which are tangibly expressed in a husband–wife relationship. In more technical terms, marriage counseling calls for a sociopsychological approach to love.

A LOVING RELATIONSHIP

Acceptance and Love

Acceptance has been associated with love by many writers from various disciplines. Erich Fromm, for example, has stressed that a person who loves someone wants this person to grow and unfold for his own sake. Overstreet says that to love someone is to grant him the full right to his unique humanhood. In other words, to love means to accept.

The old proverb "Love is blind" gives some indication of this aspect of love. It suggests that the loved one's unacceptable qualities are ignored. Actually, the test of love comes when one faces a person's undesirable characteristics and still loves him. One client explained it in this way:

I would guess from the beginning I wasn't accepted by Dad. He has made no bones about always wanting a son. He did everything he could to pretend I was one. I have a boy's name. I played the game all the way. I was a tomboy—I am sure you noticed my haircut when I first came to you. I even went to engineering school and got an engineering degree. I tried hard, but I've always known I wasn't acceptable to my Dad.

When I married, I hoped my husband would love me as a woman. Two things were wrong. I didn't know how to act like a woman or feel like one. But it didn't matter—my husband really didn't want a woman. He wanted a housekeeper and a buddy. We lived together, but I never had a chance to act the way I thought a woman should.

As I became more hopelessly lost from the world, I desperately looked for some kind of acceptance from my husband—he was the only one who gave me any attention. My efforts didn't make sense, because I became more obnoxious than ever. I was convinced I couldn't be loved.

The change came in a funny way, but it was real to me. It happened one night when I sat like a stupid mess on a small chair in the kitchen. I was ugly and miserable. I looked worse than a witch. When my husband looked in, I told him to go away. In spite of my nasty remark, he came in and emphatically yelled, "I love you regardless."

To be accepted at my absolutely worst was what I wanted. It flashed through me that at last someone loved me. I didn't question it carefully, but I realized what my longing for love involved and what my Dad had never been able to give me.

This woman's account stresses the need for acceptance as proof of love. In her case, as in many others, conditional acceptance was not enough. Love for her meant acceptance without qualification. It was only after experiencing this that she could contemplate love in terms of degrees. In other words, she could then realize that the more love there is in a relationship, the fewer will be the qualifications attached to acceptance.

That love from the social point of view cannot be a purely personal matter is also illustrated in the above example. A characteristic, a feeling, or behavior must not only be accepted by the loving person, but the loved one must agree that the factor designated for acceptance is significant. For a husband to say, "I love you," is not enough. The wife may say, "If you love me, you accept this or that about me." When they agree on what each accepts and wishes to be accepted, a love relationship exists. This wife demanded unconditional acceptance as proof of love. A less damaged personality could possibly settle for less.

This need for agreement also underlines the importance of communication in a love relationship. The assumption that a husband or a wife does not love his or her spouse cannot be accepted until the communication process has been evaluated. A man's contention that his wife doesn't love him might be a problem of this man's unwillingness to translate his wife's expression of love as love. It could also be the wife's inability to put into acceptable action her feelings of love. The relationship between love and acceptance is found in an analysis of the counseling process. The counselor's permissiveness and nonjudgmental attitude can easily be translated as acceptance. Many clients report the sense of being loved under such circumstances.

Esteem and Love

Another social dimension by which love can be identified is the esteem one individual has for another. *Esteem* was chosen as the term to be used over the synonyms of regard, respect, and admire. About these terms Webster's dictionary says, "*Regard,* the least explicit of these words, usually requires qualification to complete its meaning; *respect* implies a judgment of high valuation; *esteem* adds to respect the implication of warmth of feeling or close attachment; *admire* connotes enthusiastic appreciation, and sometimes genuine affection."

Admiration might appear to be a better term, but as the dictionary elsewhere explains, admiration does not always imply approval. Approval is a necessary aspect of love. Esteem embraces approval and adds an even more positive reaction. It means "to value or prize, especially for real or intrinsic worth; it commonly implies some warmth of feeling or attachment."

The crucial concern of the person seeking love through esteem is his real or intrinsic worth. What he is must be esteemed, rather than a projected desire of his spouse. A person who is esteemed because he represents his partner's wishes is not likely to interpret such esteem as love. The demarcation between what one views as an integral part of himself and what are the expectations of others is not always clear to each individual. Thus it is not unusual to find people confused about it. Developing clearer self-images is one approach to this problem. If a person knows "who he is," he can determine whether or not his partner holds him in esteem. Also, being able to present a relatively clear-cut picture of what he is may increase his partner's esteem for him.

Understanding and Love

The term *understanding* connotes a variety of meanings common to a loving relationship. It indicates discernment, reasonableness, familiarity, and comprehension. In an understanding relationship there are overtones of friendliness, harmony, adjustment, and mutual agreement. These attributes provide something beyond the factor of acceptance. They imply positive involvement.

When someone says, "I understand you," the person to whom he speaks can find satisfaction that he is not so complex, unique, or unreasonable that he will have to live a life of loneliness. He is also encouraged to present or develop other aspects of his personality. The reaction becomes cyclical when the processes of understanding and revealing are enhanced by each other. One person described understanding as the garden soil from which all kinds of human beings grow.

Love and Sharing

Acceptance, esteem, and understanding encourage sharing in marriage. Sharing is the fourth aspect of a loving relationship. People who are in love give to each other for use, enjoyment, or possession what originally belonged to each. Through this process of sharing, they build a reservoir of mutual possessions, feelings, and experiences.

One client explained how she felt love had developed between her and her husband. "For too many years our marriage could be characterized as a *mine* and *his* arrangement. I had *my* closet, *my* responsibilities, *my* money, *my* friends. Even at times, it was *my* children and then *his* children. He had *his* allowance, *his* car, *his* rights and responsibilities, and *his* den. Notably absent was a list of *our* things.

"Our new relationship involves a lot more use of the word *our*. I think we first started talking about *our* children. We have talked about *our* responsibilities and *our* aspirations. I even talked about *our* saw and hammer after I made a sword for our son. As the *our* list has grown and the *my* and *your* lists have shrunk, I really believe I have learned the difference between merely saying my husband and I are in love and knowing we are in love."

How far should this sharing go? Ideally, total sharing can be equated with total love. However, from a practical point of view, it is unlikely that many individuals are capable of sharing everything. The usual answer lies between the limited list of items shared in problem marriages and the ideal everything.

The value of sharing with one's partner such peripheral experiences as premarital sex relations with someone else is questionable. However, there can be no categorical rule. Such experiences may be told to test the partner's acceptance. The "worst" is presented to "see if she really loves me." It is usually better for this problem of acceptance to be worked out in therapy. In the average case, fantasies and daydreams should also probably be excluded from the sharing process.

On the other hand, the tendency of most people to share the pleasant and hide the unpleasant needs to be discouraged. This is particularly true of feelings. The advice, "Don't get angry with your spouse," is in contradiction to the fact that most people can't avoid feeling angry with their spouses. Following it prevents the development of a loving relationship by discouraging a husband and wife from sharing their anger.

This point of view is usually strange and sometimes threatening to clients. It needs considerable explanation. One approach is to ask why a person is afraid to express anger, resentment, or hostility toward his mate. The answer will probably reveal fear of the consequences—for example, "If I hate him, he won't love me." It can be explained at this point that if a spouse loves one, he can accept and understand this hatred. Thus to show hatred implies the belief that it can be accepted without consequences. To withhold a feeling implies a lack of love. Sharing negative feelings and behavior is part of a loving relationship. Furthermore, if a partner can't accept negative feelings, there is nothing to be gained by suppressing them. Suppression won't generate love and is likely to be a burden.

Sharing does not develop as a result of resolve. It is intricately interwoven with acceptance, understanding, and esteem. If any one of these four factors is to be considered the end result of the development of a loving relationship, it is sharing. It becomes the tangible and experiential aspect of love. If there is sharing in marriage, one can assume that there have been acceptance, understanding, and esteem. In this sense, sharing becomes an ultimate. The paradox of the situation, however, is that sharing enhances further understanding, acceptance, and esteem. Thus the only realistic way to analyze love is to describe its cyclical development.

LOVING ONE'S SELF

The emphasis in our culture on loving others has encouraged the neglect of self-love. Sometimes self-love is equated with selfishness and egotism. Clients talk about the danger of loving themselves too much. They complain about egotism and bragging in their partners as indications of too much self-love.

Because of this misunderstanding, it is often necessary to discuss with clients the nature and role of self-love in the development and maintenance of a loving relationship. It should be made clear to them that self-love is essential. The person who has love for himself finds it easier to give love to someone else. As one person explained, "It's easy to express love when it seems so abundant. And as long as I am not dependent on someone else for all the love I need, I don't worry about where the next expression of love is coming from."

"If I don't love myself, how can I expect someone else to love me?" There is no proof that such is the case, but clinical observations support the proposition that it is easier to love someone who loves himself than someone who doesn't. One explanation for this is that a person who doesn't love himself is his own worst enemy. He is defensive, and in his search for acceptance and understanding, he becomes aggressive or boastful. He is also resentful of others because of his dependency upon them.

A person who becomes convinced of the need to love himself will probably wonder how it can be done. The answer is not an intellectual one, but comes through the counseling process. The counselor can begin by using the factors of a loving relationship mentioned in this chapter. A person can comprehend that to love himself he must accept himself as he is and learn to understand and esteem his own personality. This philosophy alters traditional assumptions about personality growth and change. A person no longer sees himself as an entity to be modified by persistent forces of resolution and pressure coming either from himself or from others. The New Year's resolution list is a notable example of this approach.

Instead, he treats himself with consideration in the same way he would care for a plant, giving himself the things he knows are necessary for his own existence and growth. A favorable climate of self-love and self-respect will naturally promote personality change and development. Furthermore, he accepts willingly the changes in himself that such a climate produces. In other words, he will have little anxiety about what he really is and what he is becoming.

SELF-LOVE

Erich Fromm

While it raises no objection to apply the concept of love to various objects, it is a widespread belief that, while it is virtuous to love others, it is sinful to love oneself. It is assumed that to the degree to which I love myself I do not love others, that self-love is the same as selfishness.[1] This view goes far back in Western thought. Calvin speaks of self-love as "a pest."[2] Freud speaks of self-love in psychiatric terms but, nevertheless, his value judgment is the same as that of Calvin. For him self-love is the same as narcissism, the turning of the libido toward oneself. Narcissism is the earliest stage of human development, and the person who in later life has returned to this narcissistic stage is incapable of love; in the extreme case he is insane. Freud assumes that love is the manifestation of libido, and that the libido is either turned toward others—love; or toward oneself—self-love. Love and self-love are thus mutually

---

[1] Paul Tillich, in a review of *The Sane Society*, in *Pastoral Psychology*, September 1955, has suggested that it would be better to drop the ambiguous term "self-love" and to replace it with "natural self-affirmation" or "paradoxical self-acceptance." Much as I can see the merits of this suggestion I cannot agree with him in this point. In the term "self-love" the paradoxical element in self-love is contained more clearly. The fact is expressed that love is an attitude which is the same toward all objects, including myself. It must also not be forgotten that the term "self-love," in the sense in which it is used here, has a history. The Bible speaks of self-love when it commands to "love thy neighbor *as thyself*," and Meister Eckhart speaks of self-love in the very same sense.

[2] John Calvin, *Institutes of the Christian Religion*, translated by J. Albau (Philadelphia: Presbyterian Board of Christian Education, 1928), Chap. 7, par. 4, p. 622.

exclusive in the sense that the more there is of one, the less there is of the other. If self-love is bad, it follows that unselfishness is virtuous.

These questions arise: Does psychological observation support the thesis that there is a basic contradiction between love for oneself and love for others? Is love for oneself the same phenomenon as selfishness, or are they opposites? Furthermore, is the selfishness of modern man really a *concern for himself* as an individual, with all his intellectual, emotional and sensual potentialities? Has "he" not become an appendage of his socio-economic role? *Is his selfishness identical with self-love or is it not caused by the very lack of it?*

Before we start the discussion of the psychological aspect of selfishness and self-love, the logical fallacy in the notion that love for others and love for oneself are mutually exclusive should be stressed. If it is a virtue to love my neighbor as a human being, it must be a virtue—and not a vice—to love myself, since I am a human being too. There is no concept of man in which I myself am not included. A doctrine which proclaims such an exclusion proves itself to be intrinsically contradictory. The idea expressed in the Biblical "Love thy neighbor as thyself!" implies that respect for one's own integrity and uniqueness, love for and understanding of one's own self, cannot be separated from respect and love and understanding for another individual. The love for my own self is inseparably connected with the love for any other being.

We have come now to the basic psychological premises on which the conclusions of our argument are built. Generally, these premises are as follows: not only others, but we ourselves are the "object" of our feelings and attitudes; the attitudes toward others and toward ourselves, far from being contradictory, are basically *conjunctive*. With regard to the problem under discussion this means: love of others and love of ourselves are not alternatives. On the contrary, an attitude of love toward themselves will be found in all those who are capable of loving others. *Love*, in principle, *is indivisible as far as the connection between "objects" and one's own self is concerned*. Genuine love is an expression of productiveness and implies care, respect, responsibility and knowledge. It is not an "affect" in the sense of being affected by somebody, but an active striving for the growth and happiness of the loved person, rooted in one's own capacity to love.

To love somebody is the actualization and concentration of the power to love. The basic affirmation contained in love is directed toward the beloved person as an incarnation of essentially human qualities. Love of one person implies love of man as such. The kind of "division of labor," as William James calls it, by which one loves one's family but is without feeling for the "stranger," is a sign of a basic inability to love. Love of man is not, as is frequently supposed, an abstraction coming after the love for a specific person, but it is its premise, although genetically it is acquired in loving specific individuals.

From this it follows that my own self must be as much an object of my love as another person. *The affirmation of one's own life, happiness, growth, freedom is rooted in one's capacity to love,* i.e., in care, respect, responsibility, and knowledge. If an individual is able to love productively, he loves himself too; if he can love *only* others, he cannot love at all.

Granted that love for oneself and for others in principle is conjunctive, how do we explain selfishness, which obviously excludes any genuine concern for others? The *selfish* person is interested only in himself, wants everything for himself, feels no pleasure in giving, but only in taking. The world outside is looked at only from the standpoint of what he can get out of it; he lacks interest in the needs of others, and respect for their dignity and integrity. He can see nothing but himself; he judges everyone and everything from its usefulness to him; he is basically unable to love. Does not this prove that concern for others and concern for oneself are unavoidable alternatives? This would be so if selfishness and self-love were identical. But that assumption is the very fallacy which has led to so many mistaken conclusions concerning our problem. *Selfishness and self-love, far from being identical, are actually opposites.* The selfish person does not love himself too much but too little; in fact he hates himself. This lack of fondness and care for himself, which is only one expression of his lack of productiveness, leaves him empty and frustrated. He is necessarily unhappy and anxiously concerned to snatch from life the satisfactions which he blocks himself from attaining. He seems to care too much for himself, but actually he only makes an unsuccessful attempt to cover up and compensate for his failure to care for his real self. Freud holds that the selfish person is narcissistic, as if he had withdrawn his love from others and turned it toward his own person. *It is true that selfish persons are incapable of loving others, but they are not capable of loving themselves either.*

It is easier to understand selfishness by comparing it with greedy concern for others, as we find it, for instance, in an oversolicitous mother. While she consciously believes that she is particularly fond of her child, she has actually a deeply repressed hostility **towar**d the object of her concern. She is overconcerned not because she loves the child too much, but because she has to compensate for her lack of capacity to love him at all.

This story of the nature of selfishness is borne out by psychoanalytic experience with neurotic "unselfishness," a symptom of neurosis observed in not a few people who usually are troubled not by this symptom but by others connected with it, like depression, tiredness, inability to work, failure in love relationships, and so on. Not only is unselfishness not felt as a "symptom"; it is often the one redeeming character trait on which such people pride themselves. The "unselfish" person "does not want anything for himself"; he "lives only for others," is proud that he does not consider himself important. He is puzzled to find that in spite of his unselfishness he is unhappy, and that his relationships to those closest to him are unsatisfactory. Analytic work shows that his unselfishness is not something apart from his other symptoms but one of them, in fact often the most important one; that he is paralyzed in his capacity to love or to enjoy anything; that he is pervaded by hostility toward life and that behind the facade of unselfishness a subtle but not less intense self-centeredness is hidden. This person can be cured only if his unselfishness too is interpreted as a symptom along with the others, so that his lack of productiveness, which is at the root of both his unselfishness *and* his other troubles, can be corrected.

The nature of unselfishness becomes particularly apparent in its effect on others, and most frequently in our culture in the effect the "unselfish" mother has on her children. She believes that by her unselfishness her children will experience what it means to be loved and to learn, in turn, what it means to love. The effect of her unselfishness, however, does not at all correspond to her expectations. The children do not show the happiness of persons who are convinced that they are loved; they are anxious, tense, afraid of the mother's disapproval and anxious to live up to her expectations. Usually, they are affected by their mother's hidden hostility toward life, which they sense rather than recognize clearly, and eventually they become imbued with it themselves. Altogether, the effect of the "unselfish" mother is not too different from that of the selfish one; indeed, it is often worse, because the mother's unselfishness prevents the children from criticizing her. They are put under the obligation not to disappoint her; they are taught, under the mask of virtue, dislike for life. If one has a chance to study the effect of a mother with genuine self-love, one can see that there is nothing more conducive to giving a child the experience of what love, joy and happiness are than being loved by a mother who loves herself.

These ideas on self-love cannot be summarized better than by quoting Meister Eckhart on this topic: "If you love yourself, you love everybody else as you do yourself. As long as you love another person less than you love yourself, you will not really succeed in loving yourself, but if you love all alike, including yourself, you will love them as one person and that person is both God and man. Thus he is a great and righteous person who, loving himself, loves all others equally."[3]

[3] Meister Eckhart, *Meister Eckhart,* ed. and trans. by R. D. Blakney (New York: Harper & Row, Publishers, Inc., 1941), p. 204.

ALTERNATIVES TO ROMANTIC LOVE

Margaret Horton

One of the primary obstacles to a sophisticated understanding of love has been semantic problems. The same word, which is ill-defined in the first place, is used to characterize a number of qualitatively different interpersonal relationships. If that were not enough, this same word is made to cover concepts like patriotism (love of country), to need or require (plants love sunlight), and sexual intercourse (make love). In all, the Random House Dictionary (1967) lists twenty-four definitions for "love," as opposed to five for "hate" and four for "indifference."

To confine ourselves to the interpersonal aspects, however, the definition I find most useful is "Love is that condition in which the happiness of another person is essential to your own" (Heinlein, 1961). This seems to capture the essence of the emotion without being overly restrictive.

Given that definition, then, let us take a look at the functions that erotic adult love serves. First there is the social aspect. It is well known that in our society love is a highly positively sanctioned activity. "All the world loves a lover," and people "in" love are readily forgiven for violations of social norms that would otherwise be punished, such as ignoring all that is going on around them. Part of this indulgence is undoubtedly due to the fond memories lovers elicit from the individuals around them. Nevertheless, it remains that love is an activity that is sanctioned by society as such.

Love and marriage are intimately linked in our society, though this was not always true, nor is it true today in other cultures. This link between love and marriage is a key factor in its social significance. Any society, to remain stable, must have a well-regulated and reliable method for bringing up children and thereby assuring a steady flow of new citizens. There are many ways of accomplishing this goal, such as the extended family or community child-care resources, but in the United States, with its cult of individualism and resistance to government intervention, the nuclear family has been the most efficient child-rearing unit available. There are reasons other than the ones cited which are too complex for the present discussion. There is considerable evidence that this is changing and that social practices will force institutional change (Slater, 1970; Reich, 1971). In the past, the economic interdependency of the marital partners plus the stresses and rewards of large families were significant forces in cementing the marital bond. However, in the last 50 years, the advantages of having fixed roles for husband and wife have declined: women have begun to have economic power in their own right and the positive sanction for having children has been converted to a negative sanction. Love has had to carry most of the burdens for holding marital relationships together.[1] Thus, the emphasis in marriage has shifted to satisfaction with the love relationship, and the divorce rate has risen correspondingly.

A second segment of society that beams approvingly on budding lovers is the manufacturers of consumer goods. The most phenomenal rip-off of all is weddings, but that is only the beginning. One need only listen to a jeweler's ad that urges the teen-age listener to "buy her that pre-engagement ring" to realize that the eyes of merchants light up when they see lovers primarily because they hear the music of cash registers in their ears. Each individual family must have its own vacuum cleaner, blender, dishwasher, garbage disposal, and so on ad nauseam. It might conceivably be argued that if nuclear families

[1] Coppinger and Rosenblatt (1968), in a cross-cultural study, found that love was less necessary as a marital bond in societies where spouses depended upon each other for subsistence. Interestingly, Rosenblatt (1967), in another cross-cultural study of 75 societies, found romantic love to be surprisingly predominant in other societies and that "it no longer seems reasonable to state that romantic love is rare across all cultures and occurs in our own culture because of some grotesque cultural pathology" (p. 479).

need all this, then carried to its ultimate end, merchants should emphasize staying single, because then every *person* would need all this. However, single persons usually realize they don't need all that stuff; whereas in marriage each partner buys it because he thinks the other one wants it. However, businessmen succeed in capitalizing off single persons also because they are more vulnerable to the propaganda that states they are neither sexy nor lovable unless they utilize an enormous number of products ranging from deodorants and toothpaste to late-model sports cars.

A third great force in our society that nudges people into falling in love is the fact that people have to work like crazy to earn enough money to buy all the goods that they need to be lovable. Any person with minimal skills can support himself or herself adequately for a couple of thousand dollars a year. Why would anybody work harder if not for the fact that really desirable things like sexual satisfaction and love are linked in our minds with the possession of material goods. Obviously, to keep the machinery of the economy running smoothly, people must be duped into both producing and consuming these goods. Greenfield (1973) argues . . . that "love" is necessary to induce a man to give away his valued money and possessions to a strange woman and her children. I would say, instead, that the reason men work so hard for material possessions is because they think this will buy them the love they desire.

The personal reasons for being in love are more compelling and better documented than the social. As Casler (1973) points out . . . , one gains access to a sexual outlet, has some measure of security, and is allowed to express dependency needs. One also gains approval, nearly undivided attention, someone to whom it is acceptable to give, and someone to share experiences with. More significant than any of these, love brings relief from the overwhelming loneliness that our society fosters.

So far we have been talking about adult erotic love in general; romantic love is a subcategory which is distinguished by loss of conscious control over one's life and destiny. Romantic love "happens"; it is not brought about; one falls in love. The person is obsessed with the loved one and is unable to concentrate on anything else. The person loses all desire to remain independent, and instead desires to merge and subsume himself into the other. Sovereignty over one's thoughts, feelings, behavior, and destiny are all relinquished (the original escape from freedom).

The advantage to romantic love is that it is exciting; the disadvantages are numerous. A commonly cited criticism of romantic love is that it is too demanding on both the lover and the beloved. John Collier's (1954) short story "The Chaser" illustrates this point. A young man comes into a magic shop seeking a love potion which the old man guarantees him is permanent, will substitute devotion for indifference, admiration for scorn. "She'll want nothing but solitude and you," the old man assures him and continues to describe how jealous she will become, how he will be her sole interest in life, how devotedly she will care for him, and how frantically she will worry if he is a minute late. The young man is rapturous. At the same time the old man is selling him this marvelous potion for the sum of one dollar, he is careful to inform him of the existence of another elixir which will remove the effects of the first. The price of that mixture is $5000.

The second major criticism of romantic love is that it is based on illusion. After all, if you fall in love at first sight, then you cannot have a very realistic notion of the other person. The brisk sale of colognes, make-up, padded bras, padded shoulder jackets, girdles, and elevator shoes demonstrates only the physical aspect of the process of deluding others, and perhaps oneself. Germaine Greer (1971) was not the first to point out that men despise women as a class so much that these illusions are necessary for them to love at all. H. L. Mencken's (1967) statement, "Love is the delusion that one woman differs from another," represents this misogynist point of view. People regularly fall in love with idealizations, then their dreams of perfection are eroded as reality asserts itself. The maintenance of the illusion is even more disastrous to the individuals concerned than would be the consequences if their deceit were discovered. To have a lie accepted as oneself and then to have to live that lie may be poetic justice, but it is certainly a harsh punishment.

The third major problem with romantic love is

that it is predicated on a power-based relationship. Shulamith Firestone's (1971) definition of romantic love is, "Love which has been corrupted by an unequal balance of power." As previously mentioned, one of the characteristics of romantic love is the desire of the participants to lose their individuality and merge with the other person. Now if both lovers are merged, nobody is left to take care of business. So one or the other must emerge as the dominant one; in our culture it is usually the man. Furthermore, men and women have different conceptions of love, and it has vastly different significance for them. It has been traditionally accepted that women devote their lives to love and the fruits thereof, whereas this forms a relatively minor part of men's existence. Simone de Beauvoir (1961) presented a brilliant analysis of this phenomenon. This generalization is much less true now (in that men are more able to admit their emotional needs) but it is still a significant force in establishing the domination of men over women. The root problem here is not that love is a vehicle for men to subjugate women; the reverse would be just as odious; the point is that romantic love, by definition, requires that one partner hold a position of power over the other.

These criticisms alone are enough to establish the destructive nature of romantic love. Yet conditions in American society today are such that love is being called upon to fulfill tremendous needs. Popular songs suggest that if we only had enough love, everyone would be happy, there would be no more wars, and President Kennedy would not have been assassinated. A look at the phenomenal success of *Love Story*, a naive, sentimental tale, shows what a responsive chord was struck in the hearts of the public. Love cannot solve the world's problems and should not be asked to. What we need is a more realistic conception of love and its capabilities. What are the alternatives to romantic love?

One form of love that is rarely discussed, and I believe much more widely practiced than people would like to admit, is contractual love. In this, the partners have an agreement, usually unspoken, to love each other as long as the loved one continues to behave in certain ways. The "her" side of the agreement might run something

like, "As long as you provide for me and don't beat me or insult me in public, I will love you." His might go, "As long as you clean the house, take care of the kids, and are decent to me when I come home, I will love you." Contractual love can be seen in its most cynical and obvious form where one person marries another (and agrees to love) for financial gain. However, at least part of the popularity of couples living together is due to the fact that the bonds are easily dissolved and little commitment was required in the first place. The positive aspect of this model is that unrealistic promises to love one another forever are not made. However, in this particular form, neither are extensive commitments of any kind made to the other person. Granted, all love has conditional elements (or else it would be masochistic), but this form is a little too calculating for me. After all, we do not stop loving our children even if they do things we disapprove of and refuse to tolerate. While I would not deny the authenticity of a love that diminished after the loved one began behaving intolerably, I would like to see a more sophisticated model, one which places more emphasis on character and less on superficial behavior.

A form of love that is attracting more attention than adherents is various attempts at group love. Books like *Stranger in a Strange Land* (Heinlein, 1961) and *The Harrad Experiment* (Rimmer, 1967) have served as models for persons attempting to escape the restrictions of monogamy. The advantage of this arrangement is that one's emotional and sexual satisfaction need not be tied to one object and source. Of course, one must be prepared to give to an equal number of people. My reservations about this approach are more practical than theoretical. Theoretically, it is beautiful, but so is romantic love. Of course it is possible to love more than one person at a time, but to live together creates problems that are almost insurmountable for people raised in our culture. Sexual jealousy is much more easily overcome than, for example, the desire to control events and to relate in hierarchical patterns. Even those problems could be overcome if the people were committed to each other. I have seen several experimental living arrangements fail disastrously because the persons involved were committed to an ideology rather than each other. The only chance I see for such experiments to succeed is if the people involved first discover the nature of their feelings for each other, then extrapolate to the kind of living arrangement that would be appropriate for them. However, even though these attempts frequently fail, the people who are trying deserve congratulations for their bravery. Individuals in our society need to learn how to live and work together instead of retreating to their own cocoons when problems occur.

It seems appropriate at this point to say something about the love that homosexuals feel for one another. Gay liberation has made many people aware for the first time of the fact that homosexuals want, and are entitled to, dignity in their relationships. In order to discuss this conception of love, I find it necessary to make a distinction between old gay and new gay (although this distinction is not necessarily age-related). Old gay relationships are characterized by stereotyped exaggerations of some of the worst features of male-female relations, particularly role-playing and power aspects. Male homosexuals who take the feminine role appear ridiculous to us partly because we see the behavior as being inappropriate for a male, partly because it is an exaggeration, and partly because the feminine behaviors they imitate are often ridiculous in the first place. Female homosexuals who adopt the masculine role are often characterized by extreme machismo (behavior reflecting patriarchal attitudes) and a "tough guy" image. In the old gay world, relationships were based on the romantic love model and were often so game-riddled that it is doubtful if any true intimacy occurred.

The new gays are a completely different breed. Perhaps because the deficiencies of the romantic model were so blatant in their world they were better able to confront issues, and they have now emerged with a model for love that everyone could learn from. Its basic tenet is the right to love one another with freedom and dignity, a right that heterosexuals seldom have to fight for. One major premise is that role-playing is a game that is inappropriate in a love relationship. Each person should be free to do the things he or she does best without the constraints of stereotypes. The other major point is that love should not involve power plays. Neither partner should be dominant. In actual practice, as usual, the real and the ideal are separated by a considerable gap.

It has seemed to me that female homosexuals have been somewhat better able to realize this ideal than males. I attribute this phenomenon to the extra support available to females from the women's movement, though that may or may not be accurate.

Finally, I would like to discuss the model for love that I like. The word "epigenetic" seems most descriptive of the kind of love I am talking about. (Thanks to Gloria Gordon for this suggestion.) In biology, epigenetic refers to the phenomenon of modifications in an embryo due to environmental influences. Thus, epigenetic love is love that continually changes and grows with time and experience. It combines the best facets of the forms of love previously discussed.

The basic principle is that epigenetic love is founded on a realistic appraisal and acceptance of the other as that person *is*, not as that person *should be* according to someone else's ideals. Rather than falling in love, people grow into it. They gradually come to know one another and learn to love the whole person, not a public image.

A second feature is that unrealistic promises are avoided. Like contractual love, no promise to love forever are made, although other kinds of commitments are. Because epigenetic love is based on enduring aspects of the other, this love has a better chance to survive than a love based on illusion. But people change, and so do their values and goals. What is right for one time may not be right for another.

Third, epigenetic love is not possessive. It is recognized that involvement with others enriches the core relationship. This is not to say that sexual promiscuity or being in love with others is necessarily tolerated. Nor is it to say that jealousy does not exist. But jealousy occurs only when the primary relationship is seen as being threatened. The difference between romantic and epigenetic love is in the degree of involvement with others that is seen as threatening.

The fourth point is that maintaining a relationship takes work. In the past, love stories tended to end at the point where people realized they were in love and they got married; it was assumed that they lived happily ever after. But in real life, this assumption is no longer made. Thus, people now ignore these stories and instead spend hours talking together about their feelings and ironing out difficulties.

Out of the same background as the new gay model, epigenetic thinking arrived at the same conclusion: that role playing is detrimental to the person and to the relationship. Each person should be free to do what they do best and want to do. The maintenance work that no one wants to do is divided functionally, not on the basis of sex. Thus there are husbands caring for the children and wives working on the car. There are also many whose behavior conforms to role expectations, but the decision to behave that way was made after consideration of other alternatives; it was not automatically assumed.

Finally, epigenetic love is dedicated to the proposition that men and women are created equal and that neither should be dominant in the love relationship. This proposition has dual drawbacks in that it is difficult to live up to and that decision-making takes work. But these disadvantages are more than outweighed by the positive results. Every interaction that entails oppressed and oppressor results in feelings that are antithetical to intimacy. The oppressor becomes insensitive and indifferent. The oppressed one uses guilt and dependency to maintain his position. By contrast, with epigenetic love, all this is rejected in favor of true give-and-take and mutual support.

Although there have always been isolated examples of couples who have practiced these principles, the incidence is increasing hearteningly. Furthermore, they are increasingly articulate and vocal about their beliefs. John Dryden (1942) once said, "Love either finds equality, or makes it." That is an alternative to romantic love I would like to believe.

REFERENCES

CASLER, L. "Toward a Re-evaluation of Love," in M. E. Curtin, ed., *Symposium on Love*. New York: Behavioral Publications, 1973, pp. 1–36.

COLLIER, J. "The Chaser," in *Fancies and Goodnights*. New York: Bantam Books, 1954, p. 415.

COPPINGER, R., and P. ROSENBLATT. "Romantic Love and Subsistence Dependence Between Spouses," *Southwestern J. Anthropology*, 24 (1968), 310–319.

DE BEAUVOIR, S. *The Second Sex*. New York: Bantam Books, 1961, pp. 603 ff.

DRYDEN, J. In H. L. Mencken, ed., *A New Dictionary of Quotations on Historical Principles from Ancient and Modern Sources*. New York: Alfred A. Knopf, 1942, p. 1715.

FIRESTONE, S. *The Dialectic of Sex*. New York: Bantam Books, 1971, p. 130.

GREENFIELD, S. M. "Love: Some Reflections by a Social Anthropologist," in M. E. Curtin, ed., *Symposium on Love*. New York: Behavioral Publications, 1973, pp. 37–51.

GREER, G. *The Female Eunuch*. New York: McGraw-Hill Book Company, 1971, pp. 245 ff.

HEINLEIN, R. *Stranger in a Strange Land*. New York: Putnam & Sons, 1961, p. 345.

MENCKEN, H. L. In R. L. Woods, ed., *Modern Handbook of Humor*. New York: McGraw-Hill Book Company, 1967, p. 2077.

REICH, C. *The Greening of America*. New York: Random House, Inc., 1971.

RIMMER, R. *The Harrad Experiment*. New York: Bantam Books, 1967.

ROSENBLATT, P. "Marital Residence and the Functions of Romantic Love," *Ethnology*, 6(4) (1967), 471–480.

SLATER, P. *The Pursuit of Loneliness*. Boston: Beacon Press, 1970.

STEIN, J., ed. *Random House Dictionary of the English Language* (unabridged). New York: Random House, Inc., 1967, p. 849.

MULTIPLE LOVE RELATIONSHIPS

Herbert A. Otto

Small children are capable of loving several children with great intensity and devotion. The preteen and teen-ager can let themselves experience different feelings and qualities of love toward several boys or girls at the same time. We as adults are prone to dismiss these manifestations of love as "teen-age crushes." However, another possibility presents itself: that man is capable of not only one but several loving and deep relationships at the same time, if he so wishes and has the freedom to do so.

Although we may not choose to admit it, the main characteristic of these relationships of children and teen-agers to several other age mates is an emotional involvement of considerable intensity, which invariably has some sexual overtones. Similarly, a loving, emotional involvement of varying intensity, quality, and depth at the same time with several persons is not only possible, but has been experienced by many adults. The familiar triangle situation wherein one person loves two persons at the same time but with varying and different qualities of love, has been described, often celebrated, in the literature of all ages. Certainly the experienced marriage counselor has come across many instances of persons deeply, responsibly committed in love to two individuals at the same time. "I love you, you as my wife (husband) but I love her (him) in a different way." How often have these words echoed through the divorce court?

The element of deep pain and struggle in the triangular love complex is often introduced by the mental construct, whether implicit or explicit, *that love and loving should be and can be only on a one-to-one relationship.* Inseparable from this mental set is the "love-as-ownership" issue. Seemingly a carry-over from male ownership of goods and chattels (women were legally considered to be chattel in many Western countries into the early twentieth century), love is seen as conferring ownership rights. "I love you, you love me—therefore I own (should have) *all* of your love" is accepted as a basic premise. Ownership and possession have been both the delight and despair of lovers throughout the centuries. However, it is exactly these mental constructs of ownership and possession which create the barriers and griefs on which love so often flounders. Owning or expecting to own all of another person's mature heterosexual love as one's lifelong due is one of the bases of contemporary monogamy—an institution which is in difficulty. (The large divorce rate and the even larger subclinical incidence of marital unhappiness which never reaches the counselor or divorce court is a clear indication of the deep-seated problems inherent in today's modes of married relating.)

When love is conceived as bestowing ownership qualities, that which we call "jealousy" emerges in clearer perspective. Jealousy is attributed in part to outraged property rights ("I own your love—you own mine"), and in part to the formulations "I must own, have, possess, *all* of your love and attention; otherwise you are not giving me what rightfully belongs to me," and "I am afraid of losing what is mine."

Another major element in jealousy and the process of love between two people is insecurity. At the very base of much insecurity is love starvation. Everyone is starved for love—few of us have enough love in our lives. If, then, we do let love come into our lives, we often have reached such a point of starvation that, like the hungry man, we must have all. We insist on total possession, even if it kills love. Suffering from love starvation, we deeply fear that there isn't enough to go around— for that has been our experience. We must have every bit of love the other person is capable of giving. Our own feelings of insecurity, based on love starvation, demand this.

When we feel insecure, we question: "Does the person I love really love me?" The answer we give ourself is "Of course he loves me *if he gives me all of the love he is capable of giving.* But if he gives even a part of this love to another, he does not truly love me." The deeper issues here are those of self-worth and self-identity. If a woman is not sufficiently secure and fulfilled by her status as a wife and homemaker, she may reach out and supplement her sense of identity and selfhood by incorporating considerable elements of her husband's identification (including his successes, values, viewpoints) as a part of her ego structure. Her sense of self-identity may become blurred through this incorporation process and at the same time there may be an awareness and resentment of what is going on. This symbiotic process of supplementing her identity by deriving part of it from her husband (or lover) leaves the woman in a vulnerable position. A threat of loss of the man (the possibility of his sharing his capacity for affection with someone else) undermines her sense of identity and contributes materially to the end product we call "jealousy." Happily, with the advent of Women's Liberation many women are now able to attain a new sense of self-worth and identity separate and apart from their function as wife and homemaker.

A woman or man may also supplement [her/his] sense of self-worth by a strong identification with the partner. The more solid a person's sense of self-worth, the less likely he is to succumb to petty feelings of jealousy. The greater our sense of self-worth, the less easily are we hurt by actions of the beloved *which we interpret subjectively* as indicating a diminishing of his love. When the sense of self-worth of one person becomes excessively dependent on the love of another person, the entire relationship is in difficulty. Love can and does make us feel more worthy, but this should be a by-product rather than the main product of love. Love can and does give us greater self-esteem, but this is a part of the process of love, not *the* process.

Identity in love also has another aspect. Most lovers report a simultaneous blurring and heightening of their sense of self. They feel their own identity more intensely at the same time that they experience oneness with the identity of the beloved. These pulsating changes are a part of the process of love. As the lovers temporarily merge their identities in the process of love, they emerge with new permutations and growth in their personality. In the merging of identities there is a cross-pollination as subtle nuances and factors in one person's being enrich the other. Again, if one person's sense of identity is excessively dependent for its definition on the beloved, the relationship is in difficulty. A heightened sense of identity emerges from the process of love—it is not the focus of love.

One of the main doubts of most men and women when confronted with the idea that a person is capable of simultaneous multiple love relationships centers around the belief that everyone has only a limited amount of love to give. This is true if we do not have enough love inputs and positive inputs, enough caring coming in. If we become participants in the stream of love, our capacity for loving is as limitless as our capacity for vital, creative living. In the final analysis, ecstatic living is inseparable from the free flow of loving.

To many, the notion of multiple love relationships is ludicrous, bizarre, *unthinkable.* This is precisely the point. *We are what we think of ourselves,* we are what we feel, we are our mental constructs, our vision of ourselves. Today we may not feel like it or may not be ready for a multiple love relationship. Tomorrow we may change. Or we may never change.

This, then, is my main point: I may not myself have the interest or need to enter into a multiple love relationship; but I can understand, accept it (and perhaps feel a little envious) when other people are involved in such a relationship. From my point of view, love is so rare and so precious that those who are able to share love should never be discouraged from the risk taking inherent in giving their love to more than one person. Love is too rare to discourage its sharing.

If we believe in monogamy, a major question with which we are left is: "Do we believe in only monogamistic loving?" Or, to put it differently, if we encounter a married person who has entered into a love relationship with several other single or married persons, what is our attitude?

Kinsey, Cuber, and other researchers have found that the lifelong monogamistic commitment is a pious fiction for many people. An exclusive sexual (and emotional) lifelong commitment to the marriage partner is the exception rather than the rule. Having a spur-of-the moment affair or sexual encounter of some sort at some time(s) during the marriage seems to be one characteristic of the contemporary union. The extramarital liaison is rarely openly admitted to, and rarely are its implications fully explored through discussion by both marital partners. However, this type of relationship has become institutionalized to a certain extent. It is often called "an arrangement" and one or both partners feel free to engage in other sexual relationships while exercising all due discretion. Many couples who *live* according to such an arrangement have grave difficulty accepting it, do not deal with it honestly, cannot come to emotional terms with it, and cannot discuss it.

The affair or sexual encounter of the married person in most instances seems to be an act of desperation, laden with guilt feelings and a nagging sense of transgression. It appears to stem from the unacknowledged realization that the love relationship with one person exclusively and for the rest of one's life is, for most people, an unsatisfactory compact. Implicit also is the fact that in many marriages, due to a multitude of factors, the interaction between partners opposes and stifles the development of individual potential and interpersonal growth. The partners, in fact, have an investment in maintaining the relationship as it is and where it is, however unsatisfactory this reality might be. Also, since people grow at different rates and in different directions, couples often tend to grow apart and outgrow each other while at the same time they attempt to prevent each other from growing.

A loving and sexual relationship with several persons simultaneously can be a means of personality growth and self-unfoldment and seems to meet a deep and present need in many persons. In many instances, the extramarital affair is a means of reaching out for further personality growth, for fulfillment, through an emotional and sexual relationship with a person other than the spouse. Sometimes it can also be understood as an act of desperation designed to maintain the marital equilibrium. ("I love my husband dearly but I had to do it—I couldn't stand our marriage the way it was any longer. Yet I don't want a divorce. My husband and I belong together.")

I want to make clear that I am not opposed to the institution of marriage. My interest is in ex-

ploring alternatives to monogamy, as I believe that the living, loving arrangements of man in a free society should be bounded only by the limits of his imagination and needs. I am very much interested in regenerating the institution of marriage so that it can become a more viable and workable structure.*

At various phases during most people's lifelong unfoldment and growth, there may be a need to have a loving and sexual relationship with more than one individual. Conscious acknowledgment and communication of this need may open a new dimension of freedom. When multiple love relationships have become socially acceptable to a greater degree than the acceptability today accorded to the institution of divorce, it is highly probable there will be concomitant significant gains in man's capacity to accept and love both himself and his fellow man. In a society characterized by estrangement, repression, violence, generation and credibility gaps, *all possible loving relationships must be fostered to reverse the course of destruction and to make man more human.*

"COMMITMENT WITH FREEDOM" —A CREDO

One of the central issues in any deep union between two people, and particularly in marriage, involves the areas of freedom, trust, commitment, and dedication. These concepts often are not static but developmental—they may expand, broaden, deepen or change as a result of the relationship or as a result of life experience. In too many instances internal changes in attitude or viewpoint concerning these central issues by the man or woman are never communicated to the other partner. The issues are not openly discussed until triggered by a crisis event. I consider it most important that a couple about to enter into a deep union of any type mutually explore these issues which are so central to the nature and direction of

* See Herbert A. Otto, *More Joy in Your Marriage* (New York: Hawthorn, 1969), and "The New Marriage: Marriage as a Framework for Developing Personal Potential," in Herbert A. Otto, ed., *The Family in Search of a Future* (New York: Appleton-Century-Crofts, 1970).

the developing relationship. Such avoidance is part of a universal human tendency to shun confrontation and exploration of the other person's values and viewpoints because we fear conflict and disagreement. Our need for love is so great that we let our fears of conflict keep us from coming to grips with the central issues of the relationship. Yet, resolution of these very issues can open us to new dimensions of understanding and caring and bring us the measure of love called for by our need.

To me, the essence of a relationship is capsulated in the Eastern maxim, "Commitment without chains." I believe in the absolute commitment of two people to each other in love, in caring, and in dedication to each other's growth. Yet I am deeply convinced that my love must have freedom within the relationship. For example, I would consider it an infringement on my beloved's freedom to say, "You must not have a sexual relationship with anyone else." I may have my wishes and express them—but wishes are

neither imperatives, commands, nor rules. It is here that I must place the greatest possible amount of trust in my partner and our love. I trust my partner and our togetherness sufficiently to know that any relationship with another person, sexual or otherwise, is a part of the dedication and commitment of our love. It may be the result of various needs and causes within the mysterious being who is my love. I trust that whatever my partner does is done within the overriding framework of our love and with the preservation, maintenance, and continuation of our love in mind. In this sense, then, I must trust my partner's dedication to the centrality of our love and our commitment to each other. This is the freedom of responsibility—I trust my beloved to be responsible for the person she is and can be and for the creative unfoldment of our union. This to me is the freedom which we as lovers must have, to continue to grow in our love throughout the years.

TOPIC 13

Marriage

Now! At Last! The new fall lineup of the very latest plans and styles for satisfactory living together. The list includes a dazzling variety of sizes and shapes, options and accessories, never before made available to the general public, and the cost is surprisingly low. You pay your money and take your choice, and may you live happily ever after. Or at least until next Tuesday.

—preface to Man + Woman: A Consumer's Guide to Contemporary Pairing Patterns Including Marriage

There is more and more discussion these days about "alternate life styles," and the present youth generation is not so locked into the old pattern—or at least the old tempo—of completing high school, attempting college, marrying, having children, and starting off on a career path on which one more or less stays until retirement. Still, although it is challenged and changing, marriage as an institution is not going out of style.

From one vantage point, American marriage appears to be in trouble. Nearly one in every three marriages ends in divorce. In some urban areas and other sections of the country, divorce rates are sharply higher than this. In California, for example, nearly two out of every three marriages end in the courts.

Even among those who remain married, the situation seems far from perfect. Jackson and Lederer interviewed 601 couples on the West Coast and in New England for their study *The Mirages of Marriage.* They found that over three quarters of these couples had frequently and seriously considered divorce, and over half remained married only because divorce was too difficult, painful, or expensive.

Further ammunition for the critics of marriage can be found in present-day infidelity rates, which are higher now than ever before in American history. It has been estimated that 60 percent of all married men in this country have had extramarital relations. Adultery rates for married women, although not as high, are not inconsequential: 30 to 35 percent have been estimated unfaithful.

However, from another vantage point, marriage today seems better than ever. Despite its pitfalls, wedlock has lost none of its popularity. The United States is one of the most marrying countries in the world: it is estimated that for the present youth generation, 97 or 98 percent will be married during their lifetime.

Even among people who get divorced, matrimony remains a popular institution. Such people appear not to be escaping marriage but, rather, looking for a better one. Most divorcing persons remarry. And if they get divorced again, they remarry again. Today about two-thirds of all divorcing women remarry, and more than three-fourths of all divorcing men do so.

According to some experts, divorce, infidelity, and related marital phenomena are not symptoms of terminal disease, but rather signs that marriage is changing to better accommodate present-day conditions. And despite examples of group and communal life styles and a new tolerance for living alone or living together without marriage, there is little threat to monogamy as the principal kind of pairing. But the old patriarchal form of monogamy is on its way out and some newer forms are here or in the offing.

A guide to marriage models

So many different patterns of pairing are being advocated today that Carlfred Broderick, in the lead article, presents a "consumer's guide" to help bring some order out of the exuberance. As Broderick sees it, there are five key issues or choices leading to either a "ready-made" or a "customized" marriage model. As for Broderick, he elects the "ever-popular traditional marriage," which he says is "the model with the lowest maintenance costs and the sturdiest performance record."

The traditional model

In the second selection, Patricia Kroken sticks up for the traditional model of marriage. She writes, "I delight in being a woman, and even more, I delight in being a married woman, for I feel that marriage is the foundation on which my identity rests." Kroken accuses the feminists of demeaning wifely and maternal roles. "Being a wife and mother has given me as full a life as I could wish for," she says. "I'm a housewife—and I have the right to be proud."

The shared-roles model

More and more wives work outside the home these days, and more and more husbands help around the house, but in Alix Shulman's marriage (presented in the third article) the sharing of career, family, and household roles is complete. The Shulmans fell into a traditional pattern upon the arrival of their first child but this proved to be unsatisfactory. What followed was a rejection of the conventional roles that had turned them into a "lame family," a division of responsibilities carefully spelled out in a formal agreement, and a happier life.

The reversed-roles model

According to Department of Labor statistics, there are more than 200,000 male homemakers in this country today. Most of these men are widowed or divorced, but the married remainder includes Samuel Brown, who describes his life as a househusband in the fourth article. Brown and his wife have largely reversed traditional roles; she teaches, and he writes and keeps house. This role reversal came about when the Browns discovered that Ms. Brown would rather work, and Mr. Brown would rather stay home. Although it is not without its problems, this model works well for this couple.

The time-limited model

The Greenes, described by Tomi Knaefler in the fifth article, have a month-to-month marriage contract which is automatically renewed unless cancelled by either party. Both Tom and Pat Greene have been married twice before and both feel that the traditional marriage contract hinders rather than helps the marital relationship. Knaefler writes, "Tom and Pat feel their month-to-month contract helps keep their marriage 'alive' and 'in the present' because nothing is automatic. Problems are dealt with promptly and not put off on the notion that there's plenty of time later to deal with things that are hard to talk about."

The living-together model

Living together can be a combination of courtship and marriage that allows a couple an opportunity to explore their relationship and meet each other's sexual, love, and other needs but with easier ingress and egress than marriage. This kind of pairing may lead to marriage or, especially for couples who do not want children, it can be its own life style. In the sixth reading Theodora Wells and Lee S. Christie tell why they chose to live together rather than marry. In brief, they feel that marriage locks spouses into dependent roles and robs them of their personhood; by contrast, living together allows for separateness and individual growth, as well as for togetherness.

The group model

In the last article Donald Bremner discusses group marriage and presents an example in the marriage of Mike and Barbara and Bob. This marriage began with Mike and Barbara then added Bob, and there are plans for a fourth and possibly a fifth partner in the future. The advantages that some persons find in group marriage include greater companionship and opportunity for personal growth, and also more sexual variety and adult models for children. A chief disadvantage is the greater complexity in day-to-day living and problem-solving because of additional partners.

FOR PERSONAL APPLICATION

1. What kind of marriage do you have or expect to have? Why?
2. What kind of marriage would you want for yourself? Why?
3. Discuss or explain any discrepancies between your answers to the first two items.
4. Would you consider singlehood (living alone and not marrying) as a life style for yourself? Why or why not?
5. Would you consider living together as a prelude to marriage or as a semi-permanent or permanent life style? Why or why not?
6. Would you consider a group or communal marriage as a life style? Why or why not?
7. Discuss your reactions to conventional roles, shared roles, and reversed roles in marriage.
8. What do you expect the institution of marriage to be like in the next generation (20 to 25 years hence)?
9. What qualities do you feel are important in a mate? Would these qualities be more essential in some marriage models than in others? Why or why not?
10. What qualities do you see in yourself that might make for success or failure in marriage? Would these qualities be more crucial in some marriage models than in others? Why or why not?
11. Write down a dicussion item (not given above) that seems particularly relevant to this topic and you, and discuss it.

FOR SMALL GROUPS

1. *Playing marriage roles.* Several members volunteer to enact some contrasting models of marriage (for example, marriages in which there are conventional roles, shared roles, and reversed roles, respectively). Afterwards the other members relate the way these roles were enacted in the group to the way they have seen them portrayed in real pairs.
2. *Arguing marriage models.* The leader or one member of the group writes down the names of various models of marriage on cards (one model to a card). These cards are placed face down in the middle of the group. Then each member in turn picks a card and makes as strong a presentation as he can in support of this model as his personal choice; he must be persuasive and, indeed, try to convince the others that this is the model he thinks would be best for him. At the same time the other members of the group must argue against this model;

they must be equally as convincing that it is no good and would not work for the particular member. When the argument is over, and before going to the next card, everyone tells how he really feels about the model in question.

3. *Comparing mate values.* The group divides into subgroups of men and women. Each subgroup meets by itself and arrives at a written list of five qualities which members agree are important in a mate. Then the whole group reassembles, and the subgroups compare and discuss their separate lists of qualities and determine reasons for any discrepancies.

FOR FURTHER READING

Ackerman, N. W., et al. *Marriage: For and Against.* New York: Hart, 1972.

Bach, G. R., and R. M. Deutsch. *Pairing.* New York: Wyden, 1970.

Bach, G. R., and P. Wyden. *The Intimate Enemy.* New York: William Morrow, 1969.

Bernard, J. *The Future of Marriage.* New York: World, 1972.

DeLora, J. S., and J. R. DeLora, eds. *Intimate Life Styles: Marriage and Its Alternatives.* Pacific Palisades, Calif.: Goodyear, 1972.

Lederer, W. J., and D. D. Jackson. *The Mirages of Marriage.* New York: W. W. Norton & Co., Inc., 1968.

O'Neill, N., and G. O'Neill. *Open Marriage: A New Life Style for Couples.* Philadelphia: J. B. Lippincott, 1971.

Rogers, C. R. *Becoming Partners: Marriage and Its Alternatives.* New York: Delta, 1972.

MAN + WOMAN: A CONSUMER'S GUIDE TO CONTEMPORARY PAIRING PATTERNS INCLUDING MARRIAGE

Carlfred B. Broderick

Now! At Last! The new fall lineup of the very latest plans and styles for satisfactory living together. The list includes a dazzling variety of sizes and shapes, options and accessories, never before made available to the general public, and the cost is surprisingly low. You pay your money and take your choice, and may you live happily ever after. Or at least until next Tuesday.

The man-woman relationship has always been a popular but variegated commodity and the behavioral sciences have never been loath to set up guidelines for consumers. Until recently the "rational" guidelines for choosing a suitable partner and developing a fulfilling relationship were pretty much agreed upon by the large body of "experts" with only an occasional dissenting voice to add color and provide a straw man for the main position.

Today all that has changed. The tide of books and articles advocating the widest variety of styles of pairing has reached flood proportions. As if this were not enough there are a seemingly infinite choice of lectures, classes, workshops, marathons and training sessions available to help the couple enrich their relationship (each according to its own lights).

Even the most enrichment oriented couple might get confused as to whether it was best to strive toward an Open Marriage, Mini-Marriage, Multilateral Marriage or Trial Marriage, or perhaps simply Honest Sex, Total Sex, or Desensitized Intimacy (in the latter case they get to watch several hours worth of filmed heterosexual and homosexual intercourse, masturbation, and fun and games in living color). Clearly there is need for a Consumers' Guide so that you can see at a glance just what the basic issues are that differentiate one approach from another.

After considerable sifting it is possible to reduce the number of key issues to five. The anatomy of most of the New Visions and also of most of the Traditional Wisdoms can be clearly viewed when their positions on each of these five issues are determined. To plot the profile of each movement would be too great a task for one brief article. Instead we will lay out each of the five issues and some of the most frequently discussed positions on each issue. The reader can then analyze the features of competing pairing patterns or even develop his own model, tailored to his own position on all five issues.

ISSUE #1: FREEDOM FROM PARENTHOOD VS. FULFILLMENT THROUGH PARENTHOOD

Position A: Anti-Natal (Utopian or Brave New World Variety)

In the best of all possible worlds children would be the wards of the state freeing all adults to pursue careers, fulfillment, etc. without encumbrance. Whether in the Huxlean fantasy where children are conceived in a test tube, developed in a bottle and decanted in a state nursery or in the more pragmatic mode advocated by Plato and Marx and Engels where the children are born to mothers but are immediately turned over to professional caretakers, this position holds that both children and adults profit from the elimination of the parent role in society. Freed from family ties the couple is free to be infinitely flexible in its arrangements, sex is free, commitments are open, etc.

Position B: Anti-Natal (Elitist or Jet-Set Variety)

This is not a societal philosophy but a personal preference to live an unencumbered life. Research shows that children compete with pair intimacy. These couples opt for an adult-centered life style of dual careers, travel, cultural enrichment, and exciting shared experiences. Moreover, with two incomes they can afford it.

Position C: Time-Limited Parenting

These couples commit 20 to 25 years of their marriage to childbearing but before and especially after attempt to achieve the life style of the Jet-set group in Position B. Often the parenting years themselves are characterized by a conscious determination not to let the children stifle the growth of the romance or of the career goals of the wife-mother.

Position D: Parenthood as Career

These couples have parenthood as a central focus of their pair relationship. The mother only works outside the home if she can justify it as "best for the family." Much of the father's spare time is spent with the family as a whole. Family rituals and traditions develop. After the children are officially launched important ties are maintained between the families. The relationship changes as the children raise families of their own, but the older couple never fully vacate their parental role while adding the grandparental role.

ISSUE #2: PAIR AS A SETTING FOR SELF ACTUALIZATION AND INDIVIDUAL GROWTH VS. PAIR AS A MUTUAL AID SOCIETY WITH DIVISION OF LABOR AND INTERDEPENDENCY

Position A: Whole-Soul (Utopian Orientation)

The "whole soul" point of view is that the man-woman relationship (or any other relationship, for that matter) only reaches *its* full potential when it facilitates its members' reaching *their* full human potentials. There are many versions of what constitutes "full human potential" and the vocabulary of each is, to some degree, unique.

Nevertheless there are several points common to nearly all versions of the movement. Everything is focused in the here and now. The past is dead, the future may never be; it is what you are experiencing at the very moment which is real and getting in touch with it is your prime imperative if you would be whole. This has two aspects. First, it emphasizes keeping your current options open by not mortgaging your future with long range commitments. In this way you avoid getting "boxed in" or "closed minded." Secondly, *awareness* is all; for example, the couple must be absolutely honest with each other about their feelings and especially their most unacceptable feelings—anger, lust, fear, pain. The standard treatment for hung-up couples is sensitivity training or group confrontation—often on a marathon basis where barriers to emotional honesty erode under the stimulus of group pressure and physical exhaustion. Equally important is the development of sensory awareness, becoming intensely in touch with your own body and your senses of touch and taste and sight and smell. One branch of the movement is especially sensitive to the symbolic and actual defense against openness which clothes afford. For this group, at least, "letting it all hang out" is not just a vivid phrase.

One step further in the same direction is the ecstatic experience or the altered state of consciousness. This takes many forms both as to means and ends with each school defending its own mark of grace against all comers. Within the movement you may seek *satori* (the state of sublime detachment from all desire) through Eastern religious disciplines, *rebirth* through accepting Jesus, *astrotravel* through occult meditation, *grooving* through psychedelic drugs, *tranquility* through training your alpha waves with an electronic brain wave monitor and many, many more. Currently in fashion is pain as a royal road to the exalted state. Two of the most chic versions are Primal Scream therapy (based on sensory deprivation and re-experiencing all pains back to the pain of birth) and Rolfing (where each part of your body is painfully massaged until you have worked through all of the meaning attached to each pain).

But whatever the approach, the key to this position is that the pair is only valuable if it facilitates the growth of the one. Constricting relationships should be exchanged for those in which the partners are helping each other to find their full Human Potential.

Position B: Mutual Enrichment

Midway between the thoroughgoing (and often expensive) personal renovations of the whole soul movement and the more traditional "strengthening marriage" position discussed below are a variety of mutual enrichment programs. Some are aimed impartially at both partners, laying out programs of improved communication, more effective arguing, better sex or whatever. Others are aimed primarily at the woman, urging her to develop in ways that will enrich both. Prescriptions vary from recipes for becoming a "fascinating" woman (mix equal parts canny Victorian matron and behavioral mod shaping technique) to brews designed to convert any housewife into a "sensuous" woman (add Masters and Johnson to a basic blend of grandpa's racier fantasies and then lace generously with women's lib).

Position C: Strengthening Marriage

Rather than personal enrichment (let alone achieving the "full human potential") this position focuses on the institution of marriage itself. It emphasizes sacrifice, mutual support, and the traditional values of stability, exclusivity, and the fulfillment of conventional role expectations. The husband should be a good provider (steady pay check, provides the "advantages" to his family), a good father (spends time with the children, firm but understanding, backs up mother) and good husband (good leadership ability but emotionally supportive and personally gentle). The wife should be a good housekeeper (attractive home—neither too messy nor too compulsively neat, good manager), a good mother (warm, interested in children, informed on child development and applied psychology) and a good wife (warm, sexy, supportive). Books and articles on this view are less eye catching but nearly all of the mass media supply persuasive material supporting this "middle American" position.

ISSUE #3: INCLUSIVITY VS. EXCLUSIVITY

Position A: Multilateral Marriage

Marriage among three or more persons is held by many to be the ultimate expression of interpersonal maturity and openness. Everyone in the group is not married to everyone else but each person is married to at least two other persons.

This arrangement provides a broader base of intimate companionship within the marriage. In particular it includes unusual opportunity for closeness with adult members of one's own sex. Sexual life is enriched with variety in the context of commitment. Children receive the benefits of multiple parenting. And finally the whole group can become a continual encounter session with a unique combination of group support and group pressure for change.

The trouble with group marriage is that it makes heavier demands on individuals' discipline and selflessness than many can bear. Out of 20 that were followed in a study for two years only six survived that time period. Apparently pleasing two or three husbands or wives when compounded with trying to get along with two or three co-husbands or co-wives is not exactly a piece of cake.

Position B: The Commune

Although communes take many forms, all are an attempt to establish face to face intimacy with a larger circle of close associates. Most communes are more conventional in their sexual arrangements than multilateral marriages, but a few are based on open sexual patterns. Close association is always demanding and the communes that survive best are those based on common religions or ideological commitment and discipline.

Another stable form described by James Ramsey (he calls them "evolutionary" communes to distinguish them from the more radical "revolutionary" variety) is based on formal social contract (including legal incorporation more often than not). These groups band together to enable members to succeed better in the competitive American system through pooling their resources, living arrangements, etc. The least stable are the revolutionary or utopian communes which tend to resist organization and structure and thus fail to sustain themselves or their boundaries.

Position C: Swingers

These couples are traditionally exclusive with respect to most things (living arrangements, care of children, holding of property, etc.) but involve themselves with other couples in sexual exchange or in group sex. Since they swing as a couple and by mutual consent they do not view this lack of sexual exclusivity as a threat to their own relationship. Many claim their marriages have been strengthened by this style of life although others do not survive. Studies indicate that most swingers return to a more traditional marital format after two or three years simply because it is such an emotionally taxing style of life.

Position D: Open Marriage

Couples committed to the human potential philosophy (see Issue #2 above) may maintain conventional living arrangements and yet be open to intimate friendships with other couples or individuals which may include sex. This differs from swinging in that swingers typically avoid close emotional ties with their partners, and tend to view sex recreationally. Proponents of the Open Marriage (or Honest Sex, or whatever name various authors chose to give it), on the other hand, exalt sexual intimacy as an ultimate sacrament of togetherness between persons who are already in deep communion in other dimensions.

Position E: Traditional Monogamy

"Forsaking all others, till death do us part." Still popular although on the defensive as a moral position in view of the enthusiasm of the advocates of alternative positions.

ISSUE #4: PERMANENT COMMITMENT VS. PERMANENT AVAILABILITY

Position A: Universal Total Availability

Outside of the writings of a few Utopians (and also a few anti-Utopians such as Aldous Huxley, who were scared to death by the future they fore-

saw) the condition of universal total availability has never existed. There are individuals in our society committed to this principle, however.

Position B: Tentative Commitment —Options Open

The position that in the best of all possible worlds one could enjoy mutual love, trust and sexual satisfaction while avoiding marriage has been popular from ancient times. Formerly it was usually identified with the traditional male aversion to the "ball and chain," but in recent years it has become popular with both sexes and especially among college students. The rationale has both pragmatic and philosophical components. On the practical side these young people feel that their futures are too uncertain to make long range commitments. Moreover they are in a period of rapid personal development and they don't want to settle permanently on someone who may not "keep up" with their own growth. Finally, until they are settled in a job they may feel in no position to take on the commitments of home and family. From a philosophical viewpoint also they find this open ended relationship more attractive than marriage. For one thing, it is more sincere since there is no constraint against either person leaving if [he/she] tires of the arrangement. Moreover, it avoids the distasteful necessity of involving representatives of the establishment (clergy, magistrates, county registrars, etc.).

Research on this form of pairing is being done at several universities but the results are not all in yet. Early returns suggest that it seldom survives graduation and job placement. Couples either break up and go their separate ways or get married.

Position C: Time-Limited Commitments

The concept of a three or five year renewable marriage contract has been seriously suggested, although, so far as we know, it has never been put into practice anywhere. The notion is that the emotional and financial costliness of divorce could be avoided in this way along with the equally costly experience of a long term empty or destructive marriage. Certainly such an idea would necessitate a complete restructuring of modern romantic thought (try substituting "for three years" in place of "forever" in the standard romantic exchange). Also it would seem that bringing a child into the world with so tenuous a guarantee of partnership might be particularly taxing. Another variation would have a time-limited trial marriage contract to be followed (if the option were exercised) by a regular life-time commitment.

Position D: Open-Ended Marriage with Serial Polygamy

This is, in effect, our present system. California is the first state to grant divorce on a no fault, no contest basis. Either partner may end the marriage by filing for divorce. The judge's only job is to preside over the equal division of property and the assignment of custody of the children. Other states will follow. An increasing number of people will promise to "love, honor, and cherish till death do us part" more than once.

Position E: Life Long (or Even Eternal) Commitment

This traditional model is still the ideal of most Americans, even those who get divorced. Most people wouldn't believe it but despite the excitement about rising divorce rates, over two-thirds of us die married to the only spouse we have ever had. Surveys show that many believe (contrary to the doctrines of their own denomination) that their marriage will survive in after-life, as well. Curiously those who expect the most from marriage (in terms of personal growth and satisfaction) are often those most disappointed by it; marriages based on division of labor with mutual support appear to be the most enduring.

ISSUE #5: EQUALITY VS. COMPLEMENTARITY

Position A: Radical Women's Liberation

This position would settle for nothing less than the universal elimination of all social and economic distinction based on sex. Most feminists do not reject what might be called stylistic differences as long as they do not connote inferiority/ superiority but they would insist that responsibility for housework, child care, and income belong to each sex equally. Moreover, each would have equal access to the full range of economic, social and political activities available to the other. In order to achieve this, many, but not all, adopt an anti-marriage or anti-natal position.

Position B: Cake Eaters (or Moderation in All Things)

These people want a world in which women can compete successfully with men in any field and be rewarded equally for equal performance in any field, but are committed also to the woman's right not to compete with men at all. They would like traditional sex roles to be an available option for women and men who prefer that pattern.

Position C: Complementarity

This point of view is that men and women are fundamentally different in their makeup and in their relationship to society. Men are naturally more aggressive, sexual, cerebral, mechanical, etc. Women are naturally more gentle, nurturant, expressive, manually dextrous, etc. It does women and men and society at large a disservice to attempt to suppress these differences in the name of equality. Men **and** women are most fulfilled when teamed in a **complementary** coalition with each supplying strengths the other lacks.

Well—there you are. Choose your pairing profile and may you find what you seek.

As a parting service here is my own choice for

✔ BEST BUY

Although some customers may be happy to pay a little extra for some of the special models available, years of laboratory testing indicate that the model with the lowest maintenance costs and the sturdiest performance record is the ever-popular, traditional marriage (permanent, monogamous, mutual support oriented, featuring parenthood as career and optional cake-eating or complementary stance in sex roles). In fact, I've had one for twenty years myself and it's running better today than when it was new. I recommend it.

I'M A HOUSEWIFE—AND I HAVE THE RIGHT TO BE PROUD*

Patricia Kroken

I delight in being a woman, and even more, I delight in being a married woman, for I feel that marriage is the foundation on which my identity rests. I cannot discuss myself without discussing my husband and our relationship. Rather than feeling stifled, as married women frequently say they do, I am convinced that my marriage has provided me with a framework on which to build a fulfilling life, a framework that has allowed me to expand my consciousness and to enjoy being the person that I am.

My husband and I met as high-school students and were "in like" long before either of us admitted to being in love. In spite of parental protests because of our tender age, we found a relationship that endured the trauma of adolescence and the death of both his parents and that culminated in our marriage.

Bruce was a junior in college and I a sophomore. We had dissimilar fields of study, converging and diverging opinions on nearly everything, little money and a strength in our union that made us feel that as long as we were together, we could weather anything. Ours was a partnership, and we did not discuss our roles as man and woman, husband and wife, for they evolved naturally according to our personalities and the demands made upon us.

Bruce earned the money with his part-time job

and I governed its dispensation. I typed his term papers and he proofread mine. We did not see our "weaknesses" as inherent in our respective sex but rather in our individual personalities. Instead of trying to change each other to fit recognized roles, we adapted to each other's flaws and capitalized on our strengths.

When Bruce was graduated we moved quite a distance from the college we'd both been attending so that he could take his first teaching job. I resigned myself to the fact that I would get my degree "someday" when we were living closer to a college. "Someday" wasn't good enough for Bruce. He encouraged me to work as a student teacher at a nearby secondary school, thus fulfilling one of the degree requirements for my major. Later on he endured our five-day separations when I commuted to classes, living at a college during the week and driving home on weekends.

In the midst of my harried education I suffered a ruptured ectopic pregnancy and nearly lost my life. Frantically I threw myself into schoolwork as therapy. When I felt myself totter under the weight of our despair Bruce comforted me; when I felt sorry for myself he chided me; and when I finally was graduated with honors we rejoiced—together.

After graduation I turned eagerly to a new job—that of housewife. And my world expanded before me as I grabbed at opportunities my schooling had forced me to neglect for years. I joined a service club and a children's-theater board, took part in two plays, instructed a group of majorettes, began sewing most of our clothing, joined the city band and read insatiably. We were cautiously joyful when I once again became pregnant and wildly joyful when our daughter Christina was born.

Through all this I watched the Women's Liberation Movement flower. I listened to its proponents, read their articles in magazines, agreed and disagreed with them in turn. I examined my life in terms of who I was as a person, ticking off the limitations that had been imposed on me by a child, by a husband and by the rambling old home we had bought. My teaching certificate weighed on my conscience like an albatross around my neck. Why was I sitting at home when I could enjoy the rewards—not to mention the extra income—of the profession I was trained for? Why? Because I had *chosen* to live this way. I could (and can) agree with the movement in theory, but in reality being a wife and mother has given me as full a life as I could wish for.

Granted, housework implies seemingly endless janitorial duties—babies bring mounds of diapers and husbands must be fed and kept in clean shirts—but a woman's life need not end there. A housewife has time on her hands, either the long, empty hours of the complainer or the fleeting, flying minutes of the eternally curious innovator. Time can be either a wife's bane or her boon, and I use mine resourcefully, cramming each minute with the business of living, growing and learning.

I feel that feminists make a grave and perhaps fatal error when they demean the housewife and mother, depicting her life as filled with empty hours and enslavement to squalling brats. Perhaps it is because I view my home as a sanctuary rather than a prison. Yes, I work hard for "room and board," but no one can convince me that my job is inferior to anyone else's because I am not monetarily paid. I see my husband come home exhausted by the pressures of his job; I know he lacks the time to pursue many activities he would like. No, I don't want his so-called "rights."

After six years of marriage Bruce and I still are partners, and we still need each of our special talents. It's my turn to bolster him—my turn to encourage, to push and to comfort. We have given, we have endured, we have loved—we love. I am a woman, and I wouldn't have it any other way!

A CHALLENGE TO EVERY MARRIAGE

Alix Shulman

When my husband and I were first married, a decade ago, keeping house was less a burden than a game. We both worked full-time in New York City, so our small apartment stayed empty most of the day and taking care of it was very little trouble. Twice a month we'd spend Saturday cleaning and doing our laundry at the laundromat. We shopped for food together after work, and though I usually did the cooking, my husband was happy to help. Since our meals were simple and casual, there were few dishes to wash. We occasionally had dinner out and usually ate breakfast at a diner near our offices. We spent most of our free time doing things we enjoyed together, such as taking long walks in the evenings and spending weekends in Central Park. Our domestic life was beautifully uncomplicated.

When our son was born, our domestic life suddenly became *quite* complicated; and two years later, when our daughter was born, it became impossible. We automatically accepted the traditional sex roles that society assigns. My husband worked all day in an office; I left my job and stayed at home, taking on almost all the burdens of housekeeping and child raising.

When I was working I had grown used to seeing people during the day, to having a life outside the home. But now I was restricted to the company of two demanding preschoolers and to the four walls of an apartment. It seemed unfair that while my husband's life had changed little when the children were born, domestic life had become the only life I had.

I tried to cope with the demands of my new situation, assuming that other women were able to handle even larger families with ease and still find time for themselves. I couldn't seem to do that.

We had to move to another apartment to accommodate our larger family, and because of the children, keeping it reasonably neat took several hours a day. I prepared half a dozen meals every day for from one to four people at a time—and everyone ate different food. Shopping for this brood—or even just running out for a quart of milk—meant putting on snowsuits, boots and mittens; getting strollers or carriages up and down the stairs; and scheduling the trip so it would not interfere with one of the children's feeding or nap or illness or some other domestic job. Laundry was now a daily chore. I seemed to be working every minute of the day—and still there were dishes in the sink; still there wasn't time enough to do everything.

Even more burdensome than the physical work of housekeeping was the relentless responsibility I had for my children. I loved them, but they seemed to be taking over my life. There was nothing I could do, or even contemplate, without first considering how they would be affected. As they grew older just answering their constant questions ruled out even a private mental life. I had once enjoyed reading, but now if there was a moment free, instead of reading for myself, I read to them. I wanted to work on my own writing, but there simply weren't enough hours in the day. I had no time for myself; the children were always *there*.

As my husband's job began keeping him at work later and later—and sometimes taking him out of town—I missed his help and companionship. I wished he would come home at six o'clock and spend time with the children so they could know him better. I continued to buy food with him in mind and dutifully set his place at the table. Yet sometimes whole weeks would go by without his having dinner with us. When he did get home the children often were asleep, and we both were too tired ourselves to do anything but sleep.

We accepted the demands of his work as unavoidable. Like most couples, we assumed that the wife must accommodate to the husband's schedule, since it is his work that brings in the money.

As the children grew older I began free-lance editing at home. I felt I had to squeeze it into my "free" time and not allow it to interfere with my domestic duties or the time I owed my husband—just as he felt he had to squeeze in time for the children during weekends. We were both chronically dissatisfied, but we knew no solutions.

After I had been home with the children for six years I began to attend meetings of the newly formed Women's Liberation Movement in New York City. At these meetings I began to see that my situation was not uncommon; other women too felt drained and frustrated as housewives and mothers. When we started to talk about how we would have chosen to arrange our lives, most of us agreed that even though we might have preferred something different, we had never felt we had a choice in the matter. We realized that we had slipped into full domestic responsibility simply as a matter of course, and it seemed unfair.

When I added them up, the chores I was responsible for amounted to a hectic 6 A.M.–9 P.M. (often later) job, without salary, breaks or vacation. No employer would be able to demand these hours legally, but most mothers take them for granted—as I did until I became a feminist.

For years mothers like me have acquiesced to the strain of the preschool years and endless household maintenance without any real choice. Why, I asked myself, should a couple's decision to have a family mean that the woman must immerse years of her life in their children? And why should men like my husband miss caring for and knowing their children?

Eventually, after an arduous examination of our situation, my husband and I decided that we no longer had to accept the sex roles that had turned us into a lame family. Out of equal parts love for each other and desperation at our situation, we decided to re-examine the patterns we had been living by, and starting again from scratch, to define our roles for ourselves.

We began by agreeing to share completely all responsibility for raising our children (by then aged five and seven) and caring for our household. If this new arrangement meant that my husband would have to change his job or that I would have to do more free-lance work or that we would have to live on a different scale, then we would. It would be worth it if it could make us once again equal, independent and loving as we had been when we were first married.

Simply agreeing verbally to share domestic duties didn't work, despite our best intentions. And when we tried to divide them "spontaneously" we ended up following the traditional patterns. Our old habits were too deep-rooted. So we sat down and drew up a formal agreement, acceptable to both of us, that clearly defined the responsibilities we each had.

It may sound a bit formal, but it has worked for us. Here it is:

MARRIAGE AGREEMENT

I. Principles

We reject the notion that the work which brings in more money is more valuable. The ability to earn more money is a privilege which must not be compounded by enabling the larger earner to buy out of his/her duties and put the burden either on the partner who earns less or on another person hired from outside.

We believe that each partner has an equal right to his/her own time, work, value, choices. As long as all duties are performed, each of us may use his/her extra time any way he/she chooses. If he/she wants to use it making money, fine. If he/she wants to spend it with spouse, fine. If not, fine.

As parents we believe we must share all responsibility for taking care of our children and home—not only the work but also the responsibility. At least during the first year of this agreement, *sharing responsibility* shall mean dividing the *jobs* and dividing the *time*.

In principle, jobs should be shared equally, 50–50, but deals may be made by mutual agreement. If jobs and schedule are divided on any other than a 50–50 basis, then at any time either party may call for a re-examination and redistribution of jobs or a revision of the schedule. Any deviation from 50–50 must be for the convenience of both parties. If one party works overtime in any domestic job, he/she must be compensated by equal extra work by the other. The schedule may be flexible, but changes must be formally agreed upon. The terms of this agreement are rights and duties, not privileges and favors.

II. Job Breakdown and Schedule

(A) *Children*

1. Mornings: Waking children; getting their clothes out; making their lunches; seeing that they have notes, homework, money, bus passes, books; brushing their hair; giving them breakfast (making coffee for us). Every other week each parent does all.

2. Transportation: Getting children to and from lessons, doctors, dentists (including making appointments), friends' houses, park, parties, movies, libraries. Parts occurring between 3 and 6 P.M. fall to wife. She must be compensated by extra work from husband (see 10 below). Husband does all weekend transportation and pickups after 6.

3. Help: Helping with the homework, personal problems, projects like cooking, making gifts, experiments, planting; answering questions; explaining things. Parts occurring between 3 and 6 P.M. fall to wife. After 6 P.M. husband does Tuesday, Thursday and Sunday; wife does Monday, Wednesday and Saturday. Friday is free for whoever has done extra work during the week.

4. Nighttime (after 6 P.M.): Getting children to take baths, brush their teeth, put away their toys and clothes, go to bed; reading with them; tucking them in and having nighttime talks; handling if they wake or call in the night. Husband does Tuesday, Thursday and Sunday. Wife does Monday, Wednesday and Saturday. Friday is split according to who has done extra work during the week.

5. Baby sitters: Getting baby sitters (which sometimes takes an hour of phoning). Baby sitters must be called by the parent the sitter is to replace. If no sitter turns up, that parent must stay home.

6. Sick care: Calling doctors; checking symptoms; getting prescriptions filled; remembering to give medicine; taking days off to stay home with sick child; providing special activities. This must still be worked out equally, since now wife seems to do it all. (The same goes for the now frequently declared school closings for so-called political protests,

whereby the mayor gets credit at the expense of the mothers of young children. The mayor closes only the schools, not the places of business or the government offices.) In any case, wife must be compensated (see 10 below).

7. Weekends: All usual child care, plus special activities (beach, park, zoo). Split equally. Husband is free all Saturday, wife is free all Sunday.

(B) *Housework*

8. Cooking: Breakfast; dinner (children, parents, guests). Breakfasts during the week are divided equally; husband does all weekend breakfasts (including shopping for them and dishes). Wife does all dinners except Sunday nights. Husband does Sunday dinner and any other dinners on his nights of responsibility if wife isn't home. Whoever invites guests does shopping, cooking and dishes; if both invite them, split work.

9. Shopping: Food for all meals, housewares, clothing and supplies for children. Divide by convenience. Generally, wife does local daily food shopping; husband does special shopping for supplies and children's things.

10. Cleaning: Dishes daily; apartment weekly, biweekly or monthly. Husband does dishes Tuesday, Thursday and Sunday. Wife does Monday, Wednesday and Saturday. Friday is split according to who has done extra work during week. Husband does all the house cleaning in exchange for wife's extra child care (3 to 6 daily) and sick care.

11. Laundry: Home laundry, making beds, dry cleaning (take and pick up). Wife does home laundry. Husband does drycleaning delivery and pickup. Wife strips beds, husband remakes them.

Our agreement changed our lives. Surprisingly, once we had written it down, we had to refer to it only two or three times. But we still had to work to keep the old habits from intruding. If it was my husband's night to take care of the children, I had to be careful not to check up on how he was managing. And if the baby sitter didn't show up for him, I would have to remember it was *his* problem.

Eventually the agreement entered our heads, and now, after two successful years of following it, we find that our new roles come to us as readily as the old ones had. I willingly help my husband clean the apartment (knowing it is his responsibility) and he often helps me with the laundry or the meals. We work together and trade off duties with ease now that the responsibilities are truly shared. We each have less work, more hours together and less resentment.

Before we made our agreement I had never been able to find the time to finish even one book. Over the past two years I've written three children's books, a biography and a novel and edited a collection of writings (all will have been published by spring of 1972). Without our agreement I would never have been able to do this.

At present my husband works a regular 40-hour week, and I write at home during the six hours the children are in school. He earns more money now than I do, so his salary covers more of our expenses than the money I make with my free-lance work. But if either of us should change jobs, working hours or income, we would probably adjust our agreement.

Perhaps the best testimonial of all to our marriage agreement is the change that has taken place in our family life. One day after it had been in effect for only four months our daughter said to my husband, "You know, Daddy, I used to love Mommy more than you, but now I love you both the same."

I AM A HOUSEHUSBAND (BUT CALL ME MISTER)*

Samuel C. Brown, Jr.

A catchy commercial that has been running recently on television depicts a marital experiment in—where else?—Sweden. The wife goes off to work while the husband stays home to wipe the kids' noses, burn the meals and mop up the spills that result from his inevitable incompetence as a *hemmaman* (Swedish for "househusband"). At the end of the day and the commercial the calm, happy and unruffled wife returns to rescue the poor duffer with a kiss and a dose of the advertised product, a headache reliever and stomach soother.

Perhaps I should take offense at this commercial. I am a househusband, and I know perfectly well that it is my working wife, not I, who most often could use a bit of seeing to. But then again, I did blow the safety valve off our pressure cooker one night, and I have mistaken baking powder for flour (mine was the only gravy on the block that fizzed), so I can appreciate the humor.

Except for such rare blunders, however, my life as *hemmaman* is not particularly bizarre. I do not speak in a falsetto nor does my wife lift weights. (She even wears a bra.) We are not hippies (we live not in a commune but in a rented house, and neither of us uses illegal drugs), and we have never been to Sweden. Nonetheless, it is Isabel who earns a living and I who sew, cook, do the

laundry, wash the dishes and tend our four-year-old boy. Ours is a story, as the soap operas might put it, that asks the question: Can a young man with a master's degree find happiness steaming turnips and watching TV reruns?

Though, like anyone who spends much of the time in the house, I have occasional bouts of cabin fever, my answer is yes. This is primarily because that's not all I do—any more than the average housewife spends all her time with an ironing board and *The Doctors*. My extracurricular activities include membership in a civic-affairs group and a church volunteer service, and door-to-door canvassing at election time. I also write and have managed to sell nine stories and articles to various magazines, complete one children's novel (as yet unsold) and start another in the 18 months since I received my last regular paycheck. But I find that free lancing is hardly lucrative, so Isabel works, and I consequently spend more than half my time running our home.

We did not adopt our current life-style in anything like an apocalyptic manner. There was no dramatic disillusionment with conventional patterns, no waking at midnight in a sweat crying: "Oh-ho! *Now* I see the error of our ways!" It was simply that I disliked teaching English (the field in which I have a master's degree) and Isabel disliked staying home.

That old saying, "Home is where the heart is" was probably first voiced by a man who hated his job. For two years my mind and body taught at school, but my heart stayed home. I was nervous and reluctant to leave its familiar, uncomplicated warmth every morning and oh, so glad to return every night.

And for her part, Isabel literally "wanted out." She did not find her hours watching soap operas wildly absorbing, nor was she enthusiastic about spending her evenings and weekends with a bedraggled husband who was either preparing lessons in a stony silence or altering his personality with liquor. Furthermore she is trained in ballet and modern dancing, and as anyone who knows dancers will tell you, a dancer *has* to dance. (Our families refer to Isabel's affliction as "tarantism," which the dictionary defines as "a nervous affection characterized by melancholy, stupor and an uncontrollable desire to dance.")

Symptoms of her frustration increased. Perhaps you have seen the magazine advertisement in which a man frowns and says, "I suffer from menstrual cramps." In like fashion I found that I was suffering vicariously from Isabel's boredom and her longing to dance again.

And so we made the switch. Isabel landed a job teaching dance at Skidmore College, in Saratoga Springs, New York, and I became a writer and househusband.

Like an unwed mother or a secret alcoholic I do not always admit to my condition, but it exists. When a cocktail-party acquaintance politely inquires, "And what do you do?" I do not say, "I'm a househusband." I say, "I'm a writer," which is at least as true as the other reply, and much safer. For I do spend considerable time writing—Skidmore girls baby-sit regularly, neighbors invite our son Gene over to play with their youngsters, and I sometimes manage to scribble away even with Gene crashing around alone downstairs.

Still, family obligations take priority in my schedule. When Isabel has her 8 A.M. classes, the coffee and eggs must be on the table by 6:45. Gene's playmates often come to our house, where they require not a little supervision. The supper must be served hot at 6 P.M. on those days when Isabel has only half an hour between daytime classes and evening rehearsals. (At one such meal she looked at me wearily over the mashed potatoes and said, "I'm a liberated woman, Sam, but I sure am tired.")

Many domestic jobs fall naturally on me—and I like them! There is a definite warmth and satisfaction, unknown to most men, to be derived from serving one's family in this way. Chief among them, of course, is the pleasure of really knowing my son. We paint together, frost cakes together, shop together, read picture books together, roughhouse on the floor together. He resists his nap by fussing; I respond with what is euphemistically termed discipline. His best friend, Brian, accompanies us on our walk to the playground, where they spend half an hour on the swings, shrieking with delight while I push them in tandem.

What can compare with such ecstatic cries? What is more touching than a child's spontaneous kiss when his daddy "feels bad"? How many other fathers really know the exuberant confidence—

and the honest fear—with which their children greet life?

The television commercial, of course, shows none of these things. And it is unfortunate that men generally receive impressions about the life of a househusband only through such distortions. But then, they probably prefer not to be disabused. It is hard enough as it is for a man to retain his masculine self-respect in a world grown wary of authority and tradition. Even four-year-old Kurt, our next-door neighbor, had some trouble understanding my role as cook and baby sitter, and for several months he called me "Mrs. Brown." (He finally gave up after repeated correction and now calls me "Sam," which suits me just fine.)

Our role reversal has provided us with a lot of drollery. At Skidmore faculty receptions, for example, it is always fun to watch the face of a new acquaintance when I introduce myself as a "faculty husband" or "Mr. Isabel Brown." A good friend of ours, looking for volunteers for a project, recently turned to me at a party and said: "Why don't you give us a hand, Sam? You don't do anything." He, of course, was in on the joke. But not so the detergent saleslady who came to our door last fall. "Hello," she said to me. "Is your mother home?" "No," I cheerfully replied, "but my son is." Poor woman. She didn't even stay to tell me the virtues of her detergent—a good, low-phosphate one at that.

You might suppose from all I have said that I am a disciple of Women's Liberation. This would be an incorrect assumption. I do see much of value in the Movement's philosophy. I see much of value in the Roman Catholic philosophy too, but I don't plan to become a Jesuit priest. And our marital arrangement certainly testifies to the principle, repeatedly stated by proponents of Women's Lib, that it is high time women were treated by men as equals.

I disagree with the feminists, however, on one of their prime issues: that the work performed by the housewife and mother in the home for free should be done in communal kitchens and child-care centers instead, where it would be paid for. I find this suggestion appalling. In effect, these women are offering to replace familial ties with cold cash. How thoroughly our money-mad society has brainwashed them! "If we want men to value a service," they say, "we must make them buy it." Rot! How can one equate homes with hotels, nurseries with laundromats?

Far more sensible and much less crass would be a proposal based on a reverse logic that asserts not the inferiority but the equality of family life. We should not permit the career world to dictate to the family; we should demand at least that it negotiate. I do not mean merely that husbands should do more of the unpaid, home-centered work, though they should do that. I mean that men—and their working wives—should make clear to their employers that their careers will not automatically be allowed to pre-empt their family lives.

Certainly there are times when occupational demands take precedence. If the oil starts gushing from a well 200 miles away, a petroleum geologist can't stay home simply because his wife needs relief from dishwashing and child bathing. But there should be nothing to prevent a man from refusing to entertain a client after hours or to do evening paper work on exactly the same grounds.

Take "women's work" out of the home? On the contrary—bring men back into the home, where they can work with their wives to rebuild the crumbling values of family living: deep knowledge of others, mutual sacrifice and growth, spiritual comfort, appreciation, intimacy and the wonders of child rearing.

For there can be no more important task than raising a child. A man ultimately retires from his career, but he never retires from fatherhood; while several can take his place at work, no one can ever take his place in the heart of his child. So while I agree that women deserve full equality with men, I insist further that the family, which has lately been undervalued, be given full equality with the career world, which is generally overrated.

Have I, you might be tempted to ask, given my family life such priority that as a househusband I have compromised my masculinity? Well, that depends on how you define "masculinity." I've never seen it defined satisfactorily. Nonetheless, it would be dishonest for me to claim that this question has never bothered me. Perhaps that is one reason why I continue to write, for I thereby aspire to a career—and one which permits me to

stay home while pursuing it. And Isabel hasn't completely deserted her domestic role either. She still does the heavy once-a-week or -month housework. When she is at home, she is again housewife and mother.

The best of both worlds? At least I can dream. At the moment I am pleased not to be subservient to some impersonal corporate hierarchy or to the swarm of commuter traffic. And all that is required to guarantee my feeling of "masculinity" is my wife's acceptance of me as lover and helpmeet.

That's an interesting word, by the way: to be a helpmeet for another implies that one helps the other in a manner meet—suitable or fit—for that person. It means "companion" or "spouse" but is usually restricted to "wife" (the word is derived from a reference to Eve in Genesis). But why should a husband not also be a helpmeet? If both partners have an urge to hold down a job or pursue a career, why shouldn't the wife's urge be considered as worthy of attention as the husband's? Conversely, why should a man not get to stay home if he wants to and it can be arranged?

I confess that the answers are probably not as easy as I make them sound. But where there are answers—like Isabel's and mine—I believe they will be forthcoming only if a marriage means sharing, not merely bed, board and affection, but also responsibilities and privileges.

The prophets of our time would have us believe that the American family as we have always known it is caught in a revolution. No doubt my own family would be considered evidence to support this theory. Not that I think we are unique; in my bones I feel what might be called the "guerrilla instinct," that there must be others around like us. Still, changes are occurring and will continue to occur, some of them unsettling in the extreme.

In the face of such change, that television commercial is in a sense a sign of health, for it shows that Americans can still laugh at the uncertain consequences of innovation. The future should prove both rich and exciting, provided that we are able to adopt new forms of living without sacrificing the old values of life. High among the traditional values are marriage and the family; it is these that count most for me, and that I am working to sustain—as a househusband.

DO YOU, THOMAS, TAKE THIS WOMAN FOR A MONTH?

Tomi Knaefler

Psychologist Tom Greene and Patricia A. Whitesell celebrated what has got to be one of the most unusual anniversaries Sunday.

It was their first wedding anniversary month. But more than that, it marked the first renewal of their month-to-month marriage contract.

No, you didn't misunderstand anything. A month-to-month renewable marriage contract is indeed exactly what we said.

It's abundantly clear that Tom and Pat's wedding was no garden variety event. It's clear also that their definition of marriage differs from the accepted legal definition.

Among other things, the requisites for a valid marriage contract under State law calls for the filing and granting of a marriage license that takes several things into account, such as clearance of syphilis through blood tests.

Tom and Pat ignored the State's statutory requirements and chose instead to marry themselves under terms of their own marriage contract.

Their wedding ceremony took place on a bright sunny Sunday morning last Feb. 10 at San Souci Beach. It was witnessed by a gathering of friends and relatives.

Tom and Pat, alternately, read their very personal nuptial vows and their very business-like marriage contract and exchanged rings. Then the witnesses placed their signatures below that of Tom and Pat's on the marriage contract.

The contract opens with these words:

"We (James Thomas Greene and Patricia Atkinson Whitesell) wish to be married in our eyes and the eyes of the public of the legal systems. We wish this statement of intention of commitments and obligations to serve as a legal contract of marriage.

"We wish to be married according to the terms of this contract for personal reasons. We have objections to marrying according to State law and on a permanent basis. We believe that promises of lifetime commitment and obligations have more potential for injuring a relationship than for nurturing it. . . ."

The contract then spells out 13 terms, all of them negotiable and most of them pertaining to financial and property rights and obligations on a daily basis, upon one partner's death and in the event of a split.

The latter removes the need for divorce proceedings. However, it doesn't close the possibility for either party to file a civil suit in case the settlement is unacceptable.

The sociologically significant statement in the contract is contained in the following articles:

"2) This marriage commitment is for one month's duration.

"3) This contract is automatically renewed at the end of the first month of marriage, and at the end of every subsequent month of marriage, unless the contract is cancelled by either or both parties.

"4) This contract can be cancelled at the end of any month of marriage by either party by delivering the spouse a written statement of such intent. Reason must be given. Consent must be given. . . ."

Last Sunday, with the end of their first month of marriage, renewal negotiations began with Tom presenting Pat with a bunch of spring flowers.

"Everything's cool," as Pat put it, and the couple sealed the renewal of their marrage contract for the second month with a kiss.

In a recent interview, the couple explored various questions that their did-it-ourselves marriage provokes.

For instance, why did they choose this route?

Tom said: "My basic reason is that I flatly refuse to legally obligate myself to anyone permanently. I object to the concept of a permanent marriage on my personal and idealistic grounds."

They each have been married twice before and feel that the traditional marriage contract with its roots in the church-state sacraments hinders rather than helps nurture relationships.

They spoke of having looked deeply into the question of what marriage is and what marriage isn't and were surprised to conclude that "a very, very real part of marriage in this country is financial."

Tom said, "I think many people are very naive about the financial and legal obligations of a marriage and what happens when a relationship ends. For many, getting into a marriage is like buying a pig and a poke."

He said, "I see marriage more and more as a business contract. I used to say 'hogwash' when people would say that love and marriage are two different things. Now, I've turned around and I agree with that more and more."

Tom and Pat feel their month-to-month contract helps keep their marriage "alive" and "in the present" because nothing is automatic. Problems are dealt with promptly and not put off on the notion that there's plenty of time later to deal with things that are hard to talk about.

They don't believe their style of marriage is for everyone. For instance, they feel it probably wouldn't be easy for a couple wanting children. They have one child each from previous marriages and have "no intention" of having any more children in this marriage.

Tom said, "I feel it's right that the State law have a say in guaranteeing protection for children of a marriage, but I don't like the idea of the State with its vague law telling adults how to get married. I question the State's moral authority to do that."

The couple was asked why "getting married" was important to them. Why did they choose that over living together?

Tom said: "For several reasons. I'm proud of Pat and the relationship we have. I want to make a public proclamation of that. I want my friends and business acquaintances to see me as officially committed.

"I want to identify myself as a married person. I like the idea of a public proclamation of commitment for however long we remain married. I am responsive to the expectations and attitudes of society." . . .

The Greenes got ideas for their contract from various writings on the subject, including articles in "Ms" magazine and an earlier piece in "Life" magazine written by two legally married attorneys who got divorced in order to remarry under their own contract.

They said it's "amazing" how much interest there is in their contract. Pat said, "We're kept busy Xeroxing it for so many people wanting copies."

Their contract was reviewed by an attorney friend, who prefers not to be named.

The attorney feels that people can agree to just about anything by contract. He believes that Pat and Tom can legally agree to marry themselves under their own contract, provided their expectations don't extend to matters, such as filing a joint income tax return, that require government sanction of their marriage.

Another legal authority consulted by this reporter described Pat and Tom's status in the eyes of the law as a "formalized common law marriage" and he noted that under the law, Hawaii doesn't recognize common law marriages.

Asked whether their marriage enabled a base of security or did Pat, particularly, feel under a constant test, Tom said:

"For me, security lies in trust. I know she loves me and takes our relationship seriously. So many people go so blithely along believing in a forever kind of security when in truth, security can't be assumed. It exists only from day to day."

Pat said: "We talked at length about the matter of security. I was married twice before under the traditional contract and there was no security there. This marriage with its day-to-day sharing relationship is much more secure.

"The whole point is that this marriage is us. It's honest, it's business-like and it's tailored to our individual needs."

LIVING TOGETHER: AN ALTERNATIVE TO MARRIAGE

Theodora Wells and Lee S. Christie

We choose to live together rather than marry. I am Theo, 44, chronicler of the tale. My female sex-roles include daughter, daughter-in-law, wife, mother, stepmother, divorcee, aunt, grandmother, lover, and now—consort. Lee, 51, has almost as good a collection of male sex-roles. This is our position paper.

"Personhood" is central to the living-together relationship; sex-roles are central to the marriage relationship. Our experience strongly suggests that personhood excites growth, stimulates openness, increases joyful satisfactions in achieving, encompasses rich, full sexuality peaking in romance.

Marriage may have the appearance of this in its romantic phase, but it settles down to prosaic routine where detail invades ideas, talk scatters thought, quiet desperation encroaches, and sexuality diminishes to genital joining. Personhood is renewing of self; sex-roles are denigrating of self.

To us, personhood means that each person accepts primary responsibility for tending to his or her own physical, mental, emotional, sexual, and spiritual growth. It means bringing to the relationship two healthy, growing persons who want to share their strengths and who offer secondary support to each other's growth processes. Also, both persons bring human needs that can only be met with another, but they are not needy in the sense of having to make excessive or neurotic demands that the other must meet.

Personhood also means that each one can get along without the other. Temporary separation carries no strain because it has no sense of separation. Permanent separation is faced with knowing that each is richer because of the shared communion, that life proceeds by extending the richer self toward further growing.

In this quality of personhood, we experience various sensings that seem to be implicit in the process of becoming a person:

Reasonable freedom from major neurotic problems and a thrust toward growing, feeling worthwhile, valuable.

An identity, a clear, separate selfness, which one learns to sense and trust by being in touch with one's own feelings.

An inner desire to achieve, to set and reach specific goals, forming new self-concepts, experimenting with ideas.

Open-ended choice, commitment to not foreclose future choices.

Willingness to take more risks, to learn from mistakes, to expose more of one's self, to entertain change.

A certain fearlessness, courage and sureness, stemming from a deep honesty, keeping one's word, trusting one's self.

Enjoying and valuing one's body, like to be "inside my own skin"—sensing sensuality, a tensing sexuality.

Spontaneous wit springing from roving observations, sensing the ridiculous, juggling a mental "scrabble," playing a "what if" fantasy— open to wandering driftings of thought fragments.

Sense of urgency, too much to do in too little time, too much possible living that is vital, alive, some impatience.

The female sex-role is least like personhood and therefore more denigrating than the male sex-role.

On the asset side, the "truly feminine woman" is warm, nurturing, likes to please others, soft, pliable, cooperative, pretty, good at detail, giving of herself, charitable, moral, and of religious spirit.

On the liability side, she is a bit helpless, not good with figures nor conceptual thought, moody and illogical, crying to get her way, dependent, needing approval and praise, biologically defective, and subject to "penis envy."

As a girl she is brought up to find fulfillment in "her man," rather than achieve something on her own. Her name is taken from her when she marries; she becomes simply "Mrs. Him." She is not to excel, if she expects to get married. (No one asks her if she wants to marry, because marriage is the only acceptable choice.) She learns to downgrade the capabilities of her mind, and to fail. Competing with other girls for the "best catch," she learns not to trust other women and so becomes isolated from them as potential friends with genuine persons.

DISTRUSTING OTHER WOMEN, SHE IS CUT OFF FROM MEN

After she marries, she is supposed to confine herself to her husband and no other men. This effectively cuts her off from friendships with the other half of the population. When babies come, her world is home, pets, children, and repairmen. Surrounded by material comforts, she is indeed ungrateful if she complains, and proves that "you can't please a woman." If she settles cheerfully into her role, she proves that that is her "nature."

Any woman who does something on her own, who competes and excels, is subject to the charge of "not being feminine." The highest praise of all is "You think like a man!"

In short, the female sex-role defines woman by her sexual function of child-bearing and nurturing "instincts." By performing sexual and maintenance services for the male, she "earns" her way as an economic dependent. At the same time, the male sex-role prescribes the man's obligation to be achieving and responsible. These patterns, which radiate out into all aspects of living, are held as cultural values to be transmitted by all our social institutions.

Lee and I are rejecting marriage, the most basic of these institutions. As a woman, I have been through every bit of the denigrating vicious circle, while working toward personhood. I choose to keep my own unique way because I must. Anything else is self-chosen insanity, now that I know what I do. The wife role is diametrically opposed to the personhood I want. I therefore choose to live with the man who joins me in the priority of personhood.

What kind of man is he that goes for this arrangement? I do not speak for Lee, but only as I experience him. To me, he is more than just "a man." He is a person, a human being, first. He doesn't have to be defined in terms of sex. He's "got his balls," so to speak, and doesn't need me to give them to him, nor does he fear my taking them away. Therefore he doesn't need me as his sexual and maintenance services department.

He needs and wants me as a person first, and as a woman running a close second. Our sexuality serves us as persons, rather than defining us as roles. Our expressed sexuality is real peak-experiencing, not of the same order as sex-role sex.

We choose living-together, and find ourselves designing a new pattern of man-woman relatedness. We appreciate the value of a long-term, continuing, growing relationship. As we see it, we are joined in a commitment-for-growth. The commitment is to our own selves and to each other, respecting the separateness in our togetherness.

Both of us commit ourselves to:

Continue to grow, each in his or her unique way.

Retain future choices about our relationship, recognizing that the risks of growth include the risks of growing apart.

Give room for the process of growing, being patient with no-growth plateaus, being "there" when it's painful, giving space for the bursts of joy.

Provide a climate that stimulates and invites growing—confronting without judging, sensing when the most help is no help.

Take risks of self-exposure, confrontation, pain, shame; also risks of joy, fun, play.

Respect differences of belief or viewpoint, without requiring agreement but expecting a curiosity to understand, or acceptance.

We've lived together for a period approaching two years, but we don't know how long we will stay together. We feel, however, that the freedom to rechoose each other whenever we want to reduces the risk of separation. I've rechosen Lee hundreds of times already, and each time it is a real choice of stay or go.

You may ask, Why not make a commitment for growth within a marriage? Perhaps you can. You can define yourselves and the relationship within your four walls in terms of personhood. But the institution of marriage and the expectations of the outside world define it in terms of roles. An invitation to mask the real you, to dance to another's tune. We choose the harmony of personhood, inside and out.

BOB & BARBARA & MIKE & . . . ?

Donald Bromner

Barbara holds hands affectionately with Mike and glances lovingly at Bob, her other "husband," as she sits cross-legged on the couch of their Los Angeles apartment. Their "triad" family suits her fine.

Group marriage for her means more companionship, more love to give and receive, more variety in sex, as well as the prosaic benefits of living expenses divided three ways instead of just two.

As with any marriage, there are unanswered questions and potential problems which the three partners readily acknowledge.

Barbara, 28, Mike, 27, and Bob, 23, nod happily at the prospect that in a year or so, Barbara might get pregnant and add a baby to their threesome.

Does it bother them that they won't know who the father is?

No, they say. They want a normal, intelligent child, but since all three are physically normal and intellectually acute, they aren't likely to produce anything less.

But what Barbara calls just her "fantasy" may betray a significant preference.

"I want a red-haired baby," she says. "I've always had that fantasy about a red-haired baby." Barbara has dark hair and brown eyes. Mike has red hair and a bushy red beard. Bob has curly dark hair and sideburns.

It's only a passing point, but a hint that the five years Barbara and Mike lived together before Bob joined their marriage last year might put the question of parenthood in a special light for them.

They haven't really come to that bridge yet. In the meantime, they are busy with plans to move soon to a bigger house nearby, as well as adding a fourth member—a man—to the family, perhaps later bringing in another woman to help balance things.

Persons such as these trying some sort of alternative to conventional marriage and family are hoping to find something they feel is missing from ordinary living arrangements.

Group marriages are rare, involving only a few thousand persons in this country—an educated guess, since these "marriages" of three or more persons are not recognized by law and thus are not registered.

Far more Americans have taken to communes in order to share work, political or ideological interests, religious ideals, a craft, or family life— but not necessarily sex—with others in a closely knit group.

And millions who stick with the conventional marriage-family system liven it up by swinging with willing sexual partners, or try to improve life by deliberate steps to enrich, expand or extend the family.

Why do they do it? What do they get out of it? Do these variations from "normal" represent some kind of threat to society's basic unit?

The answers are almost as numerous as the participants. But there are common themes: The so-called "nuclear" family of man, wife and children, these family "experimenters" say, is too limited. There are not enough people to share ideas and interests, not enough scope for personal growth in dealing with other people.

Barbara and Mike, for instance, when they finally got married—by means of a certificate filed with a church—after a couple of years of living together, found it an important experience to write out and say their own wedding vows because it made them express exactly what they wanted their life together to be.

"We didn't want to be just a conventional family," Mike says. "We wanted to be able to love more than one person. We talked about it a long time."

And so when Barbara met Bob at work and they began taking their lunch break together and going out in the evening, Mike "really put the screws to her" to bring Bob home "so I could be friends with him, too."

How do other people react to their three-way marriage?

Neighbors in their middle-class area apparently take little notice. Their parents' attitudes range from disapproval to acquiescence. Some friends have similar life-styles and thus approve. Fellow workers generally are aware and seem to accept it. Mike's employer has even offered him a promotion.

Social pressures can be a hazard for group marriages, and may help account for their short life—a median length of 14 months, according to Larry L. Constantine, family therapist, and also director of research at a family service agency in the Boston area.

However, Constantine, coauthor with his wife, Joan, of a recent book, *Group Marriage*, based on a three-year study, says that social pressure and sex conflicts are not the critical factors in group marriages.

"The really telling part is not the intimacy or sexual involvement, but day-to-day living," he explains. "There are a lot of mechanical details—life-style, decision-making—that are more complicated (with more people)."

Family Synergy, a Los Angeles group which provides information and programs on group marriage and other alternatives, also lists the complexity of dealing with additional marriage partners as a hazard to balance the advantages of greater diversity and sharing.

Communes similarly are often troubled by the complexities of getting several or even dozens of persons to agree on things.

However, an estimated 3,000 or more communes have attracted members who want to share common beliefs in simple, self-reliant living, in religion or politics, in service projects, or child-raising within a larger "family."

What these alternative family forms offer is explored in at least one graduate-level seminar at Penn State University taught by Profs. Carl A. Ridley, Jr. and Stella Goldberg. The object, Ridley says, is to see what human needs might be filled by diverse forms of marriage and family. Each form, he adds, offers both benefits and liabilities.

"It's a funny thing. Usually the students come out of the course more committed to the nuclear type of family—not the nuclear structure but the nuclear type—than when they went in. I haven't pushed it, but when you look at these other structures, you find, my God, they've got problems, too."

In regard to group marriage, Constantine notes that people trying group marriage are looking primarily for more companionship—which, he adds, is also a major reason people get conventionally married.

Other reasons vary in importance from person to person, Constantine goes on, "but, overall, companionship is No. 1, and close behind are personal growth, sexual variety and advantages for children in having more adult models."

Arlene S. Skolnick, research psychologist at UC Berkeley's Institute of Human Development, believes that strains on the family stem from two main factors:

—Lack of community. "In early American times, there was no sense of a wall between the community and the family, no sense that the family was warming and loving while the community was harsh and cold."

—Lack of common tasks. "The family performed a lot more functions in the past. Family life now is emptied of lots of tasks that used to go on, and we're left now with this emotional function (of providing happiness), but it's difficult to service each other emotionally when we don't work together in common tasks."

Communes help fill this need, says Mrs. Skolnick, coauthor with her husband, Jerome, of *Family in Transition*. Her own book, *The Intimate Environment*, will be published this year.

"What people like best about communes," she remarks, "is this sense of meaningful participation in work, and also that their children take part in it." But Mrs. Skolnick also points out that communes frequently produce tension between the conflicting ideals of individualism and individual submergence in the group.

The fact that people now marry to find happiness makes for instability, according to Mrs. Skolnick. "If you marry to be happy, and then find you're not happy, the reason for the marriage is gone.

"Family life is inherently difficult. Sure, there's love, but also a lot of tension connected with relationships in the family. In the traditional family, this was suppressed. You had a whole series of obligations you had to fulfill no matter how you felt. In modern society, difficulties in family life are openly experienced. Family relations now depend on feelings and that's a very unstable basis."

Where does all of this leave the family? The consensus of some leading authorities is that the conventional family will continue to be the choice of most Americans, but that the experimentation with different forms may shed light on basic human relationships and thus help solve some family problems.

"There really is no such thing as *the* family," says Mrs. Skolnick. "There have been lots of variations in family forms historically and in other cultures. So when we say, 'Whither the family?' it sort of implies there has been this stable form that is now disintegrating.

"Actually, we're moving in the direction of plurality and variety in family forms. It's funny: We've always had diversity and plurality in religion and politics, and I think we're moving toward that in family life.

"I think the nuclear family will continue to dominate, but not as the only form of the family."

TOPIC 14

Family

*The family as a sacred union of husband and wife, of parents
and children, will continue to disintegrate. Divorces and
separations will increase until any profound difference between
socially sanctioned marriages and illicit sex-relationship
disappears. Children will be separated earlier and earlier from
parents. The main sociocultural functions of the family will
further decrease until the family becomes a mere incidental
cohabitation of male and female while the home will become
a mere overnight parking place mainly for sex relationship.*

—Sociologist Pitirim A. Sorokin (1941) predicts the final
disintegration of the family

*The family of the future will be larger, less narrowly defined.
No one will be childless; no one will lack for affection. The
outworn roles of "man" and "woman" will be discarded. As
high-pressure sex becomes less important, all of life will become
more erotic. Indeed, as roles and classes and even separate
nations fade in importance, we may see the emergence of a
family as wide as all humankind, a family that can weep
together, laugh together, and share the common ecstasy of a
world in transformation.*

—Educationist George B. Leonard (1973) predicts the flowering of the family in the year 2000

Almost all of us spend almost all of our life in a family setting. We begin
life in a family, grow up in it, and then marry to begin a family of our own.
Our living is family living.

Because of its great importance, the family has been extensively studied
by social scientists and commented on by social critics. Most of the
studies, comments, generalizations, and—not infrequently—overgener-
alizations have concerned the middle-class family. Over the years every
member of the middle-class family has been placed under scrutiny, and
the material that follows presents some salient criticisms.

In the 1940s the American mother, "smother love," and "momism" came under attack. According to social critic Philip Wylie, who led the charge, "mom" (about one woman in ten) and lesser mom-types ruled the roost, demeaned their spouses, and tyrannized their children, who grew up dependent or rebellious. Other observers have similarly noted the considerable power and assertiveness of the American mother and also, in fairness, the considerable demands made upon her and the little assistance she often receives.

In the 1960s the American father began to draw fire, and the fusillade has heightened in this decade. He has been accused of being an invisible, passive, or indifferent member of the family, of neglecting it for his job, business, or career, and of trying to compensate for his parental shortcomings by giving material goods in place of attention and affection. One sociologist has advocated giving fathers "paternity leave"—part-time off with an income supplement—to make it possible for them to spend more time with their children during certain critical stages of development.

The American child or adolescent appears to have escaped major criticism until recently. This is partly because our society tends to hold parents responsible for their children's behavior. And partly it has been due to our tendency to revere our young. American historian Lawrence Fuchs writes, "W. C. Fields, who knew what really mattered in America, was fond of saying that anyone who hated dogs and little children couldn't be all bad. The more typical American view, particularly since the nineteenth century, has been that the young are more important and virtuous than the old. All other major cultures have viewed the young as untrustworthy; they must be civilized by society, prepared for responsible membership in it, and defer to the wisdom of their elders."

In the 1960s there was a major falling out between adult American society and its young. In 1968 *Newsweek* put the charge against youth in a nutshell: "On the most superficial level, they wear their hair too long and their skirts too short and play their transistors too loud. Worse, some smoke pot and use obscene language. But of all the insults that the young inflict upon adult society, perhaps the most galling is that they systematically thumb their noses at authority—at the values of their parents, the precepts of their teachers and the actions of their governments."

Fuchs faults present-day American youth, or at least some of them, for being self-centered and occupied with their own feelings, and also for shirking responsibility and pursuing independence at all costs. He writes, "It seems that many of the young have replaced an older form of dependency on parents and families with a new one on psychiatrists, group-therapy sessions, fleeting relationships and drugs in their frantic search to 'live my life the way I want to.' Having been taught that dependency is a dirty word, many seem to want love without obligation, affection without responsibility."

What should be done for the family? Some authorities believe parents and especially fathers should get back into their children's lives. And some believe there has been too much permissiveness and the time has come for more control. Even Dr. Spock, whose bible *Baby and Child Care* was accused of starting the swing to superpermissiveness, has become alarmed by what he feels is a growing failure of parents to provide firm leadership. In an article published in 1974 (entitled "How Not to Bring Up a Bratty

Child") he writes, "Inability to be firm, to my mind, is the commonest problem of parents in America today."

Not everyone agrees that American parents need to exercise greater control over their children. A number of writers have depicted youth in this country as a powerless and even oppressed minority with little status at home, in school, or before the law. In the 1960s some critics were encouraging a "children's power" movement, and in the 1970s, in tune with the times, they call for a "children's liberation."

There are those who believe that the family is beyond repair or nearly so. In at least one way the family may have done its job too well, producing people until the relatively recent pronouncement that families should generally be limited to two children is being challenged by some who say that by now even two is too many. In their book *The Case Against Having Children,* Anna and Arnold Silverman argue that many people become parents for the wrong reasons and would be better off with no children at all. And some feminists have become strong opponents of the family, holding it to be an institution that has trapped and enslaved women and kept them from developing their full potential as individuals.

If there is no agreement on the present health of the family or on the medicine needed, there is even less consensus on what the future holds. In the 1940s a number of authorities were predicting the disintegration of the family and sounding its death knell, but the family survived (held together, some cynics claim, by the television set). According to the most recent set of family forecasters, there are some interesting times ahead.

In his best seller *Future Shock,* Alvin Toffler predicts a "weird and novel" future for the family. He feels that the dominant feature of family life will be temporary marriage: people will move from one spouse to another depending upon changing needs and stages of life. Parenthood may be redefined as new birth technology makes it possible to control the characteristics of offspring or even grow human embryos in a laboratory jar. Fewer couples will rear children; rather, children may be raised by specially qualified couples or families.

Sociologist Leo Davids also predicts a demise in parenthood. He foresees that by 1990 less than a third of North American marriages will produce children. In fact, in order to qualify for child rearing one would need to undergo rigorous training and a careful evaluation by a team of professionals as well as obtain a parenthood license. He writes, "All those who desire to become parents, and therefore to exercise a public responsibility in an extremely important and sensitive area of personal functioning, will have to prove that they are indeed the right people to serve as society's agents of socialization."

By contrast, in her book *The Future of the Family,* sociologist Betty Yorburg writes that "the nuclear family will not only persist into the twenty-first century, but it will be stronger than ever. She forecasts some increase in homosexual marriages, group marriages, single-parent households, and communes. "But," she insists, "ultimately for biological reasons, and more immediately for psychological reasons, the pairing husband and wife relationship and the exclusive parent-child relationship will endure."

In the readings that follow no more time is spent over the cloudy crystal ball—there are no selections on families as they will be (those who are intigued by the future should see Toffler or Yorburg's book). Instead the readings focus on families as they now are (or at least as some see them) and families as they should be (and would be if some had their druthers).

Families as they are

The first three articles on this topic present some insights into families as college students see them. Sandra D. Sandell and Jack E. Rossmann explored the perceptions that freshmen have of their parents and found these views to be quite favorable. Mothers were generally described as warm and sympathetic, while fathers were closely identified with their occupations. The major conflict areas between students and parents concerned sex, religion, and politics. Four out of five students felt that their values were different than those of their parents: specifically, students saw themselves to be less materialistic, more liberal, and living a different and more casual life style than their parents.

In the second reading, Joyce Maynard who was 18 years old when she wrote the article, describes her own family in what she calls a "portrait of one good and loving parent-child relationship." In her portrait both mother and father emerge not as TV stereotypes, but as individuals whose individuality is warmly understood and appreciated by their daughter. Her family is notable for its coherent set of values, rituals, tastes, and pressures, which she perceives to be generally beneficial for her although not completely so.

The third paper, written by a 22-year-old woman in one of the editor's classes, presents a sharply contrasting familial experience. This woman remembers her parents as rejecting, autocratic, cold, and critical. In response, she became supersensitive to criticism and rejection and avid for attention, praise, and love. At the same time, her familial experience imbued her with a deep sense of worthlessness that now makes it difficult for her to believe and accept the affection and approval of others.

Families as they should be

The second set of three articles criticizes present-day families and suggests ways to improve them. Urie Bronfenbrenner believes today's family needs more interaction between parent and child. "Children," he writes, "*used* to be brought up by their parents." But increasingly child rearing (or tending) is left to peer groups and TV. Bronfenbrenner feels that the transmission of qualities valued by our society requires more active participation by parents; otherwise there will be a "breakdown in the process of making human beings human."

While Bronfenbrenner laments that parents have withdrawn from their children's lives, Richard Farson faults parents for standing too much in their children's way. He calls for a children's liberation and drafts a child's bill of rights to provide new freedom and power to the young. In Farson's opinion, the nuclear family is difficult for parents and oppressive to children, and he advocates more multiple parenting such as multifamily communes, child-exchange programs, and children's residences.

Bruno Bettelheim (as interviewed by Jane Whitbread) advocates establishment in this country of children's homes that are patterned after those in the Israeli kibbutz. He feels American society and its mothers are failing millions of children and that homes based on the Israeli experience can provide these children with the guidance and care they now lack. This course of action is necessary, he believes, not only for the children's sake but also for the sake of mothers who are seeking more fulfillment outside the home.

FOR PERSONAL APPLICATION

1. Describe the family you were raised in and its effect on you.
2. Describe your relationship with your mother, father, or a sibling and its effect on you.
3. Compare your values with those of your parents.
4. Discuss any areas of conflict between you and your parents.
5. Describe the family you have begun yourself or the family you would like to have.
6. To what extent were you raised by your peers or television rather than by your parents? Do you consider this to be a critical problem in America today? Why or why not?
7. Do you believe that there is a need today for a "children's liberation"? Why or why not?
8. What rights or freedom were you denied as a child that might have proven desirable or beneficial? Discuss your answer.
9. What rights or freedoms were you denied as a child are you now extending or planning to extend to your own children? Discuss your answer.
10. Would you be interested in living in an American version of a kibbutz or in having your children raised in a kibbutz-like center? Why or why not?
11. How many children would you like to have? Why?
12. Do you believe that any couple should be allowed to conceive children and that anyone should be allowed to raise children? Why or why not? What restrictions, if any, would you place on the right to bear and rear children?
13. What do you expect the family will be like in the next generation (20 to 25 years hence)?
14. Write down a discussion item (not given above) that seems particularly relevant to this topic and you, and discuss it.

FOR SMALL GROUPS

1. *Positing family backgrounds.* The group, focusing on each member in turn, summarizes everything it knows or can guess about the member's home and family background. (Guesses should be accompanied by

reasons for guessing in that particular way.) The member is silent until the group has completed its summary; then he responds, correcting, supplementing, and interpreting what the group has said.

2. *Enacting family roles.* The way we behave as parents and spouses are influenced by the models that were presented by our own parents. Sometimes we deliberately model our behavior after our parents. Sometimes we deliberately attempt to be different. Or we may be unintentionally captured by the past and behave like one of our parents whether we want to or not. By playing all the roles (or getting other members of the group to assist him), each member enacts a family situation both as it would have been handled in the family in which he grew up and how it is handled or should be handled in the family he has established or will establish.

3. *Arguing family models.* Each member researches and writes on a 5 × 8 card a concise description of a present-day family model. This may be the middle-class American family, the family form in the Israeli kibbutz, or a typical family in any group or subgroup in any country. Included in the description should be the relationships between family members, their roles, and the child-rearing practices. The cards are gathered, shuffled, and placed face down in the middle of the group. Each member in turn takes a card, reads the description aloud, and indicates the extent to which this family model would be acceptable to him. Then, before proceeding to the next member and card, others in the group are invited to comment on the particular model.

FOR FURTHER READING

Bettelheim, B. *The Children of the Dream.* New York: The Macmillan Company, 1969.

DeLora, J. S., and J. R. DeLora, eds. *Intimate Life Styles: Marriage and Its Alternatives.* Pacific Palisades, Calif.: Goodyear, 1972.

Farson, R. *Birthrights.* New York: The Macmillan Company, 1974.

Fuchs, L. H. *Family Matters.* New York: Random House, Inc., 1972.

Handel, G., ed. *The Psychosocial Interior of the Family: A Sourcebook for the Study of Whole Families.* Chicago: Aldine, 1967.

Otto, H. A., ed. *The Family in Search of a Future: Alternate Models for Moderns.* New York: Appleton-Century-Crofts, Inc., 1970.

Silverman, A., and A. Silverman. *The Case Against Having Children.* New York: David McKay Co., Inc., 1971.

Toffler, A. *Future Shock.* New York: Random House, Inc., 1970.

Wylie, P. *Generation of Vipers.* New York: Rinehart, 1942.

Wylie, P. *Sons and Daughters of Mom.* Garden City, N.Y.: Doubleday & Co., Inc., 1971.

Yorburg, B. *The Changing Family.* New York: Columbia University Press, 1973.

COLLEGE FRESHMEN VIEW THEIR PARENTS

Sandra D. Sandell
Jack E. Rossmann

Is the current "generation gap" primarily a creation of the popular press, a normal phase of the human developmental process, or a new and highly significant phenomenon which is one of the by-products of a technologically oriented, rapidly changing society? In an attempt to answer this question, sections of a structured interview used in a large longitudinal study focused on the relations between Macalester College freshmen and their parents. A random sample of 31 men and 28 women—approximately 10 percent of the 627 new freshmen—was interviewed in the fall (October and November) of 1968. By the following April, 2 women and 2 men had withdrawn from Macalester, but the remaining 55 students were reinterviewed.

This sample of Macalester freshmen came from large, relatively affluent families which were largely unbroken by death or divorce. The average number of children per family was 3.75; median family income was approximately $12,000; and almost 90 percent of the students had been living with both parents prior to enrolling at Macalester.

About half of the students said their families were quite close and did things together often, and another 10 percent said that their families were close although not involved in mutual activities. Only one-fourth felt that their families were not at all close. Although picnics, outings, and vacations together were the most frequently mentioned family activities, they covered a wide range, from attending church together to playing poker or marching in anti-war demonstrations.

But even close homes can hardly be expected to be free from problems. Almost one-third of these students reported some sort of difficulty in the family while they were growing up. Of these, less than half said that the problem had had only negative consequences, and about one-third said it had had some good and some bad results. Surprisingly perhaps, 13 percent even said that the problem had had only good effects: for example, bringing the family closer together. These students mentioned marital conflicts (often related to a drinking problem) and prolonged illness or death of a family member as being the most common difficulties, and emotional and economic problems as being the most common consequences.

Students showed sensitivity and perceptiveness in their appraisals of their parents' marital problems. They were seldom hostile toward the "problem parent." Said one girl, "It was important that my parents had decided that their lives had gone different directions and that a wife needs intellectual companionship. . . . I think when it [the divorce] first happened, I went along with the idea that families should stay together. [I] accepted others' ideas about broken homes. . . . But there was a greater feeling of love flowing freely—of needing each other [among the rest of the family after the father had left]."

WHAT ARE YOUR PARENTS LIKE?

Although this girl, like other students from breaking or broken homes, had been forced to grapple with an evaluation of her parents before she came to school, many freshmen begin to make this assessment only after they are away at school for a few months. One of the questions in the interview that turned out to be most interesting was a loose one asked in both the fall and spring interviews: "What are your parents like?"

One thing discovered was that students gain a more objective, complex, and sensitive view of their parents after they have been away from home an additional four or five months. In the fall, large numbers of students looked somewhat dumb-founded when we asked this question although they did eventually respond to it. But less than half were able to discuss their parents as individuals. They spoke of them as a monolithic "they," virtual abstractions; and they tended to give short, stereotyped statements. All that one girl could say about her parents was, "Very liberal, but both of them are temperamental—about all." The response of a boy was still more terse: "Conservative, Lutheran, Republican." Although these responses were not uncommon, those that follow are a bit more typical:

Both are very kind and they think of the children rather than themselves. Mother is quick-tempered; father even-tempered.

Really wonderful people. I like them a whole lot. Really close family. Given me proper motivation and yet not too much pressure. Given me direction—not too much. Now they seem a little conservative to me; before they didn't. They're good about writing and finding opportunities for me to come home, which I appreciate.

By the time of the spring interview, more than two-thirds of the students spoke of their parents as individuals. The greater complexity and objectivity of the responses obtained during the spring interview are illustrated by the following:

Well, my mom is quiet, sensitive. She is easily hurt and keeps it inside her. She's really a wonderful person. I've learned to realize what kind of person she is and to try to understand her feelings which I didn't a few years back.

My dad? Oh, he's kind of a rough character. That's the way most people in this line of work are. He doesn't like to admit he's wrong. He hates his kids to smart off. We usually don't. Since I've been working with him, I can joke with him. He understands I'm not being smart and we get along a lot better.

Fathers and Mothers

Besides the differences between the fall and spring interviews, there was an interesting difference between descriptions of fathers and those of mothers. Mothers were warm, sympathetic, and likely to be the ones in whom both the men and women confided. Fathers, on the other hand, were often typified by their occupations. They were "businessmen," good providers, interested in the children, perhaps, but certainly not demonstrative. Several students, especially men, mentioned that they were just getting to know their fathers. One said, "Well, start with my father. He works very hard. I have no real relationship with him except that he gives me money. That's enough. My mother? She's just a mother. They're all the same—excitable sometimes." A girl described her relationship with each of her parents like this: "Mother is very liberal. [She was] brought up very strict. I can tell her things like a sister; I tell her six months afterwards. Father is very distant and temperamental and I don't think I've talked to him before." From only two interviews, it is rather difficult to tell whether students gave stereotyped responses or simply described the traditional sex roles in their homes.

The enthusiasm with which some students described their parents may be somewhat surprising. One girl said of her parents, "Two of the greatest people I've met in my life. My mother's a saint and an angel, perfect, considerate. [It's] hard to believe all she's done for me. In a way, they've kept me from doing things. I ask myself, 'Would doing this hurt my parents?' I try not to hurt them even if I may not think it wrong." This may be a somewhat extreme example; nevertheless several students spontaneously dropped statements like, "Really groovy," or "Almost overly concerned with me; very protective; ambitious for me." Then they went on to explain how much their parents cared about them. It appears that many Macalester students have parents who are highly considerate of them, perhaps to the point of overindulging or spoiling them. Frequently accompanying this concern, however, is a demand for and expectation of achievement.

Permissiveness

An impression that these freshmen perceive their parents as permissive was confirmed by the responses to a question asked in the spring: "Compared with the parents of the kids with whom you went to school, would you say your parents were more or less lenient than most about such things as hours, dating, and use of the family car, or were they about average?" About two-thirds said their parents were more lenient, and only one in six felt their parents were more strict. It is apparent that many students were surprisingly favorable in their estimations of their fathers and mothers. In fact, only three students in the fall and one in the spring gave definitely negative appraisals of both parents, although an additional two or three students disliked one of their parents. The change that occurred between fall and spring was in the degree of approval that students expressed. Whereas in the fall one-fourth of the students rated their parents in superlatives and another 40 percent with milder approval, by spring superlatives were used by only 1 student in 10.

COMPARED WITH OTHER STUDIES

Exactly what do these responses about parents signify? It is certain that this pattern of response is fairly typical. Katz and associates (1968), who conducted a study similar to the Macalester project at Berkeley and at Stanford, say this about the responses to their questions about parents:

The mildness of the description of the parents is not surprising to us in the light of the information we obtained in the interviews. First of all, it is difficult for students to talk about their parents with adequate openness. Assessment and criticism are easily confused in their minds. (In their last senior interviews, many students told us that their sexual behavior and their parents were the two topics they found it particularly difficult to talk about) [p. 61].

Westley and Epstein (1969), however, claim that among those they interviewed, both brief, cliché-ridden answers and long, rambling, shallow ones are indicative of emotional instability. It should be noted that Westley and Epstein interviewed their subjects over a period of six years, during which time a greater rapport between the interviewer and the student can be expected to take place. So the preceding statement should be modified: A tendency to *persist* in giving stereotyped or rambling statements is indicative of poor mental health. At least among those interviewed at Macalester, another factor seems to be at work. Both curt and vague responses may be an attempt to put off the interviewer. These Macalester students are no different from other people who would be unwilling to confide in virtual strangers.

Keniston (1968), who interviewed a number of young activists working in the Vietnam Summer project, would concur with Katz that late adolescents have difficulty talking about their parents with objectivity. One thing which Keniston feels distinguishes the radicals from the majority of students is the ability of the former group to be objective. His radicals "seemed unusually able to tolerate ambivalence, to explain parental failure with its probable causes, to combine praise and affection with the recognition of defects. Their life histories indicate this capacity was not achieved without struggle" (p. 67). Thus, it would appear that our freshmen are not atypical in their expressed favorable attitudes toward their parents.

Perhaps a slight part of this attitude can be attributed to a recent easing of tensions between the students and their parents. The interviewer also asked these students whether their relationships with their parents had undergone any recent changes. Although almost all the students had moved away from home, about 40 percent felt that no appreciable change had taken place in parental relationships. Apparently going away to school is an expected move, for which psychological and other preparation is made by many students so it does not radically alter family relationships.

Among those who said that the relationship with their parents had changed, interesting sex differences appeared. Men were more likely to suggest that their parents had begun to see them as more adult-like or had given them more freedom. In other words, the *parents* had tended to cut the strings. On the other hand, women who suggested that their parental relationships had changed were more likely to say that they (the students) had become more independent or self-reliant. The *women*, in this case, appeared to have cut the strings.

PARENTAL CONFLICT
AND ITS SOURCES

So far, there is an overall picture of happy homes and smooth family relations. But inevitable conflicts do exist. In an attempt to find out about communications within the family, we asked whether the students generally discussed with their parents matters that were important to them. Approximately half of the sample in both the fall and spring answered that they generally did. Another third answered that they discussed some things with both parents or most things with one parent. There was a slight shift from the "usually" to the "occasionally" categories between fall and spring, which may suggest that students became more independent of their parents during their freshman year. Incidentally, not all of those who said they seldom or never discuss important matters with their parents found themselves at odds with them; some were simply self-reliant youths who were fortunate to be independent enough (for example, financially) to make their own decisions. Nor can we say that those who usually discussed things had no conflicts, for conversation may be just an excuse for verbal confrontation.

In order to isolate these areas of conflict, the interviewer asked, "What topics can't or don't you discuss with your parents, or what topics cause conflict if they are "discussed?" Apparently the sources of tension are primarily those old controversial topics which all of us have been advised to avoid at polite social gatherings, namely, religion, politics, and sex. The latter topic clearly created more problems for women than men.

One interesting change that occurred between fall and spring was the number of students who mentioned either "sex" or "social life" as topics of potential disagreement. (In most cases, these topics were scrupulously avoided.) In the fall 29 percent mentioned social life and 15 percent sex. By spring, these percentages were nearly reversed: 14 percent and 26 percent for social life and sex, respectively.

Several alternative explanations for this phenomenon are possible. First, it appears that the term *social life* often was not used to cover a very wide range of human relationships or social activities; many seemed to use it as a synonym for dating and, of course, for the sexual aspects of dating. So perhaps the apparent increased importance of sex was merely the avoidance of euphemism during the second interview when the student felt that he could be more frank with the interviewer. But it may have indicated that during their freshman year the social life of these

students became more overtly sexual or that they were becoming aware that a subject which they were discussing more and more in the dorm with their peers was one which they had never felt comfortable discussing at home. Probably all three explanations, in part, account for this change.

After asking students about the larger topics of conflict, the interviewer asked about the little things, the "points of friction," between them and their parents. Here about one-fourth claimed that there were none. Significantly, however, the major source of friction seemed to revolve around the development of "autonomy." One student put his finger on the sore spot when he reported that the points of friction were "just things that I want to do that for them would mean that I'm breaking the ties, I guess." These freshmen did not like being asked where they were going or being told when to come home, how to spend their money, or how to wear their hair or clothes. The only significant ideological matter mentioned was that of religion, and even this in some cases might have indicated only that students resented being told or expected to attend church although there is no doubt that some doctrinal differences existed, too.

ACCEPTANCE OF PARENTAL VALUES

The final attempt to get at the sources of the generation gap was to ask, "In what way do you differ from your parents in such things as beliefs, values, goals, or life style?" Katz (1968) says of the students he interviewed: "Few define themselves as different from their parents and set out to fashion a different life style for themselves" (1968, p. 63). Only one student in five in our sample said that his values were basically the same as his parents. For the rest, some seemingly significant differences appeared to exist. The major differences were these: (a) "I'm more liberal" (in no specific way); (b) "I'm less materialistic, less interested in making money"; (c) "My life is more free and casual, less rigid"; (d) "My political beliefs are more liberal"; and (e) "My life style is 'different'" (in no particular way). Many freshmen also saw themselves as less religiously oriented than their parents. Related to the large number who claimed to be less materialistic was the near absence of those who expressed a desire to surpass their parents in education or socioeconomic status.

Of course there is no way of knowing how deeply ingrained these attitudes were or whether they would change as these students confronted the "real world." In fact, they themselves did not know, as one girl's description of the differences between her and her parents indicated: "They were probably the same way when they were my age, and I'll probably be the same way when I am theirs. . . . I don't want to work for money, and they say, 'You'll come back.'" Another indication that these attitudes might change is that many students stated that they were more "experimental" than their parents. They wanted to test different ideas, beliefs, and methods of artistic and emotional expression. In so doing, they were not wantonly rebelling against their parents. Their expressed affection for their families was only one indication of this. Indeed, their relatively permissive, nondogmatic parents have not instilled in them a rigid system of beliefs which they can easily attack. One girl said, "I'm different [from my parents] in that they had theirs [a set of beliefs, values, and goals] set up and just adopted them. I'm developing my own. They never tried to make their view mine." It is harder to rebel against vague principles than against clearly specified beliefs.

A SEARCH FOR COMMITMENT

And belief was what many of these Macalester freshmen seemed to be seeking. Along with their interest in experimentation they expressed a desire for "commitment." For what they saw as the blind, passively accepted belief of their parents they wanted to substitute an active faith, so to speak, one that would survive both the test of intellectual scrutiny and that of workability in their daily lives. For some, like the young man who had forsaken his parents' Presbyterianism to become "committed to Unitarianism," this process of experimentation and commitment had led into socially acceptable paths. But for others, it might lead to a long series of adventures and misadventures, during which they would welcome every intellectual current, every breath of passion which pushed and pulled them relentlessly. A few would never survive this ordeal. But that, unfortunately, is one of the costs of living in a world without viable traditions, the world in which these Macalester students—and their parents—find themselves.

REFERENCES

Katz, J., et al. *No Time for Youth: Growth and Constraint in College Students.* San Francisco: Jossey-Bass, 1968.

Keniston, K. *The Young Radicals: Notes on Committed Youth.* New York: Harcourt Brace, Jovanovich, 1968.

Westley, W. A., and N. B. Epstein. *The Silent Majority: Families of Emotionally Healthy College Students.* San Francisco: Jossey-Bass, 1969.

MY PARENTS ARE MY FRIENDS

Joyce Maynard

On the bus to the airport, just after leaving my parents for a summer away from home, something quite sad happened, and I haven't been able to get it out of my head. The bus stopped in some small town, and a girl about my age got on—clearly, like me, going away for the summer. Her mother was at the bus stop with her—a woman about my mother's age but very tired-looking, with her hair tied back and an apron on. The mother helped the girl with her luggage—a couple of shopping bags, cardboard boxes tied with string and a very fancy overnight case—then hugged her goodbye, and the girl stood on the steps of the bus with her arms at her sides. Then she took her seat by a window, and the mother moved so that she was standing right next to the window, with just glass between them. She was crying by this time, but trying to smile, and waving. And the girl sat stiff in her seat, looking straight ahead. Finally the bus pulled out, and the mother turned around and left. She was wearing that furry kind of bedroom slippers.

First I just felt so angry at the girl I wanted to shake her, and terribly, terribly sorry for the mother. I tried to imagine what the mother could have done to deserve that, and what the daughter felt like, and how that girl would be with her own kids—which brought me to parents and children generally, and what it was that mine did that worked so well. I missed them, but not in an unhealthy, dependent way; I just like being at home—enough, I think, so that it was important for me to get away last summer, as I did. I'm happy away from home, and not homesick, just as

I know they're happy when I'm there and happy when I'm not, and their lives don't begin and end with the children (which, when one's children are 18 and 22, is a pretty dangerous place to have them begin and end).

We've got a pretty good thing going, our family. But we are hardly typical. What worked for us can't be taken as general rules. So—not presuming to suggest that this is how things should be done, but just that this is how we did things—here is a portrait of one good and loving parent-child relationship: my parents' and my own.

First, though, some kind of explanation, because there's a danger that I'll come out of this sounding like an apple polisher—the kind I always hated when I was little. (Pollyanna, I suspected, was too dull to get in trouble. As for Shirley Temple at her sunniest—well, I always rooted for Jane Withers.) I feel dangerously close to becoming Pollyannified myself now. At an age when I should be rebelling, I'm without a cause. I think that's because my parents' standards are so reasonable; it's hard to protest principles that make sense, principles based not on tradition or prejudice or an arbitrary laying down of laws for their own sake. There is a wholeness to our way of life: What we admire in human conduct is of a piece with what we admire in poems and flower gardens. In other words, what my parents passed on to us is not a bunch of unrelated fragments but a coherent set of values, all of which speak for reason, order, symmetry. Our lives are filled with family rituals, family phrases, family tastes.

Family. We didn't have religion, we didn't have a large circle of friends close by or a cozy network of relations. But we had a family style, a distinctive way of doing things. When my sister married, the first thing she asked for was a large schefflera tree. In our family *we have scheffleras*. In our family we dislike coloring books and painting by numbers; we admire Mexican crafts, we love Mozart operas and shortbread cookies. . . . I could fill in all the blanks. Some kids don't even know what, if anything, their family represents.

We could be called opinionated. Certainly we are a hypercritical family—we don't lavish superlatives on things and places and people. I was raised to look closely, not to accept easily. My father and I took long walks together, examining mushrooms and leaves, stopping in midsentence and midstep sometimes to catch a birdcall. We went to museums together and talked about paintings, or sat side by side on the floor listening to music he conducted with a pencil in the air. My mother's training came evenings, after dinner, when she sat on the living-room couch marking papers and I sat next to her, reading her corrections. Not just marked-in commas and circled misspellings, but paragraph-long notes on how a story might be improved. We talked about the scripts of TV commercials and the designs of cereal boxes and the arrangements of people's flower beds—the opinions never let up. I couldn't suspend judgment even when I wanted to; it was as if I went through life with X-ray glasses on, seeing through not just the things I wanted to see through but the things I'd just as soon have believed in, too. I longed to wallow in a sentimental movie with my friends, to join them in the delicious Friday night tears that followed every movie we'd see—*To Sir, With Love; The Sound of Music*—but I'd always end up munching popcorn while they wept, and commenting to myself on the stiffness of an actor's speech or the corniness of the sound track.

I was old before my time, a junior sophisticate who could analyze the appeal of Barbi dolls compared to baby dolls long before I stopped playing with either. My sister and I weren't prodigies by any means; we were just raised in a household whose chief sport was conversation. While other families played basketball, we volleyed words and ideas. My parents never said "Don't talk back" (though rudeness was out), because we learned from argument. From Perry Mason and from my father, I learned how to find a loophole in a thought; from my mother, I learned how to present my case persuasively.

The criticism we applied to everything we encountered we applied to ourselves as well. Never "You are bad," but "You could do better." I like to see a job done really well, and if that means ripping out a seam and starting over, or spending all day in the library doing research for a term paper, I'll do it. My parents never let me feel satisfied with an encyclopedia-copied oral report or a hem held up with safety pins. My parents' greatest compliment to us was their high expectations. Not everything we did was wonderful to them just because we did it. They never

implied that we were the most wonderful children in the whole world, but they certainly made us feel unique. So why would we want to copy other people instead of showing what *we* saw and felt?

My father taught me to appreciate the morning. Sometimes, when I've stayed up till three A.M. and the alarm inside my head, conditioned by my father's predawn rising, wakes me at seven, I wish ours had been the kind of household where everybody slept till ten and lounged in pajamas all afternoon. My father wouldn't have kept us from sleeping in, of course, but it would have saddened him. We would have missed the birds in full song and the angle of the sun before it's high and scorching and the feel of grass when it's still damp. Getting up early may sound like an unimportant thing, but it's central to everything my family cares about. Discipline, energy, activity, distaste for wastefulness, love of sunshine, and a pretty good balance, I think, between order and freedom. There might be piles of clothes on the chairs in my bedroom sometimes—four outfits tried on and discarded—but I always felt compelled to make my bed. We had something of the same balance in relation to meals. Breakfast, comfortable and free: bathrobes, Ann Landers, *TV Guide*, but dinner at a set time (*always* at six), sit-down, really quite formal, with no reading at the table and considerable thought to the way things looked.

I have friends whose families never eat a meal together. They drift in and out of the kitchen from five to seven, cooking hot dogs and munching potato chips standing up, or sitting down in front of the TV with a bowl of salad, gulped down in the space of a commercial. I've never been much of an eater myself (though my mother is a fine, creative cook), but meals have always meant a lot to me. Even if all I'm eating is an apple, I want to eat it at the table with my family, with places set and the good silver laid out. (Why should guests get silverware while children eat with stainless steel?)

And we never eat in silence, we never need to make polite conversation. Sometimes my mother will tell about a person she met on the street—what he wore, how he walked; she doesn't simply give the facts, she tells a story. My father is a dreamier observer who will tell us that he heard something interesting today, but forgot it, or that someone we know just gave birth to triplets, but he can't remember her name. He doesn't have the knack for minute detail my mother has but—like her—he understands the way people operate, why they do things. Our dinner conversation makes the food taste better. My parents are never boring.

We serve wine with dinner. We all know it's just about the cheapest kind you can buy, but my mother keeps it in a vintage bottle from years back and serves it in chilled crystal, not just for grown-ups. I've always preferred milk, but being offered wine (and having the luxury of refusing it) made me feel trusted. It has to do with the humiliation of childhood and the dignity that every child deserves to feel. (The liberal-minded parents in *Sunday, Bloody Sunday* who offer marijuana to their children were up to something entirely different. My mother gave us wine because it was part of a pleasant ritual, not to experience drunkenness.)

I remember my first high-school drinking parties—the line outside the bathroom of people looking sick and the limp bodies sprawled in heaps along the floor. For them liquor was *booze*, gulped down in closets and bathrooms at school or late at night in cars. Scotch tasted good because it was forbidden. It never was forbidden to me—and to me, it never tasted very good.

I cannot think of a single rule my parents ever told us to obey. What they gave us were principles—a concern for property, a desire to please them. Somehow, we just *knew*. I wouldn't have wanted to toss my mother's white linen sofa cushions on the floor (and I still remember how it pained me when a friend did once) because I was proud of our house and aware (as I told my friend, in what must have seemed like a hopelessly goody-goody tone) that my mother spent a lot of time making those pillows. Good behavior comes down to a good imagination—being able to see how things will look to another person, being able to tell if something you do will hurt him, being able to predict the consequences. Not that empty phrase, "Put yourself in someone else's shoes," but my favorite childhood game—fun, not Sunday school morality: putting myself in someone else's head.

In our town, the usual punishment for high-school kids is grounding—keeping the villain at home for a few weeks and sometimes even locking him in his room. That accomplishes little except to make him more careful not to get caught next time. What it does is to humiliate. There's no dignity in being locked up or sent to bed at 6:30 or told: "You're my child. As long as you live in my house, you'll do as I say." I've never felt as though I were my parents' possession, and no child should. A child who does will realize that the only way to hurt his parents (and that's what he'll want) is to hurt himself, to break their favorite toy.

I've never felt that my fate was totally out of my hands, that no matter what I did, I could change nothing. (Parents say that so often: "I don't care what you say, I'm not changing my mind.") I always had a fairly early bedtime, but a flexible one. (Households with no bedtimes, where weary children are allowed to drag around until they finally collapse, have always saddened me. They're hard on the parents and, most of all, hard on the kids.) If I really wanted to stay up late to finish a book or watch TV, I could. I made sure I'd get that permission by not asking for it too often.

There's a distinction that has to be made between treating children with the respect adults get and treating children like adults. My parents talked to us in a grown-up way, never baby talk. They let us see fairly grown-up books and movies (censorship—like locks on the liquor cabinet—only make the forbidden thing seem more exciting), and they exposed us to grown-up ideas. But they never made the mistake of turning us into little adults—we were never dragged out to join their cocktail parties or freed from the disciplines (not rules, but structures) of our lives. What my parents did was, quite simply, to treat us as politely as they'd treat an adult. I'm always embarrassed for my friends when their parents scold them in front of me, a guest. It's humiliating to them and, most of all, it's rude. My parents allowed us the dignity that so many children lose when their parents force them to wear clothes they dislike or eat foods they hate. Parents who do that, robbing their children of the adult right to choose, aren't just treating their children like children, they're treating them like babies. A child who announces that he doesn't like green sweaters or fried chicken is asserting himself for the first time. How can he ever have opinions on books and people and politics if he doesn't first have opinions on spinach?

I think it was my parents own good manners in their relationship with me that have given me the good manners I now have in relation to other people. Simple good manners, especially among people of my generation, are so rare. Mine come quite naturally (I am the kind that everybody's grandmother loves) not because my mother ever drilled me on please and thank you, but because, even when she was angry, she was never impolite.

I remember a first-grade friend of mine who didn't know what her parents' first names were. In fact, she didn't know her parents *had* first names. What seems sad is that my friend never really thought of her parents as human beings. Except when they got mad at her, they never showed their feelings, never admitted their weaknesses, as though saying "I'm sorry" or "I'm sad" would have made them harder to respect.

My parents never presented themselves to me as perfect and infallible, so I never had that awful moment so many children face when they suddenly discover their parents can be wrong—that Superman is really just Clark Kent. The stories they told about their own childhoods weren't simply illustrations of how good they'd been, how hard the times were, and how grateful my sister and I should feel for having shoes with soles on them and schoolrooms with radiators; they were stories about the times my father played hooky and the day my mother cut off the lace from my grandmother's wedding gown.

I knew what my father's job was (so many children know a meaningless title and nothing else). I knew not only that my father was an English professor, but what his office looked like and what books he taught from, and sometimes I'd visit his class. Whenever my mother wrote a magazine article we'd all gather in the living room to hear her read the first draft and discuss the changes she should make. And even when I was very young, she consulted me ("What kinds of games do they play at recess?" "What's the name of a TV show with policemen in it?"). My parents never bought a piece of furniture that any one of us disliked. We didn't command the household, my sister and I, but we had a say in what went on. How can you have a comfortable relationship between parents and children if all the knowledge is on one side? They knew about us; it was only fair that we should know about them.

My father is a liberated man. He doesn't boss our household, nor is he bossed. My parents have no formal contract of dividing up the chores because they really don't need one—my father helps before my mother needs to ask him. Until I left home and encountered men making jokes about "never trusting a woman," and men who laughed at women drivers, I never understood what male chauvinism meant. It was a shock, discovering that not all men were like my father. (Most men with two daughters and no son would be disappointed.) But being insulated in that one area gave me something terribly valuable: complete confidence in myself. I never wished I were a boy or felt that, since I wasn't one, I would have any fewer options in my life.

Long before "recycling" was made an everyday word, we were doing it. A burned-out flashcube was a dollhouse aquarium; an old umbrella frame, trimmed and stuck on a base, became a comically ugly kitchen Christmas tree. My mother and I can't walk down the street on trash-collection day without finding some discarded treasure to bring home. We go to rummage sales for ten-cent dresses that we transform into evening gowns; we save popsicle sticks and plastic straws and aspirin bottles. We do not like to waste.

My mother's junk collecting has given me a well-trained eye that can look at a cork or a thimble and see the half dozen other things they might become. Her frugality is sometimes extreme, but it has taught me to take no amount of money lightly. I don't ever shop for the simple pleasure of spending money. My pleasure comes from saving it, and from getting something just as nice with a pot of batik dye and fabric or with a needle and thread.

Some people have nightmares about car accidents and forests full of wild animals and escaped convicts and falling from the top of a high building. My recurring nightmare is that our house burns down. I wake up, uncertain for a moment whether it happened or not, and terribly upset, not just because a house is worth a lot of money, and losing it means great expense, but because our house is so much a part of our family, so full of objects we're attached to. We never had a lot of money, but we always lived in style. Every piece of furniture we put in the house, every pillow, every bowl, is something we really care about. It's a house you can feel comfortable in—no slipcovers—but not a tumble-down house. Something happens to a family, I think, when they live in too much decorator-perfection or too much untidiness. There may be dust under the rug at our house, but the surfaces are neat, and when they begin to get messy and disorganized, so do I.

I think of one fine, earnest, committed family whose dining-room table is always cluttered with posters for the latest grape boycott or political campaign. The walls are covered with peace signs and taped-on newspaper clippings no one ever bothered to take down. Our kind of insulated comfort—our "gracious living"—would probably seem irresponsible to them. My feeling is that not until you make a reassuring, comfortable base for security can you go beyond and deal with the discomforts of the outside world. My mother never needed to put a slipcover on the sofa or tell us not to bounce or we'd break the springs—we just knew. Our house is filled with plants and paintings and Mexican pottery and comfortable big pillows and straw baskets full of fruit, and plenty of light. To lose it (and this is why the nightmare comes) would be to lose not just my roof but my foundation.

My parents made some bad mistakes, of course. Their way of doing things was so strong and definite that sometimes it was hard to keep in mind that other ways existed—just because *we* didn't like gladiolas and store-bought birthday cards and Jell-O; just because *we* poured our milk in the cereal bowl before adding the cereal—that didn't mean that plenty of good people didn't have a perfect right to like things done their way. *We:* I use that word too much. My family is too close, perhaps, too much of a club; the delineations—*us* and *them*—are too clear. The critical faculties my parents gave me have made me more demanding than I should be, given me standards that the real, flawed world can't live up to. There are things my parents did and shouldn't have done, and things they should have done and didn't. There was at times a feeling that our house was a factory of the arts, with every moment spent in what the experts call "creative play"—constant painting and writing and acting and dancing. My parents never really pushed, but they raised me to push myself too hard, to be impatient with myself when I wasn't doing something worthwhile.

I wish I'd been sent to church when I was little (if only to have had a religion to rebel against later; as is, I have nothing, plus an ignorance of the Bible that catches me up every time I read a book, almost, or go to a museum). The image of my mother playing any outdoor game besides croquet is impossible to picture. My father was more athletic, but never a player of baseball or a skier and, as a result, neither was I. I grew up dreading gym periods at school, spending more energy thinking up excuses than I would have spent out on the playing field, where teammates knew enough to keep the ball away from me. Only recently have I learned that I'm not so uncoordinated after all, but I'm years behind now, and filled with silly, irrational fears (Will I hit my head? Will I fall? Will it hurt?) that I'm only beginning to overcome.

But I can't imagine feeling bitter toward my parents, as the girl on the bus to the airport with me must have felt—not even to have blinked while her mother waved good-bye. I have friends who are embarrassed to be seen with their parents. Very occasionally I've been tempted to pretend I didn't know mine, too (when my frugal mother returns a single bruised banana to the supermarket; when my father swims with me—in a bathing cap). Mostly I'm proud of them, and sure enough of myself not to worry about what people will think. I look at their faults and their strangeness with amusement and affection—not as odd, but as unique. I could no more hide my family and my upbringing than a friend of mine who's black could hide her blackness. And I want not just to recognize my family—to hold my father's hand when we cross the street and to sit with my mother at the movies—but to tell about it, too, because I can't help boasting—I've come out pretty happy. Saturday mornings, when I'm home, I like to go grocery shopping with my father. He's supposed to carry the shopping list my mother made up, but usually he loses it, so we drift through the aisles exclaiming on the price of lettuce, examining avocados and stocking up on boysenberry yogurt. I gave up drinking whole milk four years ago and haven't touched peanut-butter sandwiches since the days when I carried a lunch box, but he still asks me, every Saturday, "Do you need any milk? How are we fixed for peanut butter?" We look at the magazines together, he picks up some new brand of vitamins he thinks I need. We finish with soup, my father pacing in front of the Campbell's wall muttering, "What fine thing shall I have for lunch today?" and arriving, each time, at the chicken noodle as if it were a new discovery. We drive home at 20 miles an hour as high-school kids, friends of mine, whiz past, honking. Sometimes I'm impatient, but my father hardly notices. He steers the car like a Viking—his back straight, both hands tight on the wheel—slowing down to ten when he spots an interesting bird. Halfway home he'll remember—*mushrooms,* the one thing my mother specially asked for, and we'll turn back. They know us well at the checkout counter.

My mother and I cook together, side by side, my gestures just like hers, only less practiced. I've learned to scoop an egg out with my thumb to get every drop of the white, and then to beat it in the center of the bowl with the dough, already mixed, forming a well around my pool of frothy liquid. We rake leaves—she makes the piles, I jump in them—and we shop, not at big department stores (our town doesn't have any) but at funny, junky little shops we descend upon like hunters in search of treasure. Sometimes we go to an auction and come back with a boxful of handmade lace scraps whose possibilities—cuffs, collars, pockets, bodices—nobody else noticed, or an ancient mimeograph machine neither of us has any use for.

We don't spend all our time together. All three of us (and my older sister, who's married now) lead fairly independent lives. Saying that we love each other doesn't tell all that much—the most hostile children and the most frustrated parents can feel love. More than that, my parents are my friends.

PARENTAL REJECTION
AND ITS EFFECT
ON ME*

My mother and father and myself (prior to my marriage) lived in a small, stagnant farming community. All my relatives, including cousins, from both my father's and mother's side lived in this community, went to the same high school and church, and shopped at the same stores. My parents had little opportunity or desire for relationships outside of this environment. They were very rigid, opinionated, and ignorant, and spent all their waking hours working on the farm. Their only diversion was gossiping and going to church. Idleness and pleasure were "a sin."

My association with other people outside of this environment was very limited. My grammar schoolmates consisted of twelve children in grades one through eight. I had two teachers throughout grammar school. My high school experiences gave me a little more opportunity for associations during school hours. However, extra-curricular activities were limited and my participation in them was hindered by the distance of my home from school.

I feel that my parents' rejection was both passive and active. They discouraged participation in activities that would have provided opportunities for my personal and social growth because it was too much trouble. Example: My father was too busy to truck my horse to the fair so I rode it twelve miles to get there. They didn't care what I did as long as I didn't bother them. This gave me the impression that their work was more important than me. I remember following

* The author's name has been withheld by her request.

my mother around the house trying to tell her something that was important to me. As I got no response my voice became louder and louder as I tried to get her attention. This loudness became a habit with all conversation. My parents never attended my piano recitals, band concerts, graduations or other activities of importance to me. They were "too busy" or "too tired."

Love and affection were never shown between any members of our family. I was a junior in college when I first kissed my father. I wanted to receive and give affection and since my parents would neither give it or receive it, I found an outlet in my dog and my horse. They were my constant companions and I felt very depressed when I left them to go to college. I even cried and kissed them goodbye.

My mother was very strict and domineering and was the authority in our house. No explanation or consideration of my desires were given. Questions of "Why can't I?" were usually answered with "Because I said so." She never had time to give constructive help or advice but would reply "Do what you want to." Then after my decision was made, she would enforce her will, desires, and opinions upon me and if I went against her wishes, I was made to feel guilty for disobeying. Today I still find it difficult to make decisions.

Work to earn your keep was stressed in my family. Praise was not given and was not to be expected. Example: The task given me was to weed the beans in the garden. I also weeded the tomatoes in hopes of receiving praise and acceptance. When I told my mother what I had done, her reply was "Go weed the corn now." It seemed that nothing I did was good enough. The statement she often used was "You haven't earned the salt in your bread."

Criticism and comparison with others were frequent. I was very proud of myself for sewing a school dress but my mother told me what a poor job I had done and proceeded to tear it apart and resew it. When I asked her for a new dress to wear, she said, "Your sister didn't have a new dress for her junior prom. Why do you think you have to have one?" She was always comparing me with my older sister.

I have looked for acceptance all my life. I sought it from everyone with whom I came in contact. "Nobody likes me—everybody hates me" has been my attitude throughout life. Affiliation with people has been a source of frustration for me. As a teenager, all my energies were directed toward getting boyfriends. I interpreted any interest shown me as "love." As an adult, if people did not reciprocate my friendship and interest, I interpreted it as a dislike for me personally. "What's wrong with me?" "What have I done wrong?" were questions I asked myself many times. I was always very defensive when friendly suggestions were given me by my acquaintances. I looked upon them as criticisms. Praise from others was assurance that I was liked and silence was criticism and dislike. Praise for a poorly done act was more important to me than my own concept of a well done act. I had all my happiness in another's keeping. I have played the organ for church services and the pleasure of playing and doing a good job was secondary to the praise and recognition I hoped to receive. When I did receive praise, my self-abasement wouldn't let me accept it. I felt guilty for having received it. I felt that I didn't deserve it.

Devising ways and means of getting attention was always an important concern of mine. Being a number in a class or a small part of a group was always dissatisfying. But my insecurity and feel-ing of worthlessness prohibited me from being anything else. All I could do was hope that someone would notice me or show me special attention. I always desired to be somebody important such as the homecoming queen, the heroine in a play, or the soloist in the choir. When I did get up courage to try for one of these important roles, I always failed because I lacked the personal qualifications, and the failure reinforced my feeling of worthlessness. I also used fantasy to get imaginary attention. I would imagine and desire bodily harm because of all the attention and concern that I would receive. One means of attention-getting that was partially satisfying concerned horses. A small child riding a big horse drew attention, and thus my interest in horses grew. I used my horse to get attention and praise by riding in parades and shows and "showing off" tricks I had taught it. Although this satisfied my attention need, it was also a source of frustration. My strong desire to win and compete caused much disappointment when I didn't succeed.

I cannot blame my parents for their rejection and its effect on me because their personal and marital adjustment was related to their own childhood. I only hope that my understanding and knowledge of myself will permit me to provide a better life for any children I may have.

PARENTS BRING UP YOUR CHILDREN!

Urie Bronfenbrenner

Many changes have occurred in ways of child-rearing in the United States, particularly since World War II, but their essence may be conveyed in a single sentence: Children *used* to be brought up by their parents. Families were bigger—not in terms of more children so much as more adults—grandparents, uncles, aunts, cousins. Those relatives who did not live with you lived nearby. You often went to their houses. They came as often to yours. Everybody minded your business. They wanted to know where you had been, where you were going, and why. And if they did not like what they heard, they said so.

And it wasn't just your relatives. Everybody on the block minded your business too. If you got into mischief, the phone would ring at your house, and your parents would know what you had done before you got back home. Sometimes you didn't like it—but at least people cared.

As the stable world of the small town or the city block has become absorbed into an ever-shifting suburbia, children are growing up in a different environment. The extended family has been reduced to a nuclear one with only two adults, and the functioning neighborhood has withered to a small circle of friends. For millions of American children, the neighborhood is nothing but a row of buildings where "other people" live. One house, or apartment, is much like another—and so are the people. They all have more or less the same income, and the same way of life. But the child does not see much of that life, for all that people do in the neighborhood is to come home to it, have a drink, eat dinner, mow the lawn, watch television and sleep. Before, the world in which the child lived consisted of a diversity of people in a diversity of settings. Today, housing projects often have no stores, no shops, no services, no adults at work or play. Rarely can a child see people working at their trades. Mechanics, tailors or shopkeepers are either out of sight or unapproachable. Nor can a child listen to the gossip at the post office or on a park bench. To do anything at all—go to a movie, get an ice-cream cone, go swimming or play ball—he has to travel by car or bus.

All that does not really matter, however, for children are not at home much. They leave early on the school bus, and it is almost suppertime when they get back. And there may not be anybody home when they get there. If their mother is not working at least part-time (and over a third of American mothers are), she is out a lot—not just to be with friends, but to do things for the community. The men leave in the morning before the children are up. And they do not get back until after the children have eaten supper.

Consequently, American parents do not spend so much time with children as they used to. This development does not imply a decrease in the affection or concern of parents for their children. Nor is it a change that we have planned or wanted. Rather, it is the by-product of a variety of social changes, all operating to decrease the prominence and power of the family in the lives of children. Urbanization, child-labor laws, the abolition of the apprentice system, the working mother, the experts' advice to be permissive, the delegation and professionalization of child care—all decrease opportunity for contact between children and parents, or, for that matter, adults in general.

If a child is not with his parents or other adults, where does he spend his time? First and foremost, he is with other children—in school, after school, over weekends and on holidays. But even this contact is restricted. Housing projects, even entire neighborhoods, cater to families in a particular stage of their life or career. Social life becomes organized on a similar basis; and, as a result, contacts become limited to persons of one's own age and station. Whereas invitations used to be extended to entire families, with all the Smiths visiting all the Joneses, nowadays, every social event has its segregated equivalent for every age group down to the toddlers. While the adults take their drinks upstairs, the children have their "juice time" in the rumpus room downstairs. In short, *we are coming to live in a society that is segregated not only by race and class, but also by age.*

It doesn't take children very long to learn the lesson the adult world teaches: "Don't bug us! Latch on to your peers!"

That is exactly what children do. In a recently completed study, 766 sixth-grade children reported spending during the weekend, an average of two to three hours a day with their parents. Over the same period, they spent about twice as much time with peers, either singly or in groups. Moreover, their behavior apparently reflects preference as well as practice. When asked with whom they would rather spend a free weekend afternoon, many more chose friends than parents. Then, the characteristics of predominantly "peer-oriented" and "adult-oriented" children were compared in an attempt to find how the peer-oriented children got that way.

The study concluded that the peer-oriented youngster was more influenced by a lack of attention and concern at home than by the attractiveness of the peer group. In general, the peer-oriented children held rather negative views of themselves and the peer group. They also expressed a dim view of their own future. Their parents were rated as lower than those of adult-oriented children both in the expression of affection and support, and in the exercise of discipline and control. Finally, the peer-oriented children report engaging in more antisocial behavior such as "doing something illegal," "playing hooky," lying, teasing other children, etc. It would seem that the peer-oriented child turns to his age-mates less by choice than by default. The vacuum left by the withdrawal of parents and adults from the lives of children is filled with an undesired—and possibly undesirable—substitute of an age-segregated peer group.

In my study of middle-class adolescents, children who reported that their parents were away from home for long periods of time rated significantly lower on such characteristics as responsibility and leadership. Perhaps because it was

more pronounced, absence of the father was more critical than that of the mother, particularly in its effect on boys. In general, father absence contributes to low motivation for achievement, inability to defer immediate rewards for later benefits, low self-esteem, susceptibility to group influence and juvenile delinquency.

In 1959, investigators studied the ages at which children turn to parents or peers for opinion, advice or company. There was a turning point at about the seventh grade. Before that, the majority looked mainly to their parents as models and companions; thereafter, the children's peers had equal or greater influence. A recent study shows a substantially greater percentage of peer "dependence" at every age and grade level than the previous one. It would appear that the shift from parents to peers occurs earlier than it did a decade ago and is now much more pronounced.

The effect of a peer group on the child depends on the attitudes and activities prevailing in that peer group. Where group norms emphasize achievement, the members perform accordingly; where the prevailing expectations call for violation of adult norms, these are as readily translated into action. In short, social contagion is a two-way street.

How early in life do children become susceptible to such contagion? Prof. Albert Bandura and his colleagues at Stanford University have conducted experiments which suggest that the process is already well-developed at the prechool level. In the basic experimental design, the child finds himself in a familiar playroom. There is a person playing with toys in another corner of the room. This other person behaves very aggressively. He strikes a large Bobo doll (a bouncing inflated figure), throws objects and mutilates dolls and animal toys, using language to match. Later on, the child who "accidentally" observed this behavior is tested by being allowed to play in a room containing a variety of toys, including some similar to those employed by the aggressive model. Without any provocation, perfectly normal, well-adjusted preschoolers engage in aggressive acts, not only repeating what they had observed but elaborating on it.

The influence that peers have on the young is rivaled, perhaps, only by television. Many American children spend as much time watching television as they spend in school, and more than in any other activity except sleep and play. As with the peer group, they are propelled there in part by parental example and parental pressure.

During his experiments, Professor Bandura made films with essentially identical scripts: one with an actor, a second of a cartoon cat. The films were presented on a television set. When the children were tested, the television films turned out to be just as effective in arousing aggression as experiences with live people.

When Bandura's work was published . . . , the television industry issued a statement, questioning his conclusions on the interesting ground that no parents were present. "What a child will do under normal conditions cannot be projected from his behavior when he is carefully isolated from normal conditions and the influences of society."

Evidence for the relevance of Bandura's laboratory findings to "real life" comes from a study of more than 600 third-graders. The children who were rated most aggressive by their classmates were those who watched television programs involving a high degree of violence.

Another study tested the reactions of various groups to violence on the screen. The subjects were shown a knife fight between two teen-agers from *Rebel Without a Cause*. Then they were asked to assist in an experiment on the effects of punishment in learning by giving an unseen person an electric shock every time he made an error. One version of the experiment employed 15-year-old high school boys as subjects. With this group, the designers wondered what would happen if no film were shown. Would the everyday environment of adolescents—who see more movies and more television programs and are called on to display virility through aggressive acts in teen-age gangs—provoke latent brutality?

The results were sobering. Even without the suggestive power of the aggressive film, the teen-agers pulled the shock lever to its highest intensities. A few of the boys made remarks that suggested they were enjoying the experience of administering pain; for example, "I bet I made that fellow jump."

The peer group need not act as an impetus to antisocial behavior—if it is properly influenced by the adult society. American children, however, are relatively cut off from the adult world, and the family, primarily because of changes in the larger social order, is no longer in a position to exercise its responsibilities. The role of the church in moral education has withered in most cases to a pallid Sunday school session. The school—in which the child spends most of his day—has been debarred by tradition, lack of experience and preoccupation with subject matter from concerning itself in any major way with the child's development as a person. The vacuum, moral and emotional, is then filled—by default—on the one hand by the television screen with its daily message of commercialism and violence, and on the other by the socially isolated, age-graded peer group, with its limited capacities as a humanizing agent.

If the current trend persists, we can anticipate increased alienation, indifference, antagonism and violence on the part of the younger generation in all segments of our society—middle-class children as well as the disadvantaged. From this perspective, the emergence of the hippie cult appears as the least harmful manifestation of a process that sees its far more destructive and widespread expression in the sharp rise recently in juvenile delinquency.

Why should age segregation bring social disruption in its wake? It is obvious that such qualities as mutual trust, kindness, cooperation and social responsibility are learned from other human beings who in some measure exhibit these qualities, value them, and strive to develop them in their children. It is a matter of social rather than biological inheritance. Transmission cannot take place without the active participation of the older generation. If children have contact only with their own age-mates, there is no possibility for learning culturally established patterns of cooperation and mutual concern.

We are experiencing a breakdown in the process of making human beings human. What is needed is a change in our ways of living that will once again bring adults back into the lives of children and children back into the lives of adults.

Some ways of accomplishing this change were

presented last month at the White House Conference on Children in a report prepared under my chairmanship. It is well within the resources of our society to act on the Conference recommendations. What will happen if we don't?

In *Lord of the Flies,* William Golding describes events among a group of boys marooned on an island. Patterns of civilized human relationships, epitomized in the boy "Piggy," are as yet too shallowly rooted in the others, and are soon destroyed by the quickly rising sadism of peer power. Piggy is brutally killed just before the adult rescuers arrive. Their first question: "Are there any adults —and grown-ups with you?"

The message of the allegorical ending is clear. If adults do not once again become involved in the lives of our children, there is trouble ahead for American society.

BIRTHRIGHTS

Richard Farson

There is no way to have a liberated society until we have liberated our children. And right now our society is organized against them. The ideal child is cute (entertaining to adults), well-behaved (doesn't bother adults), and bright (capable of bringing home report cards the parents can be proud of). Efforts of parents to produce these traits have so inhibited children that neither adults nor children can always see the remarkable potentialities that lie beyond or outside them. Because we have become increasingly alert to the many forms of oppression in our society, we are now seeing, as we have not seen before, the predicament of children: they are powerless, dominated, ignored, invisible. We are beginning to see the necessity for children's liberation.

People are not liberated one by one. They must be liberated as a class. Liberating children, giving them equality and guaranteeing their civil rights, may seem to violate the fairly recent realizations that children are not simply miniature adults, and that childhood is a special time of life, with special qualities and problems. In fact, never before in history have parents and teachers had so much "understanding" of children, or at least of their physical and social development. But the "understanding" has led not to improved conditions for children, but simply to more control of them and consequently more burdensome responsibilities of supervision for parents. So that now the best things that happen between parent and child happen by accident or by surprise, very often breaking all rules in the process. Actually, anyone who isn't bewildered by child-rearing, who doesn't find it an extremely formidable and trying experience, probably has never lived with children.

Moreover, increased understanding and concern has not been coupled with increased rights. As a consequence, children's rights have actually diminished, for we have simply replaced ignorant domination with sophisticated domination. With increased attention to children has come resentment. Our efforts to shape children, to reform them, to fix them, to correct them, to discipline them, to educate them, have led to an obsession with the physical, moral and sexual problems of children; but they have not led to our liking them more, or realizing their potential.

By holding a limited and demeaned view of children and by segregating them almost completely from the adult world, we may be subverting their capacity for genius. It has been pointed out that we no longer have infant and child prodigies—or at least that they are now much rarer than before. In the past, when children were an integral part of the community, they sometimes did show great genius. By the age of 17 months, for example, Louis XIII played the violin. He played tennis when he still slept in a cradle. He was an archer, and played cards and chess, at six. Today we might worry a bit about precocity of that magnitude, but then, people took it for granted. One wonders whether we have sacrificed genius for homogeneity and conformity.

The nuclear family (two adults and their minor children), a completely self-contained unit, not dependent upon the community, is a relatively new development. Child care once was distributed among several adults in an extended family; now it falls entirely on the parent or parents. The children do little for the family, and almost nothing for each other or themselves. Overburdened parents feel an increasing sense of both responsibility and guilt as society's expectations of what families should offer their children rise—and yet the community spends less of its money and energy on aid of children or parents.

Though technically the law no longer regards them as chattels, children are still treated as the private property of their parents. The parent has both the right and the responsibility to control the life of the child.

It will take quite a revolution in our thinking to

give some of this control back to the child. Nevertheless, the acceptance of the child's right to self-determination is fundamental. It is the right to a single standard of morals and behavior for children and adults, including behavior decisions close to home. From the earliest signs of competence, children might have, for example, the right to decide for themselves about eating, sleeping, playing, listening, reading, washing, and dressing; the freedom to choose their associates, to decide what life goals they wish to pursue.

Parents may argue that the right to self-determination will bring with it the risk of physical and psychological damage. No doubt some risks are involved. But under present conditions, many children are severely damaged—physically, socially, and emotionally. Compared to the existing system, the risks of harming children by accepting their right to self-determination may be greatly over-rated. Impossible as it seems, it may be that the situations we try hardest to avoid for ourselves and for our children, would be actually the most beneficial to us. One can make a good case for a calamity theory of growth—many of our most eminent people, for instance, have come from the most calamitous early childhood situations. Of course, we don't want calamities to happen to our children, but we can be a bit more relaxed about our protectiveness.

In any event, it's time to admit that no one knows how to grow people.

Since most concerns center on the problems of living with a self-determining child, our first thoughts focus on the home. While liberation cannot be truly accomplished at home—because the home is not separate from the rest of society—the situation illustrates in microcosm the dimensions of the problem as it might exist in society at large.

Take, for example, family mealtimes. No one should be expected to prepare a meal at a special time for children simply because they choose not to eat at the regular hour. However, most children could, with some special arrangement and training, prepare meals for themselves when necessary. Those children whose schedules demand special timetables would receive the same consideration afforded any adult member of the household in similar circumstances—but no more.

Loss of authority over a child in areas such as nutrition does not mean that the child cannot be influenced. In the absence of adult tyranny, adult judgment and information have to be the primary influence and are more likely to be accepted.

Bedtime is a case in point. Most parents know that children enjoy sleeping as much as adults do. Resistance to it comes largely from adult pressures. Because adults' sleeping habits are governed largely by the pressures to engage in productive activity during the daytime hours, we adhere to nighttime sleeping hours. Children, too, must follow daytime hours to fulfill their compulsory attendance in school.

If children came to these conclusions for themselves, by suffering the consequences, they would be capable in the long run of learning, as most adults have, that when we are too tired we pay for it the next day. This would make the ritual of going to bed less of a vehicle through which adults and children express their mutual antagonisms. Believe it or not, bedtime is not a big issue in some homes. Children either go to bed by themselves or they are simply covered up on the spot where they drop off to sleep.

What about other physical dangers, such as children playing where they might injure themselves? The first answer is that of course we cannot risk a child's death. Just as we would pull an adult out of the path of an onrushing car, we would do the same for a child. There is no double standard in an emergency situation.

In fact children are equally concerned about safety—their own and their parents'. They try, for example, to keep their parents from chain-smoking, drinking too much, getting too fat, driving dangerously, or working too hard. While they are seldom successful at this, the point is to recognize the concern and responsibility as mutual.

Life is inevitably risky and almost everyone agrees that it is important that children be given the opportunity to take risks in order to develop, to push their limits, to discover their potential. What we fail to realize is that most of the dangers that children face are "man-made" and that, not recognizing what we've done to ourselves, we've accepted the responsibility to protect our children, by constant supervision, from dangers we've created—backyard pools, electrical sockets, poisons under the sink, and speeding automobiles.

Unlike man-made dangers, natural dangers like cliffs and crashing waves usually signal their own warning.

Most sports involve some physical risks, but children *do* climb trees even if falling might hurt them; they ride horses, take gymnastics, and engage in other athletics.

Of course, the elimination of all danger in our society is certainly not a realistic nor desirable goal, but we will have come a long way in making the world safer for children if we can solve the problem of the automobile—the Number One enemy of children. Besides creating a situation requiring constant supervision, automobiles have actually decreased the mobility of children while increasing the mobility of adults. This problem is one of social design, and its solution will require some difficult choices for us in city planning, and the utilization of financial resources. We must build cities with children in mind, and devise transportation systems that work for them. It means reducing our use of and reliance on the automobile. It means reorienting our work, play, family life, and commercial activities so that they are all close to each other, which would have the additional benefit of developing stronger communities, more interpersonal activity and greater involvement.

We must find ways of protecting children as best we can from the lethal dangers, where the first lesson is the last one. In our well-meaning protective attitude, however, we must not include the idea that it is our right to have children and to raise them as we see fit. The 1970 White House Conference on Children held that the rights of parents cannot infringe upon the rights of children, and all of us may soon come to the conclusion that the ability to conceive a child gives no one the right to dominate or to abuse her or him. The decisions about a child's home environment should not belong to the parents alone. Parents will have more responsibility than they have authority. They will have to depend more heavily on judgment, advice, and persuasion.

Given the fact that child-rearing practices differ widely from country to country, it is hard to pinpoint a parent's responsibilities and a child's needs. In some cultures children are wrapped tightly, in others they are always naked; some children have close ties with their father, some do not even know their father; some are exposed to the elements as a test of maturity; some are held and fondled almost constantly.

Despite this diversity, there are certain widely shared, if debatable, views of basic needs. Children need loving care as newborns and in early infancy. They need, for what we would call normal physical growth, certain nutritive elements. For their minds to develop they need stimulation and variation. And as children grow older they need to be with adults with whom they can identify. Despite current convention, however, none of these so-called basics justifies the nuclear family as the only model of family life.

Parenting in the nuclear family is difficult, demanding, restrictive, and expensive. Having children is unbelievably burdensome. It is not just the battered children who grow up in oppressive circumstances, but to some degree *all* children. The degrees of oppression vary, but one kind is universal: that children have no alternative but to live with their parents or be housed by the government in some jail-like alternative. Even when family life is delightful, the child should have other options.

Furthermore, the truth is that more than 60 percent of Americans live in domestic arrangements other than the nuclear family: single people with or without children, married people without children or with stepchildren, couples with grown children, homosexual couples or groups, elderly people living in nursing homes, convicts in prisons, students in residence halls, children living with one parent or in institutions, communal arrangements, and so forth.

Ignoring this reality, we persist in glorifying the nuclear family instead of exploring alternate living arrangements into which the child may fit just as well—or better.

One of the few well-known alternatives which honors the child's right to self-determination is A. S. Neill's Summerhill, an English residential school where the freedom and equality of children is of paramount concern and the children's participation in the government of the institution is fundamental to its operation.

Multiple parenting is the core concept of other alternatives now in practice. It means several adults share child-rearing responsibilities through community efforts.

A CHILD'S BILL OF RIGHTS

Richard Farson outlines the specific reforms that he considers essential to the true liberation of all children.

1. **The Right to Self-Determination.** *Children should have the right to decide the matters which affect them most directly.* This is the basic right upon which all others depend. Children are now treated as the private property of their parents on the assumption that it is the parents' right and responsibility to control the life of the child. The achievement of children's rights, however, would reduce the need for this control and bring about an end to the double standard of morals and behavior for adults and children.

2. **The Right to Alternative Home Environments.** *Self-determining children should be able to choose from among a variety of arrangements: residences operated by children, child exchange programs, 24-hour child-care centers, and various kinds of schools and employment opportunities.* Parents are not always good for their children—some people estimate that as many as 4 million children are abused annually in the United States, for instance, and that a half million children run away each year.

3. **The Right to Responsive Design.** *Society must accommodate itself to children's size and to their need for safe space.* To keep them in their place, we now force children to cope with a world that is either not built to fit them, or is actually designed against them. If the environment were less dangerous for children, there would be less need for constant control and supervision of children by adults.

4. **The Right to Information.** *A child must have the right to all information ordinarily available to adults—including, and perhaps especially, information that makes adults uncomfortable.*

5. **The Right to Educate Oneself.** *Children should be free to design their own education, choosing from among many options the kinds of learning experiences they want, including the option not to attend any kind of school.* Compulsory education must be abolished because the enforced threatening quality of education in America has taught children to hate school, to hate the subject matter, and tragically, to hate themselves. Children are programmed, tracked, and certified in a process of stamping out standardized educated products acceptable to the university, military, business and industry, and community. Education can change only through the achievement of new rights for those exploited and oppressed by it—the children themselves.

In this country child-care arrangements for "normal" kids present a terrible financial burden, usually to the parent, whereas the state pays for all those incarcerated in reform schools and prisons and the 200,000 children in foster-care programs. The approximately $12,000 a year it costs the state to keep one child in an institution should certainly be enough to pay for many different kinds of state-supported institutions which are not prisons, but offer realistic placement options for those children in most serious difficulty at home.

People who want alternative living arrangements need thoughtfully designed programs which (1) place more choice in the hands of the child, (2) redistribute the costs so that neither the state nor the parents suffer the total burden, (3) make use of previously unused resources, including laypeople and paraprofessionals, teenagers, or retired people, and (4) provide a variety of arrangements for new home environments from which to choose.

Large numbers of people could be involved in a professionally managed membership network, a kind of nongeographic community to which participants pay regular dues. Alternative home environments for children which could be developed by such a network are primarily multifamily communes, child-exchange programs, and children's residences.

The multifamily commune could work if there were an organized network to help with problems

6. The Right to Freedom from Physical Punishment. *Children should live free of physical threat from those who are larger and more powerful than they.* Corporal punishment is used impulsively and cruelly in the home, arbitrarily in the school, and sadistically in penal institutions. It does not belong in our repertoire of responses to children.

7. The Right to Sexual Freedom. *Children should have the right to conduct their sexual lives with no more restriction than adults.* Sexual freedom for children must include the right to information about sex, the right to nonsexist education, and the right to all sexual activities that are legal among consenting adults. In fact, children will be best protected from sexual abuse when they have the right to refuse—but they are now trained not to refuse adults, to accept all forms of physical affection, and to mistrust their own reactions to people. They are denied any information about their own sexuality or that of others. We keep them innocent and ignorant and then worry that they will not be able to resist sexual approaches.

8. The Right to Economic Power. *Children should have the right to work, to acquire and manage money, to receive equal pay for equal work, to choose trade apprenticeship as an alternative to school, to gain promotion to leadership positions, to own property, to develop a credit record, to enter into binding contracts, to engage in enterprise, to obtain guaranteed support apart from the family, to achieve financial independence.*

9. The Right to Political Power. *Children should have the vote and be included in the decision-making process.* Eighty million children in the United States need the right to vote because adults do not vote in their behalf. At present they are no one's constituency and legislation reflects the lack of representation. To become a constituency they must have the right to vote.

10. The Right to Justice. *Children must have the guarantee of a fair trial with due process of law, an advocate to protect their rights against the parents as well as the system, and a uniform standard of detention.* Every year a million children get into trouble with the law. One out of every nine children will go through the juvenile court system before the age of 18. At any given time about one hundred thousand children are in some kind of jail. Some are held illegally, many have not committed any kind of crime, most have done nothing that would be considered a crime if done by an adult, and none has been given a fair trial with due process of law. The juvenile justice system was designed to protect children from the harsh treatment of the adult justice system—but it is more unfair, more arbitrary, and more cruel.

of autocratic leadership, to establish standards of sexual behavior and fair distribution of maintenance and other responsibilities before the experiment begins and throughout its life. Obviously children would have to participate fully in all aspects of the communal life.

A second model is child exchange where families would swap children, much like today's foreign-exchange student programs. This program would accommodate children who have created a problem for their parents, or children who would like to have the chance to experience new situations.

The problem with child exchange presently is that it is informal, haphazard, and uncommon. But the need is there. (A man took a newspaper ad offering his child in exchange for another troublesome teenager, and within the first few days he received more than 70 responses.) Within a membership network the exchanges could be arranged at the option of the children as well as the parents, and counseling and contracts would also be introduced to help safeguard the system.

A third possible alternative involves residences operated by children. Organized by the network staff and similar to those now operated by and for the elderly, these would have adults in residence as consultants or in other capacities, but would be, by and large, managed by children functioning in self-determined and self-governing ways. One of the problems is that this plan might seriously reduce children's contact with adults (though the children themselves might be far less age-segregated than they are in schools now). Another is that the financing for children's residences would have to come largely from parents and government, and that might impose parent control. Finally, infant care would require adult legal responsibility. While these problems are challenging, they are not insurmountable.

Another model, not requiring a membership network, is the day-care or day-and-night care facility financed not only by parents but by government, business and industry, and society at large.

Then there are basic changes to be made in our current living facilities. Children are simply not considered important enough by those adults who design the environment. Only in places that are used exclusively by children—classrooms, playgrounds, and the like—do we find facilities built to children's scale.

Consider the daily experiences of small children—taking a shower under an uncontrollable waterfall pouring down from several feet overhead, gripping the edges of a toilet seat that is far too high and too large, standing on tiptoe to reach a cabinet or a sink, trying to see in a mirror so high that it misses them completely. Then they must go out into the world to try to open doors too heavy for them, negotiate stairs too steep, reach food on tables and shelves that are too high, pass through turnstiles that hit them directly in the face, see a film almost totally obscured by the back of the auditorium seat in front of them, get a drink out of a fountain they can't reach, make a phone call from a pay telephone placed at adult height, bang into sharp corners just the height of their heads, and risk their safety in revolving doors. Having physical reminders that there are children in the world would help to make us more alert and attentive toward them, making their lives safer and more interesting. The real advance for children will come when adults recognize them as an integral part of the community, expecting them to be around, naturally looking out for them and scaling conveniences to their size.

We must also find a health-care solution that works—for all members of our society. A child must have the right to obtain medical treatment without parental consent. This doesn't mean that the physician is empowered to dictate the kind of treatment a child receives without having to explain it to the parent, but rather that the child is empowered to deal directly with the physician and to have some freedom and responsibility in the actions taken with respect to her or his own health. (In cases where the children are too young or uncomprehending to seek medical attention on their own they should of course be represented by a parent or advocate.) Minors should be given complete information on their condition and on the procedures that are suggested for their treatment, as well as information on a variety of health problems, notably those of birth control and venereal disease. Adopted children must also have the right to obtain their natural family's medical history.

In health, welfare, and education, a child's ignorance is a strong political ally of adult society, and adults have learned to rely heavily on it. Because children are excluded from almost every institution in our society, they don't know what to do to gain power over their own lives. They are separated from the adult world, barred from important conversations, kept out of the rooms where decisions are made, excluded from social gatherings, dinner parties, and business meetings, and denied access to information about society and themselves.

Students' school records provide a good example of this exclusion. Information—including IQ scores, teachers' or counselors' reports, personality data, and health records—is, in most cases, withheld from both parent and child. The secrecy of this system prohibits the careful evaluation of the information's accuracy. Neither parent nor child—but especially not the child—is usually permitted to challenge it. Even though we evolve and change, these records are cumulative and permanent and there is no practice of their systematic destruction at various points in a person's life. Teachers, police officers (who may be able to use the material against a child or parent), and other enforcers of society's rules have access to the file even if they cannot demonstrate a need for the information. The file is often available for medical or educational research purposes. All this may represent a tremendous threat to individual privacy and to the liberation of the child.

Students are labeled and categorized; the advantaged are secretly placed on tracks toward college or vocational training and others are damaged by derogatory material appearing on their permanent files as the result of temporary anger or prejudice of teachers. The serious flaws of all diagnostic measures recorded in these files, the questionable nature of psychological tests used, the fact that having certain knowledge and therefore certain expectations of children tend to be self-confirming, the way in which test scores prejudice teachers and administrators—all these factors combine to make the keeping of records a capricious and sometimes dangerous procedure.

Children are also systematically denied information in sexual matters. The average child sees literally thousands of filmed and televised murders, yet parents and the media strain to keep sex out of the child's thoughts.

The fact that children want information about sex does not mean they should be able to invade adults' bedrooms. Adults and children alike should have control over their private lives. At this point, however, the privacy that needs protection is the child's. Adults think nothing of entering children's private space (if indeed they have private space); of opening their mail, going through their drawers, interrogating them about associates or activities. As a result, most children have little or no private life.

Subjecting children to such prohibitions and deceptions ultimately threatens our democratic process; above all else, that process requires an independent and informed citizenry. The most potent weapon against tyranny is knowledge that is easily accessible to all. Whenever one group decides what is and what is not desirable for another to know, whenever a "we-they" condition exists, society becomes vulnerable to totalitarian controls. The acquisition of information by the child causes adults distress for exactly the same reasons; it empowers children, and makes it less easy to control and dominate them.

Our predisposition to ignore children's concerns, deal expeditiously with their questions, and deny them entry into the world of adults, is precisely the reason they tend to remain ignorant, dependent, and impotent. It's time to give up our adult privileges and make room for the autonomous child.

Individual action is vital, but it can never be sufficient. Only concerted action taken on many fronts can enable children to escape their prisons. Either we do this together—or it won't be done at all.

A NEW WAY TO RAISE KIDS*
(An Interview with Bruno Bettelheim)

Jane Whitbread

"The survival of millions of our children depends on a U.S. version of the children's homes on the Israeli *kibbutzim*, and I would do anything I could to help get experimental centers started here right now."

This, from Bruno Bettelheim, the legendary expert on children and their problems, is like the Pope coming out against marriage. For decades, the authorities have been saying that an institution is even worse for a child than a bad home. Here are Bettelheim's reasons for changing his mind, condensed from hours of talking with him at the University of Chicago.

"If all children had good mothers and good communities to grow in," he started out, "my idea would be cockeyed. But when you've seen the failures I have seen for thirty years, you wonder how many children have either."

I got a sample of some of those failures while Dr. Bettelheim and I were talking. In three hours one morning, he was interrupted 20 times by phone calls from desperate parents. Their kids had tried suicide; they were messed up with heroine or speed or acid. They had been busted or had split. The experience was horrifying to me. To Dr. Bettelheim, it was routine.

As director of the Orthogenic School at the University, he spends 12 to 16 hours a day with

50 children (he always says "our" children). Some of them were so emotionally hurt by the age of three that they'd all but given up living—not talking, eating, or lifting a finger for themselves; sometimes bent on elaborately convoluted schemes of self-destruction. Literally hundreds more wait to fill each place that opens.

These 50 are the privileged kids—they come from middleclass homes. The children who brought us together are the millions born to poverty (in New York, alone, almost one million), surrounded by ugliness and filth, kicked around by alternating waves of smothering affection and explosive rage, nourished on progressive failure and despair.

America has been failing its children for decades. Moved by the frightening evidence of that failure, Dr. Bettelheim questioned our child-rearing methods. Five years ago, he went to study a *kibbutz*—one of the communal settlements of Israel, where men and women worked side by side for the community, and children, although they see their parents daily, grow up in homes of their own. The kids sold him. He came back convinced that U.S. children's homes based on the *kibbutz* system could give normal childhoods to many millions of our boys and girls who haven't a prayer of a decent start the way things stand today.

"Parents are down on kids," he said. "Mothers are not content enough to be good mothers. Rich and poor, both lead such busy, complicated, unquiet lives that they haven't the emotional aptitude for motherhood. The woman who doesn't work feels unimportant. She makes her children her job. Their performance has to erase all her self-doubts. The mother who does work uses her children, too, to prove that she is still a good mother—and a real woman.

"Anxious mothers make unsure kids. The child thinks, 'There must be something very wrong with me that makes my mother worry so much about how I look and how I do everything.' Then he begins to worry about himself. It makes him grow up timid."

Dr. Bettelheim had letters to illustrate. A young girl who was trying to kick the drug habit said she'd started with pot because it promised a group. "I never had any friends," she wrote. A young man whom Dr. B. had met on a plane confided he'd taken LSD to "get close to a girl" for the first time. He was 26.

"These young people have a deep contempt for themselves and their bodies," Dr. B. explained. "It must have started in response to parental anxiety."

Hold on now. Don't get that drowning feeling that comes over you when high 'n' mighty experts let go on poor old mom. Dr. Bettelheim doesn't blame the old lady entirely.

"Mothers are no better or worse than they ever were. If anything, they try too hard. But they have an impossible time making up for everything that's lacking in children's lives today."

He began to turn up the past: "Once, children could escape their parents. Mother wasn't be-all and end-all to baby; and baby wasn't her sole reason for being. In frontier America, the whole village was like one big family. A child could leave the house after breakfast and not come home until supper. He didn't get a steady diet of maternal anxiety.

"Children's lives were more functional in those days. Childhood experience actually prepared them for their grown-up role.

"I remember myself during World War I. Vienna was hungry. There were breadlines. Everyone had to wait for hours every day in the cold. I was a pretty good boy and a good student, but I had the job of getting the family bread, and when I finally brought it home, it made me feel much more important than my good grades and behavior ever did.

"On the farm, when the little boy milked the cows, he knew it gave his father more time to get the hay in before the storm broke. The little girl knew the eggs from her chickens really fed the family. You didn't have to worry about what you'd do when you grew up and whether you could do it. You watched your older brothers and sisters and father and mother. You didn't get the feeling many American children still have when they are in graduate school at 24, that they are a separate breed—a non-adult, run by parents, with no will or identity of their own.

"For the slum child, it's worse. He goes from a miserable home and street life to a school where it is routine to fail, and the only defense is to drop out as soon as possible."

Granted, I say. We ask too much and too little

of our children. We exploit them. We neglect them. Their lives are pale shadows of what they might be. But don't tell me that an institution where mom and pop play very second fiddle, and even babies have no one steady to cling to, can do better.

"It certainly can if it is a good institution," Dr. Bettelheim says categorically. Then he explains: "It works in Israel because it allows parents to live full lives as adults, and children to lead full lives as children. Parents don't have to use their kids. Children have their own place and value to the community from infancy to independence. They don't depend on their parents for their self-esteem. It flows in from their lives.

"The proof is the children," he goes on. "All of them make it. Sons and daughters of poor, illiterate African refugees catch up with the native born on IQ tests. They work as hard and just as competently. When they grow up, their lives will be as good as everyone else's. The *kibbutz* has shown that you can break the cycle of poverty in one generation if you change a child's environment. This to me is the most compelling reason for starting homes here. You could take kids out of the repeater class in poverty and failure."

But that's Israel. The United States is something else. With our confused goals, sizzling conflicts of interest, how would you ever get enough people together with the fervor and singleness of purpose to start the communities we need? How would such a dreamworld ever flower in the chaos we call home?

I know for a fact how teachers, social workers and the other deskmen of our culture can stamp poor kids for the out box before they're in training pants. No plastic smile, presidential press conference or unfunded program will switch that defeatist style. Or will it?

The man doesn't waver. "It wouldn't be a Washington program," Bettelheim says. "Young people are starting communes because they've lost faith in the family's ability to satisfy its members' emotional needs. They've turned their backs on the Establishment, where there is no sense of belonging. Students are demanding day-care centers so women can be liberated from 'second-class citizenship' and have a chance for fulfillment and independence.

"Black activists, like the founders of the *kib-*

butz, are gathering young people to make a better life for themselves. These are some of the people who might join to start centers in which children can grow up with a deep commitment to their communities."

These are the leaders. Where are the followers? I want to know. People who have it hard today feel everything is wrong, and it almost is. They feel helpless, and they almost are. They're up to their necks in broken promises, and they're not buying any more. How can you change their minds?

"The biggest strike against the city poor is the paralyzing feeling that THEY—faceless all-powerful forces—rule their lives. Improving the condition of the poor—the bulldozer method of leveling their familiar lives and moving them into strange, cold structures—just adds to that sense of helplessness. Do-it-yourself is the only answer. The schools will succeed only if parents believe in them for their kids; then plan and run them; and are responsible for making them work.

"All we need is a start: a few parents to convince their neighbors. Then the centers, with the help of the children who come out of them, will sell themselves.

"A group in some inner city might set up a *kibbutz*-like community in the country, supporting itself by agriculture and light industry. But most centers would be in the cities where life is harder than it is anywhere else. There would be day centers for children whose parents wanted them home at night and over weekends, and homes where the teachers and counselors would be fathers and mothers to the kids."

I know, but I remember institutional children fading like wildflowers in the mower's wake. I can trade facts about their decline with the experts. How can an institution give a small human sensitive enough care for him to become the trusting, confident, independent person we Americans like to think all our children will be?

Before I reach the question mark, I remember the Bronx street where only one in 20 dies a natural death and nine of ten teen-agers are on hard drugs. If I were a mother there, waiting for the bell to toll for mine, I would take a chance on the *kibbutz* for my kids. And if someone asked me, "Don't you think the street and home sweet home would bring them greater personal fulfillment?"

I'd die laughing. But Dr. Bettelheim knows liberal Americans won't give up the dream of happy homes for every tot without a struggle. Besides, he says:

"Democracy needs critical, independent people, sure enough of themselves and what they believe to stand up and fight for it. That means we must bring up individuals."

In an impersonal institution?

"No! In a very personal one. We do it here at the Orthogenic School with children who start out sick. Certainly it would be possible with well babies.

"Individuality grows out of a child's relationship with the 'mothering person,' whom he depends on completely in his first years. The better she sees and responds to his unique needs, the more content and comfortable he is. This early security gives him his first sense of who he is—his identity. It lays down the base of his self-confidence.

"It takes a huge commitment for anyone to assume so much responsibility for someone else's children. But if the program and directors are good, plenty of young people will be willing to stay the three or four years each group of children will need to get a strong start. They'll line up for the chance, like they did for the Peace Corps. If they find it is phony, they'll quit."

I could tell he was sure of his case. He asked his secretary to bring our tea and cookies.

"Children get a sure sense of themselves and where they're going by playing a real part in the life around them. The *kibbutz* manages this effortlessly, and we can learn from it.

"I would have the children clean, cook and take care of their home and their belongings. I would put them in charge of getting the work done, and let them plan their own social life. When they are ready to graduate at 17 or 18, they should be fully responsible for their own lives and their life in the home.

"They would grow up with a sense of responsibility to the community around them too. They could run a neighborhood tutoring program, a baby-sitting service. They could hold story hours, put on plays, and run block parties.

"The staff would be an example, by involving themselves in the community: family counseling, parent discussion groups, a cooperative nursery that would teach mothers better child care and free them to get jobs, and independence.

"The children's home could be the most exciting, lively, attractive place in the neighborhood. Its program would promote better childhood, and better life for parents. And the children would feel capable, useful, proud and important, being part of it.

"A lot depends on the founders. If they are concerned about the quality of life in their communities, there will be a feeling of brotherhood and common purpose in the homes that will make them good places for children to grow in."

Sold, Dr. B. So, let's get started. God knows there's no time to waste. We need community children's homes for the sake of millions of American women who have a right to jobs, and a right to feel that their children are safe and secure when they're gone. We need them for the millions of Americans who want their children to grow up belonging to a community where everyone cares for every single member. We need them, especially, for the many millions of children in our overexposed and undertreated slums who will have no future at all without them.

TOPIC 15

Vocation

*I stay at the office so late that I must race home with all the
other blind drivers on the expressway to hurry with dinner and
sit with a stack of papers to be read or, too tired to think, stare
at the TV until past bedtime. My work is a series of fighting
crises . . . making a travesty out my filling in blanks of the tax
form saying that my occupation is "university professor." There
is virtually nothing intellectual about my work—I am clearly
a paper-pushing puppet in a system which deadens my spirit
perceptibly day-by-day.*

    —Robert E. Potter, *The Quality of Life Within the Rat Race*

*When I look for work I look for a way to express my existence.
If there is no fixed job that lets me do that then I have to create
my own. That's how we decided to start our own school. Creating
a job is not easy, but I want to be me, not someone else's idea
of what I should or might be.*

    —David Steinberg, *Work Notes*

*Without Bert's approval and encouragement I'm sure I would
not have resumed my career. I can't say I would have been
as zestful a wife and mother if I hadn't. For me, each segment
of life nourishes the other.*

    —Letty Cottin Pogrebin, *How to Make It in a Man's World*

Much of our adult life is spent at work. We work because we must—in
order to earn a living. We work because we want to—in order to keep
busy and fulfill ourself. And if we are lucky, we find a job that allows us
to earn a living in a fulfilling way.

    Most of us are able to get some sense of fulfillment or at least content-
ment from our work. Over the years many investigations have been made
of job satisfaction, and the results indicate that the majority of workers are

content. However, the level of satisfaction varies considerably with the people and the jobs studied. Generally speaking, minority-group members and women are less satisfied than white males, and there is less satisfaction among persons whose work is low in pay, security, or prestige, or is unsuited to their interests and abilities.

Work is a very important part of our identity. To a large extent, our job defines who we are. If one asks for information about a person, it frequently is presented in terms of what the person does for a living. "He's a teacher." "She's in real estate." "He works down at the plant."

For adolescents and young adults the search for identity is bound up with the struggle to find a career direction. And when they are unable to hit on a career or pursue the one they have elected, a full-fledged identity crisis may result. Erik Erikson, a prominent theoretician in this area, writes that "it is primarily the inability to settle on an occupational identity which disturbs young people."

The important part that work plays in the middle years of life is dramatically shown when a career in which a person has heavily invested himself proves to be unfulfilling or is interrupted in some way. Beyond the sheer economic privation that may result is the devastating loss of purpose and identity, as demonstrated in these comments by two unemployed air industry workers. A technician: "Not working for the first time since I was a kid really knocked me for a loop at first. It's the feeling of worthlessness that gets you. A man's got to do something. Can't just stand around. Drives you nuts." A supervisor: "The psychological blow of not being a breadwinner was devastating. I felt like a blemish. A failure. A flop. And when people asked me what I was doing, I just felt like a complete washout."

Other observers have noted the identity crisis that is common at the time of retirement. Suddenly, without the pattern and definition provided by one's work, a person may feel completely adrift. One retiree writes, "With your occupational identity gone, you have to find another existence for yourself." If one has spent most of a lifetime in one line of work, this is not easily done.

For a woman the work world may present special identity problems. During early adulthood she may feel pressured to subordinate career plans and seek identity in the roles of wife and mother. (Or if she enters the job market, she may find less opportunity for fulfilling or remunerative work than a man would.) Later, perhaps with her children grown and her husband engrossed in his own career, a woman may seek a vocational direction but find it involves a difficult readjustment.

Our world is undergoing rapid change, and the world of work is changing too. The future is very uncertain. With affluent times, there is more freedom to explore careers before making a commitment and also more freedom to change careers in midstream, to combine a career with other pursuits, or to pursue a life style that integrates vocation and avocation. With the advent of less prosperous times and a scarcity of good jobs, earning a living can be paramount and we may be less willing or less able to hang loose, explore, and grow.

Choosing work

In the lead article, Emanuel M. Berger points out that students are under considerable pressure to make early vocational choices, but most cannot or should not do so because they know too little about themselves and occupational demands. As a result of this pressure many students make premature choices that do not pan out and are then experienced as failure. Berger holds that all vocational decisions should be considered to be tentative: each choice is one to be explored and then confirmed or disconfirmed. More than this, every career remains to some extent exploratory since we may move from one subfield to another within our field or even change careers completely to accord with our personal development.

Choosing growth

If it is successful, liberal education causes students to examine their values and open themselves to growth; this, of course, has important implications for careers and postcollege lives. In the second reading Mildred Henry and Harriet Renaud report on four states or stages of growth in college students. "Psychically foreclosed" students come to college with predetermined careers and life styles; they are closed to growth and even threatened by it. The "situationally foreclosed" have never been exposed to alternative ways of thinking and behaving but can open themselves to change. "Moratorium" students delay making commitments to a career or life style while they seek out new ideas and experiences. And students who achieve "identity status" arrive at a definition of themselves and a career direction, but both are continually open to revision depending upon changing conditions.

Choosing to grow in work

An important distinction can be made between the "standard of living" and the "quality of life." To put it in a nutshell, the first relates to how well we eat and the second to how well we fulfill ourselves and grow. If we are fortunate, we find work that provides us with both a comfortable and a fulfilling life.

In the third reading, Robert E. Potter takes stock and finds that his standard of living is high but that the quality of his life is low. At the time he wrote the article Potter was a university administrator, a job that had once been satisfying but was no longer so, and he has since returned to teaching. He faults education for our preoccupation with our standard of living. Education, he says, must help people toward vocations which enable them to live humane as well as prosperous lives.

We all have feelings and ideas about our work or the work we will do. Taken together, these feelings and ideas might be said to make up our philosophy of work just as sometimes we talk about our philosophy of life.

For David Steinberg, work and life are inseparable, and the work notes that appear in the fourth selection present his work-life philosophy. Although his standard of living is not high (at the time of the article his monthly income was $290), Steinberg writes, "I feel glad to be whole, not pulled apart by the conflict between work and the rest of my life."

Finally, Letty Cottin Pogrebin writes from her own experience and observations about the punishments and rewards of being a career woman. She finds herself under assault from two sets of culprits: harassed housewives who want to justify their own martyrdom and men who seek to perpetuate the unequal status quo. She notes the considerable problems women face but manages her own combination of work, marriage, and motherhood very well. In her experience, each of these areas of living enriches the others, and she is a fuller person for having all three.

FOR PERSONAL APPLICATION

1. Beginning with your earliest childhood recollection, trace the development of your ideas concerning a career for yourself.
2. Discuss any pressure you have felt from others or from yourself to make an early (or too early) career choice.
3. Discuss any difficulties you have or have had in arriving at a career choice. What effect has this indecision had on you?
4. Consider your present career or career choice. What factors were involved in your selection of this career?
5. Consider your present career or career choice. What personal assets and limitations do you bring to this career?
6. Consider your present career or career choice. Is your career critical to your identity? Why or why not?
7. Consider your present career or career choice. How goal-urgent or hang-loose is your pursuit of this career?
8. Consider your present career or career choice. How open are you or have you been to changes and revisions in your career direction?
9. Consider your present career or career choice. What implications does this choice have for your future "standard of living" and "quality of life"?
10. Discuss your philosophy of work and your philosophy of life. How congruous are the two?
11. Discuss the life style you would like to have and the part your work would play in this life style.
12. Consider your marriage, family, and work careers as you foresee or experience them. What conflicts or harmonies do you see between these various areas of your life?
13. Write down a discussion item (not given above) that seems particularly relevant to this topic and you, and discuss it.

FOR SMALL GROUPS

1. *Suggesting career directions.* One member sits in the center of the group. He faces each person in turn who suggests a career that might be suitable for him along with reasons for making this suggestion. After everyone has had a chance to suggest a vocation, the person in the center comments on the suggestions. Then another member takes the center spot, and the group continues as before.
2. *Forecasting career directions.* Each member tells the group what his career and life style will (1) most likely be in 10 years and (2) what it would be if his most optimistic dreams come true.
3. *Unfreezing career directions.* Once we have selected a career direction, we may foreclose further exploration or reassessment. A volunteer gives the group the names of two careers, one that he has chosen or will likely choose, and another that is a reasonable choice. Then he is asked to present a strong case against the career he has elected to pursue and an equally strong case for the alternate one.
4. *Working and growing.* Each member tells the group his career plans and also his personal strengths and limitations which might affect his success. Then the group tells the member of other strengths they see in him and also ways he might overcome his limitations.

FOR FURTHER READING

Pogrebin, L. C. *How to Make It in a Man's World.* Garden City, N.Y.: Doubleday & Co., Inc., 1970.

Sheppard, H. L., and N. Q. Herrick. *Where Have All the Robots Gone?* New York: The Free Press, 1972.

Super, D. E., R. Starishevsky, N. Matlin, and J. P. Jordaan. *Career Development: Self-concept Theory.* New York: College Entrance Examination Board, 1963.

Tiedeman, D. V., and R. P. O'Hara. *Career Development: Choice and Adjustment.* New York: College Entrance Examination Board, 1963.

Working Loose. San Francisco: American Friends Service Committee, 1971.

VOCATIONAL CHOICES
IN COLLEGE

Emanuel M. Berger

The very freedom of our college-bound youth to choose a vocation has become an important problem and task for most of them. More so than in most other countries of the world—and more so than their grandfathers before them—young people in our country today have freedom to decide on how they want to work. At the same time that there is greater freedom to choose, there is greater difficulty in choosing because of the much-enlarged number of possibilities to choose from in an increasingly complex occupational world. This situation requires knowing much more about one's self and about possible occupations if one is to make satisfying choices.

In my work as a counseling psychologist, I see many students who are disturbed to various degrees by not knowing what their vocational goals are. According to the students' reports, this lack of vocational goals is responsible for much anxiety, low motivation in college work, poor grades, and—not just occasionally—for their leaving college until they know what they want to accomplish there. This is not a distinctly local situation, certainly, but one that exists for thousands of college people all over the country. . . .

And it is not just the students who are concerned, but also their parents. One large part of parental concern, understandably, is that their children be content in the work they choose. Another part, also understandable from their point of view, has to do with using hard-earned money to finance a college education when their children are so confused or uncertain about vocational goals that it seems doubtful that their education will have any practical, vocational value.

These concerns are nourished and aggravated by a general social pressure on students to make a vocational choice before they enter college, or soon thereafter. Other students, parents, relatives, the community in general, and even some teachers, counselors, and advisers in high school and college, are a party to the pressure. In high school, and to an increasing extent in earlier grades, there is likely to be a vocational counselor and prominently displayed occupational information—a general stimulation and prodding of the student to make a vocational choice. When he enters college he is likely to be asked what his vocational choice is, from which it is easy for students to take the implication that they are expected to be able to make one at the outset. Even among some professionals concerned with education and counseling there is a use of language that implies that there is but one grand and lasting choice to be made and that students should be able to make that choice now or very soon. They talk or write of choosing *a* career, of making *a* vocational choice.

Although the high tide of pressure seems to center on students about to begin their college experience, perhaps because this is seen as the beginning of serious professional training, the pressure continues for the more advanced students if they have not been able to make a satisfactory vocational choice.

The pressure is based on an erroneous and misleading assumption, namely, that most college freshmen are able to make a lasting and satisfactory vocational choice as freshmen or soon thereafter. The assumption is erroneous because most college freshmen have not yet learned, and will not learn in a short time, what they need to know about themselves and about occupations in order to make a first, satisfactory vocational choice. The assumption is misleading because it creates the impression that the student's vocational task is merely one of "choosing" a vocation, cafeteria style, rather than a potentially lifelong task of vocational self-discovery which may reasonably include many vocational choices, especially in the process of discovering a satisfactory occupational field. In a sense, the assumption requires that the freshman be omniscient, that he foresee his future experience and development, that he predict what his eventual vocational choice will be before he has had the experience and undergone the development out of which satisfactory choices emerge.

ILL EFFECTS

In response to the pressure to make a definite vocational choice, many students commit themselves prematurely. They tell the world they are going to be engineers or architects or nurses or whatever, before they know whether they can handle the required subjects, before they know whether they have the required talents or special aptitudes, before they know what the training is actually like, before they have any idea of how much they would like the day-to-day work possible in their chosen field. Then, when they discover that their choice was not a good one for some reason or reasons, such as the possibilities just suggested, their tendency is to view the experience as a "failure." They said they were going to become engineers, etc., and they could not do it. And to the extent that people around them share the same assumption, that they should have known better somehow when they made their choice, the feeling of failure will be reinforced. They should not see such experiences as a failure on their part. The fault is in their point of view.

Another unhappy effect of the pressure stems from a sort of corollary of the assumption underlying it. If a student doesn't know as a freshman or shortly thereafter what he wants to do vocationally, the thinking goes, then he should not be in college. How many times I have heard students say that they have no idea of a major, no vocational goals, so they plan to leave college and go into the military service or get a job. They express the vague hope that such experience will help them decide on their vocational plans, and this could be the case. But they assume that it is a waste of time and money, from a vocational point of view, to go to college when one doesn't have any definite vocational plans. It is difficult to assess the extent to which these students delay or distort their vocational development when they act on this assumption.

And when students and parents become anxious because the student has not been able to make a definite, satisfactory vocational choice as a freshman or soon thereafter, that anxiety is needless. It is needless because the assumption on which it is based is in error. Most such students have not yet learned enough about themselves or about occupations to be able to make a definite, satisfactory vocational choice. The fault again is in their point of view.

DISCOVERY—NOT "KNOWING"

A healthier and more realistic point of view recognizes that students eventually discover and confirm that a vocational choice they made is satisfactory, following experiences that permit them to do so. They cannot know in advance of such experience that they will be able to handle the academic requirements or be able to find a satisfying way of working in some chosen field. And yet, that is apparently just what our society expects of its young college people.

Even those students who eventually realize an early choice with satisfaction did not really "know," but rather discovered and confirmed that the early choice was a good one.

It then follows that every student who has made a choice at all—with little or much confidence—should consider it a *tentative* one rather than a committed one. Then his task becomes one of discovering, testing, confirming whether or not the choice was a good one in much the way a scientist goes about testing a hypothesis. He does not have to defend the presumption that he knew all he needed to know about himself and the field he chose at the time he chose it, before he had any opportunity to confirm his choice by experience. He can avoid a position where he clings unrealistically to a choice mainly because he told the world of his decision as if it were final in response to the social pressure to make a definite vocational choice.

In this perspective, the negative experiences that a student has in his efforts to confirm a choice can be seen in a different light. They can be seen as the "error" part of a trial-and-error process that is necessary and inevitable in any successful solution of a difficult problem. When a student discovers that he lacks the ability, aptitude, or talent that is required to maintain his vocational choice, this is a negative experience in relation to that choice but it has the positive aspect of eliminating an inappropriate choice, thereby narrowing the field of best looking vocational possibilities from which he is trying to make a choice. It brings him closer to a positive choice. Also, a student who sees his task as one of discovering his vocational choice through experience is more likely to accept the discovery of limitations as part of the process he must go through on his way to a satisfactory choice. But the student who has committed himself to a choice on the assumption that he should be able to choose wisely in advance of confirming experience will tend to see the interfering limitations as "incompetence" and the inappropriate choice as a kind of "failure." Of course, not all students react this way, but many do, and in a sense they are beating themselves into a loss of self-esteem because they were not omniscient enough to choose wisely from the beginning.

A broad academic experience can be helpful to a student who has not yet been able to make a first, tentative choice of vocation. Most liberal arts colleges require students to fulfill requirements in a variety of fields—sciences, social sciences, and humanities. The student has an opportunity to follow up interests he has and discover new interests in subject matter and to see how well he can handle different kinds of college courses. Learning about his abilities, limitations, and interests helps him to narrow down the field of best vocational possibilities for him. The point for those students who cannot see the vocational value of broad academic experience is that military service or a job, though they may be valuable experiences in other ways, are not likely to permit a student to learn about his interests, abilities, and limitations in relation to academic subjects. But what he can aspire to educationally and vocationally depends on just that sort of self-knowledge.

While I consider the above to be generally true, it should be recognized here that a student's performance in college sometimes improves greatly with increased maturity. Thus, a period in which he works at a job or is in the military service may contribute indirectly to improved academic performance when he returns to college. This in turn can permit him to raise his vocational aspirations. It is in view of just this sort of possibility that students might, under certain conditions, help their vocational development by leaving college for a while to work or go into military service.

Choice of a specialty within a field is also a matter of discovery and confirmation. The student who feels pretty sure that he wants to be in a certain occupational field is generally misplacing his anxiety if he worries a lot about how he wants to specialize. This is something he either confirms or discovers, something to be learned from experience rather than known in advance of experience.

ABILITIES AND LIMITATIONS

One of the primary ways in which a student needs to have learned about himself to some degree before he can begin to choose a field is with respect to his abilities and limitations at the college level. Generally speaking, a student aspires to vocational goals in the belief that he has enough of whatever abilities and talent are required to reach those goals and do well in the field.

But a college freshman's conception of his abilities as he enters college is likely to be based on his high school experience. Although there are some exceptions, most high schools in our country pitch the level of difficulty of subject matter at some medium point so that most students will be able to understand it. Also, the degree of responsibility, initiative, and effort required of students in most high schools in order to "pass" is relatively much less than that required by most colleges.

As a result, many of our high school graduates have little conception of their limitations. They tend to have one or another omnipotent attitude: (1) that they can do well at just about anything in school if they really want to and try hard enough; (2) that they are so bright that they can do well at just about anything in college with only a little effort. It is this state of affairs that I see as accounting in large measure for the unrealistic aspirations of high school students suggested by the data obtained in Project TALENT.

Project TALENT, a large-scale, continuing research on our human resources, has published a report on the American high school student that concludes on several different occasions that the aspirations of our high school seniors appear "unrealistic" (Flanagan et al., 1964). The conclusions are based on large amounts of data on the aptitudes, interests, and aspirations of our high school students. For example, it was found that 48 per cent of high school senior boys and 40 per cent of senior girls planned to enter a professional field; yet census data show that only about 15 per cent of employed males and 17 per cent of employed females between the ages of 25 and 29 are in professional and technical occupations. And in a study of the plans of those high school seniors who entered college a year after leaving high school, it was found that 37 per cent of those in the bottom quarter on a test of college aptitude planned to obtain an advanced degree!

College freshmen who learned little about their academic limitations from their high school experience are likely to get a jolt if they go to a college with relatively high standards. They will fail courses or do poorly as a result of too little effort or lack of sufficient aptitude in certain subjects. They are then forced to face their academic limitations perhaps for the first time. For some students this can be a serious problem. Their conception of what they can do in college and thereby vocationally is contradicted by their college performance. Unfortunately, many quite capable students interpret this as meaning that they are not competent. They confuse limitations with incompetence, and their self-esteem is damaged.

I believe we should have a high school system where students have an opportunity to learn about their limitations at a level of difficulty closer to that in most colleges without having to be failed out of high school if they cannot handle this level of work. This could be done if we "passed" students at different levels of difficulty, assigning grades to each—1,2,3, or whatever— with passage from one level to another being possible as the student's performance merits being raised or dropped from one level to another. This would help students to be realistic about their abilities and limitations earlier, cut down the number of unrealistic vocational plans and consequent emotional hurt that comes with their disruption at the college level, and perhaps avoid the

loss of talented youth who give up career goals in scientific fields because of poor performance due to their not having learned earlier the limitations of how well they could do with a minimum or insufficient effort.

Determining what one's specific limitations are is a tricky and uncertain business at best. In an abstract and ideal way one learns about a limitation by doing his "best," making a maximum effort to achieve something, and then evaluating the outcome of his efforts. But one's best efforts in arts or academic subjects at one stage of his development may have very different results five or ten years later when he has become more mature. And, at any particular time in a person's life, a "best" effort is limited by the circumstances of his individual life and his own attitudes about what a maximum effort is.

The question is really one of the nature of limitations. With what degree of effort and at what level of difficulty do the limitations occur? In what specific subject matter? What are the implications of the limitations for the individual's choice of vocational field?

A student's limitations due to level of difficulty may mean that an advanced degree in mathematics is out, but he may still be able to do well enough to become a competent engineer. At a somewhat lower level, he may be able to do well enough to teach high school math or go ahead with training in business.

Also, some students have an either-or attitude, which says in effect: "Either I will be among the best in my field or I won't go into it—I refuse to be mediocre." Then, getting a C in some course in a major field or doing slightly above average work is a sign to them that they cannot possibly be "among the best." They are then ready to look elsewhere to some field where they can be "at the top." They do not recognize that no one excels in every subject in a field all the time or in every way—or that there is a very large segment of people in any field who are quite competent and make a modest contribution most of the time, and some of them will eventually make an outstanding contribution despite "not being among the best" when they were doing their academic work. Given a degree of accomplishment sufficient to admit a student to an occupational field, it is the willingness to accept the risk that one's continued efforts may not result in an outstanding contribution that I see as the necessary but not sufficient condition for making an outstanding contribution in one's field.

THE DEVELOPING
COLLEGE STUDENT

The task of the student who is trying to reach a vocational decision about a field of work is a complex one. He must eventually bring together in a harmonious way his conceptions of himself that might in any way be vocationally relevant and his knowledge of occupations. But important changes in his vocational thinking may and do occur during the college years, thus complicating his problem. The student must not only be able to clarify and assess accurately the nature of his abilities, limitations, talents, interests, values, and personal dispositions, he must also be able to cope with changes that may take place in these aspects of himself at the very same time he is trying to evaluate them in relation to ways of working in some occupational field.

Some of the change can be attributed to students' difficulties with courses basic to a field they chose earlier. Would-be nurses have trouble with chemistry, etc. Naturally, such difficulty leads many students to change their vocational plans. It represents a complication due to a change in students' conceptions of their academic or creative abilities and limitations.

Students also change their vocational thinking as a result of the development of their interests and values. In general, social and aesthetic values and interests develop later in adolescence and it seems that the special stimulation of the college experience spurs their development. Not for all students, certainly, but for many.

There may be changes in students' conceptions of their nonacademic potentialities as a result of experiences they have along with the academic experience or before they complete it. It may be a summer camp experience where the student enjoyed helping young teen-agers, or working on a student newspaper and confirming a commitment to journalism, or being an officer in the service and discovering a potential for management. Many kinds of nonacademic experience can contribute to a student's developing sense of himself as a potential teacher, newspaperman, or manager, or whatever.

Another factor is that of the student's knowledge of occupations—the nature of the training, abilities, and personal qualifications required as well as the specific ways of working possible within the occupation. As things are, some students choose engineering because they want to design airplanes or are mechanically minded, only to discover from experience that engineering training emphasizes mathematics and sciences and theories, and that the design of airplanes will have to come much later, after all that, and that one's mechanical skills may not be important in engineering and certainly not a sufficient basis for choosing it. Even at a much later vocational stage, engaging in the work of an occupation, there are those who discover from that experience that they are not suited to the field in some way—not patient enough to do chemical research, more interested in people problems than they are in engineering problems, etc.

Knowledge of occupations, like other kinds of awareness and information, grows with time and experience, is an aspect of the developing person, and another complicating factor in the process of vocational development and choice.

REASONABLE EXPECTATIONS

Considering all of the potential for change in a student's vocational thinking, when could we reasonably expect a student to be able to make a stable and satisfying vocational decision about a field? There is no simple, general answer to this question although one might say what we could reasonably expect of most students, with qualifications.

We would expect most seniors in college to have matured enough so that their awareness of their abilities, limitations, interests, and values has become stable enough to permit them to make a satisfying choice of an occupational field. Then the matter of how they want to work more specifically within the field can be worked out later as they get more training and experience.

Even then it is not so unusual or necessarily a sign of some special problem if a student majors in one field, graduates from college, and then switches to some quite different field. In my own field of psychology, I can think of at least a dozen acquaintances who switched to graduate work in psychology from undergraduate majors in science, engineering, or mathematics. And in a . . . study of the career choices of scholars, Strauss (1965) found that 32 out of 96 university professors changed their field of interest, 14 of them to unrelated fields (such as from natural science to social science or humanities), although one can't tell from the study just when the changes to an unrelated field took place.

Some men manage to make rather radical changes even in their middle years without undue hardship to themselves or others. One acquaintance switched from a career in engineering to one in law in his mid-thirties. And most of us have heard about or read about the lawyer in mid-career who switched successfully to writing or to composing hit musicals or the salesman who switched in his forties to acting, with success and satisfaction.

THE LONG LOOK

The opportunity or necessity of making further vocational choices does not end with a satisfactory choice of an occupational field. With experience, what a man enjoys doing most and does best may come more sharply into focus. He may develop new skills, different aspirations. The physician who has liked his work in general practice for several years may move with equal or greater satisfaction to specializing in internal medicine or psychiatry, to editing a medical journal, to being a hospital administrator. A lawyer may similarly move from general practice to corporation law, to being a judge, to becoming a congressman.

Not that satisfying development and change will be a general matter for all professionals. Some will be content to continue to work in a certain way most of their lives; others may not be content but may not have the freedom or power to choose other ways of working.

Vocational thinking and choices, if we view them in a broad way that goes beyond the matter of earning one's livelihood, may continue throughout one's lifetime, including the retirement period. Then each of us may again consider his values, interests, abilities, and limitations in relation to the question of how he can most satisfactorily engage himself in his later years. Some retirees are content to putter around the house, go fishing, play golf, etc. Others, needing something more akin to "work," take to community projects or writing or painting or turning out fine carpentry.

The point is that as long as we live, develop, and change we can and may think about and evaluate ourselves in relation to how we use our energies in the world much in the same way we did when we made our choice of an occupational field.

REFERENCES

FLANAGAN, J. C., F. B. DAVIS, J. T. DAILEY, M. F. SHAYCOFT, D. B. ORR, I. GOLDBERG, and C. A. NEYMAN, JR. *The American High-school Student*. Cooperative Research Project No. 635, U.S. Office of Education. Pittsburgh, Pa.: Project TALENT Office, Univ. Pittsburgh, 1964.

STRAUSS, S. "Career Choices of Scholars," *Personnel and Guidance Journal*, 44 (1965), 153–159.

EXAMINED AND UNEXAMINED LIVES

Mildred Henry with
Harriet Renaud

One of the firmly held beliefs in academe is that a liberal education liberalizes and enriches. But does it accomplish this feat for everyone, and if not, then for whom?

There can be little question that the liberal arts colleges have emphasized that they mean to bring about significant changes in their students, as statements from their catalogues clearly indicate:

The program . . . has the . . . goal of developing in each individual student his ultimate potential of human worth and dignity. . . .

It is . . . a process designed to help a person understand himself, other human beings, and the society in which he finds himself. . . .

The student should develop a genuine interest in things intellectual and artistic sufficient to motivate continuing self-education. . . .

Nevertheless, some . . . years ago, Jacob (1957) was able to shock the academic world by asserting that most young people in colleges evidently did little more than learn to adjust to the campus climate, so that by their senior year they had moved, politically and intellectually, toward the views held by most of their fellow students. And . . . Feldman and Newcomb's (1969) exhaustive review of the literature showed that it is still unclear whether the liberalized attitudes that manifest themselves in college—in political, social, and religious attitudes—are merely adaptive and perhaps transient mechanisms to conform to

a campus norm, or evidence of a pervasive molding of inner disposition and character.

To explore whether colleges encourage students, for the most part, to a kind of standardized campus liberalism, or whether they enable them to consciously develop more actively held values, in the fall of 1966 the Center for Research and Development in Higher Education initiated a series of longitudinal studies on 1,580 students in five institutions, the results of which are being prepared for a final report. Those data are now being looked at in the context of the influence of faculty characteristics and campus environment on students of different attitudinal and personality dispositions. The following informal observations are based on interviews conducted to gather data for a phase of that report, and took place in generally small, experimental colleges, institutions which claim to strongly influence their students.

IDENTITY STATES AS PHASES OF GROWTH

The students interviewed seemed to illustrate six identity or "self-states" which represent different phases of growth, four of which will be discussed here. The terms used here to designate the identity states are similar to those used by Erikson (1956, 1963) and Marcia (1966).

The "Psychically Foreclosed"
Among students who come to college with a predetermined career or goal in mind (to become a lawyer; to get a credential; to find a husband), a good majority never consider any other path, and any question of alternative life styles rarely comes up for discussion. Awareness of options or the possibility of change tends to precipitate anxiety in such young people, and left to themselves they skirt the unfamiliar and place themselves in situations which do not offer choices. They thus effectively insulate themselves from meeting new people and being exposed to new ideas.

One of the implications of such a mode of operation for the college experience is that these students, already largely closed down to new experiences and ideas when they enter college, usually continue to avoid faculty whose views might challenge theirs, and choose peers who share their beliefs and values. All their encounters and experiences in college therefore tend to serve as reinforcement for the attitudes and opinions they brought with them.

It is common to find that the predetermined careers of these "psychically foreclosed" are viewed by them as being highly utilitarian, and were evidently hit upon without regard for their intrinsic interest, or for their value other than as a means toward a livelihood.

One student, who had never seriously considered going into any field but law, said,

> I decided on becoming a lawyer back in the eighth grade. I don't know how I decided on this really. But I am certain this is what I want to be. I don't feel I will dislike the law. . . . I feel it won't bore me to death and it pays adequately. . . .

An interest in Russian was given up when he decided, "It is not especially relevant to law," and when asked whether he knew what it might feel like to be a lawyer, and what was required of him, he said, "I have some phone numbers of people to call who could tell me something about it, but I haven't bothered to do this yet. Anyway, I don't expect not to like law."

Each year, this student's response to queries about his life plans varied little in content and manner. His attitudes toward law didn't change; his expressed satisfaction with the status quo never altered. To the question, *"Can you think of and describe any experience that had a big influence on you prior to coming to college?"* he answered, "Nothing stands out strongly. I was always oriented toward going to college." To the question, *"Are there any important ways you would like to change in the future?"* he answered "No." When any change is perceived as threat, even changes that come with normal growth and development are evidently precluded.

Not given to introspection, and out of touch with their own feelings, these kinds of foreclosed students accept "general opinion" as their value system, and handle difficult situations by conforming without conviction and adapting behaviorally without any internal restructuring of feelings and ideas. Asked what he found most challenging or difficult in college, the pre-law

student said, ". . . since the faculty is less conservative than the students, you have to learn to express things in their terms, and that can be difficult."

To express things in his own terms or to try to define his own terms did not seem to have occurred as a possibility to this "psychically foreclosed" student. Nor is this possibility likely to arise for him unless he is helped, with a good deal of encouragement, to recognize the value of defining himself and the world in his own way.

The perception of differences in values and style is a universal human problem; what often distinguishes between people most critically is the way in which the differences are handled. The psychically foreclosed individuals, whose instinctive response is to regard any difference as a threat of conflict, and any conflict as intolerable, move to avoid it. This response is in marked contrast to that of the other types observed.

The "Situationally Foreclosed"

Students designated here as "situationally foreclosed" also seem markedly limited in their affective lives when they come to college—but with a difference. They are for the most part young people who have never been exposed to alternative modes of thinking and behaving, and their constraints, rather than being the wounds of earlier psychic battles, are simply evidence of backgrounds characterized by lack of information and a minimal opportunity for experience.

When such students become aware of a whole new range of options and opportunities, their response can sometimes be dramatic. As old assumptions and realities are brought into question, priorities begin to take place. Some, of course, left without the firm moorings of a familiar, usually parental value system, get caught in crisis situations which they are unable to resolve. But those strong enough to make trials and risk errors, who are open to their inner experiences, and reflective about the probable consequences of unfamiliar ways of behaving and feeling, enter into the next phase of identity formation—the moratorium stage.

The Moratorium Students

In the sense that it is used here, the term "moratorium" does not imply a suspension of activity, but rather a delay in making final commitments to people, ideas, a lifestyle—during a period of experiential testing and exploration. Students in a moratorium stage of development characteristically engage in a good deal of introspection and analysis of motives—their own and others. Embarked on the adventurous task of reality-testing, they seek diverse friends and experiences, try out different modes of acting and thinking, and open everything to question. They tend to engage in a variety of apparently unrelated interests, but what seems like total involvement in Zen, or modern art, or a political movement, usually turns out to be a temporary port, simply another place to be assessed in the long itinerary of experience.

In college, these are the students who reach out to events and seize on alternatives in the academic environment. They are particularly sensitive and responsive to casual comments dropped in lectures, class discussions, and seminars, search out and read unassigned books, and find it important to talk with professors informally.

Unlike the foreclosed students, who seem wholly future-oriented, and in effect mortgaged to a prearranged future, students in a moratorium stage are engaged in a perpetual process of taking soundings on their experiences and reformulating goals. In time, their tentative, experimental pattern in relation to people and tasks is replaced by real commitment as they move toward an "achieved identity status."

Achieved Identity Status

Unlike the unchanging, unconsciously determined commitments of foreclosed individuals, the commitments of those who have achieved identity are both deeply self-involving and flexible, made with a readiness to bend, adapt, and even change with the inevitable personal changes that life, experience, and circumstances bring about. Such people's growth clearly does not end with graduation from college.

A case in point is the student from a lower middle-class Lutheran family, who provides an enlightening contrast to the psychically foreclosed pre-law student described earlier. Both young men came to college expecting to become lawyers, and both graduated with the same intention. But the second student's comments revealed that during the four years in college both he and his conception of his career had shifted, changed, been reconstituted.

As a freshman, he wanted to become a lawyer because he thought this career offered an "opportunity for significant accomplishment." In his sophomore year, he made it clear that he was trying to discover which aspect of the law he wanted to go into, and what specifically he could accomplish through the law. During his junior year, he felt that a kind of law that made for social justice was important, and saw law as combining "reality with abstract ideas—a fusion of the two." He felt this suited his "style of thinking," and he was "90 percent certain" that he would go into law. At the end of his senior year, he regarded the law not as a closed-ended choice, but rather as "a stepping-stone for other things that I might want to go into" at a later time as his life unfolded. The law, for him, had come to have a substantive value in and of itself, and he was in the process of exploring the implications of this value for himself.

Nearing graduation, he stated, "I'm going to law school. Beyond that I haven't decided. I'm leaving it wide open." Thus, as his commitment to the law sharpened and became more articulated, it also became more flexible. Going into the law had become a possible means toward other ends, and not an end in itself; a doorway hopefully opening into still other areas of life, still in the process of being discovered.

IMPLICATIONS FOR UNDERGRADUATE EDUCATION

Do liberal arts colleges and programs significantly help students to change and develop in fundamental ways? Are students liberated from the unexamined bases for their thought and action which they have carried with them into college? Do they learn to lead examined lives as a result of their undergraduate experience?

If we are to move closer to a realization of the liberal arts vision—toward increasing the individual's ability to examine the assumptions that guide his thought and action—we must devise an educational process that engages students more directly. The current study indicated what other writers also have held—that currently only those students ready to grow and develop (and who do not get caught in a crisis bind) manage to develop further in the present undergraduate system of education. Since many of these seem to need only a diverse, ideationally rich environment to nudge them into growth, the process of relatively passive exposure offered by the current formal liberal arts curriculum at least does not get in their way.

It is ironical that, although the time in college has often been described as a moratorium period —when students can make mistakes, develop, grow, and find themselves before entering the adult world—it is mainly those already capable of experiencing, acting, and reflecting (those already in what we have defined here as a moratorium phase of self-development)—who make the college experience a true moratorium. For students who are foreclosed, mere exposure to a liberal arts curriculum and faculty does not seem to be enough. In colleges where more liberal views and practices were the norm, some foreclosed students became even more defensively foreclosed, and adjusted, for the most part, by coping with academic demands in a formalistic rather than an assimilative manner. They were permitted to play the academic game without ever being forced to become involved to the point of recognizing and re-examining the assumptions by which they guided their lives.

Three suggestions might be offered to colleges seeking to make a difference in the lives of their students:

1. Students should be given more direct help and practice in learning how to think more critically and constructively about their lives. Most students listed extracurricular experiences and peers as their main sources for self-discovery and growth, and this suggests that the sources commonly presumed to have an impact on students— the faculty and the curricular structure—are not critically influential in the kind of growth students need most at this point in their lives. Asked about focal points of discussion between them and faculty members, few mentioned items such as, *Made me aware of social issues, Encouraged me to inspect my values,* or *Counseled me about career plans.* Caught in the narrow shafts of the academic disciplines in college, students more frequently named former high school teachers than college faculty as having stimulated them to think.

It is unrealistic to expect students at the outset to move from the unexamined values by which they govern their actions, or to be vitally interested in the substantive problems of an academic discipline which are not of immediate concern to them. They are involved, or ought to be involved, in the task of building a self. This is undoubtedly one of the most important tasks they will ever have to do, and it is critically important for them and for society that they do it well.

2. If students are to strive for the growth and development they are potentially capable of during their college years, then they must be given more emotional support and encouragement than they typically get from faculty or support service people such as student personnel counselors. It is customary for the faculty to ignore the affective dimension of students and only pay attention to the cognitive, and for support service people to wait for students to come to them for help and advice. At least one-third of the students in our sample could have used help from people skilled in helping to clarify emotions.

Perhaps the most important change that needs to be made in undergraduate education is to provide an educational process for individuals who are developing, growing human beings. Accordingly, both the cognitive and affective or emotional dimensions of students must be given comparable attention. Students must be involved in critical, reflective thinking, experiencing, and acting. Without a wide range of opportunities for involvement and experimentation in these areas, they will be unable to put together a picture which includes themselves, others, and the larger world.

3. Students should be responded to as particular kinds of holistic individuals. Teaching approaches and curricular tasks need to be different for the psychically foreclosed, the situationally foreclosed, those in moratorium, and those with achieved identities. *The psychically foreclosed* need to be taught that their feelings, emotions, and desires are valuable and valid, that the abstractions governing their lives are not ones they actively and consciously chose. *The situationally foreclosed* need to be exposed to a variety of options and encouraged to explore the implica-

tions of diversity. And when the presumbly stable worlds of both the psychically and situationally foreclosed start to crumble, they need encouragement to actively enter into finding, experimenting with, and critically thinking about new ways of being in the world. For the *students in a moratorium,* who are already actively thinking, exploring, and experiencing, the program provided should be diverse and allow for trial and failure without punishing failure per se. They need help in learning how to critically assess and reassess their efforts so that eventually they can learn how to make thoughtful choices and focus their energy on commitments to longer-lasting, more demanding tasks. Those who have reached an *achieved status* of identity formation need only to be allowed to pursue whatever commitments they have selected.

Failure to recognize that students are in different developmental phases when they enter college has been a factor in the failure of colleges to successfully change students in the direction of leading more examined lives.

When the affective dimension is neglected, students are left to sink or swim on their own. As indicated by the data, the results of their being left solely on their own are not heartening. Many sink. Many others barely stay afloat, clinging to the bits and pieces of former lives. Some learn how to swim. A very few learn how to swim against the current.

The results of research on the importance of colleges on students has not been encouraging, but a realistic assessment of the situation indicates that very few colleges have given serious attention to providing educational experiences that are specifically designed to touch their students' affective lives. The solutions are not easy. Further experimentation and further evaluation are needed to turn the rhetoric of the catalogues into the realities of the campus.

REFERENCES

ERIKSON, E. H. "The Problem of Ego Identity," *J. Amer. Psychoanalytical Assoc.,* 4 (1956), 56–121.

———. *Childhood and Society.* New York: W. W. Norton & Co., Inc., 1963.

FELDMAN, K. A., and T. M. NEWCOMB. *The Impact of College on Students.* San Francisco: Jossey-Bass, 1969.

JACOB, P. E. *Changing Values in College: An Exploratory Study of the Impact of College Teaching.* New York: Harper & Row, Publishers, 1957.

MARCIA, J. E. "Development and Validation of Ego-identity States," *J. of Personality and Social Psychology,* 3(5) (1966), 551–558.

THE QUALITY OF LIFE WITHIN THE RAT RACE

Robert E. Potter

At the first of the interim programs for the Governor's Conference on the year 2000, a young man in the audience asked the panel, "Aren't you confusing quality of life with standard of living?"

And the answer revealed how much the past-30 generations have confused the real issue, for he was told by two panelists, with none of the others objecting, that in effect the two expressions are interchangeable.

Those of us who lived through a depression period when we were concerned with enough of the material necessities of life to avoid hunger, loss of housing, shabby hand-me-downs as clothing, cast-off furniture, and all the other continual threats to a life of reasonable comfort and security, learned that a high income was something which marked a good life.

Boys went to school to get diplomas and degrees which would enable them to get better paying jobs.

One of the most widely circulated reports of the U.S. Office of Education was on the dollar-value of education. Girls went to high school and college to catch the man who was going to get the job that brought good money.

Vocational programs multiplied in high schools, and vocationally-oriented programs—generally called professional schools—thrived when the GIs came marching home in 1945 and 1946.

That generation and the ones before it were much concerned with making enough money to avoid the unpleasantness they saw or felt in the 1930s and remembered acutely during the 1950s. For them—most of us on the "2000" task force—"standard of living" has been synonymous with "quality of life."

But the children born to my generation are products of an affluent society. They have not learned the lessons of a depression. They have not felt the insecurity of lack of money.

Some of them who become hippies and move out of their parents' "establishment" to live on the land do so with the confidence that when they tire of the romance of "roughing it" or "making it with nature," then they can return to the establishment much as the prodigal son did.

Their poverty is scornful of the materialistic concern of their parents for a more comfortable and secure standard of living. Their education—but not their schooling—has taught them that there is a difference between "standard of living" and "quality of life."

Perhaps this distinction is the proper starting place for our task force as it looks at what education should be in the year 2000. Is there a difference between the two terms? Should formal education—schooling—be concerned with either or both? How?

What about those who have already completed their formal schooling—are they entitled to continue education which will help them face the kind of life which makes an affluent society different from the one which nurtured them to adulthood?

Without any question, my standard of living is higher now than it has ever been in my life. I have a better income than I ever dreamed I'd ever have. I have a nice home in one of the best sections of one of the finest cities in the world.

We have good furniture, ample food, good quality clothing, two cars, sufficient money so I have no worry about educating all of my children through college, enough money to go to a show or out to dinner when we want, season tickets to the opera and symphony concerts, and enough coins left over for my children to have spending money for what they want—perhaps more than is really good for them.

But right now, I'm afraid that my quality of life is lower than it has been for several years, at least lower than when I first moved to Hawaii. Then I had time to go to the beach with my family frequently, to go to the zoo a couple of times a year and to Sea Life Park and the museum as a family.

I was working on a book which I found intellectually stimulating and satisfying.

I did not have a guilty feeling when I went out with a colleague or a student and spent a leisurely hour with a cup of coffee at Atherton House or Hemenway Cafeteria as we talked over the problems of life or issues within our fields of study.

I could drive home in the late afternoon and stop at the Diamond Head lookout and watch the surf—the equivalent of my pre-dinner martini—without feeling pressed for time. We could even rise before dawn and drive out to the Blow Hole in hopes of catching sight of a comet in the pre-dawn Eastern sky.

Now life moves at such a frantic pace that I have time for few of these simple pleasures. I chafe at the hours being lost when I lie on the beach watching my children play in the water. I justify a swim by persuading myself that exercise is necessary—"sound mind in sound body," you know.

I stay at the office so late that I must race home with all the other blind drivers on the expressway to hurry with dinner and sit with a stack of papers to be read or, too tired to think, stare at the TV until past bedtime.

My work is a series of fighting crises so that this task force promises to be the only intellectually stimulating thing I will attempt this spring and summer—making a travesty out of my filling in blanks of the tax form saying that my occupation is "university professor."

There is virtually nothing intellectual about my work—I am clearly a paper-pushing puppet in a system which deadens my spirit perceptibly day by day.

I lose my temper at my colleagues, scold my children for trifles, yell at my dog when she barks to come in the house, neglect my non-duty reading, wolf down a dry sandwich at my desk while I plow through work during the lunch hour, and find less and less satisfaction in life.

Then why don't I stop? Why don't I do something else? Why don't I turn back the clock and live like it was even five short years ago? Surely no one has chained me to my desk and to the routine of my life. Or is that so sure? The chains are there. And what is worse, I'm not alone.

My personal confession can be matched by most of you on the task force, I fear. Our chains are much like those of Jacob Marley. We are chained by the demands that our advanced standard of living has placed upon us. We cannot afford to give up the good job—how else can we make the payments on the mortgage?

We can't afford to slow down—other people are depending on us to come up with certain papers by deadlines which they set and over which we have no control.

We dare not relax and take it easy—our Puritan consciences, schooled carefully, would prick us most uncomfortably. And so we plunge on, "living more now but enjoying it less," to paraphrase the cigarette commercial.

And regardless of the lip service we give to our concern for such social problems as air pollution, we are not committed to the principle enough to do something about it.

As I drive to work in the mornings on the freeway, I can rarely see the beauty of the Waianae Mountains, a sparkling view of which until a couple of years ago was like a morning coffee-break as I drove in from Kaimuki to Manoa. Now the smog hides everything [west] of downtown.

I curse the smog for depriving me of one of the joys of living in Hawaii—I accepted without much complaint the hotels hiding the blue of the ocean, but I am reluctant to give up the green of the mountains without a cry of frustration. And yet I drive a car which needs a ring-job, and I add my share to that morning smog.

And tragically I am not educated to the need to do something about it. I'll wait until a law is passed regulating exhaust fumes and drive my polluting automobiles until they cost more to run than to junk.

And this shortcoming on the part of all of us—our overwhelming preoccupation with standard of living rather than quality of life is due to our education. We must do better for our children and the children of the future.

But we cannot completely separate standard of living from quality of life, for at some point, at least, a falling standard of living does create a falling quality of life. And it should be possible to have a high quality of life and yet maintain a high standard of living.

We don't have to return to nature—even if we could—to find a way of getting more out of living. We may have taken "living" out of the "country," but we don't have to go back to the country to enjoy living.

We need to educate people—including the post-30 generations—how to restore quality of life to their high standard of living in an urban and suburban environment.

There is where our real challenge lies. We must devise an education—preschool, kindergarten, elementary, secondary, higher, continuing, adult, senior citizen and all the combinations possible—that will help people learn how to be vocationally productive enough for them to have a high standard of living and contribute to the high standard of living for others and at the same time how to be humane enough to find quality of life for themselves, for others in the world with them, and for all the unborn generations yet to come.

Would you please think about education in the year 2000 in these terms? If you think my framework is naive and unproductive, please say so and we'll look for a better analysis.

If you think it can lead to a useful series of discussions and eventually a program for achieving a desirable system of education . . . , don't waste time and words agreeing with me but sail right into the troubled waters of the decades to come and let's try to design an education to help people get more out of life every day in every way.

If I sit and perform the same job twice a minute, 120 times an hour, 5000 times a week, am I working? I can be almost asleep, repeat myself endlessly, and be paid well. Or perhaps my mind will wander awake, and then it will work while my hands earn money.

WORK NOTES

David Steinberg

I know when I'm working from the feeling I get, the work feeling. A coming alive, involvement, energy flow. Getting in tune with myself, feeling all the different parts of me coming together. Moving ahead together.

For a lawnmower, the opposite of working is being broken. And for a part of me that's also true. My work is a sign of where I am. When I'm broken I don't work.

If I confuse working with making money I'm letting other people decide when I'm working and when I'm not. When other people like my work, they buy it. Their money expresses their sense of me. But my own sense of work has no particular relationship to money or outside approval.

Often my best work is with and for myself. Like working out relationships with other people, or working out my relationship with myself. Sometimes I sit for a week by myself, thinking, feeling, sometimes writing like this. Some people see this sitting as laziness, but I know that when I'm sitting I can be being lazy or I can be working very hard. It's hard for other people to see the difference, but to me the feelings are as different as being asleep and being awake, as forest and desert.

Working and growing stand very close together. Perhaps they are completely synonymous. At least I can't think now of how to do one without the other. Learning also is the same. So is change.

I have held different jobs for as long as I had the feeling that I was working, and left them when the work feeling was gone and there was only an empty shell. With the work feeling gone I have felt my alive self retreat and shrivel, coming out only "after work." Sometimes I have held on to dead jobs from habit and inertia, but I've always come to where I feel a deathly emptiness coming over me, forcing me to choose between changing and withering away. So far I have always chosen change. Looking back at this, it makes me feel good about myself.

There is a notion called career. It says that a person should do the same basic thing for a very long time. It feels very alien to me, not fitting my rhythm of growth and change. I have had several jobs that have been both difficult and involving, but even the most interesting and difficult jobs, like editing my own magazine, lost their sense of real growing work after a while. I once stayed at one job for two and a half years, but that was only because I could change what I was doing as I went along.

Sometimes I wonder if I'm just running away, drifting, always staying close to the surface. But I know that as long as I continue to change I will move from job to job in order to stay in tune with my changing sense of work. Work each job to the limit, and when the limit becomes restrictive, move to where there are new limits. Ultimately there are no limits save those we set for ourselves.

My work grows out of my sense of myself, not the other way around. Sometimes I want to say "I am a writer" or "I am a teacher," but I feel best when I say "I write" or "I teach."

When I look for work I look for a way to express my existence. If there is no fixed job that lets me do that then I have to create my own. That's how we decided to start our own school. Creating a job is not easy, but I want to be me, not someone else's idea of what I should or might be.

How many regular jobs are there that let me add to my own energy without stealing it from the people around me? I don't see many. But in the work I create, my energy adds to the energy of others, and theirs energizes me.

When I come to the most trying and difficult work, it helps me to be working with people who add to my energy and strength. I feel their support and acceptance, and both help me face the difficulties without being consumed by the fear of failing.

If my work atmosphere adds to my fear of failure, I will only attempt safe work. Whatever energy I invest in being afraid of failure is energy diverted from working. I work best when all my energy flows into my work and not into negating side channels.

People who see our school often treat us as magical giants, to have been able to do such a thing. They look at themselves as independent, isolated individuals and can't imagine doing what we've done. In fact, a good deal of strength and courage comes from the sense of community we share. Before we started the school, we spent five months living together as four people, building a sense of trust and support, growing together into a real family. Other people may be strengthened by other supportive contexts; this is mine.

We tend to think too little about the environment in which we work. We pretend that our energy is unrelated to the inputs that surround us. When I think of work now, I look at the work environment and context as much as I do at the substance. I measure my work as much by the process as by the result.

Competition can be a form of work, but it doesn't suit the parts of me that I like best.

Work that seems cooperative on the surface is often quite competitive underneath. I have felt competitive in my work even when there was no scale of output or system of promotions. When I find myself defensive against the people I work with, creating walls and distances, isolating myself from meaningful work contact with others, then I know that I judge my work competitively.

I ask myself this question: When people around me are leaping ahead in their work much better than I am, do I feel glad or resentful? If I'm resentful then I know I'm being competitive.

Often I compete not with others, but with some expectation I have of myself. A neutral work environment does nothing to help me overcome this. I am so used to setting myself off against others that I can only cure myself of this disease by careful and conscious effort.

Working against my inner habits of competition is, for me, very good, strong, rewarding work.

When I had been working for the National Student Association for about a year, I began to feel a growing restlessness. I searched for the source in the content of my work, but nothing there matched the intensity of my feelings. Finally I realized that my uneasiness stemmed from the context: an office full of people behind closed doors, in isolated cubicles, working on unrelated programs, not helping or caring about each other, sharing no sense of common purpose or common work. Several other people felt the same way, and we came together around a racism project, trying to mold the beginnings of a co-operative work group. We felt the power of our new energy, and tried to extend our community of cooperative work, but in the wider staff group nothing changed. Finally we gave up and moved to San Francisco. I believe that the structure of the work there at NSA and the prevailing work concepts ruled out any possibility for significant change.

My experience at NSA teaches me that there is no easy way to decide to be cooperative. Working together is so contrary to American culture, so contrary to much of what we have adopted as our own natures, that we can only slowly and gradually begin to understand what real cooperation means. I see that I have begun to overcome my individualistic, competitive, defensive, isolating reflexes. But I also recognize that the reflexes are very deep and that changing them is very difficult. If I remember this, I won't be disappointed at how slowly I change.

Hierarchy says that I should give others the power to judge my work. I see now that giving away this power weakens me, that I feel best when I judge for myself what I do. I am working to take back what judgmental power I have given away, and to reject that power over others when they push it at me.

At the school there is no sense of one staff person over another, of a person who is in charge. This has not resulted in chaos, but rather in a shared sense of everybody's worth and everybody's help in making difficult decisions.

In my relationships with students this has been harder and slower, but I feel myself moving ahead. I find myself acting less and less as an authority, and the students expect less and less for me to judge, criticize, validate, and direct them.

I see rejecting work hierarchies as just one facet of rejecting all forms of master–slave, top–down, dominant–submissive relationships. I find this pattern stifling whenever I experience it. In its place, mutual relationships give me new strength and freedom, and uncover possibilities that I had never even considered before. This goes for employer/employee, teacher/student, male/female, older/younger, parent/child.

Developing new work patterns helps me become more aware of the other patterns in my life. If I don't change them too, I feel myself splitting in half. This is also true when other changing patterns in my life make me aware of contradictions which I resolve by changing my work forms.

I have turned almost full circle from the notion that earning money is a sign of doing good work. Now when I see that someone earns lots of money I assume that his work can't be worth very much. I do know a few people who are paid well for doing good work, but my experience overall has been that the better I feel about what I'm doing, the less I get paid for it.

If I have to choose between work and money, I will choose work and learn how not to need so much money. This although I'm married and expect a baby in the next two weeks. I find that the more "family responsibility" I gain, the less I want to sacrifice myself to a need for money. I see that as I have had less and less money I have been happier with my work and with myself. I think of my relationship with my parents and resolve even more strongly to give my kids an open, loving father even if that should mean fewer clothes and toys.

Neither I nor Susan believes that it is the man's responsibility to work and earn money. We take equal responsibility for providing for our collective needs.

It's not that I have anything against money. I enjoy discovering what I can do without, but I don't enjoy being poor. It's just that when I think of what I would have to give up in order to have more money, I decide that it's not worth it.

At the school we pay salaries not according to how much each person produces, or how useful others find him, but according to what he needs. Money is a real need, and the staff community resolves to take care of the needs of its members. I express my feelings about other people's work, and they give me their perspective on what I do, but this is not done through the medium of money.

Right now Susan and I together bring in about $290 a month. Recently we have managed to save about $30 a month. We've found that we can get along quite well without a car, and that stroganoff is as good made with hamburger as it is with round steak.

It hurts me to hear people say "I work for this company" or "I work for that person." I know that when I'm working best and not just attending a job I'm working only for myself.

In the end, I work for the enjoyment of working. Not that work is happy fun every minute, but when I lose that basic enjoyment of the work I'm doing, I'm best off if I stop and do something else.

The best way for me to release work energy is to find *my* work and begin doing it. This means first not doing other people's work, and so there's a middle period of no work that is very disconcerting. My best tool for surviving this vacuum has been trusting the validity of my existence.

Sometimes I find that I begin working for someone else's benefit and neglect my own enjoyment. Then my work moves under the power of some external "should." I feel my resentment growing, but unless I acknowledge my own needs, I can't find the source of the negative energy. My resentment becomes a wall between me and my work.

My needs and my work are not in conflict with each other if I'm doing good work. If I take care of myself I will be able to do my best work.

I'm not lazy. I like doing good hard work. My most basic instincts lead me to good work. Whatever resistance I feel to these ideas comes from having done other people's work for too long.

When I'm at school, everything I do is part of my work. I feel glad to be whole, not pulled apart by the conflict between work and the rest of my life. But this fusion can also become too strong. When the four of us were living and working together, it felt like the school had taken over our lives altogether. The school is important, but not the only important work I do. When one part takes over the whole, everything falls out of balance.

It is possible to see all work as art, and as an expression of who I am. The Balinese have a saying: "We do not have any art; we do everything as well as possible." I like that saying. I am what I do.

Often when my friends or parents ask me what work I've been doing, I become uneasy. I want to answer "working out some good things with Susan" or "feeling closer to Walt" or "becoming more aware of my sexual feelings." But I still have part of me that says this is not real work.

The better the sense I have of my own work values, the more completely I can shed the values of others that don't suit me and my life.

If I have high energy all day, sleep short nights, and wake rested, I know I'm working. If my energy is low and I sleep long, I know I'm resting. Both work and rest are necessary. I know friends who work without resting, and they seem as unfulfilled as those who rest without working.

I have more trouble getting myself to rest than I do getting myself to work. America teaches that we are basically lazy, and I still have some parts of that in me. It makes me call rest escape, and keeps me from trusting that when I relax I work best.

A culture that draws a strict dichotomy between work and play will have tedious jobs and trivial, unrewarding leisure.

Sometimes when I ask myself what work I've been doing, I find myself looking for products. But work is a process and only the final stage is rewarded with a product. The work I do to overcome my fear of writing, the work of thinking in bed, the work of abortive attempts, all these are as real as the one time when I produce some writing that I like.

When I'm concerned with producing I'm trying to prove to others that I am working. I know that the entire process gives me the feeling of good work, but the product is all I can show someone else.

When I go for days teaching at the school *and* doing things I enjoy *and* getting paid for it *and* being with people I like *and* getting admiration for myself and the school, I know that this is why I've been working so hard to organize my life and my work around my real needs. Then I get a big surge of energy, and strength to begin moving forward again.

IF YOU CAN'T STAND THE HEAT, GET BACK TO THE KITCHEN

Letty Cottin Pogrebin

Last New Year's Eve my husband and I went to a party in the suburbs at which were many of his old college friends and their wives. In almost each case the couples had married immediately after graduation and the wives—all college educated—had become full-time housewives and mothers. My presence at this party seemed to challenge these nice ladies. It was as though my split-level life was an affront to their single-tracked home-mindedness. At first I suspected myself of my own female paranoia. But my husband corroborated the original impression. They *resented* me because I work as well as raise children and run a household. They were hostile, self-righteous and rather defensive. It would have been convenient if I had two children on the psychiatrist's couch. Then they could have pointed to cause and effect.

It's easy to dismiss a maverick with a yes, but. "Sure, she has an exciting job and an interesting social life. Yes, but look at those poor neglected children."

Unfortunately for their egos they know my children to be happy, well-behaved, bright and spirited kids. So where's their out? Well, in this particular gathering, the forces coalesced into a phalanx with the battle cry of "I love my children and home more than you do."

My final sense of relief and triumph came not from any brilliant putdown that I thought up. It came when one of the women let slip her true feelings. The dialogue is worth reporting only because it is so classic:

WIFE A: *How's your job, Letty?*

ME: *Marvelous. It's been an exciting season in publishing.*

WIFE A: *It must be awful to leave your children for an office job.*

ME: *No, actually, I don't mind it. I work because I want to, not because I have to. The children are quite accustomed to my working.*

WIFE A: *But, I mean, you have to leave them with a virtual stranger. Someone who couldn't possibly love them as much as a mother does.*

WIFE B: *And what if some accident happened while you were working. I'd never forgive myself.*

ME: *Our baby-sitter is by no means a stranger. She's been with us since the twins were three months old. She lavishes love on them like crazy. I wouldn't leave my children with a woman unless I were absolutely positive that she would care for them just as well as I do. And as far as that illusive extra quality called mother love is concerned, the girls get that from me almost full-time when I am home.*

WIFE B: *And what about accidents?*

ME: *Naturally, I can't say they won't happen. But thus far the only accidents we've had are those that have occurred while I was home. You can never be sure your child won't be run over when he's out for a walk with his grandmother but you don't forbid her to take him out for walks, do you?*

WIFE C: *What I wouldn't like about working would be the loss of precious hours with my own children. No one can possibly contribute to my child's growth and experience the way I do. I want to be home every minute to watch my little girl develop and to teach her things and share in her discoveries. A baby-sitter can't do that!*

ME: *Tell me this: Do you ever go out shopping? Do you get your hair done? Do you clean your house, cook the meals, do the mending, visit with neighbors, read the newspaper?*

WIVES' CHORUS: *Sure we do.*

ME: *Then you're not spending every waking moment with your precious children. I'll bet you send them out to the yard or into their rooms to play when you're busy. I'll bet you tell them to keep quiet when you're on the telephone. I'll bet you deposit them at other children's homes—not just to expand their acquaintanceships but to en-*

sure yourself free time. I'll just bet that none of you spend any more uninterrupted time with your children than a working mother like me does.

WIFE C: *Ridiculous! I always watch my children play. I talk with them, play with them, sit with them at lunch.*

ME: *Sounds very busy. And what does your husband do with them when he gets home?*

WIFE C: *Oh, they're asleep by the time he gets home. Come six o'clock I can't wait to get them into bed.*

If that's a loving mother, I'm a Lebanese juggler.

The circle of wives mumbled disclaimers and murmured in discomfort. One of their number had betrayed them. Was the lid off the Pandora's box of trapped, sterile harassed housewifehood? Is each day only to be endured with one's children until they can be packed off to bed? Are these women fulfilling a role compulsively and without enjoyment?

I don't think so. Probably, their defensiveness escalated their assault. This group of women overreacted to me as a challenge to their own status. I don't really believe that all of them suffer through endless days of demanding children and bleak household duties.

HARASSED HOUSEWIVES VS. *HAPPY HOMEMAKERS*

Many women are sincerely gratified by full-time motherhood. I know only a few of them but I do know one such woman intimately. My sister, Betty, thrives on the smooth operation of her home and the busy interaction between the parents and four children in the family. Her home is very much a career to her. She runs it enthusiastically, efficiently and with utter devotion. She's a cheerful, professional homemaker. Women's magazines and home-furnishing brochures are her trade papers. Her kitchen shelf contains dozens of file folders that would put some offices to shame. (In answer to two of my current needs, Betty recently presented me with her files on "Children's Parties" and "How to Add a Powder Room." Do *you* know how to make finger paints

out of corn starch or how to fit a bathroom into forty-nine inches of space?) Because my sister *chose* to be a full-time homemaker she suffered no frustrated hindsight of what she might have been. Reading, community affairs, involvement with her husband's work in education administration gave her complete satisfaction apart from the stimulation she found in the home.

Betty went back to teaching a few years ago when her youngest child was well along in school. She's glad to be out in the world again, but she looks back on her stay-at-home years with the absolute conviction that they constituted a rich, full life.

For her and others like her, work is something you do before your children arrive and after they've grown up. This book isn't really talking to them. Because to them a career will always be a man's thing—like the Army or power tools.

What I mean to illustrate with the scene at the New Year's Eve party is the complex ambivalence that a great many women feel about working. They're the ones who chose to abandon careers or never to start them and they never feel quite right about that decision. They regret their choice but feel bound by it. They may be mildly discontented or terribly bitter but somehow they haven't gotten around to correcting the situation. Some tell themselves that they aren't equipped to "do" anything now that ten years have elapsed since they last worked or attended school. Others excuse their inertia by claiming that their children would never stand for it. Still more swear that they are shackled by a husband who insists that a woman's place is at the stove and at his service.

As I see it, a woman who desires no different life than the one she leads would not feel impelled to attack the life style of the working wife and mother. She would not need to undermine another woman's confidence in order to enhance her own.

The ones on the attack, I believe to be acting out of defensiveness. They would really like to be doing something. But for their separate reasons they aren't. So they seek to reinforce their positions by finding fault with mine. If I were to crumble in a heap of self-doubt and guilt they could be reassured that their road was the right one.

After the New Year was ushered in and the

champagne floated the party into the wee hours, it came to light that one of my questioners had been a scientist and intended to go back into research. Another wife had just taken an interview for a job as a part-time physical therapist. A third woman planned to work as a technical writer when her child started school.

I became more convinced than ever that many educated women feel stymied by household chores. They are stultified by constant child care and children's company. Not all women. But some.

Why do they perpetuate the myth of Woman Equals Mother/Wife? I've told you my theory. There are two culprits: women who want to justify their own martyred, self-sacrificing position and men who want to keep the status quo as comfy cozy as it's always been.

THE FEMINISTS MAY BE ON TO SOMETHING

I'm not obsessed with the problem. And I'm not the crusading type. For myself, my own adjustment to being a working mother is right for me. I'm not hell-bent on converting every housewife I meet at a party. But there are banner-waving feminists around and their view of the situation—though extreme—is worth some attention. One such group is the National Organization for Women whose credo is "Full equality for all women in America in truly equal partnership with men."

It's too bad that our society has made so little progress in freeing talented, aspiring women from their homes. It accounts for a tremendous waste of human potential. It causes frustration in women who value their abilities and tension in marriages where one partner feels unfulfilled. It accounts for the sad statistics cited by the National Organization for Women: of the twenty-eight million women in the job market, seventy-five per cent of them are in rock-bottom positions, ninety per cent of them earn less than $5000 a year and many of them earn up to forty per cent less than men who hold the exact same jobs.

Behind the statistics covering women in general is an important subcategory. The working wife and mother is subject to all the disadvantages common to any female looking for a job plus a whole host of special pressures and societal excuses. She is perhaps the aspirant with the most strikes against her and the most doors slammed in her face.

I could spit nails when I hear the usual condescending "explanations" for employers' dense stubbornness. There *are* answers to every allegation. The enlightened employer has discovered them for himself. The company or industry or boss who would try them on me would get a lot of back talk.

You won't be free to travel.

To this I say, partly right, partly wrong. I'm not applying for a job as a traveling salesman. If the job I do want involves constant travel, then tell me and I'll bow out. Sure, I don't care to leave my family regularly or for weeks on end. But if what you mean is an occasional overnight out-of-town conference, a weekend convention or a week abroad once every two years, just try me. If my husband and I agree that I would be happiest working, we are also implicitly in agreement that some of my duties will cause us inconvenience—like my occasional absence from home. If I take a job with full knowledge that traveling or late hours or occasional weekend work is involved, you may be sure that I'll be as faithful to my obligations as a single man who hasn't a responsibility in the world.

"You don't need the raise because you've got a husband supporting you."

Wrong. I need the raise because I deserve the raise; because in our system merit is rewarded in money; because I justify the economics of my working on the balance sheet between my income and such expenses as transportation, baby-sitters, wardrobe and lunches. I need the raise because I know that if I were a man or if I were working here without your knowing my biographical facts, I would get that raise.

"How can I be sure you'll stay?"

You can't. But neither can you be sure that any man you hire will stay. The average man stays with the same employer only four years. His reasons for moving on are probably the same as mine would be: to get a better job elsewhere. Once I am a working wife or mother I have established my desire to remain in the business world. *You* must assume that once in I'm here to stay.

"You're just working for fun and extra money."

Maybe I am. But so what? Finding fun and gaining extra money are in themselves a pretty strong incentive for succeeding in business. In fact, if I'm so clearly applying here by choice and not out of need, shouldn't you be more confident of my having a good attitude?

But maybe I'm not. Maybe the fun and extra money are just ancillary benefits. Maybe I have the same motivations common to other applicants. Maybe I really want the job, like the work and can do it exceedingly well. Maybe, just maybe, I am extraordinarily endowed with the ubiquitous talent to be my husband's lover, a good cook, a creative mother, an able housekeeper *and* a fantastic copywriter on your staff. Maybe you should think of what we have in common—a brain—instead of what differentiates us—my family responsibilities.

"We can't spare the time you'll need to take off for P.T.A. conferences or for your child's bout with German measles."

Just tell me your limit on sick days and don't second guess me on my absences. I may be absent because my child is having his tonsils out but I won't take off to fulfill my obligations at Army Reserve meetings. I might take a morning for a teacher's conference at school but I won't be out with a hangover. You don't give your male applicants a warning in advance. You don't grill them to discover if they lift weights and therefore may end up out of the office with a hernia. Don't anticipate. Just tell me the company rules and I'll abide by them.

"We want people whose first loyalty is to their jobs."

Come now. Are you telling me that your own wife and five kids don't come first? Why should a woman be any less able to split her energies than a man is? Why don't we call you "Working Fathers"? Because it's understood by sensible people that you can shoulder both lives without collapsing. Your wife can be suffering postpartum blues, your son can be palling around with a drug-taking crowd, your car payments can be two months overdue and the cesspool can have overflowed the night before—you'll still manage to get through the business day in a passable state of productivity. No one presents you with either/or loyalties. Naturally I'm going to love my husband and children a zillion times more than I love my job. So do you, I hope. Certainly, if it's a question of success on the job or the health and well-being of my family, I'd tell the job to go to hell. Wouldn't you?

It's a $95 a week, take it or leave it. And you'd be smart to take it."

You take it. I'll leave it. If I know that the assistant art director down the hall is making $150 a week and that the person who held the job up until now was making $150 a week, I want $150 a week. If I'm worth hiring, I'm worth paying the going rate. Fifty-five dollars is a stiff handicap for an applicant who happens to have a husband and a child or two. I may not be the hottest commodity in the job market place but neither am I marked-down merchandise.

The woman who encounters resistance such as this and talks her way into a desirable job deserves a pat on the back and a generous dose of sympathy. She'll be under surveillance for weeks and maybe months. If she's a working wife, her employer will watch for signs of morning sickness and a euphoric look that may signal the beginning of a pregnancy and the end of her job. If she's already a mother, he'll be keeping close tabs on her attendance record and her phone calls. After six months of punctuality, he'll pounce on her the day she leaves the office at five minutes to five because she had to get her son to the dentist by five-fifteen. Those are the breaks. Discriminatory attitudes die hard. But there does eventually come a day when the quality of a woman's work overshadows her marital or maternal status.

NEVER UNDERESTIMATE THE POWER OF A WORKING WOMAN AND A WILLING EMPLOYER

Working wives who have no strong union doing battle for them and those who find little elasticity in their management will have to break new ground. It takes only a willing boss and a workable arrangement the first time around to convert management to make wholesale policy revisions.

Everything that my boss and I devised to keep us both happy *has* worked. And much of it had never been done before. Before my children were born, there were actually few instances when an adjustment or compromise had to be made. Obviously, a woman with no children has no special demands made upon her time and energies during the workday. Her husband is also presumably holding down a job that keeps him occupied from nine to five or thereabouts. I used to talk to my husband once a day and occasionally meet him for lunch—no more of a diversion from the job than a man or a single woman might have.

Still, my boss made enough gestures that indicated to me that he was very much aware of my new marriage. I remember once in the early months when Mr. Geis overheard me asking one of the girls for a recipe suggestion. He came into my office five minutes later with one of the cookbooks from his library of other publishers' books. When Mr. Geis heard that my husband had won one of his most important cases I was given the rest of the day off. My boss gave me a guest voucher for two dinners that night at one of New York's best restaurants—a celebration meal on him.

Now, there's something that had never been done. But it worked as well as if it had initiated an official reciprocal trade agreement. Subsequently, if my boss needed me to stay late or to take a visiting foreign agent to dinner, my husband never had a beef. Bert doesn't complain (very much) when we drink ourselves blind at the airport waiting for an author on a flight that's six hours late on the very night when Bert wanted to see the Knick's game. You give a little, you get a little.

It was an easy, fair and square give-and-take when I was simply a working wife. Once I became a working mother the plot thickened. It would be safe to say that it was still give-and-take. I gave a lot of trouble and Mr. Geis kindly took it. Our particular adjustment has been so ideal, quite frankly, because of his gambling spirit. He has been a consistent proponent of the "Let's try it" philosophy.

I quit "for good" at the end of my first pregnancy. I was convinced at that time that I was meant to be a full-time mother. (See how close I came to being one of those frustrated stay-at-homes!) My boss was convinced that I'd be back. He held the job open. Six months later I was back.

When our third baby was born, Mr. Geis was wishing for a boy even more than we were. After twin girls he felt that the birth of a boy would halt my procreation by satisfying my craving for a well-balanced family. . . . When the boss was in England he saluted me with this cablegram: "HOPE YOUR YOUNGEST WILL BE A BOY AND LONG MAY HE BE YOUR YOUNGEST." It had continued to be a standing joke between us that I might retire again for six months. This time, however, I had only a six-week-paid maternity leave. When I was feeling up to it, my secretary brought paperwork to my home and I sent work back to the office by messenger. The office health-insurance policy paid the hospital bills.

CREATIVE MOTHERHOOD

Being a working mother does not interfere with my personal goals where creative motherhood is concerned. Because I have a baby-sitter who is also a housekeeper, I am able to ignore major cleaning chores on at-home days. My husband and I try to plan activities that are enjoyable for all of us and often educational to the kids. In our family, we've dubbed such activities "adventures." This can encompass something so seemingly modest as a ride on the bus or subway (a colossal adventure to a three-year-old), to a walk along the waterfront waving at the tugboats, to a full-fledged outing including a visit to the zoo or museum, perhaps a Chinese tea-lunch, a stop in the playground, ice skating or an indulgent jaunt through a toy store. On rainy days we may make papier-mâché candleholders or greeting cards for the holidays or my husband may construct complex cities out of blocks, chessmen and anything wee and wondrous that happens to be around the house.

As I said before, it isn't how much time you spend with your children but how well you spend it. The important thing is to make the time a total involvement—a family adventure.

Let's suppose you're confronted with the dilemma of giving up your job in favor of your children but you suspect that it shouldn't even be a dilemma. In the long run, you realize that you'll be a better mother if you're happy. And your work makes you happy. No sweat—or only a little. First and foremost in this situation is the complete approval of your husband. Second, and in its way just as important, is your choice of baby-sitter or housekeeper. You must trust her as you do yourself. If you don't have complete confidence in her judgment or if you doubt, in the slightest, her ability to love your kids and give them full, warm attention—then stay home until you find the right woman. *No* job, however fantastic, is worth risking a child's psychological and physical well-being. You should hire someone who understands that the children come first. The house can look like hell, the wash can pile up, eggs can be curdling in the Hollandaise but if the baby is crying, she must hold it, comfort it and minister to its discontent.

If you have school-age children, your concern will obviously lessen. Their hours at home before you return from the office will be minimal. Nevertheless, it's the nine-year-old who decides to experiment with a match so that he can play fireman. And he can get into as much trouble between 3:30 and 5:30 as the ten-month-old who crawls around the iron cord at eleven in the morning.

The mother who works has an added challenge. The precious hours she does spend with her family are compensatory. She will want to use them to make up for her time away from home. She won't spend an hour putting on her face in the morning. She'll use that hour to talk to an eight-year-old about his pitching arm. Or she'll spend it stringing wooden beads with a toddler. She won't dash in at 6 P.M. and immediately get on the telephone with a friend while the child waits for her attention. She'll perhaps order naps for the youngest children so that they'll be able to stay up to be with Mommy and Daddy for a few hours in the evening. If the office is nearby, she'll come home for lunch occasionally. And she'll use weekends for those adventures we talked about. With Daddy along on the weekend adventures to a play, picnic, long walk or family day at home, a child will never feel cheated.

By the same token, the working mother will not feel guilty about leading her double life. The point is, such a life *can* be led if you feel it's for you and you are willing to apportion your time with infinite care and judicious advance planning.

HAVING YOUR CAKE AND MAKING IT TOO

Women who are able to split their time to serve all the complex needs and commitments that matter to them are often working wives and mothers. With one foot firmly planted in the business world and the other foot sliding around on a loose marble or a waxed floor in the home, this multipurpose female is a stranger to boredom. She reads *Aviation Week & Space Technology* under the hair dryer and grows chives in her office window "because it gets more sun than at home." She can discourse for hours on rising interest rates but she's always the one woman in a crowd who has a foolproof method of separating egg yolks—"use your hands." She can recite in sequence the dates of her product's spring advertising campaign, her dinner party for twelve, her daughter's next visit to the orthodontist and her secretary's birthday—without benefit of calendar. She knows by heart her Diner's Card number, her son's locker combination and her husband's Social Security number. She translates her penchant for organization and efficiency to her home, keeping impeccable recipe files, tax records and stock market lists in the file cabinet under her dressing table.

I can only speak authoritatively about my own experience. My husband and I have a rare symbiosis in that deep down in my heart I would like to be a labor lawyer and deep down in his lurks a book publisher yearning to get out. Bert plays an integral role in the man's world that I occupy. He loves to attend National Book Awards ceremonies, trade cocktail parties, interesting television bookings and dinners with authors like Groucho Marx (no, Groucho doesn't always crouch over, chomp on a cigar and chase girls) or Jacqueline Susann. Because he is a lawyer he is especially interested in our publishing contracts. He sweats out our knotty negotiations and contributes free legal advice during our occasional bouts of litigation. He has attended copyright workshops with me. He has been to Authors League receptions and to motion-picture screenings. He's always coming up with book ideas, publicity suggestions and reliable reactions to my brainstorms (remember Scarsdale Research?). I've been to lawyers' lectures, clients' homes and top level meetings. I kibbitz, read all his briefs and know the details of all his cases.

The symbiotic relationship was never more apparent than at a recent dinner party. On one side of the table I was regaling my companions with triumphant reports about Bert's prowess at settling a school strike. On the other side of the table he was describing a publicity gimmick I dreamed up. Later in the evening when everyone was talking about children, Bert volunteered a quote from our four-year-old, Robin ("I'm starving tired!") and I contributed one of Abigail's *bon mots* ("My chest doesn't breast right"). There in microcosm is the best illustration of my point of view. Instead of the woman talking only house and kids and the man talking only business, there was six-way cross-pollination. It all adds up to a lot of shared interests, mutual respect and enormous pride in one another.

Without Bert's approval and encouragement I'm sure I would not have resumed my career. But I can't say I would have been as zestful a wife and mother if I hadn't. For me, each segment of life nourishes the other.